AF819600

Recommended by **Teachers**
Trusted by **Toppers**

All in One

ENGLISH CORE

Class 12

EVERYTHING YOU NEED TO SCORE

- Detailed Study Material for all the Three Sections
- NCERT & Other Important Questions
- CBQs; Extract Based & SA, LA
- Board Questions Upto 2025
- Sample Question Papers

CBSE Exams 2026

Recommended by **Teachers**
Trusted by **Toppers**

All in One

ENGLISH CORE
Class 12

EVERYTHING YOU NEED TO SCORE

- Detailed Study Material for all the Three Sections
- NCERT & Other Important Questions
- CBQs; Extract Based & SA, LA
- Board Questions Upto 2025
- Sample Question Papers

CBSE Exams 2026

Authors
Parneet Kaur
Neha Singh

arihant
SUCCESS AND NOTHING LESS

arihant
SUCCESS AND NOTHING LESS

ARIHANT PRAKASHAN
(School Division Series)

ADMINISTRATIVE & PRODUCTION OFFICES

Regd. Office
'Ramchhaya' 4577/15, Agarwal Road, Darya Ganj, New Delhi -110002
Tele: 011- 47630600, 43518550; Fax: 011- 23280316

Head Office
Kalindi, TP Nagar, Meerut (UP) - 250002, Tel: 0121-7156203, 7156204

SALES & SUPPORT OFFICES
Agra, Ahmedabad, Bengaluru, Bareilly, Chennai, Delhi, Guwahati, Hyderabad, Jaipur, Jhansi, Kolkata, Lucknow, Nagpur & Pune.

PO No : TXT-XX-XXXXXXX-X-XX

Published By Arihant Publications (India) Ltd.

For further information about the books published by Arihant, log on to www.arihantbooks.com or e-mail at info@arihantbooks.com

Follow us on

PRICE ₹ 500.00

PRODUCTION TEAM

Publishing Managers
Mahendra Singh Rawat & Keshav Mohan

Cover Designer
Salman Shaikh

Inner Designer
Ankit Tyagi

Project Head
Manju

Page Layouting
Lalit Chaprana

Proof Readers
Harsh Agarwal, Naina Rajya

Index *cum* Study Planner

LITERATURE TEXTBOOKS

PROSE

		Studied	Revised	Exam ready

One Book- Endless Features

to Help you Succeed

Summary of the Chapter

In each chapter of the Prose, Poetry & Supplementary, Summary of the Chapter & Explanation is given in simple and easy to understand language. It will help the students to understand theme of the chapter easily.

Summary of the Chapter

Franz's Surprise

The story starts with a young school going boy named Franz being late for school. He was scared of getting scolded by his French teacher, M. Hamel, as he had not learned participles. He also wanted to enjoy his day outside in nature. However, he had to go to school. On the way, Franz passed the town hall where a many people were reading the bad news from the bulletin board. Without paying much attention to it, he reached his school.

Franz was surprised to see that the school was quiet. He had expected to find a lot of noise. Inside the class, he saw that his classmates were seated and M. Hamel was walking to and fro. Embarrassed, Franz entered his class. He thought that he would get scolded. But, M. Hamel kindly told him to take his seat.

The Order from Berlin

In the classroom, Franz observed that M. Hamel was wearing his special attire. Further, the village elders were sitting in the back benches. They all looked sad. M. Hamel announced that it was their last French lesson. An order had come from Berlin to teach only German in the schools of Alsace and Lorraine and that it was their last French lesson.

Franz was shocked by the information. He regretted not learning his lessons on time. He also felt bad because M. Hamel was leaving. Franz realised that M. Hamel wore his special attire to honour his last lesson. Moreover, the village people had come to express their gratitude towards him. They wanted to show their respect for their country and their language.

M. Hamel's Patriotism

When it was time for Franz to recite, he was not able to speak the French participles properly. He was ashamed of himself. However, M. Hamel did not scold him. M. Hamel criticised the people of Alsace for postponing their learning. He blamed the parents for wanting their children to earn instead of study. He also blamed himself for giving them a holiday whenever he wanted to go fishing.

M. Hamel called French language- the most beautiful, the clearest and the most logical language in the world. He told the people of France to treasure their language. According to him, whenever the people of a particular nation are enslaved, as long as they are attached to their language, it is as if they have the key to their prison.

The Final Goodbye

That day Franz understood everything. He realised that he never paid much attention in the class and that M. Hamel had never explained everything with so much patience. Everyone did their work with full concentration. Even the old Hauser was focused on reading his old book. M. Hamel was sitting in his chair and observing his class. For 40 years, he had given his faithful service to the school and now he had to leave.

At the end of the lesson, everyone in the class became emotional. However, M. Hamel had the courage and patience to hear every lesson. Finally, as the church-clock struck twelve, M. Hamel stood up. He tried to speak but choked. He turned to the blackboard and wrote as large as he could 'Vive La France!' meaning 'long live France'. Hamel dismissed the class, signaling everyone to leave.

Word-Meaning

in great dread of	—	with great fear of
drilling	—	undergoing military training exercises
apprentice	—	trainee, a person who is learning a trade from a skilled employer
a great bustle	—	excited activity and movement
in unison	—	all at once, together
rapping	—	striking rapidly on a hard surface, especially in order to attract attention
counted on	—	relied or depended on
primer	—	an elementary book for teaching children to read
thunderclap	—	a crashing sound of thunder
wretches	—	villains; people deserving contempt
Saar	—	a river in North-Eastern France and Western Germany
cranky	—	bad-tempered, eccentric or strange
reproach ourselves with	—	criticise ourselves for
at one stroke	—	by a single action having immediate effect
Angelus	—	a bell rung as call to recite the Angelus–a devotional prayer in the Roman Catholic Church
bearing on	—	pressing
Vive La France	—	long live France

Formats in Writing Section

In Writing section standard format has been given. This will help students to learn proper format of each writing task.

Nehru Colony
Indore — **Sender's address**

24th February, 20XX — **Date**

The Editor
The Times of India
New Delhi 110002 — **Receiver's name/rank and his/her address**

Subject **Concerns over online teaching** — **Subject of the letter** Indicate the theme of the letter here

Sir/Ma'am — **Salutation**

Through the columns of your esteemed newspaper, I would like to draw the attention of the concerned authorities to express my concern regarding online teaching.

With the Covid-19 Pandemic affecting all of the world's different areas at large, the one to take the most hit is the education sector. The pandemic forced to fasten the acceptance of online teaching methods to sustain learning. In the need to continue effective education, online teaching- learning was accepted by all schools. However, the acceptance of online teaching came with its various limitations.

Online teaching- learning from school promoted learning from school but promoted isolation. As a result, children make almost no friends. They are stuck at home for all day and suffer from stress, anxiety and even obesity. Thus, the condition of the future of the country is deteriorating.

Hence, it is time for us to look for a fine balance between the two worlds of online learning and innocence of childhood. To do so, we can take certain steps in the form of physical activities, family time and constructive leisure time.

I hope that all of us understand the need to maintain this balance and make sure that our young minds enjoy their innocent childhood to the fullest and not sit in front of their systems all day long.

— **Body of the letter**

Thanking you
Yours truly
Manju/Manav — **Complimentary closure** Name and designation of the sender

Word Meaning

In each chapter of the Prose, Poetry and Supplementary, Difficult words are given along with their meaning. This will help students to understand difficult word easily.

One Book- Endless Features

to Help you Succeed

NCERT Folder

Here, we have covered questions of NCERT Textbook (Intext & Exercise) with their detailed answers in simple and easy language.

NCERT Folder

Think as you Read (NCERT Page 7)

1. What was Franz expected to be prepared with for school that day?

Ans. Franz was expected to be prepared with his lesson on participles. M. Hamel, his French teacher, had announced that he would question the class on participles.

2. What did Franz notice that was unusual about the school that day?

Ans. Franz noticed many unusual things about school that day. First, normally when the school began there was much commotion, which was missing that day. Second, his teacher, M. Hamel, had worn his ceremonial clothes. Third, and the most unusual, the village people were sitting quietly on the back benches, which were usually empty on other days.

3. What had been put up on the bulletin-board?

Ans. An order that had come from Berlin had been put up on the bulletin-board. The order was that from the next day onwards, only German would be taught in the schools of Alsace and Lorraine. The new teacher for German would join the school from the following day.

scold anyone. Further, the village people attended the lesson and everyone present in the class paid full attention to what was being taught.

2. How did Franz's feelings about M. Hamel and school change?

Ans. Franz's feelings about M. Hamel and school changed when M. Hamel told the students about the order from Berlin and that it was their last French lesson. Franz forgot about his teacher's ruler and crankiness; instead, he started liking M. Hamel. His feelings towards his school also changed, as he did not want to give up his books and lessons, which seemed to be his old friends.

Understanding the Text (NCERT Page 9)

1. The people in this story suddenly realise how precious their language is to them. What shows you this? Why does this happen?

Ans. When the order had come from Berlin that henceforth only German would be taught in schools, people realised that it was the last day to learn their precious mother tongue. To show their affection for the language, many elderly people came to attend the school, occupying the last benches, which had usually remained vacant earlier.

Exam Pattern Questions

Extract Based Questions

Read the extracts given below and answer the questions that follow.

1. When I passed the town hall there was a crowd in front of the bulletin board. For the last two years all our bad news had come from there–the lost battles, the draft, the orders of the commanding officer– and I thought to myself, without stopping. "What can be the matter. Now?"

   Then, as I hurried by as fast as I could go, the blacksmith, Wachter, who was there, with his apprentice, reading the bulletin, called after me, "Don't go so fast, bub: you'll get to your school in plenty of time!"

   I thought he was making fun of me, and reached M. Hamel's little garden all out of breath.

   (i) What do you think is the significance of the bulletin board and the crowd around it?

   (ii) Select the correct option from those given in brackets to fill in the blank.

   'The matter' is related to .... (language/territory)

   (iii) Complete the following suitably.

   (c) Franz did not like the blacksmith.
   (d) Franz had no idea that it was his last French lesson.

   (vi) Select the option that completes the given sentence appropriately.

   'the lost battles, the draft, the orders of the commanding officer' in the given context would refer to ....

   (a) the news that come from the bulletin board
   (b) general knowledge regarding France
   (c) government decisions regarding Alsace
   (d) the reason for the crowd

Ans (i) The bulletin board plays a significant role as it has been the source of all bad news for the people of Alsace for the last two years. The crowd presents the eagerness of people to learn the news development of the war as they may bring about a change in their lives.

Self Assessment Test

At the end of the chapter, there are unsolved questions for practice and assessment of students. By practising these questions, students can assess their preparation level for the chapter.

Exam Pattern Questions

Each chapter cover all types of questions like, Extract Based Questions, Short Answer & Long Answer Type Questions.

SELF ASSESSMENT TEST

Extract Based Questions

Read the extract given below and answer the questions that follow.

1. "Your parents were not anxious enough to have you learn. They preferred to put you to work on a farm or at the mills, so as to have a little more money. And I? I've been to blame also. Have I not often sent you to water my flowers instead of learning your lessons? And when I wanted to go fishing, did I not just give you a holiday?"

   (i) When did M. Hamel give students a holiday?

   (ii) Select the correct option from those given in bracket to fill in the blank.

   The narrator seems to be .... (angry/regretful) about losing on teaching French.

   (iii) Complete the sentence suitably.

   The speaker of the given lines blames himself for giving a .... for ....

   (iv) Rationalise, to support the given opinion.

   The parents feel guilty for not sending their children to school after listening to M. Hamel.

   (v) Why did Franz's parents put him to work?

   (a) To make him realise the importance of work (b) To earn a little more money
   (c) To punish him for his callous attitude (d) To pay his school fees

   (vi) The speaker of the given lines is giving what seems to be a/an ....

   (a) lecture (b) advice
   (c) sermon (d) judgement

Latest Course Structure

Section A (Reading Skills) **22 Marks**

Reading Comprehension through Unseen Passage

1. One unseen passage to assess comprehension, interpretation, analysis and inference. Vocabulary assessment will also be assessed via inference. The passage may be factual, descriptive or literary.
2. One unseen case-based factual passage with verbal/visual inputs like statistical data, charts etc. to assess comprehension, interpretation, analysis, inference and evaluation.

   Note: The combined word limit for both the passages will be 700-750 words.

Multiple Choice Questions / Objective Type Questions and Short Answer type Questions (to be answered in 40-50 words) will be asked.

Section B (Creative Writing Skills) **18 Marks**

Creative Writing Skills

3. Notice, up to 50 words. One out of the two given questions to be answered. (4 Marks: Format : 1 / Content : 2 / Accuracy of Spelling and Grammar : 1).
4. Formal/Informal Invitation and Reply, up to 50 words. One out of the two given questions to be answered. (4 Marks: Format : 1 / Content : 2 / Accuracy of Spelling and Grammar :1).
5. Letters based on verbal/visual input, to be answered in approximately 120-150 words. Letter types include application for a job with bio data or resume. Letters to the editor (giving suggestions or opinion on issues of public interest) . One out of the two given questions to be answered . (5 Marks: Format : 1 / Organisation of Ideas: 1/Content : 2 / Accuracy of Spelling and Grammar :1).
6. Article/ Report Writing, descriptive and analytical in nature, based on verbal inputs, to be answered in 120-150 words. One out of the two given questions to be answered . (5 Marks: Format : 1 / Organisation of Ideas: 1/Content : 2 / Accuracy of Spelling and Grammar :1).

Section C (Literature Text Book and Supplementary Reading Text) **40 Marks**

This section will have variety of assessment items including Multiple Choice Questions, Objective Type Questions, Short Answer Type Questions and Long Answer Type Questions to assess comprehension, interpretation, analysis, evaluation and extrapolation beyond the text.

7. One Poetry extract out of two, from the book Flamingo, to assess comprehension, interpretation, analysis, inference and appreciation. *(6x1=6 Marks)*
8. One Prose extract out of two, from the book Vistas, to assess comprehension, interpretation, analysis, evaluation and appreciation. *(4x1=4 Marks)*
9. One Prose extract out of two from the book Flamingo, to assess comprehension, interpretation, analysis, inference and evaluation. *(6x1=6Marks)*

10. Short answer type questions (from Prose and Poetry from the book Flamingo), to be answered in 40-50 words each. Questions should elicit inferential responses through critical thinking. Five questions out of the six given, are to be answered. *(5x2=10 Marks)*
11. Short answer type questions, from Prose (Vistas), to be answered in 40- 50 words each. Questions should elicit inferential responses through critical thinking. Any two out of three questions to be done. *(2x2=4 Marks)*
12. One Long answer type question, from Prose/Poetry (Flamingo), to be answered in 120-150 words. Questions can be based on incident / theme / passage / extract / event as reference points to assess extrapolation beyond and across the text. The question will elicit analytical and evaluative response from the student. Any one out of two questions to be done. *(1x5=5 Marks)*
13. One Long answer type question, based on the chapters from the book Vistas, to be answered in 120-150 words, to assess global comprehension and extrapolation beyond the text. Questions to provide analytical and evaluative responses using incidents, events, themes, as reference points. Any one out of two questions to be done. *(1x5=5 Marks)*

Prescribed Books

1. **Flamingo:** English Reader published by National Council of Education Research and Training, New Delhi

Prose

- The Last Lesson
- Deep Water
- Indigo
- The Interview
- Lost Spring
- The Rattrap
- Poets and Pancakes
- Going Places

Poetry

- My Mother at Sixty-Six
- A Thing of Beauty
- Aunt Jennifer's Tigers
- Keeping Quiet
- A Roadside Stand

2. **Vistas:** Supplementary Reader published by National Council of Education Research and Training, New Delhi

- The Third Level
- Journey to the End of the Earth
- On the Face of It
- The Tiger King
- The Enemy
- Memories of Childhood
  - *The Cutting of My Long Hair*
  - *We Too are Human Beings*

Internal Assessment

Assessment of Listening Skills	-	05 Marks
Assessment of Speaking Skills	-	05 Marks
Project Work	-	10 Marks

READING

01

Reading Comprehension

Marking Scheme

In the Class XII examination, two passages carrying a total of 22 marks will be asked from the reading section.

YOUR STUDY GOALS

- Types of Passages
- Sample Passages (Factual, Discursive & Literary Passages)
- Practice Questions
- Sample Passages (Case Based Factual Passages)
- Practice Questions
- Self Assessment Test

Comprehension involves a thorough understanding of a given passage consisting of one or more paragraphs. It essentially involves integrating the understanding of the passage into what we already know and drawing inferences about the writer's purpose, intent and point of view. Thus, it tests the understanding power and intellectual skills of a student.

Reading Comprehension usually includes questions that test the reader's ability to

- Find the main idea or a suitable title for the passage.
- Find information directly specified in the passage.
- Draw inferences from the given passage.
- Determine the meaning of unfamiliar words used in the passage.
- Determine the author's style, mood or point of view.

Types of Passages

The CBSE Class XII curriculum defines the two categories of passages from which questions will be asked. These are

Passage 1 will either be Factual, Descriptive or Literary.

Passage 2 will be Case based Factual Passage

A closer analysis of the sources of these passages are given below.

Type of Passages	Examples	Sources from where passages are taken
Factual Passage	▪ A set of facts ▪ Instructions ▪ Report ▪ Description	▪ Newspapers and magazines ▪ Brochures ▪ Reference books ▪ Encyclopedias
Discursive Passage	▪ Opinions ▪ Persuasive text ▪ Argumentative text ▪ Interpretative text	▪ Newspapers and magazines ▪ Reference books
Literary Passage	▪ Extracts from fiction, drama, essay, biography, etc.	▪ Novels ▪ Short stories ▪ Dramas ▪ Biographies ▪ Other literary books
Case based Factual Passage	Passage with visual and verbal imputs of ▪ Statistical data ▪ Charts ▪ Graphs	▪ Newspaper reports ▪ Magazines ▪ Reference books

Points to be Kept in Mind while Answering the Questions

- Read the passage at a reasonable pace to get the general idea of the text. Then, go through the question one.
- Next, do a second reading at a slow pace to find the answers. Underline the part where you think the answer is located.
- Underline the words you don't understand and try to guess their meaning from the context.
- Now read the passage again to counter check your answers and write your answers briefly and to the point.
- Remember answers should be based on information given/inference derived from the information in the passage.
- Make sure to use the same tense in which the questions has been asked.
- In multiple choice questions, analyse the questions and options carefully before selecting the correct option because some of the four options are closely related.

Sample Passages

Factual, Discursive & Literary Passages

Read the following passages carefully and answer the questions that follow.

Passage 1 (Factual)

1. World Conservation Day is celebrated internationally to increase awareness about the best practices needed to protect our natural resources. The Earth is supplied with a limited amount of resources that we all rely upon, like water, air, soil and trees. The World Nature Conservation Movement is a great opportunity to celebrate the progress we've made and determine to take action, wherever needed. It is time to remind ourselves that we need to give back to nature instead of just using resources without thinking about conservation. There is a need to replenish and recycle the resources we consume from nature.
2. Our forests, rivers, oceans and soils provide us with the food we eat, the air we breathe, the water we irrigate our crops with. We also rely on them for numerous other goods and services. We depend on them for our health, happiness and prosperity. We have a cycle of biodiversity which needs proper conservation.
3. The population explosion remains one of the major reasons why natural resources are getting depleted at a very fast rate. Technological advancement and luxurious lifestyles have led to several environmental problems like global warming, ozone layer depletion, river water pollution and deforestation which threaten the planet's future.
4. Humans, animals, marine creatures and the environment, all need to be protected and conserved for the planet's future well-being. There are many examples of conservation. One is a programme to try to preserve wetlands, or a programme to try and save old buildings. Another example is of an attempt to minimise the amount of electricity used by turning off lights when leaving a room, or an attempt to turn off the running tap to avoid wastage of water. There are lots of examples like these which need implementation.
5. Following these small steps in our daily lives we can help to maintain the balance of nature, thereby saving humankind from the kinds of natural disasters we may face in the near future.
6. Nature also has a profound impact on our minds and our behaviour, helping reduce anxiety, brooding, and stress and increase our attention, capacity, creativity and ability to connect with other people. So there is a need to save nature if we want to save life as the two are interconnected and need each other. If we hurt or destroy the environment, surely we will be ruined. We must create awareness among family members, and try and practise a sustainable lifestyle to protect and conserve nature. **CBSE 2023**

Questions

Based on your understanding of the passage, answer the questions given below.

(i) Complete the sentence by choosing the correct option.
There is an urgent need to conserve our natural resources because ....
- (a) we are aimlessly using the natural resources and not replenishing them
- (b) they will be replaced by manmade resources
- (c) serious efforts are needed to cut down the consumption of these resources
- (d) we must become alert before it is too late

(ii) In the opinion of the writer, which are the primary natural resources without which our life is not possible?

(iii) In Paragraph 1, the writer talks about 'celebrating the progress'. Explain in context.

(iv) The writer would not agree with the given statements based on Paragraph 6, EXCEPT
- (a) Stress can be relieved by working overtime.
- (b) Nature can affect man's emotional well-being.
- (c) Lifestyle cannot be changed permanently.
- (d) Destruction of the environment is a temporary measure undertaken by man.

(v) In the context of the given passage, what is the synonym of 'replenish' in Paragraph 1? Choose the correct option.
(a) Scarcity (b) Restore (c) Reconcile (d) Minimise

(vi) List two ways in which forests and rivers help mankind.

(vii) How can the solutions suggested in Paragraph 4 be best described?
(a) Unrealistic (b) Short term
(c) Practical (d) Challenging

(viii) Why is it fair to say that population explosion remains one of the major reasons why natural resources are getting depleted rapidly?

(ix) Complete the given sentence with an appropriate reference with respect to the following.
The writer quotes the example of family awareness in order to .... (Paragraph 6)

(x) Select the most suitable title for the above passage.
(a) Ways to Save the Environment
(b) Save Nature Save Life
(c) Nature-A Pharmacy
(d) Nature-A Food Factory

Answers

(i) (a) we are aimlessly using the natural resources and not replenishing them.

(ii) According to the writer, the primary natural resources without which our life is not possible are water, air, soil and trees.

(iii) In paragraph 1, the writer talks about 'celebrating the progress' in the context of the World Nature Conservation Movement. This day provides an opportunity to celebrate the progress made in protecting natural resources and determine to take action wherever needed.

(iv) (a) Stress can be relieved by working overtime.

(v) (b) Restore

(vi) Two ways in which forests and rivers help mankind are
- They provide us with food, air and water that are necessary for our survival.
- They play a significant role in maintaining the balance of nature by absorbing carbon dioxide from the atmosphere, controlling floods and preventing soil erosion.

(vii) (c) Practical

(viii) It is fair to say that population explosion remains one of the major reasons why natural resources are getting depleted rapidly because an increasing population leads to higher demand for resources, which puts a strain on the environment and leads to their depletion.

(ix) create awareness among family members and try to practice a sustainable lifestyle to protect and conserve nature.

(x) (b) Save Nature Save Life

Passage 2 (Discursive)

1. In a room filled with people, each face illuminated by the soft glow of their smartphones, moments drift away like autumn leaves in the wind. The constant hum of notifications fills the air, punctuating conversations like an incessant drumbeat. Every vibration or ping sends fingers flying to screens, a response ingrained by years of digital conditioning. The once-reliable tick-tock of analog timepieces has been overshadowed by the constant flicker of notifications on the wrist watch, blurring the boundaries between the virtual and the real.

2. Anxiety gnaws at the edges of consciousness when the phone is out of reach, a phantom limb syndrome that leaves us feeling incomplete without our digital appendage. The fear of missing out permeates every moment spent away from the screen, driving us to constantly check for updates and notifications.

3. Thumbs move with the speed and precision of skillful pianists, tapping out messages and scrolling through feeds with practiced ease. Yet amidst the flurry of activity, the true rhythm of life remains unheard, drowned out by the dissonance of digital noise. The weight of constant connectivity forms a hunch upon our shoulders, a physical manifestation of the burden we carry in an age of information overload. Our minds are perpetually on high alert, scanning for the next wave of excitement that comes with each like, share, or comment.

4. And yet, for all our efforts to stay connected, we find ourselves increasingly isolated in a sea of digital faces. Genuine connections are fleeting, drowned out by the constant clamour for attention. In the pursuit of digital validation, we sacrifice the wealth of lived experience, trading meaningful moments for fleeting glimpses of connection. The true essence of life lies not in the pixels on a screen, but in the depth of human connection and the richness of shared experiences.

5. As we navigate this brave new world of constant connectivity, let us not forget the value of presence and the beauty of being fully engaged in the moments that matter most. For in the end, it is not the number of likes or followers that defines us, but the depth of our connections and the richness of our experiences that truly matter. **CBSE SQP 2024**

Questions

Based on your understanding of the passage, answer the questions given below.

(i) According to Paragraph 1, what effect do smartphone notifications have on the people in the room?

(ii) How does the author use the metaphor of 'autumn leaves in the wind' to interpret the passing of time in the setting? Described.

(iii) Read and complete the following sentence suitably.

The phrase 'a phantom limb syndrome that leaves us feeling incomplete without our digital appendage' suggests that just as an amputee might feel pain in a limb they no longer have, individuals can feel a sense of loss or incompleteness when they are separated from their digital devices.

Choose the correct response from the two options to complete the sentence. The concern this analogy points towards is about ....

(a) a deep (psychological) dependence on technology for a sense of wholeness or connection

(b) excessive physical damage that can be caused due to constant use of digital devices

(iv) Complete the following suitably with one advantage, with reference to Paragraph 2. Designating specific hours each day to intentionally avoid checking digital devices can help ....

(v) Why does the writer refer to digital noise as 'dissonance' in Paragraph 3?

(a) It creates a jarring and chaotic environment that disrupts focus.

(b) It contributes to a sense of overload, overwhelming the senses.

(c) It interferes with our ability to engage with meaningful aspects of our life.

(d) It induces stress by interrupting with regular updates about the device.

(vi) Provide one textual evidence with reference to Paragraph 3, to prove the following. The need to be perpetually engaged with digital notifications manifests in the body.

(vii) In the line, 'Yet amidst the flurry of activity, the true rhythm of life remains unheard…,' what does the phrase 'true rhythm of life' refer to? (Paragraphs 3 and 4)

(viii) Complete the analogy with one word from Paragraph 4.
Whisper : Quietly :: .... : Loudly

(a) Validation (b) Fleeting
(c) Essence (d) Clamour

(ix) Why is it fair to say that the statement 'And yet, for all our efforts to stay connected, we find ourselves increasingly isolated in a sea of digital faces' from Paragraph 4, employs irony?

(a) Despite the intent to connect more effectively, the result is the opposite.

(b) The writer mocks the seriousness with which people approach digital connectivity.

(c) The writer exaggerates the effects of digital connectivity to highlight its impact.

(d) Use of 'a sea of digital faces' to symbolically represent digital platforms.

(x) Assess the potential challenges or benefits of relying on survey outcomes for designing health interventions, as outlined in Paragraph 5.

Answers

(i) According to the passage, smartphone notifications lead to constant disturbances in between conversations.

(ii) The author uses the metaphor of 'autumn leaves in the wind' with respect to the passing of time to illustrate how moments, especially significant moments go unnoticed, due to technology and the distractions of digital interactions.

(iii) (a) a deep (psychological) dependence on technology for a sense of wholeness or connection

(iv) reduce the anxiety associated with the need to constantly be connected

(v) (c) It interferes with our ability to engage with meaningful aspects of our life.

(vi) The sentence from Paragraph 3 which proves the given statement is "The weight of constant connectivity forms a hunch upon our shoulders, a physical manifestation of the burden we carry in an age of information overload."

(vii) The 'true rhythm of life' refers to the genuine, meaningful and often quieter moments that make up human existence and relationships. These moments occur away from the digital chaos in simple life experiences, such as face-to-face conversations, quiet contemplation, enjoying nature and real-world interactions. According to the writer, these moments are overlooked or drowned out by the constant noise of digital activity.

(viii) (d) Clamour

(ix) (a) Despite the intent to connect more effectively, the result is the opposite.

(x) The benefits of relying on survey outcomes for designing health interventions are

- They can offer a detailed understanding of the specific needs and preferences of various demographic groups. This can help enhance the effectiveness of health interventions by making them more targeted and relevant.

- Using data-driven insights can foster a sense of collaboration among stakeholders, promoting a unified approach towards health and sustainability.

The challenges of relying on survey outcomes for designing health interventions are

- Relying on survey outcomes may present challenges such as the risk of biases in the data collection process, which can twist results and lead to ineffective interventions.
- There's also the issue of survey fatigue among participants, potentially reducing engagement and the accuracy of the data gathered.
- Further, translating survey findings into practical interventions requires resources and continuous stakeholder commitment, which might not always be feasible.

Passage 3 (Literary)

1. "Who doesn't know how to cook rice? Cooking rice hardly takes time." said my father. So, I challenged myself. I switched from news to YouTube and typed "How to cook rice?" I took one and a half cups of rice. Since I didn't have access to a rice cooker, I put the rice in a big pot. First, the rice has to be washed to get rid of dust and starch. I thought I won't be able to drain the rice and that it will fall out of the pot. I observed the chef as I swirled the rice around and used my dexterous hands to drain it, not once, not twice, but three times. I looked down at the sink and saw less than 50 grains that made their way out of the pot. Suffice to say, I was up to the mark.
2. The video stated that the key to perfect rice is equal amounts of rice and water. I have heard that professionals don't need to measure everything; they just know what the right amount is. But as this was my first time in the kitchen, I decided to experiment by not measuring the water needed for boiling the rice. I wanted the rice to be firm when bitten, just like pasta. I don't enjoy the texture of mushy rice. It has to have that chutzpah; it has to resist my biting power just for a bit before disintegrating.
3. After what seemed like 10 minutes, all the water disappeared. I went in to give it a good stir. To my surprise, some of the rice had got stuck to the pot. I tried to scrape it off but to no avail. At the same time, there was a burning smell coming from it. I quickly turned the stove off. "What have you done to the kitchen?" shouted Mother, while coming towards the kitchen. I managed to ward her off.
4. Finally, when the time came to taste my creation, I was surprised! It wasn't bad at all. The rice had the desired consistency. Sure, a little more salt would've been better, but I just added that while eating. The experience was fairly rewarding and memorable. It taught me a new sense of respect for those who cook food on a regular basis at home or engage in gourmet creations professionally.

Questions

Based on your understanding of the passage, answer the questions given below.

(i) State the author's reaction and thoughts while eating rice.

(ii) Mention the steps taken by the author to prepare the rice to be cooked.

(iii) Complete the sentence by choosing an appropriate option.

Father's question to the author, about knowing how to cook rice, was intended to ....

(a) criticise the author's lack of abilities
(b) make the process sound simple

(iv) Complete the sentence appropriately.

According to the passage, the fact that the author risked experimentation, on his/her maiden attempt in the kitchen, shows ....

(v) Select the option that conveys the opposite of 'dexterous'.

(a) Uncomfortable (b) Clumsy
(c) Unclear (d) Clueless

(vi) What does the author say about the professionals who cook?

(vii) Provide one textual evidence with reference to Paragraph 3, to prove the following.

The writer was not a regular cook but could become one with practice.

(viii) Complete the analogy with one word from Paragraph 4.

Literature : Critic : : Food : ....

(a) Respect (b) Cook
(c) Mushy (d) Gourmet

(ix) Which option represents the correct ratio of water to rice for cooking 'perfect rice'?

(a) 50% water, 50% rice
(b) 70% water, 30% rice
(c) 25% water, 75% rice
(d) 45% water, 55% rice

(x) Assess the usage of Chutzpah in the passage with reference to the author's cooking experiment.

Answers

(i) The author thought that the rice was surprisingly not bad and he/she wasn't a bad cook. He/She thought of the experience as fairly rewarding and memorable and that it taught him/her a new sense of respect for those who cook.

(ii) The steps taken by the author to prepare the rice to be cooked are
- Take the rice in a utensil
- Wash the rice using water
- Swirl the water in and around the rice
- Drain the water
- Repeat the process three times

(iii) (b) make the process sound simple

(iv) that he/she was experimental

(v) (b) Clumsy

(vi) The author says that cooking professionals don't need to measure everything and thus just know the right amount of everything while cooking.

(vii) The fact that while the rice that the writer was cooking had got stuck to the pot and there was a burning smell coming from it indicates that the writer was not a regular cook. However, even with the burnt rice, the writer seems to find it tasty. The rice has a good consistency and just lacked some salt.

(viii) (d) Gourmet

(ix) (a) 50% water, 50% rice

(x) The word 'chutzpah' literally means courage, boldness or guts. However, in the context of the passage, the writer uses the word to indicate the perfect texture and consistency of the rice. In other words, the rice needed to have a particular texture for it to be tasty enough for the writer.

Practice Questions

Read the following passages carefully and answer the questions that follow.

Factual Passages

Passage 1

1. In the heart of a bustling city, amidst the cacophony of traffic and the incessant buzz of urban life, there lies a sanctuary of tranquility — a sprawling public park that offers a respite from the daily grind. This park, with its verdant lawns and serene water features, attracts visitors from all walks of life, seeking solace and rejuvenation.
2. A public park is an area of open space owned and maintained by the local government, providing recreational opportunities for citizens. Public parks are places of leisure integrated into the community and are generally considered safe places. They provide essential environmental, aesthetic, and recreational benefits to our cities.
3. As the Sun rises, joggers and fitness enthusiasts can be seen navigating the winding paths, their faces set with determination. Meanwhile, yoga practitioners find their own quiet corners, their movements graceful and meditative. The air is filled with the chirping of birds and the rustling of leaves, creating a natural symphony that soothes the soul.
4. By midday, the park transforms into a lively gathering spot. Families spread out picnic blankets, sharing meals and laughter, while children chase each other across the grass, their joyous shouts echoing through the trees. Elderly couples sit on benches, reminiscing about days gone by as they watch the world go by.
5. As dusk approaches, the park takes on a magical quality. The setting sun casts a golden hue over the landscape, and the water features glisten in the fading light. Street performers and musicians add to the enchantment, drawing crowds with their captivating acts. The park, now aglow with lanterns, becomes a haven for stargazers and dreamers alike.
6. In this urban oasis, people find a connection with nature and one another, a reminder that amidst the chaos of modern life, moments of peace and tranquility are still within reach. Especially in cities, parks encourage native flora and fauna to thrive.

CBSE 2025

Questions

Based on your understanding of the passage, answer the questions given below.

(i) Why does the writer refer to the park as a 'sanctuary of tranquility' in Paragraph 1?

(ii) Why is it important for governments to set up public parks?

(iii) According to the passage, what activities can be observed in the park during the early morning hours?

(iv) Describe the transformation of the park by midday.

(v) Complete the following suitably.

The park at dusk is described as taking on a magical quality because of ....

(a) the setting Sun casting a golden hue and water features glistening
(b) the bustling activities of joggers and fitness enthusiasts
(c) the lively gathering of families and children playing
(d) the quiet solitude and meditation of yoga practitioners

(vi) Provide one textual evidence with reference to Paragraph 4 to prove the following.

Elderly couples feel a sense of nostalgia.

(vii) In the line "The park, now aglow with lanterns, becomes a haven for stargazers and dreamers alike," what does the phrase 'haven for stargazers and dreamers' refer to? (Paragraph 5)

(viii) Complete the analogy with one word from Paragraph 6.

urban life : chaos : : park : ....

(a) connection
(b) reminder
(c) tranquility
(d) oasis

(ix) Why is it fair to say that the statement "In this urban oasis, people find a connection with nature and one another" from Paragraph 6 is significant?

(a) It highlights the park's role in promoting physical activities.
(b) It emphasises the park's importance as a social and natural retreat.
(c) It mocks the idea of nature within a bustling city.
(d) It underplays the park's significance in modern life.

(x) Assess the potential benefits of an urban park.

Passage 2

1. I know many friends of mine who drink coffee regularly but do not know that coffee exists in different forms other than instant coffee. There are many who swear by Nescafe Classic or Bru Gold, which they consider premium coffee. I may sound offensive but instant coffee is not the only way; in fact it's a very bad way of making coffee! Instant coffee cannot match up to brewed coffee's flavour nor does it have Arabica beans. It uses Robusta beans that are lower in flavour. Don't know the difference?! Read on...

2. That plant might be a genius! It created a chemical that would keep pests away. Fortunately for us and unfortunately for the plant – that plan did not work the way it intended to. The chemical might have averted a few pest attacks, but attracted far greater threat – human beings. The plant I am talking about is coffee and chemical is caffeine.

3. To begin from the beginning – coffee is from a more mature part of the tree – the seed – unlike other stimulants. The ripe berry is picked and de-pulped leaving us with a seed called 'green bean' or 'green coffee'. Green bean is uncharacteristically bland with a taste nowhere close to that of coffee, but it is valued for its higher antioxidant levels.

4. It's an interesting phenomenon to see how this bland green bean turns to a flavourful coffee bean. Coffee bean is a seed and like any other seed is rich in proteins, fats and all necessary ingredients for giving birth to a new plant. When exposed to heat, the fats and carbohydrates in the bean turn into essential oils, which give the characteristic taste and aroma to the coffee bean. The degree of roasting depends on the need or purpose of use.

5. These beans are ground so that the surface area of the bean is increased, which makes extraction easier. The bean can be ground or crushed but making the particles uniform will ensure equal extraction, or else the smaller particle will get over extracted and the larger one under extracted. Hence, the burr grinder is used to ensure that the coffee bean gets ground in a uniform way in which all particles are of similar sizes.

6. Does under extraction give a lighter coffee and over extraction a stronger one? No, for a lighter or stronger coffee less or more coffee powder has to be used. Why? Under extraction will not get all the flavours of the coffee as the water runs too quickly. It will not get what you want – It will taste sour. Over-extraction will bring out all unnecessary flavours rendering the taste bitter. **CBSE 2023**

Questions

Based on your understanding of the passage, answer the questions given below.

(i) Complete the sentence by choosing an appropriate option.
The author complained that his friends ....
(a) consumed only Flora classics
(b) were not aware of different forms of coffee
(c) were severely addicted to drinking coffee
(d) considered Coco gold as premium coffee

(ii) Comment on the writer's reference to the unique feature of coffee plant. (Paragraph 2)

(iii) List the reason why the author refers to humans as 'great threat to coffee' plants.

(iv) Select an option that conveys the same meaning as 'energiser' from words used in Paragraph 3.
(a) Bland (b) Mature
(c) Antioxidant (d) Stimulants

(v) Complete the given sentence with an appropriate inference with respect to the following.
Fats and carbohydrates turn into essential oils leading to ....

(vi) Comment on the writer's reference to the interesting phenomenon in Paragraph 4.

(vii) Over-extraction does not give a stronger coffee. Based on your understanding of Paragraph 6, list one method to get stronger coffee.

(viii) The writer would not agree with the given statements based on Paragraph 5, EXCEPT
(a) The burr grinder grinds coffee beans uniformly.
(b) Less surface area makes extraction easier.
(c) Grinding gives stronger aroma.
(d) Good coffee is a mix of smaller and bigger particles.

(ix) Why is it fair to say that the right degree of extraction of coffee is important?

(x) Select the most suitable title of the above passage.
(a) The Art of Coffee Making
(b) Benefits of Consuming Coffee
(c) Green Coffee - The Perfect Antioxidant
(d) The Coffee Addict

Passage 3

1. In recent years, air pollution has emerged as one of the most pressing environmental and public health issues in India. Cities like Delhi, Mumbai and Bengaluru often record Air Quality Indices (AQI) that fall isto the hazardous' category, posing several health risks to their inhabitants. The thick blanket of smog that shrouds these urban areas is composed of harmful pollutants such as particulate material (PM 2-5 and PM 10), nitrogen dioxide (NO_2) and sulphur dioxide (SO_2). These pollutants originate from various sources including vehicular emissions, industrial activities and construction dust.

2. The constant emission of pollutants from vehicles, industrial activities and construction works exacerbate the problem. Residents of these cities are often seen wearing masks and using air purifiers in a desperate attempt to mitigate the effects of polluted air. The 'urban haze not only affects physical health but also impacts mental well-being. Studies indicate that prolonged exposure to high pollution levels can lead to respiratory issues, such as cardiovascular diseases and even cognitive decline.

3. Furthermore, children and the elderly are the most vulnerable groups. Children, with their developing respiratory systems, and the elderly, often with pre-existing health conditions face the brunt of this environmental crisis. Schools frequently shut down during peak pollution periods, disrupting education and daily life. The economic cost of air pollution is staggering, with increased healthcare expenses and lost labour productivity, Businesses also suffer as employees' health issues lead to increased absenteeism and decreased efficiency.

4. Government initiatives, such as the National Clean Air Programme (NCAP) aim at reducing air pollution levels across the country. However, these measures require robust implementation and public cooperation to be effective. Simple actions like reducing vehicle use, promoting public transportation and adopting cleaner technologies can significantly alleviate the situation. Additionally, the enforcement of stricter emission norms for industries and vehicles is crucial. Public awareness campaigns can play a pivotal role in encouraging others to adopt environmentally friendly practices.

5. The role of technology in combating air pollution is also noteworthy. Innovative solutions such as air quality monitoring systems, green buildings and electric vehicles are gaining attraction. These technologies not only help in reducing pollution but also promote sustainable development. Urban

planning that incorporates green spaces can also mitigate the effects of pollution by improving air quality and providing residents with a healthier living environment.

6. As we navigate this challenge, it is imperative to remember that the solution lies not just in policy changes but also in the behavioural shifts of individuals. Embracing a lifestyle that prioritises environmental health will pave the way for a cleaner, healthier India. Collective efforts and sustained commitments are crucial for ensuring breathable air for future generations. It is a shared responsibility that requires action from every segment of society from policy makers to ordinary citizens. **CBSE 2025**

Questions

Based on your understanding of the passage, answer the questions given below.

(i) According to Paragraph 1, what components make up the 'urban haze' that envelops Indian cities?

(ii) The writer refers to air pollution as a 'public health issue' in Paragraph 1 because
(a) it is a threat to the physical well-being of the people.
(b) it disrupts the daily activities of urban inhabitants.
(c) it leads to the closure of schools during peak pollution periods.
(d) it disrupts industrial activities and construction works.

(iii) Complete the analogy with one word from Paragraph 2.
blanket : cover : : extended : ....
(a) composed
(b) attempted
(c) declined
(d) prolonged

(iv) Complete the following sentence suitably Paragraph 2.
"The prolonged exposure to high pollution levels lends to cognitive decline' indicates that it impacts ....
(a) mental health (b) economic development
(c) respiratory functions (d) mobility

(v) Provide one textual evidence with reference to Paragraph 3, to prove the following:
"Children and the elderly are the most vulnerable groups affected by air pollution."

(vi) Complete the following suitably with one advantage with reference to Paragraph 4.
Implementing stricter emission norms for vehicles can help to ....

(vii) Assess the potential challenges and benefits of promoting public transportation as a solution to air pollution, as outlined in Paragraph 4.

(viii) What is the significance of urban planning in mitigating air pollution according to Paragraph 5?

(ix) How does technology help in resolving the problem of air pollution?

(x) Why does the author say that just the policy change is not the solution?

Passage 4

1. A World Bank Group report found that globally, women earn just 77 cents for every dollar paid to men. This difference has been cited in the past as an example of the 'gender pay gap' - women earning less than men on average. Different figures have also been given over the years across various reports, with some critics even disputing the existence of such a gap. The International Labour Organisation terms the gender pay gap as a 'measurable indicator' of inequality between women and men.

2. According to the ILO, the gender pay gap is defined as the gap between the average wage level of all women and all men working in the labour market for a monthly salary, hourly or daily wage. This gap is not the wage gap between a man and a woman with the same observable characteristics, doing the same work; it is the difference between the average wage levels of all working women and men. Therefore, it is distinct from the concept of 'equal pay for equal work'.

3. What explains this gender gap? First is the simple fact that women are not involved in paying jobs as much as men are, owing to notions about gender roles. The labour force participation rate gives an idea about this. It is the number of people looking for work or working already and above 15 years of age, divided by the total population. According to ILO, the current global labour force participation rate for women is just under 47%. For men, it is 72%. In India, as per the 2011 Census, the workforce participation rate for women is 25.51% against 53.26% for men.

4. The second factor is the type of jobs women are employed in, once they join the workforce. ILO's Women in Business and Management report found that "Far fewer women than men are in management and leadership positions, especially at higher levels. When women are managers, they tend to be more concentrated in management support functions such as human resources and financial administration than in more strategic roles. This brings down the average salary of female managers compared to that of male managers."
5. A 2013 survey from Georgetown University found that the top 10 most remunerative professions - mostly in engineering and computer science - were dominated by men, while the 10 least remunerative professions - in fields like arts and education - were dominated by women. Other institutional and socio-economic issues - the view that men should be breadwinners, lower investments in women's education, and issues of safety in commute and at the workplace - also play a significant role.
6. Useful patterns can be found when one looks at employment data based on age, when men and women take career breaks, and so on. For instance, when women reach their mid-30s and 40s, it is found that their earnings dip compared with men in the same position and profession. Some critics say that the 77 percent statistic hides another interesting piece of data, that women who do not get married earn 95 cents or even more for every dollar a man makes. This is what has been called the "motherhood penalty", meaning that women are unfairly published in terms of their career growth when they take breaks to have and care for children. The pace with which the gender gap is reducing has varied over time, as policies such as maternity and paternity leaves, flexibility in work, etc. have been introduced, helping workers.

Questions

Based on your understanding of the passage, answer the questions given below.

(i) What is the difference between 'gender pay gap' and 'equal pay for equal work'?

(ii) Why are women still suffering from the gender pay gap? What are some probable reasons?

(iii) Complete the sentence suitably.

The International Labour Organisation terms the gender pay gap as .... for inequality.

(a) measurable indicator

(b) equal pay for equal work

(iv) Complete the following sentence with an appropriate inference with respect to the following.

The average salary of female managers is less as compared to male managers as ....

(v) Select the option that conveys the meaning of the word 'concentrated' as used in Paragraph 4.

(a) Focused
(b) Threat
(c) Engaged
(d) Exposed

(vi) List two observations in the patterns of profession and employment which indicate that gender pay is a common issue.

(vii) Explain 'motherhood penalty' as used by the writer in Paragraph 6.

(viii) Unmarried women earn .... cents for every dollar a man makes.

(a) 77 (b) 95
(c) 75 (d) None of these

(ix) The writer would agree with the following statements based on Paragraph 4 and 5, EXCEPT

(a) Far fewer women than men are in management and leadership positions, especially at higher levels.
(b) The top 10 most remunerative professions, mostly in engineering and computer science, were dominated by women.
(c) Many institutional and socio-economic issues add to the gender pay gap.
(d) Women are active in administrative roles and not strategic ones which reduces their pay.

(x) What kind of policies are being introduced for reducing such a pay gap?

Passage 5

1. Ghost nets aren't supernatural but they are legitimately scary. A ghost net is a fishing net that's been lost or abandoned in the ocean. They are one particularly appalling part of the global ghost fishing problem, which includes fishing gear abandoned in the water. Any net or line left in the ocean can pose a threat to marine life. Just because a net is no longer used by fishers doesn't mean it stops working. These nets continue to trap everything in their path, presenting a major problem for the health of our oceans and marine life.
2. Ghost nets entangle sea turtles, dolphins and porpoises, birds, sharks, seals and more, apart from catching fish. The nets keep animals from moving freely, cause injuries and keep mammals and birds from rising to the surface for air. Since hundreds of animals can be caught in a single net, this threat is monumental. The ghost nets harm coral reefs too-breaking corals, exposing them to disease and even blocking the reefs from needed sunlight.
3. Ghost nets are also a major contributor to the ocean plastics' crisis. Most modern nets are made of nylon or other plastic compounds that can last for centuries. According to a 2018 study in Scientific Reports, ghost nets make up at least 46 percent of the Great Pacific Garbage Patch. Those abandoned fishing lines and nets that do breakdown never go away; they just become smaller pieces of plastic. Marine animals mistake this microplastic for food and eat it, which can harm internal organs, keep them from eating and expose them to toxic chemicals.
4. Exorcising ghost nets from our oceans will require commitment, cooperation and innovation. Many groups are working to remove ghost nets from the sea and are collaborating with local fishers and governments around the world to identify target areas and remove as many nets as possible. In 2015, a single World Wildlife Fund for Nature (WWF)-led mission in the Baltic Sea hauled up 268 tons of nets, ropes and other material.
5. To stop these nets from becoming ghosts in the first place, conservation organisations advocate for fishing gear that can be traced to its owner so anyone dumping nets can be fined and for refundable deposits on nets to encourage returning or recycling rather than littering. Tools like sonar reflectors that can make ghost nets easier to find and working with small-scale fisheries to develop more sustainable fishing gear and practices are other suggestions. It is only by attacking this problem from all sides, together with conservation partners, fishers and supporters, than we can banish ghost nets and protect our oceans.

Questions

Based on your understanding of the passage, answer the questions given below.

(i) How are ghost nets a major environmental concern?

(ii) Why is it fair to say that commitment and innovation have to go hand-in-hand to rid the oceans of ghost nets?

(iii) Complete the sentence suitably.

Ghost nets have been named so because they ....

(a) are not owned by anyone

(b) act as a snare for all animals in oceans

(iv) Complete the given sentence with an appropriate inference with respect to the following.

The writer quotes the example of the WWF-led mission in the Baltic Sea Paragraph 4, in order to ....

(v) Select the option that conveys the opposite of 'negligible' from words used in Paragraph 2.

(a) Unimpressive

(b) Monumental

(c) Exposing

(d) Threat

(vi) List the two ways being entangled in a ghost net is likely to impact a walrus.

(vii) Comment on the writer's reference to the ghost nets in Paragraph 1 as a health problem for the oceans.

(viii) How can the solutions, suggested in Paragraph 5, best be described?

(a) Practical (b) Presentable

(c) Popular (d) Prejudiced

(ix) The writer would agree with the given statements based on Paragraph 3, EXCEPT

(a) Most ghost nets take a few years to completely disintegrate.

(b) Ghost nets contribute to the Great Pacific Garbage Patch.

(c) Most ghost nets provide nutrition to marine animals, upon disintegration.

(d) Ghost nets can curtail freedom of marine animals.

(x) Some records share that fishing nets used to be made of common rope using natural fibres, prior to the 1960s. Based on your understanding of Paragraph 3, list one major advantage that these had over the fishing nets being used in present times.

Discursive Passages

Passage 6

1. Marketing is all about creativity and expression, so it must be an art, right? Not necessarily. While marketers once relied purely on instinct, they now rely on data-driven insights. On top of that, cutting-edge technologies and analytics have shifted the focus of marketing farther toward the science side of the spectrum. Armed with so much data, marketers can now track the impact of money spent on their bottom line.
2. In today's world, the best approach to marketing combines both disciplines. And there's a distinct balance to the craft- a strategic mix of interpersonal empathy and tactical analysis. Neither side of the mix can be isolated or ignored, or the results will not be encouraging. Psychologists believe the brain is separated into two distinct functions– the left-brain and the right-brain. The right side of the brain is responsible for creative thinking and artistic intuition.
3. As an art, marketing is all about understanding the nuances of human behaviour and determining how to make an emotional connection with the customer. More importantly, some level of art is needed to create brand standards for your company, including the logo, messaging, and overall visual identity for a brand.
4. Right-brained marketers focus on the creative the copy, graphics and emotions tied to the message. The science side of marketing tells us to let the data guide what strategies will be most effective. Marketers are now reporting the need for digital-first expertise including digital proficiency, data analysis, and data science. With science, marketers adopt an outcome-centric mindset that helps them curate smarter campaigns. Over the past few years, there has been an evolving prioritisation on data-savvy talent. In 2020 and beyond, brands will need to focus on recruiting talent that can understand the complexities of Al and machine technologies.
5. But when we reflect on earlier times, marketing was defined as the predominance of traditional advertising, like television, newspaper, and direct mail. Today, it ropes in digital channels, social media, mobile devices, and integrated, complex campaigns. And just as consumers today are more tech-savvy, employees should be able to match-and -exceed their expertise. It's important that brands continue to prioritise creative, engaging campaign messages while also focusing on key insights and performance metrics for optimal results. **CBSE 2025**

Questions

Based on your understanding of the passage, answer the questions given below.

(i) According to paragraph 1, how does the author describe the evolution of marketing?

(ii) Choose one of the following statements that aptly reflects the point of view of the writer.
(a) In the field of marketing, there is a conflict between Art and Science.
(b) Art and Science should work in tandem to do effective marketing.

(iii) Provide one textual evidence with reference to Paragraph 3 to support that marketing is an art.

(iv) Based on the passage, assess the way data and digital platforms have transformed the field of marketing and employment.

(v) .... cutting-edge technologies and analytics have shifted the focus of marketing. (Paragraph 1)
By 'cutting-edge technologies', the writer refers to ....

(vi) Complete the analogy with one word from Paragraph 2.
included : incorporated :: .... : secluded
(a) approach (b) empathy
(c) isolated (d) intuition

(vii) 'Marketing is all about understanding the nuances of human behaviour. (Paragraph 3)
The writer uses the word 'nuances' to denote
(a) man's appreciation for art.
(b) man's preference for branded clothes.
(c) the complexities of human character.
(d) human inclination for analytical approach.

(viii) Complete the following based on your understanding of the above passage.
According to the writer, modern marketing is built on both .... and ....

(ix) '.............. exceed their expertise'. (Paragraph 5)
With reference to Paragraph 5, what skills do you think the employees should possess to match the demand of the consumers?

(x) What fascinating fart about the human brain is revealed by the writer in the above passage?

Passage 7

1. Five enterprises received approval and grants for prototype development of sustainable educational toys.
2. The government authorities, educational institutions and EdTech start-ups are planning to introduce state-of-the-art, made-in-India educational toys that not only throw light on Indian values and civilisations, but also help in developing children's critical thinking and decision-making skills.
3. One such enterprise is working on different types of projects that can teach children how electromagnets and magnetic fields work. These projects can resolve a lot of issues in many schools in tier two and three cities that don't have proper infrastructure. Another is working on an excavation site to teach children about ancient Indian civilisations. It has implanted a few artifacts at the site, which the children will have to find so that they are able to learn how to preserve and label artifacts. Another start up has proposed to create miniaturised labs for schools in tier 2 and 3 cities where children can learn concepts of Physics. "We will ensure that these prototypes are developed within a year and then the production can be scaled up," says the senior manager of the project talking about the importance of indigenously-built educational toys.
4. Playtime is vital for the cognitive development of children and toys are an essential component that helps enhance specific cognitive abilities and skill sets. "Well-designed toys ignite student's curiosity, increase focus and can be very beneficial in helping them master a skill and enhance understanding. These can be in the form of visuals, auditory aids, kinesthetic, or a mixture of all three." says HOD, Early Childhood Education.
5. Toys offer an engaging avenue to teach mathematical, verbal, problem-solving skills. "Toys that engage students in experiential learning enhance their special awareness and fine motor skills. Those designed for two or more players help students develop better social skills as they learn to negotiate, settle differences, etc. with their peers."
6. Experiential gadgets and toys enable students to learn faster and retain lessons longer. A child's interest is piqued when he is taught in a contextual framework as opposed to rote learning. The Indian education system has been witnessing several innovations with the development of toys and gadgets that can be used and felt in person or through VR platforms across subjects, be it Science, Technology, Math or Engineering. **CBSE 2024**

Questions

Based on your understanding of the passage, answer the questions given below.

(i) By tier 2 and tier 3 cities, the author refers to
(a) metro cities (b) cities with huge population
(c) underdeveloped cities (d) cities with less population

(ii) Complete the sentence with evidence from the text.
The made-in-India educational toys serves dual purpose of ....

(iii) The author's point of view that can be inferred from the above passage is that ....
(a) educational toys are the booming business
(b) educational toys are meant to entertain children
(c) educational toys will replace teachers
(d) educational toys will make education more pragmatic

(iv) Complete the following sentence appropriately.
Educational toys enhance the personality of children by ....

(v) Read the five headlines (i) - (v), given below.
(i) Sustainable Educational Toys are Developmentally Appropriate.
(ii) Sustainable Educational Toys - Promote Free play.
(iii) Sustainable Educational Toys - Free and Widespread.
(iv) Sustainable Educational Toys - Experiential Learning.
(v) Sustainable Educational Toys - Hinder Interaction with people.

Identify the option that displays the headline that does/do not correspond with what the passage highlights.
(a) Only (v) (b) (i) and (ii)
(c) (iii) and (v) (d) Only (iv)

(vi) What evidences do you gather from the passage to state that educational system is revolutionised by educational toys? Answer in about 40 words.

(vii) Explain in about 40 words, how education at grassroot level is benefitted by these projects.

(viii) As opposed to learning by heart, experiential toys
(a) ignite interest (b) challenge the teachers
(c) replace textbooks (d) confuse learners

(ix) Playing is usually considered a distraction. Is it justified on the part of the narrator to assert that playing is an important aspect of education? Write your answer in about 40 words.

Passage 8

1. As a young adult, life can be stressful and overwhelming at times. Juggling among school, work social life and other responsibilities, it can be easy to feel alone and disconnected from the world around us. Dogs are the ultimate companions for anyone looking to alleviate stress and loneliness. We'll explore many reasons why dogs make the best companions for young adults.
2. **Unconditional love** Dogs are known for their loyalty and love for their owners, no matter what. They don't judge us, criticise us, or hold grudges against us. No matter how flawed or imperfect we may be, our dogs will always love us unconditionally. This kind of unwavering support and affection can be incredibly comforting for young adults struggling to find their place in the world.
3. **Social connection** Dogs are great ice-breakers and conversation starters. Whether you're walking them in the park, taking them to the dog beach, or simply hanging out at home, dogs have a way of bringing people together. For young adults who may feel isolated or disconnected from their peers, having a dog by their side can be a great way to connect with others and form new friendships.
4. **Increase physical activity** Dogs require regular exercise in order to stay healthy and happy. This means that young adults who own dogs are more likely to engage in physical activity themselves. Whether its going for run playing frisbee, or simply taking a leisurely stroll, getting out with your dog can be a great way to boost your mood and energy levels.
5. **Emotional support** Dogs are also great emotional support animals for those struggling with mental health issues such as anxiety and depression. Their presence alone can provide a sense of calm and comfort and their ability to sense their owner's emotions can be incredibly comforting. For young adults dealing with mental health challenges, having a dog as a companion can be a life-changing experience.
6. **Improve responsibility and self-care** Owning a dog also comes with a great deal of responsibility and self-care. Dogs require regular feeding, grooming exercise and attention which can be a great way for young adults to develop a sense of responsibility and self-discipline. Additionally, having a dog as a companion can encourage young adults to take better care of themselves, such as making sure they get enough sleep, eat healthy and engage in regular exercise.
7. For all these reasons and more, dogs make fantastic companions for young adults. Whether you're looking for emotional support, social connection, increasing physical activity, or simply someone to love and be loved by, a dog can provide all these things and more. So, the next time you're feeling stressed or overwhelmed, consider finding a furry friend to take on the world with you. **CBSE 2024**

Questions

Based on your understanding of the passage, answer the questions given below.

(i) What is the significance of owning a dog for a young adult who is striving for acceptance in society?
(a) It means increased physical activity
(b) It builds a sense of responsibility
(c) It helps young adults get more sleep
(d) It is a source of unconditional love

(ii) Complete the given sentence appropriately, in about 40 words, with a characteristic or description.

A dog can encourage its owner to lead a healthier life by ....

(iii) Share evidence from the text, in approximately 40 words to support the view that dogs provide a sense of calm and comfort to those struggling with mental health issues.

(iv) Explain in about 40 words the statement that 'dogs are great ice-breakers'.

(v) Which of the following activities help(s) young adults, owning a dog build their sense of responsibility and self-discipline?
(a) Walking the dog daily
(b) Feeling it regularly
(c) Engaging the services of a dog trainer
(d) Both (a) and (b)

(vi) What does this article aim to do?
(a) Explain the benefits of owning a dog.
(b) Provide advice on how to get a dog.
(c) Discuss how to take proper care of a dog.
(d) Describe the experiences of dog owners.

(vii) Select the option that is similar in meaning to the phrase 'take on the world'.
(a) Travel the world
(b) Accept a responsibility
(c) To be pessimistic
(d) Have a global outlook

(viii) What does the underlined part in the sentence "consider finding a furry friend take on the world with you" refer to?

(ix) What is the tone of the article?
(a) Critical but supportive (b) Indifferent and bored
(c) Positive and informative (d) Humorous and casual

Passage 9

1. Very often, we do not take the first step towards a good cause because we say to ourselves, "The task is so big. What can I do alone?" So nothing gets done. There is much talk about environmental protection, air pollution and saving our forests. Do we really care? If we do, here are a few things we can do to make our surroundings more pleasant.
2. It is good to adopt a two-uses-attitude! By putting an article to a second use, we are giving it a longer lease of life and using up less raw material from nature. One of the worst things we do is the abuse of paper. The clean sides of envelopes can be used to write small notes, lists and reminders around the house. The more paper we use, the more trees will have to be cut down. For the same reason, we should avoid the use of paper napkins or paper plates. Cloth napkins are just as good, for they can be washed and used over and over again.
3. Another area which needs the most urgent attention is effective garbage disposal. People who are conscious about it follow rules and laws strictly. As a result, their neighbourhoods are clean and beautiful. Similarly, each one of us can contribute to a cleaner environment. All kitchen waste should be collected separately. Those of you who have green fingers can turn this into valuable manure. Dig a pit and put the kitchen waste into it. When the pit is a little over half full, cover it up with mud. Let nature do the rest. Within three or six months, we will have a good garden manure. It can also be done as a community project by digging a large pit in the colony). Do take help of all the members, for nothing succeeds like co-operation.
4. A lot of people don't care about the environment because they don't understand the adverse effect that society has on it. It is important to convince people to care about the environment. The first step would be to convince people to change by providing simple alternative solutions and ways of doing things. The internet is a powerful tool and a group on social media of like-minded people can be formed. People can share environmental stories and issues, as well as pool in solutions and alternatives to educate one another.

With the current state that our planet is in, it is imperative that people actively care about the environment and most importantly to act now.

CBSE 2022 Term II

Questions

Based on your understanding of the passage, answer the questions given below.

(i) Complete the sentence by choosing the correct option.
According to the author, nothing gets done because ....
(a) we do not want to do any task
(b) we do not take the first step towards the task
(c) we feel that our actions are small
(d) we do not have time for many things

(ii) Comment on the writer's statement that 'we do not take the first step towards a good cause'.

(iii) What can we do to avoid the abuse of paper? (any two points)

(iv) Select the option that conveys the opposite of 'beneficial', from the words used in Paragraph 4.
(a) Adverse (b) Alternative
(c) Imperative (d) Issue

(v) The writer would agree with the following statements, EXCEPT
(a) Awareness is the key towards change.
(b) We need to follow the 3R's- Reuse, Reduce and Recycle.
(c) Paper use needs to be significantly reduced.
(d) Individual actions triumphs community actions.

(vi) What procedure can one adopt for kitchen waste? How long does it take to make good garden manure?

(vii) How can making of garden manure be done as community project?

(viii) Complete the given sentence appropriately.
An effective garbage disposal ensures ....

(ix) Select the option that states the purpose of the passage.
(a) To warn (b) To suggest
(c) To motivate (d) To give information

(x) Which of the following will be the most appropriate title for the passage.
(a) Change Starts with 'I'
(b) Need for Environment Conservations
(c) How to Bring Environmental Awareness
(d) Becoming Environment Conscious

(xi) Select the option that defines the two-uses-attitude.
(a) Finding a multipurpose product
(b) Using a product only two times
(c) Finding two different usages of a product
(d) Reselling a product for further use

(xii) List the ways in which the internet can be used towards the cause of the environment.

Passage 10

1. Too many parents these days can't say no. As a result, they find themselves raising 'children' who respond greedily to the advertisements aimed right at them. Even getting what they want doesn't satisfy some kids; they only want more. Now, a growing number of psychologists, educators and parents think it's time to stop the madness and start teaching kids about what's really important: values like hard work, contentment, honesty and compassion. The struggle to set limits has never been tougher—and the stakes have never been higher. One recent study of adults who were overindulged as children, paints a discouraging picture of their future: when given too much too soon, they grow up to be adults who have difficulty coping with life's disappointments. They also have distorted sense of entitlement that gets in the way of success in the work place and in relationships.

2. Psychologists say that parents who overindulge their kids, set them up to be more vulnerable to future anxiety and depression. Today's parents themselves raised on values of thrift and self-sacrifice, grew up in a culture where 'no' was a household word. Today's kids want much more, partly because there is so much more to want. The oldest members of this generation were born in the late 1980s, just as PCs and video games were making their assault on the family room. They think of MP3 players and flat screen TV as essential utilities, and they have developed strategies to get them. One survey of teenagers found that when they crave for something new, most expect to ask nine times before their parents give in. By every measure, parents are shelling out record amounts. In the heat of this buying blitz, even parents who desperately need to say no find themselves reaching for their credit cards.

3. What parents need to find, is a balance between the advantages of an affluent society and the critical life lessons that come from waiting, saving and working hard to achieve goals. That search for balance has to start early. Children need limits on their behaviour because they feel better and more secure when they live within a secured structure.

4. Older children learn self-control by watching how others, especially parents act. Learning how to overcome challenges is essential to becoming a successful adult. Few parents ask kids to do chores. They think their kids are already overburdened by social and academic pressures. Every individual can be of service to others, and life has meaning beyond one's own immediate happiness. That means parents eager to teach values have to take a long, hard look at their own.

Questions

Based on your understanding of the passage, answer the questions given below.

(i) What is the balance which the parents need to have in today's world?

(ii) How do older children learn self-control?

(iii) Complete the sentence suitably.
Children who are overindulged by their parents come out to be ....
(a) unhealthy, psychotic and short tempered
(b) vulnerable, anxious and depressed

(iv) Complete the given sentence appropriately.
Today's children want much more because ....

(v) Select the option that conveys the meaning of 'wealthy', from the words used in Paragraph 3.
(a) Critical (b) Affluent
(c) Secure (d) Saving

(vi) What do the psychologists, educators and parents want to teach the children?

(vii) What are the results of giving the children too much too soon?

(viii) What is essential to become a successful adult?
(a) Values of honesty, hardwork and security
(b) Learning how to overcome challenges
(c) Learning to be satisfied with what they have
(d) Practical skills and worldly knowledge

(ix) Complete the sentence by choosing the correct option.
Why do parents not ask their children to do chores because ....
(a) they feel that they should not burdened the children
(b) they do not want their children to work
(c) they do not want their children to resent them
(d) they feel that their children are already over-burdened

(x) How are the children of the present times different from their parents?

Literary Passages

Passage 11

1. I got posted in Srinagar in the 1980s. Its rugged mountains, gushing rivers and vast meadows reminded me of the landscapes of my native place – the Jibhi Valley in Himachal Pradesh. Unlike Srinagar that saw numerous tourists, Jibhi Valley remained clouded in anonymity. That's when the seed of starting tourism in Jibhi was planted. I decided to leave my service in the Indian Army and follow the urge to return home.

2. We had two houses – a family house and a traditional house, which we often rented out. I pleaded with my father to ask the tenant to vacate the house so that I could convert it into a guesthouse. When my family finally relented, I renovated the house keeping its originality intact, just adding windows for sunlight.

3. I still remember the summer of 1992 when I put a signboard outside my first guesthouse in Jibhi Valley! The village residents, however, were sceptical about my success. My business kept growing but it took years for tourism to take off in Jibhi Valley. Things changed significantly after 2008 when the government launched a homestay scheme. People built homestays and with rapid tourism growth, the region also changed rapidly. Villages turned into towns with many concrete buildings. Local businesses and tourists continued putting a burden on nature.

4. Then, with the 2020-21 pandemic and lockdown, tourism came to a complete standstill in Jibhi Valley. Local people, who were employed at over a hundred homestays and guesthouses, returned to their villages. Some went back to farming, some took up pottery and some got involved in government work schemes. Now, all ardently hope that normalcy and tourism will return to the valley soon. In a way, the pandemic has given us an opportunity to introspect, go back to our roots and look for sustainable solutions.

5. For me, tourism has been my greatest teacher. It brought people from many countries and all states of India to my guesthouse. It gave me exposure to different cultures and countless opportunities to learn new things. Most people who stayed at my guesthouse became my repeat clients and good friends. When I look back, I feel proud, yet humbled at the thought that I was not only able to fulfill my dream despite all the challenges, but also to play a role in establishing tourism in the beautiful valley that I call home.

Questions

Based on your understanding of the passage, answer the questions given below.

(i) Give a reason for the skepticism faced by the author from the village people?

(ii) Why did the narrator leave the Indian Army?

(iii) A collocation is a group of words that often occur together.
The writer says that Jibhi valley remained clouded in anonymity.
The word that collocates with 'clouded in' is ....
(a) disgust (b) doubt

(iv) Complete the sentence appropriately.
The writer's initial thought of Srinagar and its scenic beauty fills him with ....

(v) Why did tourism become stagnant in the Jibhi Valley?
(a) The valley had no attractions.
(b) The 2020-21 pandemic and the eventual lockdown.
(c) The writer had no idea of what needed to be done.
(d) Everyone there wanted to go back to their day job.

(vi) What does the author feel at the end of the passage?

(vii) The writer mentions looking for sustainable solutions. Why does he refer to the need for sustainable solutions.

(viii) Complete the analogy with one word from Paragraph 2.
Faux : Artificial : : Genuine : ....
(a) Relented (b) Intact (c) Originality (d) Tenant

(ix) Which quote summarises the writer's feelings about the peace of growth of tourism in Jibhi Valley?
(a) We kill all the caterpillars, then complain there are no butterflies. – John Marsden
(b) Nature will give you the best example of life lessons, just open your eyes and see. – Kate Smith
(c) We do not see nature with our eyes, but with our understanding and our hearts. – William Hazlett
(d) I'd rather be in the mountains thinking of God than in church thinking of the mountains. – John Muir

(x) Write a customer review for the writer's project.

Passage 12

1. The postmaster's office was located in the village of Ulapur. He was a young man from Calcutta. Stationed here, away from the known limits of civilisation, he often felt like a fish out of water. The plantation workers nearby seemed to have their own community. Social miscegenation between two different classes of people seemed all but impossible.

2. In truth, the boy from the city wasn't good at mixing with people. Uprooted and exiled to a foreign land, his feelings oscillated between arrogance and shame. He rarely met any of the villagers. At times, he tried writing. He wrote poems: poems in which the marrow of life seemed to resonate with the faint tremble of young leaves, where the memory of existence was rejuvenated by the sight of rain clouds-and yet, in his heart of hearts, he knew that the only way he'd welcome the sight of a new life would be if some fantastical djinn from the Arabian Nights arrived at night, unawares, and secretly swept away this maze of maddening vegetation. He longed for the security of metalled roads, of tall houses which blocked the sight of clouds in the open sky. The city was spreading its tentacles, calling him back.

3. The postmaster's salary was meagre. He had to cook his own meals and his housework was under the care of an orphan girl called Ratan. Ratan was thirteen years old and called him dadababu. Her marital prospects seemed bleak. Evenings would arrive with plumes of smoke rising from the cowshed. The postmaster would light his lamp. The flame would sputter as he'd call out, 'Ratan?' Ratan would be waiting for this call. But on its arrival, she'd rush into the room, feigning surprise. "You called, dadababu?" "Are you busy?" "Well, I need to go and make the fire ..." "You can afford to do that later, can't you? Do be a dear and dress my tobacco.."

4. Ratan would enter with the coal-filled hookah, blowing on it feverishly. The postmaster would snatch it from her hands and ask, quite suddenly, "Ratan, do you remember your mother?" Memories would flow back in. Her father, she remembered, loved her more than her mother. She remembered his smile clearly, the smile he'd carry home when he returned every evening. His face would return to her like a revenant, and the little girl, still lost in thought, would proceed to sit on the floor by the postmaster's feet. Looking at the young man, she'd remember how she had a brother once. She'd remember the past like it was only yesterday; how they'd played by that old pond, using a branch as a fishing pole! She'd find herself remembering bits of insignificant things. The larger tragedies of life were murky.

5. There were days of magnetic nostalgia-sitting on the wooden plank by the hut, the postmaster would find himself remembering his own history-as he'd think of his little brother, his sister, of everyone he'd left behind. He was infinite and infinitesimal, engulfed by a gaping emptiness-if only, if only he had someone to share this with! And just like that, all of nature was echoing his abyssal vacancy. My heart is in free fall. Won't anyone catch it?

6. One afternoon during monsoons, Ratan walked into the postmaster's room and found him lying on his cot under a pile of blankets and was running a fever. Something was happening to Ratan. The pale fire of steady resolution crackled under her skin. In the force of an instant, she assumed the authority of a mother. Rushing out of the hut, she called the local doctor, stayed awake for the entirety of the night, crushing herbs and feeding them to her patient, punctuating the stillness of this frightening night with the words, "Are you feeling better, dadababu?"

7. It took the postmaster weeks to recover from his illness. When he had completely recuperated, he thought to himself, "Enough is enough!" He had to get out of here. He had to. He immediately wrote a letter to his superiors in Calcutta asking for a transfer on medical grounds. Her duties relieved, Ratan spent her days outside his room, book in hand, waiting for that old call. But the call never arrived. Finally, after weeks of waiting, Ratan was called in one evening. Nursing secret excitement and tender trepidation, she walked into the room.

"Dadababu, you called?" 'Ratan,' he began, "I'm leaving tomorrow." "Where are you going, dadababu?" "I'm going home." "When will you come back?" The postmaster pursed his lips. "I don't think I will." Ratan stood still for a while. Words seemed to be losing their way in the labyrinth of her silence. "Dadababu, will you take me with you?" The young man stared at the girl and then laughed. "That's ridiculous!" Shaken, she burst into tears. "Listen, Ratan. I never thanked you for everything you did. Now that I'm leaving, I want to give you something. Keep this. It'll make your ends meet for some time at least." The postmaster handed her a pouch. Peering inside, Ratan found that it contained all of her master's earnings. Stunned, the little girl fell onto the floor, clutching the postmaster's feet. 'Dadababu!' she stuttered, "I b-beg of you! You don't have to give me anything! Please! Please! I don't want your kindness! No one-no one has to take charge of me!" And she ran out, vanishing into the mist enveloping the hut.

8. Sighing, the postmaster picked up his bags, and walked to the riverbank where a boat was waiting for him. When the boat finally slid into the current, it was then that the postmaster felt the sudden weight of crushing grief that his heart was gravitating with. "I should turn back," he thought to himself. "Let me take her with me; she, who has always been neglected. She, who has never been welcomed." But by then, the wind had begun pushing the sails. The lukewarm heart of the voyager consoled itself with eternal philosophy: 'life was a river of partings and departings, of death and uprooting, of longing and belonging. What was the use of looking back? Who belonged to whom in this world?' But Ratan's little heart harboured no such philosophy. She had been circling the old hut cradled in the river of her own tears. Perhaps she nursed a tender hope that her dadababu would return one day. Anchored by its roots, she refused to move away from the debris of her own heartbreak.

- 'The Postmaster by Rabindranath Tagore'
- translated from the Bengali by Utsa Bose

Questions

Based on your understanding of the passage, answer the questions given below.

(i) What does the postmaster mean when he thinks, "Who belonged to whom in this world?"

(ii) What does the image of the "faint tremble of young leaves" symbolise in the excerpt? Explain in brief.

(iii) Complete the sentence appropriately.
Ratan could not reconcile herself to the postmaster's 'eternal philosophy' and therefore chose to ....

(iv) Complete the following sentence with an appropriate inference with respect to the following.
The postmaster often felt like a 'fish without water' in Ulapur because ....

(v) What literary device is used in the phrase "life was a river of partings and departings"?
(a) Metaphor
(b) Simile
(c) Hyperbole
(d) Personification

(vi) What all would Ratan recall while conversing with the postmaster?

(vii) And just like that, all of nature was echoing his abyssal vacancy." What does this tell about the mental condition of the postmaster? Answer in about 40 words.

(viii) What does the river symbolise in the final Paragraph?
(a) The postmaster's journey to a new life
(b) Ratan's grief and isolation
(c) The passage of time
(d) The inevitability of change

(ix) The postmaster's decision to leave reveal about his character shows that he is ....
(a) determined and resolute
(b) indifferent and uncaring
(c) hopeful and optimistic
(d) weak and indecisive

(x) In the last Paragraph, the author uses a phrase "debris of her own heartbreak", what do you think this means in the context of the passage. Explain your answer.

Passage 13

An Excerpt from 'A Piece of Chalk'

1. I remember one splendid morning, all blue and silver, in the summer holidays when I reluctantly tore myself away from the task of doing nothing in particular and put on a hat of some sort and picked up a walking-stick and put six very bright-coloured chalks in my pocket. I then went into the kitchen (which, along with the rest of the house, belonged to a very square and sensible old woman in a Sussex village), and asked the owner and occupant of the kitchen if she had any brown paper. She had a great deal; in fact, she had too much; and she mistook the purpose and the rationale of the existence of brown paper. She seemed to have an idea that if a person wanted brown paper he must be wanting to tie up parcels; which was the last thing I wanted to do; indeed, it is a thing which I have found to be beyond my mental capacity.

   Hence, she dwelt very much on the varying qualities of toughness and endurance in the material. I explained to her that I only wanted to draw pictures on it, and that I did not want them to endure in the least; and that from my point of view, therefore, it was a question, not of tough consistency, but of responsive surface, a thing comparatively irrelevant in a parcel. When she understood that I wanted to draw she offered to overwhelm me with note-paper, apparently supposing that I did my notes and correspondence on old brown paper wrappers from motives of economy.

2. I then tried to explain the rather delicate logical shade, that I not only liked brown paper, but liked the quality of brownness in paper, just as I liked the quality of brownness in October woods, or in beer, or in the peat-streams of the North. Brown paper represents the primal twilight of the first toil of creation, and with a bright-coloured chalk or two you can pick out points of fire in it, sparks of gold, and blood-red, and sea-green, like the first fierce stars that sprang out of divine darkness. All this I said (in an off-hand way) to the old woman; and I put the brown paper in my pocket along with the chalks and possibly other things. I suppose every one must have reflected how primeval and how poetical are the things that one carries in one's pocket; the pocketknife, for instance, the type of all human tools, the infant of the sword. Once I planned to write a book of poems entirely about the things in my pockets. But I found it would be too long; and the age of the great epics is past.

***Source** (edited): 'A Piece of Chalk', Tremendous Trifles, G. K. Chesterton*

Questions

Based on your understanding of the passage, answer the questions given below.

(i) Why did the narrator want to write poems about things in his pocket?

(ii) Why did the narrator prefer brown paper to note-paper for drawing pictures?

(iii) Read and complete the sentence appropriately.

The writer says "I remember one splendid morning, all blue and silver, in the summer holidays when I reluctantly tore myself away from the task of doing nothing in particular…"

From this we can conclude that the narrator ……… .

(a) enjoyed his time being idle
(b) suffered from a vision impairment

(iv) In accordance with the narrator's view, complete the sentence below by adding an appropriate comparison.

…but liked the quality of brownness in paper, just as I liked the quality of brownness in October woods, or in beer, or in the peat-streams of the North, or in ………………… .

(v) Which of the reader's senses does the author primarily appeal to in the first two sentences of Paragraph 2?

(a) Sight (b) Touch
(c) Smell (d) Sound

(vi) In 20-30 words, state any one trait of the narrator and justify it with an example.

(vii) Based on the passage, how can the description of the woman as 'square and sensible' be justified?

(viii) I did not want them to endure in the least; and that from my point of view, therefore, it was a question, not of tough consistency, but of responsive surface... (Paragraph 1)

What does 'them' refer to in the statement above?

(a) Parcels (b) Pictures

(c) Note-paper (d) Brown paper

(ix) Which of these best describes the narrator of the passage?

(a) Argumentative (b) Elaborate

(c) Objective (d) Ignorant

(x) Whom does the narrator compare an artist to in the statement below? Explain your answer.

...and with a bright-coloured chalk or two you can pick out points of fire in it, sparks of gold, and blood-red, and sea-green, like the first fierce stars that sprang out of divine darkness. (Paragraph 2)

Passage 14

1. The afternoon was warm and the prospect of a dull, prolonged vigil in the beer garden had made me feel vaguely uneasy and almost sad. I felt that Tom would drift on forever seeking a little wistfully for the dramatic turbulence of some irrecoverable football game. And, as I walked on, I was lonely no longer. I was a guide, a pathfinder, an original settler. He had casually conferred on me the freedom of the neighbourhood. And so with the sunshine and the great bursts of leaves growing on the trees, just as things grow in fast movies, I had that familiar conviction that life was beginning over again with the summer.
2. There was so much to read, for one thing, and so much fine health to be pulled down out of the young breath-giving air. I bought a dozen volumes on banking and credit and investment securities, and they stood on my shelf in red and gold like new money from the mint, promising to unfold the shining secrets that only Midas and Morgan and Maecenas knew. And I had the high intention of reading many other books besides. I was rather literary in college-one year I wrote a series of very solemn and obvious editorials for the "Yale News" and now I was going to bring back all such things into my life and become again that most limited of all specialists, the "well-rounded man." This isn't just an epigram-life is much more successfully looked at from a single window, after all.
3. It was a matter of chance that I should have rented a house in one of the strangest communities in North America. It was on that slender riotous island which extends itself due East of New York and where there are among other natural curiosities, two unusual formations of land.
4. Twenty miles from the city a pair of enormous eggs, identical in contour and separated only by a courtesy bay, jut out into the most domesticated body of salt water in the Western Hemisphere, the great wet barnyard of Long Island Sound. They are not perfect ovals-like the egg in the Columbus story, they are both crushed flat at the contact end-but their physical resemblance must be a source of perpetual confusion to the gulls that fly overhead. To the wingless a more arresting phenomenon is their dissimilarity in every particular except shape and size.

Questions

Based on your understanding of the passage, answer the questions given below.

(i) How does the narrator describe the appearance of the books he purchased?

(ii) What conviction did the narrator feel with the arrival of summer? How does the narrator describe his intention to become a "well-rounded man"?

(iii) In the line 'It was a matter of chance that I should have rented a house in one of the strangest communities in North America.' What made these communities strange?

(a) Unusual geographical formations

(b) Unique cultural practices

(iv) Complete the sentence suitably.

The expression "unfold the shining secrets that only Midas and Morgan and Maecenas knew" indicates an aura of ....

(v) I was rather literary in college-one year I wrote a series of very solemn and obvious editorials for the "Yale News"...

In the given expression, 'solemn' means

(a) unfold (b) thoughtful

(c) obvious (d) epigram

(vi) Why does the author say that he has 'rented a house in one of the strangest communities in North America'?

(vii) Share evidence from the text in about 40 words, to support the view that the speaker is determined to make a change in his life and what inspires him to do so.

(viii) Complete the analogy with one word from the passage.
Enormous : Huge : : Supervision : ....
(a) Vigil (b) Courtesy
(c) Pursuits (d) Conviction

(ix) According to the passage, what did the writer spend money to buy?
(a) Artwork and home decor
(b) Books on finance and investment
(c) Travel tickets and accommodation
(d) Electronic gadgets and technology

(x) "I felt that Tom would drift on forever seeking a little wistfully for the dramatic turbulence of some irrecoverable football game." Explain this line from Paragraph 1 and why the speaker feels so.

Passage 15

1. Atticus was leaving the post office when Mr. Ewell approached him, cursed him, spat on him, and threatened to kill him. Miss Stephanie said Atticus didn't bat an eye, just took out his handkerchief and wiped his face and stood there and let Mr. Ewell call him names wild horses could not bring her to repeat. Mr. Ewell was a veteran of an obscure war; that plus Atticus's peaceful reaction probably prompted him to inquire, "Too proud to fight, you nigger-lovin' bastard?"

2. Miss Stephanie said Atticus said, "No, too old," put his hands in his pockets and strolled on. Miss Stephanie said you had to hand it to Atticus Finch, he could be right dry sometimes.
Jem and I didn't think it entertaining. "After all, though," I said, "he was the deadest shot in the county one time. He could–"
"You know he wouldn't carry a gun, Scout. He ain't even got one" said Jem.
"You know he didn't even have one down at the jail that night. He told me havin' a gun arounds an invitation to somebody to shoot you."
"This is different," I said. "We can ask him to borrow one."
We did, and he said, "Nonsense."

3. Dill was of the opinion that an appeal to Atticus's better nature might work. After all, we would starve if Mr. Ewell killed him besides, he raised every child in the county but us, and we'd like to keep it that way. We thought it best to keep this among ourselves we were the first and only line of defense.

4. Atticus told us that Mr. Ewell was a coward, but he wasn't going to take any chances. We could shoot all the bluejays we wanted, but it was a sin to kill a mockingbird.
"Remember, it's a sin to kill a mockingbird."
That was the only time I ever heard Atticus say it was a sin to do something, and I asked Miss Maudie about it.

5. "Your father's right," she said. "Mockingbirds don't do one thing but make music for us to enjoy. They don't eat up people's gardens, don't nest in corncribs, they don't do one thing but sing their hearts out for us. That's why it's a sin to kill a mockingbird."

Questions

Based on your understanding of the passage, answer the questions given below.

(i) Why is it considered a sin to kill a mockingbird?

(ii) What is the significance of Mr. Ewell confronting Atticus outside the post office?

(iii) Read the extract and complete the following suitably.
In the extract, the reference to mockingbird is to ....
(a) provide worldly wisdom
(b) make a comparison between mockingbirds and Mr. Ewell

(iv) Complete the following suitably.
Miss Stephanie said you had to hand it to Atticus Finch, he could be right dry sometimes. Here, 'right dry' indicates ....

(v) According to the passage, What was Atticus's reaction to Mr. Ewell's threat?
(a) Cursed (b) Spat (c) Threatened (d) Kill

(vi) Miss Stephanie said Atticus didn't bat an eye, just took out his handkerchief and wiped his face and stood there and let

Mr. Ewell call him names wild horses could not bring her to repeat. Explain your understanding of this situation from Paragraph 1.

(vii) What does this excerpt reveal about Atticus? Give 2 qualities.

(viii) Complete the following analogy with one word from the passage.

Mr. Ewell : Disturbed : : Atticus : ....

(a) Cautious (b) Indifferent (c) Angry (d) Sad

(ix) In the line 'This emotional response provides early evidence that feeling is a vital component of language learning.' What emotional response does the author refer to?

(a) Crying and Cooing
(b) Response to human voices uttering comforting words
(c) Response to toys and movements
(d) Response to food and hunger

(x) Assess the relationship between mockingbirds and Mr. Ewell according to the excerpt.

Answers

Passage 1

(i) The writer refers to the park as a "sanctuary of tranquility" because, amidst the noise and chaos of urban life, it provides a peaceful retreat where people can relax and rejuvenate.

(ii) It is important for governments to set up public parks because they provide recreational opportunities, promote environmental and aesthetic benefits, and serve as safe and accessible spaces for people to connect with nature and each other.

(iii) During the early morning hours, joggers and fitness enthusiasts navigate the park's paths with determination, while yoga practitioners find quiet corners for meditative exercises. The park is also filled with the sounds of chirping birds and rustling leaves.

(iv) By midday, the park becomes a lively social hub where families enjoy picnics, children play and chase each other, and elderly couples sit on benches reminiscing about the past while watching the activities around them.

(v) (a) the setting Sun casting a golden hue and water features glistening

(vi) Textual evidence from Paragraph 4 that proves elderly couples feel a sense of nostalgia.

"Elderly couples sit on benches, reminiscing about days gone by as they watch the world go by."

(vii) The phrase "haven for stargazers and dreamers" refers to the park becoming a peaceful retreat at night, where people can gaze at the stars and find inspiration, solace, and a sense of wonder.

(viii) (c) tranquility

(ix) (b) It emphasises the park's importance as a social and natural retreat.

(x) Potential benefits of an urban park include are

- Providing a green space for relaxation and recreation.
- Encouraging physical activities like jogging, yoga and sports.
- Enhancing environmental quality by supporting native flora and fauna.
- Serving as a community hub where people can socialise and bond.
- Reducing stress and promoting mental well-being.

Passage 2

(i) (b) were not aware of different forms of coffee

(ii) The writer's reference to the unique feature of the coffee plant, which is its ability to produce caffeine as a chemical to protect itself from pests, adds depth to the discussion of coffee and its role in human culture and biology. The reference to this unique feature highlights the complexity of the relationship between the coffee plant and humans and how it has evolved over time to meet the needs of both.

(iii) The author refers to humans as a great threat to coffee plants because of the chemical that the plants had originally produced to ward off pests. This chemical-caffeine is happily consumed by humans all over the world leading to the increased demand of coffee. The increased demand for coffee plants can lead to deforestation, habitat loss and other environmental impacts. Additionally, it can lead to unsustainable farming practices and the use of harmful chemicals to grow and process coffee, further endangering the coffee plant and its ecosystem.

(iv) (d) Stimulants

(v) the characteristic taste and aroma of the coffee bean

(vi) The writer does an excellent job of describing the interesting phenomenon of the green bean turning into a flavourful coffee bean. The writer explains that the green coffee bean is uncharacteristically bland with a taste nowhere close to that of coffee, but is valued for its higher protein and fat content. When the bean is exposed to heat, the fats and carbohydrates turn into essential oils which give the characteristic taste and aroma to the coffee bean. This transformation is indeed an interesting phenomenon that showcases the transformative power of heat and the complexity of coffee production.

(vii) One method to get stronger coffee is to use more coffee powder. This will ensure that the water has enough time to extract all the flavours from the coffee beans, giving you a stronger cup of coffee.

(viii) (a) The burr grinder grinds coffee beans uniformly.

(ix) The right degree of extraction of coffee is important because it will determine the flavour, aroma and overall taste of the coffee. If the extraction is done incorrectly, the coffee will either taste sour or bitter and over-extracted. The right degree of extraction requires precise control over the amount of coffee and the time it is exposed to water. Only then can you create the perfectly balanced cup of coffee.

(x) (a) The Art of Coffee Making

Passage 3

(i) The urban haze that envelops Indian cities is composed of harmful pollutants such as particulate material (PM 2.5 and PM 10), nitrogen dioxide (NO_2), and sulphur dioxide (SO_2).

(ii) (a) it is a threat to the physical well-being of the people.

(iii) (d) prolonged

(iv) (a) mental health

(v) "Children, with their developing respiratory systems, and the elderly, often with pre-existing health conditions, face the brunt of this environmental crisis."

(vi) reduce the release of harmful pollutants into the air, leading to improved air quality

(vii) **Challenges** Limited infrastructure, public reluctance to shift from private vehicles, and overcrowding.

Benefits Reduced vehicular emissions, decreased traffic congestion, and cost-effective transportation.

(viii) Urban planning helps mitigate air pollution by incorporating green spaces, improving air quality, and providing a healthier living environment.

(ix) Technology helps resolve air pollution through air quality monitoring systems, green buildings, and electric vehicles, which reduce emissions and promote sustainability.

(x) The author says that just policy change is not the solution because individual behavioural shifts are also necessary. A collective effort from policymakers and citizens is required for lasting change.

Passage 4

(i) 'Gender pay gap' means women earning less than men on average. This refers to the total earnings of women as compared to men in all professions for every type of work in the labour market for a monthly salary, hourly or daily wage. However, 'equal pay for equal work' means women get an equal amount of pay for the same nature and equal amount of work they do as compared to men.

(ii) Women are suffering from gender pay because of certain socio-economic reasons. These are

- Predefined gender norms in the society, women are less involved in paying jobs as compared to men. The labour force participation rate gives an idea about this, stating that the labour force rate for women is 47% whereas for men, it's 72%.
- The types of job women are involved in vary from men. Managerial positions for women are mostly restricted to administrative roles such as human resource management. This brings down the salary of women as compared to their male counterparts.
- Most lucrative and remunerative professions of practical nature are dominated by men

(iii) (a) measurable indicator

(iv) women tend to be more concentrated in management support functions such as human resources and financial administration than in more strategic roles.

(v) (a) focused

(vi)
- According to a survey by Georgetown University, most remunerative professions, mostly in engineering and computer science, are dominated by men, while the 10 least remunerative professions, in fields like arts and education, are dominated by women.
- Age factor is a major factor in employment and wage earning capability. This happens due to many socio-economic reasons. When women enter their mid-30s and 40s, it is found that their earnings dip compared with men in the same position and profession.

(vii) 'Motherhood penalty' refers to the idea that women earn less money because of their maternal duties. When they become mothers, their attention is divided between two parts-professional and personal life. The writer means that women are unfairly published in terms of their career growth when they take breaks to have and care for children.

(viii) (b) 95

(ix) (b) The top 10 most remunerative professions, mostly in engineering and computer science, were dominated by women.

(x) There are certain policies functioning towards helping the workers. These policies include provisions for maternity leaves and paternity leaves, flexibility in work, etc. They aim at bridging the gap between unequal pay scales for men and women.

Passage 5

(i) Ghost nets are major environmental concerns because they pollute the water bodies, presenting a major problem for the health of our oceans and marine life.

(ii) It is fair to say that commitment and innovation have to go hand-in-hand to rid the oceans of ghost nets because the task requires perseverance as it will take a long time to accomplish. Further, creative ideas and strategies would be needed to address this problem effectively.

(iii) (a) are not owned by anyone

(iv) draw attention to the magnitude of the problem. The reference indicates that governments need to collaborate with such groups for addressing the problem of ghost nets.

(v) (b) Monumental

(vi) A walrus is a large marine mammal which can suffer from huge negative consequences. Being entangled in a ghost net is likely to impact a walrus in the following ways
- their movement is hindered
- they can injure themselves from the net

(vii) The ghost nets are major health problems for the ocean because these fishing nets have the capacity to trap everything in their path. As a result, marine animals cannot move freely and can injure themselves. They even harm the marine flora like the coral reef making the flora and fauna sick. Thus, if this issue is not addressed, this 'health issue' would soon become chronic.

(viii) (a) Practical

(ix) (c) Most ghost nets provide nutrition to marine animals, upon disintegration.

(x) Fishing nets made of common rope, made of natural fibres, have one big advantage over the nylon or plastic fishing nets. They are bio-degradable and can easily disintegrate in water in comparison the artificial fibre nets that do not disintegrate. This is a major advantage that they had ever the fishing nets being used in present times.

Passage 6

(i) According to paragraph 1, marketing has evolved from being based purely on instinct to a more data-driven approach. With the advent of cutting-edge technologies and analytics, marketers can now track the impact of their spending, shifting marketing towards a more scientific discipline.

(ii) (b) Art and Science should work in tandem to do effective marketing.

(iii) Textual evidence (Paragraph 2):

"Neither side of the mix can be isolated or ignored, or the results will not be encouraging."

This supports the idea that marketing is an art because it highlights the importance of creativity and interpersonal empathy.

(iv) Data and digital platforms have transformed marketing by enabling a more precise, outcome-driven approach. Marketers now rely on AI, data analytics, and digital proficiency to craft effective campaigns. Employment in marketing now requires digital expertise, data interpretation, and technological adaptability.

(v) Advanced digital tools such as artificial intelligence, machine learning, and data analytics, which have enhanced marketing strategies

(vi) (c) isolated

(vii) (c) the complexities of human character.

(viii) creativity and data-driven insights

(ix) Employees should possess digital proficiency, data analysis skills, AI knowledge, and the ability to interpret consumer behaviour to match the expertise of tech-savvy consumers.

(x) The writer reveals that the human brain is divided into two functions the right brain, responsible for creativity and artistic intuition, and the left brain, which focuses on analytical and logical thinking.

Passage 7

(i) (c) underdeveloped cities

(ii) elucidating the importance of Indian values and civilisations, and developing children's critical thinking and decision-making skills.

(iii) (d) educational toys will make education more pragmatic

(iv) helping in the development of specific cognitive abilities and skill sets

(v) (c) (iii) and (v)

(vi) It is evident from the passage that educational toys aim to transform traditional educational system by introducing initiatives that enhance cognitive skills, foster the significance of Indian values, exercise practical learning, and encourage social interactions.

(vii) The projects aim to promote technical and hands on knowledge in various fields such as Physics and ancient Indian civilisations. Some of the projects involved plan to resolve the issue of poor infrastructure in several schools of underdeveloped cities so as to impart holistic learning.

(viii) (a) ignite interest

(ix) Yes, it is justifiable. The passage mentions that educational toys promote the overall development of cognitive skills such as critical thinking, decision-making and comprehensive skills in children. Furthermore, the toys sharpen their focus and ignite the interests within them.

Passage 8

(i) (d) It is a source of unconditional love

(ii) increasing their physical activity as dogs are in need of regular exercise in order to stay healthy. Dogs are also great emotional support animals and help their owners who are struggling with mental health issues. Thus, having a dog helps in keeping the owner physically fit and mentally sound.

(iii) As mentioned in the passage, dogs provide a sense of calm and comfort to those struggling with mental health issues. In order to keep the dogs healthy, the owners are required to engage themselves in physical activities. This helps lift up one's mood and energy levels thereby increasing the mental health of the person.

(iv) Dogs have a knack for bringing people together wherever they go, whether it is at home, park or dog beach. They play a great role in connecting people and forming social interactions. Thus, dogs are indeed ice-breakers.
(v) (d) Both (a) and (b)
(vi) (a) Explain the benefits of owning a dog.
(vii) (a) Travel the world
(viii) According to the passage, a furry friend refers to a dog.
(ix) (c) Positive and informative

Passage 9

(i) (b) we do not take the first step towards the task
(ii) The given statement by the writer indicates that the writer blames each one of us as individuals for the lack of change in anything. The writer believes that our lack to take initiatives, because we feel that the task is too big and we cannot do anything alone, had resulted in our condition as far as the environment is concerned.
(iii) To avoid the abuse of paper, we can use the blank sides of any used paper like the clean sides of an envelope to write small notes, lists and reminders around the house. Further, we must avoid using paper napkins and replace them with reusable cloth napkins.
(iv) (a) Adverse
(v) (d) Individual actions triumphs community actions.
(vi) All the kitchen waste collected separately can be turned into manure. People can dig a pit and put kitchen waste into it. When the pit is half full, put some mud over it. After some time, we will have good manure to be used. It takes 3-6 months to make good garden manure.
(vii) People of an area can covert making garden manure to a community project by digging and making large pit in the colony and then throwing kitchen waste into it.
(viii) a cleaner neighbourhood and a cleaner environment
(ix) (b) To suggest
(x) (d) Becoming Environment Conscious
(xi) (d) Reselling a product for further use
(xii) The internet is a powerful tool that can be used towards the cause of the environment. A group on social media of like-minded people can be formed so that people can share environmental stories and issues, as well as pool in solutions and alternatives to educate one another.

Passage 10

(i) Parents need to find a balance between the advantages of an affluent society and the critical lessons of life that come from waiting, saving and working hard to achieve goals in today's world.
(ii) Older children learn self-control by watching how others, especially elders and parents act.
(iii) (b) vulnerable, anxious and depressed
(iv) there is so much more to want. They crave for something new. They consider even luxurious items as essential commodities.
(v) (b) Affluent
(vi) (c) Psychologists, educators and parents want to teach the children about the values of life like hard work, contentment, honesty and compassion.
(vii) When children are given too much too soon, they grow up to be adults who have difficulty in coping with the disappointments of life. Such children may develop distorted sense of entitlement that comes in the way of success in the work place and relationships.
(viii) (b) Learning how to overcome challenges
(ix) (d) they feel that their children are already over-burdened
(x) The children of the present times are different from their parents because the children want to gain as many luxuries as the world offers while the parents follow the values of thrift and self-sacrifice.

Passage 11

(i) The village people were skeptical of the author's attempt at making Jibhi Valley a place for tourism because they did not hope that any person would prefer visiting their home town.
(ii) The narrator left the Indian Army to convert his home town Jibhi Valley in Himachal Pradesh into a tourist destination.
(iii) (b) doubt
(iv) nostalgia about his native place
(v) (b) The 2020-21 pandemic and the eventual lockdown.
(vi) The author feels pride at realising that he had fulfilled his dream and made his home town a popular tourist destination.
(vii) The writer is skeptical of the economic development in Jibhi Valley in the name of tourism. He believes that after the pandemic and lockdown, it is essential to look for sustainable solutions so as to maintain the beauty of nature present in the valley. For the same, they need to avoid the existing concepts of business and stop all the environmentally destructive activities.
(viii) (c) Originality
(ix) (a) The writer of the passage very intrinsically highlights that man and his developmental activities ruin nature, the environment is destroyed and there is no place where they could get peace. Such a feeling is clearly emphasised in the quote by John Marsden where he said, 'We kill all the caterpillars, then complain there are no butterflies.'

(x) It is mentioned in the passage that the writer had ensured to add more windows to the guesthouse so that guests can get ample sunlight. In addition, the fact that the place is peaceful suggests that the writers project will have the following review.

'Comfortable and peaceful, Neat room with ample sunlight. Pleasant and warm host'.

Passage 12

(i) The postmaster is wondering about the futility of life and relationships. When he thinks "who belonged to whom in this world?", He means that man is a mortal being. No relationship in this world is permanent and nobody can bond with someone forever on this Earth because eventually death will set them apart.

(ii) The image of the "faint tremble of young leaves" symbolises the fragile nature of life. It refers to the idea that life is delicate and prone to changes. It captures the vulnerability and emotional sensitivity in the unfamiliar surroundings, perhaps mirroring his own feelings of insecurity, uncertainty and hesitancy in adapting to a life so different from his upbringing.

(iii) stay in the village, anchored by her memories and heartbreak

(iv) his urban background made him a bad mixer in an unfamiliar place like Ulapur

(v) (a) Metaphor

(vi) Ratan would often dive into the memory of certain bittersweet things while conversing with the postmaster. She recalled her father, brother and many insignificant things. She would often get lost in the murky tragedies of her life.

(vii) The phrase "all of nature was echoing his abyssal vacancy" suggests that the postmaster feels a deep, overwhelming emptiness and loneliness. His inner void is so intense that he perceives the surrounding natural world as mirroring his desolation, as if nature itself reflects his sense of isolation and disconnection. The word 'abyssal' emphasises the depth of his inner emptiness, indicating that his loneliness is vast and consuming.

(viii) (d) The inevitability of change

(ix) (b) indifferent and uncaring

(x) The phrase "debris of her own heartbreak" symbolises the emotional remnants of Ratan's deep sadness and shattered hopes after the postmaster leaves. Throughout the story, Ratan forms a close bond with the postmaster, even developing a sense of attachment and possibly seeing him as family. However, when he departs, her hopes of a meaningful connection are crushed, leaving her with the painful 'debris'—the fragments of her broken dreams and affection.

Passage 13

(i) The writer wants to write poems about the things in his pocket because he felt that they were interesting things to write about.

(ii) The narrator preferred brown paper to note-paper for drawing pictures because he loved the shade of brown colour on the brown paper.

(iii) (a) enjoyed his time being idle

(iv) earthen vessels

(v) (a) Sight

(vi) The narrator is very imaginative. We can say so because he describes the qualities of brown paper. He sees brown paper as best fitting to draw. He is observant because he identifies various shades of brown. He is also creative because he likes to draw.

(vii) The woman in the passage can be aptly described as a square and sensible due to the way she viewed the functionality of brown paper. She considered the sole purpose of brown paper to be of tying up parcels and did not understand the reason why the narrator wanted to draw on brown paper. Also, the fact that she gave thought to the toughness and endurance of brown paper to best fit the tying of parcels and that she made an effort to save brown paper for future use shows that she is sensible.

(viii) (d) Brown paper

(ix) (b) Elaborate

(x) In the given statement, the narrator compares an artist to a divine power or God. He feels that when an artist makes attractive drawings with colours like gold, red and green on brown paper, he is essentially demonstrating the same artistic creativity that a divine power or God showed when he created fiery stars out of the darkness that existed.

Passage 14

(i) The narrator likens the books to 'new money from the mint', standing on the shelf in red and gold, promising to reveal the secrets of banking and investment securities.

(ii) The narrator felt the conviction that life was beginning over again with the summer. The narrator intended to read many books and bring literary pursuits back into his life.

(iii) (a) Unusual geographical formations

(iv) mystery and thrill

(v) (b) thoughtful

(vi) The author says that he has 'rented a house in one of the strangest communities in North America, because he found two unusual formations of land near the island where he lived.

(vii) The speaker's determination to make a change is evidenced by his purchase of books on finance and investment, indicating a desire for intellectual growth. He is inspired by the prospect of renewal and possibility symbolised by the arrival of summer.

(viii) (a) Vigil

(ix) (b) Books on finance and investment

(x) The line suggests the speaker's perception of Tom's longing for past excitement, akin to the intensity of a football game. It reflects a sense of nostalgia and a belief that Tom may endlessly pursue moments of exhilaration, unable to recapture them.

Passage 15

(i) Atticus explains to Scout that it's a sin to kill a mockingbird because they don't harm anyone, they only provide beautiful music. Symbolically, this idea extends to innocent and vulnerable individuals like Tom Robinson, who should not be harmed or unfairly accused.

(ii) The confrontation highlights the tension between Atticus and Mr. Ewell. It underscores that a prejudice exists in Maycomb, as Mr. Ewell feels threatened by Atticus's actions.

(iii) (b) make a comparison between mockingbirds and Mr. Ewell

(iv) Indifference

(v) (c) Threatened

(vi) Atticus remains composed while Mr. Ewell insults him. His calm demeanour contrasts with Ewell's aggression, emphasising Atticus's strength and integrity.

(vii)
- Atticus is unflappable and composed even when faced with hostility. His moral compass leads him to defend Tom Robinson, a Black man, despite the town's racial prejudice.
- Atticus embodies justice, empathy and wisdom throughout the novel, serving as its moral guide and voice of conscience.

(viii) (b) Indifferent

(ix) (b) Response to human voices uttering comforting words

(x) Mockingbirds and Mr. Ewell are similar according to the characters present in the excerpt. Mockingbirds don't do one thing but make music for us to enjoy. They don't eat up people's gardens, don't nest in corncribs, they don't do one thing but sing their hearts out for us. Similarly, Mr. Ewell does not harm the community but just goes on a rant against Atticus. So, bothering him would be useless.

Sample Passages

Case Based Factual Passages

Read the following passages carefully and answer the questions that follow.

Passage 1

1. **Introduction** In the hasty lifestyle of today's world, the choice of snacks can greatly impact one's health and well-being. This case study aims to analyse the preference for seasonal fruits compared to packaged snacks among different age groups and the implications for overall health.
2. **Methodology** A survey was conducted among individuals across various age groups, ranging from children to seniors, to determine their snacking preferences. Participants were asked to indicate their preferred snack choices and provide reasons for their preferences. The data was then analysed to identify trends and patterns among different age demographics.
3. **Survey Examination** The survey encompassed a comprehensive examination of snacking habits, including not only preferred snack choices but also delving into the underlying motivations and influences guiding these choices. Beyond mere preference, participants were encouraged to articulate the reasons behind their selections, providing invaluable insights into the multifaceted nature of snacking behaviour.
4. **Results**

   The survey results revealed interesting insights into snacking preferences among different age groups:

Age-group	%	Preferred Snack	Reasons for Preference
Children	77	Seasonal fruits	Taste, Health benefits, Parental guidance
Teenagers	65	Packaged snacks	Convenience, Taste, Peer influence
Young adults	52	Seasonal fruits and packaged snacks	Transitional lifestyle (college, beginning careers, and establishing independence), Health consciousness, Convenience
Middle-aged	83	Seasonal fruits	Freshness, Nutrition, Health consciousness
Elderly	90	Seasonal fruits	Health benefits, Digestive ease

5. **Implications for Interventions** By discerning the diverse preferences among different age groups, policymakers and health practitioners can tailor interventions to address specific demographic needs. For instance, targeting educational campaigns towards parents could empower them to instill healthy eating habits in their children from an early age. Concurrently, efforts to mitigate the influence of advertising and peer pressure on teenagers could involve regulatory measures and educational initiatives aimed at promoting critical thinking and informed decision-making. Furthermore, the prominence of seasonal fruits as a preferred snack choice among middle-aged adults and senior's points towards the importance of promoting access to fresh produce and nutritional education across all age demographics.
6. **Conclusion** The survey outcomes serve as a roadmap for designing targeted interventions that not only cater to diverse demographic needs but also nurture a culture of health and well-being.
   By harnessing the insights gleaned from this study, stakeholders can collaboratively work towards building healthier communities and promoting sustainable practices for generations to come.

Questions

Based on your understanding of the passage, answer the questions given below.

(i) Complete the following suitably.

In the introduction, the researcher links a hasty lifestyle with the choice of snacks in the study to highlight ....

(ii) What would the following be classified as? To examine snacking preferences across various age groups in detail, and assess health implications. Select the appropriate response.

(a) Primary purpose (b) Secondary objective (c) Method of analysis (d) Research outcome

(iii) Give two points to support why it is likely that fresh fruits were given as an option to the survey participants to choose from in the study on snacking preferences.

(iv) Paragraph 3 includes words - 'motivations' and 'influences.' Classify the following sentences as 'influence' or 'motivation'.

Sentence 1 Peer pressure leads teenagers to prefer packaged snacks over healthier options.

Sentence 2 The drive to maintain health as one ages makes middle-aged adults to choose seasonal fruits.

(v) Read the following.

Seema regularly enjoys snacking on chips and cool drinks while watching movies. Mohan, her neighbour, prefers to snack on oranges and also some nuts occasionally. Arindam, who lives across, often tends to eat a mix of carrot sticks and instant noodles, in between meals.

Select the option that identifies the correct demographic Seema, Mohan and Arindam belong to.

(a) Seema - young adult; Mohan - teenager; Arindam - middle-age
(b) Seema - teenager; Mohan - middle-age; Arindam - child
(c) Seema - young adult; Mohan - child; Arindam - teenager
(d) Seema - teenager; Mohan - elderly; Arindam - young adult

(vi) Although children, middle-aged, and elderly groups all prefer seasonal fruits, why is the preference percentage highest among the elderly?

(vii) Analyse how targeted interventions based on the diverse snacking preferences of different age groups can lead to improved health outcomes in Paragraph 5.

(viii) What is the ultimate goal for stakeholders, based on the insights from the study?

(a) Increase profitability through enhanced snack marketing
(b) Building healthier communities
(c) Reducing the cost of healthcare services
(d) Expanding the range of available snack product

Answers

(i) how busy daily routines influence people to opt for quick and convenient eating options, often at the expense of nutritional value

(ii) (a) Primary purpose

(iii) Fresh fruits were given as an option to the survey participants to choose from in the study on snacking preferences because of these two reasons

- **To Indicate Health Focus** As fruits are widely recognised for their health benefits, introducing them aligns with the study's goal to analyse snacking habits and their implications for health (making fresh fruits a relevant choice for understanding healthy snacking behaviours).
- **For Comparative Analysis** Introducing fruits allows the study to compare the health implications of seasonal fruits versus packaged snacks. Including fresh fruits allows researchers to directly evaluate preferences between natural, healthier choices and processed, potentially less healthy alternatives.

(iv) Sentence 1 - influence, Sentence 2 - Motivation

(v) (d) Seema - teenager (taste and convenience); Mohan - elderly (health, digestive ease); Arindam - young adult (health and convenience)

(vi) Even though children, middle-aged, and elderly groups all prefer seasonal fruits, the preference percentage is highest among the elderly because of their increased health needs and focus on foods that are easier to digest and are nutritionally beneficial.

(vii) Targeted interventions based on the diverse snacking preferences of different age groups can lead to improved health outcomes because they can effectively address specific health needs by focusing on the unique factors influencing each demographic's snacking choices. For example, educational campaigns for parents can foster early healthy eating habits in children, while initiatives for teenagers can reduce the impact of advertising and peer pressure, promoting wiser food choices. Also, ensuring that middle-aged and older adults have access to fresh produce supports ongoing health maintenance, directly contributing to overall improved health outcomes across the lifespan.

(viii) (b) Building healthier communities

Passage 2

1. We're all familiar with the usual reasons workers cite for wanting to stay away even after lockdowns have long ended flexible schedules, not having to commute, and ofcourse, increased productivity. However, productivity isn't the only reason people want to stay away from the office. We recently surveyed 1,000 remote workers to find out what's really keeping them tied to their work from home lives.

2. The findings include : 72% want to be able to take a nap or exercise during the day. Nearly three out of four remote workers surveyed stated that the ability to take a nap or workout during the workday was one of the reasons they wanted to stay home. Though these activities may very well increase worker productivity, there's no doubt that a nap on the kitchen couch would be frowned upon in the office.

3. 73% want to be able to watch TV while they work. Three out of four respondents again say that being able to entertain themselves with TV, podcasts, music, or other media is one of the reasons they want to keep their work-from-home lifestyle.
4. 62% cite concerns about their appearance. Well over half or respondents stated that they are concerned about their co-workers seeing them in person again after such a long time apart. Whether it's weight loss or gain, not having the right clothes, or another concern about appearance, most would rather not have to worry about the way they look to their co-workers outside a zoom call.
5. When asked to choose the reason that most affects their desire to keep working from home, predictable answers like caring for children and lack of a commute were still the most common number one reasons. 14% of respondents stated that working remotely was so important to them, that they would not go back to work in person even if their employers required it. **CBSE 2024**

Questions

Based on your understanding of the passage, answer the questions given below.

(i) '...... these activities will increase productivity'. By 'Productivity' the author refers to

(a) products produced (b) efficiency of the employee
(c) time spent by the employee (d) number of activities

(ii) What change in the work place would bring those people back to office who want amusement?

(a) Giving long breaks
(b) Free coffee and tea
(c) Building entertainment lounge
(d) Spacious conference hall

(iii) As per the survey, why do health conscious people prefer to work from home?

(iv) Complete the following sentence appropriately.

The passage ends on a note that some people are resolved to ....

(v) Explain one inference that can be drawn form Paragraph 1 about the reason for people's preference to work from home.

(vi) State whether the statement given below is True or False.

The survey reveals that people deeply miss socialising in the work from home style.

(vii) Explain in your own words how appearance is one of the factors for people's preference for work from home.

(viii) As per the survey, what top priorities of people prevent them from going to office?

Answers

(i) (b) efficiency of the employee

(ii) (a) Giving long breaks

(iii) As per the survey, health conscious people prefer to work from home because this mode allows them to take a nap or exercise during the day without compromising their work efficiency. This flexibility to engage in such activities during the workday is not typically available in an office setting.

(iv) work from home, even if their employers insist upon them working from the office.

(v) One inference that can be drawn from Paragraph 1 about the reason for people's preference to work from home is that there are many reasons besides increased productivity that inspire people to continue working from home such as flexible schedules and convenience. Factors such as not having to commute, being able to set a flexible schedule, and maintaining a work-life balance play a significant role in this preference.

(vi) False

(vii) Appearance is a major factor in people's preference to work from home because the relaxed lifestyle during the lockdown period has brought changes in people's appearances. The survey found that 62% of the respondents had concerns about their physical appearance, especially their colleagues seeing them in-person again after such a long time apart. The changes could be weight gain or loss, not having the appropriate clothing for office settings, or other concerns related to their physical appearance. Working from home eliminates the stress and anxiety of how they look to their co-workers outside of a virtual meeting, making it a preferred choice for many.

(viii) Following are the top priorities of people preventing them from going to office.

- Caring for their children and lack of a commute
- Naptime and exercise
- Ability to entertain themselves with TV, podcasts or music while working
- Concerns about personal appearance in the office

Practice Questions

Read the following passages carefully and answer the questions that follow.

Passage 1

Case Study Tourism in India

1. **Introduction** India, with its rich cultural heritage, diverse landscapes, and historical sites, attracts millions of tourists each year. Tourism significantly contributes to India's GDP, generating employment and boosting infrastructure. This case study explores factors impacting tourism in India, examines seasonal patterns, and assesses tourist satisfaction through a survey.
2. **Methodology** The study involved primary data collection through a structured survey targeting 500 tourists across major destinations like Delhi, Jaipur, Goa and Kerala. Additionally, secondary data from government reports and tourism boards were used. The survey included questions about preferences, challenges and satisfaction levels, focusing on various demographics, including international and domestic tourists.
3. **Survey Examination** Tourists were surveyed on travel preferences, challenges encountered, accommodation satisfaction and cultural experiences.

   Feedback highlighted India's appeal due to its history and cultural diversity, but also noted issues like infrastructure gaps and pollution.
4. **Results** The study found that most tourists preferred historical sites and beaches. International tourists were drawn to heritage sites, while domestic tourists preferred nature destinations.

   Satisfaction was high among tourists who experienced local culture, but infrastructure issues and overcrowding at key locations were common complaints. Overall, 85% of tourists expressed a desire to revisit. **CBSE 2025**

Questions

Based on your understanding of the passage, answer the questions given below.

(i) Complete the following suitably.

In the introduction, the researcher links tourism to India's GDP to highlight ....

(ii) What would the following be classified as ?

The study involved primary data collection through a structured survey

Select the appropriate response.

(a) Primary purpose (b) Secondary objective
(c) Method of analysis (d) Research outcome

(iii) Give two points to support why the study involved primary data and secondary data.

(iv) Paragraph 3 includes words - 'preferences' and 'challenges'. Classify the following sentences as preference or challenge.

Sentence 1 Feedback highlighted India's appeal due to its history and cultural diversity.

Sentence 2 Also noted issues like infrastructure gaps and pollution.

(v) List any two points tourists were asked about in the survey.

(vi) What were the more preferred destinations?

(vii) Analyse why though there was satisfaction among tourists, there were some complaints.

(viii) What is the ultimate goal for stakeholders, based on the insights from the study?

(a) Tourists expressed a desire to revisit.
(b) Tourist will visit historical sites.
(c) Domestic tourism will increase.
(d) To promote India as a tourist destination.

Passage 2

1. **Introduction** As the world grapples with climate change, renewable energy has emerged as a crucial solution. This case study aims to analyse the increasing use of renewable energy in India, its adoption across different sectors, and the implications for society and the environment.
2. **Methodology** A survey was conducted among households, businesses, and industries across various regions in India. Participants were asked about their primary source of energy (traditional fossil fuels or renewable energy) and the reasons for their preferences. The data was then analysed to identify trends and patterns among different demographics and sectors.
3. **Survey Examination** The survey encompassed a comprehensive examination of energy consumption habits, not only focusing on the preferred sources of energy but also delving into the underlying motivations and influences guiding these choices. Beyond mere preference, participants were encouraged to articulate the reasons behind their selections, providing invaluable insights into the multifaceted nature of energy consumption.
4. **Results** The survey results revealed interesting insights into the energy preferences among different groups.

S. No.	Demographic Preferences	%	Preferred Source	Reasons for Preference
1.	Households	62%	Renewable	Environmental concerns, cost savings, government incentives
2.	Small Businesses	55%	Renewable	Cost efficiency, public image, sustainability
3.	Large Industries	48%	Renewable	Long-term savings, corporate responsibility compliance
4.	Rural Areas	71%	Rural Areas	Accessibility, reliability, local employment opportunities
5.	Urban Areas	58%	Renewable	Environmental awareness, incentives, modern infrastructure

5. **Implications for Interventions** By discerning the diverse preferences among different demographics, policymakers, and energy providers, one can tailor interventions to address specific needs. For instance, increasing government incentives and subsidies for renewable energy can encourage more households and businesses to adopt sustainable practices. Concurrently, efforts to improve the infrastructure for renewable energy can enhance its reliability and accessibility. By harnessing the insights gleaned from this study, stakeholders can collaboratively work towards building a cleaner and more sustainable future for generations to come. **CBSE 2025**

Questions

Answer the following questions, based on the given passage.

(i) Complete the following suitably

In the introduction, the researcher links climate change with the rise of renewable energy by highlighting ....

(ii) What would the following be classified as?

To examine energy preferences across various demographics in detail, and assess their implications.

Select the appropriate response.

(a) Primary purpose (b) Method of analysis (c) Secondary objective (d) Research outcome

(iii) Mention the two steps adopted in the survey methodology.

(iv) Paragraph 3 includes the words 'motivations' and 'influences'. Classify the following sentences as influence or motivation.

Sentence 1 Government incentives lead households to prefer renewable energy over traditional fossil fuels.

Sentence 2 The desire for long-term savings makes large industries choose renewable energy.

(v) Read the following text.

Rajan, a rural household head, prefers using solar panels for energy due to their reliability and the local employment opportunities they provide. His neighbour, Rama, a small business owner, values renewable energy for its cost efficiency and sustainability. Meanwhile Suresh, who runs a large industry, opts for renewable energy due to corporate responsibility and compliance with regulations.

Select the option that identifies the correct demographic they belong to.

(a) Rajan — household worker; Rama — small business owner; Suresh — large industry owner
(b) Rajan — rural employee; Rama — urban worker; Suresh — household head
(c) Rajan — rural — household head; Rama — small business owner; Suresh — large industry owner
(d) Rajan — urban worker; Rama — large industry owner; Suresh — rural worker

(vi) Although both rural and urban areas prefer renewable energy, why is the preference percentage higher among rural areas ?

(vii) Analyse how targeted interventions based on diverse energy preferences of different demographics can lead to improved environmental outcomes. (Paragraph 5).

(viii) What is the ultimate goal for stakeholders, based on the insights from the study?
(a) Increase profitability through enhanced renewable infrastructure
(b) Build a sustainable future
(c) Reduce the cost of energy
(d) Expand the range of renewable energy products available

Passage 3

1. People below the age of 20 and above the age of 50 are more likely to believe fake news. Those relatively new to the use of the internet still do not grasp the concept of fake information over these platforms, reveals a new survey 'Countering Misinformation in India'. This survey has been conducted jointly by Internet and Mobile Association of India (IAMAI).
2. At least 40% of the respondents believed in 'misinformation' received over social media if it came with leading backgrounds and evidence, while 34% of them believe the information when it is shared by a trustworthy organisation.
3. The dominant factor that drives people to forward such information is their belief that it might benefit others and help in their safety. In fact, that was the response of almost 50% of the respondents. This was compounded by the fact that at least 20% of the respondents expressed their lack of trust in conventional media thus their faith in contents shared by common people over social media.
4. But even then, newspapers still remain the top source of information for most. At least 53% of the respondents trust what is generally perceived as neutral media and only 29% trust technology and social media platforms.
5. However, what was surprising was that almost 45% of the respondents did not even know about the existence of fact-checking organisation and most did not even know that journalists had to verify data before they let it out. Only 26% of the respondents believe that it is the responsibility of the media to curb or identify fake news. Many respondents also put the responsibility of identifying such fake news on an individual.
6. The survey has found that first time or early users of the Internet platforms are more susceptible to fake news than others. There is a need for building capacities and creating a National Civic Digital Literacy Strategic Plan. **CBSE 2024**

Questions

Based on your understanding of the passage, answer the questions given below.

(i) Select the option that comes under conventional media.
(a) Instagram
(b) Newspaper
(c) Facebook
(d) E-mail

(ii) Select the correct option.
One factor that prompts people to believe fake news is that
(a) it supports their point of view
(b) they are biased
(c) it is from a reliable site
(d) it has more 'likes' and 'shares'

(iii) What according to the passage are the intentions of people who share information?

(iv) Which reason do you infer from the passage is responsible for journalists spreading misinformation?

(v) Complete the sentence appropriately.
The threat faced by the new entrants in social media is ....

(vi) Explain your understanding of the difference between 'misinformation' and 'fake news'.

(vii) As per your inference drawn from Paragraph 1, which category of people fall as victims to fake news?

(viii) What is the blame game that goes on in fixing the onus of identifying fake news?

Passage 4

1. A recent survey conducted by an independent research firm sought to measure levels of happiness among youth aged 16-24 years in seven countries. The findings revealed some intriguing insights into what makes today's youth happiest, as well as which factors influence their overall well-being. In India, an overwhelming majority of the youth reported feeling satisfied with their lives, with 87% rating of their overall happiness a 'high' or 'very high'. Financial security was identified as the primary source of happiness for 66% followed by family support (89%), having a purpose in life (50%), and work or studies (40%). Unfortunately, 65% reported feeling stress related to academic performance or workload, while 25% reported feeling lonely. These figures point to a need for increased mental health support among India's youth.
2. These surveys also revealed that family support is an important source of contentment for young people across countries. In Europe, 59% of respondents said that their families were a major source of happiness. In France this figure was 67% and 63% in Germany. In North America, 64% rated family as an important factor for well-being in Canada, while 61% did so in the United States. Similarly, 89% of survey respondents in Indian named family support as a major contributor to their overall contentment level.
3. It is clear that stress has a significant impact on the happiness of today's youth. The findings suggest that young people need better resources to manage their mental health and well-being. This may include access to counselling services, mindfulness activities and support groups to help them cope with challenging circumstances. It is also important to provide financial support so as to reduce some of the economic pressures.
4. In India, 65% of youth surveyed reported feeling anxious about their academic performance or workload, while 25% felt lonely. These figures are especially significant given how important family support is for young people's overall contentment.

CBSE 2024

Questions

Based on your understanding of the passage, answer the questions given below.

(i) What are the two findings that the survey mentioned in Paragraph 1 reveals? Answer in about 40 words.

(ii) "It is also important to provide financial support so as to reduce some of the economic pressures." Explain the statement in about 40 words.

(iii) Elaborate giving date, the statement "Stress has a significant impact on the happiness of today's youth."

(iv) Which of the following factors, with reference to the given passage does not play a substantial role in the well-being of Indian youth?

(a) Family support and strong ties
(b) Social connection and technology
(c) Books and literature
(d) Economic stability

(v) State whether True or False, with reference to the given passage.
It is not necessary to provide financial support to the youth as only academic performance plays an upper hand in deciding the stress level.

(vi) What are the top choice which are of maximum value to today's youth

I. Collectivism II. Social media
III. Individualistic society IV. Family ties

Options

(a) I and II (b) II and III (c) I and IV (d) II and IV

(vii) The mental health of today's youth can be managed by resources like .... and ....

(viii) Write the following sources that provide happiness to today's youth in descending order.

(a) Purposefulness (b) Financial status
(c) Family support (d) Stress

Passage 5

1. **How bird hits happen, why they are a concern?**

New Delhi 20th June: At least two bird strike incidents happened on Sunday. Both aircrafts returned to their airports of origin and were grounded for maintenance. An ABC aircraft, which took off from Guwahati towards Delhi, suffered damage to its left engine following a bird hit at 1600 feet. The pilots returned to Guwahati. The other strike happened on another flight from Patna to Delhi. The pilots of the aircraft suspected a bird strike during the take-off roll but continued to climb. Following the takeoff rotation, they were informed by the cabin crew of sparks emanating from the left engine. Subsequently, the pilots were also informed by air traffic control of smoke coming out of one of the engines. The pilots declared an emergency and returned to Patna.

2. **Why are bird strikes a concern?**

Bird strikes are among the most common threats to aircraft safety and they typically occur during take-off or landing. Dozens of bird-strikes happen each day but some can be more dangerous than others. Typically, when birds collide with an aircraft's airframe, it is unlikely to cause significant problems for the pilots flying. But there are instances when the aircraft engine ingests the birds. This can lead to a loss of thrust for the engine and cause maneuverability problems for the crew. In these cases, where a jet engine ingests a bird, procedures would generally call for pilots to land the plane at the closest airport. While most airframe bird strikes are not considered critical to air safety, if a collision cracks a window or a wind screen, pilots will look to land as early as possible.

3. **How critical are bird strikes to air safety?**

Smaller planes would generally be more susceptible to the dangers of bird strikes than larger ones. However, given that bird strikes mostly happen during take-off and landing, these incidents could distract the pilots during what are highly critical phases of flights that demand the complete attention of the crew.

4. **What causes bird-strikes?**

The presence of birds around an aircraft increases the chances of a bird strike. In the monsoon, as water puddles emerge on open grounds attracting insects to breed, the presence of birds increases. In some cases, bird hits also happen at higher altitudes when a plane is cruising. These are more dangerous than the low-altitude hits, given that they can cause rapid depressurisation of cabins. Other reasons for bird activity around the air field could be the presence of landfills or waste disposal sites that can attract a large number of birds.

Questions

Based on your understanding of the passage, answer the questions given below.

(i) Complete the sentence appropriately with one/two words.

In cases where the aircraft engine infests the bird, it leads to the loss of thrust and causes problems in ....

(ii) Select the option that displays the most likely reason for bird hits.

(a) When the aircraft is overloaded
(b) At the time of landing or taking off
(c) When the crew becomes negligent
(d) When the passengers become panicky

(iii) Which are the areas more prone to bird hits?

(iv) The passage mentions causes and concerns. Classify the following statements as causes and concern.

Statement 1 - Fear of air accidents.

Statement 2 - Migration for breeding.

(v) Complete the sentence by selecting the most appropriate option.

When the window or the windscreen of the air plane is cracked due to a bird hit, ...

(a) the crew must rush to the cockpit
(b) the pilot must land at the nearest airport
(c) the pilot must inform the maintenance engineer
(d) the pilot must get instructions from the aviation

(vi) In some cases, bird hits also happen at higher altitudes when a plane is cruising. These are more dangerous. How?

(vii) Based on the reading of the text, state a point to challenge the given statement.

The area around air fields should be clear of any waste disposal sites.

(viii) Based on the reading of the text, state a point to further the statement.

Dozens of bird hits take place every day ....

(a) but only a few are dangerous
(b) all of them are fatal
(c) but after every bird hit, it is imperative to land the aircraft
(d) the pilot should ignore them

Passage 6

1. A recent study cites around 37.15% of children experienced reduced levels of concentration due to smartphone use, and 23.80% of children use smartphones while they are in bed, before going to sleep. Increased usage of mobile phones among children during the Covid-19 pandemic is resulting in internet addiction. The use of smartphones before sleeping is not the only ill-effect of such devices having an adverse impact on children. Checking mobile phones while studying is another menace that is a prominent source of lapses in concentration and weakening of attention span, among children, the study said.
2. The study's data showed that 42.9% of children confessed to having a social networking account. Among those children are those who have accounts on the major social networking apps/sites which they use. In the age-wise distribution of children having social media accounts, it was found that children of all ages operate social media accounts. A large proportion of 10-year-olds have such accounts. As per the data collected. 78.90% of children said that they spend between 0-2 hours on smartphones using the internet, playing games, listening to music, chatting, etc.
3. When asked about the features/facilities that children like to use or enjoy using on smartphones, internet devices, 52.9% answered as chatting. While the most common purpose is using internet-enabled device for online learning/classes, only 10.1% of children like to use smartphones for online learning and education.
   The data showed that the most prominent means to access smartphones and the internet for the children is through their parents' phones (62.6% of all valid respondents used their parents' phones). It is also interesting to note that 30.2% of the children of all age groups (8 to 18 years) already possess their own smartphones and use the same for all purposes.
4. "Experts working for early detection and prevention of internet addiction at AIIMS Behavioural Addiction clinic suggest that parent's supervision of their child is of paramount importance. Parents must introduce other life skills to children to ensure a reduction in screen time. The parents can encourage social interaction of the child. More internet de-addiction centers need to be established in the country.

*(**Source:** The federal/25 March/2022/350 word)*

Questions

Based on your understanding of the passage, answer the questions given below.

(i) Complete the following suitably.

An appropriate title of the passage can be ....

(ii) Which does the increasing usage of phone 'with age' indicate?

(a) Internet addiction among children.
(b) Internet requirement among children.
(c) Concentration and focus among children.
(d) Internet literacy among children.

(iii) "children of all ages operate social media accounts". What concerns does this finding raise?

(iv) The given passage presents the inference drawn from a study as well as adverse effect it can have. On the basis of the passage, categorise the following statements as inference and effect.

Statement 1- Loss of sleep

Statement 2- 10 years old have social media accounts

(v) Identify an internet addict child from the following statements.

(a) Sania - I turn off my notifications when studying or spending time with friends and family.
(b) Adil - Gosh! I can't keep my hands off from checking my notifications.
(c) Kanti - My screen timer alerts me when it's time to stop watching.

(vi) The survey mentions ill-effects of increased usage of mobile phones among children. What are they? Give any two.

(vii) How parents can play a pivotal role in curbing the rising menace of internet addiction among children?

(viii) Complete the sentence appropriately.

The real intended reason for promoting access to mobile phone: during COVID pandemic was to facilitate .... among children.

(a) online chatting (b) online music listening
(c) online learning (d) online gaming

Passage 7

1. Nowadays companies demand an outstanding job performance by every single employee to be better than that of their competitors because there is competition among enterprises. The employers make efforts to motivate the employees and optimise performance.
2. There are numerous factors affecting job performance. These can be divided into external and internal factors. The internal factors are team spirit, competent boss, respect from colleagues and job satisfaction. The external factors are chance for personal development, job security, promotion prospects and monetary incentives. The decisive determinant is that the employees remain highly motivated. One possible method to increase motivation is the salary. Employees are willing to stay longer hours in the office and perform better, when they have the chance to get financial rewards, for instance, a higher salary or bonuses.
3. The bar graph (given below) shows the result of a survey conducted among workers in a company to analyse their work performance across ten different factors that contribute to make their work environment pleasant. The workers are grouped into two categories - those between the ages of 18-30 and those between 45-60. Interestingly, in six out of the ten factors surveyed, the 18-30 age group is shown to be more affected than the 45-60 age group. Factors, besides the salary, which affect the work performance of the two different age groups are interesting. These factors are the chance for personal development, relaxed working environment, promotion prospects, job satisfaction and monetary incentives. Furthermore, two out of the remaining four factors namely, team spirit and work environment have been equally influential among the two groups. The 45-60 years workers are impacted a lot by 'respect from colleagues' whereas the prospect of a promotion is an important reason that drives younger employees to work better.
4. Job performance of happy employees is 31% more productive and they show three times more creativity than their unhappy counterparts. They are more resilient and more likely to stay in the same company for a longer period. Consequently they drive the company towards long-term goals by being more productive and efficient.

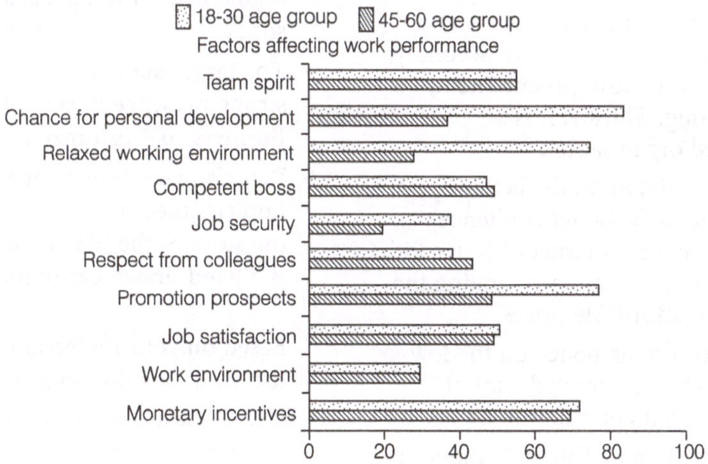

CBSE 2023

Based on your understanding of the passage, answer the questions given below.

(i) Does the following statement agree with the information given in Paragraph 1?

When the company has a lot of competitors, it tries to invent the most efficient technology to stay ahead.

Select from the following.

True If the statement agrees with the information

False If the statement contradicts the information

Not Given If there is no information on this

(ii) Why do you think the companies demand an exemplary performance from their employees? Support your answer with reference to the passage.

(iii) Select the option that displays the most likely reason for employees to perform better.
(a) Companies demand an outstanding performance
(b) If the company grows, their growth is assured
(c) When there are chances to get financial gratification
(d) To drive the company towards long-term goals

(iv) Select two factors that display that work performance of both the categories of workers remains the same.

(v) Based on the bar graph, complete the following statement.
The 18-30 age group is shown to be more affected than the 45-60 age group in most factors.
We can say this because ....

(vi) Complete the given sentence by selecting the most appropriate option.
Loyalty as an attribute is there in employees who are ....
(a) senior (b) healthy (c) motivated (d) happy

(vii) The 45-60 age group workers are motivated by ....

(viii) Based on the reading of the passage, state a point to challenge the given statement.
Increase in salary is the only motivation for better job performance.

(ix) Complete the sentence.
The internal factors affecting work performance are ..... .

(x) Complete the given sentence by selecting the most appropriate option.
The concluding sentence of the passage makes a clear case for .... by listing it as a core component of steering the company towards long-term goals.
(a) collaboration (b) flexibility (c) happiness (d) adaptability

Passage 8

1. Ratan, a global brand in Dairy products, works on a business model popularly known as, 'The Ratan Model'. This model aims to provide value for money to the customers and protect the interests of farmers simultaneously.
2. The Ratan Model is a three-tiered structure that is implemented in its dairy production: Firstly, Ratan acts as a direct link between milk producers and consumers that removes the middlemen. Secondly, farmers (milk producers) control procurement, processing and marketing. Thirdly, it is a professionally managed organisation.
3. One can understand the Ratan Model better by taking cognizance of 'Ratan's Target Audience', where it has targeted the mass market of India with no premium offerings and works on providing the best quality products at affordable prices.
4. So Ratan formulates its pricing policy on the low cost price strategy which has attracted a lot of customers in the past and it continues to do so.
5. Another stance used by Ratan's Target Audience is based on customer-wise targeting and industry wise targeting. This strategy divides the target audience on the following two bases.
6.

Segment wise break down to Customer-Based target Audience

Customers	Ratan products
Kids	Chocolate, Ratan cool, Ratan milk
Youth	Ratan Pizza cheese, Cheese spread
Health Conscious	Ratan Shakti, Ratan Lite, Butter

The above table showcases how Ratan has a diversified customer base.

7. Industry Based Target Audience: Ratan has segmented milk for various industries such as ice-cream manufacturers, restaurants, coffee shops, and many similar- industries. Further, it has segmented butter, ghee and cheese for bakeries, snack retailers, confectioneries and many more.
8. The target audience study tells us that Ratan has a strong presence in both Business-to-Business and Business-to-Customers.
9. Ratan's marketing campaigns and strategies are implemented in a very attractive way. For example, the story of the 'Ratan Girl' is a popular 'ad' icon. It is a hand drawn cartoon of a young girl.

CBSE 2022 Term II

Based on your understanding of the passage, answer the questions that follow.

(i) Does the following statement agree with the information given in the passage.
Ratan has created a new business model named the 'Ratan Model'.
Select from the following.
True if the statement agrees with the information
False if the statement contradicts the information
Not Given if there is no information on this.

(ii) What does 'The Ratan Model' aim at?

(iii) Select the option that states the purpose of the table given along with the passage.

(a) To show how Ratan diversified customer base
(b) To show the Ratan model's focus
(c) To point out how Ratan's model is customer oriented
(d) To show how Ratan dairy became popular

(iv) Complete the sentence appropriately.
The Ratan Model is a .... that is implemented in its dairy production.

(v) Which of the following products can be targeted for health conscious people.
(a) Coconut milk (b) Cold coffee
(c) White butter (d) Flavoured curd

(vi) Select the most appropriate title for the passage.
(a) Ratan's business model
(b) Ratan's three-tiered structure
(c) Ratan the dairy company
(d) Both (b) and (c)

(vii) Which word in the passage means the same as awareness?
(a) Implemented (b) Premium
(c) Procurement (d) Cognisance

(viii) 'Ratan acts as a direct link .... '. Explain.

(ix) 'Ratan Target Audience' is described as a diversified market. Explain with reference to the given table.

(x) Name the two basis on which Ratan divides the target audience.

(xi) In which two spheres does Ratan have a strong presence?
(a) Business to Business
(b) Business to Customers
(c) Business to Government
(d) Both (a) and (b)

(xii) Which is the most loved ad icon of Ratan?

Passage 9

1. Our history makes it evident that the Indian Plastics Industry made a vigorous beginning in 1957 but it took more than 30 years for it to pervade Indian lifestyles. In 1979, 'the market for plastics' was just being seeded by the state-owned Indian Petro-Chemicals and it was only in 1994 that plastic soft drink bottles became a visible source of annoyance.

2. In the same year, people in other cities were concerned about the state of public sanitation and also urged regulatory bodies to ban the production, distribution and use of plastic bags. However, the challenge was greater than it appeared at first.

3. The massive generation of plastic waste in India is due to rapid urbanisation, spread of retail chains, plastic packaging from grocery to food and vegetable products, to consumer items and cosmetics.

   The projected high growth rates of GDP and continuing rapid urbanisation suggest that India's trajectory of plastic consumption and plastic waste is likely to increase.

   Global plastics production 1950 to 2020

   Annual global polymer resin and fiber production (plastic production), measured in metric tonnes per year.

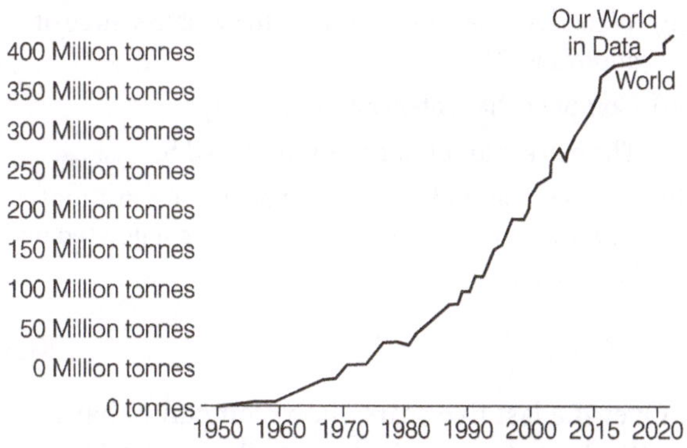

Source Geyeretal (2017)

4. According to the United Nations Environment Programme (UNEP) report of 2018, India stands among few other countries like France, Mongolia and several African countries that have initiated total or partial national level bans on plastics in their jurisdictions.
   On World Environment Day in 2018, India vowed to phase out single-use plastics by 2022, which gave a much needed impetus to bring this change.

5. In this context, thereafter ten states (Andhra Pradesh, Chhattisgarh, Gujarat, Himachal Pradesh, Karnataka, Madhya Pradesh, Meghalaya, Odisha, Rajasthan and Tamil Nadu) are currently sending their collected waste to cement plants for

co-processing, twelve other states/UTs are using plastic waste for polymer bitumen road construction and still four other states are using the plastic waste for waste-to-energy plants and oil production. A world of greater possibilities has now opened up to initiate appropriate and concrete actions to build up the necessary institutions and systems before oceans turn, irreversibly into a thin soup of plastic.

6. However, there is no one single masterstroke to counter the challenges witnessed by the staggering plastic waste management in the country. The time is now to formulate robust and inclusive National Action Plans and while doing so, the country will establish greater transparency to combat the plastic jeopardy in a more sustainable and holistic way.

CBSE 2022 Term II

Questions

Based on your understanding of the passage, answer the questions that follow.

(i) Does the following statement agree with the information given in the passage.

Pollution as a menace came into limelight in early 1990s.

Select from the following.

True if the statement agrees with the information

False if the statement contradicts the information

Not Given if there is no information on this.

(ii) What does the writer mean by the visible source of annoyance?

(iii) Complete the sentence appropriately.

The market for plastic was introduced by ....

(iv) The fact that India's trajectory of plastic consumption and plastic waste is likely to increase is suggested by ....

(a) high growth rates of GDP
(b) rapid urbanisation
(c) Industrialisation
(d) Both (a) and (b)

(v) Complete the sentence appropriately.

The last Paragraph of the passage ....

(a) states the need for effective garbage disposal
(b) states the need for effective plastic waste management
(c) states the need for urgent government action
(d) states the need for an effective implementation of strategies

(vi) What stepas are being taken to combat the challenges of plastic waste management? What will be its impact?

(vii) What does the upward trend of the graph indicate?

(viii) What does the line, 'oceans turning irreversibly into a thin soup of plastic' suggest?

Passage 10

1. Over the last five years, more companies have been actively looking for intern profiles, according to a 2018-19 survey by an online internship and training platform. This survey reveals that India had 80% more internship applications — with 2.2 million applications received in 2018 compared to 1.27 million in the year before that. The trend was partly due to more industries looking to have fresh minds and ideas on existing projects for better productivity. What was originally seen as a Western concept, getting an internship before plunging into the job market, is fast gaining momentum at Indian workplaces.

2. According to the survey data, India's National Capital Region has been the top provider of internships, with a total of 35% internship opportunities, followed by Mumbai and Bengaluru at 20% and 15%, respectively. This includes opportunities in startups, MNCs and even government entities. The survey also revealed popular fields to find internships in (Fig. 1).

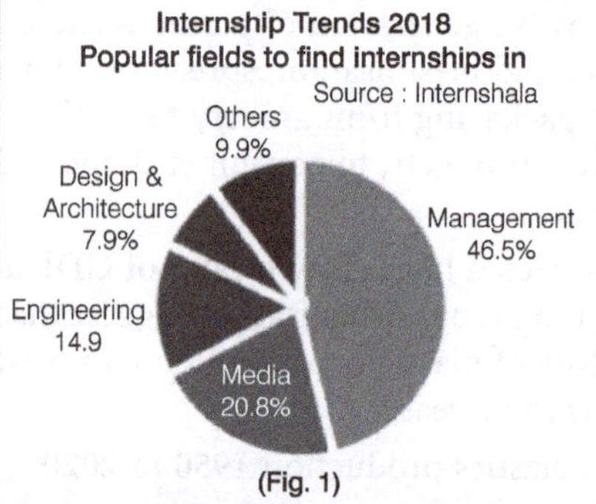

(Fig. 1)

3. There has been growing awareness among the students about the intern profiles sought by hiring companies that often look for people with real-time experience in management than school masters.

The stipend has been an important factor influencing the choice of internships. The survey data reveals that the average stipend offered to interns was recorded as ₹ 7000 while the maximum stipend went up to ₹ 85,000.

4. According to statistics, a greater number of people considered virtual internships than in-office internships. Virtual internships got three times more applications than in-office, since a large chunk of students were the ones already enrolled in various courses, or preferred working from home.

5. Internship portals have sprung up in the last three to four years and many of them already report healthy traffic per month. Reports suggest that on an average, an internship portal company has around 200,000-plus students and some 8,000 companies registered on it.
It gets around two lakh visits online every month.

6. The Managing Director of a leading executive search firm says that though these web platforms are working as an effective bridge between the industry and students, most established companies are still reluctant to take too many interns on board for obvious reasons.

Questions

Based on your understanding of the passage, answer the questions given below.

(i) Complete the following suitably.
.... are reluctant to take too many interns on board.

(ii) Select the correct inference with reference to the following.
Over the last five years, more companies have been actively looking for intern profiles.
(a) The past five years have seen active applications by interns to several companies.
(b) The activity for intern profiling by the companies has reached a gradual downslide over the past five years.
(c) There were lesser companies searching for intern profiles earlier, as compared to those in the recent five years.
(d) Several companies have initiated intern profiling five times a year in the recent past.

(iii) State a reason for an increase in internship applications?

(iv) Select the option which is not true in regard with internship portals.
(a) They have sprung up in the last three to four years.
(b) Many of them do not report a healthy traffic every month.
(c) On an average, an internship portal has 2,00,000 students and 8,000 companies.

(v) The survey statistics mention the average stipend, indicating that
(a) 50% interns were offered ₹ 85,000.
(b) 7,000 was the lowest and ₹ 85,000 was the highest.
(c) most interns were offered around ₹ 7,000.
(d) no intern was offered more than ₹ 7,000.

(vi) Why is virtual internship preferred?

(vii) Why do you think companies do not prefer taking many interns?

(viii) Complete the sentence appropriately. There was an increase of .... internship applications received in 2018 as compared to the year before.
(a) 60% (b) 57.7% (c) 56% (d) 58.1%

Passage 11

1. Changing food preferences have brought about rapid changes in the structure of the Indian diet. The rapid proliferation of multinational fast-food companies and the influence of Western culture have replaced traditional home-cooked meals with ready-to-eat, processed foods thus increasing the risk of chronic diseases in urban Indians. Therefore, nurturing healthy eating habits among Indians from an early age would help to reduce health risks. To date, little is known about the quality and quantity of foods and beverages consumed by urban Indian adolescents. This lack of evidence is a significant barrier to the development of effective nutrition promotion and disease prevention measures.

2. Therefore, a self-administered, semi-quantitative, 59-item meal-based food frequency questionnaire (FFQ) was developed to assess the dietary intake of adolescents. A total of 1026 students (aged 14–16 years) attending private, English-speaking schools in Kolkata completed the survey. A sample percentage of the food consumption pattern is displayed (Fig. 1).

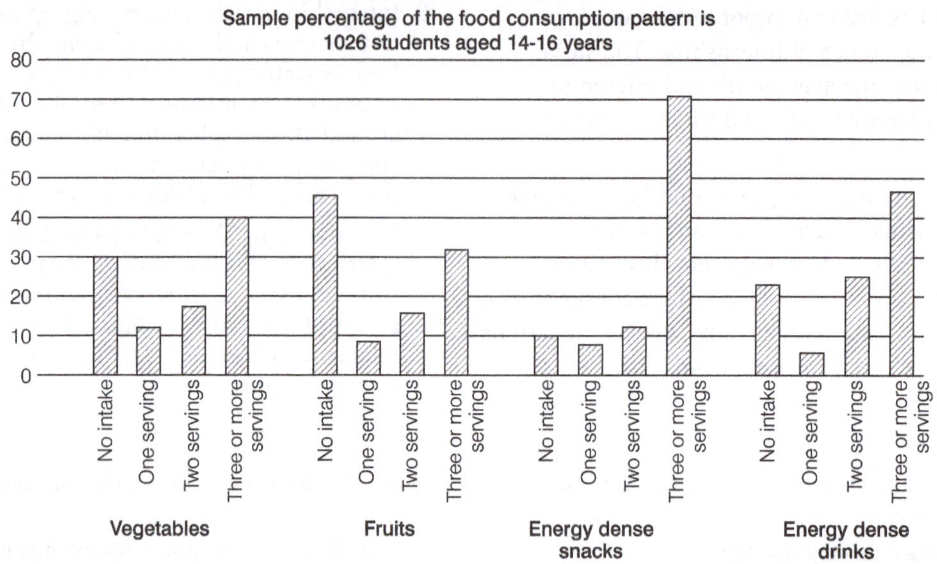

3. The survey results report poor food consumption patterns and highlights the need to design healthy eating initiatives. Interestingly, while there were no gender differences in the consumption of legumes and fried snacks, the survey found more females consumed cereals, vegetables and fruits than their male counterparts. In conclusion, the report suggested that schools ought to incorporate food literacy concepts into their curriculum as they have the potential of increasing the fruit and vegetable intake in teenagers. Additionally, healthy school canteen policies with improved availability, accessibility, variety and affordability of healthy food choices would support the consumption of nutritious food in students.

Questions

Based on your understanding of the passage, answer the questions given below.

(i) Complete the following sentence appropriately.
.... acts as a barrier in developing effective nutrition promotion and disease prevention measures?

(ii) Why is 'affordability' recommended as a significant feature of a school canteen policy?
(a) Because consumers are children
(b) Because food is a basics necessity
(c) Because children want to save
(d) Because it would promote balanced intake of food

(iii) Why was this survey on the food consumption of adolescents undertaken?

(iv) State True or False.
There were gender differences observed in the consumption of healthy foods, according to the survey.

(v) What can be said about the food choices of students on the basis of the figure?
(a) Childred do not like to eat fruits and vegetable.
(b) Children prefer eating energy boosting foods.
(c) Children eat only selective food items daily
(d) Children prefer energy drinks to energy dense foods.

(vi) What does the researcher mean by 'changing food preferences'?

(vii) What can be concluded by the 'no intake' data of fruit consumption versus energy dense snacks, with reference to Fig. 1?

(viii) Which of the following things can a school do to ensure consumption of nutritions food?
(a) Offer healthier varieties of food
(b) Offer affordable fresh meals
(c) Offer variety for balanced mea
(d) All of the above

Passage 12

1. The term Internet Addiction (IA) was first introduced in 1996 by Goldberg, who related it to substance dependence. IA can be defined as the maladaptive pattern of internet use which is time-consuming and leads to clinically significant impairment or distress. The symptoms of IA include tolerance, withdrawal and lack of control, relapse, and a large amount of time spent online. Internet Addiction generally consists of four elements namely, excessive use, withdrawal, tolerance and negative social repercussions.
2. Considering the recent report on the addiction of internet in India, in 2018, All India Institute of Medical Sciences (AIIMS) claimed that the number of people visiting with the complaints of internet addiction has almost doubled since the launch of the facility two years ago. It is not only about the internet but is the symptomatic expression of other psychological problems such as anger, low self-esteem, isolation and depression.

   World Health Organisation (WHO) in June 2018 classified gaming disorder as a mental health condition, thus, establishing the concern for the technology-oriented era on people. Further, as per the news, a London Hospital is also preparing to launch the first-ever internet addiction centre for young people and adults funded by the National Health Service (NHS).
3. Smartphones represent the edge of the evolution of information technology. As per the New Zoom's Global Market Report 2018, smartphone penetration in India is 28.5%, which constitutes 386,934,000 smartphone users.
4. The survey indicated the presence of addiction for 1·3% for internet (2% males and 0.6% females) and mobile phone overuse (4.1% – 2.5% males and 1.5% females).
5. Recent researches have shown a positive correlation between internet addiction and frequent use of smartphones, indicating a higher frequency of internet-based use of smartphone applications, priority being social networking sites and gaming applications.
6. As more and more people are getting involved in the internet and are getting addicted; thus, they have adopted the practice of 'Internet fasting' by deliberately spending time offline. Internet fasting can be defined as the re-evaluation of one's lifestyle to learn appropriate ways to use the internet by maintaining the distance from digital life.

Questions

Based on your understanding of the passage, answer the questions given below.

(i) Complete the following sentence appropriately.

The concluding paragraph conveys the message that ....

(ii) According to the author of the passage, the outcome of the advent of smartphones in the market is that

(a) it marked the evolution of information technology.

(b) the number of smartphone users exploded in the recent years.

(c) it triggered an increase in the number of people suffering from internet addiction.

(d) it encouraged more people to become tech-savvy.

(iii) How would you define internet addiction?

(iv) Read the following statements and state which is True.

1. Social networking sites and gaming applications are the root cause of Internet Addiction.
2. Internet addiction can save people from many psychological problems.

(v) WHO in June 2018 classified gaming disorder as a mental health condition. The above statement indicates that

(a) WHO is against the use of Internet.

(b) gaming disorder is a recognised global health issue.

(c) there is a need for ban on mobile games.

(d) there is a need to dissuade people from using smartphones.

(vi) How many smartphone users recorded in India?

(vii) London Hospital is preparing to launch the internet addiction centre. What does this statement mean?

(viii) State True or False.

Twitter is more popular than instagram among people.

Passage 13

1. An Increase in the Tiger population in India
   The fourth quadrennial report on the status of tigers released by the Government of India revealed that the number of tigers in India increased by 74% between 2010 and 2018, and by more than 33% between 2014 and 2018.
2. Certain methodological changes along with tiger conservation programmes have contributed to the increase. The tiger population has been estimated in three phases, wherein phase three made extensive use of camera traps. The 2018 data has been lauded since 83% of the tiger population was individually camera trapped. Additionally, in this data, all tigers above the age of one have been included while in all the previous surveys (in 2010 and 2006), only tigers above 1.5 years of age were included.
3. The estimate of tiger population may not be accurate owing to the limitations in counting the highly secretive carnivore. Hence, the survey provided not a specific number but the range of tiger numbers i.e., between 2,603 and 3,346. This data has a possible error of 14%. Currently, India is home to 75% of the global tiger population.
4. To estimate the tiger population pragmatically (since tigers keep moving within forests and are not restricted to any one state), India's states have been classified into five different regions: Shivalik Hills and Gangetic plains, North-East Hills and Brahmaputra Plains, Sunderbans, Central India and Eastern Ghats, and Western Ghats. The graph shows the region-wise distribution of India's tiger population.

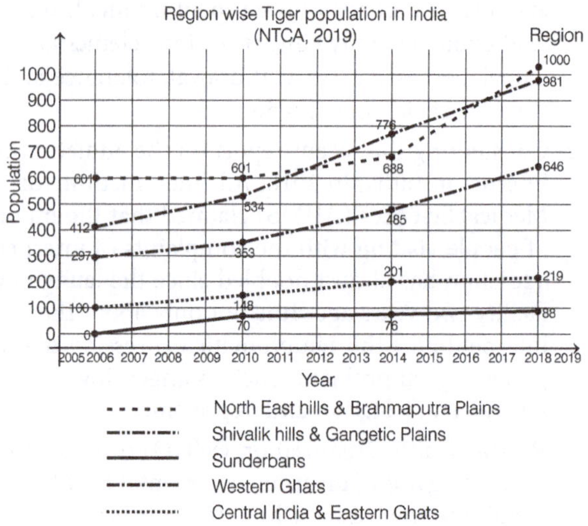

Questions

Based on your understanding of the passage, answer the questions given below.

(i) Complete the following statement with an appropriate inference from the passage.
It is appropriate to refer to India as the Land of Tigers because ....

(ii) Why is it a challenge to accurately estimate the total number of tigers present?
- (a) People who are skilled at estimating without errors are few.
- (b) Tigers are difficult to be spotted since they are good at hiding.
- (c) Tigers are dangerous since they are prone to attacking humans.
- (d) People find it difficult to keep up with the fast growing number of tigers.

(iii) Why does the author state that the increase in the tiger population between 2010-2018 is 'a step in the right direction'?

(iv) Which of these does the phrase 'wildlife trafficking' in Paragraph 5 refer to?
- (a) Organised relocation of endangered wildlife to their natural habitats
- (b) Illegal gathering, transportation and distribution of protected wildlife

(v) Based on the graph given, which of these regions showed a trend different from other regions between 2006 and 2010?
- (a) Sunderbans
- (b) Central India and Eastern Ghats
- (c) Shivalik Hills and Gangetic Plains
- (d) North-East Hills and Brahmaputra Plains

(vi) What does it mean when Paragraph 2 states that '83% of the tiger population was individually camera trapped'? Answer in 20-30 words.

(vii) State ways in which each of us can contribute to the conservation of tigers.

(viii) Which of these factors contributed to the increase in the number of tigers in the fourth quadrennial report?
I. Programmes designed to protect tigers
II. A change in the category of tigers considered
III. An improved methodological design to spot tigers
IV. A change in the total number of tigers above the age of one

Options

(a) I and III (b) III and IV
(c) I, II and III (d) II, III and IV

Passage 14

1. Virtual Reality (VR) technology has witnessed significant growth and adoption across various sectors worldwide. As of 2023, the global VR market size is estimated to be around $7.5 billion, with projections indicating substantial expansion in the coming years.

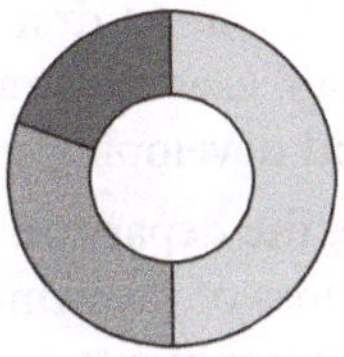

2. One of the primary drivers of VR adoption is the gaming and entertainment industry, which accounts for a significant portion of VR usage. In 2022, the global revenue from VR gaming alone amounted to approximately $4.5 billion. Popular VR gaming platforms like Oculus Rift, HTC Vive, and Playstation VR have amassed large user bases, with an increasing number of immersive gaming experiences being developed.

3. Beyond gaming, VR is making inroads in areas such as education, healthcare, and training. In education, VR enables immersive learning experiences, allowing students to explore historical sites, conduct virtual dissections, and engage in interactive simulations. Healthcare professionals utilise VR for medical training, surgical simulations, and therapeutic interventions.

4. Moreover, VR is revolutionising the way businesses conduct training and simulations. Companies are leveraging VR technology to train employees in realistic virtual environments, reducing costs and minimising risks associated with traditional training methods.

5. The adoption of VR is also driven by advancements in hardware technology, with more affordable and accessible VR devices entering the market. As of 2023, there are approximately 171 million active VR users worldwide, a number expected to grow as VR technology becomes more mainstream and diversified across industries.

Questions

Based on your understanding of the passage, answer the questions given below.

(i) Complete the following sentence with correct facts from the passage.

As of 2023, the global VR market size is estimated to be around ....

(ii) Which industry is the primary driver of VR adoption?

(a) Education (b) Healthcare

(c) Business (d) Gaming and entertainment

(iii) How is VR utilised in healthcare, and what are the benefits of using VR in business training?

(iv) Select the correct antonyms for 'leverage' as used in the following context.

Companies are leveraging VR technology to train employees in realistic virtual environments, reducing costs and minimising risks associated with traditional training methods.

I. Advantage II. Weakness

III. Rank IV. Disadvantage

Choose the correct option

(a) I and II (b) III and IV (c) II and III (d) II and IV

(v) The passage mentions the various uses of VR. Classify the following uses as Business and Medicine

Statement 1 Training

Statement 2 Therapy

(vi) Why is the adoption of VR technology expected to grow in the coming years?

(vii) From "VR is making inroads in areas such as education, healthcare, and training," what can be inferred about the versatility of VR technology? What does "immersive learning experiences" mean in the context of VR in education?

(viii) Which of the following is not a VR gaming platform?

(a) Oculus Rift

(b) HTC Vive

(c) Playstation VR

(d) Xbox

Passage 15

1. In 2024, the tech sector witnessed a significant phenomenon termed "brain drain", where skilled professionals migrated from one region to another, predominantly from developing countries to developed ones.
2. The tech industry, known for its rapid advancements and lucrative opportunities, became a magnet for talented individuals worldwide. However, disparities in economic opportunities, political instability, and limited career growth prospects in their home countries prompted many skilled workers to seek greener pastures abroad. For instance, countries like India and Nigeria experienced a notable exodus of tech talent to tech hubs such as Silicon Valley and Singapore.

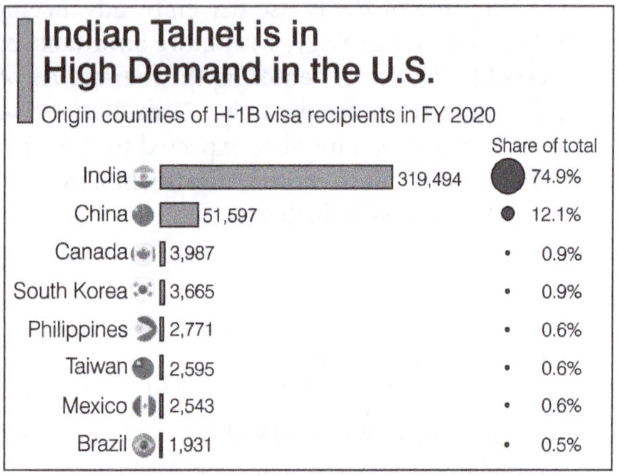

• The H-1B is a non-immigrant, i.e. temporary visa that allows U.S. companies to employ foreign workers in high-skilled speciality occupations.
Source: U.S. Citizenship and Immigration Services

3. This migration of skilled workers had multifaceted repercussions. While destination countries benefited from a diverse talent pool and enhanced innovation, source countries faced a depletion of their intellectual capital, hindering their own technological advancement and economic growth. Additionally, the brain drain widened the global technology gap, exacerbating inequalities between developed and developing nations.
4. Furthermore, the departure of skilled workers often resulted in a loss of investment in education and training, as governments and private sectors struggled to retain talent and foster innovation domestically.
   1.8 million Indians will be spending close to $85 billion on studying abroad by the year 2024. This perpetuated a cycle of underdevelopment in source countries, exacerbating socio-economic inequalities and impeding progress towards sustainable development goals.
5. In conclusion, the phenomenon of brain drain in the tech sector in 2024 underscored the urgent need for global cooperation and equitable policies to mitigate its adverse effects on both source and destination countries. Efforts to address the root causes of brain drain, such as improving economic opportunities and promoting inclusive growth, are essential for fostering a more balanced and sustainable global tech ecosystem.

Questions

Based on your understanding of the passage, answer the questions given below.

(i) Complete the following sentence with correct facts and figures from the table.
US granted majority H1B visas to indian skilled workers, the number was as high as .... In FY 2020.

(ii) What multifaceted repercussions did the migration of skilled workers have, according to the passage?
(a) Enhanced innovation in destination countries
(b) Depletion of intellectual capital in source countries
(c) Widened global technology gap
(d) All of the above

(iii) After reading the passage, give a brief explanation on how brain drain has impacted the education industry in India. Give statistics.

(iv) The given passage presents the causes and the result of brain drain. Classify the following statements as such.
Statement 1 depletion of intellectual capital
Statement 2 political instability

(v) Who is more likely to leave his/her country for better opportunities?
(a) Joseph from Canada (b) Moana from Brazil
(c) Shivanya from India (d) Jay from China

(vi) In what way did the brain drain phenomenon impact source countries?

(vii) What is the writer referring to by the phrase 'greener pastures'?

(viii) Efforts to address the root causes of ...., such as improving economic opportunities and promoting inclusive growth, are essential for .... a more balanced and sustainable global tech ecosystem.
(a) brain drain, fostering (b) economising, favourable
(c) studying, no (d) exodus, many

Answers

Passage 1

(i) its economic significance in terms of employment generation and infrastructure development

(ii) (c) Method of analysis

(iii) The study involved primary data and secondary data as

(a) Primary data was collected through a structured survey of 500 tourists, ensuring firsthand insights into their experiences and preferences.

(b) Secondary data was obtained from government reports and tourism boards, providing broader industry trends and statistics.

(iv) **Sentence 1** Preference, **Sentence 2** Challenge

(v) Two points tourists were asked about in the survey are

(a) Travel preferences (e.g. choice of destinations)

(b) Challenges encountered (e.g. infrastructure and pollution issues)

(vi) The more preferred destinations were historical sites and beaches.

(vii) While tourists enjoyed India's cultural richness and historical sites, complaints arose due to infrastructure gaps, overcrowding, and pollution, which affected overall travel experience.

(viii) (d) To promote India as a tourist destination.

Passage 2

(i) its crucial role in reducing carbon emissions and promoting sustainability

(ii) (a) Primary purpose

(iii) The two steps adopted in the survey methodology are

(a) Conducting a survey among households, businesses, and industries across various regions in India.

(b) Analysing the data to identify trends and patterns in energy preferences and the reasons behind them.

(iv) **Sentence 1** Influence, **Sentence 2** Motivation

(v) (c) Rajan - rural household head; Rama - small business owner; Suresh - large industry owner

(vi) The preference percentage is higher among rural areas because of the accessibility, reliability, and local employment opportunities provided by renewable energy sources. In rural areas, conventional power supply can be inconsistent, making renewable sources a more dependable option.

(vii) Targeted interventions based on diverse energy preferences can lead to improved environmental outcomes by

- Increasing government incentives to encourage wider adoption of renewable energy.
- Enhancing infrastructure to make renewable energy more accessible and reliable.
- Encouraging industries to adopt renewable energy by enforcing sustainability policies.
- Raising public awareness through media and educational programs.

(viii) (b) Build a sustainable future

Passage 3

(i) (b) Newspaper (ii) (c) it is from a reliable site

(iii) According to the passage, people share information because they believe that it might benefit others and help in their safety.

(iv) From the passage, it can be inferred that journalists spread misinformation unintentionally as they are not aware of the existence of fact checking organisation.

(v) that they are more prone to fall victims to fake news as they do not grasp the concept of fake information that are spread on these platforms.

(vi) Misinformation refers to false content that is unintentionally or unknowingly disseminated while fake news is deliberately fabricated as an agenda to achieve some purpose.

(vii) People below the age of 20 and above the age of 50 are most likely to fall victims to fake news. Early users or new entrants in social media are also susceptible to fake news than others who have been active on social media for some time.

(viii) The blame game goes on between media houses and individuals in fixing the onus of identifying the fake news. Individuals are asked to take the responsibility of verifying information before spreading it. However, it is believed that the media should also be equally responsible in curbing the spread of fake news by carrying out fact-checking process.

Passage 4

(i) The survey delves into the factors that make today's youth the happiest and what uplifts their overall well-being. It is reported that majority of the youth are satisfied with their lives. However, their stress level is also high due to academic pressures or workload and a quarter of the population reported feeling lonely.

(ii) As it is mentioned in the passage, more than half of the youth surveyed reported to have stress problems. In order to have access to counselling services, mindfulness activities and support groups, they would need financial support. This will in turn help them to manage their mental health and well-being better.

(iii) Reportedly, 65% of youth are in stress although a majority of the youth have also claimed to lead happy and contended lives which points out the need to provide mental health support to the youth.

(iv) (c) Books and literature (v) False (vi) (c) I and IV

(vii) counselling services, mindfulness activities and support groups

(viii) (c) Family support, (b) financial status, (a) purposefulness, (d) stress

Passage 5

(i) maneuverability of the crew

(ii) (b) At the time of landing or taking off

(iii) The sites of landsfills or waste disposals can attract a large number of birds. Further, in the monsoon, as water puddles emerge on open grounds attracting insects to breed, the presence of birds increases.

These increase the chances of bird hits making landfills prone to bird hits.

(iv) **Statement 1** Concern, **Statement 2** Cause

(v) (b) the pilot must land at the nearest airport

(vi) In the cases where bird hits happen at higher altitudes when a plane is cruising, the fear of air accident increase. This is so because the bird hits can cause rapid depressurisation of cabins.

(vii) The given statement is true because there are waste disposal sites nearby, there will be an increase in number of birds, thereby increasing the chances of bird hits.

(viii) (a) but only a few are dangerous

Passage 6

(i) "Effects of Use of Mobile Phone and Other Devices with Internet on School Children"

(ii) (a) Internet addiction among children.

(iii) The given findings indicate that while children are becoming tech savvy which is the need of the times, they are also becoming vulnerable to internet scams and addiction. With almost all children having social media accounts, there is a loss of health and good social relationships as well as interactions. Further, they lose concentration and focus.

(iv) **Statement 1** Effect, **Statement 2** Inference

(v) (b) Adil - Gosh! I can't keep my hands off from checking my notifications.

(vi) The survey mentions many ill effects of increased usage of mobile phones among children. Two of them are

- lapses in concentration
- weakening of attention span

(vii) Parents can play a pivotal role in curbing the rising menace of internet addiction among children. Parents must introduce other life skills to children to ensure a reduction in screen time and they can encourage social interaction of the child.

(viii) (c) online learning

Passage 7

(i) False. According to the passage, when the company has a lot of competitors, it tries to demand an outstanding job performance by every single employee to be better than that of their competitors.

(ii) The companies demand an exemplary performance from their employees because they want them to be better than that of their competitors due to the competition among enterprises.

(iii) (c) When there are chances to get financial gratification

(iv) According to the data given in the bar graph, team spirit and work environment are the two factors that display that work performance of both the categories of workers remains the same.

(v) the affect of the work performance of the 18-30 age group, due to factors such personal development, relaxed working environment, promotion prospects, job satisfaction and monetary incentives are more profound.

(vi) (c) motivated

(vii) respect from colleagues

(viii) The given statement is false as there are many factors other than increase in salary such as job satisfaction, relaxed working environment and promotion prospects that motivates an employee to perform better.

(ix) are team spirit, competent boss, respect from colleagues and job satisfaction

(x) (c) happiness

Passage 8

(i) Not Given

(ii) The Ratan model aims to provide value for money to the customers and protect the interests of farmers simultaneously.

(iii) (a) To show how Ratan diversified customer base

(iv) three-tiered structure

(v) (a) Coconut milk

(vi) (a) Ratan's business model

(vii) (d) Cognisance

(viii) The given phrase indicates that Ratan closely connects milk producers and customers through the three-tiered structure of the Ratan Model, which is used in its dairy operations. As a result, farmers (milk producers) have control over purchasing, processing and marketing. The farmers receive the entire benefit as a result and intermediaries cannot earn from a commission.

(ix) The 'Ratan Target Audience' is said to as a diverse market because every sort of client is taken into consideration while releasing the items. Age group and health are also important factors in segmentation. For example, chocolate, Ratan cool, and Ratan milk are marketed to children; pizza cheese and cheese spread are marketed to young people; and Ratan Shakti and RatanLite butter are marketed to consumers who are health conscious.

(x) The basis on which Ratan divides the target audience are
- Customer-wise targeting
- Industry-wise targeting

(xi) (d) Both (a) and (b)

(xii) One of Ratan's most well-known 'commercial' icons is the tale of the 'Ratan Girl.' It features a young girl in a hand-drawn cartoon.

Passage 9

(i) True. The passage states that plastic soft drink bottles became a visible source of annoyance in 1994. In the same year, people in other cities were concerned about the state of public sanitation and also urged regulatory bodies to ban the production, distribution and use of plastic bags.

(ii) The writer means that only in 1994 the plastic bottles could be seen in such numbers that it became annoying for the common man. Earlier it was not much of a nuisance.

(iii) Indian Petro-Chemicals (iv) (d) Both (a) and (b)

(v) (b) states the need for effective plastic waste management

(vi) Following steps being taken by some states for plastic waste management are

(a) Ten states of India are sending their plastic collected waste to cement plants for co-processing, (b) 12 other states are using plastic waste for polymer bitumen road construction and others use it for waste to energy plants and oil production.

Its impact would be seen on oceans with less plastic waste and this would help combat plastic jeopardy in a sustainable and holistic way.

(vii) India's trajectory of plastic consumption and waste would increase.

(viii) The phrase means that there is a lot of plastic floating in the oceans.

Passage 10

(i) Established companies

(ii) (c) As per the given lines, it can be said that earlier lesser companies were searching for interns as compared to those in the last five years.

(iii) There has been a rise/increase in internship applications because more and more companies today are looking for fresh minds and ideas for better productivity.

(iv) (b) Many of them do not report a healthy traffic every month.

(v) (c) As the passage states, the average stipend offered to interns was recorded as ₹ 7000.

(vi) Virtual internships are preferred because most of the applicants are students who are already enrolled in various courses and so prefer working from home.

(vii) I believe that companies do not prefer taking many interns because too many interns would reduce the number of people with expertise. The lack of expertise and effective training then would reduce productivity.

(viii) (b) 57.7%

Passage 11

(i) Lack of information about quality and quantity of fast foods consumed by adolescents

(ii) (a) Because consumers are children

(iii) The survey on the food consumption of adolescents was undertaken to understand the food consumption pattern of urban adolescents and to make recommendations based on the data.

(iv) True

(v) (b) Children prefer eating energy boosting foods.

(vi) By 'changing food preferences' the researcher means to say that the urban population is transitioning from healthy home-cooked meals to ready-to-eat processed food.

(vii) With reference to the given figure the 'no intake' data of fruit consumption versus energy dense snacks, nearly half the respondents (45%) did not consume any servings of fruit but in contrast to that, 95% had some form of energy dense snack.

(viii) (d) All of these

Passage 12

(i) it requires will of the people to lead a healthy life.

(ii) (c) it triggered an increase in the number of people suffering from internet addiction.

(iii) Internet addiction can be defined as the maladaptive pattern of internet use which is time consuming and leads to clinically significant impairment or distress.

(iv) Statement 1 is true.

(v) (b) gaming disorder is a recognised global health issue.

(vi) 386,934,000 smartphone users have been recorded in India.

(vii) The given statement means that internet addiction in same in all parts of the world and affect the young and adults alike.

(viii) False

Passage 13

(i) India is home to 75% of the tiger population in the world.

(ii) (b) Tigers are difficult to be spotted since they are good at hiding.

(iii) The writer states that the increase in the tiger population between 2010-2018 is 'a step in the right direction' because the outcome contributes towards the success of the Sustainable Development Goal 15 established by the United Nations. The goal focuses on the prevention of threatened species. Since tigers are an endangered species, the increase in the tiger population is aligned to this goal.

(iv) (b) Illegal gathering, transportation and distribution of protected wildlife

(v) (b) Central India and Eastern Ghats

(vi) The statement that 83% of the tiger population was individually camera trapped means that 83% of the tigers that were identified through special cameras that were set up in the tigers' natural habitats.

(vii) We can contribute to the conservation of tigers by not purchasing products that are made from tigers or their parts, by spreading awareness and sharing news about the tiger population, by volunteering for tiger conservation programmes, by donating for wildlife conservation projects and by carefully driving in the natural habitats of tigers.

(viii) (c) I, II and III

Passage 14

(i) $7.5 billion

(ii) (d) Gaming and entertainment

(iii) In healthcare, VR is used for medical training, surgical simulations and therapeutic interventions. In business training, VR reduces costs and minimises risks by providing realistic virtual environments for employees.

(iv) II and IV

(v) **Statement 1** Business

Statement 2 Medicine

(vi) The adoption of VR technology is expected to grow due to advancements in hardware and increasing affordability and accessibility of VR devices.

(vii) VR technology is versatile and applicable across various sectors beyond gaming and entertainment. It means using VR to create engaging, interactive environments that simulate real-life experiences for enhanced learning.

(viii) (d) Xbox

SELF ASSESSMENT TEST

Factual, Discursive & Literary Passages

Passage 1 (Factual)

1. 'Lifestyle' is a way used by people, groups and nations and is formed in specific geographical, economic, political, cultural and religious text. Lifestyle is referred to as the characteristics of inhabitants of a region in special time and place. It includes day to day behaviours and functions of individuals in job, activities, fun and diet.
2. In recent decades, lifestyle as an important factor of health is more interested by researchers. According to WHO, 60% of related factors to individual health and quality of life are correlated to lifestyle. Millions of people follow an unhealthy lifestyle. Hence, they encounter illness, disability and even death. Problems like metabolic diseases, joint and skeletal problems, cardio-vascular diseases, hypertension, overweight, violence and so on, can be caused by an unhealthy lifestyle. The relationship of lifestyle and health should be important considered.
3. Today, wide changes have occurred in life of many people. Malnutrition, unhealthy diet, smoking, alcohol consuming, drug abuse, stress and so on, are the representations of unhealthy lifestyle that are used as the dominant form of lifestyle. Besides, the lives of citizens face new challenges. For instance, emerging new technologies within IT, such as the internet and virtual communication networks, lead our world to a major challenge that threatens the physical and mental health of people. The challenge is to control the overuse and misuse of the technology.
4. Therefore, according to the existing studies, it can be said that: a person's lifestyle has a significant influence on their physical and mental health. There are different forms of such influences. Consanguinity in some ethnicity is a dominant form of lifestyle that leads to the genetic disorders. Reformation of this unhealthy lifestyle is a preventing factor for decreasing the rate of genetic diseases. In some countries, the overuse of drugs is a major unhealthy lifestyle. Iran is one of the 20 countries using the most medication.

   They prefer medication to other intervention. Furthermore, in 15–40% of cases they use medications without prescription. Pain relievers, eye drops and antibiotics have the most usage in Iran. While self-medications such as antibiotics have a negative effect on the immune system, if the individual would be affected by infection, antibiotics will not be effective in treatment. Overall, 10 per cent of those who are self-medicated will experience severe complications such as drug resistance. Sometimes drug allergy is so severe that it can cause death.

Questions

Based on your understanding of the passage, answer the questions given below.

(i) Paragraph 4 states Iran is one of the countries using most medication. Justify.

(ii) How would you relate health and lifestyle on the basis of your reading of the passage?

(iii) Problems like metabolic diseases, joint and skeletal problems, cardio-vascular diseases cannot be caused if

(a) we eat lots of fruits, green vegetables and dairy products daily.

(b) we avoid malnutrition, unhealthy diet, smoking, alcohol consuming, drug abuse, stress, etc.

(iv) Complete the sentence appropriately.

According to WHO, 60% of health factors are related to ....

(v) Assonance refers to the resemblance of sound in nearby words or syllables. It is a figure of speech.

From the given options, choose a phrase from the above passage that can be an example of assonance.

(a) "the overuse and misuse"

(b) "it can be said"

(c) "health and quality of life"

(d) "referred to the characteristics of inhabitants"

(vi) Do you think that Iran is medically careless? Give reasons for your answer.

(vii) What is a preventing factor for decreasing the rate of genetic diseases?

(viii) Complete the analogy using one word from paragraph 4.

Dominant : Superior : : Prevalent : ....

(a) Influence (b) Existing (c) Genetic (d) Lifestyle

(ix) Which of the following statements is not substantiated in Paragraph 4?

(a) Our lifestyle is responsible for our mental and physical health.

(b) Iran relies mostly on the medicines to cure most of the illnesses and diseases.

(c) Drug overdose causes allergy that becomes fatal sometimes.

(d) If any person is infected, it can only be treated by antibiotics.

(x) Which medication(s) has/have the most usage in Iran?

Passage 2 (Discursive)

1. When we think of the game of cricket, we come to the conclusion that it is primarily a game that depends on outstanding physical activities, good hand-eye co-ordination, speed, skill and strength. It provides entertainment and generates strong feelings of excitement. A good match of cricket or of any other game neither adds to the existing stock of human knowledge nor reveals any secret of existence. It does not carry any deep meaning but most people, particularly the lover of sports, attach deep emotions and numerous meanings to it. Games are thought of as a metaphor for life. They are supposed to teach many lessons. In fact, more is said and written about a cricket match than about scientific findings or great philosophy.

2. This is because games, like a morality play, in which settings and rules are made by us can easily make people test their fair and foul conduct, principles of reward and punishment, and emotions of joy and disappointment. They can make us experience the thrill of war without exposing us to its dangers. A man watching a cricket match on T.V. and munching popcorn is like a surrogate warrior. In fact, games provide us with a safe outlet for our aggressiveness. If games become aggressive, they lose the very purpose of providing entertainment and purging us of our aggressiveness. They can calm our impatience without creating any conflict.

3. Commentators, journalists, politicians and analysts can do a great favour to the competing teams by keeping the excitement within limits. The teams should play without being dominated by feelings of national honour and shame. Excellent performance of the players of both teams should be enjoyed and appreciated. Winning or losing in a game should not be taken seriously. A game is fun if it is played with true spirit of sportsmanship.

Questions

Based on your understanding of the passage, answer the questions given below.

(i) Comment on the writer's reference to that cricket does not reveal any secret of existence.

(ii) List two responses which watching a game of cricket gives rise to.

(iii) With reference to the passage, a spectator is compared to a 'surrogate warrior'.

Choose the option that best describes this phrase.

(a) A spectator who is paid to watch.

(b) A spectator who enjoys the match as an armchair soldier.

(iv) Complete the sentence suitably.

Most people conclude that cricket is primarily a game because ....

(v) Select the option that conveys the opposite of 'destroy' from words used in the passage.

(a) Reveals (b) Experience

(c) Generate (d) Purging

(vi) Why does the writer compare games to a morality play?

(vii) The writer says that games can calm our impatience. How?

(viii) The writer would agree with the given statements based on Paragraph 2, EXCEPT

(a) Rules of any game are made by people.

(b) Watching a cricket match makes the viewer believe that he is fighting a battle?

(c) It is necessary for a game to be aggressive in order to build excitement.

(d) A game can test people's sense of fair judgement.

(ix) Select the most suitable title for the above passage.

(a) Excellent Performance by Cricketers

(b) The Benefits of Playing Cricket

(c) Cricket-The King of Games

(d) The True Spirit of Playing Games

(x) A game is fun if it is played with true spirit of sportsmanship. How can this sportsmanship be maintained?

Passage 3 (Literary)

1. There are some places which seem as cute and welcoming, some formal and intimidating. And weren't we glad that Potboiler fell into the first category. We had dived into the coffee shop after being caught in a sudden sharp shower. High ceiling supported by old-fashioned columns, daylight pouring in from the wide windows, fairy lights, simple but comfortable seating arrangements and we were instantly struck by its inviting ambience.
2. As we were shown to our seats, we discovered there was more to the coffee shop than coffee. There were shelves of books around us, framed photographs of well-known authors and wall decoration sporting quotes from famous books. We could pick up any book (it was quite an eclectic collection) and read it while we sipped and munched, we were informed by the service staff.
3. As we scanned the menu and tried to figure out what to order, up walked a young girl to help us choose. Patiently she walked us through the varieties of coffee, about the journey of the beans from the farm to the cup, how it is roasted and brewed. Much later into the conversation we realised we were talking to the owner Sonali Lakhotia, who also happens to be a certified barista. And it is her love for books and coffee which forms the heart and soul of Potboiler. Even the brews and the food on the menu have been tweaked to give a literary turn.
4. "I am an avid reader who loves cafe hopping," Lakhotia would say later. "I always wanted to create a safe, escapist space where each and everyone felt like they belong to. A place they could step into to keep their worries away."
5. Incidentally, Potboiler showcases three to four coffee bean options from different roasters for a wholesome experience. It being a relatively uncrowded afternoon, we learned about where and how the coffee is grown, how it is roasted and brewed and what impacts the final cup. How one should be careful about the brewing method, the water temperature, the size of the ground coffee beans and their storage and the water-coffee ratio. And it is not only the coffee. While the beverage menu has been designed with some coffee experimentation, the food menu too has been revamped to suit a wide range of palate.

Questions

Based on your understanding of the passage, answer the questions given below.

(i) What forms the heart and soil of the Potboiler?

(ii) The writer mentions- the food menu too has been revamped to suit a wide range of palate. What does this mean?

(iii) Pick the option that correctly states what did not happen after the writer checked in the coffee shop.

(a) The writer found the ambience of the shop very appealing and inviting.

(b) The writer was welcomed by the owner of the shop who was an entrepreneur.

(c) The writer did not like the stuffy and dilapidated look of the shop.

(iv) Complete the following appropriately.
Potboiler can be defined as ....

(v) The use of the word 'intimidating' in the first line of the above passage suggests that the place is

(a) friendly (b) unapproachable
(c) responsive (d) distant

(vi) What things are to be taken care of in the brewing method?

(vii) "As we were shown to our seats, we discovered there was more to the coffee shop than coffee." Explain.

(viii) Complete the analogy with one word from Paragraph 5.
Changed : .... : : Taste : Palate

(a) Brewed (b) Revamped
(c) Uncrowded (d) Roasters

(ix) Which of the following statements is/are not true in the context of the passage?

1. Sonali Lakhotia, the owner of Potboiler coffee shop, was a certified barista.
2. The owner of the coffee shop was an avid reader of books and a lover of coffee.
3. Potboiler showcases three to four coffee bean options from different roasters for a wholesome experience.
4. The writer had to wait their turn to have a cup of coffee in the packed and congested crowded places.

Options

(a) Only 1 (b) Both 1 and 2
(c) Both 1 and 3 (d) Only 4

(x) What happened after the writer checked in the coffee shop?

Passage 4 (Factual)

1. Dinosaurs died gradually from climate change caused by a series of severe volcanic eruptions in the Deccan traps in India at the end of the Cretaceous period, says Gerta Keller, professor at Princeton University. This theory debunks the long-held notion that dinosaurs died due to climate change when a giant meteor hit the Yucatan region of Mexico. "The Chicxulub impact hit the Yucatan about 300,000 years before the mass extinction that included dinosaurs and therefore could not have caused it," Keller says.
2. Research by volcanologists shows that lava eruptions in the Deccan were not continuous but occurred in pulses, with each pulse lasting about 10 to at most a 100 years, and the pulses were separated by short periods of quiescence. New results from eight subsurface cores drilled by the Oil and Natural Gas Corporation of India, a public-sector undertaking, in the Krishna-Godavari Basin of Eastern India, reveal that at least nine lava flows mark the critical volcanic phase that ended in the mass extinction. This ending phase may have occurred over as little as 10,000 to 100,000 years. During each lava eruption, fire shot up in tall columns from fissures in the Earth's surface and lofted gases into the stratosphere while the oozing lava flow as sheets, or in rivers, up to 1046 kilometers across India, and formed the longest lava flows on Earth. "Their destructive nature is evident in the marine life record: the population of marine life decreased by about 50 percent after the first of these long lava flows," says Keller. "By the time of the last lava flow, the mass extinction was complete." The sulfur dioxide gas injected into the stratosphere converted to sulfate aerosols that caused climate cooling. The cooling lasted until the sulfate aerosols were washed out as acid rain and caused the ocean to acidify in the process.
3. Keller doesn't disagree with scientists who believe that the Chicxulub impact affected the climate. The event would certainly have caused earthquakes, tsunamis, regional fires and injected huge quantities of sulfur dioxide into the stratosphere, causing cooling and acidification of the land and oceans. "The difference is that the quantity of gas injection from the main phase of Deccan eruptions was 30 to 100 times larger than the Chicxulub impact and occurred over a shorter geological period of time, with each pulse lasting about 10 years or more."
4. Up until now, sceptics have doubted whether gas from Deccan-like eruptions can reach the stratosphere, but the relatively small 1783? 1784 Laki eruption in Iceland revealed that even rather small eruptions loft gases into the stratosphere. Field research by Keller and her collaborators has revealed that the mass extinction coincided with the end of the main phase of Deccan eruptions, suggesting that volcanism killed dinosaurs.

Questions

Based on your understanding of the passage, answer the questions given below.

(i) The passage mentions two differing views regarding the extinction of dinosaurs. Which global phenomenon is the underlying cause of dinosaurs' extinction in both these views? Answer in one sentence.

(ii) Cite a point from the passage that shows that the lava flows from the Deccan eruptions were extensive.

(iii) Based on the passage, choose an option to aptly complete the sentence below.

The research by Keller and her collaborators showed that the .... of mass extinction and the Deccan eruptions overlapped with each other.

(iv) Complete the sentence suitably.

The theory proposed by Gerta Keller was based on observations from a real, natural environment and not a controlled environment. This statement can be catergorised as ....

(a) field research (b) hypothesis

(v) Which of these best describes the author's tone in the passage?

(a) Sarcastic (b) Concerned
(c) Awestruck (d) Compelling

(vi) Cite a point of evidence which shows that the lava eruptions in the Deccan caused great damage to Earth's ecosystem.

(vii) According to Gerta Keller, how did the effect caused by the Chicxulub impact differ from that of Deccan eruptions?

(viii) Which of the following does not reflect Gerta Keller's viewpoint on the Chicxulub impact?

(a) It contributed to climate change.
(b) It caused the emission of sulphur dioxide.

(c) It caused acidification of land and oceans.

(d) It led to the phenomenon of mass extinction.

(ix) Which of these can be another suitable title of the passage?

(a) Reinventing the Life and Characteristics of Extinct Species

(b) The Current Theory of Dinosaur's Extinction Looks to India

(c) The Chicxulub Impact and its Environmental Consequences

(d) Understanding Major Mass Extinctions that Shaped the Earth

(x) In 30-40 words, state a point of evidence from the passage to show India's contribution to Keller's research work on Deccan eruptions.

Passage 5 (Literary)

1. As we speed our way from Guwahati towards Sualkuchi, vivid images of colourful silk mekhela chadars flood my mind. This is my second visit to Sualkuchi. Sualkuchi is endearingly referred to as the Manchester of the East. Situated on the Northern banks of the Brahmaputra, it is famous for its centuries-old heritage of weaving.

   When I reach Sualkuchi, I can hear the rhythmic click-clack of the traditional throw-shuttle loom.

2. Here, weaving is not just a tradition handed down by generations, but a way of life and a labour of love. The majority of the families have hand operated looms, which they call 'taatxaal'. "I've been weaving for more than 25 years now; I still love the craft," says Binita Roy, a weaver working here. As I ask Binita about the different designs used in the silk garments, I'm amazed at the sheer beauty of the motifs. A popular design used in mekhela chadars is the 'kinkhaap'. It is believed that this design has been used since the days of the Ahom kings and consists of two front-facing lions.

   Other popular designs include those inspired by Assamese jewellery like the 'gaamkharu' (a wrist band) or 'joonbiri' (a half moon-shaped pendant) and the kaziranga design inspired by the wildlife at Kaziranga National Park. These days, coloured silk threads are bought from South India as it is not commercially viable to dye the silks before weaving here.

3. Assam's flora and fauna often sneak into its mekhela chadars. Creepers are woven into borders, peacocks prance about the chadars and delicate, geometric flowers dot the bodies of the mekhelas. Occasionally, pots and lions too make an appearance. The more I learn about the tedious procedure of weaving, the more my respect for the craft grows.

4. There are mekhela chadars in different colours: red, blue, green, purple and blue as well as white, beige, black and grey. The 'paat' silk mekhela chadars have intricate designs made out of golden silk threads or guna all over. In some of them, different coloured threads are also used.

5. The white 'paat' silk, warm 'eri' and the golden 'muga' silk threads are made into exquisite chadars, saris, shawls, dress materials, rihas and 'gamochas'. The 'paat' fabric is often described as one that dries in the shade and hides in a fist. The crisp, bright, gold 'muga' silk, exclusive to Assam, is of superior quality and very costly. Mekhela chadars made from 'muga' are gracefully draped by dancers during Rongali Bihu, the traditional festival of Assam. 'Muga', the golden silk of Assam, was given the Geographical indication status in 2007 and the GI logo in 2014.

Questions

Based on your understanding of the passage, answer the questions given below.

(i) What is special of Sualkuchi?

(ii) What was the intention behind the writer's question to Binita's knowledge about the different designs?

(iii) Complete the given sentence appropriately.
The rhythmic click-clack that the writer hears indicates ....

(a) sewing

(b) movement of machines

(iv) Complete the sentence by choosing an appropriate option.
The 'gaamkharu' and the 'joonbiri' designs have been inspired by ....

(v) Which of the following words is closest in meaning to 'exquisite' as used in the above passage?

(a) Elegant (b) Crude (c) Rudimentary (d) Primitive

(vi) Cite a reason for the high cost of muga silk.

(vii) "The more I learn about the tedious procedure of weaving, the more my respect for the craft grows." What does this mean?

(viii) Select the option that lists central idea of Paragraph 5.
(a) Muga, the golden silk of Assam.
(b) Assam's flora and fauna depicted in the mekhela chadars.
(c) The famous golden tea of Assam.
(d) Mekhela chadars- the identity of Sualkuchi in Assam.

(ix) Select the most suitable title for the above passage.
(a) The Golden Silk of Assam
(b) The Assamese Textiles
(c) Visiting Sualkuchi
(d) A Trip to Remember

(x) The passage states 'Assam's flora and fauna often sneak into mekhela chadars'. Elucidate.

Passage 6 (Discursive)

1. From the moment a baby first opens its eyes, it is learning. Sight and sensation spark off a learning process that will significantly shape the person they become. Among all the tools of learning, language stands out as the most crucial. It gives humans an edge in intelligence over other creatures. No other species can assemble ideas, consider them, draw conclusions and then explain their reasoning. Man can do all this because of language.
2. Even very young babies respond to human voices uttering comforting words close to them. This emotional response provides early evidence that feeling is a vital component of language learning. Children learn to use language through interaction with other human beings, especially against a backdrop of affectionate feedback from those closest to them. The interaction between parent and baby, with eyes locked together, sets the pattern for their relationship.
3. Before they can even speak, children engage in a two-way communication process that lays the foundation for their later use of language. Surrounded by language, they unconsciously build mental structures into which their speech and reading will later fit-grammatical constructions, tense sequences, and more. The forms of these structures depend on the complexity of the speech they hear. Children who listen to articulate adults expressing ideas and defending opinions are fortunate. They understand that relationships are forged through speaking and listening, where warmth, humour and other emotions play a role.
4. Using books is essential for a child's language development. While adults can't endlessly initiate and maintain speech with very young children, books provide a rich source of language exposure. Through reading, children absorb vocabulary, grammar and various forms of expression. Thus, language plays a critical role in shaping thought and understanding, making it a powerful tool for lifelong learning.

Questions

Based on your understanding of the passage, answer the questions given below.

(i) Explain how humans can use language and do things that other species cannot.

(ii) "Language plays a critical role in shaping thought and understanding, making it a powerful tool for lifelong learning." Explain with examples from Paragraphs 3 and 4.

(iii) In the line "This emotional response provides early evidence that feeling is a vital component of language learning." What emotional response does the author refer to?
(a) Crying and Cooing
(b) Response to human voices uttering comforting words

(iv) Complete the following sentence with an appropriate word "Sight and sensation spark off a learning process that will significantly shape the person they become."
In the above sentence, the author talks about the .... process in humans.

(v) Find the word in Paragraph 3 which means 'express'.
(a) Process (b) Articulate
(c) Construction (d) Sequence

(vi) Children engage in a two-way communication process that lays the foundation for their later use of language. Elaborate.

(vii) Share evidence from the text in about 40 words, to support the view that surroundings and external factors play an important role in language development.

(viii) Read the five headlines (i)-(v) given below.
1. Language - The Key to Human Intelligence
2. Children - A Rebellious Generation
3. Early Language Development - From Infancy to Childhood
4. Teacher - A Nation Builder
5. The Role of Interaction in Language Acquisition

Identify the option that displays the headlines that correspond with the occurrences in the text.

(a) 1, 3 and 5 (b) 3 and 5 (c) Only 2 (d) 1 and 3

(ix) According to the passage, why do children who listen to articulate adults expressing ideas have an advantage?

(a) They learn to use language more quickly.
(b) They develop stronger relationships.
(c) They understand the importance of warmth and humour.
(d) They build complex grammatical structures.

(x) Explain in about 40 words why books are essential for children's language development.

Case Based Factual Passages

Passage 1

1. With the enormous amount of information potentially available to travellers, the Internet constitutes an important platform for information exchange between the consumer and industry suppliers (e.g. hotels, transportation sectors, attractions), intermediaries (e.g. travel agents), controllers (e.g. governments and administrative bodies), as well as many non-profit organisations such as destination marketing organisations.
2. Different technological interfaces, such as search engines, online travel booking sites, and websites of destination marketing organisations facilitate the information exchange between online travellers and the so-called 'online tourism domain'.
3. Particularly, it has been argued that understanding the nature of the online tourism domain, i.e. the composition of online tourism related information potentially available to travellers, provides an important stepping-stone for the development of successful marketing programs and better information systems in Tourism.
4. The importance of social media is identified by Xiang & Gretzel (2010). Their analysis showed that social media constitutes a substantial part of the search results, indicating that search engines linked the travellers directly to social media sites. Since more and more travellers seem to tap into this 'collective intelligence' available on the Web, this will challenge the established marketing practices of many tourism businesses and destinations.
5. The relation between social interaction, communication media and content can provide various supplementary advantages. It is more convenient and efficient way of spreading information compared to traditional media and thus, more and more companies are utilising it as a marketing channel. Furthermore, through media visibility companies are able to create more approachable image, and possibly bring awareness among new customers as well as retain existing consumer relationships.
6. One of the popular travel social media site Expedia Media Solutions partnered with ComScore, shed some insightful details of how travellers consume and share content prior to, during and after a trip.

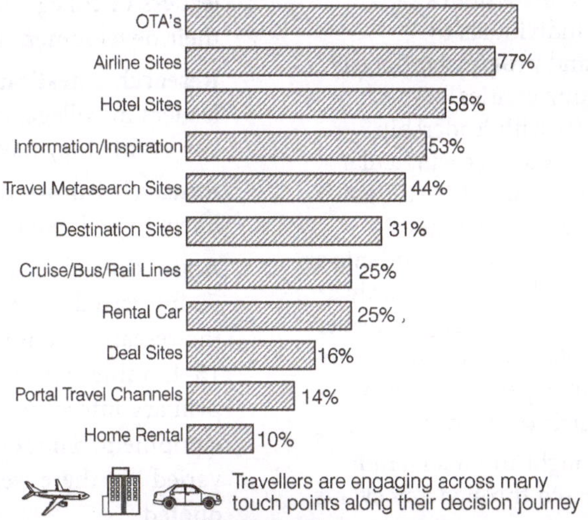

Travel Buyer Reach

7. It shows that the field of online content consumption is growing at a rapid pace. Another interesting point was that content is available and being accessed by consumers across more platforms and channels than ever before. Not surprisingly coming from an Expedia Solutions study, online travel agencies were found to be an important source across all platforms and throughout all stages of the booking process. It is no wonder that destinations, airlines, hotels and most travel marketers are embracing social networks such as pinterest, photo/video applications such as Instagram and Vine, as part of their storytelling toolkit, reaching out to growing crowds of travellers.

Questions

Based on your understanding of the passage, answer the questions given below.

(i) Complete the sentence appropriately.
Online tourism domain can be understood as ....

(ii) What does the given passage focus on?
- (a) The increasing role of social media in tourism.
- (b) The increasing demand of tourism.
- (c) The need to boost tourism in India.
- (d) The Indian Tourism marketing needs.

(iii) How is media visibility important to tourism?

(iv) Does the following statement agree with the information given in the Passage 5.
The relation between social interaction, communication media and content can be very advantageous.
Select from the following.
True if the statement agrees with the information
False if the statement contradicts the information
Not Given if there is no information on this

(v) Which of the following statements is not substantiated by information in Paragraph 4?
- (a) The established marketing practices of many tourism businesses and destinations are challenged by the online media.
- (b) Social media constitute a substantial part of the travel search results.
- (c) Search engines link the travelers directly to social media sites.
- (d) None of the above

(vi) Who are the controllers in the field of tourism?

(vii) According to Expedia solutions, what facilitates the exchange of information between online travellers and online tourism domain?

(viii) According to the given data graph, which marketing field shows the greatest influence of tourists?
- (a) Deal sites of make my trip
- (b) Site of Malibu
- (c) OTA's
- (d) Air India

Passage 2

1. It is generally accepted that leadership development should be a part of the education system's responsibility for preparing individuals to participate in a democratic and progressive society. Many schools, colleges and universities, across nations, provide their students with leadership courses, curricular programmes and co-curricular programmes that are designed to develop students' formal knowledge about leadership as well as opportunities and experiences to develop students as leaders and actually practise leadership. Yet, only a handful of studies have sought to understand leader development from the students' point of view, with students describing their own experiences and what they learned from them in their own words.

2. A recent descriptive study sought to understand student leadership with research through key events via the following research questions:

Research Question 1 What key events do student leaders in college, report as significantly impacting their development as a leader?

Research Question 2 What lessons do student leaders in college, report learning as a result of the key events they have experienced?

Research Question 3 Are certain key events more likely to be linked to particular lessons?

Approximately 130 students were contacted and the 72 interested, were interviewed. Two members of the research team were present for each 15-45 minute interview. One member served as the primary interviewer while the second ran the audio equipment. The results for lessons learned were varied but there were a few that were frequently quoted.

Lessons Learned	Responses
Identity	
Self Identity	58
Leadership Identity	54
Professionalism	30
Balancing Roles	19
Individual Competencies	
Delegation	17
Decision Making	15
Adaptability/Flexibility	38
Resilience/Persistence/Hard Work	18
Taking Initiative	36
Accountability/Responsibility	29
Big Picture	27
Learning to Teach/Learn	18
Support Systems	
Developing and Using Support Systems	36
Being a Support System	28
Working with Others	
Communication	59
Teamwork	26
Conflict	21
Diversity	32
Inspiring and motivating others	17
Other working with others	30
Getting the job done	
Task skills	55
Environment	54

3. This study described the rich array of leadership lessons that students are learning through their experiences. It revealed that student leaders are learning foundational leadership skills and competencies that have positively impacted how to accomplish work, how to work with others and how to be both supported by and support others.

Questions

Based on your understanding of the passage, answer the questions given below.

(i) Complete the sentence appropriately.

More than 50% of the identified student respondents were keen to participate in the 2014 study. We can say this because ....

(ii) Select the option that displays the most likely reason for including Research Question 3 in the 2014 study.

In order to find out if...

(a) learning opportunities shape students' overall personality
(b) leadership lessons are the result of the designed learning opportunities
(c) all learning opportunities cater to a specific lesson
(d) certain lessons are common in more than one learning opportunity

(iii) Do you think the researchers of the study aimed to change the students' outlook towards the development of leadership skills, directly or indirectly? Support your answer with reference to the text.

(iv) Fill in the blank by choosing the correct words from the brackets.

The concluding sentence of the text makes a clear case for .... (collaboration/observation) by listing it as a core competency for student leadership.

(v) Give one reason why having the least number of responses for 'Decision Making', is a matter that needs attention. This is because

(a) there were least number of responses for 'Decision Making'
(b) Students were indecisive during the survey.
(c) Decision making was selected as the least practiced skill.
(d) Students did not consider decision making as important.

(vi) Does the following statement agree with the information given in Paragraph 1?

The researcher believes that educational institutions have ideal resources to study impact of leadership skills on young adults.

(vii) Based on the reading of the text, state a point to challenge the given statement.

When theoretical knowledge about leadership suffices, it is a waste of funds by educational organisations, to organise leadership camps and programmes.

(viii) Complete the given sentence by selecting the most appropriate option.

The 2014 study attempts to understand student leadership by focussing on ....

(a) experiences that shaped students' overall personality
(b) lessons gained by students as they grew up
(c) relationship of key events with particular lessons
(d) students in leadership roles

Passage 3

1. A new poll of global experts by the Thomson Reuters Foundation published on Tuesday suggests that India is perceived as the most dangerous country for women. India's rise to the top place (it occupied the fourth place in a similar survey in 2011) is driven by the perception about rising sexual violence in the country, Thomson Reuters Foundation reported.

2. But a Mint analysis of data from Demographic and Health Surveys (DHS) conducted across developing nations of the world shows that the incidence of sexual violence reported by women is lower in India than in most other countries for which such data is available.

3. The DHS surveys that are conducted periodically by the respective governments of these countries with funding from the United States Agency for International Development and UN agencies are considered to be the official source of data on health, nutrition and status of women for the respective nations.

4. According to the data provided by the DHS, the incidence of such violence against women has declined over time of the 43 countries for which recent data on sexual violence is available, India ranks 32 when it comes to the share of women, aged 15-49, who experienced such violence in their lifetime.

Not the most dangerous place

The incidence of sexual violence is lower in India compared to several other developing nations

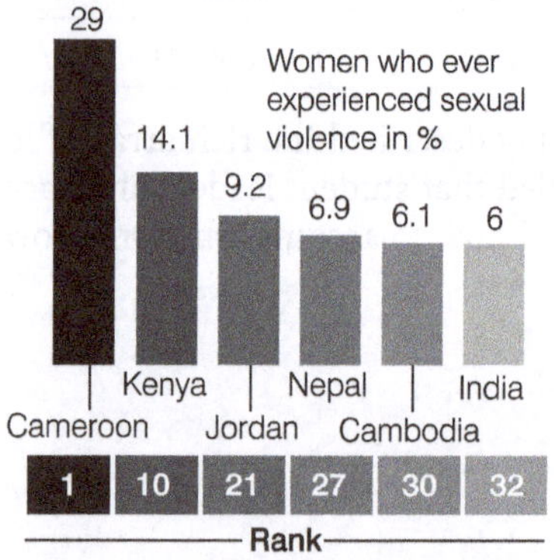

Countries for which DHS data is available for 2010 and later have been considered here.

5. From the details given above, there seems to arise a dissonance between the perception about India, as recorded by the Thomson Reuters Foundation poll of around 550 global experts, and the actual experiences of millions of women across the world, as recorded by the DHS surveys.
6. While it is possible that the DHS surveys underestimate the true extent of sexual violence faced by women, there is little reason to believe that the bias, if it indeed exists, is higher for India than for other countries. While the risk of sexual violence in India is undeniable, India does not seem to be the most dangerous place when it comes to the risk of sexual violence.
7. The nature of sexual violence that women face, however, has a unique dimension in India. Chances that the perpetrator of sexual violence is known to the victim are among the highest. Most offenders tend to be husbands or partners of the victims.
8. The high share of known offenders might also partly explain why most sexual assaults go unreported in the country. As pointed out, 99% of sexual assaults in the country go unreported. Even if one excludes marital rape, 85% of sexual assaults go unreported. Even among crimes that are reported, most perpetrators are known to the victims.
9. The silver lining in the data is that the actual incidence of sexual violence, as recorded by NFHS (the DHS of India), has declined over the past decade even as the reporting of sexual assaults has risen.

Questions

Based on your understanding of the passage, answer the questions given below.

(i) Complete the sentence appropriately.
The countries that participate in the DHS are ……………

(ii) According to the Thomson Reuters Foundation, India is the most dangerous country for women because of
(a) the patriarchal system
(b) rising cases of sexual violence
(c) the number of unreported cases in India
(d) the apathy of government to the cause of women

(iii) Give a brief description of the DHS on the basis of the given passage.

(iv) State True or False.
99% of the sexual assaults on women go unnoticed.

(v) The Thomson Reuters Foundation recorded the data from
(a) real experiences of women
(b) global experts
(c) Both (a) and (b)
(d) the institutions commissioned for women safety

(vi) With reference to the figure, write one conclusion about the perception of rising sexual violence in the world.

(vii) The nature of sexual violence women face, however, has a unique dimension in India. Explain.

(viii) What does the passage tries to claim?
(a) India is not the most dangerous country for women.
(b) The surveys often take incorrect data.
(c) India has been subduing the patriarchal structure.
(d) There are discrepancies in various surveys regarding women's health.

Passage 4

1. The 21st century will be ruled by data. Data Science has become an indispensable part of many businesses and industries. It provides valuable insights into customer behaviour that can lead to increased conversions, more detailed market analysis for competitive advantage in pricing strategies or product development, improved operational efficiency and minimised risk exposure through accurate forecasting models. The emergence of disruptive technologies like IoT, digital media platforms, smartphones, artificial intelligence, big data analytics, blockchain and quantum computing has ushered in an era where Data Science will be central to organisational success.
2. As organisations are turning towards Machine Learning, Big Data and Artificial Intelligence, the demand for Data Science roles is seeing a sustained and accelerating upward surge. Since 2012, the Data Science sector has witnessed a massive hike of 650%, far outpacing other sectors.
3. Therefore, transitioning to Data Science is a smart move as it fetches far higher comparative returns. For instance, transitioning from a marketing analytics job to a Data Science job leads to a 37% salary growth on average.

4. Similarly, the expected salary growth when people switch from digital analytics to Data Science is 31% on average. For someone transitioning from a Data Engineering role to a Data Science role, the salary hike could be as high as 44%. According to recruitment firm Michael Page's 2021 India Talent Trends report, Data Science professionals with 3-10 years of experience get annual salaries in the 25-65 lakh range, while those with more experience can command pay packages upwards of 1 crore.
5. Professionals with over 15 years of experience can get paid up to 1.8 crores. Similarly, the average annual pay hike for Data Science professionals falls between 20-30% compared with 15-20% for professionals from other backgrounds. India Inc. is witnessing the rapid digitisation of businesses and services, making it the second-largest hub for Data Science in the world. Analysts predict that the country will have more than 11 million job openings by 2026. In fact, since 2019, hiring in the Data Science industry has increased by 46%.
6. Data Science and Machine Learning have a steep learning curve. Even though there is a huge influx of data scientists in India every year, very few people have the required expertise and specialisation. As a result, there is a surging demand for professionals with specialised data skills.

Questions

Based on your understanding of the passage, answer the questions given below.

(i) Complete the sentence appropriately.
There is a demand for professionals with specialised data skills ....

(ii) Select the central idea of the paragraph preceding Paragraph 4.
(a) The transitioning to Data Science is not a smart move and should not be encouraged.
(b) The transitioning from a marketing analytics job to a Data Science job leads to a plunge in the salary on average.
(c) The transitioning from a marketing analytics job to a Data Science job leads to a boost in the salary on average.
(d) The transitioning to Data Science leads to organisational success by minimising the attrition rate.

(iii) What does the author mean by 'steep learning curve' in the context of the passage?

(iv) Identify the term in Paragraph 2 that indicates that certain technologies are becoming popular.

(v) The demand for .... is seeing a sustained and accelerating upward surge.
Which demand is being referred to here?
(a) Robotics' learning
(b) Design thinking
(c) Nanotechnology
(d) Data Science

(vi) "Transitioning to Data Science is a smart move". Substantiate.

(vii) On the basis of the passage, write any two conclusion about the scope in the field of data and analytics.

(viii) Select the correct inference with reference to the following.
"...the average annual pay hike for Data Science professionals falls between 20-30% compared with 15-20% for professionals from other backgrounds."
(a) There is a lot of scope of annual increment for professionals from any other background than Data Science.
(b) There isn't much scope of annual increment for professionals from any other background than Data Science.
(c) There is a lot of scope of annual increment for Data Science professionals.
(d) There isn't much scope of annual increment for Data Science professionals.

Passage 5

1. The Olympic Games, hailed as the pinnacle of athletic excellence and international camaraderie, present an unparalleled platform for showcasing talent and promoting sportsmanship. However, ensuring equitable access to the Games, particularly among youth demographics, remains a pressing concern.
2. In recent years, efforts have been made to democratise access to the Olympic Games, particularly among youth cohorts, through various initiatives aimed at increasing participation and engagement. One such initiative is the Youth Olympic Games (YOG), introduced in 2010 by the International Olympic Committee (IOC). The YOG serves as a platform for young athletes aged 15 to 18 to compete in Olympic sports, providing them with invaluable experience and exposure on an international stage.

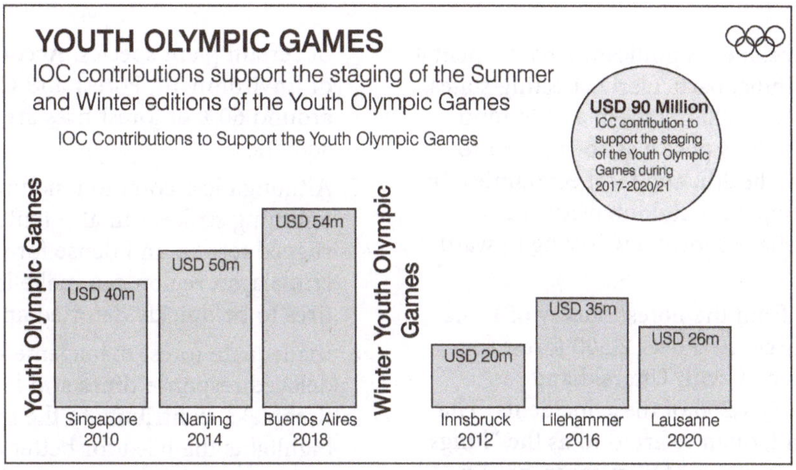

3. Furthermore, advancements in digital technology and media have played a pivotal role in expanding youth access to the Olympic Games. With the proliferation of livestreaming platforms and social media channels, youth audiences now have unprecedented opportunities to engage with Olympic events in real-time, regardless of geographical barriers. Moreover, the IOC's emphasis on youth-oriented content and interactive experiences has resonated with younger demographics, fostering a sense of ownership and belonging within the Olympic movement.

4. Despite these strides, challenges persist in ensuring comprehensive youth access to the Olympic Games, particularly in marginalised communities with limited resources and infrastructure.

   Addressing these challenges requires concerted efforts from stakeholders across the Olympic ecosystem, including policymakers, sports organisations, and community leaders, to implement targeted interventions and foster a culture of inclusivity and accessibility for future generations.

Questions

Based on your understanding of the passage, answer the questions given below.

(i) Complete the following sentence with correct facts and figures from the table.

IOC contributed .... to support the staging of Youth Olympic Games during 2017-2020/21.

(i) What inference can be made regarding youth participation in Olympic Games in India?

(ii) Which of the following best describes the role of digital technology in increasing youth participation in the Olympic Games?

(a) Reducing the cost of attending the games in person.
(b) Replacing traditional sports with e-sports competitions.
(c) Increasing the number of youth athletes who can compete in the games.
(d) Providing real-time access and engagement through livestreaming and social media.

(iii) What initiatives have been introduced to increase youth participation in the Olympic Games and what challenges still hinder this participation in India?

(iv) Based on the given data, select which nation funded $40 Million and $20 Million.

(v) What has the IOC's emphasis on youth-oriented content done?

(a) Foster health
(b) Foster belonging
(c) Foster responsibility
(d) All of these

(vi) What is the writer referring to by 'culture of inclusivity'?

(vii) List two functions of Youth Olympic Games (YOG).

(viii) Fill in the blank by selecting the correct option.

The .... Games, hailed as the pinnacle of .... excellence and international camaraderie, present an unparalleled platform for showcasing talent and promoting sportsmanship.

(a) Olympic, athletic
(b) Olympus, intellectual
(c) Ogilvy, sports
(d) Summer, textbook

Passage 6

1. Forest fires have become a significant environmental concern in North India, particularly affecting states like Uttarakhand, Himachal Pradesh and Jammu and Kashmir. These fires pose a serious threat to biodiversity, human health, and local economies. In recent years, the frequency and intensity of forest fires in this region have shown a worrying upward trend.
2. According to data from the Forest Survey of India (FSI), North India reported over 2,500 forest fire incidents in 2023 alone, with Uttarakhand accounting for nearly 1,200 of these incidents. The fires in Uttarakhand, often referred to as the "lungs of India" due to its extensive forest cover, have had devastating impacts. The 2023 fires burned over 4,000 hectares of forest land, causing significant loss of flora and fauna.
3. Several factors contribute to the increasing incidence of forest fires in North India. Rising temperatures and prolonged dry spells have created more favourable conditions for wildfires. The region has experienced an increase in average temperatures and reduced precipitation, exacerbating the dryness of forest floors and making them more susceptible to ignition.
4. Human-induced factors are a major cause of forest fires. These include agricultural practices like slash-and-burn (shifting cultivation), accidental fires from picnickers or trekkers, and intentional fires set by locals for land clearing or improving the growth of certain plant species. According to the Ministry of Environment, Forest and Climate Change, around 60% of forest fires are caused by human activities.
5. Although less common, natural causes such as lightning strikes can also ignite forest fires. The rugged terrain and dense forest cover in the Himalayan region can make it difficult for natural fires to be quickly detected and controlled.
6. Inadequate forest management practices, including delayed response times and lack of proper firebreaks, contribute to the spread of fires. The FSI highlights the need for better early warning systems and increased investment in firefighting infrastructure and training.
7. The impact of these fires extends beyond the immediate destruction of forest cover. They lead to loss of wildlife habitat, reduced air quality due to smoke and particulate matter and increased carbon emissions, further exacerbating climate change. The economic cost is also significant, affecting tourism, agriculture, and local livelihoods dependent on forest resources.
8. Addressing forest fires in North India requires a multifaceted approach, including improving forest management practices, increasing public awareness and enhancing coordination between state and central agencies to mitigate and respond to fires effectively.

Questions

Based on your understanding of the passage, answer the questions given below.

(i) Complete the following sentence appropriately.

Rising temperatures and .... have created more favourable conditions for wildfires.

(ii) According to the Ministry of Environment, Forest and Climate Change .... percentage of forest fires in North India are caused by human activities.

(a) 30% (b) 45%
(c) 60% (d) 75%

(iii) What are the primary climatic and human-induced factors contributing to forest fires in North India?

(iv) State whether the statement given below is True or False.

Inadequate forest management practices do not contribute to the spread of forest fires in North India.

(v) Which state in North India reported the highest number of forest fire incidents in 2023?

(a) Uttarakhand
(b) Himachal Pradesh
(c) Jammu and Kashmir
(d) Punjab

(vi) How many forest fire incidents were reported in North India in 2023 according to the FSI?

(vii) What are the impacts of forest fires on the environment and local economies in North India?

(viii) What is a significant natural cause of forest fires in the Himalayan region?

(a) Lightning strikes
(b) Tourismz
(c) Cigarette butts
(d) Camping fires

CREATIVE WRITING SKILLS

01 CHAPTER

Short Composition

Notice

A notice is a very important form of written communication used by individuals and organisations to convey into about functions, events and occasions or to make an announcement about something that has happened or is about to happen.

Marking Scheme

Format	1 Mark
Content	2 Marks
Expression	1 Mark
(Accuracy of Spelling and Grammar)	

Points to be Kept in Mind While Writing a Notice

- The language used must be simple and clear.
- Use third person pronouns. Use of personal pronouns like I, me, you, mine, your, etc. should be avoided.
- Always write the content of the notice in present or future tense.
- Remember that the content of the notice must answer the questions - 'What?', 'When?', 'Where?', 'How?', 'Why?' etc. and provide all the necessary details required.
- Always write the notice in a box.
- Adhere to the word limit, if given in the question.

Types of Notice

We write various types of notices for various purposes. Some notices that are asked in Class XII examination are

(i) Notice for Meeting

(ii) Notice for events like Competition/Celebration/Cultural events, etc.

(iii) Notice for tours/visits

(iv) Notice for Lost or Found

(v) Notice for Seminar/Workshop/ Debate/Other Literary Events

(vi) Notice for Appeal

(vii) Notice for Change of Name/Residence/Company, etc.

(viii) Notice for warning to the general public

(ix) Notice for giving general information

Format of a Notice

You are Aakrati of Class XII. As the Cultural Secretary of your school, draft a notice for a Robotics Workshop to be held in your school.

KSNN International School, Delhi — Name of the Organisation/Institution/Office issuing the notice

NOTICE — The word 'Notice' to be written in capitalisation

1st February, 20XX — Date of issuing the notice on the left side

Robotics Workshop — Subject of the Notice

This is to inform all the students that a Robotics Workshop is being organised on 12th February, 20XX at school auditorium. Those willing to participate in the workshop can give their names to their respective class teachers latest by 10th February. Only students who submit their names will be allowed to attend the workshop. The workshop is for Class VI to XII students.

For further details, contact the undersigned.

— The content of the notice

Aakrati
(Cultural Secretary)

— Name & Designation of the person issuing the notice

Type 1 Notice for Meeting

Details Required

- Who has called the meeting
- Date and time/duration of the meeting
- Venue
- If requiring further details, contact person with designation
- Purpose or agenda of the meeting
- People/departments who are required to attend the meeting
- Specific instructions for the people called for the meeting

Sample Notice 1 You are Abhishek/Avantika of Class XII, Swami Vivekanand Public School. Being an Activity Coordinator, draft a notice to all the other Activity Council members to attend a meeting to discuss and plan the activities for 25th December (Christmas Day) celebrations.

Ans.

Swami Vivekanand Public School, Delhi

NOTICE

6th December, 20XX

Activities for Celebration of Christmas Day

All the Activity Council members are hereby informed to attend a meeting tomorrow at 10:30 a.m. in the Biology Lab. The meeting is called to discuss the activities to be organised for Christmas Day celebrations. Members are expected to come up with their suggestions and ideas along with the estimated cost and all other necessary requirements. For further details, please contact the undersigned.

Abhishek/Avantika
Class XII
(Activity Coordinator)

Type 2 Notice for Events
(Competition/Celebration/Cultural Event etc.)

Details Required

- Who is organising
- Occasion
- Venue
- Contact person with designation
- Who can participate
- Time, Date and Day
- Any specific instructions

Sample Notice 2 You are the Secretary of the Environment Club of Dharmik Sandhya Public School. Write a notice to invite students of Class XII to the tree plantation drive organised by the Club on the World Environment Day.

Ans.

Dharmik Sandhya Public School

NOTICE

25th May, 20XX

Tree Plantation Drive

All the students are hereby informed that the Environment Club of the school is organising a tree plantation drive on the occasion of World Environment Day on 5th June, 20XX. The club needs volunteers to make the drive meaningful and successful. Interested students of Class-XII may register their names with the undersigned by 2nd June, 20XX. For further details, contact the undersigned.

XYZ
(Secretary, Environment Club)

Sample Notice 3 Write a notice to be published in your school magazine about a charity show in aid of cancer patients. Do not forget to give the details regarding the date, venue, time, etc. You are Amar/Amrita.

Ans.

Aryamba Public School, Kochi

NOTICE

12th June, 20XX

Charity Show for Cancer Patients

This is to inform all the students that a charity show is being organised by the Cultural Club of the school, in aid of cancer patients. The details are as follows
Date 20th November, 20XX
Venue School Cultural Hall
Time 3:00 p.m. to 6:00 p.m.
All the interested students may give their names to their respective class teachers latest by 15th November, 20XX. Kindly cooperate and participate to make this show a great success. For any other details, you may contact the undersigned.

Amar/Amrita
(Secretary, Cultural Club)

Sample Notice 4 Arts Club of your school is going to organise a drawing and painting competition. Write a notice in not more than 50 words to be displayed on the school notice board inviting students to participate in it. Give all the necessary details. You are Rishabh/Ridhima, Secretary, Arts Club, Sunrise Public School, Gurugram, Haryana.

Ans.

Sunrise Public School, Gurugram, Haryana

NOTICE

11th January, 20XX

Drawing and Painting Competition

All students of the school are invited to participate in a Drawing and Painting Competiton on Saturday, 21st January, 20XX at 11 a.m. in the school auditorium. Interested students may submit their names to their respective class teacher latest by 15th January, indicating the category (Drawing or Painting) in which they want to participate. For further details, contact the undersigned.

Rishabh/Ridhima
(Secretary, Arts Club)

Type 3 Notice for Tours/Visits

Details Required

- Who is organising
- Who can be a part of the tours
- Fare cost
- Last date for deposit
- Purpose
- Number of days
- Itinerary

Sample Notice 5 Your school has planned an excursion to Lonavala near Mumbai during the autumn holidays. Write a notice in not more than 50 words for your school notice board, giving detailed information and inviting the names of those who are desirous to join. Sign as Naresh/Namita, Head Boy/Head Girl, DV English School, Thane, Mumbai.

Ans.

DV English School, Thane, Mumbai

NOTICE

2nd October, 20XX

Excursion to Lonavala

This is to inform all the students that our school is organising an excursion to Lonavala near Mumbai during the autumn holidays. The details of the excursion are as follows
Duration 12th October, 20XX to 17th October, 20XX
Fare cost 5500/-
Itinerary Stay at a 4-star hotel. Adventurous activities like trekking, zip-living, rock climbing etc. followed by bonfire and DJ at night.
All the interested students must submit the fare along with the consent form latest by 7th October, 20XX to their respective class teachers. For further details, contact the undersigned.

Naresh/Namita
(Head Boy/Girl)

Type 4 Notice for Lost or Found

Details Required

- Article/Object lost or found
- Where you lost or found it
- Description of the article like colour/size/model, etc.
- Date/Time/Day when you lost it/found it
- Whom to contact
- A suitable gift/reward for the person who returns that article/product
- Writer's name and designation/class

Sample Notice 6 Ira Sachdeva is the Head Girl of Vanasthali Public School, Ludhiana. She lost her hall ticket for the Board Examinations. She has to put up a notice on the school notice board. Draft the notice in not more than 50 words.

Ans.

Vanasthali Public School, Ludhiana

NOTICE

25th February, 20XX

Lost-Hall Ticket

This is to inform all that Ira Sachdeva has lost her hall ticket for Class XII Board Examinations in the school playground during lunchtime. It has her photograph along with her Roll no. 1234567. Anybody who finds it is requested to give it to her in Class XII or to the Administrative Officer. The person finding it and handing it over will be rewarded.

Ira Sachdeva
Class XII

Sample Notice 7 You have found a plastic bag in the park near your house. Write a notice for the same in about 50 words. Invent the necessary details.

Ans.

Shiv Vatika Park, Janakpuri

NOTICE

5th February, 20XX

Found

This is to inform all that a small black plastic bag containing some documents and cash was found in the park premises on 2nd February, 20XX around 10 a.m. The genuine owner is requested to collect it from the undersigned after proper identification.

XYZ
(The Secretary)

Type 5 Notice for Seminar (Workshop/ Debate/Other Literary Events)

Details Required

- Organising Body
- Who can attend
- Subject of the seminar/debate/workshop
- Duration of the programme
- Speakers/Chief Guest/Honourable Persons
- Date/Time
- Specific instructions
- Contact Person/Designation, etc.

Sample Notice 8 You are Vikram, School Captain of Meerut Public School, Shastri Market, Varanasi. Write a notice informing the students of Class XII about a guest lecture by Mr. Rajiv, an environmentalist, on the topic 'Conservation of Water'. Write the notice in not more than 50 words.

Ans.

Meerut Public School, Shastri Market, Meerut

NOTICE

31st October, 20XX

Guest Lecture by An Environmentalist

All the students of Class XII are informed that a guest lecture on the topic 'Conservation of Water' by a renowned environmentalist Mr. Rajiv is organised by the school. The seminar/lecture will be held on the coming Saturday, i.e., 3rd November in the school auditorium from 10:30 a.m. onwards. Attendance of Class XII students is compulsory. For more information, contact the undersigned.

Vikram
(School Captain)

Type 6 Notice for Appeal/Invite

Details Required

- Whom to appeal/warn
- A slogan or message
- Issuing authority (if different from the person signing the notice)
- Important instructions

Sample Notice 9 Recently it was in the news that a cyclone hit Orissa. Being the Head Girl of your school, draft a notice for the students and staff appealing for donations of relief products like clothes, money, books and other articles in not more than 50 words.

Ans.

Vijay Public School, Vijay Nagar

NOTICE

8th December, 20XX

Appeal for Donations

This is to inform that the Student Council of our school is organising a rehabilitation drive for the victims of the recent cyclone in Orissa. All the students are appealed to donate clothes, books and other articles like blanket, blazer, quilt, etc. to help the poor and affected. By doing this, we will show our humanitarian nature. Certificates will be given to the major contributors. For other details, contact the undersigned.

XYZ
(Head Girl)

Sample Notice 10 You are Nidhi/Nihal, student editor of your school magazine 'Jyoti'. Write a notice for the school notice board inviting short stories, poems, articles, etc. from students of all classes for the school magazine. Invent all necessary details. **CBSE 2024**

Ans.

Eklavya Secondary School, Hoshangabad

NOTICE

16th July, 20XX

Contributions Required

All the students are invited to send articles, poems, short stories, etc. for publication in school magazine 'Jyoti'. Entries should reach the Editor latest by 31st August, 20XX. Each entry should be neatly written and must carry the name and class of the contributor. For further details, contact the undersigned.

Nidhi/Nihal
(Editor, 'Jyoti' school magazine)

Type 7 Notice for Change (Name/Residence/Company, etc.)

Details Required

- Whom to inform about the change
- Existing/Current and changed information
- Reason for change
- Your name and signature

Sample Notice 11 You are the proprietor of a company which has changed its office address from 2A Phool Bagh Colony to Mangal Pandey Nagar. Draft a notice to be inserted in the local newspaper informing about the change in not more than 50 words. You are Rajat Sharma.

Ans.

Rajat Enterprises, Meerut

NOTICE

13th October, 20XX

Change of Address

This is to inform all that XYZ organisation has changed their office address from 2A Phool Bagh Colony to 334/3, Mangal Pandey Nagar. Anyone needing their services is requested to contact them at their new address. Their phone no. 0121-28XXXXX remains unchanged.

Rajat Sharma
(Proprietor)

Type 8 Notice for Warning to the General Public

Details Required

- Name of the issuing authority
- Punishment if warning not heeded
- Warning

Sample Notice 12 A sea storm is expected to hit the states on the East Coast of the country within 72 hours. As Rohit/Reema, Director General, Coast Guard, Odisha, write a notice in 50 words to warn fishermen, tourists and general public to take all safety precautions and not venture into the sea. Mention relevant details.

Ans.

State Government, Odisha

NOTICE

2nd January, 20XX

Warning

All fishermen, tourists, and members of the general public are informed that a sea storm is anticipated to hit the East coast of the country within the next 72 hours. Everyone is asked not to go into the sea and to take all required safety precautions. Please visit the Odisha government's website for more details.

Rohit/Reema
(Director General, Coast Guard, Odisha)

Type 9 Notice for Giving General Information

Details Required

- Name of the issuing authority
- Sorry for Inconvenience, if any
- Information

Sample Notice 13 You are secretary of the Residents Welfare Association of Sahyog Colony, Delhi. Write a notice in not more than 50 words informing the residents of the colony that there will be no water supply in their area for about a day due to maintenance work.

Ans.

Residents Welfare Association

NOTICE

28th July, 20XX

No Water Supply

This is to inform all the residents that due to maintenance work that is going on, the water supply would remain affected on 29th July, 20XX. Please make a note of it. In case of urgent need of water please contact association officer for water tanker. For further details please contact the undersigned.

XYZ
(Secretary)

PRACTICE QUESTIONS

1. Your school is organising an Education Fair in the school premises. As the Head boy/Head girl of Sunshine Public School, Agra, draft a notice informing students of Classes IX-XII about the fair. Include other necessary details. You are Muskan/Manoj. Put your notice in a box. **CBSE 2025**

Ans.

XYZ School

NOTICE

12th January, 20XX

Inter-House Maths Quiz Competition

All students of Classes IX to XII are invited to participate in the Inter-House Maths Quiz Competition on 1st February, 20XX at 11:00 am in the Auditorium. Each house must nominate a team of 3 students. Register with your House Captain by 27th January, 20XX. For details, contact the undersigned.
Akhila/Akhil
(President, Quiz Club)

2. The School Mountaineering Club is organising a weekend trek to Mussoorie. As President of the club, write a notice informing students of Classes XI-XII about the forthcoming trek and invite registrations for the same. Include all other necessary details. Put your notice in a box. **CBSE 2025**

Ans.

XYZ School, Dance Club

NOTICE

22nd March, 20XX

Auditions for Annual Ballet

The Dance Club is holding auditions for the annual ballet performance. Students of Classes XI and XII are invited to participate.

- **Date** 25th March, 20XX
- **Time** 3:00 PM onwards
- **Venue** School Auditorium
- **Selection Criteria** Grace, technique, expression and stage presence

Interested students must register by 24th March, 20XX.

Ananya Verma
President, Dance Club

3. Bharat Public School, I.P. Nagar, has recently constructed a Science Park, a dedicated area where specific equipments based, on principles of science are setup. As Rashi Kapoor, President of Science Club, draft a notice for the school notice board, informing students of the same. Mention relevant details. **CBSE 2024**

Ans.

Bharat Public School, I.P. Nagar

NOTICE

27th February, 20XX

Science Park

This is to inform all the students that the Science Park has been officially opened. This facility is set-up to impart experiential knowledge and foster considerable expertise on the working of various scientific phenomena. The park is equipped with Barton's Pendulum, Revolving Periscope, Principle of Lever equipment, Crystal Structure, DNA, Gaussian theorem and Pythagoras theorem models.

Opening hours for the park are as follows- Monday to Saturday 9:00 a.m. to 4:00 p.m.

We look forward to your active engagement. For further details, contact the undersigned.

Rashi Kapoor
(President, Science Club)

4. P.S. Public School, Aram Nagar has opened a gym for the benefit of students. As Sports Captain, draft a notice informing students about the facilities available in the gym along with the timings and other details. **CBSE 2024**

Ans.

P. S. Public School, Aram Nagar

NOTICE

12th March, 20XX

School Gym

This is to inform all the students that the school gymnasium has commenced operation. This facility is designed to foster physical well-being and fitness among our student body. The gym is equipped with state-of-the-art facilities, including cardio machines, free weights, and exercise mats to cater to various fitness needs.

Operating hours for the gym are as follows.

Monday to Friday 8:00 a.m. to 5:00 p.m.
Saturday 9:00 a.m. to 1:00 p.m.

We look forward to your active participation. For further details contact the undersigned.

XYZ
(Sports Captain)

5. Your school is planning to conduct an Inter-Class seminar on the topic 'The Importance of Mental Health' to create awareness in adolescents. As the head of the organising committee, write a notice to inform all students about the seminar and invite registrations from Classes XI and XII. Include other necessary details. Put your notice in a box. **CBSE SQP 2024**

Ans.

XYZ School

NOTICE

12th August, 20XX

Seminar on the topic 'The Importance of Mental Health'

This is to inform all the students of Class XI and XII that our school is organising a seminar on the topic 'The Importance of Mental Health, to create awareness in adolescents. The seminar will be held on 16th August, 20XX in the Auditorium hall from 12:00 p.m. onwards. Interested students may register to participate in the seminar by giving their names to their class teachers latest by 14th August. For further details, contact the undersigned.

PQR

President

(Academic Committee)

6. Your school is organising an Inter-House webinar on enhancing coding skills. As the President of the Computer Club, write a notice to inform all House members from Classes IX to XII about the webinar and specify the number of registrations invited per House. Include other necessary details. Put your notice in a box. **CBSE SQP 2024**

Ans.

ABC School

NOTICE

18th August, 20XX

Inter-House Webinar On Enhancing Coding Skills

This is to inform all the House members from Classes IX to XII that the Computer Club of our school is organising webinar on enhancing coding skills. The webinar will be held on 26th August, 20XX on an online platform from 12:00 p.m. onwards. Each House can register up to 40 members by 24th August, 20XX. Interested students are requested to give their names to the House Prefects. For further details, contact the undersigned.

XYZ

President

(Computer Club)

7. The Literary Society of Gloria Public School is setting up a Creative Writing Club to encourage and develop the habit of creative writing. Draft a notice in not more than 50 words for the school notice board inviting students from Classes VI-X to join the Writer's Society. The members would be expected to stay back after school for 2 hours once a week. Mention day, date, time and venue. You are Ragini/Rakesh, President of the society. **CBSE 2023**

Ans.

Gloria Public School

NOTICE

25th April, 20XX

Membership of Writer's Society

This is to inform all the students of Classes VI to X that the Literary Society of our school is setting up a Creative Writing Club known as Writer's Society to encourage and develop the habit of creative writing among students. Students must know that the members of the society will have to stay back after school for 2 hours once a week in the Speaking Laboratory. Interested students can give their names to Ms. Mridula in Room No. 204. For further details, contact the undersigned.

Ragini/Rakesh

(President, Literary Society)

8. The RWA of Ganga Society, Pushp Nagar has planned to start free yoga classes for its residents. You are Sharmila Tiwari, the President of RWA. Draft a notice informing residents about the proposal, timing, venue and other details. **CBSE 2024**

Ans.

Residents Welfare Association, Ganga Society, Pushp Nagar

NOTICE

10th March, 20XX

Free Yoga Classes

This is to inform all the residents of our society that our organisation is going to conduct free yoga classes every Sunday at the common hall. The timing for the same will be 6:30 a.m. to 8:30 a.m. All the interested participants are requested to join the classes and obtain its benefits. For further details about the yoga classes, feel free to contact the undersigned.

Sharmila Tiwari
(President, RWA)

9. You are Neelam/Nitesh, Secretary of the school Library Club. The club is organising an Inter-School 'Let's Read a Book' week to help develop and encourage the habit of reading among children. Draft a notice in about 50 words, for the school notice board inviting club members from Classes X to XII to be student volunteers for the event. Mention day, date, time and venue. **CBSE 2023**

Ans.

XYZ Public School

NOTICE

25th June, 20XX

Volunteers for Event

This is to inform all the students of Classes X to XII that the Library Club of our school is organising an Inter-School 'Let's Read a Book' week to help develop and encourage the habit of reading among children. The details of the camp are as follows

Dates 3rd July to 10th July
Time 9:00 a.m. onwards
Venue School Auditorium

Students are requested to volunteer for the event and make it a success. Interested students can give their names to the undersigned.

Neelam/Nitesh
(President, Student Council)

10. You are Secretary of Vishal Housing Society, Prem Nagar. Draft a notice for the society notice board informing and inviting residents to the annual get-together to be held in the society compound, followed by dinner, on 28th March, 2024 from 7 p.m. onwards. Invent other details like contribution per family guest charges, etc. **CBSE 2024**

Ans.

Vishal Housing Society, Prem Nagar

NOTICE

20th March, 2024

Annual Get-together

This is to inform all the residents of the society that the annual get-together is being held in the premises of the society compound. The details of the get-together are as follows

Day Thursday
Date 28th March, 2024
Time 7:00 p.m. onwards
Venue Society compound

All residents are requested to attend the get-together. This will help the residents bring closer and build a healthy and supportive society.

Sunita
(Secretary)

11. Your school is planning to organise a Water Conservation Awareness Programme for the students. As school captain of SLV Public School, Lucknow, draft a notice in about 50 words informing the students about the programme mentioning day, date, time and venue. You are Sanjay/Sanjana. **CBSE 2023**

Ans.

SLV Public School, Lucknow

NOTICE

24th February, 20XX

Water Conservation Awareness

This is to inform all the students that our school is organising a Water Conservation Awareness Programme to create awareness about the importance of water conservation and sustainable use of water resources. The details of the event are

Day Thursday
Date 3rd March, 20XX
Time 10:00 a.m. to 12:00 p.m.
Venue School Auditorium

We encourage all students to attend this informative workshop. For further details contact the undersigned.

Sanjay/Sanjana
(School Captain)

12. As the Secretary of Sahar Group Housing Society, draft a notice in 50 words calling for the Annual General Meeting to discuss issues of Security and maintenance of public spaces. Specify the day, date, time and venue. Request the members to attend the meeting and give the benefit of their valuable suggestions on the issues in the given agenda. You are Razia/Rashid. **CBSE 2023**

Ans.

Sahar Grouping Housing Society

NOTICE

5th May, 20XX

Annual General Meeting

This is to inform all the residents of the society that a meeting is being held to discuss issues of security and maintenance of public spaces. The details of the meet are as follows

Day Sunday
Date 10th May
Time 9:00 a.m. onwards
Venue Community Hall

All residents or at least one member from each house is requested to attend the meeting.

Razia/Rashid
(Secretary)

13. The Literary Society of your school is setting up an Editorial Board for the forthcoming academic session. Draft a notice in 50 words to be put up on the school notice-board, inviting students from Classes IX-XI to join the Board. The members would be expected to stay back after school for 2 hours once a week to work on the school magazine. You are Shiela/ Sameer, Secretary of the Literary Society. **CBSE 2023**

Ans.

XYZ Public School

NOTICE

25th April, 20XX

Setting up Editorial Board

This is to inform all the students of Classes IX to XI that the Literary Society of our school is setting up an Editorial Board for the forthcoming academic session. Members of the Board would be expected to stay back after school for 2 hours once a week to work on the school magazine. Interested students can give their names to Ms. Sukriti in room 204. For further details contact the undersigned.

Sheila/Sameer
(Secretary, Literacy Society)

14. There has been an increase in the number of cyberbullying cases in our schools. This has led to parents and students getting very anxious. As the school counsellor, you are organising a talk during the morning assembly by Mr. Kakkar, Director, Cybercrime Department inviting both students and parents. Draft a notice in about 50 words informing students of the same mentioned day, date, time and venue. **CBSE 2023**

Ans.

ABC International School

NOTICE

24th February, 20XX

Cyber Bullying Talk

This is to inform the students of all classes that our school is organising a talk on Cyber bullying to address the issue of increase in the number of cyber bullying cases in our schools. The details of the event are

Day Friday
Date 17th March, 20XX
Time Morning assembly
Venue School Auditorium

Mr. Kakkar, Director of Cybercrime Department, has accepted to address this issue. The talk is open to both students and parents. All students and parents are requested to attend the talk.

PQR
School Counsellor

15. As the House Captain of A.B.M Public School, Telangana, draft a notice in not more than 50 words for the school notice board, informing house members from Classes X to XII about the change in topic and submission dates for Round 1 of 'Discovery' - the upcoming Inter- House Reasearch-based Paper Presentation Competition. Do not forget to issue an apology for the above. You are Kruthika Reddy. **CBSE SQP 2023**

Ans.

A.B.M Public School, Telangana

NOTICE

25th September, 20XX

Change in Topic and Submission Dates For Discovery

This is to inform all the house members of Classes X to XII that there has been a change in the topic and submission dates for Round 1 of 'Discovery' - the upcoming Inter-House Reasearch-based Paper Presentation Competition. The details of the competition are as follows

Topic	Ancient ruins of Hampi
Date of Submission	4th October, 20XX
Time	12 noon
Venue	Room No. 14

For further details contact the undersigned.

The inconvenience caused by the sudden change is deeply regretted.

Kruthika Reddy
(House Captain)

16. As Librarian of Crescent International School, Gwalior, draft a notice in not more than 50 words asking all students to return the library books they have borrowed by two days before the commencement of the examination. You are Neeta Gupta, Librarian.

Ans.

Crescent International School, Gwalior

NOTICE

25th February, 20XX

Return of Library Books-Last Date

This is to remind all the students to return the books borrowed from the library latest by 1st March, 20XX. Students will not be allowed to sit for the final examination if they do not return the books by the specified deadline. Your prompt action will be appreciated. For any other query, contact the undersigned.

Neeta Gupta
(Librarian)

17. You lost your Titan wrist-watch in your school. Draft a notice in not more than 50 words to be placed on your school notice board. You are a student of Class XII. Sign as Rani.

Ans.

XYZ International School Gwalior

NOTICE

7th August, 20XX

Lost Wrist Watch

This is to inform all that Rani of Class XII has lost her metallic strap, round dial Titan wrist-watch in the school playground during the 7th period yesterday. Anyone who finds it please contact the undersigned in Class XII A. Finder will be rewarded with a treat in the canteen.

Rani
(Class XII)

18. You have found an expensive geometry box in the school playground. Draft a notice in not more than 50 words for the school notice board. You are Vineet, Class XII, Angel School, Faridabad.

Ans.

Angel School, Faridabad

NOTICE

31st October, 20XX

Found Geometry Box

This is to inform all that Vineet of Class XII has found a red-coloured 'Faber-Castle' Geometry Box in the school playground during the 8th period yesterday. Owner may please contact the undersigned between the 6th and the 7th period in Class XII.

Vineet
(Class XII)

19. You are an executive at Samsung. Recently your service center caught fire and you had to temporarily shift your center to a nearby locality. Write a notice to all informing them of the same. Mention all the necessary details.

Ans.

Samsung Service Centre

NOTICE

7th October, 20XX

Change of Address

This is to inform all that due to a recent fire that engulfed the service center, the Samsung facility has been temporarily shifted to Second Floor, A-19 XYZ Complex. If you have any query, kindly contact us at 98XXXXXXXX. We deeply regret any inconvenience caused.

PQR
(Samsung Executive)

20. Your organisation has recently changed its name to Stardust Technologies. Draft a notice informing every one of the same. Mention that your address and contact number remains the same.

Ans.

Stardust Technologies

NOTICE

7th October, 20XX

Change of Name

This is to inform all that the PQR organisation is now legally known as Stardust Technologies. Hence, all correspondence should be done with that name. It is noted that the address and the contact details of the organisation remains unchanged.

ABC

SELF ASSESSMENT TEST

1. You are Ram/Rajani, Secretary, Social Service Club, Sun Public School, Nagpur. Your club is organising a book fair for your school students. Draft a notice for your school notice board giving all relevant information about the event in not more than 50 words.
2. RJ Public School is located in a Central Government employees' residential colony. Cultural Society of the school has decided to organise a fancy dress show on 25th January in which each participant will wear the dress particular to his/her region. The aim is to show the cultural diversity of India. As Secretary, write a notice in about 50 words inviting the names of those who want to participate.
3. After the rains, cases of dengue, chikungunya, etc., are on the rise in your city. As Principal, Sunshine Public School, Manu Vihar, you have decided to allow your students to wear full sleeve shirts and trousers in the school for a period of one month. Write a notice regarding the same in about 50 words.
4. Every year in the central park of the city a flower show is held in the month of February. Your school has received a circular from the District Collector inviting your students to visit it. Write a notice in about 50 words informing the students about the show and advising them to go and enjoy it. You are Navtej/Navita, Head Boy/Girl, Sunrise Public School, Surat.
5. You are Tripti/Trilok Lahiri, Secretary, ABL School Cricket Association. It has been decided that a meeting of all the members of the school cricket team be held to discuss plans and strategies for the coming Zonal Tournament. Write a notice in not more than 50 words informing the members of the team about the meeting and requesting them to attend it.
6. You have lost your leather wallet, containing your examination entry ticket for Class XII, while travelling by a bus from Banshankari to MG Road in Bengaluru. Write a notice in not more than 50 words, to be published in the 'Deccan Herald'. You are Pranav/Parveen, 12 Gandhi Road, Bengaluru.
7. Due to a sudden landslide and inclement weather, St Francis School, Vasco has to be closed for a week. As Principal of that school, draft a notice in not more than 50 words to be displayed at the school main gate notice board.
8. As Sports Secretary of GDG Public School, Pune, draft a notice in not more than 50 words for your school notice board informing the students about the sale of old sports goods of your school.
9. As Principal of Sardar Patel Vidyalaya, Lucknow, draft a notice in not more than 50 words informing students of the change in school timings with effect from the 1st of October. State valid reasons for the change.
10. You are Krati of St. Xavier's School, Noida. You have found an I-Card in the school premises. Draft a notice for the school notice board for the same.
11. You are Smitha/Sunil, Secretary of AVM Housing Society. You are going to organise a Blood Donation Camp. Write a notice in not more than 50 words urging the members of your society to come in large numbers for this noble cause. Invent the necessary details.
12. Very soon your school is going to be a center for CBSE examinations. You have seen that during lunch break students of junior classes keep going around the examination rooms and make all kinds of noises. You are Navtej/Navita, Head Boy/Girl, Akash Public School, Ajmer. Write a notice in about 50 words warning such students not to go near the examination rooms.
13. As Principal, Kendriya Vidyalaya, Kanpur, write a notice in about 50 words informing the students of Class XII about the use of unfair means in the Pre-board examinations.
14. You are Raman/Suman of R.V. Public School, Narayanpet. Your school has planned to organise an educational tour of Hyderabad. As a Head Boy/Girl, write a notice informing students about an educational tour to Hyderabad.
15. You are Nand/Nandini, teacher in charge of picnic of your school. You are planning to take your students to 'Statue of Unity - Sardar Sarovar'. Write a notice that is to be pinned on Notice Board of your school informing the students about the same.

02 CHAPTER

Invitations and Replies

An invitation is a request, a solicitation or an attempt to get another person or group of people to join you for some special occasions. These include birthdays, house-warming parties, inauguration ceremonies, conferences, shows, etc.

There are two types of invitations

(i) Formal invitations

(ii) Informal invitations

Marking Scheme

Format	1 Mark
Content	2 Marks
Expression	1 Mark

(Accuracy of Spelling and Grammar)

Formal Invitations

Formal invitations are polite, pleasant and courteous. All printed invitations cards are generally considered formal invitations. They are also written as letters.

Points to be Kept in Mind While Writing Formal Invitations

- Formal invitations do not include the name of the addressee.
- They are always written in third person i.e. he, she or it are used in place of I, you or we.
- The occasion, name of the invitee, name of the host, date, day, time, venue, etc. are written in a proper sequence.
- Some more details like name, designation, address, etc. of the organiser, sponsor or host should be included.
- If a VIP is invited, then the name of that VIP should appear prominently.

Types of Invitations and Replies

I. Formal Invitations

- Formal Invitations in the form of Invitation Card
- Formal Invitation in the form of Letter

II. Informal Invitations

Replies to Invitations

- Formal Replies
- Informal Replies

Formal Invitation in the Form of Invitation Card

You are opening a new fitness club. Draft a formal invitation for its inauguration with the necessary details.

M/S PIONEERS	Name/Designation of the Host/Organiser
announce the opening of their new fitness club	Occasion
at 80, Mall Road, Gurugram	Venue
Cult Fit	
On Saturday, the 18th June, 20XX at 11:00 a.m.	Date and time
By Supercricketer **Virat**	Name of the VIP attending the event
All are Cordially Invited	
Free one-month membership for the first 15 customers!	
RSVP Manya Singh Phone: 059422-61XXX	Contact details

Formal Invitation in the Form of Letter

PQR International School is organising its Annual Literary Day. The Principal wishes to invite the famous writer and mythologist Devdutt Pattanaik as the Chief Guest to preside over the event. Draft a formal letter of invitation to be sent to the above mentioned dignitary.

PQR International School E-7 New Model Town Mumbai-400002	Sender's address/ Letterhead
12th August, 20XX	Date
Devdutt Pattanaik Andheri East Mumbai-400005	Receiver's name and address
Subject Invitation for Annual Literary Day	Subject
Respected Sir,	Salutation
It is a matter of great pride that our school is celebrating its 25th Annual Literary Day on 25th September, 20XX from 10 a.m. in the school auditorium. We shall consider it a great honour if you could grace the occasion by presiding over the function as the Chief Guest to share your experiences with students and give away the prizes.	Event/ Occasion; Date/Time/Venue
Soliciting a line in reply or an e-mail at admin@pqrinternational.in	
Thanking you	
Yours sincerely	Subscription
Principal **PQR International School**	Sender's name and designation

PRACTICE QUESTIONS

Invitation in Card Form

1. Draft an invitation card on behalf of the Principal of J.B. Bhatia Public School for the launch of 'Yoga for Life' programme in the school. Mention a compelling highlight of the programme along with other necessary details. **CBSE 2025**

J.B. Bhatia Public School
Cordially invites you to the launch of

'Yoga For Life' Programme
on
21st June, 20XX
at 11:30 am
in the School Sports Ground

Highlight of the Programme Special interactive session on *'Yoga for Holistic Well-being'* by renowned Yoga Guru XYZ.

Join us as we embark on a journey towards a healthier mind and body through the power of yoga! Your presence will truly encourage our students in embracing this transformative practice.

RSVP
R S Saxena
Principal, J.B. Bhatia Public School
011–2033XXXXX

We look forward to your gracious presence!

2. Draft an invitation in not more than 50 words from Vani Gopalan, Chief Project Officer of an NGO, for the launch of the 'Each One Teach One' programme, addressed to School Principals and Coordinators. Mention a compelling highlight of the programme along with other necessary details. **CBSE SQP 2024**

Ans.

The Literate Indian NGO
requests the pleasure of School Principals
and Coordinators at the launch of

Each One Teach One Programme
On

Monday, 15th October, 20XX
at 11:00 a.m.

XYZ Auditorium, New Delhi

Chief Guest-Honourable Education Minister
Dharmendra Pradhan

RSVP
Vani Gopalan
Chief Project Officer
ABC, Delhi
Phone: 98210XXXXX

3. You are Mr. Anmol Gupta. You are planning to celebrate your sister's silver jubilee wedding anniversary. Draft an invitation card to be sent to relatives and friends, sharing all relevant details. **CBSE 2024**

Ans.

Mr. Anmol Gupta
solicit your esteemed presence
on the auspicious occasion of

25th Wedding Anniversary Celebration

of his
Beloved sister and brother-in-law
on

Saturday, 12th of March, 20XX

at our parents' residence
21, Shivaji Vihar, New Delhi
from 6 p.m. onwards, followed by dinner.
Please accept the cordial invitation and oblige.

RSVP
Anmol Gupta
Phone: 7500XXXXX

4. You are the President, Literary Society of Hans Public School, Railpura. Draft a formal invite to the renowned author Ms. Savita Patil, requesting her to conduct a workshop on 'Creative Writing' in your school, Invent necessary details you are Anita/Amit. **CBSE 2024**

Ans.

Hans Public School, Railpura

requests your presence for a workshop on

'Creative Writing'

In the school campus
On the occasion of

Rabindranath Tagore's 163rd birthday

on Tuesday, 7th May, 20XX
at 11:00 a.m.
Kindly preside the one-day workshop as the Speaker.

RSVP
Anita/Amit
(President, Literary Society of HPS)
Phone: 96254XXXXX

5. You are Sarla Dutta, proprietor of Child's Planet, a showroom of children's educational toys. Draft a formal printed invitation in 50 words to be sent to your patrons, friends and relatives inviting them to the opening of the new showroom. Give details such as day, date, time and venue. **CBSE 2023**

Ans.

Child's Planet

announces the opening of a showroom of children's educational toys
at 23, Gandhi Marg, Kolkata

Inauguration

on Sunday, 18th February, 20XX
at 11 : 30 a.m.
by the famous toymaker, Mr. Shrey Narayan
All are cordially invited
Free gifts for the first 100 chidlren!

RSVP
Sarla Dutta
Phone: 033 (2934XXXX)
Phone: 96254XXXXX

6. You are a student of Chandrayan Public School, Mirzapur. The school is holding its Annual Function on 8th September, 2022. The Education Minister of State Mr. Chetak Singh has consented to be the Chief Guest. Design an invitation card to be sent to parents and other invitees. Mention necessary details of date, time and venue. Do not exceed 50 words.

Ans.

The Principal, Staff and Students

of Chandrayan Public School, Mirzapur solicit the pleasure of
your company on the auspicious occasion of

THE ANNUAL FUNCTION

of their school on
Saturday, 8th September, 20XX
at 11:00 a.m.
in the school auditorium
Mr. Chetak Singh, The State Education Minister will
preside as the Chief Guest

RSVP
Principal
Chandrayan Public School, Mirzapur
Contact no: 011-23XXXXX

7. M/S Aggarwal and Sons are opening a new general store 'Super Saver Mart', in Geeta Enclave, ABC Nagar, Delhi. The inauguration ceremony is fixed for Sunday, the 19th June, 20XX at 11:00 a.m. The store will be inaugurated by Mr. Roshan Sethi, councellor of the area. Draft an invitation card for the residents in not more than 50 words. Mention day, date, time and other details. **CBSE Term II 2022**

Ans.

M/S Aggarwal and Sons announce the opening of

SUPER SAVER MART

a general store in Geeta Enclave, ABC Nagar, Delhi

Inauguration on

Sunday, the 19th of June, 20XX at 11:00 am

By **Mr. Roshan Sethi**, Councellor of the Area

All are cordially invited to increase the grace of the occasion

Visit for all kinds of Grocery & Domestic items

Avail 10% inaugural discount on all items

RSVP

Super Saver Mart

Contact: 011-23XXXXX

8. Draft an invitation in about 50 words, on behalf of your aunt, Meghna Menon, which she has to share to invite prior work colleagues to the inaugural event of her own investment consultancy firm, in the Acer Mall, Kozhikode, Kerala. **CBSE SQP 2023**

Ans.

Meghna Menon requests the pleasure of your esteemed presence at the

Inaugural Event

of her own

Investment Consultancy Firm

located in Acer Mall, Kozhikode, Kerala on

5th October, 20XX

at 12:00 noon

RSVP

Meghna Menon

Contact : 98XXXXXXXX

9. As the President of the Spastic Society of India, invite all its members on 10th March, 20XX, to a dance programme by 'Hema Ratna' at 6:30 p.m. at Siri Fort Auditorium. Famous film personality Mrs. Madhuri Mani has consented to be the Chief Guest in about 50 words.

Ans.

The President Staff and Members of

Disha

The Spastic Society of India,
cordially seek the pleasure of your inspiring presence at the
Dance Programme

by Hema Ratna

in the aid of spastic children

JOIN US

on Monday, 10th March, 20XX
at **Siri Fort Auditorium**
from
6:30 p.m. onwards

Famous film personality Mrs. Madhuri Mani has kindly consented to be the
Chief Guest

RSVP Admin Officer
Phone: 011-233743XX

Tickets available online and at the venue.

www.dishatheevent.com

Invitation in Letter Form

1. Draft a formal invitation letter in not more that 50 words from Dr. Singh, Director of the Clean Water Initiative, for a panel discussion on 'Access to Safe Drinking Water', inviting Dr. Rajesh Gupta to be one of the panelists. Mention a compelling highlight of the panel discussion along with other necessary details. **CBSE 2025**

Ans. Dr. Singh
Director, Clean Water Initiative

22nd March, 20XX

Dr. Rajesh Gupta

Subject **Invitation, for a panel discussion on 'Access to Safe Drinking Water'**

Dear Dr. Gupta

We are honoured to invite you as a panelist for a discussion on 'Access to Safe Drinking Water' on 5th April, 20XX, at 10:00 am at Taj Convention Hall, New Delhi. The panel will explore innovative solutions for clean water accessibility. Looking forward to your valuable insights.

Sincerely
Dr. Singh
Director, Clean Water Initiative

2. Send a formal letter of invitation in 50 words to Dr. Mehra, noted novelist and educationalist, to speak on 'The Importance of Books'. You are Lena/Sanjay, Secretary, Literary Club, S.S. Public School. Mention day, date, time and venue. **CBSE 2023**

Ans. S.S. Public School
Nagpur, Maharashtra

28th August, 20XX

Dr. Mehra
Mumbai

Subject **Invitation to speak on 'The Importance of Books'**

Respected Sir,
This is to inform you that Literary Club, S.S. Public School is organising a session on the Importance of Books for the students. For the same, we shall be honoured if you could grace us with your presence on the occasion of Teachers' Day at 12 p.m. to speak on the Importance of Books. Kindly confirm your acceptance by 1st September and oblige.

Yours sincerely
Lena/Sanjay
(Secretary, Literary Club)

3. Sunrise Global School, Agra is going to organise a one-act play competition in the school auditorium. You have decided to invite noted stage artiste, Nalini, to grace the occasion. Draft a formal invitation for her in about 50 words. You are Karuna/Karan, Cultural Secretary.

Ans. Sunrise Global School
Hari Parvat, Near Delhi Gate
Agra - 282002

5th August, 20XX

Ms. Nalini
New Delhi

Subject **Invitation for the School One-Act Play Competition**

Respected Ma'am,
This is to inform you that Sunrise Global School, New Delhi is organising a One-Act Play Competition. In this light, we shall be obliged if you could spare some time from your busy schedule to be the Chief Guest at our school's One-Act Play Competition to be held on 20th August, 20XX in the school auditorium 2 p.m. onwards.
We will be highly honoured if you grace the occasion with your presence. We solicit a line in reply or an e-mail at sunriseglobal@gmail.com.

Thanking you

Yours respectfully
Karuna/Karan
(Cultural Secretary)

4. You are Shahneela/Sameer Malik living at No. 4, Zakir Bagh, Meerut. You and your friends decide to host a dinner to honour the teachers who have taught you in Class XII. Draft a formal invitation in 50 words to all your teachers to a grand dinner at your residence.

Ans. No. 4, Zakir Bagh, Meerut

5th November, 20XX

Class XII teachers
XYZ school,
Meerut

Subject **Honorary Dinner**

Respected Teachers,
You all are cordially invited by the students of Class 12th to the dinner party organised as a token of gratitude and honour for the great sacrifice you all have made to bring us to this position. We request you to kindly grace the evening of 14th November with your presence at No. 4, Zakir Bagh, Meerut at 6:00 p.m. Your presence shall be eagerly awaited.

Shahneela/Sameer Malik

5. You have been asked by your Director to invite a team of students and teachers from SD Public School, Modinagar for a workshop on changes in CBSE syllabus being conducted by a reputed publisher of educational books. Write the invitation as the Secretary, English Literary Society of the publisher in 50 words. You are Sukanya/Satish.

Ans. The English Literary Society
XYZ Publications
Ghaziabad–201007

20th September, 20XX

The Principal
SD Public School
Raj Chowk
Modinagar–201204

Subject **Invitation for Workshop on Changes in the Syllabus 2024-2025**

Respected Sir,
The English Literary Society of XYZ Publications has arranged a two-day workshop on the topic of 'Changes in the Syllabus 2024-2025' on 28th and 29th September, 20XX at Shiva Auditorium, Station Road, Ghaziabad. Professor, Dr. Manorama Trikha, an eminent linguist and resource person, has kindly consented to conduct the workshop.
Kindly depute a team of four teachers and 12 students (3 each from Class IX, X, XI and XII) of your school to attend the workshop and send their names to us latest by 25th November, 20XX.
Looking forward to a prompt reply.

Yours sincerely
Sukanya/Satish
(Secretary)
The English Literary Society

6. You are Nainai/Nachaobi Kom, Head Boy/Girl of Loktak High School, Manipur. Your school wishes to honour an old student of your school, the famous boxer Mary Kom for all her numerous achievements by inviting her to the school Annual Day as the Chief Guest. Write a formal invite in not more than 50 words to be sent to Mary Kom requesting her presence on the occasion.

Ans.

Loktak High School
Imphal, Manipur

15th November, 20XX

Ms. MC Mary Kom
Imphal

Subject **Invitation as the Chief Guest for the School's Annual Day**

Respected Ma'am,
With utmost pleasure, the Loktak High School would like to inform you that it is hosting an Annual Day event.
For the same, we shall be honoured if you could spare some time from your busy schedule to be the Chief Guest at our school's Annual Day to be held on 30th November, 20XX from 2 p.m. onwards in the school auditorium.
Kindly confirm your acceptance by 23rd November and oblige.

Yours respectfully
Nainai/Nachaobi Kom
(Head Boy/Girl)
Mobile no. 88046XXXXX

7. On 30th November your school is going to hold its annual sports day. You want Mr. Dhanraj Pillai, a noted hockey player, to give away the prizes to the budding sportspersons of the school. Write a formal invitation in about 50 words requesting him to grace the occasion. You are Karuna/Karan, Sports Secretary, Sunrise Global School, Agra.

Ans.

Sunrise Global School
Hari Parvat, Near Delhi Gate
Agra - 282002

15th November, 20XX

Mr. Dhanraj Pillai,
New Delhi

Subject **Invitation for the School Annual Sports Day**

Respected Sir,
It is with great pleasure that Sunrise Global School would like to inform you that it is organising the school's Annual Sports Day. Our pleasure would trifold and we would be honoured if you could spare some time from your busy schedule to be the Chief Guest at our school's Annual Sports Day to be held on 30th November, 20XX 2 p.m. onwards at the school's sports field. It would be a matter of great pride for us if you grace the occasion and give away the awards for the day. We solicit a line in reply or an email at sunriseglobalagra@gmail.com

Thanking you

Yours respectfully
Karuna/Karan
(Sports Secretary)

Informal Invitations

Informal invitations are sent to invite close friends or relatives to personal occasions. They are written in the form of personal letters. The style is relaxed and informal.

Example of an Informal Invitation

Your mother has recently purchased a franchise of Tinkle Tea Ltd. For advertising, you are organising a tea tasting event at your house for your family and friends. Prepare an informal invitation for the same. You are Anurag/Anuradha.

Ans.

161, Vasant Kunj
Delhi — Sender's Address

6th November, 20XX — Date

Dear family and friends, — Salutation

It gives me and my mother a great pleasure to tell you that we have recently purchased a franchise of Tinkle Tea Ltd. In order to advertise the franchise, we are organising a small tea-tasting event and snacks party on 10th November, 20XX at 4:00 p.m. at our residence. You will get to taste a widespread variety of teas and we are offering a special discount of 25% just for that day.

It will be our great pleasure to have you as a part of the small celebration.

(Occasion, Date, Venue and Time)

Warm regards — Subscription

Anuradha — Sender's Name

PRACTICE QUESTIONS

1. You are Mr. Srikanth Sharma. You have recently built a new house in the hills of Uttarakhand. Draft a letter inviting your brother and his family to spend a few days with you in your new home. Include relevant details. **CBSE 2024**

Ans.

4, Subhash Road
Uttarakhand Secretariat
Dehradun, Uttarakhand
Pin code-248001

6th March, 20XX

Dear Ramakanth,

How are you? Hope your vacation has started and hope you are free. The construction of my new house in Uttarakhand has finally been completed! I am officially inviting you to come to my new house with your family to spend your summer vacation. It's been a really long time since we have met up. I've thought of many exciting things for the vacation. We can go swimming, trekking and sight-seeing. There are some really beautiful sunrise and sunset points near my home.

We could have such amazing picnics! The hills of Uttarakhand are really beautiful. It feels like I finally have my own piece of heaven, and I'm excited to share it with you my dearest brother. You can take the bus to Uttarakhand from ISBT. Please let me know as early as possible whether you can make it or not. And do not forget to bring me some berries!

Looking forward to seeing you again.

Lots of love
Srikanth Sharma

2. Your family is celebrating the 50th wedding anniversary of your grandparents. Draft an informal invitation in 50 words inviting your close friends and relatives to grace the occasion. Mention the day, date, time and venue. You are Roy/Rosie. **CBSE 2023**

Ans.

New Delhi

6th March, 20XX

Dear family and friends,

It gives me and all of the PQR family great pleasure to tell you that my grandparents Sh. Radheyshyam and Shrimati Sharda are celebrating their Golden Jubliee on 21st February, 20XX. In their honour, we are hosting a grand celebration at Hotel Seven Seas, Rohini at 7:00 p.m. The event will be filled with a small performance by us, followed by an extravagant dinner.

It will be our greatest pleasure to have you as a part of the celebration.

Yours lovingly

Roy/Rosie

3. You have bought a new house in Meerut. Write an informal letter of invitation inviting your friends and relatives to the housewarming ceremony. Mention the day, date, time and venue. As Rajesh Sharma, draft an invitation in about 50 words. **CBSE 2023**

Ans.

XYZ Road
ABC City

24th February, 20XX

Dear PQR,

I hope this letter finds you in good health and in high spirits. I am writing to inform you that with the grace of God, I have recently bought a new house in Meerut. To celebrate it, I have organised a house-warming ceremony and would be delighted if you could join us for the same. The ceremony will be held on Sunday, 6th March, 2023, from 11:00 a.m. to 2:00 p.m. at my new residence: LMN Apartments, ABC city.

I am looking forward to having you over and sharing this special occasion with you. Please do let me know if you are able to attend.

Warm regards

Rajesh Sharma

4. Amit is planning to invite his friends and relatives for the celebration of the 80th birthday of his grandmother. Draft an invitation letter in about 50 words on his behalf. Mention the day, date, time and venue. **CBSE 2023**

Ans.

XYZ Road
ABC City

24th February, 20XX

Dear PQR,

I hope this letter finds you in good health and in high spirits. I am excited to invite you to join us in celebrating the 80th birthday of my beloved grandmother. We will be hosting a small get-together at our home on Friday, 21st February, 20XX from 7:00 p.m. onwards. It would be an honour to have you be a part of this special occasion and share in the joy with our family.

Please join us at our residence PQR Society, ABC City for some great food, drinks and entertainment. Looking forward to seeing you there!

Warm regards

Amit

5. Rohit has successfully cleared the NEET admission test. He wants to celebrate his admission to Shivaji Medical College, Nagpur by throwing a party for his friends. Write an informal invitation in 50 words giving details of the venue, time and date.

Ans. 33/472, Krishna Nagar
Delhi

28th June, 20XX

Dear Rakshit,
It gives me immense pleasure to tell you that I have secured the 80th rank in the NEET exam and got admission in Shivaji Medical College, Nagpur. I really want to share this memorable moment and celebrate it with the company of all my friends. So, I invite you to a celebratory dinner at the Imly's at 6:30 p.m. on 1st July, 20XX.
Please join the celebrations and merry-making.

Yours affectionately
Rohit

6. You are Neena/Naveen of 21, Shakti Vihar, Delhi. You have opened a departmental store in Chandni Chowk. Draft an informal invitation in 50 words to invite your friend in the inauguration ceremony.

Ans. 21, Shakti Vihar Delhi

27th November, 20XX

Dear Varun,
With the grace of God and your blessings, I am opening my first ever business venture, a departmental store, by the name of ESSENTIAL GROCERY. I would like to invite you to the inauguration of my store in Chandni Chowk on 5th December, 20XX at 9:00 a.m.
Please come in time to join the ceremony and shower your blessings on us.

Yours sincerely
Neena/Naveen

7. You are Sooraj Dwivedi. Your friend, Manav from Mumbai is staying in a paying guest accommodation. Invite him to join Diwali celebrations with you at your residence in 50 words.

Ans. 417/2, Block B-1, Janakpuri
New Delhi-110058

11th November, 20XX

Dear Manav,
I am so excited for the upcoming festival of lights, Diwali. I know that you are excited too. So, let's double up our excitement and celebrate Diwali together. I know you won't be able to go home this Diwali and so I am inviting you to celebrate it at my house. We will have loads of fun with widespread sweets and Diwali gifts. Looking forward to your arrival.

Yours affectionately
Sooraj

8. You are Pihoo Sengupta. The wedding of your sister Aarohi Sengupta is going to be held on 24th November, 20XX at Hotel Palace, Udaipur. Draft an informal invitation in 50 words to your friend Malini requesting her to attend the functions.

Ans.

4357, Vasant Vihar
Raj Nagar

24th October, 20XX

Dear Malini,
You will be pleased to know that the wedding of my elder sister, Aarohi Sengupta is going to be held on 24th November, 20XX at Hotel Palace, Udaipur. The whole family will be leaving for the functions on 20th November and I invite you to join us for the same. It will be great fun as we will enjoy all the wedding festivities together.
I do hope you will join us on the auspicious occasion.

Yours affectionately
Pihoo Sengupta

Replies to Invitations

Whenever we receive an invitation, it is considered a good etiquette to confirm or decline your presence in the event.

Formal Replies

Formal replies involve a certain standard and form. They are usually very short and to the point. In a formal reply, the invitation is acknowledged, and a note of thanks is written in third person. Acceptance is communicated or regret is shown if the person is unable to attend the occasion. In case of not attending, a specific reason is to be given.

(i) If the invitation comes in the form of a printed card, one can simply RSVP the status on the given number.

(ii) In other cases, you send a reply to the host.

Examples of Formal Replies

Reply to an Invitation in the Form of a Card

You have received an invite to the wedding of your dear friend's son. Write a reply in line of the invitation.

Accepting the Invitation

Mr. Rakesh Rana has much pleasure in accepting the kind invitation of Mrs. & Mr. KL Shastri for the marriage of their son, Mohit on 15th October, 20XX at 7 p.m.

Declining the Invitation

Mr. Rakesh Rana sincerely thanks Mrs. & Mr. KL Shastri for their kind invitation to the wedding of their son, Mohit on 15th October, 20XX at 7 p.m. but regrets his inability to attend because of a prior engagement. He wishes Mohit a blissful conjugal life.

Reply in the form of a Letter

In many official formal replies like that within an organisation, sometime, we also write a reply in the form of a letter.

An invitation had been issued by Mr. Cherian, the HR Head of your company inviting you for the company picnic. As Joseph Vijayan, Asst. Manager, Operations, draft a reply in not more than 50 words, consenting to attend. **CBSE SQP 2024**

Ans. XYZ Organisation
New Delhi

5th September, 20XX

Mr. Cherian
The HR Head
XYZ Organisation
New Delhi

Subject **Office Picnic**

Respected Sir,
It was a great pleasure to receive the invitation to attend the company's picnic celebration on 13th September, 20XX at PQR Gardens. I would love to attend it, and be a part of the fun and frolic with my colleagues.

Thanking you
Yours sincerely
Joseph Vijayan
Asst. Manager, Operations

Informal Replies

In informal replies, simple language is used and the invitation is acknowledged in first or second person. Acceptance is communicated or refusal is regretted with a specific reason.

Examples of Informal Replies

You have received an informal invitation to the graduation party of your dear friend's daughter. Draft a suitable reply to the invitation.

Accepting the Invitation

15, Doctors' Colony Bhopal-462004	Sender's address/ Letterhead
18th September, 20XX	Date
Dear Singh and Bhabhi,	Salutation
Thanks a lot for your invitation to Vaidehi's graduation party. I am really stumped! Has she grown so big? I still remember her as a little girl competing with other kids, pestering me for chocolates! Anyway, it is really a happy occasion and I will definitely join the festivities. I am coming with Ranjana and the kids. See you soon.	Expressing gratitude Accepting the invitation
Yours affectionately	Subscription
Rakesh	Sender's name

Declining the Invitation

15, Doctors' Colony Bhopal-462004	Sender's address
16th September, 20XX	Date
Dear Singh and Bhabhi,	Salutation
Thanks a lot for your invitation to Vaidehi's graduation party.	Expressing gratitude
It is a happy occasion and I would have loved to join in all the festivities, but Shaurya, our little son, is not keeping well and needs our constant care and attention. I really feel bad for missing the event. Please accept my best wishes.	Declining invitation
Yours affectionately	Subscription
Rakesh	Sender's name

PRACTICE QUESTIONS

1. You are Mrs. Sonali Gupta, a nutritionist. You are invited by the Principal of Radiant Public School, Jammu to address the students on 'Forming Healthy Food Habits'. Write a formal letter of reply accepting the invitation. **CBSE 2025**

Ans. 47, Jayanti Society
Guwa Road
Shimla 220XXX

12th May, 20XX

The Principal
Radiant Public School
Jammu

Subject **Acceptance of Invitation**

Sir/Madam
I sincerely thank you for inviting me to address the students on 'Forming Healthy Food Habits'. I am pleased to accept this invitation and look forward to interacting with the students on 20th May, 20XX at 1:00 pm.
Warm regards
Sonali Gupta
(Nutritionist)

2. You are Mr. Shyam Sundar, Professor of Psychology. You are invited by S.K.M. College, Mehboob Nagar to be the keynote speaker at its Annual Conclave on 'Student Health - The Emotional Impact of Social Media'. Draft a reply letter expressing your inability to accept the invitation and also cite a reason for refusal. **CBSE 2024**

Ans. K-159, Shastri Nagar
New Delhi - 110092

8th March, 20XX

S.K.M. College
Mehboob Nagar

Subject **Inability to Accept the Invitation**

Respected Sir/Ma'am,
I am honoured to have received your invitation as the keynote speaker at your Annual Conclave on Student Health 'The Emotional Impact of Social Media'. However, I regret to inform you that I am unable to accept the invitation due to a scheduling conflict. Please accept my sincere apologies for any inconvenience my absence may cause. While I am unable to participate as the keynote speaker, I am more than willing to explore alternative ways to contribute to the event, such as providing written materials or participating in a panel discussion. I hold your organisation in high regard and am eager to support its endeavours in any way I can. Thank you for your kind understanding and consideration.

Warm regards,
Mr. Shyam Sundar
Professor of Psychology

3. You are Ankur Pandey a student counsellor of N.J. Public School. You are invited by S.M. International School, Kala Puram, to address Class XII students on 'Goal Setting & Time Management'. Write a formal letter of reply accepting the invitation and confirming your presence at the stated time, include relevant details. **CBSE 2024**

Ans. K-55, Kurnool
Andhra Pradesh - 515775

10th April, 20XX

S.M. International School
Kala Puram

Subject **Acceptance of Invitation**

Respected Sir/Ma'am,
I am honoured to be on the receiving end of your invitation as a speaker at your esteemed school on the topic 'Goal Setting and Time Management'. I would be delighted to share critical insights and tactics with the students of Class XII. I, hereby, confirm my availability and acceptance of the invitation to speak on 23rd April at 10 a.m. Thank you for this wonderful opportunity and I look forward to the interaction with the students.

Best regards
Ankur Pandey
Student Counsellor, N.J. Public School

4. You are Dr. Suchitra Mukherjee. You have received an invitation from the Director, Health Services, Kharagpur, W.B, to preside over a gathering of leading medical practitioners attending a workshop on mental wellness on 9th November, 2023, at 11 am in the Public Hospital, Jammu, J & K. Respond to accept the invitation in about 50 words. **CBSE SQP 2023**

Ans. The Director
Health Services
Kharagpur, W.B.

5th November, 20XX

Subject **Acceptance of Invitation**

Sir/Ma'am,
Dr. Suchitra Mukherjee feels honoured and grateful to have received an invitation from your esteemed organisation to preside over a gathering of leading medical practitioners attending a workshop on mental wellness on 9th November, 20XX at 11 a.m. in the Public Hospital, Jammu, J & K. She would like to use this opportunity to engage the medical industry in a much open conversation about the mental health problems of the present day world. Therefore, she is delighted to confirm her participation in the workshop.

Yours sincerely
Dr. Suchitra Mukherjee

5. You have been invited to inaugurate the art and craft exhibition at Rashida Public School on the occasion of the school's Annual Day on 20th March, 2023 in the school auditorium. Write a formal letter of regret in about 50 words expressing your inability to attend due to a prior engagement. You are Salil/Reena. **CBSE 2023**

Ans. Rashida Public School

24th February, 20XX

Sir/Ma'am,
This refers to your invitation to attend your prestigious school's Annual Day on 20th March, 2023 in the school auditorium at 10:00 a.m. I thank you for the invitation. However, due to some previous commitments, I would not be able to attend the event.
My heartiest congratulations to you!

Thanking You
Yours sincerely
Salil/Reena

6. Your friend, PV Sathish, has invited you to attend the wedding of his sister, Jaya. You find that you have an important paper of pre-board examination on the day of the wedding. Thus, you cannot attend the event. Write in about 50 words a formal reply to the invitation expressing your regret. You are Puneet/Puneeta Vij, M-114, Fort Road, Chennai. **CBSE 2017**

Ans. Puneeta Vij sincerely thanks PV Sathish for their kind invitation to the wedding of his sister Jaya on 15th October, 20XX at 7 p.m. but regrets her inability to attend because of a prior engagement. She wishes Jaya a blissful conjugal life.

7. You are Pankaj Gupta and have received an invitation card from Sh. AK Sinha, Principal of St. Xavier's School, Dehradun to attend the school's annual function. Draft a formal reply of acceptance in 50 words.

Ans. Mr. Pankaj Gupta thanks Mr. AK Sinha, Principal, St. Xavier's School, Dehradun for his kind invitation to the annual function to be held on 1st March, 20XX in the school ground. He is pleased to accept the invitation and will attend the same.

8. Draft a formal reply in 50 words refusing an invitation to be present on the occasion of the wedding of Ankush S/o Mr. and Mrs. Shankar of 24, Green Park Road, Kanpur. Your are Vikram Gaur, Raja Marg, Agra.

Ans. Mr. and Mrs. Vikram Gaur thank Mr. and Mrs. Shankar for inviting them on the occasion of the wedding of their son at 24, Green Park Road, Kanpur on 24th June, 20XX and assure them that they will be present on the occasion to wish the couple a happy married life. The details of their arrival will be shared with them soon.

Vikram Gaur
5th June, 20XX

9. You are a social activist. You have been invited to take part in the discussion concerning the tobacco habits initiated by your friend who is the Manager of Tobacco Association. Write a acceptance in not more than 50 words.

Ans. PQR has much pleasure in accepting the kind invitation of Manager of the Tobacoo Association for the discussion concerning the tobacoo habits on 23rd September, 20XX at 5:00 p.m.

10. You have received an invitation on the wedding of your friend, Akshat. As Radhika/Rakesh, write a letter expressing your extreme happiness at the news and explaining your inability to attend the function. Convey your best wishes for the future to the couple. **CBSE 2024**

Ans. K-366, Greenpark Society
New Delhi - 110013

23rd November, 20XX

Dear Akshat,
It was a great pleasure to have received your invitation to attend your wedding. I would have been delighted to be a part of the wedding but unfortunately my business trip has been arranged in the same week. Hence, I would not be able to attend the wedding. I express my sincere regret and wish you and your partner the best in your married life.

Yours sincerely
Radhika/Rakesh

11. You are Manoj/Meena. You have received an invitation from your friend Vijay to a party to celebrate his admission in a prestigious Management Institute. Write an informal letter in about 50 words accepting the invitation. Mention the day, date, time and venue. **CBSE 2023**

Ans. XYZ Road
ABC City

24th February, 20XX

Dear Vijay,
I was delighted to receive your invitation to your party to celebrate your admission in the prestigious Management Institute. Thanks for the same. I am really happy for you and I would love to be a part of your celebrations. The day, date, time and venue you have mentioned in the invitation suit me perfectly. So, I will be there at your party on Saturday, 4th March, 2023, at 7:00 p.m., at your residence: LMN Apartments, ABC city. I am looking forward to meeting you and sharing this special occasion with you.

Warm regards
Manoj/Meena

12. You are Natasha, residing in Pune. Your cousin, from the same city is hosting your grandmother's eightieth birth anniversary and has extended an invite to you. He has also requested your assistance for arrangements needed. Draft a reply of acceptance, in not more than 50 words. **CBSE SQP 2022, Term II**

Ans.

XYZ Apartments
Pune

17th January, 20XX

Dear Mayank,
I am delighted to hear about the celebrations being held in the honour of grandmother's eightieth birth anniversary. Thank you so much for extending the invitation to me and my family. I would love to be a part of the celebration and nothing could stop me from attending our grandma's birthday on 27th January at our old residential home in Mumbai. It goes without saying that I would be glad to help you out in the arrangement. Just let me know when we can discuss the details for the celebrations and I would be there for help.

Yours lovingly
Natasha

13. You are Avantika, residing in Jamshedpur. Your friend from the same city is hosting her parents 50th marraige anniversary and has extended an invite to you. Draft a letter of reply of acceptance in not more than 50 words mentioning date, venue and time. **CBSE SQP 2022, Term II**

Ans.

XYZ Apartments
Jameshedpur

4th May, 20XX

Dear Sukriti,
I am delighted to receive the invitation to the celebrations being held on the occasion of your parents 50th Wedding Anniversary. Thank you so much for extending the invitation. I would love to be a part of the celebration held at Hyatt Hotel on 15th May at 8:00 p.m. Looking forward to meeting you.

Yours lovingly
Avantika

14. You are invited by a friend of yours, Naina to spend some days at his/her village near Manali during the summer vacation. Respond to his/her invitation in not more than 50 words. Mention day, date, time and venue. You are Mishika/Manik. **CBSE 2023**

Ans.

XYZ Road
ABC City

24th May, 20XX

Dear Naina,
I am pleased to accept your offer to spend a few days in your village during the summer vacation. I will arrive by train at 1:30 p.m. on the 2nd of June, Sunday and stay for a week. I would love to spend some time with you and your family. Looking forward to meeting you.

Warm regards
Mishika/Manik

15. Your friend, Manish Tripathi has invited you to attend his wedding anniversary. You cannot attend it as you have a family get-together on the same day. Write a polite letter, in not more than 50 words, expressing your inability to attend the function and wish him all the happiness on this joyous occasion. You are Mita/Mahendra Juneja of 5, Vasundra Colony, Patna. **CBSE 2014**

Ans. 5, Vasundra Colony
Patna – 800009

16th May, 20XX

Dear Manish,
It was a great pleasure to receive the invitation to attend your wedding anniversary on 23rd May. I would have loved to attend it, but I have a family get-together on the same day in which many relatives are coming from outside Patna. Thus, I will not be able to attend the wedding. Please convey my best wishes to Anuja Bhabhi for the anniversary.

Yours friendly
Mita/Mahendra Juneja

16. Your friend is hosting a class reunion at his newly built resort. He has invited you to join this celebration on Saturday, 22nd March. Write an informal letter of reply in 50 words, expressing your inability to attend due to a family function. Mention day, date, time and venue. You are Sehaj/Sahil. **CBSE 2023**

Ans. PQR Apartments
New Delhi

25th May, 20XX

Dear Rohit,
I feel honoured to have been invited to attend the class reunion at the newly built XYZ Resort on Saturday, 22nd March. I would have loved to meet everyone and catch up with them. However, due to some unavoidable previous commitments, I shall not be able to attend the reunion.
Hope you all enjoy the day.

Yours lovingly
Sehaj/Sahil

SELF ASSESSMENT TEST

1. Vikrant Public School, Patiala is celebrating its Annual Prize Distribution Function on 14th August. Dr. Akhil Raj, the renowned author, is the Chief Guest for the occasion. Draft an invitation card in not more than 50 words to be sent to the parents and guests, mentioning the date, time and venue. **CBSE Term II 2022**

2. Your school is planning to organise a talk on the 'Importance of Promoting Art Education' at all levels. You plan to invite the Director, Delhi School of Art, as a Keynote Speaker. As CCA Coordinator of Vidya Mandir Vidyalaya, draft an invitation for the same giving all the necessary details in about 50 words.

3. As Secretary of the Literacy Club of St. Anne's School, Ahmedabad, draft a formal invitation in not more than 50 words for the inauguration of the club in your school.

4. You are Jaya. The wedding of your Brother Ajay Sengupta is going to be held on 24th November, 20XX at Hotel Palace, Udaipur. Draft an informal invitation in 50 words to your friend Malini requesting her to attend the functions.

5. Rohit has successfully cleared a prestigious international Management exam. He wants to celebrate his admission and farewell by throwing a party to his friends. Write an informal invitation in 50 words giving details of the venue, time and date.

6. You have opened a beautiful resort in your city. Draft a formal letter of invite to the Chief Minister of your city inviting him to inaugurate the event.

7. You are Rajneesh/Rajee Mehta, an eminent educationist. You have been invited to Nav Nirmaan School, Sucheta Vihar, Kolkata to attend and speak at a workship on the topic 'The Importance of Time Management' on 5th June, 2022 at 10:00 am. Draft a letter of acceptance to the Cultural-in-Charge, Piyush, in about 50 words. **CBSE 2022, Term II**

8. You are Anshika Kapoor, 646, Defence Colony, New Delhi and have received an invitation from the Secretary, Bharat Vikas Parishad to attend a function on 15th July, 20XX. Draft a formal reply of refusal in not more than 50 words.

9. You are Dr. B.L. Kapoor from Pratibha Kapoor Hospital, Patiala. You have been invited to speak on 'Health-a dietary journey', for Senior Secondary School students. Draft a reply accepting the invitation in not more than 50 words. Request for the time, date and venue where the meeting has been organised.

10. You are Manoj/Meena. You have received an invitation from your friend Vijay to a party to celebrate his admission in a prestigious Management Institute. Write an informal letter in about 50 words accepting the invitation. Mention the day, date, time and venue. **CBSE 2023**

03 CHAPTER

Long Composition

Letter Writing

Letter writing is one of the most effective ways of communication. Today, although telephone, fax and e-mail have replaced personal (informal) letters, formal letters are still in use. Commerce, trade, official correspondence, complaints, transactions and communication with people are still conducted through formal letters.

Marking Scheme

Format	1 Mark
Organisation of ideas	1 Mark
Content	2 Marks
Expression	1 Mark
(Accuracy of Spelling and Grammar)	

Main Elements of a Formal Letter

Before we move into the main aspects of the formal letter, it is important to note that formal letters have set patterns and are written using a crisp and clear language in a matter-of-fact style. The language should be kept simple without including any unnecessary expressions.

1. Sender's Address

According to the latest format, sender's address is written at the top along with the pin code. Do not write sender's name with the address.

e.g. K-127, Ashok Nagar
New Delhi-110092

Note While writing the address (both sender's and receiver's), one must not use 'comma' at the end of each line. If the address is not provided in the question, then you may create a fictitious address, but writing an address is mandatory.

2. Date

It appears directly below the sender's address, after leaving a one line space. It is advisable to always write the full date in the following format.

e.g. 25th December, 20XX

3. Receiver's Address

It appears directly below the date and comprises the receiver's name, designation and the complete address.

e.g. The Editor
The Hindustan Times
47/ 1567, Daryaganj
Delhi-110002

4. Subject

Subject is generally used in writing a formal letter. It can be written after the receiver's address or after the salutation. It should be short and to the point.

e.g. **Subject** Application for the Post of Content Writer

5. Salutation

This consists of words of greeting and is written on the left hand side of the page just after the subject after leaving a line. The form of greeting depends upon your relation to the person to whom the letter is being written. In case of formal letters you use only Sir/Ma'am.

6. The Body

The body is the main part of any letter. This is written in response to the given topic, in a simple and direct language. The body includes three main parts

1. Introductory paragraph/sentence → States the purpose of writing the letter
2. Informative paragraphs → Details about the subject of the letter
3. Concluding paragraph/sentence → The closure of the letter/conclusion stating hope, request or comment.

7. Complimentary Close

It is a courteous way of ending the letter. The expression used must match the salutation. In case of formal letter, we use Yours sincerely/Yours faithfully.

8. Name

It is written just below the 'complimentary close' and includes the sender's name and designation (if applicable).

e.g. Ankita Chakravarti
Editor

A. Letters to the Editor

Letters to the Editor of a newspaper or magazine form an important part of the paper. Such letters voice the opinion of the people and provide them with a platform to express their agreement, disagreement or reaction to the social issues or issues concerning the common masses.

Some Useful Expressions to be Used in Letter to the Editor

- Through the columns of your esteemed newspaper, I wish to bring to the notice of the concerned authorities ....
- In my opinion ....
- I hope that ....

Format

The recent increase in online teaching is of great concern for both parents and teachers. A fine balance needs to be maintained between the two. Using the given clues and your own ideas, write a letter to the editor on this topic and give suggestions. You are Manju/Manav. Word limit is 120-150 words. You can use the following clues.

Impact Social isolation, Loneliness, Obesity, Stress and Anxiety.

Solutions Physical activity, Family time, Hobbies

Nehru Colony
Indore — **Sender's address**

24th February, 20XX — **Date**

The Editor
The Times of India
New Delhi 110002 — **Receiver's name/rank and his/her address**

Subject **Concerns over online teaching** — **Subject of the letter** Indicate the theme of the letter here

Sir/Ma'am — **Salutation**

Through the columns of your esteemed newspaper, I would like to draw the attention of the concerned authorities to express my concern regarding online teaching.

With the Covid-19 Pandemic affecting all of the world's different areas at large, the one to take the most hit is the education sector. The pandemic forced to fasten the acceptance of online teaching methods to sustain learning. In the need to continue effective education, online teaching- learning was accepted by all schools. However, the acceptance of online teaching came with its various limitations.

Online teaching- learning from school promoted learning from school but promoted isolation. As a result, children make almost no friends. They are stuck at home for all day and suffer from stress, anxiety and even obesity. Thus, the condition of the future of the country is deteriorating.

Hence, it is time for us to look for a fine balance between the two worlds of online learning and innocence of childhood. To do so, we can take certain steps in the form of physical activities, family time and constructive leisure time.

I hope that all of us understand the need to maintain this balance and make sure that our young minds enjoy their innocent childhood to the fullest and not sit in front of their systems all day long.

— **Body of the letter**

Thanking you
Yours truly
Manju/Manav — **Complimentary closure** Name and designation of the sender

PRACTICE QUESTIONS

1. **You are Sheetal/Shailesh Khanna of 42, Model Town, Khushnagar. Write a letter to the editor of a local daily expressing your concern about the cutting down of trees in your city to make space for huge commercial complexes. Discuss the environmental impact of the cutting of trees. Also, suggest effective ways to raise awareness about the importance of a green environment. You may use some of the given cues along with your own ideas.** **CBSE 2025**

- Loss of biodiversity, increased temperatures, poor air quality
- Prioritise green infrastructure and sustainable urban planning
- Create 'green spaces'
- Spread awareness through programmes, public messages, media

Ans. 42, Model Town
Khushnagar

11th November, 20XX

The Editor
The Times Daily
Khushnagar

Subject **Concern over deforestation for commercial complexes**

Sir/Madam

Through the columns of your esteemed newspaper, I wish to draw attention to the rampant cutting down of trees in our city to accommodate large commercial complexes. This destruction of greenery is leading to loss of biodiversity, rising temperatures and deteriorating air quality, making our city less liveable.

To address this issue, authorities must prioritise green infrastructure and sustainable urban planning. Spaces for trees and parks should be integrated into commercial projects. Additionally, public awareness campaigns, media messages, and community programmes should be used to educate people about the importance of preserving greenery. Schools and organisations can also initiate tree-planting drives.

A balance between development and nature is crucial for a healthier environment. I urge the authorities to take immediate action to protect our city's green cover.

Yours sincerely
Sheetal Khanna

2. **Write a letter to the editor of a local daily about the 'Importance of Mental Health Awareness among Teenagers'. You are Ragini/Rajan a school counsellor, living at 17/235, Sector 5, Newpur. You may use the following cues along with your own ideas to draft the letter.** **CBSE 2025**

- What are the mental health issues among teenagers?
- Examples highlighting the problem.
- Importance of early intervention.
- Role of schools, parents and counsellors.
- Suggestion of awareness programme and support system.

Ans. 17/235, Sector 5
Newpur

16th September, 20XX

The Editor
The Daily News
Newpur

Subject **Importance of mental health awareness among teenagers**

Sir/Madam

Through the columns of your esteemed newspaper, I wish to highlight the growing need for mental health awareness among teenagers. With academic pressure, social media influence, and peer expectations, many teenagers struggle with stress, anxiety, depression, and low self-esteem. Cases of cyberbullying and Fear Of Missing Out (FOMO) further add to their emotional distress.

Early intervention is crucial in preventing long-term mental health issues. Schools, parents, and counsellors must work together to create a supportive environment. Schools should integrate mental health awareness programmes, while parents should encourage open conversations. Regular counselling sessions and peer support groups can also help.

I urge authorities to implement awareness campaigns and provide accessible mental health resources in schools. Addressing these concerns will ensure a healthier future for our youth.

Yours sincerely

Ragini/Rajan

(School Counsellor)

3. You are Jyoti/Jagan of Park Avenue, Karampur. You feel sad to notice that people litter the roads with utter disregard for sanitation and cleanliness. As a responsible citizen, write a letter to the editor of a national daily highlighting the need for educational institutions to instill civic responsibility among the school children. You may use the following clues along with your own ideas to compose this letter. **CBSE 2024**

- Cleanliness drive
- Spreading awareness campaigns
- Eco club activities in schools
- Volunteer for cleanup
- Workshops, seminars

Ans. 472, Park Avenue
Karampur

20th March, 20XX

The Editor
The Times of India
New Delhi - 110001

Subject **The lack of civic responsibility among school children**

Sir/Ma'am

Through the medium of this letter, I wish to bring the attention of the common masses towards the matter of growing concern in our community, the lack of civic responsibility among school children. It saddens me to witness the disregard for sanitation and cleanliness, as evident in the rampant littering on our roads and public spaces.

Educational institutions play a pivotal role in shaping the values and behaviours of young individuals. It is imperative that they prioritise the installation of civic responsibility among students. By incorporating lessons on environmental stewardship, waste management, and community involvement into the curriculum, schools can nurture a sense of ownership and accountability towards maintaining a clean and hygienic environment.

Moreover, fostering partnerships between schools, local authorities and community organisations can provide opportunities for students to actively participate in clean-up drives and awareness campaigns, thus instilling lifelong habits of responsible citizenship.

It is my hope that through concerted efforts, we can empower our youth to become proactive agents of positive change in our society.

Thanking you
Yours sincerely
Jyoti/Jagan
(A Concerned Citizen)

4. To maintain 'work life' balance, there is a surge of people going on short and budgeted vacations. Seizing this opportunity more people are offering 'the home stay' option. Write a letter to the editor of a national daily sharing your views on this trend. You may use the following clues along with your own ideas to compose this letter. You are Ankit/Ankita. **CBSE 2024**

- Home Stay
- Home cooked meals
- Emerging opportunities for locals
- Budgeted travel option
- Opportunity to enjoy local culture, cuisines, life-style
- Opportunity to showcase indigenous communities in villages/small towns

Ans. 14, Paschim Vihar,
New Delhi - 110034

7th March, 20XX

The Editor
The Indian Express
New Delhi - 110002

Subject **Surge in short, budgeted vacations and home-stay**

Sir/Ma'am

Through the column of your esteemed newspaper, I would like to draw the attention of the masses towards the matter of growing trend of short, budgeted vacations. As each and every individual is running in a rat race, maintaining a healthy work-life balance is of prime importance. This new trend offers individuals a chance to explore new destinations to de-stress and have a glimpse of different lifestyles lived by individuals in remote areas.

The most significant outcome of this trend is the rise of home stays as a preferred accommodation option rather than hotels or resorts. People start to seek for more affordable yet authentic travel experiences and what could be a better option than a home stay?

By providing home-cooked meals, home stays allow travellers to savour the taste of the local cuisines in a cosy ambience thereby establishing meaningful connections with the locals. The travellers also get a chance to get insights of the various cultural activities or festivals. Thus, home stays not only act as a source of income to the locals but also contribute to the economic growth of their communities. Moreover, they are able to promote their rich cultural heritage on a bigger scale.

In conclusion, the surge of budgeted vacations and home stays represents a positive shift towards a more balanced and enriching approach to travel and also contributes to the prosperity of the communities they visit.

Thanking you
Yours sincerely
Ankit/Ankita

5. You are a resident of Pranihar Colony and a member of the Resident Welfare Association. During your morning walks, you have noticed that the parks are in a dismal condition. Due to the neglect, the parks are no longer safe for residents to walk or children to play. Write a letter to the editor of your local newspaper in about 120-150 words expressing your views on the situation and suggesting ways to improve and maintain the park. You may use the following clues given below. You are Sunaina/Satish, Member of the RWA. **CBSE 2023**

Condition of Parks		Suggestions
- overgrown trees/grass	→	- prune trees
- broken walking tracks		- repair tracks, replace tiles
- open pits		- covering of open potholes and pits
- no boundary walls		- build boundary wall
- no lights		- install solar lights
- no dustbins		- put benches and dustbins

Ans. Pranihar Colony,
New Delhi

16th April, 20XX

The Editor
XYZ Times
New Delhi

Subject **Misuse and poor maintenance of public park in our colony**

Sir/Ma'am

Through the column of your esteemed newspaper, I would like to draw attention of the concerned authorities towards the problem of misuse and poor maintenance of the public park of our colony.

The park in our area has fallen into a miserable state due to its misuse and poor maintenance. The gardeners don't come regularly and do not take care of the plants properly. As a result, many trees and plants are either overgrown or decaying. The walking track is broken and there are many open pits. Even the boundary walls are broken and there are no security guards, making it an easy pathway for thieves and other bad influences. There are no lights or dustbins which makes the park more of a dumping ground for all. Therefore, senior citizens and children have nowhere to go for relaxing and playing.

Hence, it is time that the authorities look into the matter and work towards hiring responsible gardeners. They should also repair the tracks, cover the open potholes, build a proper boundary wall, install solar lights and put benches and dustbins so that the lost glory of the park can be renewed.

I hope that this issue reaches the concerned authorities and they will take necessary actions as soon as possible.

Thanking you
Yours sincerely
Sunaina/Satish
(Member, RWA)

6. You are Sujoy/Sujata of Nehru Colony, Indore. You recently visited Shimla with your family. You were perturbed to see the tourist throwing empty bottles and cans all over the place. Write a letter to the editor The Times of India in about 120-150 words expressing your concern and offering suggestions to improve the situation. Use the given clues with your own ideas to compose the letter. **CBSE 2023**

Eco-Friendly Travel

- Create less waste
- Dispose garbage properly
- 40% pollution increase during the tourist season
- Do sustainable travel
- Waste and pollution have far-reaching impacts on wildlife, the environment, visitors and communities, create - a clean and healthy vacation destination
- Ecological Conservation - A Need of the hour

Ans. Nehru Colony
Indore

24th February, 20XX

The Editor
The Times of India
Delhi - 110002

Subject **Concerns over increasing pollution and waste during tourist season**

Sir/Ma'am

Through the column of your esteemed newspaper, I would like to draw the attention of the concerned authorities to express my concern over the increasing pollution and waste during the tourist season. The realisation of this concern dawned on me during my visit to Shimla with my family. It was disheartening to see tourists throwing empty bottles and cans all over the place, spoiling the natural beauty of pristine hill station.

Tourism, today, has become an important source of income for many places, but it also has many negative impacts on the environment. Waste and pollution have far-reaching impacts on the ecological balance of the region as it adversely affects all flora and fauna, communities and environment of the region. Hence, ecological conservation of the place is a need of the hour. We can create a clean and healthy vacation destinations by following some easy steps and measures. First, we should encourage eco-friendly travel by promoting public transport, cycling, and walking. Second, we should create less waste by carrying our own reusable water bottles and avoiding single-use plastics. Last, we should dispose of garbage properly by using designated bins.

I believe that sustainable travel is the key to preserving the beauty of tourist destinations. We must ensure that tourism does not come at the cost of environmental degradation. I urge the concerned authorities to take immediate action towards ecological conservation and create a safe and healthy environment for tourists and locals.

Thanking you
Yours truly
Sujoy/Sujata

7. Financial literacy is increasingly recognised as a crucial 21st-century skill for young individuals. Write a letter to the editor of a local daily discussing the benefits of providing financial literacy education to children. Also, suggest effective ways to raise awareness about the importance of this education among parents and guardians. You may use some of the given clues along with your own ideas to draft the letter. You are a counsellor, Chitra Mahapatra from Puri, Odisha.

- What are the long term benefits of learning financial independence from a young age?
- Why is understanding the power of finances beneficial for young learners?
- Why skills learned during childhood tend to have a lasting impact?

Ans. Examination Hall
New Delhi

12th August, 20XX

The Editor
The Times of India
New Delhi

Subject **The need of financial literacy for youth**

Sir/Ma'am

Through the column of your esteemed daily, I would like to draw the attention towards the need of financial literacy for youth.

In the age where money is king, it is crucial for all of us to effectively be able to manage money. Gone are the days when managing money was in the hands of an adult. With digital payment becoming a fad, even children today have to become responsible for how they use their money they get as pocket money. Hence, it is not surprising that financial literacy is increasingly recognised as a crucial 21st-century skill for young individuals.

Financial literacy is the knowledge and skills needed to manage personal finances effectively and efficiently. It includes understanding how to budget, save, invest, and manage credit and debt. Being financially literate means having the ability to make informed decisions about financial matters and navigating the complex world of personal finance. For students, even without any earnings, learning financial basics is invaluable. It includes finding income sources, utilising skills for earnings, and understanding how to multiply even modest incomes. Early knowledge about management and multiplication of money can pave the way for financial freedom. It helps in making intelligent financial choices and shapes a financially wise mindset, promoting sound decision-making. Further, financially literate individuals are more likely to avoid debt traps and manage debt responsibly, resulting in lower levels of debt and interest payments. Overall, financial literacy is a valuable life skill that can lead to greater financial stability, security and success.

Hence, parents, guardians and all educational institutes must talk and discuss finances to make a child financially literate.

Thanking you
Yours sincerely
Chitra Mahapatra

8. **You are Minu Sen, an intern in a software company in Hyderabad. You feel that the growing relationship of companies with non-profit organisations have made Corporate Social Responsibility (CSR) the buzzword today. Your own involvement in one such project for your company has convinced you that CSR looks beyond the company profits and focuses on benefitting the greater community.**

Write a letter to the editor of a national daily in about 120-150 words, sharing your opinion about CSR and its advantages and provide suggestions to make it an integral part of every organisation. Use the given clues along with your own ideas to compose this letter.

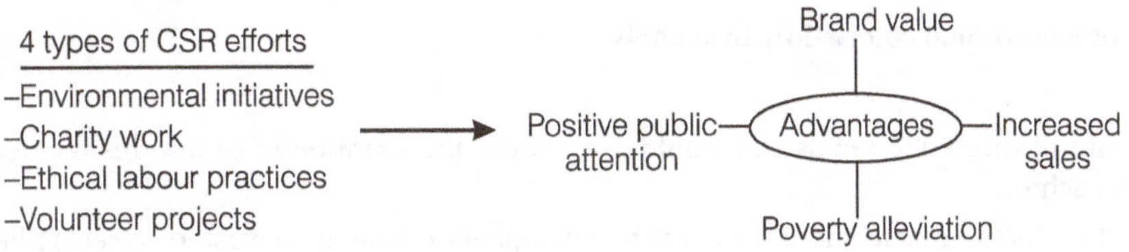

CBSE SQP 2023

Ans. 112, Taj Road
Delhi - 110065
25th September, 20XX

The Editor
The Times of India
New Delhi-110002

Subject **Increasing focus on Corporate Social Responsibility**

Sir/Ma'am

Through the column of your esteemed newspaper, I would like to draw the attention of all towards the increasing trend of Corporate Social Responsibility (CSR) amongst private conglomerates. I had recently been a part of large project that made me realise that organisations today are looking beyond company profits.

In the present day world, we are witnessing the growing relationship of companies with non-profit organisations. The result is the new buzzword called Corporate Social Responsibility (CSR). CSR refers to all those initiatives through which organisations focus on bettering their society without any selfish interest.

Many large MNC's today, are taking up environmental initiatives, doing charity work and participating in volunteer projects. They are not only changing to a more sustainable way of working but have also been introducing more ethical labour practices. Their actions play a large part in poverty alleviation, conservation of environment and growth of the society. While these organisations do not expect any profit, they are indirectly profited. As their works come into limelight, their brand value increases and they receive positive public attention. Consequently, they gain increased sales.

However, there are still some organisations that ignore CSR. The need of the hour is to make CSR a norm. To do so, we must spread awareness regarding the benefits of CSR. Laws mandating companies to include CSR along with introduction of some privileges to companies that show some positive change in society can urge more and more organisations to take up their CSR.

I hope that readers are urged to follow CSR in their work places so our world is a better place to live in.

Thanking you
Yours sincerely
Minu Sen

9. **Write a letter to the editor emphasising on the need of educational counsellors for guidance in matter of choosing a career in each school.**

You can use the following clues

- Modern and competitive time
- Make a very difficult choice
- Students are misguided
- No valid mechanism to assess the suitability of candidates for a particular stream
- Peer or parental pressure
- Regret their decisions
- A special post of educational counsellor

Ans. 48, Agra Fort
Agra

2nd March, 20XX

The Editor
The Times of India
Fort Road
Agra

Subject **The need of educational counsellors in schools**

Sir/Ma'am

Through the columns of your esteemed daily, I would like to draw the attention of all towards the need of educational counsellors in every school.

In this modern and competitive time, there is a cut throat competition among youngsters to secure better marks. After passing the secondary school examination, a candidate has to make a very difficult choice from a number of streams available to him or her for further studies. Students are often misguided by others who are ready to cheat the unsuspecting students and their parents. There is no valid mechanism to assess the suitability of candidates for a particular stream. Students opt for subjects under the influence of peer or parental pressure without considering their own preferences and capabilities. As a result, many students, later, regret their decisions, which by then has already affected their career and psyche.

The ministry of HRD should be serious towards the career of the students. A special post of educational counselor should be created in every school so that the students and parents can discuss their issues and concerns, and clarify their doubts regarding further education. This will certainly give them some relief from the unnecessary worries.

Hoping for favourable consideration for the welfare of students.

Thanking you
Yours sincerely
XYZ

10. **Recently, the paper leaking of the esteemed NEET and NET exam have created an uproar regarding the efficiency of our education system. In order to increase the reliability of such competitive exams, the Government of India has introduced the Public Examinations (Prevention of Unfair Means) Act, 2024. You recently researched upon the act while preparing for an inter-state debate competition. Write a letter to the editor of your local daily, expressing your views on this act. Use the given clues along with your own ideas to form the letter.**

- **Key Features**
  - Transparency, credibility and fairness in examinations
  - Anti-cheating law
  - Punishment in the form of imprisonment and fine for fifteen crimes listed in the Act
  - Exams conducted by UPSC, SSC, RRB, IBPS, NTA are covered
- **Impact**
- **Your suggestions**

Ans. A4, Ecovillage 1
Noida

8th November, 20XX

The Editor
Jagran Daily
Sector 52
Noida

Subject **Regarding Public Examinations (Prevention of Unfair Means) Act, 2024**

Sir/Ma'am

Through the columns of your esteemed daily, I would like to draw the attention of all towards the new act passed by the government of India regarding 'unfair means' used in public examinations.

Time and again, we have heard about the news of leaking of question papers and bypassing security measures in public examinations by the students. The issue has become critical and relevant in today's competitive world where every student is fighting for their better future. The problem involves the nuisance created around exams by paper leaking, surpassing the authorities, tempering with admit cards and merit lists, issuing fake documents and marksheets and deliberate violation of security measures set up by the conducting authority. The act recently passed will allow the government to keep a check on any unfair means being used in the examinations by students, or any other person responsible. The act sets up a severe punishment structure for the offenders which involves imprisonment and financial liability. This ensures the integrity and fairness in these examinations.

Nations was outraged by the unfair means that happened in the national level examinations, a series of scams and frauds undermining public trust in the educational process was uncovered. Exams were being conducted without a proper framework. The new act will uphold the value of merit by reassuring the students that their hard work will be fruitful and rewarding. Successful implementation of the act will require collaboration between authorities and exam conducting bodies. Public awareness and continuous improvement will be required to maintain the standards.

I hope that the act is properly implemented considering the favourable welfare of the students.

Thanking you
Yours sincerely
XYZ

11. Write a letter to the editor of a local daily urging people to use public transport and to have patience while driving. You can take help of the following image. (120-150 words) **CBSE 2020**

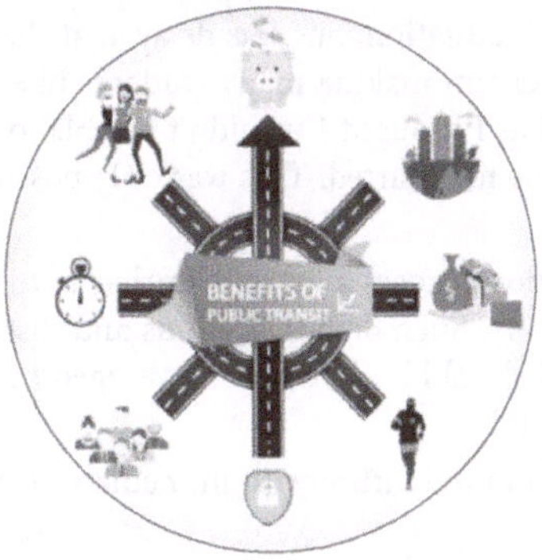

Ans. 4, Raja Road
Karnal

5th July, 20XX

The Editor
The Hindustan
Karnal

Subject **Use of public transport**

Sir/Ma'am

Through the columns of your esteemed newspaper, I would like to inform everyone about the various advantages of using the public transport.

Everybody knows that the increase in the number of private vehicles on the road is the major cause of pollution. Furthermore, vehicles mean more congestion and traffic jams. Everybody tries to move first and fast which not only increases the chance of accidents but also causes a lot of noise pollution because people continuously blow horn during the waiting moments.

An easy and quick solution of the problem is that we make use of the rapidly increasing public transport. It will prove more beneficial as it will save our energy, money and time and we can use that energy in doing other tasks efficiently.

Therefore, I hope that people realise the depth of this issue and I urge them to try and use public transport as much as they can.

Thanking You
Yours sincerely
XYZ

12. **Public demonstration causes a lot of disturbance in daily routine of common man. You almost missed your important entrance examination as people blocked the highway. As Tarun/Taruna, a student aspiring to be a doctor, write a letter to the editor of The Times of India highlighting the need to discourage such demonstrations and disturbance by public on highways which cause a great loss of time and opportunity for many. You may use the following clues given below**

- Delay
- Disturbance in daily routine
- Loss of time and opportunity
- Need for preventive action

Ans. 44/7, Sarvodaya Colony
Mohan Nagar, Ghaziabad

10th March, 20XX

The Editor
The Times of India
New Delhi - 110002

Subject **Public protests and demonstrations cause inconvenience**

Sir/Ma'am

Through the columns of your esteemed newspaper, I wish to bring the attention of the concerned authorities towards the inconvenience caused by public protests and demonstrations.

Recently, I myself had to go through a hassle because of these protests and demonstrations. A few days back, I was going to take the medical entrance test for my post-graduation, but was delayed at the border due to a public protest by farmers. They damaged many cars and held a chakka jam making many students like me, office goers and other people wait for a long time. With the level of protests, I panicked as I thought I wouldn't be able to give my exam. However, after great difficulty, I reached the examination hall just when the test started. This was only possible because I had started one hour earlier than normal.

Everybody is aware that public demonstrations causes a lot of disturbance to the daily routine of the common man. Emergency services are also affected adversely. Such demonstrations and disturbances by people on highways, cause a great loss of time and opportunity for many and should be actively discouraged by the authorities. They should take suitable preventive action so that traffic flows smoothly.

Hoping that such situations will be avoided in the future with immediate action by the concerned authorities.

Thanking you
Yours sincerely
Tarun/Taruna

B. Letters of Job Application

These are letters that are written to apply for a job or a service. It is the primary means of introducing the applicant or the job seeker to the employer. Therefore, it acts as a personal advertisement with an appeal for a job with a letter and a bio-data.
A job application thus contains.

(i) A covering letter (ii) A Bio-data/Curriculum Vitae

The Curriculum Vitae or Bio-data refers to a person's life and his/her achievements. It has a very specific format.

Some Useful Expression to be Used in Letters of Job Application

- In response to your advertisement in.... I offer my candidature for your consideration.
- I would like to apply for the post of....... in your organisation, advertised today in.... of ....

Format

You are Maya Syiem from Shillong. You read the given advertisement and wish to apply for the post advertised. Write a job application along with your bio-data for the provided advertisement.

Join our Creative Team!
A renowned publishing house in Shillong
A NEW WORLD
is seeking a talented illustrator for children's books.
Creative individuals with a passion for storytelling through art, welcome.
Experience, not mandatory.
Team players with degree/ diploma in Fine Arts/ Graphic Design may apply with 5 samples from portfolio illustrating a variety of work.
Write to the Project Lead, 23-C Rosewood Lane, Shillong-793005

XYZ Apartments — Sender's address
Shilong
11th September, 20XX — Date

The Project Lead — Receiver's name/rank and his/her address
23-C Rosewood Lane
Shilong - 793005

Subject **Application for the post of an illustrator for children's books** — Subject of the letter

Sir/Ma'am — Salutation

This is in response to your advertisement in 'The Times of India' dated 10th September, 20XX for the post of an illustrator for children's books, I wish to apply for the same.

I possess requisite qualifications and experience. In my previous capacity as a Junior Illustrator for a Marketing organisation, I have created logos and social media posts for various big brands. I am enclosing my detailed resume for your perusal. You may call me for an interview on any date as per your convenience. I shall be able to join my duties at one month notice
if appointed. I hope for a positive reply.

(Body of the letter)

Thanking you — Complimentary Closure
Yours sincerely
Maya Syiem

Enclosure Detailed Resume

Resume

Name	Maya Syiem
Father's Name	Mr. Shivank
Date of Birth	15th September, 1994
Age	28
Address	XYZ Apartments, Shillong
Email-id	MayaS@gmail.com
Nationality	Indian

Educational Qualifications

Name of the Exam	College/Board/University	Year of Passing	Percentage
Degree in Graphic Design	MAAC	2017	-
Fine Arts	ABC University	2015	73%
Senior Secondary (Class XII)	CBSE	2012	96%
Secondary (Class X)	CBSE	2010	95%

Certification	Classical dance and Music for 12 years in Pandit Birju Maharaj Dance and Music Academy
Hobbies	Music, Photography, Reading and Dancing
Languages Known	Hindi, English and Spanish
Experience	Working as an Junior Graphic Designer, PQR Marketing
References	1. Mr. Arun Agarwal, MAAC 2. Mrs. Rashmi Sharma, PQR Marketing

PRACTICE QUESTIONS

1. **You are Radha/Ram living at 18, Jan Vihar, Nayapur. You have read the given advertisement and wish to apply for the post of Marketing Executive. Write a job application along with your bio-data.** **CBSE 2025**

> **ABC Corporation**
> **Requires**
> **Marketing Executive**
> **Qualification** BBA in marketing with 4 - 5 years work experience
> **Skills** Proficiency in digital marketing
> — Good communication skills
> — Market research and analysis
> — Strategic thinker
>
> Apply with details to:
> Director ABC Corporation, Nayapur

Ans. 18, Jan Vihar
Nayapur

16th August, 20XX

The Director
ABC Corporation
Nayapur

Subject **Application for the Post of Marketing Executive**

Sir/Madam

This is in response to your advertisement in the daily newspaper dated 13th August, 20XX for the position of Marketing Executive at ABC Corporation, as advertised. I hold a BBA in Marketing and have over five years of experience in the field. My expertise lies in digital marketing, market research, and strategic planning. With strong communication skills and an analytical mindset, I have successfully developed and implemented marketing campaigns that boosted brand visibility and customer engagement.

I am confident that my skills and experience align well with your company's requirements. I have attached my bio-data for your kind consideration. I look forward to the opportunity to discuss my application further.

Yours sincerely

Radha/Ram

Bio-data

Name Radha/Ram

Address 18, Jan Vihar, Nayapur

Mobile 0XX - 2958XXXX

Email marrket93@gmail.com

Educational Qualification

Name of the exam	College/Board/University	Year of Passing	Percentage
BBA in Marketing	ABC University	2014	88%

Work Experience

Marketing Executive XYZ Pvt. Ltd. (20XX-20XX)

- Managed digital campaigns, increasing engagement by 30%.
- Conducted market research for product positioning.

Assistant Marketing Manager PQR Ltd. (20XX-20XX)

- Developed strategic marketing plans.
- Led a team to execute promotional activities.

Skills

- Proficiency in digital marketing
- Market research and analysis
- Strong communication and strategic thinking

References Available upon request

2. You are Sujata/Suresh, a qualified fashion designer. You came across the given advertisement in a newspaper and wish to apply for the position advertised. Write a letter of application along with bio-data for the same. **CBSE 2024**

> We are Hiring!
>
> **Apparel Designer**
>
> **Required Qualification** Graduation in fashion design.
>
> **Experience** Minimum 2 years in relevant field.
>
> **Skills** Creativity, computer designing of apparels, aptitude for sewing, business sense, in depth knowledge of fabric drafting.
>
> Apply to the Director, Estella House of Fashion 26, M.G. Road, Kanthapuram

Ans. B-94, Fort Road
Kanthapuram

20th March, 20XX

The Director
Estella House of Fashion
26, M.G. Road
Kanthapuram

Subject **Application for the post of apparel designer**

Sir/Ma'am

In response to your advertisement in 'The Indian Express' dated 19th March, 20XX, requiring an Apparel Designer, I wish to be considered for this post. With a passion for fashion design and a proven track record of creating innovative and trend-setting apparel, I am confident in my ability to contribute effectively to your team.

Having graduated with a degree in Fashion Design from the New York Fashion School, I have acquired a solid foundation in design principles, garment construction and textile technology. My previous experience at Bella Bridals has further honed my skills in conceptualising, sketching, and executing designs that resonate with target demographics.

I am particularly drawn to Estella House of Fashion's commitment to quality craftsmanship and cutting-edge design. I am eager to bring my creative vision and technical expertise to contribute to the development of your apparel line.

I am enclosing my biodata and attested copies of my certificates. I hope to receive a positive response from your side.

Thanking you
Yours faithfully
Sujata/Suresh

Enclosure Bio-data

Bio-data

Name Sujata/Suresh Agarwal
Father's Name Mr. Shivank Agarwal
Date of Birth 15th September, 1991
Address B-94 Fort Road, Kanthapuram
Email-id sunami102@gmail.com
Nationality Indian

Educational Qualifications

Name of the exam	College/Board/University	Year of Passing	Percentage
Masters in Fashion Designing	New York School of Fashion	2015	69%
Bachelors in Fashion Designing	New York School of Fashion	2013	73%
Senior Secondary (Class XII)	CBSE	2010	96%
Secondary (Class X)	CBSE	2008	95%

Hobbies Music, Photography and Painting
Languages Known Hindi, English and French
Experience Bella Bridals (2016-2024)
References 1. Mr. Sandesh Dhupia - Bella Bridals
2. Ms. Sandy D'souza - New York School of Fashion

3. **You are Dinesh/Deepa of M.G. Nagar, Pratap Nagar. You are a pharma graduate. You saw the given advertisement in a newspaper and wish to apply for the position advertised. Write a letter to Ideal Pharma, along with your bio-data, expressing your interest in the advertised post.** **CBSE 2024**

Ideal Pharma
Requires
Sales Representatives

Qualification Graduation in Pharmacy
Experience Min. 3 years in the relevant field
Skills Product Knowledge, Communication Skills, Computer Compentency
Apply to the Manager, Ideal Pharma, 55, Ajit Arcade, Tenalipuram within a week.

Ans. M-14, M.G. Nagar
Pratap Nagar

16th March, 20XX

The Manager
Ideal Pharma
55, Ajit Arcade
Tenalipuram

Subject **Application for the post of sales representative**

Sir/Ma'am

In response to your advertisement in 'The Hindustan Times' dated 14th March, 20XX, requiring a Sales Representative, I wish to be considered for this post.

I have completed my B. Pharm with a First class division from Panjab University. I have work experience of three years as a Medical Representative at Apollo Pharmaceuticals. I have dealt with numerous clients and got exposure to various types of medicines and surgical instruments. From my work experience, I have acquired good communication skills and am able to work efficiently on computers. I believe that my qualifications and experience align with the job responsibilities and requirements mentioned in the advertisement.

As requested, I have enclosed my resume with this letter. I shall be available for an interview call as per your convenience. I shall be able to join my duties at one month notice if appointed. Hoping to hear a positive response from your end.

Thanking you
Yours sincerely
Dinesh/Deepa

Enclosure Bio-data

Bio-data

Name Dinesh/Deepa Kumar

Father's Name Mr. Suresh Kumar

Date of Birth 20th August, 1998

Email-id kumardask12@gmail.com

Nationality Indian

Educational Qualification

Name of the Exam	College/Board/University	Year of Passing	Percentage
B. Pharm	Panjab University	2017	76%
Senior Secondary	CBSE	2014	78%
Secondary	CBSE	2012	82%

Work Experience Working for last 3 years in 'Apollo Pharmaceuticals' as a Medical Representavtive.

Languages Known Hindi, English and Telugu

Hobbies Reading and gardening

References
1. PS Kapoor, Manager, Apollo Pharmaceuticals, Telangana
2. Gopal Gupta, Team Lead, Apollo Pharmaceuticals, Telangana

4. **You are Neeta/Neeraj of Rainbow Nagar, Shakti Ganj, a qualified basketball coach. You saw the advertisement given below and wish to apply for the position advertised.** **CBSE 2024**

> **R.J. Sports Academy**
> Requires
> **Basketball Coach**
> **Qualification** Master's Degree in specific game with NIS diploma.
> **Work Experience** Minimum 2 years in the relevant field.
> **Skills** Patience, empathy, leadership qualities, attention to detail.
> Apply with complete bio-data to the Director R.J. Sports Academy, 43, L.M. Square, Shakti Ganj expressing your interest in the advertised post.

Ans. B-94, Rainbow Nagar
Shakti Ganj

20th March, 20XX

The Director
R.J. Sports Academy
43, L.M. Square, Shakti Ganj

Subject **Application for the post of basketball coach**

Sir/Ma'am

This is with reference to your advertisement in 'The Hindustan Times' dated 15th March, 20XX for the post of basketball coach. I wish to apply for the same. I am enclosing the details of my educational qualifications and experience in my resume.

As per your requirement, I have a Master's degree in Basketball with NIS Diploma. I also possess 3 years of industry experience. I am a confident, empathetic and attentive individual. I am confident that I will not disappoint you and I will produce some champion athletes to bring pride to your academy.

I shall be available for an interview at any time convenient to you. I am enclosing my biodata and attested copies of my certificates. I hope to receive a positive response from your side.

Thanking you
Yours faithfully
Neeta/Neeraj

Enclosure Bio-data

Bio-data

Name Neeta/Neeraj
Father's Name Mr. Rohan
Date of Birth 15th September, 1991
Address B-94 Rainbow Nagar, Shakti Ganj
Email-id neetuni11@gmail.com
Nationality Indian

Educational Qualification

Name of the Exam	College/Board/University	Year of Passing	Percentage
M. P. Ed. (Physical Education)	University of Delhi	2007	69%
B. P. Ed. (Physical Education)	University of Delhi	2005	73%
Senior Secondary (Class XII)	CBSE	2002	96%
Secondary (Class X)	CBSE	2000	95%

Experience Working as Physical Education Instructor in Saraswati Public School, New Delhi since March, 20XX.

Languages Known English, Hindi and Punjabi
References
1. Mr. Sandesh Dhupia - Senior coach, Sports Authority of India (7803XXXXXX)
2. Ms. Sandy Desouza - Vice Principal, Saraswati Public School (8076XXXXXX)

5. **You are Radhika/Rahul, currently working on probation as an Assistant Manager in Romy Chain of Restaurants. You saw the given advertisement in the newspaper and wish to apply for the position advertised. Write a letter of application along with your bio-data in 120-150 words to the Director Personnel, Rose Restaurant.** **CBSE 2023**

Rose Restaurant

Required – A Gourmet Delight
– Senior Manager
– Food & Beverage Department

Job Responsibilities
- Oversee Finances of the Food & Beverage Department
- Supervise Restaurants

Preferred Skills & Qualifications
- Degree in Hotel Management
- 5 years work experience
- Strong Interpersonal & Communication Skills (Verbal and Written)

Ans. XYZ Apartments
Mumbai

11th March, 20XX

The Director Personnel
Rose Restaurant
Mumbai

Subject **Application for the post of a senior manager, food and beverage department**

Sir/Ma'am

This is in response to your advertisement in 'The Times of India' dated 11th March, 20XX for the post of a Senior Manager, Food & Beverage Department, I wish to apply for the same.

I possess requisite qualifications and experience. In my previous capacity as a Assistant Manager I had overseen the finances of the department and supervised restaurants. I am enclosing my detailed resume for your perusal. You may call me for an interview on any date as per your convenience. I shall be able to join my duties at one month notice if appointed. I hope for a positive reply.

Thanking you
Yours sincerely
Radhika/Rahul

Enclosure Bio-data

Bio-data

Name	Radhika/Rahul
Father's Name	Mr. Vishal
Date of Birth	15th September, 1994
Age	28
Address	XYZ Apartments, Mumbai
Email-id	Ra234@gmail.com
Nationality	Indian

Educational Qualification

Name of the Exam	College/Board/University	Year of Passing	Percentage
Hotel Management	PQR University	2015	73%
Senior Secondary (Class XII)	CBSE	2012	96%
Secondary (Class X)	CBSE	2010	95%

Certification Classical dance and Music for 12 years in Pandit Birju Maharaj Dance and Music Academy

Hobbies Music, Photography and Reading

Languages Known Hindi, English and French

Experience Working as an Assistant Manager in Romy Chain of Restaurants since 2016

References 1. Mr. Ashok Kumar, PQR University
2. Mrs. Rashmi Sharma, Chief HR, Romy Chain of Restaurants

6. You are Minal/Mrinal. You saw the given advertisement in the newspaper and wish to apply for the position advertised in about 120-150 words. Write a letter of application for the same. CBSE 2023

ROYAL INTERNATIONAL SCHOOL

Required English Teacher for Primary Classes

Skills and Qualifications

- Graduate Montessori trained
- Strong interpersonal and communication skills
- Experience 3-5 years
- Competency in computers
- Send your bio-data within 10 days to Mr. Shams, Principal, Royal Public School.

Ans. XYZ Apartments
Delhi

22nd February, 20XX

Mr. Shams
Principal
Royal Public School
New Delhi

Subject **Application for the post of english teacher**

Sir/Ma'am

In response to your advertisement in the national daily 'The Express-Times' dated 21st February, 20XX for the post of English Teacher, I want to offer my candidature.

I possess the requisite qualifications and experience. Having my B.ed degree from Delhi University, I have two years of experience in teaching. I am also working with an NGO in the field of education.

I am enclosing my detailed resume for your perusal. You may call me for an interview on any date as per your convenience. I shall be able to join my duties at one month notice if appointed. I hope for a positive reply.

Thanking you
Yours sincerely
Minal/Mrunal

Enclosed Resume

Resume

Name	Minal/Mrinal
Father's Name	Mr. Ashok
Date of Birth	11th July, 1996
Nationality	Indian
Email-id	Minal123@gmail.com
Permanent Address	XYZ Apartments, Delhi

Educational Qualification

Name of the Exam	College/Board/University	Year of Passing	Percentage
B. Ed	Delhi University	2019	65%
B. Com	Delhi University	2017	73%

Interests & Hobbies	Reading, singing and pottery making
Languages Known	Hindi, English and German
Work Experience	Working as an English teacher for primary classes at PQR school
References	1. Mr. Ravi Sharan Singh, Project Head, ABC NGO 2. Mrs. Saakshi Sharma, Project Head, PQR School

7. You have recently come across an advertisement for the post of a software engineer in S.K. Global Solutions. Write an application with bio-data in about 120-150 words to The Manager, S.K. Global Solutions, J.P. Nagar, Bangalore. You are Ranjan/Ritu of Indra Nagar, Bangalore. **CBSE 2023**

SK GLOBAL SOLUTIONS

Required Software Engineer

Job Responsibilities

- Write well-designed software
- Develop layouts
- Execute software development cycle

Preferred Skills and Qualifications

- B. Tech Computer Science
- Experience 3-5 Years.

Ans. Indra Nagar
Bangalore

22nd February, 20XX

The Manager
S.K. Global Solutions
J.P. Nagar, Bangalore

Subject **Application for the post of software engineer**

Sir/Ma'am

In response to your advertisement in the national daily 'The Express-Times' dated 21st February, 20XX for the post of Software Engineer, I want to offer my candidature.

I feel that my qualifications and experience make me a suitable candidate for this position. I am a B. Tech Graduate in Computer Science from Bangalore University and have been working as a software development at PQR firm. I have attached my resume, which highlights my educational qualifications, work experience and skills. I am confident that my skills and experience align with the job responsibilities and preferred qualifications mentioned in the advertisement.

You may call me for an interview on any date as per your convenience. I shall be able to join my duties at one month notice if appointed. I hope for a positive reply.

Thanking you
Yours sincerely
Ranjan/Ritu

Enclosed Bio-data

Bio-data

Name Ranjan/Ritu
Father's Name Mr. Ashok
Date of Birth 11th July, 1988
Nationality Indian
Email-id ran246@gmail.com
Permanent Address Indra Nagar, Bangalore
Educational Qualification

Name of the Exam	College/Board/University	Year of Passing	Percentage
B. Tech	Bangalore University	2012	73%
Senior Secondary	CBSE	2009	84%
Secondary	CBSE	2007	87%

Interests & Hobbies Reading, singing and pottery making
Languages Known Hindi, English and German
Work Experience Working as a software development at PQR firm since 2012
References 1. Mr. Ravi Sharan Singh Manager, HOD, Bangalore University
2. Mrs. Saakshi Sharma, Project Head, PQR firm

8. **You are Minu Sen, employed as an Assistant Manager for Corporate Social Responsibility (CSR) in your current company in Hyderabad. You saw the given advertisement in the newspaper and wish to apply for the position advertised. Write a letter to Credit Sage Pvt. Ltd. along with your bio-data, expressing your interest in the situation vacant.**
CBSE SQP 2023

SAGE

CREDIT SAGE Pvt. Ltd

Required- Corporate Social responsibility Manager (CSR) Head

Job Responsibilities :

- Define strategy for Credt sage's CSR value of 1% of people's time, 1% of products and 1% of profits to the society.
- Develop various CSR initiatives in the company's adopted village
- Strategise and initiate various community benefit schemes and liason with NGO's, Govt. Bodies etc.

Preferred Skills and Qualifications

- Bachelor or Master's degree in Socialogy/Public Relations
- Strong interpersonal and communication skills (verbal and written)
- Proven experience in CSR project management and execution
- Proven experience working with non-profit organizations of Corporate CSR

Send your bio-data within 10 days to Gagan Vij, HR Head, Credit sage Pvt. Ltd., Nashik
For further details please check our website-www.sage.com/careers/csr

Ans. 56, A Block, PQR Colony
Hyderabad

10th March, 20XX

Gagan Vij
HR Head
Credit Sage Pvt. Ltd.
Nashik

Subject **Application for the post of Corporate Social Responsibility Manager (CSR) head**

Dear Sir/Ma'am

In response to your advertisement in the Indian Express dated 5th March, 20XX for the position of the Corporate Social Responsibility Manager (CSR) Head, I hereby offer my candidature for the same. I believe that my experience and background fit your requirements for the position.

I have completed my Masters in Public Relation from the reputed Y.M.C.A. located in Delhi. During my Masters, I worked with Smile NGO in Delhi and then, joined my current place of employment. Since then, I had been working as the Assistant Manager for Corporate Social Responsibility at a renowned firm in Hyderabad. In my role, I have managed various CSR projects and executed them effectively.

As requested, I have enclosed my resume with this letter. You may call me for an interview on any date as per your convenience. I shall be able to join my duties at one month notice if appointed.

Thanking you
Yours sincerely,
Minu Sen

Enclosure Resume and certificates

Resume

Name	Minu Sen
Father's Name	Mr. Krishna Sen
Date of Birth	28th September, 1989
Marital Status	Married
Address	56, A Block, PQR Colony, Hyderabad
Phone	98XXXXXXXX
Email-id	minu321@gmail.com
Hobbies	Music, Reading and Photography

Educational Qualification

Name of Exam	College/Board/University	Year of Passing	Percentage
M.A. (Public Relations)	Y.M.C.A.	2012	7.5 GPA
B.A. Hons. (Sociology)	University of Delhi	2010	82%
Senior Secondary	CBSE	2007	93%
Secondary	CBSE	2005	92%

Experience Working as an Assistant Manager for Corporate Social Responsibility in PQR Firm

References 1. Miss Malvika Ray, HR Manager, PQR Firm

2. Mrs. Dipti Chandra, Manager, Smile NGO

9. **You are Siddharth, of 46, Krishi Apartments, Lucknow. You read the given advertisement and wish to apply for the post advertised. Write a job application along with your bio-data.** **CBSE 2025**

> **Rajan Readymade Cloth Mart**
> **requires**
> **Store Manager**
>
> **Qualifications** Graduate
>
> **Skills** Knowledge of textiles, trending fashions, customer service skills, sales skills, organisational and leadership abilities.
>
> **Experience** Minimum 5 years in store keeping
>
> **Write to**
>
> **The Manager,**
>
> **Rajan Readymade Cloth Mart, 14 M.G. Road, Lucknow**

Ans. 46, Krishi Apartments
Lucknow

29th September, 20XX

The Manager
Rajan Readymade Cloth Mart
14, M.G. Road
Lucknow

Subject **Application for the Post of Store Manager**

Sir/Madam

I am writing to apply for the position of Store Manager at Rajan Readymade Cloth Mart. I am a graduate with five years of experience in store management, possessing strong knowledge of textiles, fashion trends, customer service, and sales. My leadership and organisational skills make me a suitable candidate for this role.

I have attached my bio-data for your kind consideration. I would appreciate the opportunity to discuss my qualifications in detail.

Thank you for your time and consideration.

Yours sincerely
Siddharth

Enclosure Bio-data

Bio-data

Name Siddharth
Address 46, Krishi Apartments, Lucknow
Phone 9985XXXXXX
Email siddarth1997@gmail.com

Educational Qualification

Name of the Exam	College/Board/University	Year of Passing	Percentage
BBA	ABC University	2018	86%

Work Experience

- 5+ years in store management
- Expertise in inventory management, sales, and customer relations

Skills

- Knowledge of textiles and fashion trends
- Leadership and organisational skills
- Strong customer service and sales abilities

Languages Known Hindi, English

References Available upon request

10. **You are Ashish/Nimmi Dhar, B-94 Fort Road, Jammu. You have read the advertisement given below. You are qualified for the job. Write an application in 120-150 words along with a resume.**

Indian Chemical Industries, Delhi Requires Accounts Officers	
Qualification	B. Com
Experience	Minimum 4 years
Job requirement	Maintaining books of accounts, preparation of Balance Sheet, etc.
Salary	Best in the industry
Apply to	Managing Director, ICI B-12 Barakhamba Road, New Delhi

Ans. B-94, Fort Road
Jammu – 180006

20th March, 20XX

The Managing Director
Indian Chemical Industries
ICI B-12, Barakhamba Road
New Delhi – 110001

Subject **Application for the post of accounts officer**

Sir/Ma'am

In response to your advertisement in 'The Indian Express' dated 19th March, 20XX, requiring Accounts Officers, I wish to be considered for this post. I have completed my B. Com (Honours) with a First Class from University of Delhi. In addition, I possess a Diploma in Tele-Accounting from NIIT, Delhi.

I have a work experience of 5 years in maintenance of books of accounts, preparation of trial balance and preparation of Balance Sheet in a commercial organisation. I also have hands-on working experience in the line and am well versed in account procedures.

I am enclosing my resume and attested copies of my certificates. I hope to receive a positive response from your side.

Thanking you
Yours faithfully
Ashish/Nimmi Dhar

Enclosures Resume, testimonials, attested copies of certificates

Resume

Name	Ashish Dhar
Father's Name	Mr. Ram Saran Dhar
Address	B-94 Fort Road, Jammu – 180006
Phone No.	98589XXXXX
Email-id	ashish22@yahoo.com
Date of Birth	22nd March, 1990

Educational Qualifications

Name of Exam	College/Board/University	Year	Percentage
Diploma in Tele-Accounting	NIIT, Delhi	2011	–
B.Com Honours	ARSD College, Delhi University	2010	78%
Sr. Sec. School	CBSE	2007	80%
High School	CBSE	2005	75%

Work Experience	Working as an Account Officer in CPA Global Company, NOIDA Expressway since 2012 April till date
Languages Known	Hindi and English
References	1. Mr BS Negi (Mobile No. 98765XXXXX) Asstt. Manager, CPA Global, NOIDA
	2. Dr. Piyush Goyal (Mobile No. 88047XXXXX) 190, MGB House, Kailash Hills, New Delhi

11. **The Gandhi Foundation is recruiting graduates for an Intensive Leadership Training Programme during the summer, in villages across India. You are Anjana/Benji from 21, Ratnapur Village, Bilaspur. You are very excited to see the advertisement and decide to apply for the same. Draft a letter in 120-150 words applying for the advertised programme. Include a biodata showing how suitable you are for the training. You can use the following clues**

- Good communication skills
- Suitable qualifications
- Age limit and criteria
- Anticipation of early response to my application

Ans. 21, Ratnapur Village
Bilaspur

14th March, 20XX

The Gandhi Foundation
Bilaspur

Subject **Application for intensive leadership training programme**

Sir/Ma'am

This refers to your advertisement published in 'The Times of India' dated 12th March, 20XX for the Intensive Leadership Training Programme to be conducted by you from 10th April, 20XX onwards. I wish to apply for the same. My detailed resume indicating my suitability is enclosed here for your kind consideration.

As required by you, I have excellent command over English, both in speaking and writing. I also meet your requirements of qualifications, age limit and other criteria given in your advertisement.

Hoping an early response to my application.

Thanking you
Yours sincerely
Anjana/Benji

Enclosure Resume

Resume

Name	Anjana
Father's Name	Mr. Akshat
Address	21, Ratnapur Village, Bilaspur
Phone no.	98562XXXXX
Email id	anjana198@gmail.com
Date of Birth	20th October, 19XX

Educational Qualifications

Name of the Exam	College/Board/University	Year of Passing	Percentage
BA (Honours)	English University of Delhi	2017	62%
SSCE	CBSE	2014	72%
High School	CBSE	2012	75%

Work Experience Working as TGT (English) in Surjit Singh Public School, Bilaspur since July 2017

Languages Known Hindi, English and Punjabi

References 1. Dr. GS Sidhu (94326XXXXX), HOD English, University of Delhi, Delhi

2. Mr. RM Singh (94483XXXXX), Advisor, Surjit Singh Public School, Bilaspur

SELF ASSESSMENT TEST

Letters to the Editor

1. Write a letter to the Editor of 'The Hindustan Times' New Delhi, about water shortage in your colony. You are Ida Pandit. Use the following hints

- water supplied for 10 minutes
- dependance of tankers
- unhygienic water
- cases of water borne diseases
- purchasing water daily
- no action taken need for connections from the main water line which is 200m away.

2. The concept of working from home has been a significant shift in the world today. Write a letter to the editor of a national daily, sharing your views on this trend and examining both, the benefits and the negative effects of remaining indoors for work. Use the given clues along with your own ideas to compose this letter. You are Rachit/Rachana, a concerned citizen.

Benefits

- flexible hours
- relief from travel hours

Disadvantages

- isolation and loneliness
- communication challenges
- digital fatigue

3. You are Tanvi of Rosewood Colony, Sagar Nagar. You have recently observed that people waste a lot of food in hotels, at marriages and parties. You are upset at the casual attitude of people towards wastage of food. Write a letter to the editor to a national daily expressing your concern and suggest ways to improve the situation. Use the given clues along with your own ideas to compose this letter.

Suggestions

- order only what can be consumed
- prepare less items
- donate unconsumed food
- create food banks

4. The newspapers today have full page advertisements promoting luxury items. With increase in consumerism, people find it difficult to resist and soon find themselves trapped in a world of social one-upmanship. Write a letter to the editor expressing your views on the consequences of this consumerism giving suggestions on how to control this habit. You are Renu/Rajan. Use the given clues along with your own ideas to compose this letter.

Consequences

- trapped in a competitive world
- social acceptablity
- living beyond budgets
- mental trauma

Solutions

- responsible role of media
- make informal decisions

5. You are Shubha/Krushna Mohanty, residing in Subhadra Apartments, Bhubaneswar, Odisha. You have observed, with increasing concern, that garbage collection continues to be done without segregation in your neighbourhood. Write a letter to the editor of 'The Real Times', Bhubaneswar, in about 120-150 words, explaining your concern along with the rationale behind the importance of garbage segregation. Suggest ways in which the RWAs can participate in this programme.

6. On Teacher's Day, you read in a newspaper that privately owned and managed schools in small towns or even in the suburbs of metropolitan cities exploit their teachers by paying them just a fraction of their authorised salaries. This affects their performance in the classroom and thus, the lives of their students. Write a letter in 120-150 words to the editor of a national daily raising your voice against such exploitation. Suggest ways to solve this problem. You are Navtej/Navita, 112, Taj Road, Agra.

7. When cricket teams go abroad, the members are allowed to take their wives, even friends along with them. Does this fact distract them or help them to focus on their game in a better way? If it is good, why don't we allow our athletes to enjoy the same privilege? Write a letter to the editor of a national daily in 120-150 words giving your views on the issue. You are Akash/Akansha, M-114, Mount Kailash, Kanpur.

8. You are Harsh/Harshita, Secretary, Environment Club, Akash Public School, Agra. You, along with a group of students, went on a 3-day tour through Corbett National Park. You found how the tourists abuse the available facilities and thus, endanger the environment. Write a letter in 120-150 words to the editor of a national daily highlighting the situation. Suggest ways through which the environment of the park can be saved.

Job Application

9. You are Amit/Amita, a resident of Sujata Towers, Khelnagar. You came across the following advertisement and consider yourself an ideal candidate for the same. Apply for the job giving all details.

Upkar Transport Ltd.
Requires HR Manager
Whom Do We Need

- Qualified MBA
- Minimum 5 years experience
- Willing to travel

Skills

- Excellent verbal and written skills
- Excellent interpersonal negotiation and conflict resolution skills
- Organisational ability

Contact Director, Upkar Transport Ltd. 76/A2-Prabha Nagar, Vayubagh

10. You are Pawan/Preeti Gupta residing at Uttam Vihar, New Delhi. You read the following advertisement in 'The Delhi Today'. Write a letter to the Principal in about 120-150 words applying for the advertised post. **CBSE 2022 Term II**

Nav Vihar Public School
Urgently Need Part Time Counsellors

- Able to handle online queries and provide support on mental and emotional needs of students
- Post Graduate in Psychology
- Minimum 5 years experience
- Computer literate

Contact Principal, Nav Vihar Public School

11. You are Sameera/Sameer. Write a letter of application for the mentioned post in 120-150 words. Include a detailed bio-data.

SITUATION VACANT

Nav Jeevan Public School requires Senior Computer Teacher. Eligibility requirements- Post graduate in Computer Science with minimum 5 years work experience as a Computer teacher. Mention additional skills, interests and achievements.

Contact Principal, Nav Jeevan Public School

12. **You are Shantanu, residing at Ghar B-94, Balimela Road, Malkangiri. You come across the following classified advertisement in a local daily. Write a letter in about 120-150 words, applying for the position of a volunteer for the Each One Teach One campaign.**

> **Situation Vacant**
>
> Wanted committed volunteers, aged 18 years and above, to teach underprivileged children, for one hour a week, in the district of Malkangiri. Ability to speak, read and write Odiya fluently, important. Experience not necessary. All volunteers to receive training.
>
> **Contact** Nethra N, Coordinator (Each One Teach One), 4 Literacy, Ambaguda, Malkangiri, Odisha -764045.

13. Mitali Kedia sees the following advertisement and wishes to apply for the position advertised. Write a letter of application in 120-150 words along with a detailed bio-data. **CBSE 2023**

> **Skill Development Institute**
>
> - Requires Part-time Trainers for Computers/Car Mechanics
> - The applicant must be professionally Qualified
> - Must be competent in basic Computer Skills
> - **Experience** minimum 5 years as trainer
>
> Apply within 10 days to the Director. Skill Development Institute, Meerut

14. Write an application (including a resume) for the post of receptionist advertised in a national newspaper by JKL Publishers, Peshwa Road, Pune. You are Karuna, M114, Mall Road, Pune, a graduate from SNDT University and have done a Secretarial Practice Course from Y.W.C.A, Mumbai. (120-150 words)

15. You are Ram/ Rajani, living at 1, Raja Ram Marg, New Delhi. Read the following advertisement and apply for the job that suits your qualification, giving your bio-data.

> **Sun University**
>
> **Requires**
>
> - Lecturers in English and Demonstrators in Physics, Chemistry and Botany for their new campus at Panipat.
> - Candidates with a minimum of 5 year experience alone can apply.
> - Excellent command of English is a must.
> - Excellent salary for experienced persons.
>
> Those interested may e-mail to sununiversityjobs@gmail.com or mail their response to: Box no. 123, 'The Harbinger', New Delhi.

04

CHAPTER

Very Long Compositions

An article is a highly structured and directional piece of writing, written to inform, to persuade, to entertain or to convince the reader about something. It essentially has several paragraphs containing a distinct beginning, a middle and an end.

Marking Scheme

Format	1 Mark
(Heading and Writer's Name)	
Organisation of ideas	1 Mark
(Coherence and relevance of ideas and style)	
Content	2 Marks
(Introduction causes, effects and suggestions)	
Expression	1 Mark
(Accuracy of spelling and grammar)	

Article Writing

Elements of an Article

1. **Title/Heading** There are no predetermined rules as such, but it may comprise a single word, a phrase or a sentence of 4-6 words. The title should be thought-provoking, catchy and should highlight the theme.
2. **Name of the writer** Sign off your article with your name towards the end. Alternatively, the name can come immediately after the heading in the form of a byline.
3. **Introduction** Keep the topic in perspective; specify it keeping the reader's interest intact by providing some surprising information or interesting facts related to the context.
4. **Description of the topic** Highlight various facets of the topic like the causes and effects, advantages and disadvantages, etc.
5. **Conclusion** End the article with suggestions, an appeal or a warning.

Points to be kept in mind while Writing an Article

- Give an appropriate title to the article.
- Understand the hints/information given in the verbal input.
- Divide your article into several paragraphs when necessary.
  - **Paragraph 1** The first few sentences (comprising the first paragraph) should introduce the topic and its main idea.
  - **Paragraph 2** The second paragraph should highlight the main facts of the topic like the causes and effects, advantages and disadvantages, etc.
  - **Paragraph 3** The last few sentences (comprising the last paragraph) should state a conclusion of the topic.

- All the sentences in the paragraphs should logically lead to the objective for which the article is being written. Every sentence should be linked with the rest into a single whole.
- Use sentence linkers to ensure continuity - e.g. consequently /similarly/finally/moreover, etc.
- Language used should always be simple and grammatically correct. It should be straightforward and to the point.
- Adhere to the word limit of 120-150 words.

Expert Tip

To write a good article create a rough draft. First, jot down all the ideas. Second, make sequence and third, join all the ideas with linkers and cohesive words. Further, to develop good ideas, listen to radio shows, panel discussions, explore latest data and newspaper.

Sample Article

Digital India is an initiative by Government of India, intending to create technologically literate and connected India. Write an article in about 120-150 words for a magazine, providing information about the initiative. You are Neha.

Use the cues given below to frame your article.

- Transforming the entire ecosystem of public services
- Launched by Narendra Modi on 1st July, 2015
- Objective- connecting rural areas with high-speed Internet networks and improving digital literacy
- Focus points- Digital Infrastructure as a Utility to Every Citizen, Governance and Services on Demand and Digital Empowerment of Citizens

Digital India — Title/Heading

by Neha — Byline (Name of the Writer)

Content:

In order to transform the entire ecosystem of public services through the use of information technology, the Government of India has launched the Digital India programme with the vision to transform India into a digitally empowered society and knowledge economy.

Digital India was launched by the Prime Minister of India, Narendra Modi on 1st July, 2015 with an objective of connecting rural areas with high-speed Internet networks and improving digital literacy. The vision of Digital India programme is inclusive growth in areas of electronic services, products, manufacturing and job opportunities etc. and it is centre on three key areas - Digital Infrastructure as a Utility to Every Citizen, Governance and Services on Demand and Digital Empowerment of Citizens.

The Digital India programme has witnessed a consistent upward growth trajectory, achieving numerous milestones and flagship initiatives. These achievements cover a wide plethora of sectors and include development of broadband highways, universal access to mobile connectivity, public internet access programmes, e-governance to name a few. Many major schemes and projects such as Aadhaar, Smart Cities Mission, BHIM UPI, RuPay, GSTIn, GeM (Government e-Marketplace), DigiLocker come under the aegis of the Digital India programme.

PRACTICE QUESTIONS

1. Development and urbanization lead to deforestation which leads to bio-diversity loss. This results in extinction of species and further leads to ecological imbalance which adversely impacts man's survival. Write an article for your school magazine stressing on the need to prevent bio-diversity loss and suggest ways and solutions to prevent bio-diversity loss. You may use some of the given cues along with your own ideas to compose the article. **CBSE 2025**

- You are Akash of class XII ?
- What is bio-diversity loss?
- Why is it necessary to prevent bio diversity loss?
- What needs to be done to preserve habitat?
- Practice the 'Reduce, Reuse, Recycle principle in daily life.
- What are the benefits of preventing bio-diversity loss?

Ans.

Preserving Biodiversity: A Call to Action

by Akash, Class XII-B

Biodiversity, the foundation of life on Earth, is rapidly declining due to urbanisation, deforestation, and human activities. The loss of plant and animal species disrupts ecosystems, leading to severe consequences such as climate change, food shortages, and an imbalance in nature. If not addressed, it can threaten human survival itself.

To prevent biodiversity loss, we must take immediate steps to protect habitats. Afforestation, conservation of wildlife, and sustainable land use are essential. The 'Reduce, Reuse, Recycle' principle should be practiced daily to minimise waste and pollution. Additionally, promoting eco-friendly alternatives and responsible consumption can help conserve resources.

Preventing biodiversity loss ensures a stable climate, rich ecosystems, and sustainable living conditions for future generations. If we act now, we can restore balance to nature and safeguard our planet for years to come. It is our responsibility to protect the incredible diversity of life on Earth.

2. Rapid urbanisation is taking over parks and green spaces meant for young children to play in. This is leading to children staying indoors and getting addicted to gadgets and social media. Write an article exploring the phenomenon of lost playgrounds in metro cities. Provide examples to illustrate your points wherever necessary. You may use some of the given cues along with your own ideas. You are Sangeeta/Saket, a concerned citizen. **CBSE 2025**

- playgrounds shape character, foster friendships, ignite creativity.
- opportunities for physical activity and social interaction.
- vanishing playgrounds resulting in sedentary activities and lifestyle.
- rise of obesity and related health issues, addiction to social media.
- government should make policies to save parks and green spaces.

Ans.

Lost Playgrounds : A Vanishing Childhood

by Sangeeta/Saket, Concerned Citizen

Metro cities are rapidly losing their playgrounds to urbanisation, leaving children with fewer spaces for outdoor play. Once bustling with laughter and energy, parks are now being replaced by towering buildings and commercial complexes. This lack of open spaces is pushing children indoors, leading to increased screen time and addiction to gadgets and social media.

Playgrounds play a crucial role in shaping a child's character, fostering friendships, and igniting creativity. They provide opportunities for physical activity and social interaction, essential for a child's development. However, the decline in these spaces is contributing to rising obesity, poor mental health, and a sedentary lifestyle among children.

It is imperative that the government prioritises green infrastructure, ensuring parks and playgrounds remain intact. Strict policies must be implemented to preserve these vital spaces. A balance between urban growth and environmental well-being is necessary to safeguard the health and happiness of future generations.

3. With the advancement of science and technology, basic communication has adversely impacted the social skills of today's youth. You are Girish/ Girija of Class XII. Write an article for your school magazine highlighting the adverse effects of technology and the ways to enhance social skills among the younger generation to prevent social awkwardness. You may use the following cues along with your own ideas to draft the article. CBSE 2024

Impact
- Decrease in face to face communication
- Lack of engagement
- Inability to converse and poor inter-personal skills

Suggestions
- Improve conversational and communication skills
- Personal interaction, develop collaborative skills
- Outdoor sports and activities

Ans.

Nurturing Social Skills in the Digital Age

by Girish/Girija

In the age of smartphones and social media, the art of face-to-face communication is gradually fading away, leading to a concerning rise in social awkwardness among today's youth. The impact of technology on interpersonal skills is undeniable, with many young individuals experiencing difficulty in engaging in meaningful conversations and establishing genuine connections. The adverse effects of technology on social skills are evident in various aspects of daily life, from classrooms to social gatherings. Decreased face-to-face communication has resulted in a lack of engagement and an inability to converse effectively, leading to feelings of isolation and discomfort in social settings.

To address this growing concern, it is imperative to implement strategies aimed at nurturing social skills among the younger generation. Schools and parents must prioritise the development of conversational and communicative abilities through interactive learning activities and open dialogue. Encouraging personal interaction and collaboration in both academic and extracurricular pursuits can also help in fostering essential social competencies. Additionally, promoting outdoor sports and activities provides opportunities for young people to engage in team-building exercises and develop crucial social skills such as teamwork and leadership.

By acknowledging the adverse effects of technology on social skills and actively implementing measures to combat social awkwardness, we can empower today's youth to navigate social situations with confidence and forge meaningful connections in an increasingly digital world.

4. Television has great educational value. It can be used as a tool for learning, both at home and in classrooms. There is a range of channels, that offer educational content.

You are Gopal/Geeta of Class XII. Write an article for your School magazine describing how television can be used as a tool for education.

You may use the following cues along with your own ideas to compose this article. CBSE 2024

- Easy access to T.V.
- Documentaries, panel discussions
- National Geographic, astronomy, etc.
- Informative, news
- Programme on new technologies, science, history
- Exposure to foreign culture, food, architecture, art, etc.

Ans.

Television as a Learning Tool

by Gopal/Geeta

The education sector has been swept by a sudden change to use television as a learning tool to impart knowledge and upgrade the learning process. Claims have been made that it makes learning more effective and interesting.

With an increase in the number of TV channels and advancement in education technology, the amount of content being telecast has skyrocketed. Channels like Discovery, Aljazeera, National Geographic, etc. provide contents which are fit for children while providing insights in various fields simultaneously. Its use has reduced the learners' dependence on the teacher and has filled the classroom with excitement and interest.

It can be correctly said that the invention of television has revolutionised the information technology. This is the power of the television that many a time an incident happening in any part of the globe is seen directly by millions of viewers instantaneously. Students can see for themselves many scientific principles that govern nature. Live examples on the screen simplify the complex nature of definitions. Television takes us to different countries and shows us various civilisations and people. Children become familiar with different cultures and rituals. It has been proved that the number of students increases if television is used as a medium of instruction by the school authorities.

We can thus say that the use of television for education has revolutionised the very concept of teaching. Television lessons make the students more attentive, observant and interactive.

5. With constant emphasis on improvement of road infrastructure, there is a widening of roads to accommodate the growing traffic, yet leading to traffic congestion and incidents of road rage. Write an article to the editor of a local newspaper expressing your observations, concerns and suggestions. Support your ideas with the outline cues given below. You are Sucheta/Sanjay. CBSE 2024

Infrastructure Development		
Benefits	**Disadvantages**	**Suggestions**
▪ Wide roads	▪ Air pollution	▪ Organised development
▪ Increased connectivity	▪ Traffic jams	▪ Manned signals
▪ Smooth traffic	▪ Road rage	▪ Meeting timelines

Ans.

Widening of Roads: A Lurking Peril

by Sucheta/Sanjay

In the modern world, the number of public and private vehicles are constantly on the rise in order to accommodate the large population. On that account, there has been perpetual emphasis on improving road infrastructure. While it is undeniable that wider roads will bring about increased connectivity and smoother traffic flow, it also becomes a source of issues that demand the concerned authority's attention.

Although, wider roads provide various advantages, it comes at a cost. The increased vehicular movement contributes to air and noise pollution, while ironically leading to traffic jams and incidents of road rage. In order to control these issues, a more organised approach to development is the need of the hour. The traffic signals can be manned which will allow it to function more effectively by reducing congestion and preventing confrontations among commuters. The concerned authority should also look after the adherence to timelines in construction projects to minimise disruption to commuters.

It is of utmost importance to strike a balance between development and sustainability. By prioritising solutions that not only enhance connectivity but also prioritise the well-being of our communities, we can achieve this balance.

6. In an era of rapid globalisation and technological advancement, the preservation of cultural heritage remains a vital challenge, particularly for the youth. India continues to navigate the complexities of maintaining tradition alongside modernity. Write an article exploring the role of cultural heritage in shaping the identities of today's Indian youth. Provide examples to illustrate your points wherever necessary. You may use some of the given cues along with your own ideas. You are Arti Nirula of Class XII-A. CBSE SQP 2024

- How have global interactions and technologies influenced or changed these traditional practices among today's youth?
- What are the benefits of preserving cultural heritage for young people? How does it contribute to their sense of identity?
- Suggest ways on which young people and institutions can work together to ensure preservation of cultural heritage.

Ans.

Cultural Heritage-Shaping Today's Indian Youth

by Arti Nirula, Class XII-A

Culture and heritage shapes human society. We all grew up on stories- mythologies, fables; historical events glorifying our past roots which helped us construct the identity of an individual, a nation, a region, a community or a group. Human race has always relied on its past to build the present and construct its future. Generations have lived before us and have shaped the world we reside in.

However, in an era of rapid globalisation and technological advancement, we are consistently favouring Western ideals over our culture. Consequently, global interactions and technologies have influenced these traditions to the point that we need to make consistent efforts to preserve them. In order to do so, the youth must remember that exposure to one's own and other cultures promotes tolerance and appreciation, which are vital in today's globalised society. This helps one navigate diverse social environments with respect and empathy.

To preserve our heritage, one needs to engage with traditional arts, crafts, and practices as they can inspire creativity and innovation, allowing us to reinterpret cultural expressions in ways that resonate with contemporary life. Active participation in cultural festivals, rituals, and community events strengthens social bonds and enhances social cohesion, making cultural heritage a pivotal part of daily life for youth. Incorporating cultural studies in education can increase awareness and pride among young people, encouraging them to become advocates and preservers of their traditions. By using technology to create appealing and accessible cultural content, such as virtual museum tours, digital storytelling, and social media campaigns, youths can be engaged with their heritage in formats they find relatable and exciting.

Remember, we can easily preserve our cultural heritage, if we are a little more aware. We need to understand that the destruction of our cultural heritage is the destruction of our identity.

7. Wearing the school uniform gives the student an identity, pride and a feeling of discipline. Write an article on, 'Importance of Wearing a Uniform in School'. Your are Jagan/Jagriti. You can use the hints given below to form your article. CBSE 2020

- Unity
- Identity
- Discipline
- Stability

Ans.

Importance of Wearing a Uniform in School

by Jagriti/Jagan

School is the place where all of us step in at a very tender age. In one word, our life begins at school. In every school, there are students from different backgrounds but with the school uniform everybody becomes one. The only identity that dominates at that moment is that all of them are the representative of the same school. Then there exists a great feeling of togetherness and unity. This also helps students to overcome inferiority or superiority complex which sometimes children can develop.

Uniform makes the child more conscious about his individuality which in turn helps in building self-confidence. It instills a deep rooted sense of discipline in the subconscious mind. It also helps the school officials to recognise their students much faster in case of emergency. A school uniform brings stability in a student's day-to-day life which provides the right direction for a bright future.

When school students from different places, different environments with difference in opinions stand together in the same uniform, the maxim 'Unity in Diversity' becomes reality.

8. There is a shift from content based to skill based education. In addition to foundational subjects, interesting courses such as design, digital competency and entrepreneurship are bing offered to students. The breaking away from conformity has brought out the latent potential in students as they are new selecting courses based on choice/interest and talent. Write an article in 120-150 words expressing your views on the topic 'Changing Trends in Education'. You may use the given input CBSE 2023

CHANGING TRENDS IN EDUCATION

Then	Now
• Limited subjects	• Diverse subjects
• Rigid subject streams	• Integrated syllabus
• Academic focus	• Interest/Aptitude focus
• Rote learning	• Technology based
• Pen and paper	• Competency based

Ans.

Changing Trends in Education

by PQR

The formative years of a student are spent acquiring knowledge mostly through books in schools and colleges. And, although this knowledge helps the students develop their personalities, it fails to arm them with practical skills that give them a better chance at the job market. It is not unknown that 90% of employment opportunities need the youth to be skilled in some vocation. However, the youth are lacking in these required skills.

The reasons for this lack are many. The education system, that has been accepted and has been the norm for many years, has rigid subject streams and limited subject for students. In addition, the sole focus on academics and examination had made children resort to rote learning wherein children learn things without actually understanding them. The result of such a system is evident in the youth lacking the practical skills.

Understanding this need for inculcating skills, the education system of the country is undergoing a shift from content based to skill based education. In addition to foundational subjects, interesting subjects as well as courses such as design, digital competency and entrepreneurship are being offered to students. The breaking away from conformity has brought out the latent potential in students as they are new selecting courses based on choice/interest and talent. The integrated syllabus is now more technology and competency based making the new system more effective.

9. You are Rahul/Rekha. There are frequent power cuts in your locality. You strongly feel that it is time to shift to solar power. Write an article in about 120-150 words on the topic 'Solar Power : An Apt Global Solution for Energy Crisis'. Support your ideas with the cues given below. **CBSE 2023**

- Renewable energy
- Reduce energy bill
- Completely clean no arrow water pollution no greenhouse gas effects carbon
- Free no emissions
- Low maintenance cost

Ans.

Solar Power: An Apt Global Solution for Energy Crisis

by Rahul/Rekha

In the modern world wherein population and requirements are always increasing, the demand for energy has been on a constant rise. In this light, it is not unknown to us that our conventional sources of energy are depleting at an alarming rate. Consequently, the need of the hour to switch to renewable energy sources has time and again been taken up. Finally, we have a solution- solar power.

Solar power or Solar energy is the most abundant and readily available source of energy on Earth. As a renewable source of energy, solar power offers various benefits to its users. First, it helps to reduce energy bills significantly. Once the initial installation cost is covered, solar energy is virtually free. Second, solar energy is completely clean and creates no pollution. It is carbon-free and emits no harmful gases. Hence, it is environmentally friendly and sustainable. Furthermore, solar panels which produce solar energy, requires low maintenance. It only needs to be cleaned periodically to remove dust and dirt. It is a one-time investment that has long-term benefits. Solar panels have a lifespan of 20-30 years and they can be used to generate electricity for a long period.

To conclude, solar power is an apt global solution for the energy crisis. It is renewable, environmentally friendly and cost-effective. Governments and individuals must take necessary steps towards shifting to solar power to ensure a sustainable and greener future. It is high time we realise the importance of renewable energy sources and take action towards creating a brighter and cleaner future.

10. **"The return of the cheetahs will help in the restoration of open forests and grassland ecosystems in India." Write an article in 120-150 words expressing your views on how this will help conserve biodiversity, wildlife and soil conservation. You Bela/Bhanu. Use the following cues along with your own ideas to compose your article.** CBSE 2023

- Ecological balance of nature
- Maintains ecological stability
- Cultural significance
- Helps keep the food chain in place
- Diversity ensures healthier ecosystems
- Good for mental health

Ans.

Return of the Cheetahs

by Bela/Bhanu

In the times where the world is all focused in preservation and conservation, ideas regarding the flora and fauna, environment and ecological balance of the world, the return of the Cheetahs is a great milestone. The return of the Cheetahs, to put simply is a huge success on the path towards the restoration of open forests and grassland ecosystems in India which will further help maintain the ecological balance of nature. In September 2022, Government of India brought the first batch of cheetahs from Namibia to the Kuno National Park, in an effort to reintroduce cheetahs which disappeared from Indian forests for nearly 70-years now. The return of the cheetahs has awakened the nature-loving consciousness of India. The country offers a wonderful opportunity for the cheetahs in terms of protected space.

Cheetahs also keep the food chain in place. The big cat typically hunts the weak and slowest of several species of animals. If cheetahs no longer existed, there would be too many herbivores resulting in loss of vegetation, greater soil erosion, less available water and a negative impact on the health of the ecosystem.

To conclude, when a healthy environment is maintained, the world becomes a better and a happy place for all.

11. **The construction sector is believed to be quite hazardous and has the maximum number of fatal work injuries because apart from other causes, stakeholders in this sector tend to ignore safety regulations.** CBSE SQP 2023

As a columnist for an e-zine, draft an article in about 120-150 words, on the theme of the importance of worker safety in construction zones. Explore possible reasons for the prevailing situation and include suggestions for addressing it. Support your ideas with clues given below.

- Construction workers: Risk of accident due to fatigue
- Construction workforce health challenges in extreme weather conditions
- Construction worker fatality buried under soil heap
- Are construction managers from mars and workers from venus?
- Will Training programmes revamp the safety standards?

Ans.

Importance of Safety in Construction Zones

by XYZ

The present day highly developed world is expanding at an exponential rate and so is its infrastructure. Everyday we come across new developments and new constructions being undertaken with the purpose of growth and development of our society. However, as the number of construction sites increase, so does the number of construction sites accidents. It is not uncommon for us to hear a headline presenting a massive construction accident. It does not come as a surprise to any one of us as we all are aware of the lack of safety measures taken at the construction sites.

While we all know that this lack of occupation safety at sites is illegal, we do not seek to find why this lack exists. The reasons for this lack are many. First and foremost, the key stakeholders or the construction companies ignore safety regulations to save money. They exploit poor people to work in dingy and unsafe conditions without much pay. These people work without any consideration to the extreme weather conditions or even the health risks that the job poses. Further, they even ignore the fatigue and injuries of workers all the while overworking them to get the job done as early as possible.

It is high time that these organisations ensure that safety standards are maintained at their construction sites. To do so, the first step is to spread awareness about safety and the laws associated with it to not only construction companies but also the workers so that they are able to fight for their rights. Further, we need to enforce stricter laws and penalties that ensure that workers receive frequent training programmes to work efficiently and safely. We must also make policies that bridges the gap between the worker and the manager.

Only when these requirements are met, we can think of a safe workplace for construction workers- a workplace which is a reality for educate.

12. **Rising prices of essential commodities make life difficult for the common man. You are Nalini/Ranbir. Write an article in 120-150 words describing the causes, possible solutions and how students can help their parents to cope with the problem.** **CBSE 2020**

Clues

- Varying demand and supply
- Monitoring and controlling prices
- Action against hoarders
- Artificial shortages in the market
- Lack of effective measures

Ans.

Rising Prices

by Nalini

The world today is faced with many maladies that adversely affect common man. One of these maladies is the price rise or inflation. The continuous rise in prices of essential consumer products, such as grains, vegetables, cooking oil, etc. had been the cause of the many woes that the people especially the poor of the country face today. This problem is two-fold, to check the rising prices and to bring the prices down. Both these aspects require us to understand the causes of price rise. The inflation is partly due to varying demand and supply the major reason for rising prices is the lack of timely effective measures taken by government departments to check malpractices of unscrupulous traders. Such traders create artificial shortages and charge exorbitant prices from needy persons. It is a shame that even life-saving drugs are not spared. The worst affected is the middle-class, especially the salaried working-class having a fixed income, as they have to maintain a reasonable standard of living and at the same time manage to pay more for essential commodities.

This problem can be solved by the government installing an effective system of monitoring and controlling prices through suitable measures. Strict control over commodities and strict actions against hoarders must be taken. If they do not do so, sudden and acute rise in prices can cause an all-round spiral effect on prices that makes the life of common people miserable. India is the fastest-growing large economy in the world. However, in order to preserve its position it would need to enhance private investment, create incomes and propel growth. Although rising prices are an integral part of economic growth, they must be carefully managed to prevent detrimental effects on the economy. Understanding the causes and effects of inflation is essential for devising effective strategies to maintain economic stability. It calls for refocusing attention on policies such as asset monetisation and disinvestment for instance to harness resources and leverage its demography.

13. **Using the following clues, write an article titled 'Education and awareness are the critical pillars for the success of a democracy'.**

Clues

- Significance of Indian Democracy
- Role of Education in discharging duties
- Endangering of individual freedom and dignity
- Shaping the fabric of nation

Ans.

Education and Awareness are the Critical Pillars for the Success of a Democracy

by PQR

India has declared itself as the Sovereign Democratic Republic and takes an enviable credit for being the largest democracy in the world. It is a way of life and not just a form of government. In fact, it is the rule of the people, by the people, for the people and with the people. But, unless the people are observant, aware and conscious of their rights and responsibilities, it can have no meaning and liberty cannot be safe-guarded. The result of this will be that individual freedom and dignity would be endangered, and corruption, oppression and dictatorship would be widespread in the country. Education is, thus, integral in making people alert and capable of discharging their duties efficiently.

The role of education is not limited to the circulation of knowledge. Its purpose is also to shape the very fabric of a nation. It should make people aware of what is happening around them while making them skilled and knowledgeable enough to challenge and question practices that are unjust, discriminatory and unlawful.

Education instills the ideas of freedom, self-independence, equality and justice in people which are integral to a democratic government. Moreover, properly educated individuals prove to be better voters and decision makers and, thus, will choose better representatives for themselves, further strengthening the very core of democracy.

14. Write an article titled 'Development of Cottage Industries in India'. You can use the following hints to frame your article.

- Impact of Industrialisation
- Importance of the industry
- Problems - lack of capital, funding, marketing, etc.
- Efforts - Technology, assistance, government programmes, etc.

Ans.

Developing the Cottage Industries in the Villages

by PQR

With the introduction of industrialisation, the small scale manufacturing industry or cottage industry had taken a severe hit. In a country like India, where the enormous number of ancient cottage enterprises in India is well known, the cottage industry is frequently defined by its huge potential for job creation. While the industry is of critical importance to the economy and heritage of the nation, it is not wrong to say that the cottage industry faces severe problems. Starting from a scarcity of capital and a great supply of labour, lack of access to access to low-cost, easy-to-get financing to marketing problems, the industry needs great support to survive. As a result, there is a pressing need to employ strategies that address their issues.

Efforts should be put toward the advancement of technology so that workers can live comfortably. The government could also offer subsidiaries to help cottage industries flourish, particularly in their early stages. A variety of agencies needs to be established assist small businesses and villages. Financial funding and raising the capital investment ceiling for small businesses should be a chief concern. The Department of Industries and Commerce should administer and effectively implement a number of programmes to aid existing and new industries with financial assistance, technical support, and direction.

India's cottage industries are culturally and economically significant. They preserve ancient traditions while simultaneously employing a large number of people. Because these industries confront intense competition from other economies, society should provide support to prevent exploitation and further develop them.

15. Cybersecurity is becoming the pressing need of the hour due to increasing cyber crimes. Cyber warfare is one negative aspect of this digitally empowered world. Write an article explaining the advent of cyber civilisation and the need for developing a secure cyber atmosphere. You are Sayonika/Saksham. Use the following clues to frame your answer.

- Internet has revolutionised the society
- Speed of change
- Access to information
- Cyber threat and attack
- Cybersecurity measures
- Safer internet space

Ans.

Cybersecurity and Cyberwarfare

by Sayonika/Saksham

The internet has transformed society into a cyber civilisation, revolutionising the way we communicate with each other and access information. The speed and scale of this transformation has made a pressing cornerstone of life in the 21st century. But, with the advent of this cyber world, there comes a monster in the form of cyber warfare.

Cyber warfare among nations has become an urgent topic of debate among the people of the world. Cyber warfare is usually defined as a cyber attack or series of attacks that target a country. It has the potential to wreak havoc on government and civilian infrastructure and disrupt critical systems, resulting in damage to the state and even loss of life. Cyber warfare along with an increasing rate of cyber crimes has introduced the need to rebuild a safe structure of cybersecurity.

Cybersecurity has therefore become the number one means of preventing cybercrime and cyber-attacks by maintaining safe inter-industry and social interactions. As the digital landscape continues to expand and integrate with almost every aspect of our lives, ensuring a secure online environment has far-reaching implications for individuals, businesses and nations to improve cyber security. Internet security has become an integral part of the development of new technologies, services, and government policies. Fighting cybercrime requires a comprehensive and safer approach.

16. In this modern world of computers, Artificial Intelligence (AI) has taken an upper hand in every aspect of life. With the introduction of new softwares like ChatGPT, human life has been replaced by artificial chatbots. Write an article on Artificial Intelligence and its impacts. You are Mukul/Mukulika. You can use the following clues to frame your answer.

- What is Artificial Intelligence?
- How does it function?
- The launch of ChatGPT
- Impacts of AI
- Positive and Negative aspects
- Suggestions, if any

Ans.

The Advent and Rise of Artificial Intelligence

by Mukul/Mukulika

Artificial Intelligence (AI) is a wide-ranging tool that enables people to rethink how we integrate information, analyse data, and use the resulting insights to improve decision-making. It has permeated into our modern society and spread its roots in almost every aspect. These software systems make decisions which normally require human level of expertise, help people anticipate problems or deal with issues as they come up. As such, they operate in an intentional, intelligent, and adaptive manner.

AI has entered the uncharted territories of literary and experimental research by the launch of softwares like Chat Generative Pre-trained Transformer (ChatGPT). Using ChatGPT creates the illusion of conveniently having an expert readily at hand to answer one's questions at all times. This has introduced wide-ranging possibilities that computers can exceed human intelligence. The smart systems functioning on the Artificial Intelligence models have reduced complexities in various working spaces, saves time and makes human life easy. However, this also threatens the human capacity to think and make decisions.

The long term impact of this new technology has to be analysed in detail. This includes figuring out both the positive and the negative sides of the debate. Society can harness the transformative potential of AI while mitigating its negative impacts, ensuring a more equitable and prosperous future for all.

17. On the threshold of being a world super power, India does have a large young workforce but unfortunately not many in this force are employable for want of necessary skills. Write an article for a newspaper on the topic 'Skill Development is the need of the hour'. You are Anita/Arnav.

- **Research by Tata Institute of Social Sciences** Growth is hindered by unskilled workforce, more than thirty five per cent of the Indian youth in cities unskilled.
- Demand of the new era
- Practical experience

Ans.

Skill Development is the Need of the Hour

by Anita

India is one of the fastest growing economies but according to a recent research by Tata Institute of Social Sciences, India is also one of the countries whose growth is hindered by unskilled workforce. The survey mentioned that more than thirty five per cent of the Indian youth in cities are unskilled. This makes them fall short of the qualities that are wanted by companies and as a result the job is filled in by others. The status of Indian villages is even worse.

More than seventy five per cent of the Indian youth in villages are struggling because of lack of skills. Basically, it needs to be clearly understood that mere educational certificates will not suffice. Men have to accept the fact that it's not about how many thick and complicated books that one has read. The new era demands skill -the ability to produce productive output.

And productive output is possible only when skills are enhanced along with proceeding age.

It is now necessary for the government to make more and more awareness campaigns about initiatives like 'Skill India' and other such courses which deal in a specific area of work. Practical experience is the only thing that can help India overcome such a situation. Let's walk forward to make India skilled.

SELF ASSESSMENT TEST

1. The rising obesity amongst youth today is a grave cause of concern. Addiction to technology, inactive life-style and eating sugary, and highly processed foods are among the leading causes.

Write an article for the school magazine, sharing the importance of a healthy lifestyle and nutritious diet. You may use the given cues along with your own ideas to compose this article. You are Shivani/ Satish of Class XII B. **CBSE 2024**

- Reasons for Obesity
- Consequences-ill health
- Suggestions
  - active lifestyle
  - regular exercise
  - change in eating habits
  - support and encouragement

2. Recently you read about an incident in a newspaper in which a child tried to imitate the stunts shown on television and sustained serious injuries. Write an article in 120-150 words on the hazards of unsupervised television viewing by kids and how parents should guide them in this matter.

Clues

- TV for overall well-being of children
- Entices mind-effect greater than ever
- Ruin eyesight-lack of concentration
- Bad habits-copy actors-hero worship

3. The word 'father' is synonymous with strict discipline etc. but it is not completely true. The father fulfills his responsibilities affectionately for the family. Write an article in 120-150 words on the topic, 'Role of father in the family'. You can use the following clues.

Role of father-traditional image- teacher- counsellor- promoting equality- influence decisions- prepare for reality- providers and protectors- fulfill necessities- strict- enforce discipline- pillar of strength

4. The world today is no longer governed by the morals and values of the past. The society has denigrated into a system wherein nothing is valued. Write an article on this denegation of values using the hints given below.

5. You are Ravi/Rajni, a Class XII student. Write an article for a youth magazine on selfie safety, advising youngsters to be more cautious and careful. Use the following cues along with your own ideas to draft the article. **CBSE 2024**

- Don't pose near moving train or other vehicles.
- Don't pose with wild animals.
- Be aware of your surroundings.
- Keep away from stairs, drop-offs.

6. You are Praveen/Prerna, Secretary, Eco-club of Bharti School, Lucknow. You write an article on the hazards of environment pollution for the school magazine. You may use the clues given below. **CBSE 2023**

Causes - dumping of industrial waste in water bodies, improper disposal of e-waste and medical waste, indiscriminate construction work

7. While reading about new places and searching for them online has its merits, the advantages of actually travelling to various destinations far exceed them. Write an article for the magazine 'Travel Times', evaluating both these options. You may use the clues given below along with your own ideas. You are Amrit/Amrita. **CBSE SQP 2021**

- Builds confidence
- Make friends and memories
- Experience new cultures
- Expands knowledge

8. Teachers are regarded as nation builders. They are responsible for developing the character of students and transforming them into responsible citizens. Write an article on the topic, 'Role of the Teacher in Society'. You are Gaurav/Gauri. **CBSE 2020**

- Shape the mindset
- Support system
- Role models
- Passion for educating
- The backbone of the society.

05

CHAPTER

Report Writing

A report is a description or a brief account of an event that had already taken place. It is a piece of writing that helps in recording events of importance that occurs in our day-to-day lives.

Marking Scheme

Format	1 Mark
Organisation of ideas	1 Mark
Content	2 Marks
Expression	1 Mark

(Accuracy of Spelling and Grammar)

Report attempts to give a first-hand information of an event with a scope of reporting one's ideas, opinions and impressions about the event as well. Reports are generally written in case of accidents or cultural events related to social issues. Both these reports require different information as given below.

Points to be Kept in Mind While Writing a Report

- A good report should present all the necessary information as clearly as possible.
- Write in **indirect speech** and **passive voice**.
- Write in **third person** form and avoid using **pronouns** like I, me or you.
- A report should contain 3 paragraphs providing all necessary details.
  - **Paragraph 1** Mentions the incident, its day, date, time, place and objective.
  - **Paragraph 2** It goes into details and includes causes, consequences, effects, activities, etc.
  - **Paragraph 3** It concludes the report with reactions, statements of people, promises and steps taken.
- Always provide a proper heading to your report.
- Adhere to the word limit of 120-150 words.
- Include information collected from people affected or around the event.

Important Details in Accident Reports

- What happened
- When
- Why (if known)
- Loss of life and property
- Details of accident site
- Police action/ enquiry ordered
- Warning/ recommendations/ action required
- Where
- How
- People/ vehicles involved (if any)
- Eye-witness account (if any)
- Details of rescue and relief operations
- Details of casualties - dead/ injured/ hospitalised
- Compensation to families of those killed or injured

Event Based Reports

- Type of function or its name
- Date, time and place
- Objective and main highlight of the programme
- Description of the event
- Prize distribution (if any)
- Conclusion
- Comments about the quality of the programme
- Occasion
- Name/Designation of the Chief Guest
- Inauguration, (if any)
- Chief Guest's address to audience
- Vote of thanks
- Contribution of the writer (if any)

Sample of Newspaper Report

You are Sakshi Chand and Abhay, reporters with 'The Times of India'. You witnessed a fire accident in Mundka in Delhi. Write a report to be published in the newspaper. Invent necessary details.

27 Killed in West Delhi Fire — **Heading with Byline** (What)

by Sakshi Chand and Abhay

New Delhi, 14th July, 20XX — Place and Date

A massive fire engulfed a four storey commercial building in West Delhi, Mundka on 12th July, Friday killing at least 27 people and leaving dozens injured.

The fire broke out around 4.30 p.m. causing a huge uproar in the locality. The cause of the fire is said to be a loose wire which had heated up in the summers. Fire brigade and police arrived at the venue within half an hour. About a dozen firemen battled past midnight to bring the fire under control. The loss incurred is estimated to be about five crore rupees.

The injured persons were rushed to a nearby hospital. Many people sustained minor burns. The PMO has tweeted that ₹ 2 lakh would be given to the next of kin of all the victims who died. The injured will receive ₹50,000. The police is investigating the matter and has advised everyone to avoid overheating of appliances and closing all such open wires.

Content

Sample of Magazine Report

You are Hina Aziz, student of Class XII-D and a member of the school magazine editorial board. Write a comprehensive report detailing the activities undertaken by students as part of the celebrations on Yoga Day. Include descriptions of the events, participation details, and the overall impact of these activities on the school community. You may organise your report by following - Who - What - When - Where - Why - How. **CBSE SQP 2024**

Yoga Day Celebrations

by Hina Aziz, Class XII-D

Heading with Byline

21st June saw a much anticipated day as students and teachers of the XYZ International School dressed in comfortable exercise attires stood on the yoga mats to celebrate the ancient Indian science of mind and soul called Yoga. Organised in the school playground at 7:00 a.m. to commemorate Yoga Day, the half day event saw much peace along with pomp and show. The event was presided by the esteemed National Yoga Organisation, whose member took on the role of teachers who taught important yoga asanas to the students. The event started with a small prayer and then a yoga session targeting the overall health of students. The member of the organisations also focused on some common health concerns and handed information pamphlets to all. Then, there was a presentation about yoga, Patanjali and how yoga has become a popular means of maintaining health. This was followed by a discussion on how yoga is beneficial for students and how they can do yoga anywhere even for 5 minutes.

The success of the event can be measured by its impact on those present. Participants showed their eagerness to participate in Yoga every day and students requested the school to organise yoga as a regular activity in the mornings.

Content

PRACTICE QUESTIONS

Newspaper Reports

1. **You are Suraj, reporter of The Times of India. You are sent to cover the Mango Festival organised at the farmer's market. Write a comprehensive report detailing the activities at the festival. Include descriptions of the events, participation details, the overall impact of these activities on the local community.** **CBSE 2025**

You may organise your report by following

Who — What — When — Why — How

Ans.

Mango Festival Brings Joy to the Farmer's Market

by Suraj, Reporter, The Times of India

Pune, 21st March, 20XX

The annual Mango Festival was held at the Farmer's Market yesterday, attracting mango lovers from across the city. Organised by the State Agricultural Board, the festival aimed to promote local farmers and celebrate India's rich mango diversity.

The event featured over 50 mango varieties, including Alphonso, Kesar, Dasheri, and Langra. Farmers set up stalls offering fresh mangoes, mango-based delicacies, and organic products. Visitors enjoyed tasting sessions, mango-eating contests, and interactive workshops on mango cultivation.

The festival saw active participation from local farmers, traders, and food enthusiasts, boosting their sales and exposure. The event also highlighted sustainable farming practices and encouraged direct farmer-to-consumer connections.

The Mango Festival proved to be a delightful celebration of India's 'King of Fruits', providing economic benefits to farmers while preserving traditional agricultural heritage. The overwhelming response ensured the festival's continued success for years to come.

2. **Due to heavy rainfall, the river near your town started overflowing its banks. As a result, your town was flooded. It led to a great loss of life and property. Many NGOs came forward to help the people with food, shelter and medicines. Write a report in 120-150 words for a local newspaper on the tragedy and rescue efforts. You are Raghav/Ritika.** **CBSE 2020**

Ans.

Heavy Rains Cause Flood in Kanpur

by Ritika/Raghav

13th September, 20XX, Kanpur: The city of Kanpur faced a grim situation on Saturday as the continuous rainfall resulted in the overflowing of Ganges river. The river water flooded the city and left innumerable people stranded on the rooftop of their houses. The continuous rains along with the floods have taken the lives of 54 people till now while 13,000 families have been displaced.

Rescue operations were launched by the government but incessant rainfall made it difficult to conduct the rescue operations smoothly. However, after much efforts, relief camps have been set up by the government to provide shelter to the flood victims.

Many NGOs and NGO workers volunteered to rescue people stuck in the flooded areas. The NGOs mainly work towards providing a hygienic shelter, food and medicines for the victims. The loss of life and property has been very high but the NGOs along with the government are trying to combat with the situation with great efforts.

3. **Your school is situated near a road intersection. Last week, in the morning, a bus coming at a great speed overturned when it braked suddenly. Senior students of your school rushed out and did everything to save the passengers. You were part of the rescue efforts. Write a report on the accident and your friends' role, for your school newsletter. You are George/Mary.**

Ans.

Bus Accident Victims Saved

by George/Mary

20th January, 20XX, Indore: Last week, a school bus was coming at a great speed near the intersection in front of our school. Another bus was coming from the opposite direction. The driver applied the brakes to avert the accident but due to overspeeding, the bus overturned. There were about 35 students and two teachers in this bus.

Hearing the shouts for help, many of our senior students, including me who had arrived early, immediately came and tried to break open the windows of the bus so that the passengers could be taken out safely. The students and teachers who were seriously injured were rushed to a nearby hospital immediately. Around 25 students sustained minor injuries and were given first-aid in the school itself. The principal and other staff members highly appreciated the 'good samaritan' efforts of our senior students.

Next day, all of us were awarded 'selfless social service' certificates by the Principal and our efforts were applauded during the assembly.

4. As you were travelling by train, you happened to witness an accident at an unmanned level crossing. As the reporter of a newspaper, write a report on the accident including details of the number of people injured and the extent of damage caused.

Ans.

36 Injured in Train- Tractor Trolley Collision

by Sanjeev Kumar, Times News Network

18th January, 20XX, Uttar Pradesh: One more accident at an unmanned crossing! The Railways are to be blamed as they do not have guards posted at such crossings to prevent such accidents.

The Lucknow Shatabdi was travelling to Kanpur when it hit a tractor-trolley at an unmanned level crossing after Khurja station on 17th January around midnight. The train driver was handicapped due to the heavy fog prevailing in the morning hours. The train stopped and relief measures were undertaken by the passengers.

Apparently, the trolley was full of a marriage party returning to their village after solemnising the marriage. 14 passengers of the trolley were seriously injured and were shifted to Khurja Civil Hospital by ambulances. The tractor and trolley were smashed beyond repair. The local administration has announced suitable compensation to the injured. The train resumed its journey after 4 hours.

5. You are Jessica/John, a budding journalist for a local daily. You covered the symposium on 'Play Time- The Vanishing Joy of Childhood'. The event was attended by students and teachers from different school. The group discussions were on how playing makes children fitter, unstructured playing vs. high tech toys, and how spontaneous group play helps build life skills. Write a report in 120-150 words for the local daily on the event. You may use the above given input. CBSE 2023

Revive Playtime

- Shapes better personalities
- Builds physical and mental health
- Develops life skills
- Keeps them in touch with nature

Ans.

Play Time-The Vanishing Joy of Childhood

by Jessica/John, Journalist, XYZ daily

23rd March, 20XX, Mumbai: In a bid to present the need to go back to having playtime, an extraordinary symposium was hosted by PQR Organisation on Saturday, 21st March, 20XX. The event, which saw the participation of students and teachers from different schools, started with a diya lighting ceremony by the Chief Guest, the Honourable Education Minister of the State. It was followed by a delightful dance performance on Ganesh Vandana.

Soon after, the event saw great group discussions on topics such as how playing makes children fitter, the debate of unstructured playing vs. high tech toys, and how spontaneous group play helps build life skills.

An eminent psychologist and professor from ABC University pointed out how playing sports and games shapes our personality and builds the physical and mental strengths of children. A presentation was shown to highlight that sports and games boost the development of life skills and keeps the children in touch with nature.

6. The members of your school Drama Club, recently put up a street play at the Central Park of your city. The theme of the play was Education - An Equal Opportunity. As President of Drama Club, write a report on the event to be published in your school newsletter. Use the following cues along with your own ideas to compose the report. CBSE 2024

- Date, venue, time
- Performance followed by interactive session with spectators response
- No. of participants
- Star actors
- People's feedback/response

Ans.

Education-An Equal Opportunity

by Prachi Rawat, President of Drama Club

11th August, 20XX, Indore: On the invigorating afternoon of 14th July, the members of our esteemed Drama Club engaged the park-goers with a stellar performance at Central Park, scheduled at 5:00 pm. The theme of the play was 'Education - An Equal Opportunity' and Central Park provided the perfect backdrop for the performance, attracting a diverse audience from across the city.

With 15 enthusiastic members of the Drama Club participating in the play, showcasing their talents and dedication to spreading an important message, the play was captivating and thought-provoking, highlighting the significance of providing equal educational opportunities for all. Following the performances, the club conducted an interactive session with the spectators, encouraging them to share their thoughts and ideas on the theme of the play. This engagement fostered meaningful discussions and raised awareness about the importance of education as a fundamental right for everyone.

Overall, the street play event was a resounding success, due to the hard work and dedication of the Drama Club members. We look forward to organising more such impactful events in the future to continue spreading awareness and advocating for social change through the arts.

7. As part of community outreach programme, a group of 40 students from your school identified a neighbourhood slum and took up the initiative to teach basic language and numerical skills, environmental cleanliness and personal hygiene awareness to the slum children. As Head of the team, write a report on the programme to be published in your school newsletter. Use the cues given below, along with your own ideas to draft the report. You are Rahul/Radhika. **CBSE 2024**

- Date, venue, duration
- Activities carried out
- No. of children who attended
- Books distributed
- Feedback of people

Ans.

Community Outreach Programme

by Radhika/Rahul

11th March, 20XX, Delhi: XYZ Public School organised an extraordinary community outreach programme a group of 40 students embarked on a noble initiative to educate children from a nearby slum area. The programme took place on 12th March, 20XX at the Paharganj slums and lasted for 6 hours. As part of the initiative, the school team distributed books and teaching materials to the children, aiming to enhance their basic language and numerical skills. Additionally, they conducted sessions on environmental cleanliness and personal hygiene awareness, emphasising the importance of a clean and healthy living environment.

The feedback from the residents was overwhelmingly positive, with many expressing gratitude for the efforts in uplifting the community. A total of 360 children attended the programme, actively participating in the activities and showing enthusiasm for learning.

Overall, the programme was a resounding success, reflecting the school's commitment to serving and making a positive impact on the community.

8. The construction sector is believed to be quite hazardous and has the maximum number of fatal work injuries. A safety fair was organised by 'Building Safely', an NGO in Mysuru, Karnataka with the overarching theme pertaining to the importance of worker safety in construction zones. You were asked to cover this event as the junior correspondent of a Local Daily. Write a report covering this event in about 120-150 words. Support your ideas with outline clues given below, to craft your newspaper report. **CBSE SQP 2023**

Safety Fairs Programmes

- Toolbox talks
- Speeches
- Safety demonstrations
- Emergency response drill
- Video dedication for the deceased
- Safety games
- Inaugurating special insurance programme
- Vote of thanks

Ans.

The Enlightening Safety Fair

by XYZ

25th September, Mysuru: A safety fair was organised by 'Building Safely', an NGO in Mysuru, Karnataka on 23rd September with the overarching theme pertaining to the importance of worker safety in construction zones. The idea behind the fair was simple- to reduce the construction accidents and deaths that are rapidly increasing because of a lack of safety standards. The event was attended by all employees and workers of the local and international construction companies with the focus of increasing the practice of safety standards in the state.

The event started with a simple introduction by the CM of the state discussing the centrality of safety in all fields. After his speech, a video dedication for all the deceased was shown so that the audience could understand the gravity of the issue. It was followed by some toolbox talks and some awareness speeches along with the inauguration of the special insurance programme by the NGO. Afterwards, the entire audience was up for a surprise with some fun yet enlightening games and demonstrations. The audience learnt a lot through the emergency spot drill which was followed by a gap-bridging lunch with the bosses. The programme ended with a vote of thanks from the NGO and the government with a promise that we all will follow safety rules and standards. All in all the event was an enlightening one and a wonderful experience for everyone.

9. You are Parvi/Parinay, special correspondent for 'The Times of India'. You attended a programme organised by the Rotary Club of your district on 'Increasing need for Retirement Homes', Mr. Rajesh Kher, 'The Chairman of Twilight Homes' was the Chief Guest on the occasion. The programme included a question and answer session followed by poster making, group discussions and a short play written and directed by students. Write a newspaper report on the programme in 120-150 words mentioning date, time, venue, activities and response of participants. CBSE Term II 2022

Ans.

Increasing Need for Retirement Homes

by Parinay, Special Correspondent

17th January, 20XX, Chennai: A programme on the topic 'Increasing need for Retirement Homes' was organised by the Rotatory Club of the Chennai district on 15th January, 20XX. The programme was organised in the Vivekananda Cricket Ground and lasted for 3 hours, starting at 4 o'clock in the evening. The Chief Guest of the programme was the Chairman of Twilight Homes, Mr. Rajesh Kher.

The programme intended to make the attendees understand the need for retirement homes in our society. Several sessions including a question and answer session, a poster making event, group discussion and a short play written and directed by children were organised in the programme. The play performed by children was especially praised by Mr. Kher, who in his speech, maintained that such homes are required to uphold the dignity and choices of the older generation.

The function was definitely a success; consequently, the club received a lot of donations and funds to commence the process.

10. A daylight robbery took place in Gorakhpur in Khurda Tank police station limits when the Branch Staff of PNB were on their way back after collecting ₹ 50 lakh from the regional office of the Reserve Bank. As staff correspondent for 'The Indian Express', write a report in 120-150 words.

Ans.

₹ 50 Lakh Looted in Armed Robbery

by Staff Correspondent Himanshu Sareen, The Indian Express

Gorakhpur, 5th April, 20XX : In a daring robbery, armed criminals shot at employees of the Punjab National Bank (PNB) and looted ₹ 50 lakh from them on 4th April, Friday. A security guard of the bank sustained a bullet injury in the incident. He is recovering in the city hospital and has identified one of the dacoits as being an employee of the bank.

The incident took place at about 1:40 p.m. when the Branch Staff of PNB were on their way back to the branch carrying the cash withdrawn from the regional office of the Reserve Bank in a metal trunk. Their vehicle was intercepted by a Bolero and at least five miscreants got down and fired in the air. They then smashed one side glass window of the bank's vehicle, dragged the driver out and thrashed him.

Other security personnel and the cashier were also roughed up and shot at. Terrorising the PNB staff, the dacoits fled after snatching their mobile phones and the metal trunk containing the cash. Khurda SP said that a hunt is on for the dacoits who had prior knowledge about the cash movement.

11. The efforts of 400 volunteers working with the NGO, 4 Literacy, in the district of Malkangiri, Odisha, was lauded by the District Collector, Shri V. Singh (IAS). As a staff reporter of 'The Odisha Bhaskar', write a report about this in 120-150 words covering all the details of the event, such as training, teaching and infrastructure involved in the 'Each One Teach One Campaign', initiated by the district administration in association with the NGO. CBSE SQP Term II, 2022

Ans.

Working Towards Education : Each One Teach One Campaign

by XYZ, Staff Reporter, The Odisha Bhaskar

16th August 20XX, Malkangiri, Odisha : Moving towards the goal of 100% literacy in the country, the efforts of 400 volunteers in the 'Each One Teach One Campaign' organised by 4 Literacy, in the district of Malkangiri, Odisha was lauded by the District Collector, Shri V. Singh (IAS). The event, which focused on teaching the under-privileged children of the district and motivate them to go to school, was undertaken by volunteers from all over the country. Started from 1st August, the two week long event was handled by volunteers.

The volunteers of the project has been taken to task since the middle of July wherein they were provided with training to be able to effectively communicate and motivate people. The sports grounds of the district of Malkangiri that was brought under construction last year and the 2 storeyed building that was erected was used as the teaching centre.

The equipment required were bought with the help of the Indian Government which had kindly allowed us some funds to fulfill the aim of the project. With the funds, different rooms were equipped with blackboards, notebooks, pens and all other things required to make the environment comfortable for learning. The event ended on a successful note as most children and parents had promised to further their education.

12. The Ministry of Transport, New Delhi organised a one day 'Auto-Mela' at the Institute of Driving, Saket to motivate women drivers to take up commercial driving. The day-long event was inaugurated by the Commissioner of Police, Mr. S.P. Mehra.

The event started with an introduction to commercial driving- its rules and regulations. This was followed by a basic training session in self defence, a run through of the licensing procedures and a sale of second hand cars. You are Anita/Anil, Staff Reporter of 'The Daily News'. Write a report in 120-150 words mentioning date, main features, purpose and response of participants. **CBSE 2022 Term II**

Ans.

Auto-Mela

by Anita, Staff Reporter

4th April, 20XX, Delhi: In the bid to increase employment opportunities for women in the public transportation system and to motivate women to take up commercial driving, the Ministry of Transport, New Delhi organised a one day 'Auto-Mela' at the Institute of Driving, Saket on 2nd April, 20XX. The event was presided by the Commissioner of Police, Mr. S.P. Mehra who not only inaugurated the event with the diya lighting ceremony but also commended the efforts of the Ministry for the cause.

After the words of encouragement by the honored Chief Guest, the event started with a powerful presentation about commercial driving, its rules and regulations and how it would be a great step towards women empowerment. The presentation was followed by a basic training session in self-defence hosted by the Women's cell of the Department of Police and then by a run through of the licensing procedures.

The event also saw a grand sale of second hand cars at great prices for all women who wanted to take up commercial driving. All in all, the event was a great success.

School Magazine Reports

1. You are Seema/Sarvesh Khanna of Class XII-A and a member of the school magazine editorial board. Write a comprehensive report on the Community Service Programme organised by the school. Include description of events and activities organised. **CBSE 2025**

You may organise your report by the following

Who — What — When — Why — How

Ans.

Community Service Programme: A Step Towards Social Responsibility

by Seema/Sarvesh Khanna, Class XII-A

Our school recently organised a Community Service Programme on 15th March, 2025, aimed at fostering social awareness and responsibility among students. The event was a collaborative effort by the Social Welfare Club and the Student Council, involving students from Classes IX to XII.

The programme included a cleanliness drive, where students cleaned public parks and school surroundings. A health and hygiene awareness campaign was conducted in a nearby slum, where volunteers distributed sanitary kits and educated residents on hygiene practices. Additionally, a visit to an old-age home was arranged, where students interacted with the elderly, engaging them in storytelling and musical performances.

The initiative not only helped the underprivileged but also instilled a sense of empathy and responsibility in students. The overwhelming participation and positive feedback from beneficiaries made the event a resounding success. Such programmes reinforce the values of kindness and active citizenship.

2. Your school recently organised Y-20 Chaupal under G-20 initiative. The theme chosen for the event was Health and Wellness. Nearly 20 speakers from Classes IX to XII participated and presented their innovative ideas.

You are Neeraj/Nirvita, student editor of your school magazine. Write a report the event to be published in your school magazine. Use the following cues along with your own ideas to draft the report. CBSE 2024

- Wellness - holistic and multidimensional
- Physical fitness/yoga
- Revival of alternative medicines, etc.
- Date, venue, time
- Emotional and intellectual well-being
- Importance of social interaction

Ans.

Health and Wellness Event Organised under Y-20 Chaupal

by Neeraj/Nirvita

Our school recently organised an event of Y-20 Chaupal, focusing on the theme of 'Health and Wellness' under the initiative of G-20. The main purpose of this event was to create awareness among the students as well as people regarding the crucial aspects of holistic well-being.

Both the students and teachers emphasised the importance of maintaining a healthy body. Yoga, in particular, emerged as a powerful tool for achieving physical well-being. It was highlighted that yoga not only enhances flexibility and strength but also helps in maintaining mental clarity and emotional balance. Through interactive sessions, attendees explored the profound connection between emotional well-being and academic performance, emphasising the need for holistic support systems within educational environments.

The Chaupal also shed light on the benefits of incorporating traditional practices such as Ayurveda, acupuncture and herbal remedies into modern healthcare approaches. From group activities fostering teamwork to open dialogues addressing social stigma surrounding mental health, the Chaupal emphasised the transformative power of collective support. Participants were encouraged to prioritise meaningful connections.

In conclusion, the Y-20 Chaupal on 'Health and Wellness' ended on a positive note, further highlighting the importance of fostering holistic well-being within our school community.

3. You are a Kanika/Kavish student reporter for Galaxy School. Your school celebrated Annual Sports Day recently. Write a report in about 120-150 words on it to be published in your school magazine.

You may use the cues given below CBSE 2023

– Date – venue – time – Chief Guest – opening ceremony – sports events – prize distribution

Ans.

Annual Sports Day

by Kanika/Kavish, Student Reporter

Galaxy School celebrated its Annual Sports Day on 21st September, 20XX at the XYZ Stadium with great enthusiasm and energy. The event began at 8:00 a.m. with the arrival of the Chief Guest, Mr. Kumar, a renowned sportsman in the field of athletics. The opening ceremony included a march-past by all the students, accompanied by the school band. This was followed by an inspiring speech by the Chief Guest, who encouraged the students to be physically active and participate in sports.

The sports events included races, long jumps, shot put, and other track and field events. Students from all grades participated with great zeal and enthusiasm, showcasing their talents and skills. The atmosphere was electric as students cheered for their friends and classmates. The highlight of the day was the prize distribution ceremony, where winners were awarded medals and certificates by the Chief Guest. It was a moment of great pride for both the winners and their families.

Overall, the Annual Sports Day was a huge success and a testament to the school's commitment to promoting physical fitness and sportsmanship. The event provided an opportunity for students to showcase their talents, develop teamwork skills and have fun with their peers.

4. Your school recently conducted an inter school heritage quiz contest as a student reporter write a report of the event in about 120 to 150 words to be published in your school magazine you are Amit/ Archana mention day, date, time and venue. CBSE 2023

> **Know Your Heritage**
>
> *An Inter School Quiz Contest*
>
> - History
> - Mythology
> - Culture
> - Monuments
> - Handicraft
> - Attractive prizes for audience question
> - Friday 14th March, St. Marks School

Ans.

Know Your Heritage

by Amit/Archana

In a bid to make students aware of their heritage, culture and history of the nation, St. Marks School hosted an exciting Inter-School Quiz Contest called 'Know Your Heritage' on Friday, 14th March. The contest, focused on topics related to history, mythology, culture, monuments, and handicraft, saw a great participation of students from various schools in the city.

The quiz contest consisted of multiple rounds of challenging questions. Each round tested the participant's knowledge and awareness of Indian heritage. The questions were based on various aspects of Indian culture and tradition, which made the event informative and interesting. Apart from the quiz, there was an audience question round where the audience could win attractive prizes. The quiz was conducted in a fun, and interactive manner, which kept the participants and the audience engaged throughout the event.

The students' enthusiasm and eagerness to participate made the event a great success. The winners were awarded exciting prizes, and all the participants were appreciated for their efforts. All in all, 'Know Your Heritage' was a successful and informative event that educated the participants and audience about the rich heritage of India.

5. A programme on 'Swachh Bharat Mission' was organised in your school on Mahatma Gandhi's birthday. Posters were prepared and pasted in the colony near your school. A procession was taken out. School premises and its surroundings were cleaned by the students. Public was advised to make the mission successful. Write a report on the programme in 120-150 words. You are Srinivasan/Latha.

Ans.

Cleanliness Drive Organised Under Swachh Bharat Mission

by Latha/Srinivasan

A cleanliness drive was organised by our school under the Swachh Bharat Mission on the occasion of Gandhi Jayanti. The main purpose of this event was to create awareness among the students as well as people regarding cleanliness and its benefits. Posters sharing the importance of cleanliness and hazards related to dirty surroundings were prepared and pasted in the colonies near the school.

A procession was also arranged in which students carried banners highlighting the importance of clean surroundings. A skit was also performed by the students that depicted the health hazards of living in unclean surroundings. Thereafter, the school premises and surroundings were cleaned. Our principal started by cleaning the playground. Then, the teachers and the students followed suit. Some students did the dusting of the rooms while the others cleaned the ground using brooms.

Our principal also delivered a speech in front of a public gathering telling the importance of cleanliness and sanitation. He urged the public to take efforts to make Swachh Bharat Mission successful. He also honoured the sweepers of the school for their noble job. In the end, we all took oath of keeping our home, locality and city clean. It was a learning experience for all of us.

6. With a view to create awareness regarding health, St. Anne's school organised 'Health Mela' in the school premises. Various charts, models fitness equipments were displayed. Lectures, debates, discussions, plays were organised. A workshop on low calorie cooking was also organised. Write a report in 150-200 words on the 'Health Mela' for the school magazine. You are Neha/Nikhil, Secretary of the Health Club of school.

Ans.

Health Mela' at St. Anne's School

by Neha/Nikhil (Secretary, Health Club)

A 'Health Mela' was organised by the initiative of St. Anne's School in the school premises. According to Principal Mathew, the school took this initiative as a recent survey made by the teachers proved that most of the parents were not health conscious. This was because of the immense work-load in office that they were going through. Because of the lag in energy levels, the children too were becoming unaware of good health habits. When the teachers noticed this and reported to Fr. Mathew, he decided to organise this health camp.

The event was distributed into segments of three days. Each day had an event of attraction. Day one was glorified by the display of various fitness equipment which were extremely easy to use and user-friendly. There were people who volunteered to explain the functions of the machine to everyone who was interested. A free demo session too was conducted.

Day two was a fun filled day for the students. Everyone took part in debates and plays to showcase the importance of good health practices and exercises. Day three was a day for parents. A 'cook healthy' training was held for the mothers and fathers. Every parent enthusiastically took part in it and the entire event was a great success.

7. An NGO, 'Health for All' organised a health check-up camp in a slum at Amritsar. You are Ruchika/Raunak, and you visited the camp. Write a report covering arrangements such as registration, check-up, tests carried out, etc. with the help of verbal clues given below. **CBSE 2019**

A health check-up camp in a slum -infant mortality rate was too high-event details- step-by-step procedure- first register at the counter by giving his name and age- submit the forms at the registration desk- visit a general physician, a dentist, and an optometrist - a basic work-up - requesting specific tests to understand the severity of the condition

Ans.

Health Check Up Camp in a Slum

by Ruchika/Raunak

An NGO, 'Health for All' organised a health check-up camp at Amritsar in a slum recognised to have poor hygiene because of which the infant mortality rate was too high. The event was scheduled on 15th of March at 12:00 p.m. and the registration started 1 hour prior. Once the check-up was completed, the people were requested to submit the forms at the registration desk. Upon registration, the people were required to visit a general physician, a dentist, and an optometrist. Once the available doctors had examined them, the participants were required to get a blood test done. For most people tested, it was a basic work-up of their non-fasting blood sugar and other related tests. However, for those who suffered from other diseases, the doctors made a note of it in the form given to them, requesting specific tests be done to understand the severity of the condition. Financing for additional tests were also covered by the medical laboratories associated with the NGO.

The next day another batch of patients were checked. On the 3rd day of the camp, all the test reports were examined and proper medicines were prescribed. Also, the village hospital was supplied with emergency medicines. People came in large numbers and the 3- day camp was a huge success. The people were very satisfied and suggested us to carry out such camps every month. The NGO were able to do justice to their motto 'Health for All'.

8. MMD School, Nashik, recently organised a science symposium on the topic: 'Effect of Pollution on Quality of Life'. You are Amit/Amita Raazdan, editor of the school magazine. Write a report on the event for your school magazine. (120-150 words) **CBSE 2018**

Ans.

Effect of Pollution on Quality of Life

by Amit/Amita Raazdan

The two days Regional Level CBSE Science Symposium with the theme 'Effect of Pollution on the Quality of Life' was hosted by MMD School, Nashik on 2-3rd December. The event saw young enthusiastic participants from different parts of the state putting up 72 participatory exhibits displaying how environmental pollution is impacting our life. The programme was inaugurated by Ramdas Kardam, Maharashtra's Environment Minister. He was very impressed by the presentations and congratulated the participants.

The students not only expressed their concern about the environmental pollution but also suggested various effective solutions which if executed will lengthen the life of the Earth. In the Valedictory Function organised on 3rd December, the eminent judges comprising Dr. Narendra Singh (Research Scientist) and Dr. Vikram Sisodia (Associate Professor and Dean-Faculty Welfare, SDIT) gave their judgments after inspecting each project on their own merit. All the participants were presented with certificates.

The judges applauded the students for their noble ideas which would help the world to become a much better place to live in. Mrs. Sushmita Narayan, Principal, MMD School, thanked all the participating teams for making this event a success and appreciated their noble projects.

9. Last week you visited a two-day long youth festival organised by YWCA at Bhopal. Students from all over India participated in it. Programmes included poetry recitation, staging of one-act plays, classical dance recitals, etc. There was a perfect atmosphere of national integration. Write a report on the festival. Emphasise the significance of such festivals in our national life. You are Nalini/Ravindra. CBSE 2020

Ans.

Youth Festival

by Nalini/Ravindra

The YWCA, Bhopal celebrated the 'Youth Festival' on 7th January, 20XX at the renowned YWCA association stadium. More than 2000 students from various states participated in various competitions like poetry recitation, drawing, staging of one-act plays, singing, essay writing, classical dance, recitals, etc., themed on national Integration. The bubbling enthusiasm exhibited by the participants has been tremendous. There was a perfect atmosphere of national integration. After the performances, the honourable PM of India, Narendra Modi, addressed the students.

He mentioned that the number of participating students are increasing every year. He advised the students to develop personal discipline and give due respect to parents and teachers. He also advised the students to remember that the country we live in is one of the most colourful ones. It is full of life with festivals and various cultures. The gathering was felicitated by Kamla Bhasin, a renowned feminist. She advised the students to never forget their culture in the process of westernisation.

The next day was reserved for prize distribution and light fair for everyone to enjoy. The function came to a close in the late afternoon with a vote of thanks proposed to the Chief Guest and other guests and participants. This event witnessed a grand success.

10. You are Sunil/Megha, School Leader of Sudheer Public School, Chennai. On the completion of 25 years of meritorious service to the cause of education, your school celebrated its Silver Jubilee with great pomp and show. The celebrations lasted three days and in the true tradition of the school, each day was devoted to a noble cause of service. Special attention was paid to Children with Special Needs, Old Age Homes and Orphanages. Students shared experiences of voluntary services and the Theatre Club put up short skits highlighting social concerns. Write a report in 120-150 word about the event to be published in your school magazine. CBSE 2022 Term II

Ans.

Silver Jubilee Celebrations

by Sunil/Megha

Celebrating the 25 years of excellence and great service to the cause of education, our school celebrated its Silver Jubilee with much pomp and show. The three-day celebrations took place from 25th April to 27th April, 20XX in the school premises and in keeping with the spirit of the school, each day was devoted to a deserving act of service.

Children with special needs, old age homes, and orphanages received special attention. The Theatre Club performed a series of quick sketches addressing social issues on the first day. A large festival was planned for the following day. In addition to some fun games, the students set up some fast food carts. Through this event, ₹ 75,000 in total was raised which was divided into be given to organisations that helped the Children with special needs, old age homes, and orphanages.

The students shared experiences of voluntary service performed by them and the Principal, John D'Mello gave a token of appreciation to all the participants of various activities and congratulated everyone for making it a noble, memorable and noteworthy event.

11. You are Abhishek/Abhilasha, the President of the Writer's society in your school. Your school recently conducted a session with Mr. Akshat Negi, an officer in the Ministry of Corporate Affairs, Government of India, where he explained the various Pradhan Mantri Youth Internship benefits available to the young minds of the country. Write a report on the event for your school magazine.

Ans.

PM Youth Internship Benefits

by Abhishek/Abhilasha, President of Writer's Society

The eminent officer, Mr. Akshat Negi recently visited our school campus on 5th November, 20XX and spoke to our senior students of Classes IX-XII about the PM Internship Scheme. He spoke in a lively manner and explained the benefits of the scheme without leaving any information out. He conveyed the idea of the scheme clearly when he told that the Ministry of Corporate Affairs has launched the Prime Minister's Internship Scheme, which was announced in the Union budget 2024. The scheme aims to provide students with internship opportunities to address youth unemployment. It seeks to provide internships to 1 crore young people over the next five years.

He emphasised that the applicants will get a monthly stipend of ₹ 4,500 from the government, and an additional ₹ 500 by companies as part of their Corporate Social Responsibility initiatives consisting of one year. He added that the internship will not only provide financial support to the students but also offer practical skills and their real-world application. With the scheme's structured financial support and emphasis on diverse sectors, students can benefit from practical training while exploring various career paths. The session was very enlightening for the young minds of our nation.

12. You are Shweta/Sahil. Head Boy/Girl of Rukmi Public School, Janak Puri, Delhi. Your school celebrated World Autism Day in your school to create awareness regarding needs and necessities of autistic children. Write a report on this programme in about 120-150 words.

Ans.

World Autism Day

by Shweta/Sahil

World Autism Day was celebrated by Rukmi Public School. Janak Puri, Delhi on 2nd April, 2023 from 10 a.m. to 2 p.m. in the School Auditorium. The school was well decorated with posters of various facts related to Autism. Mrs. Deepa Department of Psychology of Delhi University was the Chief Guest. Around 200 students attended the programme.

The programme began by lighting of the ceremonial lamp by the Chief Guest. After that a skit was presented by the students of Class XI showing the importance of knowledge of Autism and to upkeep the needs of autistic students. The Chief Guest gave a very motivating and thought provoking speech about the inclusion of autistic students with the mainstream students. She also highlighted the role of Youth in accomplishing this task. The Principal presented Vote of Thanks after which light refreshment was served.

It was a very interesting programme and aroused lots of questions in the minds of all participants, which were very well satisfied by the Speaker. It gave a lot of food for thought to the minds of students.

SELF ASSESSMENT TEST

1. You are the President of RWA, Preeti Nagar. Your society recently organised a cooking competition for the residents on the occasion of Women's Day. Eminent Chef Sanjay Kumar was invited to be judge. Write a report on the event to be published in a local daily.

   Clues

   - Date, venue, time
   - No. of participants
   - Variety of dishes displayed
   - Winner

2. Your school has organised a seminar on cyber-bullying and online safety. It was attended by counsellors and students from ten different schools. As a student reporter, write a report in about 120-150 words to be published in the school weekly. You are Rajshri/Rishi. You may use the following cues along with your ideas to compose it. **CBSE 2023**

   Day, date, time, venue, Speakers Dr. Rao, Dr. Sen, Dr. Sidh, discussion on perils of cyber bullying, measure to control it, legal aid (120-150 words)

3. Ranikhet district, Uttarakhand, on the occasion of Basant Panchami celebrations had organised a three-day cultural festival. You are Bhupinder/Priyanka Bhisht. Your newspaper had deputed you to cover the inaugural event of this festival. As a newspaper reporter, use the given clues along with your own ideas to write a report about the same in 120-150 words.

   - Big crowds at main grounds of the marketplace
   - Colourful decorations
   - Inauguration-local panchayatmember to inaugurate.
   - Folk dance and songs
   - Speeches

4. In your locality, a blood donation camp was organised by the NGO- 'For Your Health'. Many people visited the camp and donated blood. Write a report in 120-150 words for a local newspaper covering the arrangement, doctors' team, refreshment served, etc.

5. You are Akshita/Akshay, staff correspondent for the 'BRIGHT STAR' newspaper. A daylong seminar was organised by Nirmaan Public School on the 'Benefits of Yoga- A Healthy Hear'. Students from 20 school participated in the event. Renowned Yoga exponent Guru Shivang addressed the students on the benefits of yoga. Students of the Yoga Club demonstrated basic 'asanas' and breathing exercises.

   Write a report on it for the newspaper in about 120-150 words mentioning date, venue, Chief Guest, activities and response of the participants. **CBSE 2022 Term II**

6. Some students of the senior wing of Nav Vihar Public School, Coimbatore have collectively authored a book 'Life in a Boarding School'. The book was released by Smita Das, a renowned writer. This was followed by book reading, a question and answer session and a short play adaptation. You are Ankit/Ankita, a student editor for the school magazine, 'perspectives'. Write a report in 120-150 words on the event mentioning date, participants, activities and responses of participants

7. On your way to school, right in front of the school gate, you saw a verbal dispute leading to a physical fight between an auto rickshaw driver and his passenger. A teacher of your school intervened, found out the cause of the quarrel and amicably resolved the issue (problem). Write a report on the incident in 120-150 words. You are Balbir/Bimla.

   Clues

   People gathering in front of school gate.... Verbal dispute....rickshaw driver charging more....slapped the driver...physical fight....one of the teachers intervened.... Brought them to compromise.....driver apologised...appreciation for sense of responsibility and initiative.

8. You are Akhil/Anjana, a resident of Kailash Colony, Fort Road, Patna. Recently your city experienced a lot of rain and consequently people living in the low-lying areas suffered a lot of difficulties. NDRF rescue teams reached the affected areas in time. The marooned people were taken to safer places and provided with shelter, food and medicines. Write a report on the floods and rescue efforts with the help of the details given above.

9. A one-day cricket match was played by your school, Ratan Public School against Wali Public School. Ratan Public School won the match by 14 runs. Write a report on the same for your school magazine. You are Sanakshi/Sohan.
You can use the following cues

- Finals of Inter-school tournament
- Ratan Public School is defending champion
- Venue, day, date, time
- Highlights
- Result-Chief Guest closing speech

10. You are Rohini/Rehan. Your school KRM Senior Secondary School, Gurgaon (now Gurugram) organised a workshop on how to conserve energy. A number of CBSE schools participated in it. Many eminent personalities addressed the students. Write a report in 120-150 words for your school magazine.

11. A mock drill of earthquake was conducted in your school, SBV West Vinod Nagar. Write a report for school magazine giving the detailed report of the drill.

12. You are Deepak/Deepika, Secretary of Ahimsa Club, Parsva Public School, Delhi. On 2nd October, your school observed 'International Day for Peace and Non-violence', organising various activities such as visit to Raj Ghat, Charkha spinning, lectures by eminent Gandhians, etc. Write a report on the same in 120-150 words.

13. Your school has recently arranged a musical night in the school auditorium. Write a report in 120-150 words on this programme for your school magazine. You are Mahima/Mahesh, Cultural Secretary of Vasant Vihar Public School, Itarsi. Invent the details.

14. You school conducted a seminar on 'How to prevent cruelty towards animals' in which 40 city CBSE schools took part. As coordinator of the programme, write a report in 120-150 words for the school magazine. You are Vikram/Vidhi of CPS Senior Secondary School, Bengaluru.

LITERATURE TEXTBOOKS

- PROSE
- POETRY
- SUPPLEMENTARY

PROSE

01

The Last Lesson

About the Author

Alphonse Daudet (1840-1897) was a French novelist and short-story writer who is remembered for his sentimental tales of provincial life in France. He wrote his first poem and his first novel at age of 14. His literary career grew as he wrote poems, plays and even editorial for newspapers. During the Franco-Prussian War, Alphonse joined the army but he soon left it after viewing its horrors. His short period in the army had a deep impact on his writing which is visible in his works.

YOUR STUDY GOALS

- Chapter Sketch
- About the Characters
- Summary of the Chapter

YOUR PRACTICE GOAL

- NCERT Folder
- Extract Based Questions
- Short Answer Type Questions
- Long Answer Type Questions

Chapter Sketch

The Last Lesson is set in the days of the Franco-Prussian War (1870-1871). Led by Bismarck, Prussia defeated France and the French districts of Alsace and Lorraine passed into the Prussian hands. As a result, the new Prussian Government discontinued the teaching of French language and imposed German. The story revolves around how this decision proves to be a life-altering event for the people of Alsace including the young Franz as well as M. Hamel, a French language teacher who had to leave his old school. It shows how M. Hamel teaches the last French lesson with sincerity, dedication and courage.

About the Characters

Franz He is a young school going boy who loves spending his time in nature. He is a sensitive and observant child who feels regretful for his neglect of his studies.

M. Hamel He is Franz's French teacher. He is a strict but sincere teacher who has spent 40 years of his life teaching French to people of Alsace. He is a patriotic man who gets emotional on leaving his nation behind.

Watcher He is the blacksmith of the village who makes fun of Franz when he is hurriedly going to school.

Village people The village people includes many village residents including Old Hauser, Mayor and Postmaster. These people express their regret as well as respect for the French teacher.

Prussian Soldiers The background characters whose presence indicate the change of authority and how the lives of the people of Alsace would change.

Summary of the Chapter

Franz's Surprise

The story starts with a young school going boy named Franz being late for school. He was scared of getting scolded by his French teacher, M. Hamel, as he had not learned participles. He also wanted to enjoy his day outside in nature. However, he had to go to school. On the way, Franz passed the town hall where a many people were reading the bad news from the bulletin board. Without paying much attention to it, he reached his school.

Franz was surprised to see that the school was quiet. He had expected to find a lot of noise. Inside the class, he saw that his classmates were seated and M. Hamel was walking to and fro. Embarrassed, Franz entered his class. He thought that he would get scolded. But, M. Hamel kindly told him to take his seat.

The Order from Berlin

In the classroom, Franz observed that M. Hamel was wearing his special attire. Further, the village elders were sitting in the back benches. They all looked sad. M. Hamel announced that it was their last French lesson. An order had come from Berlin to teach only German in the schools of Alsace and Lorraine and that it was their last French lesson.

Franz was shocked by the information. He regretted not learning his lessons on time. He also felt bad because M. Hamel was leaving. Franz realised that M. Hamel wore his special attire to honour his last lesson. Moreover, the village people had come to express their gratitude towards him. They wanted to show their respect for their country and their language.

M. Hamel's Patriotism

When it was time for Franz to recite, he was not able to speak the French participles properly. He was ashamed of himself. However, M. Hamel did not scold him. M. Hamel criticised the people of Alsace for postponing their learning. He blamed the parents for wanting their children to earn instead of study. He also blamed himself for giving them a holiday whenever he wanted to go fishing.

M. Hamel called French language- the most beautiful, the clearest and the most logical language in the world. He told the people of France to treasure their language. According to him, whenever the people of a particular nation are enslaved, as long as they are attached to their language, it is as if they have the key to their prison.

The Final Goodbye

That day Franz understood everything. He realised that he never paid much attention in the class and that M. Hamel had never explained everything with so much patience. Everyone did their work with full concentration. Even the old Hauser was focused on reading his old book. M. Hamel was sitting in his chair and observing his class. For 40 years, he had given his faithful service to the school and now he had to leave.

At the end of the lesson, everyone in the class became emotional. However, M. Hamel had the courage and patience to hear every lesson. Finally, as the church-clock struck twelve, M. Hamel stood up. He tried to speak but choked. He turned to the blackboard and wrote as large as he could 'Vive La France!' meaning 'long live France'. Hamel dismissed the class, signaling everyone to leave.

Word-Meaning

in great dread of — with great fear of
drilling — undergoing military training exercises
apprentice — trainee, a person who is learning a trade from a skilled employer
a great bustle — excited activity and movement
in unison — all at once, together
rapping — striking rapidly on a hard surface, especially in order to attract attention
counted on — relied or depended on
primer — an elementary book for teaching children to read
thumbed at the edges — with pages worn out or soiled due to frequent handling
thunderclap — a crashing sound of thunder
wretches — villains; people deserving contempt
Saar — a river in North–Eastern France and Western Germany
cranky — bad-tempered, eccentric or strange
reproach ourselves with — criticise ourselves for
at one stroke — by a single action having immediate effect
Angelus — a bell rung as call to recite the Angelus–a devotional prayer in the Roman Catholic Church
bearing on — pressing
Vive La France — long live France

Important Themes of the Chapter

Culture and Language The central theme of the story is the importance of language and culture to an individual's identity. In a situation wherein one culture overpowers another, language can be a way to preserve the culture while paving a path towards freedom. This is highlighted in M. Hamel's speech.

Patriotism, Authority and Chauvinism The given story presents how the change of authority in the form of German authority leads to language chauvinism. The German authority want the people of Alsace and Lorraine to learn German and forgo their mother tongue. Such chauvinism raises patriotic feelings as seen in M. Hamel. He shows his patriotism by delivering his last lesson and by writing the words 'Vive La France!' on the blackboard. The village people too show their patriotism by being present for M. Hamel's last French lesson.

Pain and Regret One of the sub-themes of the story is pain and regret wherein the order raises the feeling of pain and regret in everyone. The people of Alsace are pained as their right to speak and write in their mother tongue is taken away from them. There is regret in not learning their mother tongue on time. This regret is heavily associated with education. Franz, the village people and even M. Hamel himself regrets not giving priority to studying French. This leads to the feelings of regret as the opportunity will now be lost to them.

NCERT Folder

Think as you Read (NCERT Page 7)

1. What was Franz expected to be prepared with for school that day?

Ans. Franz was expected to be prepared with his lesson on participles. M. Hamel, his French teacher, had announced that he would question the class on participles.

2. What did Franz notice that was unusual about the school that day?

Ans. Franz noticed many unusual things about school that day. First, normally when the school began there was much commotion, which was missing that day. Second, his teacher, M. Hamel, had worn his ceremonial clothes. Third, and the most unusual, the village people were sitting quietly on the back benches, which were usually empty on other days.

3. What had been put up on the bulletin-board?

Ans. An order that had come from Berlin had been put up on the bulletin-board. The order was that from the next day onwards, only German would be taught in the schools of Alsace and Lorraine. The new teacher for German would join the school from the following day.

Think as you Read (NCERT Page 8)

1. What changes did the order from Berlin cause in school that day?

Ans. The order from Berlin caused the French language to be stopped from being taught in the schools of Alsace and Lorraine from that day. It stated that only German will be taught in the schools from the next day.

As a result, that day, everyone was attending the last French lesson. M. Hamel was gentle in class and did not scold anyone. Further, the village people attended the lesson and everyone present in the class paid full attention to what was being taught.

2. How did Franz's feelings about M. Hamel and school change?

Ans. Franz's feelings about M. Hamel and school changed when M. Hamel told the students about the order from Berlin and that it was their last French lesson. Franz forgot about his teacher's ruler and crankiness; instead, he started liking M. Hamel. His feelings towards his school also changed, as he did not want to give up his books and lessons, which seemed to be his old friends.

Understanding the Text (NCERT Page 9)

1. The people in this story suddenly realise how precious their language is to them. What shows you this? Why does this happen?

Ans. When the order had come from Berlin that henceforth only German would be taught in schools, people realised that it was the last day to learn their precious mother tongue. To show their affection for the language, many elderly people came to attend the school, occupying the last benches, which had usually remained vacant earlier.

Franz regretted not having learnt the participles, when M. Hamel suddenly made them aware of the fact that they would become a laughing stock before the Germans. Their language was their identity, the 'key' to their prison. The strongest evidence of how important their language was can be taken from M. Hamel's mesmerising last lesson.

Everyone was extremely attentive. Franz too found the lesson quite easy to understand, whereas earlier he had found the French classes very difficult.

2. Franz thinks, "Will they make them sing in German, even the pigeons?" What could this mean? (There could be more than one answer.)

Ans. Franz's thought could have any of the meanings given below.

(a) He may have meant that they all had grown up using French as their language. Now, taking it away from them would be unfair and unkind. The language was as natural to them as cooing is to pigeons. Robbing them of it and forcing German on them would be not only difficult but also next to impossible.

(b) It is difficult for people to accept a language which is imposed on them. French was their mother tongue and they were comfortable using it as their own. It would not be easy to switch to a different language.

(c) Language is a tool for communication. Adopting a new language causes pain and discomfort. It was not going to be easy for them to adapt to the new situation, that is, adopt German that was forced on to them. Moreover, they identified with the French language. It was a factor that helped them bond with their countrymen.

Talking about the Text (NCERT Page 9)

1. "When a people are enslaved, as long as they hold fast to their language it is as if they had the key to their prison." Can you think of examples in history where a conquered people had their language taken away from them or had a language imposed on them?

Ans. There are many examples in history where conquered people had their language taken away from them or had a language imposed on them. Some of them are

(a) The Germanic tribes conquered the native Brythonic people of what is now England and imposed their culture and language upon them.

(b) When Puerto Rico became a possession of the United States as a consequence of the Spanish-American War, its population used the Spanish language. The Americans imposed English as the co-official language.

(c) The conquests of territories by Napoleon led to an imposition of French language on the people of the conquered areas as the official language in all the territories.

2. What happens to a linguistic minority in a state? How do you think they can keep their language alive? For example: Punjabis in Bangalore, Tamilians in Mumbai, Kannadigas in Delhi or Gujaratis in Kolkata.

Ans. A linguistic minority in a state cannot exercise linguistic skills like the natives of the state. At the workplace and educational organisations, English/Hindi or any other link language helps cope with the work and learning process. But, when it comes to understanding the basic norms of society, in order to socialise and communicate, they face linguistic barriers.

To keep their language alive, the linguistic minorities can form small communities where they can celebrate their festivals as per their traditions. They can also continue to speak their native language in their homes and make their children learn the language. They should also try to visit their native places at regular intervals to stay close to their roots.

3. Is it possible to carry pride in one's language too far? Do you know what 'linguistic chauvinism' means?

Ans. Yes, it is possible to carry pride in one's language too far. This happens when one is so fond of their language that they do not consider the other languages as important. They insult people who speak other language and try to impose their own language on others.

When the sense of belonging to one's own language crosses the line between 'pride' and 'being proud', it becomes linguistic chauvinism. If people feel good about their languages and traditions, they must have tolerance for other languages too.

Everybody has the right to follow the religion as well as speak the language as per their desire. In fact, it is denigrating to distort the names of communities, like Bongs for Bengalis, Gujjus for Gujratis and so on.

Working with Words (NCERT Page 9)

1. English is a language that contains words from many other languages. This inclusiveness is one of the reasons it is now a world language. For example

Petite	—	**French**
Kindergarten	—	**German**
Capital	—	**Latin**
Democracy	—	**Greek**
Bazaar	—	**Hindi**

Find out the origins of the following words.

(i) Tycoon	**(ii) Tulip**
(iii) Logo	**(iv) Bandicoot**
(v) Barbecue	**(vi) Veranda**
(vii) Robot	**(viii) Zero**
(ix) Ski	**(x) Trek**

Ans.

Words	**Origin**
(i) Tycoon	Japanese (*taikun*)
(ii) Tulip	French (*tulipe*)
(iii) Logo	Greek (*logos*)
(iv) Bandicoot	Telugu (*pandikokku*)
(v) Barbecue	Spanish (*barbacoa*)
(vi) Veranda	Portuguese (*varanda*)
(vii) Robot	Czech (*robota*)
(viii) Zero	Arabic (*sifr*)
(ix) Ski	Norwegian (*ski*)
(x) Trek	Dutch (*trekken*)

2. **Notice the underlined words in these sentences and tick the option that best explains their meaning**

(i) **"What a thunderclap these words were to me!"**

The words were

(a) loud and clear.

(b) startling and unexpected.

(c) pleasant and welcome.

(ii) **"When a people are enslaved, as long as they hold fast to their language, it is as if they had the key to their prison".**

It is as if they have the key to the prison as long as they

(a) do not lose their language.

(b) are attached to their language.

(c) quickly learn the conqueror's language.

(iii) **Don't go so fast, you will get to your school in plenty of time.**

You will get to your school

(a) very late (b) too early (c) early enough

(iv) **I never saw him look so tall.**

M. Hamel

(a) had grown physically taller

(b) seemed very confident

(c) stood on the chair

Ans. (i) (b) startling and unexpected

(ii) (b) are attached to their language

(iii) (c) early enough

(iv) (b) seemed very confident

Exam Pattern Questions

Extract Based Questions

Read the extracts given below and answer the questions that follow.

1. **When I passed the town hall there was a crowd in front of the bulletin board. For the last two years all our bad news had come from there–the lost battles, the draft, the orders of the commanding officer– and I thought to myself, without stopping. "What can be the matter. Now?"**

Then, as I hurried by as fast as I could go, the blacksmith, Wachter, who was there, with his apprentice, reading the bulletin, called after me, "Don't go so fast, bub: you'll get to your school in plenty of time!"

I thought he was making fun of me, and reached M. Hamel's little garden all out of breath.

(i) **What do you think is the significance of the bulletin board and the crowd around it?**

(ii) **Select the correct option from those given in brackets to fill in the blank.**

'The matter' is related to .... (language/territory)

(iii) **Complete the following suitably.**

Franz was late for his lesson because ....

(iv) **How do you understand Watcher, the Blackmith's advice to Franz?**

(v) **Based on the above extract, choose the statement that is true for Franz.**

(a) Franz wanted to stop by the bulletin board.

(b) Franz was irritated upon going to school.

(c) Franz did not like the blacksmith.

(d) Franz had no idea that it was his last French lesson.

(vi) **Select the option that completes the given sentence appropriately.**

'the lost battles, the draft, the orders of the commanding officer' in the given context would refer to ....

(a) the news that come from the bulletin board

(b) general knowledge regarding France

(c) government decisions regarding Alsace

(d) the reason for the crowd

Ans (i) The bulletin board plays a significant role as it has been the source of all bad news for the people of Alsace for the last two years. The crowd presents the eagerness of people to learn the news development of the war as they may bring about a change in their lives.

(ii) language

(iii) he was distracted by his surroundings and wanted to enjoy the day outside instead of going to his lesson

(iv) Watcher, the Blacksmith's advice to Franz seems genuine for he knows that by going so fast, Franz could fall and hurt himself. Further, as he had read the bulletin board, he was aware that Franz's attempt will be futile as it was his last French lesson.

(v) (d) Franz had no idea that it was his last French lesson.

(vi) (a) the news that come from the bulletin board

2. **Usually, when school began, there was a great bustle, which could be heard out in the street, the opening and closing of desks, lessons repeated in unison, very loud, with our hands over our ears to understand better, and the teacher's great ruler rapping on the table. But now it was all so still! I had counted on the commotion to get to my desk without being seen; but, of course, that day everything had to be as quiet as Sunday morning. Through the window I saw my classmates, already in their places, and M. Hamel walking up and down with his terrible iron ruler under his arm.**

(i) **How would you judge the atmosphere of the school on the day of the last lesson?**

(ii) **Select the correct option from those given in brackets to fill in the blank.**

M. Hamel can be understood to be .... (strict/stoic) as he is standing in the given extract.

(iii) **Complete the following suitably.**

There was usually a great bustle and noise when school began, but it was all very quiet. This observations brings out the feelings of .... in Franz.

(iv) **Did Franz succeed in entering the class without getting noticed?**

(v) **Why was Franz afraid to enter the class?**

(a) Because he was not prepared
(b) Because the villagers had gathered over there
(c) Because he was late and saw M. Hamel walking up and down
(d) Because he was not dressed properly

(vi) **What was observed when the school began usually?**

(a) A lot of activity leading to noise
(b) Cleanliness of the school premises
(c) Lessons of the patriotism
(d) Focus on the language

Ans. (i) The atmosphere of the school on the day the last lesson was strange and quite. It was the last French lesson and everyone in the school was sad and sombre which was reflected in its atmosphere.

(ii) strict

(iii) disappointment and anxiety

(iv) No, Franz could not succeed in entering the class without getting noticed because he expected the class to be noisy but it was very quiet.

(v) (c) Because he was late and saw M. Hamel walking up and down

(vi) (a) A lot of activity leading to noise

3. **What a thunderclap these words were to me! Oh, the wretches; that was what they had put up at the town-hall! My last French lesson! Why, I hardly knew how to write! I should never learn anymore! I must stop there, then! Oh, how sorry I was for not learning my lessons, for seeking birds' eggs, or going sliding on the Saar! My books, that had seemed such a nuisance a while ago, so heavy to carry, my grammar, and my history of the saints, were old friends now that I couldn't give up. And M. Hamel, too; the idea that he was going away, that I should never see him again, made me forget all about his ruler and how cranky he was.** **CBSE SQP 2024**

(i) **What was the writer's purpose in using the metaphor of a 'thunderclap'?**

(ii) **Select the correct option from those given in brackets to fill in the blank.**

The use of exclamatory marks in the first five sentences of the extract serves to express the speaker's .... (hidden/intense) emotions.

(iii) **Complete the following suitably.**

The activities of seeking birds' eggs and sliding on the Saar reveal two things about Franz's character before his change in perspective. First, his youthful carefree nature and second, his preference for ....

(iv) **What is reflected through the shift in the speaker's perception of M. Hamel, conveyed through his readiness to forget the ruler?**

(v) **Select the textual option that is closest to indicating a sense of panic.**

(a) Oh, how sorry I was for not learning my lessons...
(b) Why, I hardly knew how to write!
(c) Oh, the wretches; that was what they had put up at the town-hall!
(d) And M. Hamel, too;

(vi) **What does the following line from the extract, showcase?**

My books, that had seemed such a nuisance a while ago, so heavy to carry, my grammar, and my history of the saints, were old friends now that I couldn't give up.

(a) Realisation
(b) Confusion
(c) Expectation
(d) Affirmation

Ans. (i) The writer's purpose in using the metaphor of a 'thunderclap' is to emphasise the suddenness and shock of Franz's understanding about the importance of his education.

(ii) intense

(iii) play over study

(iv) The shift in the speaker's perception of M. Hamel, conveyed through his readiness to forget the ruler reflects a newfound respect and appreciation, overshadowing past fears of discipline and strictness.

(v) (b) Why, I hardly knew how to write!

(vi) (a) Realisation

4. **My Last French Lesson! Why, I hardly knew how to write! I should never learn any more! I must stop there, then! Oh, how sorry I was for not learning my lessons, for seeking birds' eggs or going sliding on the Saar! My books, that had seemed such a nuisance a while ago, so heavy to carry, my grammar, and my history of the saints, were old friends now that I couldn't give up and M. Hamel, too; the idea that he was going away, that I should never see him again, made me forget all about his ruler and how cranky he was.**

Poor man! It was in honour of this last lesson that he had put on his fine Sunday clothes, and now I understood why the old men of the village were sitting there in the back of the room. It was because they were sorry, too, that they had not gone to school more. It was their way of thanking our master for his forty years of faithful service and of showing their respect for the country that was theirs no more. **CBSE 2025**

(i) **Choose the correct option.**

What is the tone of the speaker in the expression I hardly knew how to write.... how sorry I was for not learning my lessons'?

(a) Confused (b) Regretful
(c) Surprised (d) Happy

(ii) **Choose the correct option.**

The speaker refers to 'seeking birds' egg' and 'sliding on the Saar' as

(a) part of his routine
(b) his daily routine
(c) source of distraction from learning
(d) fun time with friends

(iii) **What is reflected through the shift in the speaker's perception of his books through his expression of calling them his 'old friends' rather than considering them as 'nuisance'?**

(iv) **Select the correct option from those given in bracket to fill in the blank.**

"It was because they were sorry too...."

They were sorry for .... (not following the government order/not learning their language).

(v) **What is inferred from the expression 'the country that was theirs no more'?**

(vi) **What does M. Hamel's ruler reflect about his image?**

Ans. (i) (b) Regretful

(ii) (c) source of distraction from learning

(iii) The shift in the speaker's perception of his books reflects his deep regret and newfound appreciation for education. What once felt like a burden now feels invaluable, as he realises the importance of learning only when it is too late.

(iv) not learning their language

(v) The expression 'the country that was theirs no more' refers to the loss of their homeland to the Prussians, meaning that the people of Alsace and Lorraine would no longer be able to learn or use their native French language freely.

(vi) M. Hamel's ruler reflects his strict and authoritative image as a teacher. It symbolises discipline, but by the end of the lesson, it also represents his deep commitment to teaching and his sorrow for the loss of the French language.

5. **I heard M. Hamel say to me, "I won't scold you, little Franz; you must feel bad enough. See how it is ! Every day we have said to ourselves. Bah! I've plenty of time I'II learn it tomorrow. And now you see where we've come out. Ah, that's the great trouble with Alsace; she puts off learning till tomorrow. Now those fellows out there will have the right to say to you. 'How is it; you pretend to be Frenchmen, and yet can neither speak nor write your own language?' But, you are not the worst, poor little Franz. We've all a great deal to reproach ourselves with."** **CBSE 2024 Modified**

(i) **Identify the line from the text that reinforces the theme of patriotism in the story.**

(ii) **Select the correct option from those given in brackets to fill in the blank.**

She puts off learning till tomorrow. The phrase 'Puts off' suggests .... (to become sad/ delaying)

(iii) **Complete the sentence appropriately.**

'You must feel bad enough'. Through these words M. Hamel urges the people that ....

(iv) **State whether the following statement is True or False with reference to the extract.**

M. Hamel endorses the belief that there is plenty of time to learn their language.

(v) **'And now you see where we've come out.'**

The tone of M. Hamel in the above line is that of

(a) kindness
(b) happiness
(c) regret
(d) enthusiasm

(vi) **'We've all a great deal to reproach ourselves with'**

Select the option, which conveys the meaning of 'reproach' as reflected in the above line.

(a) The player received a reprimand for breach of rules.

(b) The students approached the management with a demand for new canteen.

(c) The clerk received a letter of appreciation for his innovative ideas.

(d) She could not find a way to broach the subject with her boss.

Ans. (i) The line that reinforces the theme of patriotism in the story is the line where M. Hamel wrote on the blackboard - 'Vive La France!'. This phrase translates to 'Long live France' highlighting M. Hamel's patriotism towards his country, France, even in such a dire situation where French language had been prohibited in Alsace and Lorraine.

(ii) delaying

(iii) they let the chance of learning their language slip away, and they might never get that opportunity again.

(iv) False. M. Hamel endorses the belief that we should learn our language as soon as possible.

(v) (c) regret

(vi) (a) The player received a reprimand for breach of rules.

6. **M. Hamel went on to talk of the French language, saying that it was the most beautiful language in the world — the clearest, the most logical; that we must guard it among us and never forget it, because when a people are enslaved, as long as they hold fast to their language it is as if they had the key to their prison. Then he opened a grammar book and read us our lesson. I was amazed to see how well I understood it. All he said seemed so easy, so easy!**

(i) **What do the given lines tell us about M. Hamel?**

(ii) **Select the correct option from those given in brackets to fill in the blank.**

Franz was able to understand the grammar lesson easily because he was .... (introspective/receptive)

(iii) **Complete the sentence suitably.**

According to M. Hamel, Language plays an important role in the freedom of a nation because ....

(iv) **Comment on the tone of the given extract.**

(v) **Select the option that completes the given sentence appropriately.**

'Prison' in the given context would refer to ....

(a) discrimination due to community

(b) enslavement by a different nation

(c) lack of freedom to enjoy your own culture

(d) ban from participation is festivities

(vi) **Based on the above extract, choose the statement that is TRUE for M. Hamel.**

(a) M. Hamel does not want to leave his school.

(b) M. Hamel adores Franz.

(c) M. Hamel wants the people to guard their language.

(d) M. Hamel wants to fight the German leaders.

Ans. (i) The given lines show us that M. Hamel was a courageous and a patriotic man. Even though, he was overwhelmed with his sadness, he took his last lesson sincerely.

(ii) receptive

(iii) as long as people hold on to and use their native language, they have the key to their freedom

(iv) The tone of the given extract is full of patriotism and emotion as the speaker applauds their mother tongue and requests the listener to practice the language. He also presents the importance of language for an individual and a community.

(v) (b) enslavement by a different nation

(vi) (c) M. Hamel wants the people to guard their language.

Short Answer Type Questions

1. **Why did Franz not want to go to school that day?**

Or What tempted Franz to stay away from school?

Ans. Franz did not want to go to school that day because he feared that he would be scolded as he had not prepared his lesson on participles, on which his French teacher M. Hamel was to question the class that day. Besides, the warm and bright weather, the chirping of birds and the sight of the marching of Prussian soldiers also tempted Franz to stay away from school.

2. **What was more tempting for Franz than the rule for participles? Did he get tempted?** CBSE 2024

Ans. The chirping of birds and the sight of the marching Prussian soldiers was more tempting for Franz than learning about the rule for participles. Moreover, the weather was bright and warm which tempted Franz to run away and spend the day outside. No, he suppressed the temptation.

3. **What surprises awaited Franz as he entered the classroom?**

Or What did Franz wonder about when he entered the class that day?

Ans. When Franz entered class that day, he was expecting a scolding from M. Hamel but he spoke very kindly to Franz and asked him to sit. Franz also wondered about the presence of senior villagers occupying back benches of the class.

4. How did Franz plan to turn the commotion in the classrooom to his favour? CBSE 2025

Ans. Franz planned to take advantage of the noise and distraction in the classroom by slipping unnoticed into his seat. He was late for school and afraid of being scolded by M. Hamel, so he hoped the commotion would divert the teacher's attention from his tardiness.

5. How different did M. Hamel look that particular morning in 'The Last Lesson'?

Or What was unusual about M. Hamel's dress on his last day in the school?

Ans. M. Hamel's dress on his last day in the school consisted of his beautiful green coat, frilled shirt, and a little black silk cap, all embroidered, that he never wore except on inspection and prize days.

6. Why was M. Hamel dressed in formal clothes in school? CBSE 2023

Ans. M. Hamel was dressed in formal clothes in school on that day because it was his last French Lesson and he wanted to make it special.

7. Comment on the significance of the villagers sitting at the back in M. Hamel's classroom. CBSE SQP 2021

Why did the elders of the village attend the last lesson? CBSE 2020

Or Why did the village elders occupy the back benches in the classroom to attend the last lesson delivered by M. Hamel?

Ans. The village elders occupied the back benches in the classroom to attend the last lesson delivered by M. Hamel because they were sorry that they had not attended school more often. They also wanted to thank their teacher for his forty years of faithful service and to show their respect for the country that was no longer theirs.

8. "This is your last French lesson." How did Franz react to this declaration of M. Hamel?

Or "What a thunderclap these words were to me!" (Franz) What were those words and what was their effect on Franz?

Ans. The announcement made by M. Hamel that there was an order from Berlin to stop teaching French, and that this was their last French lesson, seemed to be a thunderclap to Franz. He was shocked and sad to realise that he would no longer be able to learn French, his mother tongue anymore.

9. What changes came over little Franz after he heard M. Hamel's announcement?

Ans. After hearing the announcement, Franz was very sad and he regretted not learning his lessons, and suddenly being deprived of the opportunity to learn his own mother tongue. His books suddenly became his 'old friends' whom he could not abandon.

10. Who did M. Hamel blame when Franz was unable to answer a question on French participles? CBSE SQP 2020

Or Who did M. Hamel blame for the neglect of learning on the part of boys like Franz?

Or "We've all a great deal to reproach ourselves with," said M. Hamel. Comment.

Ans. M. Hamel blames both the children's parents and himself for the neglect of learning on the part of boys like Franz. The parents sent the children out to work instead of sending them to school. He blamed himself for making the students do his personal work during school time and giving them a holiday when he wanted to go fishing.

11. How did M. Hamel praise the French language?

Ans. M. Hamel called French the most beautiful language in the world. According to him, it was the clearest and the most logical language. He wanted the people of France to guard or preserve it amongst themselves and never forget it.

12. What shows M. Hamel's love for the French language?

Ans. M. Hamel had taught the French language in the school for forty years and was overwhelmed with emotions when he realised that the villagers would not be able to learn it any more. He wanted them to preserve the language with them, thus showing his love for the language.

13. How is the mother tongue important to a person? What does M. Hamel, the teacher say about it? CBSE 2020

Ans. The mother tongue is the representative of a nation's true identity and character. It acts as a binding force, creating unity among the countrymen. M. Hamel rightly said that when people are enslaved, as long as they hold fast to their language, it is as if they had the key to their prison.

14. Franz was able to understand everything that day. Why?

Ans. Franz thought that probably he had never paid much attention in the class, and that M. Hamel had never explained everything with so much patience. Perhaps, these were the very reasons that he was able to understand everything that day.

15. What did M. Hamel teach the class in his 'last lesson'?

Ans. In his 'last lesson', M. Hamel taught the class about grammar, then about writing and finally a lesson in history. More than this, he made his students realise the importance of their mother tongue, and taught them to take pride in their language.

16. **Explain the inference that can be drawn from the line.**
'Will they make them sing in German, even the pigeons?' CBSE 2024

Ans. The given statement by Franz shows that the Frenchmen were full of hatred against the Germans. Besides, they feared German atrocities. They thought that they would be forced to read German and no one will be spared.

17. **What was M. Hamel's contribution to the school in Alsace?**

Ans. M. Hamel had given forty years of long and faithful service to the school. Though the students found him cranky, he was a true Frenchman at heart, who took immense pride in teaching his mother tongue. He loved the school and wanted the children to love their language.

18. **What does the contrasting imagery of the church clock and the Prussian trumpets represent, in 'The Last Lesson'?** CBSE SQP 2024

Ans. The contrasting imagery of the church clock and the Prussian trumpets represents the tension between local traditions and foreign occupation. The church clock is a symbol of local, everyday life and continuity. In contrast stands the Prussian trumpets, which symbolise disruption, military power and the enforcement of foreign rule. This contrast highlights the theme of loss and the struggle to preserve one's cultural heritage against overwhelming odds.

19. **How did M. Hamel say farewell to his students and the people of the town?**

Ans. Towards the end of his 'last lesson', M. Hamel stood up to say farewell to his students and the people of the town. He then turned to the blackboard and wrote, 'Vive La France'. Then he dismissed the class with a gesture of his hand.

20. **When do the residents of Alsace realise how precious their language is to them?** CBSE 2023

Ans. The residents of Alsace realised the importance and preciousness of their language when the order from Berlin stating that only German would be taught in schools came.

21. **If this had been M. Hamel's first lesson, how do you think the school experience of the students might have been impacted?** CBSE Question Bank 2021

Ans. If this lesson had been M. Hamel's first lesson, the school experience of the students would have been different. M. Hamel would be just a stranger for them. They would not have become attached to him as they are now. In his first lesson, he wouldn't get such a good and respectful response from students as well as the elders as he was getting now.

22. **Little Franz is the narrator of the story. The name 'Franz' means 'from France'.**
In what way does the story being told as a first-person narrative of Franz impact your reading and understanding of the story? Provide at least one evidence from the text to support your opinion. Competency Based

Ans. Using the first person narrative of a child from the village, the reader is made to experience what the protagonist is experiencing.

This is very evident when Franz gets to know about the order and feels that the words were a 'thunderclap'. We, as readers, can feel the shock and surprise felt by Franz as if it is happening to us.

23. **'You realise the true value of a thing only on losing it'. Comment on this statement in the light of the story, 'The Last Lesson'.**

Ans. The given statement stands true for Franz and all the people of Alsace. The residents of Alsace did not give any importance to their native French language and their teacher M. Hamel. They preferred everything over sending their children to school for learning their language.

They never took M. Hamel or his classes were not taken seriously. It is only after Prussians put a ban on the French language and M. Hamel was ordered to leave the country that people realised the importance to holding onto their mother tongue and started respecting their teacher.

24. **"...when a people are enslaved, as long as they hold fast to their language it is as if they had the key to their prison."**
Do you agree or disagree with the above statement from 'The Last Lesson'? Support your opinion in 40-50 words with a reason that is factual or based on your experiences. Competency Based

Ans. I disagree with the given statement. I think if people are enslaved, they need a lot more than preservation of their language in order to be free. For instance, during Apartheid in South Africa, non-white people only got freedom and equality when a democratic government was formed and new laws were enacted. In such situations, policy level changes to need to be made for people to actually be free.

Further, while language is an important part of our identity, there are other aspects like religion which can help us preserve our culture.

25. **"I' ve plenty oftime. I' ll learn it tomorrow. And now you see where we've come out".**
What does M. Hamel mean to convey through these lines? CBSE 2025

Ans. Through these lines, M. Hamel conveys the regret of neglecting one's duty. He emphasises that procrastination leads to loss, as the students never valued their language lessons until it was too late. Now, when French is being banned, they realise the importance of learning it.

Long Answer Type Questions

1. The order from Berlin created a great enthusiasm in the school. Comment. CBSE 2020

Or The order from Berlin banning teaching of French stunned everyone. Comment.

Ans. The order from Berlin had stunned everyone because it stopped the teaching of the French language in the schools of Alsace and Lorraine. French was the mother tongue of the residents of these provinces so this development was unthinkable. Instead of French, they would now be taught German. This shocking development suddenly aroused a lot of zeal in various people in the story to learn their native language. M. Hamel, the French teacher, changed his behaviour from being a cranky and strict teacher to that of a very kind person, as it would be his last lesson, and he would be going away the next day. He also taught with more understanding and patience.

Franz was not interested in learning the language earlier but now suddenly realised what he had been missing and became very attentive in class. The villagers regretted that they did not utilise the opportunities given to them for learning French when it was possible; so, they had turned up in full strength for the last lesson.

2. The last lesson reflects the flaws in human character that led to the sad plight of people in Alsace. Substantiate your answer with evidence from the text. CBSE 2023

Ans. 'The Last Lesson' by Alphonse Daudet is a story about the loss of a language and culture due to war and political conflicts. The story highlights the flaws in human character that lead to the sad plight of people in Alsace.

One of the key flaws is the tendency of people to take their language and culture for granted. The protagonist, Franz, was a young boy who did not take his French lessons seriously, believing that he could always learn them later on. He only realised the importance of his language when it was too late and he was about to lose it.

Another flaw highlighted in the story is the tendency of people to prioritise their personal interests over the greater good. The German officials were more concerned with asserting their power and control over the region than with preserving the local language and culture. They did not consider the emotional and cultural impact that their actions would have on the people of Alsace.

In conclusion, 'The Last Lesson' portrays the tragic consequences of human flaws such as taking language and culture for granted and prioritising personal interests over the greater good. The story serves as a cautionary tale about the importance of valuing and preserving one's language and culture, and the dangers of political conflicts that threaten to destroy them.

3. Educating children is the responsibility of society. Justify the statement in view of 'The Last Lesson'. CBSE 2020

Ans. It is true to say that educating children is the responsibility of a society as teaching and learning cannot take place in an isolated situation. Teachers play an important role in the society as they impart the education that makes us a social and responsible citizens of a country. Often students don't take interest in the subject when the teacher becomes unreasonably strict. A teacher who is very understanding and sympathetic can instill confidence in students and encourage learning.

Little Franz had less interest in his lessons as M. Hamel was very strict and often scolded him. But in his last lesson, he doesn't scold Franz for reaching the class late. When he got confused while reciting, the teacher was very understanding and patient. After that, whatever he taught in the class was well understood by Franz. He took great interest in the class and felt pity that the teacher was going away. This shows that the change in Franz's attitude was genuine and realistic.

Further, apart from teachers, parents are also responsible in promoting education. M. Hamel criticised the people of Alsace because he knew that in his society the people give education a secondary position. Instead of sending their children to school, they send them to earn money. Therefore, it is in his last lesson that the village society realises the importance of education.

4. Everybody during the last lesson is filled with regret. Comment.

Ans. It is true to say that everybody was filled with regret in the last lesson. M. Hamel is filled with regret because he had not taken enough interest in teaching French, as he often sent students for petty errands and gave them a holiday when he didn't want to teach. Franz regretted that he had not been learning his lessons, but skipping school for enjoying other activities. He also regretted that M. Hamel was going away, and that he would never see him again, despite his strictness and crankiness. The villagers regretted that they did not utilise the opportunities given to them for learning French when it was possible. Hence, they had turned up in full strength for the last lesson. Thus, all of them regretted that this was their last lesson in French.

5. After reading the chapter, you realise that man has an intense desire to subjugate others. You feel that in the modern world, there is a strong need for brotherhood. Write an article in 120-150 words for a national magazine on this. Competency Based

Ans.

What will You Conquer?

by Sunil

The modern world is a world of selfishness and exploitation. In this world, to fulfill our need to be superior, we commit acts which harm others. As a result, wars, tensions, turmoil and conflicts are a common feature of this world. A very poignant example is present in Daudet's story 'The Last Lesson' which is set in the background of the Franco-Prussian war. After the war, France lost two of its provinces to Germany. The Germans passed the order in these provinces, Alsace and Lorraine, that from now on only German will be taught in the schools. The imposition of German over French was humiliating for the local residents. It filled the people with great patriotic feelings. Suddenly, on the roof when the pigeons coo in a low tone, Franz asks himself whether they will make the pigeons also sing in German.

This remark is a Frenchman's typical reaction to the imposition of learning German. The attitude of the French is full of hate and desperation as they realise that their mother tongue and a well-respected personality of the society is being banned from their land. M. Hamel has to leave the country so that the new German teacher can teach the language of the subjugators. This shows that the Germans can go to all lengths to show their power to French people. Such acts undermine national identity, kindness and humanity. Thus, in today's world, only the feeling of compassion, tolerance and brotherhood towards our fellow beings can lead us towards peace and prosperity.

6. One's culture, language and art can be a way to exercise one's freedom when one is oppressed. Comment with reference to 'The Last Lesson' and 'Aunt Jennifer's Tigers'. **Competency Based**

Ans. It is true to say that culture, language and art can be a way to exercise one's freedom when one is oppressed. They provide an agency to fight back against all forms of suppression. In fact, language and many art forms have been used by artists to present their views on cases of oppression. Two such pieces of literature are 'The Last Lesson' and 'Aunt Jennifer's Tigers'.

In 'The Last Lesson', Daudet present how a community is suppressed through language and how language itself is the means of their freedom. M. Hamel is the key character who presents how language can be used to maintain one's identity and can be the key to any prison.

In the poem 'Aunt Jennifer's Tigers', the Aunt is oppressed under the male dominated concept of marriage. She finds her voice and expresses her freedom in the forms of her embroidery of tigers. Her tigers represents what she wants to become as they stand in stark contrast to her own character.

Thus, one can find many such instances wherein language and art has been used to exercise one's freedom.

7. At the end of his last lesson, M. Hamel decides to leave a little note for each of his students for them to find the next day at their desks. Based on your reading of the story, what might his note to Franz read?

You may begin like this

Dear Franz, I know you have always preferred to run in the open fields... **Competency Based**

Ans. Dear Franz, I know you have always preferred to run in the open fields, collect birds' eggs and spend time in nature. But you must also realise the fact that there are some things that we are responsible about. For example we have duties to our family, society and nation.

Learning our mother tongue is one of our prime responsibilities. We, the people of Alsace and Lorraine, have not done this duty sincerely. As a result, we have been invaded by the Prussians. Now that they have imposed their language on us, we have realised how much we love our language.

But mere love without commitment is nothing.
I saw in my last lesson that you were greatly hurt at the loss of the freedom to learn French. I appeal to you not lose heart. Keep making efforts to learn French. Soon, we will be free again.

Sincerely,
M. Hamel

8. Comment on regret as a theme with any two examples from the story 'The Last Lesson'. In the examples, do you think the characters' regret is justified? Explain in 120-150 words. **Competency Based**

Ans. The theme of regret runs through the story 'The Last Lesson'. The atmosphere of regret can be felt in the school's environment. When Franz enters the school, he can feel a sense of sorrow and regret. The school is completely quiet when it is full of hustle and bustle on the other days. Even when Franz enters the classroom, he notices the elders from his village sitting in the class. When M. Hamel finally announces that was their last French lesson, Franz himself is filled with regret.

He realises that the villagers regret not only learning their language well enough but also are now afraid of losing their identity as Frenchmen. Franz is distressed as well and feels regret for not taking his French lessons seriously. He wishes that he could get another chance to learn the language.

Besides, Franz and the villagers, M. Hamel is also regretful. He regrets and blames himself for giving too many holidays to the students and sending them on errands.

No, I don't think regret is justified. No one could have predicted how things would turn out and it is not correct to blame oneself for little things in the past.

Or Yes, I think that the regret is justified because it is important to establish one's identity as a citizen of a country. It is important to learn one's language and know about one's culture

SELF ASSESSMENT TEST

Extract Based Questions

Read the extract given below and answer the questions that follow.

1. "Your parents were not anxious enough to have you learn. They preferred to put you to work on a farm or at the mills, so as to have a little more money. And I? I've been to blame also. Have I not often sent you to water my flowers instead of learning your lessons? And when I wanted to go fishing, did I not just give you a holiday?"

(i) When did M. Hamel give students a holiday?

(ii) Select the correct option from those given in bracket to fill in the blank.

The narrator seems to be .... (angry/regretful) about losing on teaching French.

(iii) Complete the sentence suitably.

The speaker of the given lines blames himself for giving a .... for ....

(iv) Rationalise, to support the given opinion.

The parents feel guilty for not sending their children to school after listening to M. Hamel.

(v) Why did Franz's parents put him to work?

(a) To make him realise the importance of work
(b) To earn a little more money
(c) To punish him for his callous attitude
(d) To pay his school fees

(vi) The speaker of the given lines is giving what seems to be a/an ....

(a) lecture
(b) advice
(c) sermon
(d) judgement

Short Answer Type Questions

Answer the following questions in 40-50 words.

1. Franz was not scolded for reaching the school late that day. Explain the reason.

2. What did Franz wonder about when he entered the class that day?

3. How is the title 'The Last Lesson' appropriate?

4. Comment on the old Hauser's act of reading an old primer.

5. Franz's reaction to the news of the order is justified. Elucidate

6. M. Hamel is choked at the end of the class. Give reasons for the same.

Long Answer Type Questions

Answer the following questions in 120-150 words.

1. Our native language is part of our culture and we are proud of it. How does the presence of village elders in the classroom and M. Hamel's last lesson show their love for French?

2. Discuss how the story provides strategies for resistance and protection of one's identity and community through its events and characters. Provide relevant textual details to support your argument.

02

About the Author

Anees Jung

is an Indian author, journalist and columnist. Born into a family of scholars and poets, Anees started her career in writing with the Youth Times, a Times of India publication, where she worked as a journalist and editor. As an author, she had worked to bring out the stories of the marginalised and oppressed communities in India. She has written several books, including 'Unveiling India' and 'Beyond the Tigers : Tracking Rajan'.

YOUR STUDY GOALS

- Chapter Sketch
- About the Characters
- Summary of the Chapter

YOUR PRACTICE GOAL

- NCERT Folder
- Extract Based Questions
- Short Answer Type Questions
- Long Answer Type Questions

Lost Spring

Chapter Sketch

These excerpts are taken from the author's book Lost Spring : Stories of Stolen Childhood. This chapter is divided into two parts containing the author's first-hand-experience with poverty and traditions prevailing in some parts of India. The first part describes the plight of the poor ragpickers of Seemapuri. The second part describes the miserable conditions of the bangle-makers of Firozabad.

About the Characters

The Narrator Anees Jung herself is the narrator who in a simple and straightforward manner presents of vivid image of poverty that affects childhood in the nation. Her writing style is powerful which encourages people to work to better their conditions.

Part 1 - Sometimes I Find a Rupee in the Garbage

Saheb He is a young ragpicker from Seemapuri. He is simple and hopeful of the better future. He believes in the false promises made by powerful people.

Other Young Ragpickers They are some other boys who roam around the streets with Saheb.

Pandit and his Boy These are the characters of a story that the narrator had heard. These characters present how the situation had changed from past to now.

Part 2 - I Want to Drive a Car

Mukesh He is a young boy from Firozabad. He is a daring and a hopeful boy who wants to break free from the fate of bangle-making. He wants to become a motor-mechanic and seems to be determined to do so.

Mukesh's Father He is a bangle maker by profession who regrets not being able to send his sons to school.

Mukesh's Grandmother She represents the generation which thinks that bangle-making has been their destiny.

Mukesh's sister-in-law She is a frail young woman. She seems to be a traditional wife who cooks and practices all marital customs like veiling before male elders.

Savita She is an innocent young girl who is practicing bangle-making with an old women.

Other characters This includes the old lady with Savita and her husband along with some characters who Anees talks to. They present how their situations are bad as they practice bangle-making and live in poverty without any hope of betterment.

Summary of the Chapter

The given chapter comprises of two different interactions with boys who live in poor and dismal condition.

Part 1- Sometimes I Find a Rupee in the Garbage

Saheb: The Ragpicker

The author meets Saheb and his friends when they were looking through the garbage of her neighbourhood. Saheb and his family had come from Dhaka, Bangladesh after their fields were destroyed by storms. They had come to Delhi to find a better livelihood.

When the author asks Saheb about not going to school, she gets to know that his locality has no school. So, the author promises to build a school for him. After some days, when Saheb asks her about the school, the author is embarrassed.

Saheb's real name is Saheb-e-Alam which the author finds ironical. The name means Lord of the Universe which is in contrast with his real situation.

Poor Condition

Saheb and his friends remain barefoot throughout the day. When the author enquires about it, the boys give various reasons. However, the author feels that these are excuses to hide their poverty.

The author then remembers a story told by a man from Udipi. As a boy, he had noticed the priest's son praying for a pair of shoes. This wish was fulfilled as thirty years later, the priest's son has a pair of shoes.

Seemapuri and Ragpickers

The author goes to Seemapuri, a place at Delhi's border. Seemapuri is a home to many Bangladeshi refugees who came here in 1971 and are ragpickers. They live in mud structures with roofs of tin and tarpaulin. There is no water or drainage facility. The ragpickers have been living in 30 years with only valid ration cards. They do not have stable homes and live in areas where they can find food. Children are born in them and become ragpickers.

Over the years, rag-picking has become an art. Garbage is similar to gold for the ragpickers as it provides them income. For children, garbage is filled with wonder as they find different things in it.

Saheb's Lost Childhood

A winter morning, the author sees Saheb outside the neighbourhood club. He was watching a game of tennis. He told the author that he likes the game and sometimes the guard lets him enter the club to ride the swing. That day, the author noticed that Saheb was wearing tennis shoes that were discarded by some rich boy.

Another morning the author sees Saheb at a milk booth. He was carrying a steel canister. He informed the author that now he worked at the tea stall and was paid Rs. 800 and all his meals. The author feels that Saheb is not happy as he has no freedom now.

Part 2- I Want to Drive a Car

Mukesh and Firozabad

In Firozabad, the author meets Mukesh, who wishes to be a motor mechanic and to learn to drive a car. She feels that Mukesh's dream is displaced from his reality.

Firozabad is the center of India's glass-blowing industry. Most families here work in the bangle-making. Even children work in this industry and lose their eyesight. This is so because people do not know that it is illegal for children to work in the glass furnaces with high temperatures, in dirty rooms cells without air and light.

Mukesh's House and Family

Mukesh takes the author to his home. They walk down a path covered in garbage, crossing small and dirty houses with wobbly doors and no windows. Finally, they enter a half-built shack. In the house, the wife of Mukesh's elder brother is cooking the evening meal.

Mukesh's father enters the house and tells the author that he has worked hard all his life. However, he could not educate his sons or build his house. He could only teach them bangle-making. Just then, Mukesh's Grandmother states that bangle-making is their God-given lineage and they could do nothing but make bangles.

Poor Conditions in Firozabad

In Firozabad, the author sees dark houses with flames of flickering oil lamps. Boys and girls are sitting with their parents, making-bangles. The author notices a young girl, Savita, sitting beside an elderly woman. Author wonders about the irony of Savita's life. The old lady tells her how she had not eaten properly in her entire life. Her husband tells her that he had only made a house for his family. This makes author think about if he had achieved something that others have not yet achieved.

Loss of Hope

Nothing has changed in Firozabad and people have lost all their hopes and dreams. When the author asks a group of young men to organise themselves in cooperatives, she learns that even if they do, they are taken to jail for doing something illegal and beaten up. As a result, there is no leader among them.

The author finds two distinct worlds in Firozabad. One is the exploited family which lives in poverty and the other is a vicious circle of sahukars, the middlemen, the politicians, the lawmakers, the policemen and the bureaucrats, who exploit them. These powerful people have created a situation wherein a child accepts bangle making as a profession without much thought.

A Ray of Hope

The author is filled with joy when she finds that Mukesh thinks differently. The boy is filled with hope. His dream of being a motor-mechanic is still alive in his eyes. He is willing to dare. Anees asks Mukesh if he also dreams of flying a plane. Mukesh replies in the negative. He is content to dream of cars, as few planes fly over Firozabad.

Word-Meaning

Word	Meaning
scrounging	seeking or looking for
dumps	heaps
looking for	dreaming of
glibly	fluently but thoughtlessly
hollow	insincere, superficial
shuffles	walks by dragging one's feet along
perpetual state of poverty	being always poor
drowned	overcome or overpowered by
desolation	a state of complete emptiness or destruction
ragpicker(s)	a person who collects and sells rags and other discarded things from garbage
squatter(s)	a person who unlawfully occupies an unused/ uninhabited land or building
wilderness	an uninhabited or abandoned region
tarpaulin	a heavy, hard-wearing waterproof cloth coated with paint
permit(s)	an official document authorising someone to do something
transit homes	temporary homes
proportions	shape or dimension
canister	a round or cylindrical container for storing things
looms	appears
mirage	appearing possible, but not actually so
furnace(s)	an enclosed fireplace for heating metals or materials to a very high temperature
dingy	dark and gloomy
cells	very small rooms

slog their daylight hours	—	work hard throughout the day
brightness of their eyes	—	eyesight
beam	—	shine brightly
hovels	—	a small, dirty and simply constructed building
wobbly	—	moving unsteadily from side to side
primeval	—	ancient, primitive
platters	—	a large flat dish or plate for serving food
impoverished	—	made poor
lineage	—	ancestry
shanty town	—	a town full of, crudely-built huts without sanitation
dark hutments	—	dimly lit huts
welding	—	joining together by heating the surface to the point of melting
soldering	—	joining
tongs	—	movable arms of an instrument, used for holding and picking up things
lament	—	complaint, passionate expression of grief
mind-numbing	—	so extreme or intense as to prevent normal thought
stigma	—	a mark of disgrace; shame
sahukars	—	moneylenders
hurtling	—	moving at high speed

Important Themes of the Chapter

Poverty and Exploitation The prominent theme of the stories presented in 'Lost Spring' is the prevalence of harsh realities faced by underprivileged children in India. Due to poverty and lack of proper resources, children are forced into child labour to support their families, continuing the cycle of poverty.

Denied Childhood Another theme evident in the stories is the denial of the joys and innocence of childhood to the underprivileged. Children are robbed of their childhood by being forced to work in hazardous conditions instead of enjoying their formative years in school and play.

Callousness of Society A subtheme of the story is the selfish and ignorant nature of powerful political people and the society. Powerful people suppress the marginalised, offer incentives and make promises to maintain their power. However, in the end no promises are fulfilled which further increases the hardships of the poor.

NCERT Folder

Think as you Read (NCERT Page 16)

1. What is Saheb looking for in the garbage dumps? Where is he and where has he come from?

Or What does Saheb look for in the garbage dumps?

Ans. In the garbage dumps, Saheb looks for useful items which can be sold for cash. As these items can be traded for money, they are just like 'gold' for him. Saheb and his family live in Seemapuri, a slum on the periphery of Delhi. His family had migrated from Dhaka, Bangladesh.

2. What explanations does the author offer for the children not wearing footwear?

Or What explanation did the children offer the writer for not wearing footwear? Did she agree to it? CBSE 2020

Ans. The author offers various explanations given to her by the children for not wearing shoes. These include simply not caring to take the trouble of taking their slippers down from the shelf to wear them, not wearing footwear is a tradition, and so on. However, she feels that it is simply an excuse to hide a perpetual state of poverty, as many families cannot afford to buy footwear for their children.

3. Is Saheb happy working at the tea-stall? Explain.

Or What job did Saheb take up? Was he happy?

Ans. Saheb took up the job of performing odd jobs at a tea stall. However, he was unhappy because he was tied down by the work he had to do. Thus, he had lost his independence which he earlier had as a ragpicker.

Think as you Read (NCERT Page 19)

1. What makes the city of Firozabad famous?

Ans. Firozabad is the centre of India's glass-blowing industry where families have spent generations working around furnaces to make bangles. Hence, Firozabad is famous for its bangles.

2. Mention the hazards of working in the glass bangles industry.

Ans. There are many hazards of working in the glass bangle industry. The most common of them is the loss of eye sight over a period of time. Bangles are manufactured in glass furnaces with high temperatures, in dingy cells without air and light. Consequently, the children, who spend their day in a closed room near to these hot furnaces often lose the brightness of their eyes. Other hazards are developing lung and brain related diseases.

3. **How is Mukesh's attitude to his situation different from that of his family?**

Or **"It is his karam, his destiny." What is Mukesh's family's attitude towards their situation?**

Or **'When I sense a flash of it in Mukesh. I am cheered.' How is Mukesh's attitude of life different from that of his family and friends?** CBSE 2024

Ans. Mukesh's attitude to his situation is different from that of his family because he is determined to become a car mechanic. His father, a bangle-maker, could not do anything for his family except teach them the art of making bangles. His grandmother accepted her husband's going blind from polishing bangles as 'his karam, his destiny'. She believes that they cannot break their 'God-given lineage'. However, Mukesh does not want to pursue trade.

Understanding the Text (NCERT Page 20)

1. **What could be some of the reasons for the migration of people from villages to cities?**

Ans. People migrate from villages to cities primarily in search of a better livelihood. Most of them leave behind their unproductive fields to find some or the other ways of earning money. Further, people believe that cities offer many opportunities to alleviate poverty while providing facilities that they wouldn't get in the villages.

2. **Would you agree that promises made to poor children are rarely kept? Why do you think this happens in the incidents narrated in the text?**

Ans. I fully agree that the promises made to the poor children are rarely kept. Promises are made both at the national and international levels to provide healthy lives, quality education, protection against abuse, exploitation and violence, etc. Yet, it is estimated that 246 million children are still engaged in child labour, most of them working in hazardous conditions.

In the text, the author asks Saheb half-jokingly if he will enrol in a school that she starts. In reality, the author was not at all serious about starting the school but Saheb thought that she had promised to start one. She did not keep her promise because it was not seriously made.

3. **What forces conspire to keep the workers in the bangle industry of Firozabad in poverty?**

Or **Why does the author say that the bangle-makers are caught in a vicious web?**

Ans. The forces that conspire to keep the workers in the bangle industry of Firozabad in poverty are the people who are in power. These people include the sahukars, the bureaucrats and the policemen who do not allow the people to form cooperative to change their living. Such people use their power and get those who rebel against them arrested. Hence, no one dares to rebel and people continue to live in the perpetuating state of poverty.

Talking about the Text (NCERT Page 20)

1. **How, in your opinion, can Mukesh realise his dream?**

Ans. Mukesh belongs to a family of bangle-makers, but his attitude to his situation is different from that of other family members. He dreams of becoming a motor -mechanic and learning to drive a car. His determination regarding his dreams seems to be very strong.

With his determination, sincere efforts, hard work and the guidance of a garage owner, Mukesh can attain the skills of a mechanic and gradually that of car driving. In this way, he can surely realise his dream.

2. **Mention the hazards of working in the glass bangles industry.**

Ans. Refer to the answer of Q. 2 in 'Think as you Read' (NCERT Page 19) above.

3. **Why should child labour be eliminated and how?**

Ans. Child labour should be eliminated to bring back the 'spring' in the lives of poor children like Saheb and Mukesh. We can do this by inculcating the values to

(i) have a strong will to ensure that all children get basic education. This may be done by helping them join the 'open school' system if they are not able to attend a regular school.

(ii) have a sense of commitment of wanting to help these children. An example can be to find better employment for the adults in their families.

(iii) say 'No' to child labour in any work related to us.

(iv) feel the need to do something for such children, exemplifying the saying, 'where there is a will, there is a way'.

(v) create awareness in society about the plight of the underprivileged so that people in power can help them.

Thinking about Language (NCERT Page 20)

1. **Carefully read the following phrases and sentences taken from the text. Can you identify the literary device in each example?**

(i) Saheb-e-Alam, which means the Lord of the Universe, is directly in contrast to what Saheb is in reality.

(ii) Drowned in an air of desolation.

(iii) Seemapuri, a place on the periphery of Delhi, yet miles away from it, metaphorically.

(iv) For the children it is wrapped in wonder; for the elders it is a means of survival.

(v) As her hands move mechanically like the tongs of a machine, I wonder if she knows the sanctity of the bangles she helps make.

(vi) She still has bangles on her wrist, but not light in her eyes.

(vii) Few airplanes fly over Firozabad.

(viii) Web of poverty.

(ix) Scrounging for gold.

(x) And survival in Seemapuri means rag-picking. Through the years, it has acquired the proportions of a fine art.

(xi) The steel canister seems heavier than the plastic bag he would carry so lightly over his shoulders.

Ans. (i) Irony (ii) Hyperbole
(iii) Contrast (iv) Contrast
(v) Simile (vi) Contrast
(vii) Alliteration (viii) Metaphor
(ix) Hyperbole (x) Hyperbole
(xi) Hyperbole

Exam Pattern Questions

Extract Based Questions

Part 1 : Sometimes I Find a Rupee in the Garbage

Read the extracts given below and answer the questions that follow.

1. "Why do you do this?" I ask Saheb whom I encounter every morning scrounging for gold in the garbage dumps of my neighbourhood. Saheb left his home long ago. Set amidst the green fields of Dhaka, his home is not even a distant memory. There were many storms that swept away their fields and homes, his mother tells him. That's why they left, looking for gold in the big city where he now lives.

"I have nothing else to do," he mutters, looking away.

"Go to school," I say glibly, realising immediately how hollow the advice must sound.

"There is no school in my neighbourhood. When they build one, I will go." **CBSE 2024 Modified**

(i) Explain one inference that can be drawn from the line "......... realising immediately how hollow the advice must sound".

(ii) Select the correct option from those given in brackets to fill in the blank.

The expression 'when they build one, I will go' indicates Saheb's .... (longing/stubbornness) to go to school.

(iii) Complete the sentence with an appropriate word.

Saheb's conversation with the narrator draws .... of readers towards Saheb.

(iv) State whether the following statement is True or False.

'............ his home is not even a distant memory' states that Saheb sees his home often in his dream.

(v) What does the expression 'scrounging for gold' refer to?

(a) Searching for gold items
(b) Looking for something that can fetch money
(c) Rummaging the garbage
(d) Digging to find food to eat

(vi) The influence of nature in Saheb's life was that it

(a) brought prosperity
(b) yielded food for them
(c) gave them home
(d) brought disaster

Ans. (i) It can be inferred from the above line that the narrator's advice was impractical and insensitive as Saheb's circumstances would not allow him the luxury of going to school.

(ii) longing (iii) attention or sympathy

(iv) False. '............ his home is not even a distant memory' states that Saheb remembers his as they had migrated recently.

(v) (b) Looking for something that can fetch money

(vi) (d) brought disaster

2. 'It takes longer to build a school,' I say, embarrassed at having made a promise that was not meant. But promises like mine abound in every corner of his bleak world. After months of knowing him. I ask him his name, 'Saheb-e-Alam,' he announces. He does not know what it means. If he knew its meaning-Lord of the Universe-he would have a hard time believing it. Unaware of what his name represents, he roams the streets with his friends, an army of barefoot boys who appear like the morning birds and disappear at noon. Over the months, I have come to recognise each of them. **CBSE 2021, Term I Modified**

(i) What view does the author express on the fact that 'Saheb-e-Alam' means lord of the universe?

(ii) Select the correct option from those given in brackets to fill in the blank.

The literary device used in the expression 'an army of barefoot boys who appear like morning birds' is .... (Simile/Metaphor)

(iii) Complete the sentence appropriately.

The word .... matches the meaning of 'embarrassed', in meaning with its usage in the extract.

(iv) Why do you think the author says that Saheb would have a hard time believing the meaning of his name?

(v) Select the option that explains the appropriate reason for the narrator's embarrassment.

(a) She was not able to build the school in time.
(b) She does not know the name of the boys.
(c) She is guilty of giving a false hope to the boy.
(d) She is not aware of his bleak world.

(vi) What does the author mean by 'his bleak world'?

(a) The world of children
(b) His aspirations for future
(c) Life with no hope for the future
(d) His dark world

Ans. (i) The author finds the situation to be ironical upon learning that Saheb's name is 'Saheb-e-Alam' which means lord of the universe.

(ii) Simile (iii) uncomfortable

(iv) The author says that Saheb would have a hard time in believing the meaning of his name because his name stands in stark contrast to his reality. His name means 'the lord of the universe' but his reality does not correspond with it.

(v) (c) She is guilty of giving a false hope to the boy.

(vi) (c) Life with no hope for the future

3. And survival in Seemapuri means rag-picking. Through the years, it has acquired the proportions of a fine art. Garbage to them is gold. It is their daily bread, a roof over their heads, even if it is a leaking roof. But for a child it is even more "I sometimes find a rupee, even a ten-rupee note," Saheb says, his eyes lighting up. When you can find a silver coin in a heap of garbage, you don't stop scrounging, for there is hope of finding more. It seems that for children, garbage has a meaning different from what it means to their parents. For the children it is wrapped in wonder, for the elders it is a means of survival. (Lost Spring : Stories of Stolen Childhood) CBSE SQP 2024

(i) What does Saheb's statement about finding money in the garbage reveal about his daily life and aspirations?

(ii) Select the correct option from those given in brackets to fill in the blank.

Describing garbage as 'gold' metaphorically elevates its value to the children, helping the reader understand the .... (dynamic/desperate) conditions under which these children live, where even garbage can represent crucial economic resources.

(iii) Complete the following with a suitable reason. Children continue to scrounge in the garbage because ....

(iv) How does the perception of garbage differ between children and adults in Seemapuri?

(v) What is implied by the description of rag-picking as having 'acquired the proportions of a fine art' in the excerpt?

(a) Rag-picking is an undesirable and simple task that anyone can do without effort.
(b) Rag-picking has evolved into a complex skill that is valued within the community.
(c) Rag-picking is a temporary activity that does not significantly impact the community.
(d) Rag-picking has the status of an artistic hobby that children pursue for enjoyment.

(vi) What is the reason for Saheb's eyes 'lighting up'?

(a) The immediate experience of finding something valuable
(b) Discussing his findings with others
(c) Reminiscing about past findings in the garbage
(d) Planning future scavenging expeditions

Ans. (i) Saheb's statement about finding money in the garbage highlights his sad economic situation and his dependence on chance finds for small joys and possibly essential income. This reflects the dire poverty and limited opportunities available to him.

(ii) desperate

(iii) finding valuable items like coins gives them hope of finding more

(iv) The perception of garbage differs between children and adults in Seemapuri. For children, garbage represents a source of wonder and potential treasure, whereas for adults, it is primarily a means of survival.

(v) (b) Rag-picking has evolved into a complex skill that is valued within the community.

(vi) (c) Reminiscing about past findings in the garbage

4. **"Children grow up in them, becoming partners in survival. And survival in Seemapuri means rag-picking. Through to the years, it has acquired the proportions of a fine art. Garbage to them is gold. It is their daily bread, a roof over their heads, even if it is a leaking roof. But for a child it is even more."** **CBSE 2024**

(i) Why does the author say 'survival in Seemapuri means rag-picking'?

(ii) Select the correct option from those given in brackets to fill in the blank.

The children and their parents have left .... (Dhaka/Nepal) for better livelihood.

(iii) Complete the sentence appropriately.

Children become partners in survival suggests that ....

(iv) What does the phrase "for a child it is even more" reveal about the children's dreams?

(v) Rag-picking has acquired the proportion of a fine art means ....

(a) artistic bend of mind is required
(b) it has proportionately displaced art
(c) it has become a highly skilful activity
(d) it has discovered pieces of art

(vi) Which of the following headlines suggests the central idea of the extract?

(a) Seemapuri, A Pot of Gold
(b) Rag-picking - Different Perspectives
(c) Art in Delhi and in Seemapuri
(d) Saheb-e-Alam in Seemapuri

Ans. (i) The author says the given phrase because the people residing in Seemapuri rely on rag-picking to afford food, clothing and shelter.

(ii) Dhaka

(iii) the kids are trying to survive in the same situation, they come to help one another, and face all the difficulties and hardships together.

(iv) The phrase is an indication that the children's dreams are not only to survive, which shows their lost childhood in the face of poverty.

(v) (c) it has become a highly skilful activity

(vi) (b) Rag-picking - Different Perspectives

5. **"I sometimes find a rupee, even a ten rupee note", Saheb says, his eyes lighting up when you can find a silver coin in a heap of garbage, you don't stop scrounging, for there is the hope of finding more. It seems that for children, garbage has a meaning different from what it means to their parents. For the children it is wrapped in wonder, for the elders, it is a means of survival.**

One winter morning I see Saheb standing by the fenced gate of the neighbourhood club, watching two young men dressed in white, playing tennis. "I like the game", he hums, content to watch it standing behind the fence. "I go inside when no one is around" he admits. "The gatekeeper lets me use the swing." **CBSE 2023**

(i) Which emotion of Saheb is revealed in the phrase 'his eyes lighting up'?

(ii) Select the correct option from those given in brackets to fill in the blank.

'Scrounging' in the passage most nearly means .... (digging/searching)

(iii) Complete the sentence suitably.

For the elders garbage is .... and for children it is a ....

(iv) "There is hope for finding more". Explain with reference to the above extract.

(v) Saheb found a rupee

(a) on the street
(b) in the garbage dump
(c) in Firozabad
(d) on the tennis court

(vi) On the basis of the extract, choose the correct option with reference to I and II given below.

I. Saheb watches the game from outside.
II. Saheb had lost the previous match.

(a) I is true and II is not
(b) II is true but I is not
(c) Both I and II are true
(d) Both I and II are false

Ans. (i) The given expression reveals saheb's happiness.

(ii) searching

(iii) means of survival, treasure hunt

(iv) The given lines indicates that children like Saheb and other ragpickers keep on searching the garbage dumps to look for something that could earn them money or livelihood.

(v) (b) in the garbage dump

(vi) (a) I is true and II is not

Part 2 : I Want to Drive a Car

1. **"I will learn to drive a car," he answers, looking straight into my eyes. His dream looms like a mirage amidst the dust of streets that fill his town Firozabad, famous for its bangles. Every other family in Firozabad is engaged in making bangles. It is the centre of India's glass-blowing industry where families have spent generations working around furnaces, wielding glass, making bangles for all the women in the land it seems.**

Mukesh's family is among them. None of them know that it is illegal for children like him to work in the glass furnaces with high temperatures, in dingy cells without air and light; that the law, if enforced, could get him and all those 20,000 children out of the hot furnaces where they slog their daylight hours, often losing the brightness of their eyes. Mukesh's eyes beam as he volunteers to take me home, which he proudly says is being rebuilt. Competency Based

(i) Identify the lines that indicate of the legality of occupations.

(ii) Select the correct option from those given in brackets to fill in the blank.

'I will learn to drive a car,' he answers, looking straight into my eyes. This sentence highlights Mukesh was .... (ambitious/sincere)

(iii) Complete the sentence suitably.

The simile 'dream looms like a mirage amidst the dust of streets' indicates that his dream was ....

(iv) Do you think that Mukesh will be able to fulfill his dream?

(v) Which of the following statements is not true with reference to the extract?

(a) Children work in badly lit and poorly ventilated furnaces.

(b) The children are unaware that it is forbidden by law to work in the furnaces.

(c) Children toil in the furnaces for hours which affects their eyesight.

(d) Firozabad has emerged as a nascent producer of bangles in the country.

(vi) Every other family in Firozabad is engaged in making bangles. What does this indicate?

(a) Bangle-making is the only industry that flourishes in Firozabad.

(b) The entire population of Firozabad is involved in bangle-making.

(c) Majority of the population in Firozabad is involved in bangle-making.

(d) Bangle-making is the most loved occupation in Firozabad.

Ans. (i) "It is illegal for children like him to work in glass furnaces with high temperature, in dingy cells without air and light ......"

(ii) ambitious

(iii) illusory and indistinct

(iv) Yes, I think that Mukesh will be able to fulfill his dream because he seems to possess the courage required to fight the boundations put on him by his family to join the family profession.

(v) (d) Firozabad has emerged as a nascent producer of bangles in the country.

(vi) (c) Majority of the population in Firozabad is involved in bangle-making.

2. And in dark hutments, next to lines of flames of flickering oil lamps, sit boys and girls with their fathers and mothers, welding pieces of coloured glass into circles of bangles. Their eyes are more adjusted to the dark than to the light outside. That is why they often end up losing their eyesight before they become adults. CBSE 2023 Modified

(i) What can be said about the tone of the given extract?

(ii) Select the correct option from those given in brackets to fill in the blank.

'Flickering oil lamps' suggests a lack of .... (electricity/day)

(iii) Complete the sentence with reference to the extract.

Their eyes are more adjusted to the dark than to the light outside because ....

(iv) Why do the bangle makers lose their eyesight before they become adults?

(v) Which of the following would not be true?

(a) The hutments were shining and inviting.

(b) The children's lives were as bleak as their surrounding.

(c) There were no electricity connections.

(d) The boys and girls had got used to the dark.

(vi) Which of the following most nearly means 'adjusted' in the context of the extract?

(a) Conditioned (b) Favoured

(c) Accepted (d) Reconciled

Ans. (i) The tone of the given extract is dismal as it presents the hazards of the bangle-making industry.

(ii) electricity

(iii) they used to spend their entire day working inside in darkness

(iv) The bangle-makers lose their eyesight before they become adults as they work in dim light for most part of their day.

(v) (a) The hutments were shining and inviting.

(vi) (a) Conditioned

3. She still has bangles on her wrist, but no light in her eyes. "Ek waqt se bhar khana bhi nahin khaya." She says, in a voice drained of joy. She has not enjoyed even one full meal in her entire lifetime-that's what she has reaped! Her husband, an old man with a flowing beard says, "I know nothing except bangles. All I have done is make a house for the family to live in."

Hearing him one wonders if he has achieved what many have failed in their lifetime. He has a roof over his head! The cry of not having money to do anything except carry on the business of making bangles, not even enough to eat, rings in every home. The young men echo the lament of the elders. Little has moved with time, it seems in Firozabad, years of mind-numbing toil have killed all initiative and the ability to dream.

CBSE Question Bank 2021, Modified

(i) Why is there no ability to dream in the town of Firozabad?

(ii) Select the correct option from those given in brackets to fill in the blank.

The tone of the man when he says 'All I have done is to make a house for the family to live in' is .... (regretful/dreadful)

(iii) Complete the sentence appropriately.

'He has a roof over his head!' The tone of the author is ....

(iv) 'Years of mind-numbing toil have killed all initiative and the ability to dream.' What does this show?

(v) 'She still has bangles on her wrist, but no light in her eyes.' This implies that

(a) she is married but has lost the charm in her eyes.
(b) she is a married woman who has lost her grace and beauty.
(c) though she is married, her eyes are devoid of happiness.
(d) she is a married woman who has lost her eyesight.

(vi) Which term best matches the statement "The young men echo the lament of their elders"?

(a) Acceptance (b) Reflection
(c) Reiteration (d) Doubtfulness

Ans. (i) There is no ability to dream in the town of Firozabad because all those dreams are oppressed by the authorities who make people work endlessly and punish those who revolt or take initiative.

(ii) regretful (iii) optimistic

(iv) The given expression shows that the drudgery of work has destroyed their willingness to improve their lives.

(v) (c) though she is married, her eyes are devoid of happiness.

(vi) (c) Reiteration

4. Listening to them, I see two distinct worlds–one of the family, caught in a web of poverty, burdened by the stigma of caste in which they are born; the other a vicious circle of the *sahukars*, the middlemen, the policemen, the keepers of law, the bureaucrats and the politicians. Together they have imposed the baggage on the child that he cannot put down. Before he is aware, he accepts it as naturally as his father. To do anything else would mean to dare. And daring is not part of his growing up. When I sense a flash of it in Mukesh I am cheered. "I want to be a motor mechanic," he repeats. He will go to a garage and learn. But the garage is a long way from his home. "I will walk," he insists. "Do you also dream of flying a plane?" He is suddenly silent. 'No,' he says, staring at the ground.

(i) Which two worlds has the narrator divided the people of Firozabad?

(ii) Select the suitable word from the extract to complete the following analogy.
Disdain : Respect :: Honour : ....

(iii) Complete the sentence with an appropriate explanation, as per extract.

The given extract holds importance with respect to the larger picture of Firozabad because ....

(iv) "Before he is aware, he accepts it as naturally as his father." Explain.

(v) Select the correct option to fill in the blank.
The first step towards change is ....

(a) to file a complaint (b) to dare to dream
(c) to talk to the person (d) to be the change

(vi) What is the role of Sahukars?

(a) To establish to bangle industry
(b) To empoly the people
(c) To lend money on higher rate of interest
(d) To share the burden of the working class

Ans. (i) The narrator has divided the world of Firozabad into the world of the exploited and the exploiters.

(ii) Stigma

(iii) it shows hope in the form of Mukesh who dares to dream. This dream and its success can initiate further dreams and change the state of Firozabad.

(iv) The given line indicates that the profession of bangle-making has been naturalised in the community of Firozabad. Children now do not even think of any other profession and only work in the bangle-making industry.

(v) (b) to dare to dream

(vi) (c) To lend money on higher rate of interest

Short Answer Type Questions

1. Describe the irony in Saheb's name.

Ans. Saheb is a poor ragpicker who lives in Seemapuri. His full name is 'Saheb-e-Alam', which means. 'Lord of the Universe'. The irony lies in the meaning of his name itself.

According to his name, he should be a king and he should enjoy all the luxuries of life. But unfortunately, he is a barefoot ragpicker, who lacks even the basic necessities of life.

2. Rapickers like Saheb had migrated to Seemapuri. Elucidate.

Ans. Once Saheb's parents and many other ragpickers lived in Bangladesh, amidst the green fields of Dhaka. There were many storms that swept away their fields and homes. That's why they migrated to Delhi and settled down in Seemapuri looking for an occupation.

3. Explain the sentence "an army of barefoot boys who appear like the morning birds and disappear at noon." CBSE 2024

Ans. The given sentence implies that the boys are a large, unified group who are energetic and move around quickly and unpredictably.

Due to their unfortunate circumstances, they couldn't afford shoes or slippers so they roam around barefoot. And they get up early in the morning to search for food and shelter and have to scatter away when it gets crowded during noon time.

4. What did garbage mean to the children of Seemapuri and to their parents?

Or In what sense is garbage gold to the ragpickers?

Ans. Garbage means 'gold' to the poor ragpickers because some of it can be sold for cash, thus, becoming a means of survival for the children of Seemapuri and for their parents.

It essentially provides them their daily bread and a roof over their heads.

5. The description of Seemapuri creates a very dismal picture. Explain. CBSE 2023

Ans. The given statement stands true as Seemapuri, though exists at the periphery of Delhi, is very far from it in terms of facilities and opportunities. It is a home to poverty stricken ragpickers who live together in slums without any proper sanitation or drainage facilities and without any educational or employment opportunities.

6. What kind of gold did the people of Seemapuri look for in the garbage?

Ans. The people of Seemapuri look for items in the garbage which can be traded for money so that they are able to earn their daily bread and have a roof over their heads.

7. For Saheb, how was work at the tea stall different from rag-picking? CBSE 2020

Ans. When Saheb started working at the tea stall, his face lost the carefree look which he used to have when he was a ragpicker. He was no longer his own master now. He had to do what the owner of the tea stall asked him to do. He carried heavy metal canisters, instead of light plastic bags. He was not happy working at the tea stall as he had lost his freedom.

8. Why does Anees Jung spend a significant portion of 'Lost Spring' talking about shoes? Explain any one reason in 30–40 words with relevant examples from the story. Competency Based

Ans. Anees Jung spends a significant portion of 'Lost Spring' talking about shoes to highlight the difference between the rich and the poor and how differently they respond to basic necessities. It also shows the level of challenges faced by the poor people like Saheb. The rich take their shoes for granted but poor people have to come up with justifications for not having shoes. Anees Jung tries to highlight how shoes are a luxury to Saheb and his friends who either don't own them or wear them only occasionally.

9. Describe Mukesh as an ambitious person.

Ans. Mukesh is an ambitious person because he wants to become a motor-mechanic by breaking free from the vicious web of generations of families being involved in bangle-making. He has the courage to dream of becoming a motor-mechanic, thus breaking free from destiny.

10. How bad were living conditions in which Mukesh and his family survived? CBSE 2020

Ans. Mukesh and his family were living in terrible conditions with extreme poverty. They work in high temperature in badly lit and poorly ventilated glass furnaces. There was no development or progress in their lives. But they had no choice but to work in such inhuman conditions.

11. Identify an instance of hope or resilience in 'Lost Spring' and analyse how it reflects one of the story's themes. CBSE SQP 2024

Ans. An instance of hope or resilience that can be found in Saheb's story is his continued search in the garbage.
His search is driven by the occasional discovery of a rupee or a ten-rupee note, symbolising his hope and resilience against his harsh life. This reflects the theme of the human spirit's capacity to dream and hope, even amidst poverty and destitution or the terribly dire circumstances.

12. In spite of despair and disease pervading the lives of the slum children, they are not devoid of hope. How far do you agree? Competency Based

Ans. In spite of growing up amidst despair and disease, children who live in slums have the desire to achieve something big in life. This shows that they are not devoid of hope. Saheb, a ragpicker, is eager to go to a school and learn. Mukesh, who works in dark, dingy cells making-bangles, dreams of becoming a motor-mechanic against his family tradition.

13. What does the title 'Lost Spring' convey?

Ans. Spring is associated with childhood. Just as spring is the season when flowers bloom, similarly, childhood is the period when an individual blooms and grows. Anees Jung here presents the horrific truth about the life of children in India who are victims of child labour and are not allowed to grow and bloom freely. Their childhood or springtime is lost.

14. Why do you think Mukesh is content to dream of cars and doesn't dream of flying a plane? CBSE Question Bank 2021

Ans. Mukesh is content only to dream of cars because he knows that his journey towards becoming a mechanic is a difficult one. To go any further than that is a thing that he has not thought of. As a realistic boy, he dreamt of something that he could achieve.

His dream of becoming a motor-mechanic is reasonable. Thus, he doesn't dream of flying a plane.

15. What do we come to know about the author of 'Lost Spring' Anees Jung, through her interactions with Saheb and Mukesh? Competency Based

Ans. From the stories presented in 'Lost Spring', we get an idea of observant and compassionate nature of Anees Jung- the author. Anees is observant for she observes her surroundings and the behaviour of the ragpicker boys and the bangle-makers to come to her own conclusions which we, as readers, know are truths. She is very sensitive and empathetic as the plight of the poor affects her deeply and she feels helpless about her inability to do anything for them.

16. How do you think the author's life might have been impacted after her interactions with the children and their families mentioned in 'Lost Spring'? Competency Based

Ans. The author's life may have been severely impacted after her interactions with the children and their families mentioned in 'Lost Spring'. She must have realised the depth to which poverty had impacted the Indian society. Jung must have developed an urge to do something for the betterment of the downtrodden and underprivileged people. Her writing of the chapter 'Lost spring' is itself an endeavour by her to bring their miserable conditions to light. She also raised the issues that are responsible for not improving their life.

17. Despite the difficulties that Mukesh's family goes through, his grandmother believes that their occupation is their destiny. What could be the reason behind this belief? State your response in 30–40 words with evidence from the text 'Lost Spring'. Competency Based

Ans. The reason behind Mukesh's grandmother's belief that their occupation is their destiny is their means of justifying their way of life. Their poverty and lack of awareness about other occupations prevent them from doing anything else. The belief is a denial of their cruel reality wherein they are conditioned to believe that bangle making is the only thing they are capable of doing.

We can find many evidence from the text to prove this. One of the main evidence is a woman's husband says that he knows nothing besides making bangles. Mukesh's grandmother also saw her husband go blind from polishing glass.

18. Years of mind-numbing toil have killed all initiative and the ability to dream. In the above line from 'Lost Spring', why has bangle-making been described as 'mind-numbing toil'? Answer in 40-50 words. Competency Based

Ans. In the given line, bangle making has been described as a 'mind-numbing toil' because it is mindless work that doesn't require any intellectual engagement. Since the bangle makers have no need of creativity or even thinking, their minds go numb from under-use as their actions grow automated due to muscle memory.

Long Answer Type Questions

1. "Seemapuri, a place on the periphery of Delhi, yet miles away from it, metaphorically." Explain.

Ans. Seemapuri is a place on the outskirts of Delhi where 10,000 ragpickers and their families live. The people living there are squatters who migrated from Bangladesh in 1971. The ragpickers live in structures of mud with roofs of tin and tarpaulin devoid of sewage, drainage or running water. No one can imagine that such a place exists on the periphery of Delhi, the capital of India. It stands in stark contrast to the metropolitan city of Delhi. The main city of Delhi, and Seemapuri at its periphery provide an exemplary case of contradiction.

In Delhi, there is luxury and affluence, a host of opportunities and dreams and in Seemapuri there is squalor, hopelessness and despair. There is no chance for the inhabitants of this area to strive towards the attainment of the prospects offered by Delhi.

Thus, although Seemapuri is located at the periphery of Delhi, in the real sense, it is many miles away from Delhi.

2. 'Saheb is no longer his own master.' Comment.

Ans. It is true to say that when Saheb is working in the tea stall, he is no longer his own master. Earlier as a ragpickers, he was free to do whatever he wanted. Rummaging through garbage did not only provide him with a regular income but also gave him freedom. He has all the liberty in the world to roam with his friends in the streets without any worries to bother him. Also, he could hunt for 'gold' in the garbage dumps. It provided him a hope and a thrill every day in the form of a rupee or a ten-rupee note.

In contrast, the job he takes up at a tea stall enslaves him. He is now not free to roam aimlessly in the streets. His new occupation binds him to serve somebody else. He has regular income and food. However, the steel canister took away the joy and freedom he had as a ragpicker.

3. "It is his karam, his destiny" that made Mukesh's grandfather go blind. How did Mukesh disprove this belief by choosing a new vocation and making his own destiny?

Ans. Mukesh disproved this belief that bangle-making was his destiny by choosing a new vocation and making his own destiny. He decided to become a motor-mechanic and learn to drive a car. As he had seen his parents and others suffer because of the vicious circle of poverty and exploitation by the *sahukars*, middlemen, politicians and the police, he did not want to remain in the bangle-making profession. He had the courage to break free from the family lineage of bangle-making and was ready to walk a long distance to reach a motor garage to learn the vocation of car mechanic. He had even thought that he would request the garage owner to hire him initially as a helper and learn the trade. Finally, he also wanted to learn to drive a car. Thus, Mukesh was ready to make his destiny by choosing a new vocation and break the age old belief.

5. 'Lost Spring' explains the grinding poverty and traditions that condemn thousands of people to a life of abject poverty. Do you agree? Why/why not? **Competency Based**

Ans. Yes, I do agree that 'Lost Spring' narrates the grinding poverty and traditions to which thousands of people have succumbed.

The story written by Anees Jung revolves around the pitiable condition of poor children who have been forced to live in slums and work hard in conditions which endanger their health. The first part gives the writer's impression about the life of poor ragpickers who have migrated from Bangladesh but now are settled in the Seemapuri area of Delhi. The second part narrates the miserable life of the bangle-makers in Firozabad. The stark reality of these families is that, in spite of back-breaking hard work that they put in, they cannot even afford two square meals a day. Besides, false and blind belief in traditions does not let their children take up other respectable and better paying jobs which will improve their financial situation.

6. Most of us do not raise our voice against injustice in our society and tend to remain mute spectators. Anees Jung in her story, 'Lost Spring' vividly highlights the miserable life of street children and bangle-makers of Firozabad. She wants us to act. Which qualities does she want the children to develop? **Competency Based**

Ans. Anees Jung wants the children to become free from the vicious cycle of poverty into which they have fallen due to the middlemen, *sahukars* and law enforcement officials. She wants them to be bold enough to raise their voice against their oppressors. She wants them to be fearless and optimistic so that they can dream of taking up other occupations, just like Mukesh who wants to be a motor-mechanic. She wants them to become free from their traditional occupation so that they can realise their life's ambitions. She sees the spark of such a quality in Mukesh who is willing to go to any lengths to become a motor-mechanic. She wants some people to help them develop these qualities so that they can be free from injustice and exploitation, take up other respectable and better paying jobs which will improve their financial condition.

7. How do the stories 'The Last Lesson' by Alphonse Daudet and 'Lost Spring' by Anees Jung illustrate the impact of socio-political factors on education? **CBSE 2025**

Ans. Both 'The Last Lesson' by Alphonse Daudet and 'Lost Spring' by Anees Jung highlight the profound impact of socio-political factors on education, though in different contexts. In 'The Last Lesson', the Franco-Prussian War leads to the imposition of German in Alsace and Lorraine, replacing French in schools. This sudden policy shift deprives students like Franz of their linguistic and cultural identity, making them realise the value of education only when it is too late. The story emphasises how political power can control and restrict access to education.

Similarly, 'Lost Spring' explores the harsh realities of poverty and child labour that prevent underprivileged children from receiving an education. The story of Saheb, a ragpicker, and Mukesh, a child labourer in the bangle industry, illustrates how systemic poverty and exploitation force children into labour, depriving them of learning opportunities. Both stories underline how war, oppression, and economic disparity act as barriers to education, limiting the future of young minds.

8. Analyse how freedom is curbed in the context of Franz in 'The Last Lesson' and Saheb in 'Lost Spring'. **CBSE 2025**

Ans. In 'The Last Lesson', Franz experiences the curbing of freedom when the Prussian authorities impose German as the mandatory language in Alsace and Lorraine. His right to learn and use his mother tongue, French, is taken away, symbolising the loss of cultural and personal identity. This sudden imposition makes him realise the value of education, which he had previously taken for granted.

Similarly, in 'Lost Spring', Saheb's freedom is restricted by poverty and socio-economic constraints. Born into a family of ragpickers, he is deprived of education and the right to dream beyond his circumstances. Although he aspires to a better life, he is forced into child labour, first as a ragpicker and later as a servant at a tea stall. His loss of independence and dignity reflects the harsh reality of child exploitation.

Both Franz and Saheb suffer from different forms of oppression-one through political control and the other through economic hardship-limiting their freedom and choices in life.

SELF ASSESSMENT TEST

Extract Based Questions

Read the extracts given below and answer the questions that follow.

1. Food is more important for survival than an identity. "If at the end of the day we can feed our families and go to bed without an aching stomach, we would rather live here than in the fields that gave us no grain," say a group of women in tattered saris when I ask them why they left their beautiful land of green fields and rivers. Wherever they find food, they pitch their tents that become transit homes. Children grow up in them, becoming partners in survival. And survival in Seemapuri means rag-picking. Through the years, it has acquired the proportions of a fine art. Garbage to them is gold. It is their daily bread, a roof over their heads, even if it is a leaking roof. But for a child it is even more. **CBSE SQP 2021**

(i) Identify the figure of speech used in the sentence 'Garbage to them is gold'.

(ii) Select the correct option from those given in bracket to fill in the blank.
The phrase 'transit homes' refer to the dwellings that are .... (unhygienic/temporary)

(iii) Complete the following sentence appropriately.
The ragpickers .... their migration.

(iv) What does 'acquired the proportions of a fine art' mean?

(v) Choose the term which best matches the statement.
"Food is more important for survival than an identity"?
(a) Immorality (b) Necessity
(c) Obligation (d) Ambition

(vi) Choose the statement that is not true about ragpickers in Seemapuri.
(a) Children are equally involved in rag-picking as their parents.
(b) The ragpickers settle down in a place permanently.
(c) Rag-picking has accomplished itself as a skill and form of art.
(d) Ragpickers live in unsteady shanties on the outskirts of Delhi.

2. The cry of not having money to do anything except carry on the business of making-bangles, not even enough to eat, rings in every home. The young men echo the lament of their elders. Little has moved with time, it seems, in Firozabad. Years of mind-numbing toil have killed all initiative and the ability to dream.

"Why not organise yourselves into a cooperative?" I ask a group of young men who have fallen into the vicious circle of middlemen who trapped their fathers and forefathers.

(i) Rationalise, to support the statement. "Little had moved with time".

(ii) Select the correct option from those given in brackets to fill in the blank.
The cry of not having money to do anything except .... (look forward to/carry on) the business of making-bangles.

(iii) Complete the sentence appropriately.
People of Firozabad are .... of authority.

(iv) Replace the underlined word with its antonym from the extract.
Young men of Firozabad have fallen into the <u>benevolent</u> company of the middlemen.

(v) Why does the narrator ask the young men to organise them into a co-operative?
   (a) To derive some indirect benefit from them
   (b) To help them come out of the vicious circle of middlemen
   (c) To face the police bravely
   (d) To shut bangle-making industry

(vi) Why does a cry ring in every home of Firozabad?
   (a) Middlemen exploiting the people
   (b) Police hauling them for illegal acts
   (c) Not having enough money to look beyond bangle-making
   (d) Lack of education for the youth

Short Answer Type Questions

Answer the following questions in 40-50 words.

1. Why does the author say that rag-picking has become an art?
2. Garbage has an important meaning for the children who are ragpickers. Why?
3. How are bangles important to an Indian woman? How is it used to present an irony in the chapter?
4. What does the reference to the chappals in 'Lost Spring' tell us about the economic condition of the ragpickers?
5. How would you judge the act of shuffling by the boy?
6. "Listening to them, I see two distinct worlds..." In the context of Mukesh, the bangle maker's son, which two worlds is Anees Jung referring to?
7. Do you believe that 'God-given lineage can be broken'? Support your position with a rationale.

Long Answer Type Questions

Answer the following questions in 120-150 words.

1. Give a brief account of life and activities of the people like Saheb-e-Alam settled in Seemapuri, Delhi.
2. Mukesh is not like the others. His "dreams loom like a mirage amidst the dust of streets that fill his town Firozabad". Justify the statement in the light of contrast in the mindsets of Mukesh and the people of Firozabad.
3. How is Mukesh's attitude towards his situation different from that of Saheb? Why?

03

About the Author

William Orville Douglas

(1898-1980) was an American jurist. He served as an associate justice of the Supreme Court of the United States. He was also known as a champion of civil liberties and the rights of minorities. Douglas was a prolific writer, especially on conservation, history, politics and foreign relations. Most of his writings, comprised elements that showed his love for nature and the valuable insights he had learned over the years.

YOUR STUDY GOALS

- Chapter Sketch
- About the Characters
- Summary of the Chapter

YOUR PRACTICE GOAL

- NCERT Folder
- Extract Based Questions
- Short Answer Type Questions
- Long Answer Type Questions

Deep Water

Chapter Sketch

Deep Water is an excerpt taken from 'Of Men and Mountains' by William O Douglas, a leading advocate of individual rights and a Justice in the courts of USA. It reveals how, as a young boy, he nearly drowned in a swimming pool. He talks about his fear of water and thereafter how he finally overcame it.

About the Characters

Douglas William Douglas himself is the main character of the story. We see his growth from a young and thin boy to a man determined to overcome his fear.

Douglas' mother She is a loving and caring mother who supports her son and wants him to be safe.

Bully He is an 18 year old well-built boy who throws Douglas in the deep end of the pool for a prank. He seems to be arrogant and stupid in his actions.

Douglas' instructor He is an organised, strategic and a determined man. He understood what to do to get Douglas over his fear of water and planned his classes accordingly.

Summary of the Chapter

The Narrator's Aversion to Water

The narrator was 10 or 11 years old when he developed his fear of water. He had decided to learn swimming and the YMCA pool gave him the opportunity as it was safe. In comparison, the Yakima river was dangerous and had many drowning incidents.

The narrator developed an aversion to water at the age of three or four when his father took him to the beach in California. He almost drowned in the waves and was frightened but his father had only laughed at him. The other incident happened in the YMCA pool. He was just beginning to feel comfortable in the water when one day an 18 year old boy threw him into the deep end of the pool. Douglas went into the pool in a sitting position and went to the bottom.

Attempts to Save his Life

Douglas was frightened but was able to make a plan to save himself. He decided that when his feet would hit the bottom, he would make a big jump, come to the surface, lie flat on it and paddle to the edge of the pool. When he reached the bottom of the pool, he used all strength to make the jump. However, he failed and started to panic. He tried to breathe but swallowed water. Douglas screamed but no sound came out and he started to go down again. He started to lose consciousness when he remembered his strategy.

The Terror

When Douglas opened his eyes, he saw nothing but water with a yellow glow. He was filled with an uncontrollable terror. As a result, Douglas was paralysed and only his heart and the pounding in his head showed that he was still alive. However, Douglas remembered his plan to jump when he reached the bottom. He again jumped but was unsuccessful.

Douglas, then, looked for ropes, ladders and water wings to save himself but found nothing. This frightened him even more. He tried to call for his mother, but nothing happened. Then, he started going down for the third time. By this time, all his efforts stopped and he fell unconscious.

The next thing Douglas remembers was lying by the pool. The boy who threw him into the pool was justifying his actions while getting scolded. Several hours later, Douglas walked to his home. After that, he started fearing water and avoided it whenever he could.

Learning How to Swim

The fear of water ruined Douglas' fishing trips and deprived him of the joys of water activities. Finally, in October, he decided to get a swimming instructor. He practised five days a week, an hour each day. The instructor put a belt with a rope around Douglas. This rope went through a pulley and the instructor held its other end. Each time the instructor relaxed his hold on the rope and Douglas went under water, which filled him with fear. It took him three months to get over this fear.

Then, the instructor taught him to breathe while swimming. Next, he taught him to move his legs. Thus, piece by piece, he built a swimmer out of Douglas. Finally, the fear and panic that filled Douglas went away.

Getting over the Fear

After the training was finished, Douglas wondered if he would be terror-stricken when he would be alone in the pool. He tried and some old terror returned but he was not afraid. However, Douglas was not satisfied. So, he went to Lake Wentworth in New Hampshire as well as the Warm Lake to test his swimming skills. He successfully swam to the other shores and back. He was thrilled with joy as he had conquered his fear of water.

This experience had a deep meaning for Douglas. He explains that it is the fear of death that affects a person. Then, he quotes President Roosevelt's saying, 'All we have to fear is fear itself.' Because he had experienced death and the terror that it could produce, his will to live somehow grew in intensity.

Word-Meaning

treacherous	—	dangerous, unreliable
water wing (s)	—	an apparatus in the shape of inflated waterproof bags that can be fixed to the arms to help someone learn swimming
subdued my pride	—	overcame feeling ashamed
surf	—	a mass of foam formed by waves breaking on a seashore
stirred	—	aroused
paddled	—	moved through the water
aping	—	imitating, copying
bruiser	—	bully
specimen	—	example
rippling	—	swelling, bulging
ducked	—	pushed under water
bob to the surface like a cork	—	move up quickly to the water surface like a piece of cork
panicky	—	afraid, alarmed
flailed at the surface	—	swung arms or legs violently on the surface
expending	—	spending or using up
irresistible	—	overwhelming
strike out	—	hit sharply
pounding	—	rhythmical beating or throbbing
oblivion	—	unconsciousness
curtain of life fell	—	as if life ended
fishing for landlocked salmon	—	fishing for edible fish trapped by being cut off from the sea
bass	—	a common term for many different species of fish
trout	—	a freshwater fish
slack	—	lessen or reduce
integrated	—	composite
crawl stroke	—	a stroke in which the swimmer lies flat on the water with face submerged, and takes overhand arm strokes, while moving his legs up and down
vestiges	—	traces or remains of something that is disappearing or no longer exists

Important Themes of the Chapter

The autobiographical account focuses on the themes associated with fear.

Conquering Fear The main theme of the story is the author's struggle to overcome his fear of water. The story demonstrates how to overcome fear through willpower and strength of mind. Its shows the narrator's determination and relentless pursuit of mastering the ocean's depths.

Psychological Analysis of Fear The subthemes of the story is a psycho-analytical study of fear and how to overcome it. The author realises what fear essentially is and how we need to fear the idea of fear itself. He understands that we need to conquer our fear to expand our horizons and grow as an individual.

NCERT Folder

Think as you Read (NCERT Page 27)

1. What is the 'misadventure' that William Douglas speaks about?

Or What shocking experience did Douglas have at the YMCA pool?

Ans. William Douglas speaks about the 'misadventure' which happened at the YMCA swimming pool when he was about ten or eleven years old. A big bully threw Douglas into the deep end of the pool when no one was around. As a result, Douglas almost drowned.

2. What were the series of emotions and fears that Douglas experienced when he was thrown into the pool? What plans did he make to come to the surface?

Ans. When Douglas was thrown into the pool, he was much scared but he did not lose his mind. He planned that he would make a big jump when his feet would touch the bottom. Thus, he would come to the surface. Unfortunately, the plan failed. Consequently, Douglas was frightened and he panicked. He felt paralysed and screamed to get help, but in vain.

3. How did this experience affect him?

Ans. The near drowning experience had a very deep meaning for and impact on Douglas. It left a haunting fear lurking in his heart. He was extremely scared of water and avoided going near it whenever he could. The fear deprived him of the joys of boating and fishing and destroyed his social life.

Think as you Read (NCERT Page 29)

1. Why was Douglas determined to get over his fear of water?

Ans. Douglas regretted being deprived of enjoying water-based activities and sports like canoeing, boating, fishing and swimming. His ardent wish to enjoy such activities and regain his lost confidence while staying in water were the reasons for his determination to get over his fear of water.

2. How did the instructor 'build a swimmer' out of Douglas? CBSE 2020

Ans. The haunting fear of the water followed Douglas in all of his fishing trips, and activities like swimming, boating and canoeing activities. To get rid of this fear, he employed an instructor who practiced with him five days a week, an hour each day. To build a good swimmer out of Douglas, the instructor trained him slowly and step by step.

First, the instructor made him shed his initial fear of water by making him cross a pool suspended by a rope attached through a pulley to his belt. This went on for three months. Then, Douglas was taught to exhale under the water and raise his nose above water and inhale. In the next step, Douglas was made to kick his legs until they were relaxed. Finally, after seven months, the instructor told him to swim the length of the pool. By performing all the steps that he had learned at the time, Douglas became a swimmer.

3. How did Douglas make sure that he conquered the old terror?

Ans. To make sure that Douglas had in fact conquered the old terror, he tested his skills at different water bodies. He swam alone in the pool, went to Lake Wentworth in New Hampshire and swam two miles across the lake. Further, he went to the Warm Lake and swam to the other shore and back.

Understanding the Text (NCERT Page 29)

1. How does Douglas make clear to the reader the sense of panic that gripped him as he almost drowned? Describe the details that have made the description vivid.

Ans. Douglas tells us about the fear that gripped him as he almost drowned by providing a vivid image of the situation. The use of words creates a clear picture in our mind about how the event took place and how Douglas felt and reacted to it.

The descriptions show how initially not panicked, Douglas plans to save himself. His panic and terror emerges when his plans fails and he saw nothing but water with a yellow glow. As a result, Douglas was screaming under water. He seemed to have been paralysed. He tries to look for ropes, ladders and water wings to save himself but found nothing. This frightened him even more. His arms and legs stopped moving. He tried to call for his mother, but nothing happened.

2. How did Douglas overcome his fear of water?

Ans. Refer to the answer of Q.3 in 'Think as you read' (NCERT Page 29).

3. Why does Douglas as an adult recount a childhood experience of terror and his conquering of it? What larger meaning does he draw from this experience?

Or What lesson did Douglas learn when he got rid of his fear of water?

Ans. Douglas, as an adult, recounted the horrific experience and his conquering of it as it had completely changed his life.

He felt that the sensation of dying somehow intensified his zest for life. The fight against the terror taught him the very important lesson that 'All we have to fear is fear itself.' When he finally shed his fear, it proved that nothing is impossible for one with a firm will and determination.

Talking about the Text (NCERT Page 30)

1. "All we have to fear is fear itself". Have you ever had a fear that you have now overcome? Share your experience with your partner.

Ans. Like Douglas, I too had a terrible experience in my life, but now I have overcome the fear of drowning which started due to an incident.

A small river flows near our village. During the summer vacation, we used to go there for bathing and learning swimming. Very often, we were cautioned by the villagers not to bathe in it, as there is a deeper part near the bank where we swam. Being children, we never really bothered. One day my brother and I took off our clothes and plunged into the river.

By chance, the water was overflowing the bank and the current was fast. While diving, both of us were stuck in the deeper portion and started drowning. We cried out loudly as we thought that it was the end of our lives. When one of my friends saw us, he shouted to the other villagers to call them. They soon came and brought us out of the water.

Since then, we shifted our bathing to another part of the river and took the guidance of another villager who was an expert in swimming. Soon, I became an expert swimmer and overcame the fear of drowning.

Exam Pattern Questions

Extract Based Questions

Read the extracts given below and answer the questions that follow.

1. I went to the pool when no one else was there. The place was quiet. The water was still, and the tiled bottom was as white and clean as a bathtub. I was timid about going in alone, so I sat on the side of the pool to wait for others.

I had not been there long when in came a big bruiser of a boy, probably eighteen years old. He had thick hair on his chest. He was a beautiful physical specimen, with legs and arms that showed rippling, muscles. He yelled.

(i) Why did the narrator sit on the side of the pool?

(ii) Select the suitable word from the extract to complete the following analogy.

Specimen : Sample :: Apprehensive : ....

(iii) Complete the sentence with an appropriate explanation, as per the extract.

Douglas decided to wait for the others because ....

(iv) What do you think is the purpose of the description of the bully in the extract?

(v) How did the pool look like when the narrator went there?

(a) Pleasant and lively (b) Thrilling and attractive
(c) Timid and indifferent (d) Still and clean

(vi) What did big bruiser of a boy do?

(a) He flashed his rippling muscles.
(b) He frightened the narrator.
(c) He picked the narrator and tossed him into the deep end.
(d) He took the narrator along to make him learn swimming.

Ans. (i) The narrator sat on the side of the pool because he was afraid of entering the pool alone.

(ii) Timid

(iii) he was fearful of swimming alone

(iv) The description of the bully in the extract is central to understanding the low confidence of the narrator. Douglas as a child was a skinny and lean boy. In contrast the bully was muscular and was handsome.

(v) (d) Still and clean

(vi) (c) He picked the narrator and tossed him into the deep end.

2. My breath was gone. I was frightened. Father laughed, but there was terror in my heart at the overpowering force of the waves. My introduction to the YMCA swimming pool revived unpleasant memories and stirred childish fears. But in a little while I gathered confidence. I paddled with my new water wings, watching the other boys and trying to learn by aping them. I did this two or three times on different days and was just beginning to feel at ease in the water when the misadventure happened.

(i) Why do you think the father laughed at the narrator?

(ii) Select the correct option from those given in brackets to fill in the blank.

The author was finally comfortable with water at .... (YMCA pool/Yakima river)

(iii) Complete the sentence appropriately.

The purpose of the water wings is to ....

(iv) Do you think calling Douglas' aversion to swimming as 'childish fears' is correct?

(v) The misadventure that took place right after the author felt comfortable was that

(a) the author slipped and fell into the swimming pool.
(b) a bully tossed him into the pool for the sake of fun.
(c) his coach forgot to teach him how to handle deep water.
(d) his father couldn't help him from drowning into the water.

(vi) "My introduction to the YMCA swimming pool revived unpleasant memories and stirred childish fears." It can be inferred that this was a clear case of

(a) suppression (b) oppression
(c) depression (d) repression

Ans. (i) Father laughed at the narrator because he found the situation of the narrator being swept by the wave to be amusing. He did not think that the incident would scare the narrator so much that he would develop a fear of water.

(ii) YMCA pool

(iii) protect the narrator from drowning

(iv) No, I do not think that the calling Douglas' aversion to swimming as 'childish fears' is correct as Douglas was deeply impacted by his fear.

(v) (b) a bully tossed him into the pool for the sake of fun.

(vi) (d) repression

3. **Then all effort ceased. I relaxed. Even my legs felt limp; and a blackness swept over my brain. It wiped out fear; it wiped out terror. There was no more panic. It was quiet and peaceful. Nothing to be afraid of. This is nice... to be drowsy... to go to sleep... no need to jump... too tired to jump... it's nice to be carried gently... to float along in space... tender arms around me... tender arms like Mother's... now I must go to sleep... I crossed to oblivion, and the curtain of life fell.**

CBSE Question Bank 2021

(i) Why do you think Douglas stopped attempting to come out of the pool?

(ii) Select the correct option from those given in brackets to fill in the blank.

The 'curtain (of life) fell' corresponds to an aspect of .... (history/drama)

(iii) Complete the sentence appropriately.

The efforts referred to in the extract is ....

(iv) Do you think Douglas accepted his death by drowning?

(v) Which option indicates that the poet lost consciousness?

(a) 'It was quiet and peaceful'
(b) 'I crossed to oblivion'
(c) 'Tender arms like Mother's'
(d) 'It wiped out fear'

(vi) The purpose of using "..." in the above passage is to

(a) show omission
(b) indicate pauses
(c) shorten a dialogue
(d) replace an idea

Ans. (i) Douglas stopped attempting to come out of the pool because he was tired and his body had stopped working. His mind as well as body felt paralysed due to his fear.

(ii) drama

(iii) regarding jumping up to the surface of the pool

(iv) Yes, the given extract tells us that Douglas had accepted his fate of death by drowning.

(v) (b) 'I crossed to oblivion'

(vi) (b) indicate pauses

4. **The next I remember I was lying on my stomach beside the pool, vomiting. The chap that threw me in was saying, "But I was only fooling." Someone said, "The kid nearly died. Be all right now. Let's carry him to the locker room."**

Several hours later, I walked home. I was weak and trembling. I shook and cried when I lay on my bed. I couldn't eat that night. For days a haunting fear was in my heart. The slightest exertion upset me, making me wobbly in the knees and sick to my stomach.

I never went back to the pool. I feared water. I avoided it whenever I could. **CBSE 2023**

(i) What physical problems did the narrator face after recovery?

(ii) Select the correct option from those given in bracket to fill in the blank.

After the incident, the narrator never went back to the pool as he was ...... (afraid of/allergie to) of to water.

(iii) Complete the sentence with an appropriate explanation as per the extract.
The slightest exertion upset the boy because ....

(iv) Identify the textual clue that allows the reader to infer that the chap threw the boy into the pool for fun.

(v) On the basis of the extract, choose the most correct option with reference to the two statements I and II given below.

I. The boy did not know how to swim.

II. The boy took long time to recover from his fear.

(a) I can be inferred from the extract, but II cannot
(b) II can be inferred from the extract, but I cannot
(c) I is true and II is false
(d) Both I and II are true

(vi) With reference to the extract, Douglas was vomiting because

(a) he had got severe food poisoning.
(b) he had just been rescued from nearly drowning in the pool.
(c) he was frightened when he saw the big man.
(d) he had gone for a swim on an empty stomach.

Ans. (i) After recovery, the narrator felt very weak and couldn't stand as he was trembling. He couldn't eat food properly. Even the slightest exertion would upset him, making him wobbly in the knees and sick to his stomach.

(ii) afraid of

(iii) he was not only tired and scared but also his fear has increased.

(iv) 'But I was only fooling'

(v) (d) Both I and II are true

(vi) (b) he had just been rescued from nearly drowning in the pool.

5. **Tiny vestiges of the old terror would return. But now I could frown and say to that terror, 'Trying to scare me, eh? Well, here's to you! Look!' And off I'd go for another length of the pool. This went on until July. But I was still not satisfied. I was not sure that all the terror had left. So, I went to Lake Wentworth in New Hampshire, dived off a dock at Triggs Island, and swam two miles across the lake to Stamp Act Island.**

I swam the crawl, breast stroke, side stroke and back stroke.

Only once did the terror return. When I was in the middle of the lake, I put my face under and saw nothing but bottomless water. The old sensation returned in miniature. CBSE SQP 2022 Term I

(i) What was the reason for the 'return' of terror?

(ii) Select the correct option from those given in bracket to fill in the blank.

Douglas mentions that the old sensation returned in miniature.

He means that he felt the familiar feeling of fear .... (at irregular intervals/on a small scale)

(iii) Complete the sentence suitably.
Douglas went to swim at Lake Wentworth to ....

(iv) What do the given lines tell us about Douglas's swimming ability?

(v) Select the option that lists the correct inference based on the information in the extract.

(a) Triggs Island and Stamp Act Island are both located in Lake Wentworth.

(b) Lake Wentworth is a part of Triggs Island.

(c) Stamp Act Island is two miles away from New Hampshire.

(d) Lake Wentworth is connected via docks to New Hampshire.

(vi) How did Douglas handle the 'old sensation'?

(a) He addressed it (b) He avoided it

(c) He submitted to it (d) He stayed indifferent to it

Ans. (i) The terror returned in Douglas because of his prior drowning experiences.

(ii) on a small scale

(iii) know for sure that he had overcome his fear of drowning in water

(iv) The given lines tells that with sincerity, dedication and practice, Douglas had become an expert swimmer with no fear of water.

(v) (a) Triggs Island and Stamp Act Island are located in Lake Wentworth.

(vi) (a) He addressed it

6. **The experience had a deep meaning for me, as only those who have known stark terror and conquered it can appreciate. In death there is peace. There is terror only in the fear of death, as Roosevelt knew when he said, "All we have to fear is fear itself." Because I had experienced both the sensation of dying and the terror that the fear of it can produce, the will to live somehow grew in intensity.** CBSE 2021 Term I Modified

(i) What was the impact of 'the experience' on the narrator's life?

(ii) Select the correct option from those given in brackets to fill in the blank.

The given words can be referred to as ....
(a paper presentation/words of wisdom)

(iii) Complete the sentence appropriately.
Roosevelt's opinion on fear is that ....

(iv) How had the narrator experienced 'the sensation of dying and the terror that fear it can produce?

(v) Choose the correct option which refers to 'only those' as intended by the narrator.

(a) Those who have the experience of drowning

(b) Those who have learnt swimming in YMCA pool

(c) Those who have experienced bullying

(d) Those who have experienced and conquered fear

(vi) Choose the option that best explains the expression 'deep meaning' in the extract.

(a) The experience left a deep scar in the narrator's life.

(b) The narrator drowned at the deep end of the pool.

(c) The narrator learnt a life lesson through that experience.

(d) The experience was still painful in the memory of the narrator.

Ans. (i) 'The experience' enhanced the narrator's survival instinct.

(ii) words of wisdom

(iii) one should not let fear enter one's mind.

(iv) The narrator had experienced 'the sensation of dying and the terror that fear of it can produce' while he was 10 or 11 years old at the YMCA. He had almost drowned in the deep end of the pool which had increased his fear of water.

(v) (d) Those who have experienced and conquered fear

(vi) (c) The narrator learnt a life lesson through that experience.

Short Answer Type Questions

1. 'It happened when I was ten or eleven years old.' Well-known author Ursula K. Le Guin once said, "First sentences are doors to worlds." In 20–30 words, describe how the first sentence of 'Deep Water' given above sets the tone of the text. Competency Based

Ans. It is true to say that the first sentences are doors to worlds. The first sentence of the lesson 'Deep Water' creates a sense of fear and mystery about an event that had caused a significant change in the narrator's life that the readers would soon get a glimpse into.

2. What factors made Douglas decide in favour of the YMCA pool?

Ans. Douglas' mother recommended that he should learn swimming at the YMCA swimming pool because it was safe, being only two or three feet deep at the shallow end with a gradual drop to nine feet at the other end. In contrast, the Yakima river was quite deep and several cases of drowning in it had been reported.

3. How did Douglas' introduction to the YMCA pool revive his childhood fear of water?

Ans. Douglas' introduction to the YMCA pool revived his childhood fear of water as when he had not yet learnt swimming, he was thrown into the pool's deep end by a bully wherein he sank to the bottom despite his best efforts.

4. "I was frightened, but not yet frightened out of my wits." says Douglas. Which qualities of the speaker are highlighted in the above statement? CBSE 2024

Ans. The speaker Douglas, despite being thrown into a terrifying situation at the YMCA pool, remained composed, stating, "I was frightened but not yet frightened out of my wits." Although submerged and swallowing water, the incident demonstrated Douglas' resilience and determination, despite his past trauma with water, showcasing his unwavering resolve to confront his fears.

5. "Father laughed, but there was terror in my heart." What does the above statement speak of the father? CBSE 2024

Or **"Father laughed, but there was terror in my heart at the overpowering force of the waves".**

Why did the narrator and his father have such contrasting emotions here? In 20-30 words, explain with reference to the story 'Deep water'. Competency Based

Ans. The statement "Father laughed, but there was terror in my heart" from 'Deep Water' suggests the difference between the experiences of the father and the child and how they both react to an event. The father thought his son was having fun. Further, the father was an adult who knew that the waves, which developed a deep fear in the narrator's heart, wouldn't harm him.

6. How did Douglas' experience at the beach in California affect him? CBSE 2020

Ans. Douglas developed an aversion to water in his early childhood due to his experience at a beach in California. When he was three or four years old, his father took him to the beach. The waves knocked him down and swept over him. This experience developed a fear of water in his mind.

7. What did Douglas experience when he went down to the bottom of the pool for the first time? CBSE 2011, 10

Ans. As Douglas went down to the bottom of the pool for the first time, he felt that the way down the pool was very long and that his lungs were ready to burst.
He summoned all his strength and jumped up but could not reach the surface and began to sink again.

8. When Douglas realised that he was sinking, how did he plan to save himself?

Ans. When Douglas realised that he was sinking, he thought that when his feet would hit the bottom, he would make a big jump, come to the surface and lie flat on it. Then he would easily paddle to the edge of the pool.

9. What sort of terror seized Douglas as he went down in the water with a yellow glow? How could he feel that he was still alive?

Ans. When Douglas went down in the water with a yellow glow for the second time, a stark terror seized him. It was beyond control or understanding. Douglas was paralysed with fear and could not move his limbs. Only his throbbing heart and the pounding in his head made him feel that he was still alive.

10. How did Douglas get rescued when he was thrown in the pool?

Ans. The narrator does not mention how Douglas was rescued. However, we, as readers are shown that when Douglas regained consciousness, he was vomiting while lying on his stomach beside the pool. Apparently, he had been rescued by someone.

11. Mention any two long term consequences of the drowning incident on Douglas.

Ans. Two long term consequences of the drowning incident on Douglas were

(i) Douglas always felt terrified when near water. Fear gripped him when he came near any water body.

(ii) He was deprived of enjoying any water related activities like fishing, swimming, canoeing, boating, etc.

12. What qualities turned Douglas into a good swimmer?

Ans. William Douglas' determination, sincerity, courage and will to get rid of his fear of water were the qualities that turned him into a good swimmer. Douglas regretted being deprived of enjoying water-based activities and sports. His ardent wish to enjoy such activities and regain his lost confidence while staying in water were the reasons for his determination to get over his fear of water. As he hired an instructor, he showed sincerity and courage in his practice to become a swimmer.

13. Seemingly small everyday wins are actually the greatest learning's of life. Comment on the statement with reference to the chapter 'Deep Water'. Competency Based

Ans. It is true that seemingly small everyday wins are actually the greatest learning's of life. This is true for Douglas when he was learning how to swim with the help of the instructor. The instructor took very small steps in teaching Douglas how to swim. Gradually, these small steps turned Douglas into a successful swimmer.

14. If you could give the chapter a new title, what would it be? Support your answer with reference to the chapter 'Deep Water'. Competency Based

Ans. If I could give the chapter a new title, I would call it 'Fear of Fear'. This is so because Douglas himself accepts that we need to fear the idea of fear itself.

As the narrator of the story, he recounts his experience of how he got over his fear inspiring his readers to get over their fears themselves.

15. Discus the significance of the references to the natural world in the chapter 'Deep Water'. CBSE Question Bank 2021

Ans. The natural world holds a special significance in the lesson as it indicates the growth of Douglas as a swimmer. In the beginning, we know that Douglas would not go to the Takima river but in the end he swims across various lakes and water bodies. This contrast shows the development of Douglas as an individual.

16. What handicap did Douglas suffer from? How did he overcome that? CBSE 2023

Ans. The handicap that afflicted Douglas was his fear of water which he had developed after a traumatic experience in a pool. This deprived him of the basic joys of life.

He overcame this fear by gradually exposing himself to water with the help of an instructor who taught him how to swim. He eventually conquered his fear and swam in various places to challenge himself and overcome his fear completely.

17. Based on your reading of 'Deep Water', describe how childhood memories impacted Douglas as an adult. Answer in 40-50 words. Competency Based

Ans. Douglas went through traumatic experiences of being bullied and almost drowning in his childhood. The trauma caused by these powerful memories deeply impacted his experiences as he grew up. He developed a fear of water and could not enjoy activities like fishing and boating. The fear caused by the childhood memories of terror thus continued to limit his experiences well into adulthood.

Long Answer Type Questions

1. How did Douglas develop a fear of water?

Ans. Douglas initially developed a fear of water when he was three or four years old. It happened when his father took him to the beach in California. He and his father stood together in the surf. The waves of the water knocked the author down and swept over him. He was frightened and his breath was gone.

Later, the fear of water strengthened its hold on Douglas' mind and personality when the author was about ten or twelve years old. He went to YMCA pool to learn swimming. There, a terrible incident occurred with him which increased his fear of water. When he reached the swimming pool, no one else was there. He was scared of going in water alone and sat on the side of the pool to wait for others. Just then, a big boy threw him into the pool. He did not know how to swim and, thus, felt that he was going to drown.

2. Douglas fully realised the truth of Roosevelt's statement 'All we have to fear is fear itself'. How did this realisation help him brush aside his fear and become an expert swimmer?

Ans. Roosevelt said, "All we have to fear is fear itself". Douglas had experienced both the sensation of dying and the terror that fear of it can produce. As a result, he realised that a strong will, hard determination, courage and toil as well as honest labour win over all our terrors and fears.

This realisation made him resolve to learn swimming by engaging an instructor. This instructor, gradually, built Douglas into a swimmer. Then, he went to Lake Wentworth, dived at Triggs Island and swam two miles across the lakes to Stamp Act Island. Finally he had conquered his fear of water.

3. Douglas has a near-death experience in his childhood which has a negative as well as a positive outcome. Justify the statement with evidences from the text.

Ans. The near death experience in the YMCA swimming pool had both positive as well as negative outcomes for Douglas. The negative outcome was that for many days and months, a fear of water haunted Douglas. The slightest exertion upset him and he stayed away from the pool. Even after a few years, whenever Douglas wanted to swim or wade into waters of different rivers, his old fear would return and would grip his mind and body badly. His legs would not move as if they were paralysed and a chilling horror would surround him making him motionless. As a result, he was devoid of pleasures of swimming, rafting, fishing, canoeing and other water sports. He used every possible way to overcome his fear but it would haunt him again and again.

The positive outcome of this experience was that finally he decided to get a swimming instructor and learn to swim. He went to a pool and under his guidance he practiced five days a week, an hour each day. After seven months of intense practice, Douglas overcame his fear of water and practiced on his own by swimming across various lakes.

4. 'Deep Water' and 'Indigo' bring out the importance of overcoming fear. Discuss the two texts with reference to the above statements. **CBSE 2025**

Or The prose selections, 'Deep Water' and 'Indigo', bring out the importance of overcoming fear, in order to be able to lead our lives successfully.

Imagine yourself to be a motivational speaker who has to address high school students. Write this address in 120-150 words elaborating on occurrences from the two texts to inspire your audience and to convince them about the importance of overcoming fear.

You may begin like this ...

Good morning, students!

We all know what it's like to be afraid. Fear is our body's natural response to a perceived threat or danger. But when ... **Competency Based**

Ans. Fear is our body's natural response to a perceived threat or danger. But when we are determined to learn to face our fears, we win at life and become a champion.

It is no hidden fact that fear immobilises us and prevents us from progressing. We have read the story of William Douglas. Due to his fear of water he could not lead a normal life. He could not go fishing, canoeing, etc. with his friends. But he decided to get over his fear. Rather than giving into it, he learnt swimming and practiced it with full, persistence determination and sincerity till his fear dissipated.

Much like Douglas, we also have read about the peasants of Champaran who could not take a stand for their rights due to their fear of the Britishers. It was when they gathered around the courthouse in Motihari that they realised that the main hurdle in them getting justice was their fear. Once, they understood the need to overcome their fear, they came together and relentlessly worked towards getting justice. Thus, we need to face our fear, devise a plan and work through it.

It is important to remember that fear does not get dispelled in an instant. It takes months and even years of persistence to get over it. It takes time but once the fear fades away, one is free to live life to the fullest.

5. Imagine that the bully who threw Douglas into the pool, reads this chapter and realises his mistake. As the bully, write a diary entry penning down your response to Douglas' perseverance and your own feelings of guilt and regret. **Competency Based**

Ans. Tuesday, 12th November, 20XX

Dear Diary

Today I remembered something that completely shook my world. I read the story 'Deep water' written by William Douglas.

I do not remember the man but I think he remembers me and for a reason that I am not proud of. To think of it, I remember I was a mischievous boy.

My sister tells me I was a bully but I never believed her until today. Now that I think of it, I remember, I threw a young timid looking boy in the deep end of the pool wherein he could have drowned.

I am ashamed of myself for the act and now feel guilt ridden, realising how a simple fun act like this could have destroyed Douglas. At the same time, I am in awe of the chap's perseverance.

He did not lose hope and learned swimming, knowing fully well the intensity of his fear. Today, I only hope to meet him and apologise to him.

XYZ

6. Douglas' mother writes to the YMCA authorities holding them accountable for the mishap as well as demanding that the authorities employ a team of guards near the pool for supervision of the children. As the mother, write a letter to the authorities with reference to the case of your son.

You may begin like this. **CBSE Question Bank 2021**

Sir

Subject: Negligence on Premises

This is with reference to the incident of near fatal drowning of my son, William on your premises. We were...

Ans. Sir

Subject Negligence on Premises

This is with reference to the incident of near fatal drowning of my son, William on your premises. We were great admirers of the way the YMCA Cooperation taught children swimming under expert guidance. We posed our confidence in you that your organisation will ensure that no accident happens with any child in your premises.

All those expectations, however, met with a massive failure, when my child was heedlessly thrown in the deep end of the pool without any instructor around. My child, William, could have died.
It is with deep regret that I have to mention that your carelessness had made me skeptical of sending my child to your organisation.

I, as a parent, hold your organisation accountable for the mishap since my child was your responsibility.

I hope that my complaint and experience is the last one in your organisation. To make sure this does not happen again, I would suggest that you employ a team of guards near the pool for supervision of the children. Hoping the best for your organisation.

Thanking you

Mrs. Douglas

7. The excerpt 'Deep Water' presents the growth of Douglas from a fearful boy to a courageous wise man. Elucidate mentioning the growth qualities of Douglas. Mention his growth as well as his constant qualities.

Ans. It is true to say that the 'Deep Water' presents the growth of Douglas from a fearful boy to a courageous wise man. The excerpt starts with Douglas remembering himself as a small boy who feared water. He was a conscious child who had faced two misadventures-one with his father and the other at the YMCA pool which lead to the development of Hydrophobia. His fear had impacted Douglas so much that he could not bear to be near water or enjoy any water activities. Hence, he hired an instructor and learned swimming.

In his learning curve, Douglas showed determination, courage, will and sincerity that he had developed to get over the fear. When he finally gets over his fear, we see Douglas as a wise man imparting wisdom regarding the psychology of fear.

One constant thing about Douglas that does not change is that he is a great strategist and planner. Even as a child, when he was thrown into the YMCA pool, he plans how to save himself. Later, he plans exactly how to test his fear and overcome it finally.

8. Courage is not the absence of fear but the triumph over it. In 100–120 words, comment on the statement above with reference to the text 'Deep Water'. State two ways in which the narrator strives to overcome his fear.

Ans. It is true that courage is not the absence of fear but the triumph over it. When we overcome our fears, we become confident and take on a journey towards self-awareness. In the story 'Deep Water', Douglas learns this lesson when he finally swims across the lake.

To become a swimmer, Douglas accepts his fear and decides to get professional assistance to gain the required skills. He not only acknowledges his fear but also does everything to overcome it. Even when he becomes a competent swimmer, the voice of fear inside him is still present. He confronts his fear repeatedly and in challenging ways. He chooses to look it in the face and triumph over it. So the fear did not become weaker but it is the narrator who became stronger.

Thus, with courage, Douglas faces his fears until it no longer has any effect on him. He successfully swims in a difficult place on his own until he observes the fear inside him vanish.

SELF ASSESSMENT TEST

Extract Based Questions

Read the extract given below and answer the questions that follow.

1. And then, strangely, there was light. I was comming out of the awful yellow water. At least my eyes were. My nose was almost out too.

Then I started going down for third time. I sucked for air and got water. The yellowish light was going out.

Then all effort ceased. I relaxed. Even my legs felt limp; and a blackness swept over my brain. It wiped out fear; it wiped out terror.

There was no more panic. It was quiet and peaceful. Nothing to be afraid of.

(i) Why did all efforts come to cease?

(ii) Select the correct option from those given in brackets to fill in the blank.

The narrator in the given extract is referring to a .... (trauma/misadventure).

(iii) Complete the sentence with an appropriate explanation as per the extract.

Douglas felt quiet and peaceful because ....

(iv) Analyse "There was no more panic. It was quiet and peaceful. Nothing to be afraid of."

(v) What strange thing is the narrator talking about?

(a) That he was coming out
(b) That the water had receded
(c) That it was getting dark
(d) That he had fallen asleep

(vi) What did the narrator feel?

(a) He must try again
(b) His legs felt limp
(c) He must seek revenge from the big bully
(d) His mother must come to help him

Short Answer Type Questions

Answer the following questions in 40-50 words.

1. Why was Douglas' plan to come up in the water of the pool a failure?

2. Why didn't Douglas dare to learn swimming in the Yakima river?

3. What lesson did Douglas learn when he got rid of his fear of water?

4. Describe both the physical and emotional impacts that the misadventure at the YMCA pool had on the narrator.

5. Getting rid of fear is an extremely difficult task. Elucidate with reference to the chapter 'Deep Water'.

Long Answer Type Questions

Answer the following questions in 120-150 words.

1. Fear is something that we must learn to overcome if we want to succeed in life. How did Douglas get over his fear of water?

2. The childhood experience of terror made Douglas stronger and more determined. Elucidate the above statement supporting it with evidences from the text.

04

The Rattrap

About the Author

Selma Lagerlof (1858-1940) was a Swedish author and teacher, who became the first woman writer to win the Nobel Prize in Literature. She did not publish anything until 1890, when a Swedish weekly gave her the first prize in a literary competition and published excerpts from the book which was to be her first, best and most popular work, 'Gösta Berlings Saga'. During her lifetime, she was loved throughout the world because of both her gift for storytelling and her

YOUR STUDY GOALS

- Chapter Sketch
- About the Characters
- Summary of the Chapter

YOUR PRACTICE GOAL

- NCERT Folder
- Extract Based Questions
- Short Answer Type Questions
- Long Answer Type Questions

Chapter Sketch

The Rattrap is based on the theme that the essential goodness in a human being can be awakened through understanding and love. The story is set amidst the iron mines of Sweden. The author has beautifully brought out human loneliness and the need to bond with others.

About the Characters

The Peddler A poor man who sold rattraps for a living and was a petty thief.

The Crofter A simple trusting person who is robbed by the peddler.

The Ironmaster A stern taskmaster and law-abiding person. He trusts the peddler due to his daughter's persuasion.

Edla The ironmaster's daughter who is a kind and compassionate lady.

People at the Ironworks This includes the master blacksmith and his helper. They seem to be hardworking people who do not mind helping the poor with shelter.

Captains We have two captains in the story- Nils Olof and Von Stahle. These captains represent honesty and sincerity which the peddler accepts at the end.

Summary of the Chapter

The Rattrap Peddler

Once upon a time, there was a vagabond who went around selling small rattraps. He made them from the material he got by begging in stores or at farms. However, his business was not profitable and so, he had to beg and steal to survive. He wore dirty and torn clothes, was thin in stature and his eyes showed that he was hungry. All-in-all, he lived a sad and monotonous life.

The Peddler's Amusing Thought

One day, while he was engrossed in his thoughts about rattraps, a very amusing idea came to his mind that the world was a big rattrap. It offered comforts and joys just like the rattrap offered cheese and pork. As soon as a rat was tempted to touch the bait, it trapped him.

This philosophy made the peddler happy as the world had not treated him right.

Stealing From the Crofter

One evening, the peddler went to a small grey cottage to seek shelter for the night. To his surprise, the owner, an old crofter invited the peddler in. He served food, offered him tobacco and played card games with him.

The crofter was very talkative. He informed the peddler that he used to work at the Ramsjö Ironworks. Now, he had earned thirty kronor by selling his cow's milk. Then, the crofter showed him the money.

Next day, both men left the cottage at the same time. But, half an hour later the peddler went to the window, took out the thirty kronor and left. He avoided the public highway and went into the woods, as he felt he would be safer and no one would be able to catch him. The peddler was lost in the forest. Soon, he realised that he had been fooled by the bait and thus, trapped by the rattrap.

The Ramsjö Ironworks

It was late December and the forest had become dark. The peddler was exhausted and felt that he would die. Just then, he heard the sound of the regular thumping of a hammer. When he realised that the sound was coming from an iron mill, he reached the Ramsjö Ironworks.

The peddler entered the ironworks while the people in the ironworks were working. The ironworks was so noisy that no one noticed the peddler entering the forge. However, he was given permission to stay the night there.

The Ironmaster

Ramsjö Ironworks was owned by a popular ironmaster who did regular inspections. On that night, the ironmaster came into the forge for his inspection and noticed the peddler. In the dim light, he mistook the peddler for an old regimental comrade, Nils Olof. The peddler didn't try to clear his doubt as he thought the ironmaster might give him some money. However, the ironmaster invited him home. The peddler declined the invitation.

Christmas Invite

The ironmaster assumed that the peddler felt embarrassed. He tried to comfort the peddler and told him that his wife Elizabeth was dead, his sons were settled abroad and he lived with his daughter Edla. He added that they did not have any company for Christmas and wanted him to enjoy the festival with them. But the peddler constantly refused to go with him.

The ironmaster left the mill. Soon, Edla, the ironmaster's daughter came to the Ironworks and went to the peddler. Edla was a simple, kind and shy girl. When she saw the peddler, she somehow sensed that the peddler was either a thief on the run or an escaped prisoner. Still, she was very friendly and kind to him. The peddler felt confidence in her and accepted the invitation.

Edla's Doubt

During the journey to the ironmaster's home, the peddler regretted stealing the money. The next day was Christmas Eve, and the ironmaster was happy to meet his old regimental comrade. He told Edla that they needed to feed him well and provide him with a better business.

However, Edla expressed her doubt about the peddler, as he didn't display the slightest sign of being educated.
To this, the ironmaster told her to have some patience. Just then, the peddler entered the room. He was now wearing clothes which belonged to the ironmaster.

The Peddler's Reality

When the ironmaster saw the peddler, he realised that he had made a mistake and was very angry. The peddler was not his friend. The peddler explained that he never said to the ironmaster that he was Nils Olof. He had even pleaded and begged for not coming to the manor house. He added that he could put on his rags and go away.

The ironmaster decided to take the peddler to the Sheriff. This angered the peddler and he told the ironmaster his philosophy of the world being a big rattrap. Hearing this, the ironmaster started laughing and asked the peddler to leave.

Edla's Kindness

Just as the peddler was about to leave, Edla told her father that she did not want him to leave. She felt that they had promised the peddler Christmas cheer and it would be wrong to send him away. Edla further added that the peddler must have been through a bad time and could not even sleep unafraid. The ironmaster gave in and the peddler was allowed to stay on for Christmas.

At ironmaster's house, the peddler did nothing but sleep. The ironmaster and Edla gifted him the suit that he was wearing as a Christmas present. Edla also told him that he was welcome to spend the next Christmas with them.

The Christmas Present

The next morning the ironmaster and his daughter went to the church, leaving the peddler at home. When they were returning home and Edla was very sad. At the church, they learned that a rattrap seller had robbed an old crofter.

The ironmaster was furious and thought that by the time they would reach home, the peddler would have escaped with all their valuables.

When the ironmaster and his daughter reached home, they got to know that the peddler had left with nothing. In fact, he had left behind a little Christmas present for Edla.

Edla opened the package and found a rattrap with three wrinkled ten kronor notes and a letter.

The peddler had written that since Edla had treated him like a real captain, he also wanted to be nice to her. He wanted the money to be returned to the crofter. He even signed the letter as 'Captain Von Stahle'.

Word-Meaning

rattraps	— traps for catching rats
at odd moments	— in his free time
keep body and soul together	— survive, especially in difficult circumstances
sunken	— hollow
vagabond	— a person who wanders from place to place without a home or job
plods along the road	— walks slowly with heavy steps on the road
fallen into a line of thought	— started thinking about something
set baits	— offering temptations
trudging	— walking slowly with heavy steps
sour	— hostile
mjölis	— a card game played in Sweden
confidences	— secrets, private matters
crofter	— small farmer
bossy	— (here) cow
creamery	— a factory that produces butter and cheese
kronor	— the currency of Sweden
peddler	— a person who goes from place to place selling small goods
summoned	— gathered
smelter	— an establishment for producing a base metal from its ore
forge	— a furnace where metals are heated or wrought
barges	— long flat-bottomed boats for carrying heavy goods on canals or rivers
scows	— flat-bottomed boats for transporting cargo to and from ships in harbour
pig iron	— crude iron first obtained from a smelting furnace
maw	— mouth or opening
nodded a haughty consent	— arrogantly agreed
ironmaster	— the master or proprietor of an ironworks
ragamuffin	— a person in ragged, dirty clothes
eased his way	— came in slowly and carefully
deigned	— condescended
slouch hat	— a hat with a wide flexible brim or edge
undeceive	— reveal his real identity to
regiment	— a unit of an army commanded by a lieutenant colonel
manor house	— a large country house with lands
valet	— personal attendant
apprentice	— a person who is learning a trade from a skilled employer
things have gone downhill	— matters have deteriorated or worsened
tramp	— homeless person who lives by begging or doing casual work
puckered	— wrinkled
dissimulate	— pretend
Sheriff	— the chief executive officer of a district having administrative and judicial powers
parson	— priest
interceded	— intervened or spoke on behalf of somebody else
fare	— a range of food
in good season	— on time

Important Themes of the Chapter

Power of Human Kindness 'The Rattrap' is a short story that centers around the transforming power of human kindness. A peddler goes from seeing the world as 'one big rattrap' and engaging in robbery to returning his stolen money and proclaiming himself free-all as a result of experiencing true kindness and generosity from Edla Willmansson on Christmas Eve. By showing the peddler's potential for positive change, the writer expresses a belief that there is a core of goodness in all people, and that this goodness can be unlocked through compassion and kindness.

The Human Need For Companionship 'The Rattrap' also explores the basic human need for companionship and community, and shows the negative effects of loneliness. Most of the characters in the story live a sad and lonely life. The peddler, the old crofter and the ironmaster seek companionship.

The Human Tendency to Fall into Material Gain The story also presents the human inclination to gain material wealth. It uses the metaphor of a rattrap to show how people are tempted by material benefits like riches, shelter, food and clothing.

The Role of Identity 'The Rattrap' also concerns itself with issues of identity, especially the construction of identity through actions and choices, and the role that names can play in this process. Ultimately, the story suggests that identity is a fluid thing, and people can change or be changed to inhabit different identities based on their choices and the actions of others.

NCERT Folder

Think as you Read (NCERT Page 34)

1. From where did the peddler get the idea of the world being a rattrap?

Or In what sense was the world a big rattrap, according to the peddler?

Or Explain the metaphor of 'The Rattrap' as explained by the peddler. CBSE 2022 Term II

Or Explain the metaphor of the rattrap. CBSE 2023

Ans. The peddler was a vagabond who went around selling rattraps made by him. One day, as he was just thinking about his own rattraps, he was struck by the idea that the world was a big rattrap. In this rattrap, riches, food, joys and shelter served as baits to tempt people, just like a rattrap offered cheese or meat to tempt rats. As soon as one was tempted to touch the bait, the rattrap closed and everything came to an end.

2. Why was he amused by this idea?

Ans. Wherever the peddler went, people were hostile to him and chased him away. So, he was amused by the idea of the world being a big rattrap. He was also happy that those who chased him away would also be tempted and caught up in the rattrap one day.

3. Did the peddler expect the kind of hospitality that he received from the crofter?

Or Why was the peddler surprised when he knocked on the door of the cottage?

Ans. No, the peddler did not expect the kind of hospitality that he received from the crofter. Wherever the peddler went, people were hostile to him and chased him away. So, the peddler was surprised when he knocked on the door of the cottage and the crofter welcomed him and also gave him food and shelter.

4. Why was the crofter so talkative and friendly with the peddler?

Ans. The crofter was talkative and friendly with the peddler because he was an old man with no wife or children and lived alone in his cottage. He was happy to get someone to talk to and share his feelings with. So, he welcomed the peddler, gave him food and even played a game of cards with him.

5. Why did he show the thirty kronor to the peddler?

Ans. The crofter showed the thirty kronor to the peddler because he felt proud that he had earned this money from selling the cow's milk to the creamery. Further, he thought that the stranger didn't believe him, so he showed him the money.

6. Did the peddler respect the confidence reposed in him by the crofter?

Ans. No, the peddler didn't respect the confidence reposed in him by the crofter. The crofter had showed him the thirty kronor which he had earned and where it was kept in a pouch near a window. The next day, when the crofter had gone out to deliver the cow's milk to the creamery, the peddler came back, broke the window pane and stole the thirty kronor from the pouch which was kept near the window.

Think as you Read (NCERT Page 37)

1. What made the peddler think that he had indeed fallen into a rattrap? CBSE 2022 Term II

Ans. After stealing the crofter's money, the peddler went into the woods because of the fear of getting identified and caught on the public highway. It was a big and confusing forest, and the peddler lost his way in it. Suddenly, he realised that he himself had fallen into a rattrap.

He thought that the forest was a big rattrap and the thirty kronor were like a bait which had been set to tempt him. He had allowed himself to be fooled and so, was caught in the rattrap.

2. Why did the ironmaster speak kindly to the peddler and invite him home?

Ans. The ironmaster, the owner of the Ramsjö Ironworks, spoke kindly to the peddler and invited him home because he mistook the peddler for his old regimental comrade, Nils Olof, who had fallen on evil days.

3. Why did the peddler decline the invitation?

Or Why was the peddler hesitant to accompany the ironmaster to the manor house? CBSE 2023

Ans. The peddler declined the invitation of the ironmaster because he was carrying the crofter's money which he had stolen. He thought that he would be handed over to the police if the ironmaster discovered the theft.

Think as you Read (NCERT Page 41)

1. What made the peddler accept Edla Willmansson's invitation? CBSE 2022 Term II

Ans. Edla Willmansson's kindness made the peddler feel that he could trust her and this made him accept her invitation. Edla talked to him compassionately assuring him that no harm would come to him and that he would be at liberty to leave whenever he wanted.

2. What doubts did Edla have about the peddler?

Ans. When Edla met the peddler, he became afraid. This made Edla doubtful of the peddler and his identity. She thought that either he had stolen something or he had escaped from jail.

Later, she even told her father that there was nothing about him which shows that he was once an educated man.

3. When did the ironmaster realise his mistake?

Ans. The ironmaster realised his mistake the next day when he saw the peddler in broad daylight with a fine haircut and a well-shaven face. When the ironmaster had first seen the peddler in the dim light from the furnace, he had mistaken him for an old colleague. Now, he realised that this man was somebody else.

4. What did the peddler say in his defence when it was clear that he was not the person the ironmaster had thought he was?

Or The iron master accuses the peddler of not being quite honest. What does the peddler say to justify the situation? CBSE 2022 Term II

Ans. In his defence, the peddler told the ironmaster that he had never pretended that he was the ironmaster's friend. He made no further efforts to deceive the ironmaster. He said that it was not his fault as he had begged to be allowed to stay on at the mill for the night. He had even declined the ironmaster's repeated invitation. He further said that he was ready to put on his rags again and go away.

5. Why did Edla still entertain the peddler even after she knew the truth about him?

Or Why did Edla plead with her father not to send the vagabond away?

Ans. Edla still entertained the peddler even after she knew the truth about him as it was Christmas Eve and Edla wanted to keep the spirit of Christmas by providing him with a day of comfort and solace. She justified it as they had invited him against his will. So, she pleaded with her father not to send the vagabond away.

Think as you Read (NCERT Page 42)

1. Why was Edla happy to see the gift left by the peddler?

Ans. Edla was happy to see the gift left by the peddler because it was unexpected. Earlier, Edla was shocked to learn that their guest was actually a thief. She had pleaded with her father to let the peddler stay. She held herself responsible for offering shelter to a thief.

But when she found the stolen thirty kronor in a rattrap, she was overjoyed to understand that her kindness and compassion had changed the peddler and brought out his essential goodness.

2. Why did the peddler sign himself as Captain Von Stahle? CBSE 2022

Ans. The peddler signed himself as Captain Von Stahle because he had been treated at the ironmaster's home like a real captain despite of knowing about his real identity.

He wanted to repay Edla for her kindness just as a real captain would have done. It was an indication that he wanted to retain the dignity and respect accorded to him.

Understanding the Text (NCERT Page 43)

1. How does the peddler interpret the acts of kindness and hospitality shown by the crofter, the ironmaster and his daughter?

Ans. The peddler interpreted the acts of kindness and hospitality shown by the crofter, the ironmaster and his daughter in different ways.

Initially, the peddler is shocked by the crofter's hospitality but later, he heartily accepts the generosity. However, this hospitality does not change him. He robs the crofter of his hard-earned money just because it was easy to do so.

With the ironmaster, the peddler is cautious. When the ironmaster mistakes him to be his old regimental comrade, the peddler does not disclose his true identity in the hope of getting a few kronor. However, when the ironmaster invites him home, he rejects it persistently.

The change in the peddler comes with Edla. Upon Edla's request, the peddler goes to the ironmaster's home. Edla's warmth, sympathy and hospitality transforms him in the end. She elevates him to the status of a captain, which makes him redeem himself from being a petty thief. It stirs the innate goodness of his heart. He no more feels trapped but regards her kindness as an act of nobility.

2. What are the instances in the story that show that the character of the ironmaster is different from that of his daughter in many ways?

Or Give examples from the story, 'The Rattrap' to show how the ironmaster is different from his daughter.

Or Edla is a contrast to her father, the ironmaster. Explain.

CBSE 2023

Ans. The father-daughter duo, the ironmaster and Edla are different people with very different personalities.

The ironmaster was a man of power and ambition. He was so hardwarking, disciplined and sober that he did rounds in his mills to make sure that everything was working properly. But he was also impulsive and completely non-persuasive. He invited the peddler home without confirming his identity and even when the peddle refused, he sent his daughter to convince the latter to come to his home.

The ironmaster is also a realist. He is practical and morally strict. As soon as he sees the peddler's true identity, he orders him to leave. While he does not show any softness with the peddler, he does so with his daughter whose wishes he accepts.

On the other hand, Edla, the ironmaster's daughter, was a kind and compassionate lady who was really sympathetic and considerate towards the peddler right from the beginning. She is observant and suspicious of the peddler's identity.

She treated him with respect and dignity even after knowing that was not a captain. It was her generous attitude which finally changed the peddler, bringing out the essential goodness of his nature.

3. The story has many instances of unexpected reactions from the characters to others' behaviour. Pick out instances of these surprises.

Ans. The instances of unexpected reactions from the characters to others' behaviour are

- The old crofter welcomes the tramp for shelter and food at night. He even reposes his trust in him by showing him the money and the place where it was kept. The peddler's act of stealing the crofter's hard-earned thirty kronor is unexpected.
- The peddler seeks refuge in the forge, meets the ironmaster and the latter mistakes him to be his old regimental comrade. His invitation to the tramp to come for Christmas Eve to the manor house leaves one astounded.
- The peddler's act of accepting Edla's invitation, in spite of his guilt about the stolen money and thoughts about entering the lion's den, is surprising.
- When the peddler, left to himself in the manor house, has every opportunity to slip out with the valuables, he does not do so. Even the ironmaster expects something like this to happen. However, the peddler goes away, leaving behind a small rattrap as a Christmas gift and the thirty kronor he had stolen to be returned to the rightful owner. This is also unexpected.
- The peddler's letter addressed to Edla, expressing his gratitude for elevating him to the status of captain, giving him a chance to free himself from the rattrap of the world and redeeming him, also gives us a pleasant surprise.

Thus, the story is replete with instances of unexpected reactions and surprises.

4. What made the peddler finally change his ways?

Ans. Edla's kindness, compassion and caring behaviour finally made the peddler change his ways. The peddler believed in giving back to the world what he received from it. He was always treated with contempt and hostility and so he never did anything good. However, as Edla had treated him with the love and respect befitting a captain when she knew that he was a poor vagabond, he decided to change his ways and live with dignity and respect.

5. How does the metaphor of the rattrap serve to highlight the human predicament?

Ans. The peddler, in the course of his wandering, suddenly thinks about the whole world as a big rattrap. Just as cheese and meat are baits in the rattrap, similarly the riches, joy, shelter and food that the world offers are baits to entrap and ensnare people.

Being an embittered man, shunned by everybody, these thoughts give 'unwonted joy' to the tramp. He thinks of all the people around him who have fallen into the trap.

The musings of the tramp do have an iota of truth in them. We are tempted by temptations, desires and needs. We go all out to satisfy them. In this desire to amass and accumulate more and more, we are entrapped by the world.

Just in case we do not get the things we want, we are plunged into despair and gloom. In this way, the metaphor of the rattrap highlights the human predicament.

6. The peddler comes out as a person with a subtle sense of humour. How does this serve in lightening the seriousness of the theme of the story and also endear him to us?

Ans. It is true to say that the peddler comes out as a person with a subtle sense of humour. His humour is derived from his circumstances and makes us realise the various serious themes of the story. The peddler, with his subtle sense of humour, equates the rattraps he makes to the world, which he believes is a huge rattrap offering baits like comfort, food, shelter and material benefits. One day the rattrap traps us and there is no way out. His humour is further revealed during his interactions with the ironmaster and his daughter after the truth about him becomes known. He is neither afraid of being turned out in cold in rags nor of being sent to prison. He makes the ironmaster laugh with his metaphor of the rattrap.

This philosophy of the rattrap point us to the concept of obsession over material gains that drives human actions.

Exam Pattern Questions

Extract Based Questions

Read the extracts given below and answer the questions that follow.

1. "It offered riches and joys, shelter and food, heat and clothing, exactly as the rattrap offered cheese and pork, and as soon as anyone let himself be tempted to touch the bait, it closed in on him, and then everything came to an end.

The world had, of course, never been very kind to him, so it gave him unwanted joy to think ill of it in this way."

(i) How will the peddler describe the world?

(ii) Select the correct option from those given in bracket to fill in the blank.

The peddler developed his philosophy while he was .... (working/walking) along the road.

(iii) Complete the sentence with an appropriate explanation, as per the extract.

The peddler said that the world was not very kind to him because ....

(iv) How had the peddler come across the philosophy elucidated in the given extract?

(v) Select the option that matches the reference to 'riches and joys, shelter and food'.

(a) Deceit
(b) Temptation
(c) Materialism
(d) Luxury

(vi) The given extract does not talk about

(a) how people treated the peddler
(b) the philosophy of the rattrap seller
(c) the characteristics of the peddler
(d) the monotony of peddler's life

Ans. (i) The peddler described the world as unjust and hostile because it had never been kind to him.

(ii) walking

(iii) he was a poor rattrap seller. He wore rags, had sunken cheeks and overall looked very dirty.

(iv) The peddler had come up with the world being a rattrap while sitting and thinking about his own rattraps.

(v) (b) Temptation

(vi) (b) the philosophy of the rattrap seller

2. As he walked along with the money in his pocket he felt quite pleased with his smartness. He realised, of course that at first he dared not continue on the public highway, but must turn off the road, into the woods. During the first hours this caused him no difficulty. Later in the day it became worse, for it was a big and confusing forest which he had gotten into. He tried, to be sure, to walk in a definite direction, but the paths twisted back and forth so strangely! He walked and walked without coming to the end of the wood, and finally he realised that he had only been walking around in the same part of the forest. All at once he recalled his thoughts about the world and the rattrap. Now his own turn had come.

(i) How would you judge the rattrap sellers being pleased with his smartness?

(ii) Select the correct option from those given in brackets to fill in the blank.

All at once he recalled his thoughts about the world and the rattrap. This expression indicates .... (suddenness/anxiety)

(iii) Complete the sentence appropriately.

The rattrap seller did not stay on the public highway because ....

(iv) 'Now his own turn had come.' What statement reflects this?

(a) He had become confused in the forest.
(b) He had been feeling guilty of what he has done.
(c) He had fallen prey to the rattrap.
(d) He had become a criminal.

(v) Why did the narrator feel quite pleased?

(a) For his smartness resulting in his favour
(b) For deceiving his ownself
(c) For befooling his friends
(d) For robbery in the supermarket

(vi) On the basis of the extract, choose the correct option with reference to the two statements given below.

I. The Peddler was scared of the police.
II. The Peddler had recently committed a theft.

(a) I can be inferred from the extract but II cannot.
(b) I cannot be inferred from the extract but II can.
(c) I is true but II is false
(d) II is the reason for I.

Ans. (i) As a reader, I feel disgusted by the fact that rattrap seller was pleased with his smartness in stealing someone's hard earned money. Further, the fact that he had broken the trust and faith shown to him by the crofter, intensifies the feelings of disgust.

(ii) suddenness

(iii) he feared that he would be identified as the thief and caught by the police

(iv) (c) He had fallen prey to the rattrap.

(v) (a) For his smartness resulting in his favour

(vi) (d) II is the reason for I.

3. During one of the long dark evenings just before Christmas, the master smith and his helper sat in the dark forge near the furnace waiting for the pig iron, which had been put in the fire, to be ready to put on the anvil. Every now and then one of them got up to stir the glowing mass with a long iron bar, returning in a few moments dripping with perspiration, though, as was the custom, he wore nothing but a long shirt and a pair of wooden shoes.

(i) What was the master Smith waiting for?

(ii) Select the suitable word from the brackets to complete the following analogy.

Adversity : Misfortune :: Tradition : ... . (Forge/Custom)

(iii) Complete the sentences with an appropriate explanation, as per the extract.
The given lines describes the scene inside Ramjso Ironworks. The description is significant because ....

(iv) What can we say about the workers of the Ironworks based on the given extract?

(v) How were they stirring the glowing mass?

(a) By shovelling the charcoal
(b) By heating the furnace
(c) By using a long iron bar
(d) By blowing the fire hard

(vi) What was the custom?

(a) To sit with the helper in the dark forge
(b) To wear nothing but a long shirt and a pair of wooden shoes
(c) Shovelling the charcoal into the maw of the furnace
(d) Dripping with perspiration

Ans. (i) The master Smith was waiting for the pig iron to be ready to put on anvil.

(ii) Custom

(iii) it indicates that the peddler would find shelter in the warmth of the Ironworks.

(iv) Based on the given extract, we can say that the workers at the iron works were hardworking people who were dedicatedly doing their task even on Christmas Eve.

(v) (c) By using a long iron bar

(vi) (b) To wear nothing but a long shirt and a pair of wooden shoes

4. "I am thinking of the stranger here", said Edla "He walks and walks the whole year long and there is probably not a single place in the whole country where he is welcome and can feel at home. Wherever he turns, he is chased away. Always he is afraid of being arrested and cross-examined. I should like to have him enjoy a day of peace with us here-just one in the whole year."

CBSE 2023

(i) In the context of the given extract, which day is referred to in the expression 'just one in the whole year'?

(ii) Select the correct option from those given in brackets to fill in the blank.

Edla is .... (defending/arguing with) the peddler.

(iii) Complete the sentence suitably.

Edla wished the peddler to have a peaceful day because ....

(iv) What does the expression 'he is cross examined' suggest?

(v) In the above extract, Edla comes across as
(a) conscientious (b) pretentions
(c) compassionate (d) selfless

(vi) Based on the above extract, choose the statement which is True.
(a) Relationships are rattraps.
(b) Money is important in the world.
(c) Criminal is not born but made.
(d) Christmas is a time of charity.

Ans. (i) The day referred to in the extract as 'just one in the whole year' is the day of Christmas.
(ii) defending
(iii) the peddler has always been looked with suspicion
(iv) The phrase suggests that peddler was always looked at with suspicion and cross-examined to check if he was true and honest.
(v) (c) compassionate
(vi) (d) Christmas is a time of charity.

5. **"Since you have been so nice to me all day long, as if I was a captain, I want to be nice to you, in return, as if I was a real captain — for I do not want you to be embarrassed at this Christmas season by a thief; but you can give back the money to the old man on the roadside, who has the money pouch hanging on the window frame as a bait for poor wanderers.**

The rattrap is a Christmas present from a rat who would have been caught in this world's rattrap if he had not been raised to captain, because in that way he got power to clear himself.

"Written with friendship and high regard, Captain Von Stahle." CBSE Question Bank 2021 Modified

(i) What is the significance of the letter written to Edla?

(ii) Select the correct option from those given in bracket to fill in the blank.

This communication includes ....
(a promise/regret)

(iii) Complete the sentence suitably.

Captain Von Stahle presents the ....

(iv) Do you think the peddler would have changed if Edla would not have been nice to him?

(v) Which of the following cannot be attributed to the peddler, according to the above extract?
(a) Indebtedness (b) Reform
(c) Self-pity (d) Self-awareness

(vi) Why did the peddler gift a rattrap as a Christmas present?
(a) It was all the peddler had that he could give away, and represented his turn to honesty.
(b) It symbolised his successful escape from entrapment as he returned the stolen money.
(c) It served as a reminder for Edla to be wary of the dangerous temptations of the world.
(d) Both (a) and (b)

Ans. (i) The letter written by the peddler to Edla holds significance because it highlights how Edla brought about a change in a petty peddler.
(ii) a promise
(iii) real name of the peddler
(iv) I do not think that the peddler would have changed if Edla's compassion had not impacted him. it was just because of Edla's kind treatment that the peddler changed.
(v) (c) Self-pity
(vi) (b) It symbolised his successful escape from entrapment as he returned the stolen money.

Short Answer Type Questions

1. **Explain how the rattrap symbolises the dual aspects of human nature.** CBSE SQP 2024

Ans. The rattrap symbolises the dual aspects of human nature. On one hand, the rattrap presents the tendency towards greed and deceit. In a society, driven by wealth and gain, the rattrap ensnares individuals, reducing their existence to a constant struggle to escape from materialistic enticements. On the other hand, it presents the potential for redemption through empathy and kindness, as shown by the ironmaster's daughter, Edla.

2. **What do we learn about the crofter's nature from the story 'The Rattrap'?**

Ans. The crofter was a lonely person without a wife or children. He was happy to get someone to talk to in his loneliness. He was also generous and trusting person because he hosted the peddler for a night and even showed him where he had kept his money.

3. **How did the peddler's feelings change after robbing the crofter and why? With reference to 'The Rattrap', state your response in 20–30 words.** Competency Based

Ans. The peddler's feelings undergo a change after robbing the crofter. Initially, the peddler was quite pleased with his ingenuity. Driven by greed, he had committed the theft and was happy with it thinking that he was very smart. Later, however, when he was lost in the forest, he became reflective and regretful. Eventually, he recalled his thoughts about the world being a rattrap and how he had let himself be fooled by a bait and would now be caught.

4. **How did the crofter entertain the peddler?** CBSE 2020

Ans. The crofter entertained the peddler by sharing his feelings, giving him food and even playing a game of cards with him. He behaved in a friendly manner with the peddler and welcomed him warmly to his house.

5. **Why did the stranger not tell the ironmaster that he was not Nils Olof?**

Ans. The stranger did not tell the ironmaster that he was not Nils Olof because he thought that if the gentleman believed that he was an old friend or acquaintance of his, then he might take pity on him and help him by giving him some money.

6. **Why did Edla invite the peddler?** CBSE 2022 Term II

Ans. Edla had initially invited the peddler to spend Christmas at her home on her father's behalf. Her father had mistakenly identified the peddler to be an acquaintance from his regiment by the name Captain Nils Olof and had invited him home. But the peddler had declined the invite. So, he sent his daughter Edla to convince the peddler to accept the invite.

7. **Why did Edla decide to entertain the peddler?**

Or **Why did Edla invite the peddler?** CBSE Term II 2022

Ans. Edla invited the peddler and entertained him because she wanted to celebrate Christmas in the true spirit of the festival by having a guest over for Christmas supper. She also wanted to give the peddler a day of peace. Further, she believed that it was not fair to turn away a guest on the eve of Christmas.

8. **Why did the iron master compare Edla to a parson?** CBSE 2023

Ans. The ironmaster compared his daughter Edla to a parson as she preached to him just like one when she asked him to let the vagabond stay in the house even though he was not an acquaintance.

She reinforced the Christian value of celebrating Christmas by helping others. She didn't want to chase away a human being whom they had asked to come and to whom they had promised Christmas cheer.

9. **Edla sat and hung her head even more dejectedly than usual. Which two reasons forced her to behave in that manner?**

Ans. Edla had shown kindness to the peddler even after knowing that he was not a captain. This was the reason why she felt all the more dejected when she came to know that the peddler was actually a thief who had recently robbed a crofter.

She felt that she had done wrong in offering shelter to a thief. Further, she felt bad because the peddler had not measured up to the faith which she had shown in him.

10. **What was the content of the letter written by the peddler to Edla?** CBSE SQP 2020

Ans. The peddler wrote that he wanted to be nice to Edla as she had treated him nicely and like a captain. He further stated that he did not want her to be embarrassed by a thief at Christmas and requested her to return the money he had stolen to the crofter.

11. **What Christmas present did the peddler give Edla? Explain its significance.** CBSE 2022 Term II

Ans. The Christmas present left by the peddler for Edla comprised a small rattrap with three wrinkled kronor notes in it along with a letter.

The gift present left by the peddler is significant as it indicates how Edla's kindness and compassion affected the peddler. He changed for the better and now wants to live an honest life like a captain.

12. **The lesson. 'The Rattrap' is both entertaining and philosophical. Do you agree with the statement? Give reasons.** CBSE 2024

Ans. The lesson 'The Rattrap' is indeed both entertaining and philosophical. The fast-paced narrative in the third person, generous use of dialogue, different characters with varying mindsets and locales make the story interesting. Furthermore, the peddler's theory of the world being a rattrap adds a philosophical element to it. The story teaches us that human beings are not above temptations.

13. **If the world is 'nothing but a big rattrap', as the tramp seated in the story 'The Rattrap', who might the rattrap peddler be? Discuss.** CBSE Question Bank 2021

Ans. If the world is 'nothing but a big rattrap', as per the tramp, then the rattrap peddler can become someone who sells the baits of the world. However, he is just another human being in the world, who is tempted into the rattrap as he steals money from the old crofter. He is reduced to just a person who conceptualised the idea but is not saved from it.

14. **Despite his philosophical insights, the vagabond fails to resist temptations. What would you attribute this to? Explain with reference to any instance from the text.** CBSE Question Bank 2021

Ans. Despite his philosophical insights, the vagabond fails to resist temptations simply because of his humanness.

The vagabond is a poor and a deprived man who is treated unkindly by the social world around him. Just like every other individual, he is also vulnerable to the baits of food, shelter, luxury, etc.

Hence, the bait comes to him when the old crofter shows him his money. Blinded by the bait, he also falls in the rattrap.

15. A mistaken identity led to a discovery of a new one for the rattrap peddler. How did this impact him? **CBSE SQP 2020 Term II**

Ans. It is true that the mistaken identity led to a discovery of a new one for the rattrap peddler. The mistaken identity of the Captain and the resultant goodness received by the peddler gave him the power to clear his conscience. It brought out the latent goodness that was hidden due to the cruel treatment he had received from the world. The kindness and compassion he saw lent him the conviction to become a better human and allowed him the opportunity to behave in a dignified manner befitting a Captain.

16. If the Christmas spirit is about selflessness, forgiveness and becoming 'better' versions of ourselves amongst other things, Edla Willmansson is the epitome of this spirit. Justify with two points of evidence from 'The Rattrap'. **CBSE SQP 2022**

Ans. If the Christmas spirit is about selflessness, forgiveness and becoming 'better' versions of ourselves amongst other things, Edla Willmansson is the epitome of this spirit. This is so because despite knowing the truth about the peddler not being a Captain, Edla convinces her father to give him shelter and treats him with full respect.

She forgives him for not telling his true identity to them and further invites him for future Christmas celebration showing that even the peddler had the chance of becoming a better version of himself.

Long Answer Type Questions

1. The peddler's story speaks on a general level to society, urging for a different outlook towards those maligned individuals who can be redeemed by compassion and understanding. In the light of the story 'The Rattrap', how do you think society can help individuals, specially juvenile delinquents, from falling prey to petty crimes and bad habits? **Competency Based**

Ans. The peddler in the story, 'The Rattrap', used to earn his living by selling small rattraps. Since his business was not profitable, he resorted to petty thefts. Nobody treated him with kindness or respect. But when he was showered with affection and respect by Edla, he was highly touched.

The act of concern and compassion impacted him so much that he left the stolen money at her home. This shows that goodness is latent in the human heart which can be brought out by love, care and understanding.

The peddler's instance, thus, urges society to change its outlook towards those maligned individuals who can be redeemed by compassion and understanding. Society can help such individuals by being sympathetic and compassionate.

It should treat these individuals, particularly juvenile delinquents, with love and kindness and help them from falling prey to petty crimes and bad habits. Society should thus develop an empathetic attitude towards them and try to understand human nature.

2. 'The Rattrap' focuses on human loneliness and the need to bond with others. Comment.

Ans. All the characters in the story, 'The Rattrap', suffer from loneliness and are dreary souls. First of all, the tramp appears to lead a sad, monotonous existence, left to his own musings. He is always greeted by sour faces and cold words wherever he goes.

Next, the old crofter lives all alone in a cottage by the roadside. He is happy to get someone to talk to and get over his sense of loneliness. That's the reason why he is so generous and hospitable as a host.

Then, the ironmaster and his daughter Edla also have no company for Christmas. The ironmaster takes the tramp home, mistaking him to be his old comrade. He, with his daughter, is happy to play the perfect host to his former colleague.

Thus, all of them have a strong desire for bonding and comradeship. The crofter is happy to be friends with the peddler, although only for a night. Similarly, the ironmaster and his daughter have an opportunity to practise their Christian virtues of kindness, sympathy and hospitality. The compassion and sincerity shown by Edla changes peddler into a man who is one of the members of society.

3. A good deed or an act of kindness can change a person's view of the world. What characteristics of Edla's conduct inspire the peddler to redeem himself and change his ways? **CBSE 2020**

Or In Edla's dealing with the peddler, she was compassionate and generous. Discuss with reference to the story 'The Rattrap'. **CBSE 2022 Term II**

Ans. There is great transforming power in the act of kindness. There are many fictional and real life stories which reveal us how compassion and kindness changed bad people into good human beings; these stories teach us the lesson of being kind. Edla's empathy and kindness changed the life of the vagabond rattrap seller.

Edla restored his dignity and self-worth and treated him like a Captain of the army though she was aware that he was a common tramp. She was empathetic towards the peddler and the kindness and concern she showed towards him touched the core of his heart and transformed his way of thinking. Her kindness and caring nature transformed the unscrupulous vagabond into a good human being.

This shows that the peddler was not a bad man at heart, but was only bound by his poor and unfortunate circumstances which forced him to steal things. But the love, trust and understanding shown by Edla brought out his basic human goodness.

4. In the lesson 'The Rattrap' the narrator takes an empathetic approach towards the rattrap seller. Considering the above statement, discuss the narrator's portrayal of the peddler. CBSE 2022 Term II

Ans. It is true the narrator takes an empathetic approach towards the rattrap seller who leads a life of deprivation. When we first see the rattrap peddler, we find him to be a tall man who had his own imagination and mediation. However, to meet his livelihood, he had to resort to petty thievery and begging. He wore rags and hunger gleamed in his eyes. He went round selling self-made small rattraps of wire. Mostly he came across sour faces and was a victim of his cruel circumstances. People would not talk to him respectfully or kindly let alone give him shelter or work so that he could live an honest life.

The peddler is so affected by his situation that he even philosophises his existence. His philosophy takes him to understand the world as a big rattrap. According to him all the riches, joys, food, clothing and shelter are just baits. Anyone who touches the bait, the rattrap closes on him. He himself becomes entrapped in this rattrap. His behaviour which could have been seen as immoral, now receives sympathy from the readers who understand that he is product of his situation. He could only change when he comes across compassion and kindness which happens when he meets Edla.

The latter's presence, had a significant impact on the peddler. He changes for the better. Hence, throughout the story, we cannot help but sympathise with the peddler just as the narrator had expected us too.

5. 'She gave a little cry of joy. She found a small rattrap, ...'

'Saheb-e-Alam received a pair of discarded shoes with a hole in one of them. In spite of this he was very happy.'

Compare the joy that both Edla and Saheb experience after receiving their respective gifts. Competency Based

Ans. Receiving gifts has always been loved by everyone. Be it birthday or other special occasion, getting gifts adds to the joy one feels. This joy can be a result of a number of reasons just like the joy felt by the two characters-Saheb-e-Alam from 'Lost Spring' and Edla from 'The Rattrap' are different. Both these characters receive gifts and are happy to receive them but their joy are of very different nature.

Edla's joy is a result of the realisation of how her compassion has helped transform a person's life. In the lesson 'The Rattrap', everyone except Edla, the daughter of a rich family, treats the peddler poorly. Even when his real identity and the news of theft is revealed, everyone curses the peddler except Edla. She was sad for her trust was broken but when she receives the peddler's gift, she realised how she had transformed a man to a honest citizen.

Saheb-e-Alam, on the other hand, is a ragpicker. He lives a deprived life where he has to struggle to even feed himself. He had hoped to get a lot of things which included shoes which was an item of luxury for him. In this light, getting even discarded and torn shoes were a huge gift for him and his joy knew no bounds.

Thus, the life experience of both Edla and Saheb make their joy different.

6. Franz from 'The Last Lesson' and the peddler from 'The Rattrap' learn from their mistakes. Discuss with reference to the above texts, the human tendency to make mistakes and learn from them. CBSE 2025

Or Franz from 'The Last Lesson' and the peddler from 'The Rattrap' demonstrate the importance of learning from one's mistakes and rising up to evolve as a better person.

Write an article based on the two texts on how a man evolves after learning from his mistakes. Competency Based

Ans. In 'The Last Lesson' by Alphonse Daudet and 'The Rattrap' by Selma Lagerlof, the protagonists Franz and the peddler respectively, exemplify the transformative power of learning from one's mistakes. Initially, Franz is indifferent to his studies until it is too late, realising the value of education only after losing the opportunity to learn. Similarly, the peddler initially resorts to deceit and thievery but undergoes a profound transformation after experiencing kindness and compassion.

Both characters evolve into better individuals through their experiences, demonstrating the importance of self-reflection and personal growth. Franz's regret over his past indifference motivates him to continue learning despite adversity, while the peddler's newfound integrity and gratitude lead him to a more honest and fulfilling life. These stories highlight the resilience of the human spirit and the potential for redemption, emphasising that true evolution stems from acknowledging one's mistakes and striving to become a better person.

7. The story 'The Rattrap' shows the loneliness of many characters and the human need to bond with others in society. In 100–120 words, explain any three instances to prove the above statement. Competency Based

Ans. One of the main themes of the story is loneliness. All the characters of the story — whether it was Edla, the ironmaster, the crofter or the peddler — were victims of loneliness.

The peddler is a lonely man who has always been shunned by society's cold and bitter attitude. When he goes knocking at the old cottage door, little does he expect the hospitality that he eventually receives. The crofter welcomes him with open arms, as he is thrilled to have someone to talk to, after so long. He serves the peddler hot food, gives him tobacco for his pipe and plays a game of cards with him as well. He is an excellent host who goes on to share some secrets with the stranger as well.

The ironmaster and his daughter, on the other hand, miss having company and this makes Edla extend this invitation to the peddler. Thus, the need for human bonding emerges as one of the main themes of the story.

8. In the story 'The Rattrap', explain what the rattrap symbolises with an example from the story. What can you infer about the nature of human suffering from this symbol? Answer in 120–150 words. Competency Based

Ans. In 'The Rattrap', the rattrap symbolises the deceptive allure of material wealth and the entrapments of life's temptations. The protagonist, a peddler, views the world as a giant rattrap, enticing individuals with riches and comforts only to trap them in hardship and suffering. This symbolism is exemplified when the peddler himself is tempted by the stolen money from the old crofter. Initially, the money seems like an escape from his impoverished life, but it quickly leads him into a web of guilt, fear, and eventual entrapment at the ironmaster's mansion.

This symbol of the rattrap suggests that human suffering often stems from the pursuit of superficial desires and the illusion of easy gain. The peddler's experiences illustrate how succumbing to these temptations can lead to a cycle of misery, reinforcing the idea that true contentment comes from integrity and moral strength, rather than material possessions.

9. Do the following statements about life apply to the peddler in 'The Rattrap'? Why or why not? Do you think you are similar to the peddler in this regard? Answer in 120–150 words.

We are responsible for our own lives; every choice we make shapes the life we lead. Competency Based

Ans. The statement "We are responsible for our own lives; every choice we make shapes the life we lead" applies to the peddler in 'The Rattrap'. Throughout the story, the peddler's choices significantly impact his circumstances. His decision to steal the crofter's money is a pivotal moment that leads to a series of troubles, demonstrating how his actions shape his fate. However, his eventual redemption, influenced by Edla's kindness, also highlights that making better choices can lead to positive changes in life. Reflecting on this in my own life, I recognise similarities with the peddler. Like him, my decisions have shaped my experiences and outcomes. The peddler's journey underscores the importance of personal responsibility and the potential for change through conscious choices. Acknowledging this empowers us to steer our lives towards better paths, learning from mistakes and striving for integrity.

SELF ASSESSMENT TEST

Extract Based Questions

Read the extract given below and answer the questions that follow.

1. Every now and then one of them got up to stir the glowing mass with a long iron bar, returning in a few moments, dripping with perspiration, though, as was the custom, he wore nothing but a long shirt and a pair of wooden shoes.

All the time there were many sounds to be heard in the forge. The big bellows groaned and the burning coal cracked. The fire boy shovelled charcoal into the maw of the furnace with a great deal of clatter. Outside roared the waterfall, and a sharp North wind whipped the rain against the brick-tiled roof.

(i) State the location and characters present in the extract.

(ii) Select the correct option from those given in bracket to fill in the blank.

The characters in the extract are working to .... (melt the iron/mould the iron)

(iii) Complete the sentence suitably.

The custom referred in the extract is regarding ....

(iv) What is the significance of the extract?

(v) What can be said about the weather from the extract?

(a) It is winters (b) It is windy

(c) It is hot (d) All of these

(vi) The situations presented indicates

(a) noise (b) hard work

(c) weather (d) None of these

Short Answer Type Questions

Answer the following questions in 40-50 words.

1. The crofter was happy with the peddler's behaviour during his stay. But he may have been disappointed afterwards. Why?

2. How did the peddler feel after cheating the crofter? How do you feel about the peddler's reaction?

3. Why did the ironmaster behave sternly towards the peddler after seeing him properly at home?

4. To be grateful is a great virtue of a gentleman. How did the peddler show his gratitude to Edla?

5. The Ironmaster was materialistic. Justify.

6. The crofter was 'generous with his confidences'. Comment.

Long Answer Type Questions

Answer the following questions in 120-150 words.

1. There is a saying 'Kindness pays, rudeness never.' In the story, 'The Rattrap' Edla's attitude towards men and matters is different from her father's attitude. How are the values of concern and compassion brought out in the story, 'The Rattrap'?

2. Edla proved to be much more persuasive than her father while dealing with the peddler. Comment.

05

About the Author

Louis Fischer (1896-1970) was a Jewish -American journalist. He began his career as a school teacher but later became a journalist and a famous international reporter. In June 1942, he was permitted to stay for a week in the guest house near Mahatma Gandhi's ashram and conducted daily interviews with the great leader.

YOUR STUDY GOALS

- Chapter Sketch
- About the Characters
- Summary of the Chapter

YOUR PRACTICE GOAL

- NCERT Folder
- Extract Based Questions
- Short Answer Type Questions
- Long Answer Type Questions

Indigo

Chapter Sketch

This chapter is an excerpt from Fisher's book. 'The Life of Mahatma Gandhi'. The book has been reviewed by the Times Education Supplement as one of the best books ever written on Gandhi. The author visited Gandhi in 1942 and Gandhi narrated him the incident which prompted him to fight against the British. Rajkumar Shukla, a poor peasant came to Gandhi with the problem of exploitation in his district. Gandhi visited the place and freed the people of Champaran from tyranny.

About the Characters

Louis Fischer He is the narrator of the story. He convinces Gandhi to tell him about the incident at Champaran.

Gandhi He is the powerful figure who not only freed the peasants from the tyranny of the Britishers but also helped them gain self-sufficiency.

Rajkumar Shukla He is a resolute man who persistently waited to take Gandhi so that he can help the peasants of Champaran.

Peasants They are the peasants from the nearby regions of Champaran. They are exploited by the Britishers and with Gandhi's help realised their freedom and self-sufficiency.

Lawyers They are Indians who come to help the peasants but are selfish and money hungry in nature.

British Officials They are exploitative people who get confused when the Indian peasants understand their rights and revolt against them.

Rajendra Prasad A lawyer in Patna who helped Gandhiji in his case against the Britishers. He later became the president of Congress and the independent India.

Summary of the Chapter

Rajkumar Shukla- A Resolute

Gandhi narrated the incident that made him decide to start the exit of the British from India when Louis Fischer visited Gandhi in 1942. Gandhi had gone to the December 1916 annual convention of the Indian National Congress Party in Lucknow when Rajkumar Shukla, a poor sharecropper of Champaran, approached him. He wanted Gandhi to visit his district and look into the condition of the peasants there.

Gandhi had other commitments. However, Shukla accompanied him everywhere, which impressed Gandhi. Consequently, Gandhi told him to come to Calcutta and take him from there. When Gandhi went to Calcutta after some months, Shukla was already present there, waiting for him.

Obtaining Information

Shukla and Gandhi went to Patna, Bihar, to meet a lawyer named Rajendra Prasad. But, Rajendra Prasad was out of town. The servants knew Shukla and as Gandhi accompanied him, they thought him to be another farmer. So, Gandhi was not allowed to drink water from the well.

From there, Gandhi decided to visit Muzaffarpur to obtain more information about the conditions prevalent in the area. He sent a telegram to Professor JB Kriplani, who received them at the station at midnight on 15th April, 1917. Gandhi stayed in Muzaffarpur for two days in the home of Professor Malkani. This according to him was a big thing.

The Real Relief

The news of Gandhi's arrival spread quickly and as a result, sharecroppers from Champaran began arriving in large numbers. Muzaffarpur lawyers met Gandhi and told him about their cases as well as the size of their fee. Gandhi scolded them for it and stated that the peasants were so fear-stricken that going to law courts was useless. The real relief for them would be to be free from fear.

The Champaran Arrangement

The Champaran peasants were sharecroppers. Most of the land fit for cultivation in the region was divided into large estates owned by Englishmen. They forced the Indian tenants to plant 15% of their land with indigo and surrender the entire indigo harvest as rent. This was done according to a long term contract between the tenants and the landlords.

After the landlords learned that Germany had developed synthetic indigo, they asked for compensation for being released from the 15% arrangement. The sharecropping arrangement was problematic and so, many peasants signed willingly. However, when the news of synthetic indigo reached the sharecroppers, they felt cheated. They wanted their money back.

Gandhi's Investigation

At this point, Gandhi arrived in Champaran. He visited the Secretary of the British landlord's association in order to get all the facts. However, he got no information. Then, Gandhi visited the British Commissioner where he was asked to leave Tirhut. Instead of leaving, Gandhi along with several lawyers went to Motihari.

At the railway station, a huge crowd of peasants greeted Gandhi. Using a house as headquarters, Gandhi continued his investigations. When a report that a peasant had been maltreated in a nearby village came, Gandhi decided to check the matter himself. Next day, when he was on the way, he was served with an official notice to quit Champaran. Gandhi signed a receipt and further wrote that he would disobey the order. As a result, he was summoned to appear in the court the next day.

The Revolt of the Peasants

That night Gandhi telegraphed Rajendra Prasad to come from Bihar, sent instructions to the ashram and wired a full report to the Viceroy.

Next day, several thousand peasants reached Motihari and started demonstrating around the courthouse. Gandhi felt that this was the beginning of their liberation from fear of the British.

Seeing the demonstration, the officials felt powerless. So, Gandhi helped them regulate the crowd. However, when the trial was postponed, Gandhi protested. He told the court that he was in a 'conflict of duties'. On one hand, he did not want to set a bad example as a lawbreaker; on the other, he wanted to render the 'humanitarian and national service' for which he had come.

Later, Gandhi asked for the penalty while the magistrate asked Gandhi to get a bail prepared for a 120 minutes of recess. Gandhi refused. The judge didn't deliver the judgement for days and Gandhi was allowed to remain at liberty.

Gandhi's Advice

Rajendra Prasad, Brij Kishor Babu, Maulana Mazharul Huq and several other prominent lawyers had arrived to discuss the situation with Gandhi. When Gandhi asked them what they would do if he was sent to jail, they replied that they would go home. Gandhi reprimanded them about the injustice to the sharecroppers.

The lawyers discussed among themselves and told Gandhi that they were ready to follow him to jail. Gandhi exclaimed, 'The battle of Champaran is won'. Then, he took a piece of paper and divided the group into pairs and put down the order in which each pair was to court arrest.

The Official Inquiry

Several days later, the case against Gandhi was dropped. Civil disobedience had triumphed for the first time in modern India. Later, official inquiries into the grievances of the farmers began. Testimonials were reported, notes of the evidence were made and documents were collected. All the while, the landlords protested against the inquiries.

In June, the Lieutenant-Governor, Sir Edward Gait, summoned Gandhi. Soon, they appointed an official commission to enquire into the situation with Gandhi was the sole representative of the peasants.

The Compensation

At the end of the investigation, the evidence against the landlords was overwhelming. They thought Gandhi would demand full repayment of the money which was illegally and deceitfully taken from the sharecroppers. Gandhi asked for only 50%. However, the landlords offered to refund 25%.

To everybody's surprise, Gandhi agreed. He explained that the amount of the refund was not important. What mattered was that the landlords were obliged to surrender part of the money, and a part of their prestige. After this incident, the peasants saw that they had rights and persons to defend them.

Within a few years the British planters abandoned their estates, which were given back to the peasants and indigo sharecropping disappeared.

Improving Living Conditions

Gandhi wanted to do something about the cultural and social backwardness in the Champaran villages. So, he called for volunteers to help. Many volunteers including teachers and two young men - Mahadev Desai and Narhari Parikh along with their wives, Gandhi's wife Kasturba and his youngest son arrived to help. Soon, primary schools were opened in six villages. Kasturbai taught the ashram about the rules on personal cleanliness and community sanitation. A doctor was hired to provide castor oil, quinine and sulphur ointment to the ailing.

The Turning Point of Gandhi's Life

During his stay in Champaran, Gandhi sent regular instructions by mail and asked for financial accounts.

The Champaran episode was a turning point in his life. He explained that now the British could not order him about in his own country.

Gandhi's aim was to mould a new free Indian, who could stand on his own feet. In the early days of the Champaran episode, Charles Freer Andrews, Gandhi's follower, came to bid him goodbye. Gandhi's lawyer friends wanted Andrews to help them. Gandhi strongly opposed the suggestion, stating that asking for Andrews' help was showing the weakness. He assured them the cause was just and they must rely upon themselves to win the battle.

Gandhi in this way taught them a lesson on self-reliance. Self-reliance, Indian independence and help to the sharecroppers were all bound together.

Word-Meaning

urge the departure	—	spur the exit (from India)
convention	—	a meeting or formal assembly
emaciated	—	abnormally thin or weak, especially because of illness or lack of food
towering	—	very tall or high
sharecroppers	—	tenant farmers who give a part of each crop as rent
yeoman	—	peasant or farmer
indigo	—	a dark blue dye obtained from the indigo plant
harbour a man like me	—	give shelter to a person who advocated freedom
advent	—	arrival
champion	—	a person who defends or fights for a cause
chided	—	scolded
crushed	—	suppressed
holdings	—	areas of land held on lease or rent
synthetic	—	indigo obtained from a chemical indigo process which is just like the natural product
irksome	—	irritating, annoying
thugs	—	criminals
summons	—	an order to appear before a judge or magistrate
conflict of duties	—	having two duties opposing each other
reconvened	—	met again after a break in proceedings
conferred	—	consulted or discussed
deposition(s)	—	out-of-court oral testimony of a witness that is reduced to writing for later use in court
associates	—	companions
protracted	—	longer than expected
entreaty	—	earnest request, appeal
unlettered	—	illiterate
defenders	—	protectors
sanitation	—	cleanliness and other conditions relating to public health
eruptions	—	rashes or spots
alleviate	—	reduce or lessen
intertwined	—	closely linked or connected
pacifist	—	one who believes in adopting peaceful means rather than war or violence
seek a prop	—	look for support

Important Themes of the Chapter

Unequal Economic System One of the prominent themes presented in the excerpt is the prevalence of the unjust and unequal economic system in British India. The chapter through the Champaran episode highlights the exploitation of indigo farmers by British landlords who forced them to grow indigo on their land and sell it at low prices. This led to extreme poverty and hardship for the farmers.

Importance of Good Leadership The chapter 'Indigo' emphasises the fact that effective leadership can solve any kind of problems without any harm to anybody. This chapter deals with the way Mahatma Gandhi solved the problem of poor sharecroppers of Champaran in a non-violent way.

Self-Sufficiency The chapter also presents the need for self-sufficiency for all to gain full freedom. It also highlights how the community together can realise their rights and freedoms, and fight back against the oppressive Britishers.

NCERT Folder

Think as you Read (NCERT Page 47)

1. Strike out what is not true in the following.

(i) Rajkumar Shukla was
(a) a sharecropper
(b) a politician
(c) a delegate
(d) a landlord

(ii) Rajkumar Shukla was
(a) poor
(b) physically strong
(c) illiterate

Ans. (i) (b) a politician (c) a delegate (d) a landlord
(ii) (b) physically strong

2. Why is Rajkumar Shukla described as being 'resolute'? CBSE 2025

Ans. Rajkumar Shukla is described as being resolute as he went along with Gandhi everywhere until Gandhi agreed to help him. He was adamant to take Gandhi to Champaran to solve the problems faced by the sharecroppers there and so, he resolutely went everywhere with Gandhiji until, impressed with his tenacity, Gandhiji agreed to go to Champaran.

3. **Why do you think the servants thought Gandhi to be another peasant?**

Ans. Gandhi came along with Rajkumar Shukla, a peasant, to Rajendra Prasad's house. He was dressed very simply, so the servants thought Gandhi to be another peasant and he was treated like an untouchable peasant by not being allowed to drink water from the well.

Think as you Read (NCERT Page 49)

1. **List the places that Gandhi visited between his first meeting with Shukla and his arrival at Champaran.**

Ans. After his first meeting with Shukla, Gandhiji did not visit Champaran immediately because he had prior commitments in other parts of the county. He was expected to visit Cawnpore after which he returned to his ashram near Ahmedabad. It was only after his visit to Calcutta that he was able to attend to the problem highlighted by Shukla. After his first meeting with Shukla, Gandhi did not visit Champaran immediately. He first went to Muzzafarpur to get more information about the issues regarding the agreement.

2. **What did the peasants pay the British landlords as rent? What did the British now want instead and why? What would be the impact of synthetic indigo on the prices of natural indigo?** **CBSE 2022 Term II**

Ans. The British landlords forced all tenants to plant 15% of their holdings with indigo and surrender the entire indigo harvest as rent.

When the landlords learned that Germany had developed synthetic indigo, they wanted to dissolve the agreement. However, they asked the sharecroppers to pay them compensation for being released from the 15% arrangement.

The presence of synthetic indigo would obviously impact the price of natural indigo. The synthetic indigo would be cheaper and more readily available bringing down the price of natural indigo.

Think as you Read (NCERT Page 51)

1. **The events in this part of the text illustrate Gandhi's method of working. Can you identify some instances of this method and link them to his ideas of satyagraha and non-violence?**

Ans. Gandhi made efforts to learn the complete truth about the injustice done to the peasants in Champaran. His waiting for the response of the authorities, his refusal to quit Champaran and his acceptance of the meagre 25% refund to the farmers, are all based on his principle of '*satyagraha*'. He was merely requesting for truth and justice.

Gandhi helping the officials to regulate the crowd during the spontaneous demonstration and his willingness to court arrest are instances of his non-violent methods.

Think as you Read (NCERT Page 53)

1. **Why did Gandhi agree to a settlement of 25% refund to the farmers?**

Ans. Gandhi agreed to the settlement of 25% refund to the farmers because he believed that the amount of refund was less important than the fact that the landlords had been obliged to surrender part of their money and, with it, a part of their prestige.

2. **How did the episode change the plight of the peasants?**

Ans. The episode changed the plight of the peasants by helping them immensely. It removed their mortal fear of the British. They were made aware of their rights and developed courage to fight for them.

Understanding the Text (NCERT Page 54)

1. **Why do you think Gandhi considered the Champaran episode to be a turning-point in his life?**

Ans. Gandhi considered the Champaran episode to be a turning point in his life because it was the first successful civil disobedience movement for him. Though it began as an ordinary attempt to free the poor peasants from injustice and exploitation, it was important because it wiped out the mortal fear of the Britishers from the hearts of the simple farmers. The farmers realised their rights and learnt to fight for them.

2. **How was Gandhi able to influence lawyers? Give instances.**

Ans. There are three instances where Gandhi's presence and words influence the actions and decisions taken by the lawyers. These are

(i) When Gandhi got to know that the lawyers were charging a heavy fee from the poor peasants to fight their cases, he scolded them for burdening the poor. Also, he made sure that the cases were taken back as according to him, going to court was useless in the situation.

(ii) Later, when Gandhi decided to oppose his eviction order from the district and asked the lawyers what they would do then, their response was to go back. This got them another scolding. As a result, the lawyers realised that it will not be good to not do anything for their own people, whereas an outsider like Gandhi was prepared to go to jail for them. Consequently, they decided to accompany Gandhi to jail if he was arrested.

(iii) The last instance was seen when the lawyers thought it would be a good idea for CF Andrews, one of Gandhi's followers to stay in Champaran and help them. But Gandhi opposed this idea because he wanted the lawyers to be self-reliant and know their own strengths. Thus, he influenced the lawyers to work on their own.

3. What was the attitude of the average Indian in smaller localities towards advocates of 'home rule'?

Ans. An average Indian in smaller localities was afraid to show sympathy for advocates of 'home rule' openly. They probably feared negative consequences. It is for this reason that Gandhi recalls Professor Malkani's offering him shelter in his own home as an extraordinary matter.

4. How do we know that ordinary people too contributed to the freedom movement?

Ans. Ordinary people stood by and supported Gandhi in their own little ways. Rajkumar Shukla and Professor Malkani defied all odds to contribute in the movement.

Professor JB Kriplani motivated a large number of students and welcomed Gandhi at the Muzaffarpur railway station at midnight. The spontaneous demonstration outside the court was also a significant contribution, as it showed the Britishers the unity of the Indians. Civil Disobedience could triumph in India only because of the courage and unity of ordinary people.

Exam Pattern Questions

Extract Based Questions

Read the extracts given below and answer the questions that follow.

1. The news of Gandhi's advent and of the nature of his mission spread quickly through Muzaffarpur and to Champaran. Sharecroppers from Champaran began arriving on foot and by conveyance to see their champion. Muzaffarpur lawyers called on Gandhi to brief him; they frequently represented peasant groups in court, they told him about their cases and reported the size of their fee.

(i) **What does 'their cases' refer to in the extract?**

(ii) **Select the correct option from those given in bracket to fill in the blank.**

The farmers found .... (Rajkumar Shukla/ Gandhi) to be their 'Champion'.

(iii) **Complete the sentence with an appropriate explanation as per the extract.**

Muzaffarpur's lawyers called on Gandhi because ....

(iv) **What was Gandhi's mission?**

(v) **Gandhi's protest in Champaran is most appropriately a great model of**

(a) power (b) leadership
(c) charity (d) sponsorship

(vi) **Select the option that list the feelings and attitudes the sharecroppers attached to Gandhi.**

(a) Hope
(b) Courage
(c) Leadership
(d) Both (a) and (c)

Ans. (i) In the given extract 'their cases' refers to the case that the lawyers are fighting for the sharecroppers against the tyrannical British landlords.

(ii) Gandhi

(iii) they wanted to brief him about the plight of the peasants in the region

(iv) Gandhi's mission in the given extract is to help the sharecroppers get justice as well as their hard earned money back.

(v) (d) sponsorship

(vi) (d) Both (a) and (c)

2. They had merely heard that a Mahatma Gandhi who wanted to help them was in trouble with the authorities. Their spontaneous demonstration, in thousands, around the courthouse was the beginning of their liberation from fear of the British. The officials felt powerless without Gandhi's cooperation. He helped them regulate the crowd. He was polite and friendly. He was giving them concrete proof that their might, hitherto dreaded and unquestioned, could be challenged by Indians.
The government was baffled. The prosecutor requested the judge to postpone the trial. Apparently, the authorities wished to consult their superiors.

(i) **Why did the officials feel powerless?**

(ii) **Select the correct option from those given in bracket to fill in the blank.**

Gandhi behaviour towards the British prior to the proposal of postponement of the trial was that of .... (irritated solution/polite helpfulness).

(iii) Complete the sentence suitably.

The demonstration proved that the ....

(iv) Identify the textual clue that allows the reader to infer that the government was scared of the demonstrations.

(v) Which style, from those given below, is being used by the author, when he says, "Apparently, the authorities wished to consult their superiors"?

(a) Humourous (b) Dramatic
(c) Sarcastic (d) Persuasive

(vi) The crowd in the extract shows ....

(a) power of unity (b) their fighting spirit
(c) Non-Violent Movement (d) All of these

Ans. (i) The officials felt powerless because of Gandhi's refusal to cooperate with them.

(ii) polite helpfulness

(iii) dread instilled in the hearts of Indians had begun to lessen

(iv) 'The spontaneous demonstration of the people in thousands around the courthouse was the beginning of their liberation from fear of the British.'

(v) (c) Sarcastic

(vi) (d) All of the above

3. They thought he would demand repayment in full of the money which they had illegally and deceitfully extorted from the sharecroppers. He asked only 50 percent. "There he seemed adamant", writes Reverend JZ Hodge, a British missionary in Champaran, who observed the entire episode at close range. "Thinking probably that he would not give way, the representatives of the planters offered to refund to the extent of 25 percent, and to his amazement Mr. Gandhi took him at his words thus breaking the deadlock."

CBSE 2024 modified

(i) What do we infer about the attitude of planters towards sharecroppers?

(ii) Select the correct option from those given in bracket to fill in the blank.

'Then he seemed adamant,' reflects Gandhi's trait of being .... (courageous/uncompromising)

(iii) Complete the sentence suitably.

Gandhi surprised them by ....

(iv) What inference can be drawn from the statement "Mr. Gandhi took him at his word"?

(v) .... deceitfully extorted from the sharecroppers.

The status of sharecroppers as inferred from the above line is

(a) law abiding citizens (b) followers of Gandhi
(c) victims of exploitation (d) contract labourers

(vi) What does 'deadlock' in the last line means ....

(a) a debatable situation
(b) a situation where no progress can be made
(c) a trick
(d) an arrogant statement

Ans. (i) From the given extract, it can be inferred that the planters had an exploitative attitude towards the sharecroppers. They felt that the poor peasants could do nothing against them and that their action or words are superior.

(ii) uncompromising

(iii) accepting the offer to refund 25% of the extorted money.

(iv) The given expression indicates that Gandhi made him fulfill his promise

(v) (c) victims of exploitation

(vi) (b) a situation where no progress can be made

4. This settlement was adopted unanimously by the commission Gandhi explained that the amount of the refund was less important than the fact that the landlords had been obliged to surrender part of the money and, with it, part of their prestige. Therefore, as far as the peasants were concerned, the planters had behaved as lords above the law. Now the peasants saw that he had rights and defenders. He learned courage.

CBSE 2024 modified

(i) What was Gandhi's purpose in agreeing to the settlement, even at a lesser amount?

(ii) Select the correct option from those given in bracket to fill in the blank.

The phrase 'lords above the law' suggests that .... (a group of individuals has special or exclusive privileges/a group of individuals who make the law).

(iii) Complete the sentence with one word.

The commission agreed by common consent, or in other words, they agreed to the settlement ....

(iv) Explain the impact on the landlords as a result of the settlement.

(v) Based on the content provided in the extract, select the most likely option about the behaviour of the landlords?

(a) The landlords were sorry for their behaviour.
(b) The landlords were obstinate and refused Gandhi's suggestion.
(c) The Landlords had to refund the money.
(d) The landlords and the planters became partners in the Indigo plantation.

(vi) What did the peasants realise from the Champaran incident?

(a) They were the original resident
(b) They were fooled and tricked
(c) They had rights and freedoms
(d) They had Gandhi to support him

Ans. (i) Gandhi's purpose in agreeing to the settlement is because it was more significant that the landlords were made to return some of their money, along with a part of their prestige, rather than the percentage of refund.

(ii) a group of individuals has special or exclusive privileges

(iii) consensually

(iv) As a result of the settlement, the British planters abandoned their estates and returned them to the peasants for good.

(v) (c) The landlords had to refund the money.

(vi) (c) They had rights and freedoms

5. Gandhi never contented himself with large political or economic solutions. He saw the cultural and social backwardness in the Champaran villages and wanted to do something about it immediately.

He appealed for teachers. Mahadev Desai and Narhari Parikh, two young men who had just joined Gandhi as disciples, and their wives, volunteered for the work. Several more came from Bombay, Poona and other distant parts of the land. Devadas, Gandhi's youngest son, arrived from the ashram and so did Mrs. Gandhi. Primary schools were opened in six villages.

Kasturbai taught the ashram rules on personal cleanliness and community sanitation.

(i) What never satisfied Gandhi?

(ii) Select the suitable word from the extract to complete the following analogy.

Deprivation : Backwardness :: Requested :

(iii) Complete the following sentence.

Kasturbai taught ....

(iv) What does the given lines tell us about Gandhi?

(v) Why did Gandhi appeal for teachers?

(a) To enhance literacy rate
(b) To teach the kids
(c) To spread awareness about cultural and social backwardness
(d) To bring economic prosperity

(vi) Whose wives had volunteered for the work?

(a) Devdas's
(b) Mahadev Desai and Narhari Parikh's
(c) Mahadev Desai and Devdas's
(d) None of the above

Ans. (i) Gandhi was never satisfied with the large political or economic solutions.

(ii) Appealed

(iii) ashram rules on personal cleanliness and community sanitation.

(iv) The given lines show us that Gandhi wanted the Indian society to grow and develop. His aim was not limited to just getting freedom of the nation.

(v) (c) To spread awareness about cultural and social backwardness

(vi) (b) Mahadev Desai and Narhari Parikh's

Short Answer Type Questions

1. Describe the role of Rajkumar Shukla in 'Indigo'. CBSE 2023

Ans. Rajkumar Shukla plays a very significant role in the Champaran Movement presented in the chapter 'Indigo'. He was the poor farmer who resolutely followed Gandhi and convinced him to look into the problems faced by the indigo farmers. If he had not been resolute or visited Gandhi, the Champaran sharecroppers would have suffered for longer duration and the freedom struggle would have started late.

2. Why did Gandhi feel that taking the Champaran case to the court was useless?

Ans. Gandhi felt that taking the Champaran case to the court was useless because after discussion with the lawyers, he realised that the peasants were crushed and fear stricken. As a result, they would not fight their case and the court would favour the Britishers. Hence, going to court was useless and the people needed to be free from fear.

3. What were the terms of the indigo contract between the British landlords and the Indian peasants?

Ans. The terms of the indigo contract between the British and the peasants was related to the arable land. The arable land in the Champaran district was divided into estates which were owned by Englishmen and worked by Indian tenants. The chief commercial crop was indigo. The landlords compelled all tenants to plant 15% of their holdings with indigo and surrender the entire indigo harvest as rent.

4. How did the invention of German synthetic indigo affect the peasant-landlord relationship in Champaran? CBSE 2020

Ans. The invention of German synthetic indigo affected the poor peasant-landlord relationship adversely. The landlords/ Britishers wanted to get free from the agreement and demanded compensation. As a result, poor farmers were further pushed into poverty. Further, when the news of synthetic indigo reached the peasants, they felt cheated and hired lawyers so that they could get justice.

5. Explain the possible reasons for Gandhi's quick popularity among the peasants of Champaran.

Ans. Gandhi very quickly became popular among the peasants because he had come to help them fight for justice without any fee. Further, he had gone against the British law and authority to do so.

Consequently, without any knowledge about Gandhi they had come to protest against his trail.

6. What conflict of duty was Gandhi involved in? CBSE 2022 Term II

Or What does Gandhi refer to as a 'conflict of duties'? CBSE 2023

Ans. Gandhi told the court that he was involved in a 'conflict of duties', i.e. he must not set a bad example by breaking the law (by refusing to comply with the eviction order), but he must also render humanitarian and national service for which he had come to Champaran.

7. What made the Lieutenant-Governor drop the case against Gandhi?

Ans. The Lieutenant-General dropped the case against Gandhi because thousands of peasants held a spontaneous demonstration in Motihari leaving the government helpless and baffled. The judge did not want to aggravate the situation and decided to hold the result of several days. Finally Gandhi was released without bail and in the end, the case was dropped.

8. The peasants were themselves the most crucial agents in the success of the Champaran Civil Disobedience. Explain. CBSE Question Bank 2021

Ans. The peasants were the most crucial agents in the success of the Champaran Civil Disobedience because without their presence in such large numbers, the British authority and the landlords would have continued their tyranny in Champaran. If the peasants had not stood with Gandhi or placed trust in him, then the movement will have been a great disaster. Gandhi alone could not have achieved success of Champaran. The support of the peasants made the movement a success.

9. Though the sharecroppers of Champaran received only one-fourth of the compensation, how can the Champaran struggle still be termed a huge success and victory?

Ans. Though the sharecroppers of Champaran received only one-fourth of compensation, the struggle was a huge success and victory because the objective of Gandhi in his Champaran campaign was to mould a new free Indian who could stand on his own feet and thus make India free. The peasants found confidence in fighting their own battles and they were liberated from fear of the British. They not only made the landlords surrender part of money along with their prestige but the peasants also gained courage.

10. Gandhi makes it clear that money and finance are a secondary aspect of the struggle in Champaran. Comment on aspect that you think was most important for Gandhi. CBSE Question Bank 2021

Ans. Gandhi made it clear that money and finance are secondary in the struggle in Champaran. For Gandhi, it was the removal of the fear amongst the peasants that was central. His persistent efforts, firm determination and resolution taught courage to the peasants who realised that they too, had certain rights. For him, a successful challenge to the British tyranny was more important than the money and finance involved in the agreement.

11. Gandhi firmly devied CF Andrew's help during the Champaran campaign. Substantiate with his reason.

Ans. Gandhi was opposed to CF Andrews helping him in Champaran because he wanted the lawyers to be self-reliant and know their own strengths. He told them that their cause was just and they must rely upon themselves to win the battle. He did not want them seek a prop in Mr. Andrews because he happened to be an Englishman.

12. Gandhi was a lawyer himself. Examine how his professional expertise helped in Champaran. CBSE Question Bank 2021

Ans. The fact that Gandhi was professionally a lawyer worked to his benefit in the Champaran episode. When Gandhi came to understand the sharecropping agreement, his first action was to view the entire situation. In midst, he realised that there was no point in getting into cases as law courts would hardly be able to do justice to the peasants.

He felt that it was necessary to remove the terror of Britishers and teach the peasants how to be courageous. Once he was able to do so, the British authority had no choice but to review the case justly and provide justice.

13. As the host of a talk show, introduce Rajkumar Shukla to the audience by stating any two of his defining qualities.

You may begin your answer like this

Meet Rajkumar Shukla, the man who played a pivotal role in the Champaran Movement. He ……

Competency Based

Ans. Meet Rajkumar Shukla, the man who played a pivotal role in the Champaran Movement. He is that resolute man who did not leave Gandhiji's side knowing fully well that he was the only one who could help the situation with the farmers.

He is a determined and dedicated man who was always present wherever he was required.

14. Gandhi effectively managed to redress the problems of the indigo sharecroppers with the Lieutenant Governor. What did he achieve? CBSE 2022 Term II

Ans. Gandhi successfully dealt with the Lieutenant Governor to resolve the issues facing the sharecroppers of indigo.

The estates were returned to the farmers once the landlords abandoned their claims to them. The farmers gained confidence and understood that they had supporters as well. The landlords were forced to give up some of their wealth and status. Gandhi, therefore, intervened to end the impasse between the farmers and landlords.

15. What factor/s were largely instrumental in the victory of the peasants in 'Indigo'? CBSE SQP 2024

Ans. There are various factors that were instrumental in the victory of the peasants in 'Indigo'. The most important of them all was the leadership and advocacy provided by Mahatma Gandhi. Gandhi's involvement brought national attention to the plight of the peasants. Further, Gandhi's strategic approach to negotiations and his insistence on non-violent protest empowered the peasants to stand up against oppressive landlords. This ultimately led to their immediate victory and inspired a broader movement for social and economic justice across India.

16. In smaller localities, the Indians were afraid to show sympathy for advocates of home-rule.

Based on the statement above from 'Indigo', what inference can be drawn about the political climate in India at that time? State your answer in 20-30 words. Competency Based

Ans. Based on the statement, it can be reasonably inferred that the political climate in India was marked by feelings of apprehension and anxiety. The Indians, specifically in smaller localities lived in fear of being surveilled by the British authorities and as such did not wish to commit any acts that could put their lives in jeopardy.

17. With reference to 'Indigo', describe one action by Gandhi to prove that he was concerned about the social well-being of the Champaran people. Answer in 20-30 words. Competency Based

Ans. Gandhi had taken many initiatives that prove he was concerned about the social well-being of the Champaran people. Gandhi tried to improve the lives of the Champaran people by requesting teachers to volunteer their services. He also set up primary schools for the children in the villages.

18. Read the following line from 'Indigo' and answer the question that follows.

'They thought, amongst themselves, that Gandhi was totally a stranger, and yet he was prepared to go to prison for the sake of the peasants...'

In 40-50 words, state the significance of this event to the sharecroppers' court case and to India's freedom from British rule. Competency Based

Ans. The event of Gandhi going to jail for unknown peasants is significant because it bolstered the confidence of the masses in Gandhi's commitment towards the betterment of the Indian population oppressed by Britishers. This event also fostered a sense of unity and kinship among the masses. With the strength of their unity, the peasants could then overpower the corrupt Britishers and gain at least some of their money back. This event is also important because it was the first instance of Civil Disobedience in India.

19. How was self-reliance intertwined with the Champaran incident? CBSE 2025

Ans. The Champaran incident demonstrated self-reliance as Mahatma Gandhi encouraged the peasants to take control of their situation. Instead of relying on others, he urged them to fight for their rights against the British landlords. His leadership taught them to be courageous and assertive in seeking justice.

Long Answer Type Questions

1. Why is the Champaran episode considered to be the beginning of the Indian struggle for independence? CBSE 2019, 2023

Or How did civil disobedience triumph for the first time in India? CBSE 2022 Term II

Ans. The Champaran episode was one of the major events in the struggle for independence. It was in the course of this small but significant movement that Gandhi decided to spur the exit of the British from India. A close examination of the problem of the Champaran peasants opened up Gandhi's eyes to the unjust policies of the British. He realised that people had to be made free from fear and only then could they be freed from foreign oppression. The spontaneous demonstration of the people proved that Gandhi had the people's support in his fight against the Britishers.

The triumph of the civil disobedience at Champaran motivated the launching of the movement on a large scale during the freedom movement.

Gandhi winning the case of the sharecroppers proved that British authority could be challenged. Hence, the Champaran episode served as a stepping stone to the Indian struggle for independence.

2. Gandhi's stay was not a loyalty to abstractions; it was loyalty to living, human beings. Why did Gandhi continue his stay in Champaran even after indigo sharecropping disappeared?

Or What changes occurred in the lives of farmers after Gandhi's visit to Champaran? CBSE 2022 Term II

Or Gandhi worked for the social backwardness in the Champaran village. Elaborate. CBSE 2022 Term II

Or Gandhi not only alleviated the economic conditions of the Champaran people but also their social and cultural background. Justify. CBSE 2022 Term II

Ans After the Champaran battle was won and the land reverted to the peasants, Gandhi continued to stay in the region. His loyalty was to living human beings and he realised that a lot needed to be done for the upliftment of the peasants in the villages of Champaran. Gandhi took the initiative and began the work of eradicating their cultural and social backwardness.

Primary schools were started so that the poor peasants and their children could be educated. Gandhi appealed to teachers and many of his disciples, including his wife and son, volunteered for the work.

Health conditions in the area were also miserable. Gandhi got a doctor to volunteer his services for six months.

All this goes to prove that Gandhi's loyalty was not to abstractions; his politics was always intertwined with the practical day-to-day problems of the millions.

3. Gandhi said, "Freedom from fear is more important than legal justice for the poor." How does it become clear from the lesson 'Indigo' that freedom from fear is an essential condition for justice ?

Ans. Gandhi's statement that "Freedom from fear is more important than legal justice for the poor" stands true. We get a glimpse of how true that statement is from the Champaran episode.

The peasants of Champaran were so exploited by the foreign rulers that they were scared of the British landlords. In the Champaran episode, in spite of fighting endless legal battles, the results were inconclusive. When Gandhi learned about the conditions of the peasants of Champaran, he concluded that the peasants were so crushed and fear-stricken that going to the law courts was useless. The real relief would come if they were free from fear and to teach these peasants to be courageous.

So, Gandhi helped the peasants face their situation boldly. He not only refused to go to the court but also got arrested for being the Champion of sharecroppers. Seeing his example, multitudes gathered at the court, which the Britishers couldn't control. Consequently, the trial was postponed and Gandhi was released without Bail. Later, Gandhi made the landlords surrender the money as well as their prestige, thus, making the peasants shed their fear.

In this way, it becomes clear from the lesson 'Indigo' that freedom from fear is an essential condition for justice.

4. Gandhi, Father of our Nation, is a great leader whose values have been admired by one and all. Describe at least three characteristics of Gandhi you get to know from 'Indigo', which you wish to adopt into your own life quoting suitable instances from the story.

Ans. The characteristics that Gandhi displays in the lesson 'Indigo', which we can adopt into our own lives are

(i) **Humility and Simplicity** Gandhi was a simple and humble man. He did not object to being treated as a peasant at Rajendra Prasad's house by the servants.

(ii) **Non-violent Attitude** He used peaceful means to bend the British law. He was prepared to go to jail for subverting the order for his eviction from the district.

(iii) **Fellow Feeling** Gandhi believed in the equality and brotherhood of all Indians. Hence, he worked for the people of Champaran even though he did not belong to the area and was not familiar with them.

(iv) **Humanitarian Approach** Gandhi's work was not just associated with politics or power. He wanted the betterment of the Indian society at large. Hence, he called upon teachers and his disciples to work for social and medical upliftment as well as literacy of the peasants of Champaran.

(v) **Determination** Gandhi was a determined man. In spite of the challenges he faced in Champaran, he stayed there for about a year to ensure that justice for the peasants there was accomplished.

(vi) **Self-reliance** Gandhi was a self-reliant man and wanted the Indians to be self-reliant too. Hence, he worked to liberate the peasants from their fear and even scolded the lawyers for believing that CF Andrews, a British pacifist's help would make their struggle easy.

5. Imagine Gandhi were to deliver a speech to students in present day India showing them the path to becoming responsible world leaders. Based on your understanding of Gandhi's own leadership skills, write a speech, as Gandhi, addressing the students about the qualities that every leader and politician should nurture.

Dear students, you are all leaders of social change. I see many bright and enthusiastic faces that assure me that our future is in good hands. I have learnt from my own experience....................... Competency Based

Ans. Dear students, you are all leaders of social change. I see many bright and enthusiastic faces that assure me that our future is in good hands. I have learnt from my own experience that emptying away all the biased thoughts and prejudices gives new values that enhance living.

I stress upon the importance of Truth and Non-violence and call you to 'Be Fearless' on all endeavors. It is you who is the future, the tomorrow of the nation and the instruments of social change that we want to see in the nation.

The modern youth and students have the spiritual and ethical values to become the means to form idealistic thoughts, that aim for greatness.

I encourage young minds about self-reliance as a crucial necessity to success. The young leader of today must be flexible, self reliant, independent and open-minded.

Simplicity, kindness, truth and non-violence should be the life's mantra of youth. These are the essential things that you as students have to learn and follow. Morality and spirituality of course cannot be forgotten.

6. Biographies include features of non-fiction texts-factual information and different text structures such as description, sequence, comparison, cause and effect, or problem and solution. Examine Indigo in the light of this statement, in about 120-150 words. **Competency Based**

Ans. Biographies include features of non-fiction texts – factual information and different text structures such as description, sequence, comparison, cause and effect, or problem and solution. 'Indigo' by Louis Fischer is in fact an excerpt from a biography. However, it has features of fiction as well as non-fiction texts.

It includes factual information. We know about the interview carried out by the author in order to write on about Gandhi. Louis Fischer visited Gandhi in 1942 at his ashram- Sevagram where he was told about the Indigo Movement started by Gandhiji.

We also know about the December 1916 annual convention of the Indian National Congress Party in Lucknow. Apart from this, there are many structural evidences in the text that point to its non-fictional nature.

Almost each and everything is explained without any scope of loopholes. We know clearly what the Sharecropping Agreement in Champaran was. We also get a brief background of almost all the important people in the event starting from Rajkumar Shukla to JB Kripalani. Even when the author displays (astonishment) at Kripalani's act of housing Gandhi, we know exactly why such an emotion is expected.

Further, the entire episode is present in a chronological order. We know when Gandhi went to Champaran and why. We are told what his next steps were and with what insight were they taken. In the correct order, we know how Gandhi's act garnered support from the farmers and how it resulted in the enquiry and resolution.

Thus, we can state that Indigo includes the features of a fiction as well as a non-fiction text.

7. 'Lost Spring' and 'Indigo' highlight the apathy of society and exploitation by those in power. Elaborate. **Competency Based**

Ans. 'Lost Spring' by Anees Jung and 'Indigo' by Louis Fischer, both shed light on the harsh realities of societal apathy and exploitation by those in power. In 'Lost Spring', Jung exposes the plight of impoverished children like Saheb and Mukesh, forced to scavenge for a living amidst the affluence of urban India. The story highlights the indifference of society towards the struggles of marginalised communities, perpetuating cycles of poverty and exploitation.

Similarly, 'Indigo' explores the exploitation of Indian peasants by British colonialists during the indigo cultivation period. Fischer portrays the ruthless exploitation of farmers by British indigo planters, who prioritise profits over human welfare.

Both narratives serve as powerful indictments of social apathy and systemic exploitation, urging readers to confront and address the injustices faced by marginalised communities. They emphasise the importance of empathy, activism, and collective action in challenging oppressive systems and fostering a more equitable society.

8. How did Gandhi use Satyagraha and non-violence at Champaran to achieve his goal? **CBSE 2020**

Ans. It is true to say that Gandhi used Satyagraha and non-violence at Champaran to achieve his goal. Gandhi had wished to obtain more information about the conditions in Champaran than Shukla could impart. So, he visited Muzaffarpur to inquire from the lawyers there about the issue. When he was collecting all the facts and met the Commissioner, he was advised to leave Champaran. Gandhi did not leave and decided to launch a peaceful 'Satyagraha' and Non-Violent Movement.

Next morning, there was a spontaneous demonstration by the peasants. Gandhi helped the officials in regulating the crowd, as he did not want any form of violence. After showing some early hesitation, prominent lawyers also declared their unqualified support, which resulted in dropping of the case. On the basis of the evidence collected after a thorough investigation, Gandhi succeeded in making the landlords agree to refund 25% of the compensation money.

Thus, Gandhi's peaceful and Non-Violent Civil Disobedience and Satyagraha helped him in achieving his goal.

9. 'Lost spring' and 'Indigo' bring out how the common man is a victim of exploitation. Explain. **Competency Based**

Ans. It is true that both 'Lost Spring' and 'Indigo' bring out the fact that the common man is a victim of exploitation. In the stories presented in 'Lost Spring', little children and poor ragpickers are shown to be exploited for the betterment of the authority. People in Seemapuri do not have any facilities and live in abject poverty.

However, they have ration cards which they have been provided by those in authority for votes. Similarly families in Firozabad are exploited and cannot raise their voices for being imprisoned by those in authority.

A similar picture is presented in 'Indigo' wherein the poor sharecroppers of Champaran were being exploited by the Britishers for their own benefits. First, their land was taken from them. Then, they were made to work hard and when a new cheaper version of Indigo was found, the sharecroppers were to compensate for the losses.

10. The prose selections, 'Deep Water' and 'Indigo', bring out the importance of overcoming fear, in order to be able to lead our lives successfully.

Imagine yourself to be a motivational speaker who has to address high school students. Write this address in 120–150 words elaborating on occurrences from the two texts to inspire your audience and to convince them about the importance of overcoming fear.

You may begin like this ...

Good morning, students!

We all know what it's like to be afraid. Fear is our body's natural response to a perceived threat or danger.

But when ... **Competency Based**

Ans. Good morning, students! We all know what it's like to be afraid. Fear is our body's natural response to a perceived threat or danger. But when we are determined to learn to face our fears, we win at life and become a champion.

It is no hidden fact that fear immobilises us and prevents us from progressing. We have read the story of William Douglas. Due to his fear of water he could not lead a normal life. He could not go fishing, canoeing, etc. with his friends.

But he decide to get over his fear. Rather than giving into it, he learnt swimming and practiced it with full persistence, determination and sincerity till his fear dissipated. Much like Douglas, we also read about the peasants of Champaran could not take a stand for their rights due to their fear of the Britishers.

It was when they gathered around the courthouse in Motihari that they realised that the main hurdle in them getting justice was their fear. Once, they understood the need to overcome their fear, they came together and relentlessly worked towards getting justice. Thus, we need to face our fear, devise a plan and work through it.

It is important to remember that fear does not get dispelled in an instant. It takes months and even years of persistence to get over it. It takes time but once the fear fades away, one is free to live life to the fullest.

SELF ASSESSMENT TEST

Extract Based Questions

Read the extract given below and answer the questions that follow.

1. The official inquiry assembled a crushing mountain of evidence against the big planters, and when they saw this they agreed, in principle, to make refunds to the peasants.

"But how much must we pay?" they asked Gandhi. They thought he would demand repayment in full of the money which they had illegally and deceitfully extorted from the sharecroppers. He asked only 50%. "There he seemed adamant," writes Reverend JZ Hodge, a British missionary in Champaran who observed the entire episode at close range. "Thinking probably that he would not give way, the representative of the planters offered to refund to the extent of 25%, and to his amazement Mr. Gandhi took him at his word, thus breaking the deadlock."

(i) The given extract indicates Gandhi's intention of coming to Champaran. Elucidate.

(ii) Select the correct option from those given in bracket to fill in the blank.

The crushing mountain of evidence was of .... (extortion/exploitation).

(iii) Complete the following sentence.

The Britishers thought that Gandhi would deny the payment because ....

(iv) Why did the officials feel threatened by the inquiry?

(v) What did the official inquiry reveal?

(a) Violation of the principles
(b) Illegal repayment
(c) Evidence against the landlords
(d) Breaking to deadlock

(vi) Why did Mr. Gandhi take reverend JZ Hodge at his word?

(a) To his amazement
(b) To break the deadlock
(c) To demand repayment
(d) To establish inquiry

Short Answer Type Questions

Answer the following questions in 40-50 words.

1. Was Gandhi correct in chiding the lawyers? Why?

2. Gandhi came to the conclusion that the peasants should stop going to law courts. Explain.

3. Why did Gandhi tell Prof. Malkani, a teacher in a government school, 'It was an extraordinary thing in those days for a government professor to harbour a man like me'?

4. How did the settlement of 25% refund to the farmers change the plight of the peasants?

Long Answer Type Questions

Answer the following questions in 120-150 words.

1. Gandhi considered the Champaran episode a turning point in his life. Do you agree? Substantiate.

2. Give an account of Gandhi's efforts to secure justice for the poor indigo sharecroppers of Champaran.

06

About the Author

Asokamitran (1931-2017) was the pen name of Jagadisa Thyagarajan, an Indian writer regarded one of the most influential figures in post-independence Tamil literature. Born in Secunderabad in 1931, Asokamitran moved to Chennai in 1952 following an invitation from his father's friend, the film director SS Vasan, to work at Gemini Studios. After working at the Studios for more than a decade, he began writing about his experiences of working in the film industry in a set of columns for the Illustrated Weekly of India; these columns later became his book, 'My Years with Boss'.

YOUR STUDY GOALS

- Chapter Sketch
- About the Characters
- Summary of the Chapter

YOUR PRACTICE GOAL

- NCERT Folder
- Extract Based Questions
- Short Answer Type Questions
- Long Answer Type Questions

Poets and Pancakes

Chapter Sketch

'Poets and Pancakes', an excerpt from Asokamitran's book 'My Years with Boss', is a humourous and interesting account of his experiences while working at Gemini Studios in Madras. The chapter comprises the descriptions of personalities popular in the early days of Indian cinema. The focus of the chapter is on the various eccentric personalities and the vain behaviour of people in the industry.

About the Characters

Boss He is Mr. SS Vasan, the founder of Gemini Studios. He had a liking for erudite and scholarly people.

Subbu He is the no. 2 at Gemini Studios. He always looked cheerful and was highly resourceful, charitable and of a loving nature. He was also an amazing actor, poet and novelist.

Legal Advisor He was a lawyer working in the Story Department of Gemini Studios.

Office Boy He is in the make-up Department of Gemini Studios and does the make up of the players in the crowd scenes of films. He aspired to be a top film star, screen writer, director or lyric writer but was a highly frustrated man because he could not become any of them.

Summary of the Chapter

The Make-up Department

The make-up department of the Gemini Studios was located in a building which was said to be Robert Clive's home. The make-up room looked like a hair-cutting salon, with large mirrors and lights at all angles. The make-up product with the brand name 'Pancake' was used in the Studios. Thus, it was not a very pleasing experience to get the make-up done here.

The make-up department of Gemini Studios was a symbol of National integration. Initially, it was headed by a Bengali, then by a Maharashtrian who was assisted by a Dharwar Kannadiga and others from different states of India.

Heirarchy and the Office Boy

There was a hierarchy in the make-up studious. The chief make-up man dressed up the leading actors and actresses. His senior assistant looked after the 'second' hero and heroine while the junior assistant took charge of the main comedian. The actors who played the crowd were looked after by the office boy of the department. The office boy was a man in his early forties, who had joined the studio to be a top film star, screen writer, director or lyric writer.

The Office Boy's Frustrations

The narrator's work in the studio was to cut newspaper clippings and store them in files. So, everybody thought that he did nothing and continuously lectured him. Even the office boy came to tell him about his frustrations regarding his failures.

The narrator mentions that the office boy felt that the source of his problems was a man named Kothamangalam Subbu, the No. 2 at Gemini Studios. According to the office boy, Subbu did not deserve anything because he was neither well educated nor had any exceptional talent. His only virtue was being a Brahmin, due to which he got opportunities readily.

Subbu's Talents

According to the author, Subbu was a cheerful man who was loyal to the Chief. He could offer countless solutions to the problems of the film producer. Subbu was also a poet who wrote poetry for the masses. He composed 'story poems' in folk refrain and diction. He recreated the mood and manner of the Devadasis of the early 20th century and even wrote a novel Thillana Mohanambai. In addition, Subbu was an amazing actor too.

Subbu was also a flatterer. He always said nice things about everything and everyone. His house was always crowded with acquaintances and relatives. He was really close and intimate with the Boss and so, had many enemies.

The Lawyer of Gemini Studios

The Story Department of the Studio comprised of a lawyer and a group of writers and poets besides Subbu. The lawyer was the illegal Advisor who had unintentionally brought about a sad end to the career of a talented actress by recording her outburst against the producer.

The lawyers looked different from the other members of his department as he wore pants and tie while they wore khadi dhotis and white khadi shirts. He was close to the Boss and was allowed to produce a film which flopped. The lawyer lost his job when the Boss closed the Story Department.

The Political Ideology of the Studio

Gemini Studios was a favourite place of the poets of that time. It had an excellent mess which supplied good coffee at all times. At that time, the Congress government had implemented prohibition and people enjoyed their leisure time over a cup of coffee. Almost everybody seemed to have ample leisure time at the studio.

Most of the people at the studio greatly appreciated Gandhi. They opposed Communism and thought Communists to be violent with no filial or conjugal feelings.

Studio Hosts Frank Buchman's MRA (Moral Re-armament Army)

The Gemini Studios was a host to Frank Buchman's Moral Re-armament Army or The MRA which visited Madras in 1952. It presented two plays- 'Jotham Valley' and 'The Forgotten Factor', which were seen repeatedly by the members of the studio. The Tamil and Madras drama community were really impressed by them. The sunrise and sunset scenes of 'Jotham Valley' were reproduced in almost all Tamil plays in a similar fashion as that play.

The Mysterious Visitor

Soon another visitor was going to visit the Gemini Studios. The staff did not have any idea about him. He was rumoured to be a poet or editor. However, the guest arrived and the Boss read out a very long speech that did not have much to say about the visitor. When the guest's turn came to address the audience, his accent could not be understood by anybody.

Recognising the Mystery Man

The narrator, then, refers to another event- a short story contest to be organised by a British periodical by the name 'The Encounter'. The narrator wanted to have an idea about the periodical's credentials before participating in the contest and spending on the postage. Hence, he checked at the British Council Library and found no information except that the editor's name was Stephen Spender. He recalled that this was the same editor who was a guest at the Gemini Studios.

The God that Failed

Some years after leaving his job at the Gemini Studios, the narrator bought a copy of a book 'The God that Failed' which was re-released on the 50th anniversary of the Russian Revolution. It was a compilation of six essays by six different authors on their journey into Communism and their disappointed return. When the narrator found that Stephen Spender was one of the contributors, he realised the purpose of his visit to the Studious.

Word-Meaning

pancake	— powdery material used for make-up
maiden	— young woman
incandescent	— glowing white hot
hierarchy	— system in which people are ranked based on their importance
crowd-shooting	— film shooting requiring a crowd to be shown in the scene
cubicle	— small area partitioned off
French windows	— glazed doors in walls
enlightened	— given greater knowledge
ignominy	— public disgrace
flop	— totally failed
refrain and diction	— style
improvident	— not bothered about the future
demeanour	— outward behaviour
sycophant's	— flatterer's
direst	— worst
temperamental	— changing mood in an unreasonable way
blew over	— spoke angrily
incriminating	— guilty of a crime
unmentionably foul	— insult which is so dirty that it cannot be mentioned
tirade	— long angry speech of criticism
was struck dumb	— was shocked into silence
catapulted into	— suddenly facing
unwittingly	— unknowingly

a coat of mail	— it had many holes in it
raw stock	— fresh unused rolls of cinematographic film
favourite haunt	— place which is frequently visited
radiated leisure	— showed that they were free
filial or conjugal	— related to the family or the wife/spouse
Gemini family	— persons who worked in Gemini studios
homilies	— dull talks on moral issues
played into their hands	— did something without realising that it will hurt him and help them
surmise	— assumption
precious little	— hardly anything
peppered	— scattered in various parts
bafflement	— confusion
cultivating a taste for	— appreciating
incongruity	— unsuitability
travails	— hardships
drudge	— person doing dull or routine work
Gemini literati	— employees of Gemini studios interested in literature
heard a bell ringing	— realised that I had solved the mystery
eminent	— famous
men of letters	— literary personalities
assumed tremendous significance	— became important

Important Themes of the Chapter

Inner working of the Industry The excerpt vividly portrays a film company's inner workings and personalities during the early days of Indian cinema. The narrative focuses on Gemini Studios and its mix of individuals, including poets, writers, actors and film-makers. It provides insights into the dynamics, hierarchy, and daily activities within Gemini Studios, shedding light on the roles played by various individuals and their interactions.

Poets and writers in a film company environment The excerpt explores the presence and influence of poets and writers within Gemini Studios. It delves into their backgrounds, creative pursuits, and interactions with other studio members. Asokamitran's narrative skillfully captures the atmosphere of Gemini Studios, offering readers a glimpse into the cultural and creative milieu of early Indian cinema.

NCERT Folder

Think as you Read (NCERT Page 59)

1. What does the writer mean by 'the fiery misery' of those subjected to make-up?

Ans. By 'the fiery misery' of those subjected to make-up, the narrator/writer refers to the suffering faced by those who got their make-up done in Gemini Studios. This suffering, in the form of heat and flashy light, was a result of the design of the make-up room which was crowded with bright lights at all angles.

2. What is the example of national integration that the author refers to?

Or How was the make-up room in the Gemini Studios a fine example of national integration? CBSE 2020

Or How was there a great deal of national integration in the make-up department? CBSE 2024

Ans. The make-up room of the Gemini Studios was an example of national integration. According to the author, this is so because people from different regions and religious groups worked together in the same department.

The department was headed by a Bengali who was succeeded by a Maharashtrian. The other helpers included Dharwar Kannadiga, an Audura, a Madras Indian Christian, an Anglo-Burmese and the local Tamils.

3. What work did the 'office boy' do in the Gemini Studios? Why did he join the studios? Why was he disappointed?

Ans. The 'office boy' was responsible for the make-up of the players who played the crowd. On the days of crowd-shooting, one could see him mixing his paint in a giant vessel and "slapping it" on the crowd players.

The office boy had joined the studio years ago in the hope of becoming a star actor or a top screen writer, director or lyric writer.

The 'office boy' was disappointed because he had not achieved any of his dreams. He was also a poet and felt that his talent was not being recognised. He was doing a job which was much below his actual calibre.

4. Why did the author appear to be doing nothing at the studios?

Ans. The author's job involved scanning the various news items and articles that appeared in different newspapers and keeping a record of them in files. So, he was always seen at this desk tearing up newspapers. This gave the impression that he was doing next to nothing at the studios.

Think as you Read (NCERT Page 61)

1. Why was the office boy frustrated? Who did he show his anger on?

Ans. The office boy was highly frustrated because he was not able to achieve any of his dreams of becoming an actor or a top screen writer, director of lyric writer and he directed all his anger on Kothamangalam Subbu, the number 2 at the Gemini Studios. He thought of Subbu as his enemy.

He was thoroughly convinced that all his woes, ignominy and neglect were due to Subbu.

2. Who was Subbu's Principal?

Ans. SS Vasan, the founder of the Gemini Studios, was Subbu's Boss and Principal.

3. Subbu is described as a many-sided genius. List four of his special abilities.

Ans. Four of Subbu's special abilities were

(i) Looking cheerful at all times.

(ii) A sense of intense loyalty to the Boss which made him focus his entire creativity towards benefiting the Boss. Thus, film-making was quite easy as long as Subbu was available to give his ideas.

(iii) He was literally inclined as he was a good poet, novelist and actor.

(iv) Charitable and of loving nature.

4. **Why was the legal Advisor referred to as the opposite by others?**

Ans. The legal Advisor was referred to as an illegal advisor because he was a man of cold logic.

He never put his legal knowledge to use and even destroyed the career of a budding talented actress.

5. **What made the lawyer stand out from the others at Gemini Studios?**

Ans. The lawyer stood out from the others at Gemini Studios because in a 'crowd of dreamers', he was a man of cold logic. He took a politically neutral ideology whereas everyone else in the Gemini Studios were mostly Gandhiites and Khadiites. Moreover, he wore tie and pants and sometimes a coat which made him stand out in the midst of khadi wearers.

Think as you Read (NCERT Page 64)

1. **Did the people at Gemini Studios have any particular political affiliations?**

Ans. The majority of people at Gemini Studios wore khadi and venerated Gandhi. Beyond that they did not have "the faintest affectation" for political thought of any kind. They were vehemently against Communism and called themselves Gandhiites.

2. **Why was the Moral Rearmament Army welcomed at the Studios?**

Ans. The Moral Rearmament Army was a kind of counter movement to international Communism. Because of this they were welcomed at the Gemini Studios. The Boss, Mr. Vasan, simply played into their hands because they opposed those who spread unrest and violence among the innocent and the ignorant.

3. **Name one example to show that Gemini Studios was influenced by the plays staged by MRA.**

Ans. 'Jotham Valley' and 'The Forgotten Factor', the two plays put up by the MRA, were so impressive that the Gemini family consisting of six hundred people saw them over and over again. They liked the play so much that the scene of sunrise and sunset enacted in the play 'Jotham Valley' with a bare stage, a white background curtain and a tune played on the flute was reproduced by Madras and Tamil drama community.

4. **Who was the Boss of Gemini Studios?**

Ans. Mr. SS Vasan, the founder of Gemini Studios was called 'The Boss'. He was also the editor of the popular Tamil weekly 'Ananda Vikatan'.

5. **What caused the lack of communication between the Englishman and the people at Gemini Studios?**

Ans. The lack of communication between the Englishman and the people at Gemini Studios was a result of two things. First, nobody knew anything about the antecedents of the visitor. Mr. Vasan, the Boss made a welcome speech in his honour but that did not dispel any doubts or gave clarifications about the visitor. Secondly, when the visitor spoke, nobody could comprehend what he talked about. His accent could not be understood by the 'dazed' audience.

6. **Why is the Englishman's visit referred to as unexplained mystery?** CBSE 2025

Ans. The Englishman's visit baffled everybody in the Gemini Studios. They neither knew anything about the credentials of the visitor nor could they comprehend anything from his speech due to his accent. All of them were 'dazed and silent'. They could not understand what an English poet was doing in a film studio which made Tamil films for the masses who had no taste for English poetry. So, his visit is termed as an unexplained mystery.

Think as you Read (NCERT Page 65)

1. **Who was the English visitor to the studios?**

Ans. The English visitor to the Gemini Studios was found to be Stephen Spender—the editor of 'The Encounter'.

2. **How did the author discover who the English visitor to the studios was?**

Ans. The identity of the English visitor was revealed to the author only when he read the editor's name in 'The Encounter'.

3. **What does 'The God that Failed' refer to?**

Ans. 'The God that Failed' refers to a book that was a compilation of essays by six eminent essayists. It dealt with the author's disillusionment with Communism.

Understanding the Text (NCERT Page 66)

1. **The author has used gentle humour to point out human foibles. Pick out instances of this to show how this serves to make the piece interesting?**

Or **After reading this story, you are impressed by the author's use of gentle humour to point out human foibles. Evaluate.** CBSE Question Bank 2021, Modified

Ans. 'Poets and Pancakes' has instances of gentle humour interspersed in it. They highlight human foibles without pointing fingers or having malice against anyone.

Some of the various instance are as follows

- The description of the make-up department and its transformation of decent-looking individuals into hideous monsters with truck-loads of pancake and other potions and lotions.
- The portrayal of the 'office boy' in the make-up department who harboured dreams of becoming a star actor or a top screenwriter, director or lyrics writer

despite being in his early forties. This adds a touch of irony to his character. The narrator's work itself point to some of the useless roles prevalent in the Studio.

- Asokamitran's humour reaches its peak in depiction of Subbu. Subbu's inefficiency and dependence on others is highlighted by the author's comment, "He always had work for somebody-he could never do things on his own". Further, Subbu's demeanour and his ability to always look cheerful, even after facing difficulties, contrasts with the frustrations of the make-up department employee.
- Further, the fact that the lawyer inadvertently ends a brilliant acting career by recording an actress's tirade, makes us laugh.
- The 'Boss', Mr. Vasan's weakness for being seen amongst erudite and scholarly people and the resultant invitations to unknown poets and editors is hilarious.
- The author's comment on himself that anything at a reduced price attracted his attention makes us laugh at the apparent idiosyncrasies of human nature.

Thus, the author showcases humour in every situation and almost every character, but this is only meant to make the piece a gripping one.

2. Why was Kothamangalam Subbu considered number 2 in Gemini Studios? **CBSE 2025**

Or Account for Subbu's importance in Gemini studios.

Ans. Kothamangalam Subbu has many positive qualities that made him number 2 in Gemini Studios. Although he was neither brilliant nor out-of-the-ordinary, he had an inherent smartness in him that led him to outwit everybody. He was a sycophant and always close and intimate with the Boss. He always had ready and instant solutions for problems and had the knack of getting the work done from others.

3. How does the author describe the incongruity of an English poet addressing the audience at Gemini Studios?

Ans. The author describes the incongruity of an English poet addressing the audience at Gemini Studios by highlighting the stark differences in cultural context and audience interests. The Gemini Studios primarily produced Tamil films for a simple audience whose lives didn't afford them the luxury of cultivating a taste for English poetry.

The author and others at the studio were still trying to understand the presence of the English poet, reflecting the sheer mismatch between the audience's expectations and the poet's speech. This mismatch highlights the situation's absurdity and adds a layer of irony to the narrative.

4. What do you understand about the author's literary inclinations from the account?

Ans. From the account, it's evident that the author has literary inclinations and a keen interest in exploring the intersection of literature, cinema and human experiences. The author's engagement with literature is reflected in his curiosity about British publications, recognition of Stephen Spender's significance and his own desire to send his entries to short story writing contests. The author's observations on the dynamics within Gemini Studios, including the roles of individuals like Subbu and the encounters with visiting poets and editors, highlight his interest in exploring the complexities of human interactions and creative endeavours.

Exam Pattern Questions

Extract Based Questions

Read the extracts given below and answer the questions that follow.

1. Those were the days of mainly indoor shooting, and only five percent of the film was shot outdoors. I suppose the sets and studio lights needed the girls and boys to be made to look ugly in order to look presentable in the movie. A strict hierarchy was maintained in the make-up department. The chief make-up man made the chief actors and actresses ugly, his senior assistant 'second' hero and heroine, the junior assistant the main comedian and so forth.

The players who played the crowd were the responsibility of the office boy. (Even the make-up department of the Gemini Studio had an 'office boy').

On the days when there was crowd-shooting, you could see him mixing his paint in a giant vessel and slapping it on the crowd players. The idea was to close every pore on the surface of the face in the process of applying make-up. **CBSE 2025**

(i) What does the writer mean by the phrase 'indoor shooting' in the first line of the extract?

(ii) Pick up one sentence from the extract that reflects the sarcastic tone of the writer.

(iii) The hierarchy in the make-up department puts the 'office boy' in the .... (lowest/top) rung of the ladder.

(iv) Complete the following suitably.

On the days when there was a 'crowd-shooting'. By the phrase crowd-shooting, the author refers to

(v) Choose the correct option.

".....mix his paint in a giant vessel and slapping it on the crowd players."

The choice of words like 'paint' and 'slapping' by the author reflects

(a) author's intention to degrade the office boy's role in the make-up department.
(b) the office boy's lack of seriousness.
(c) author's sarcastic and humorous writing style.
(d) author's dislike of the office boy.

(vi) Choose the correct option.

What does the following line from the extract showcase?

"A strict hierarchy was maintained in the make-up department."

(a) The office boy took all the decisions in the make-up department.
(b) A system of ranks according to importance of work was followed.
(c) Everyone was given an equal share of work in the department.
(d) Nepotism was prevalent in the make-up department.

Ans. (i) The phrase 'indoor shooting' refers to filming inside a studio using artificial sets and lights instead of shooting in natural outdoor locations.

(ii) "I suppose the sets and studio lights needed the girls and boys to be made to look ugly in order to look presentable in the movie."

(iii) lowest

(iv) the scenes in the film that required a large number of extras or background actors

(v) (c) author's sarcastic and humorous writing style.

(vi) (b) A system of ranks according to importance of work was followed.

2. **Film-making must have been and was so easy with a man like Subbu around and if ever there was a man who gave direction and definition to Gemini Studios during its golden years, it was Subbu. Subbu had a separate identity as a poet and though he was certainly capable of more complex and higher forms, he deliberately chose to address his poetry to the masses.**

(i) What was Subbu's contribution to Gemini Studios?

(ii) Select the correct option from those given in bracket to fill in the blank.

The expression 'he deliberately chose to address his poetry to the masses' indicates that Subbu's poetry was .... (nonsensical/genius).

(iii) Complete the sentence suitably.

By 'during its golden years', the writer means ....

(iv) On the basis of the given extract do you think that the narrator is appreciative of Subbu?

(v) What is Subbu likely to say when a film director faces a problem?

(a) Hold on, call Asokamitran.
(b) Let me think of it.
(c) You should have thought about it earlier.
(d) Waste of time it is.

(vi) What is the author's tone when talking about Subbu?

(a) Pleasing (b) Praising
(c) Sarcastic (d) Insulting

Ans. (i) Subbu's contribution was that he gave 'a new direction and definition' to the Gemini Studios during its golden years. Subbu directed all his energies and creativity to his boss, Mr. Vasan's advantage. If his boss was dissatisfied with one scene, Subbu would offer him many alternatives.

(ii) nonsensical

(iii) when the studios was the most successful

(iv) No, I do not think that the narrator is appreciative of Subbu. The narrator is sarcastically highlighting the qualities of Subbu to show how vain he is.

(v) (b) Let me think of it.

(vi) (c) Sarcastic

3. **His success in films overshadowed and dwarfed his literary achievements-or so his critics felt.**
He composed several truly original 'story poems' in folk refrain and diction and also wrote a sprawling novel Thillana Mohanambal with dozens of very deftly etched characters.

He quite successfully recreated the mood and manner of the Devadasis of the early 20th century. He was an amazing actor-he never aspired to the lead roles-but whatever subsidiary role he played in any of the films, he performed better than the supposed main players. He had a genuine love for anyone he came across and his house was a permanent residence for dozens of near and far relations and acquaintances.

(i) With what tone does the narrator talk about Subbu's literary genius?

(ii) Select the correct option from those given in bracket to fill in the blank.

The extract highlights that Subbu was .... (a pushover/vain) in nature.

(iii) Complete the sentence suitably. The phrase 'deftly etched' shows that Subbu ....

(iv) Why does the narrator say that Subbu never aspire to be a lead actor even though he was an amazing actor?

(v) Which of these statements is not true about Subbu?

(a) His literary accomplishments stole the limelight from his films.
(b) He was a gifted poet and writer and his literary works were noteworthy.
(c) He was selfless in nature and was empathetic towards others.
(d) He never hankered after lead roles and performed minor roles in films.

(vi) Pick the option that best describes Subbu according to the extract.

1. benevolent 2. powerful
3. accomplished 4. witty
5. generous 6. temperamental
(a) 4, 5 and 6 (b) 2, 3 and 4
(c) 1, 3 and 5 (d) 3, 4 and 6

Ans. (i) The narrator talk about Subbu's literary genius in a sarcastic tone.

(ii) vain

(iii) was skillful in creating the characters.

(iv) The narrator says that Subbu never aspired to be a lead actor because he was not an amazing actor. By calling him an amazing actor, the narrator is actually mocking Subbu.

(v) (a) His literary accomplishments stole the limelight from his films.

(vi) (c) 1, 3 and 5

4. **A girl from the countryside, she hadn't gone through all the stages of worldly experience that generally precede a position of importance and sophistication that she had found herself catapulted into. She never quite recovered from the terror she felt that day. That was the end of a brief and brilliant acting career — the legal advisor, who was also a member of the Story Department, had unwittingly brought about that sad end. While every other member of the department wore a kind of uniform — khadi dhoti with a slightly oversized and clumsily tailored white khadi shirt — the legal advisor wore pants and a tie and sometimes a coat that looked like a coat of mail. Often, he looked alone and helpless ...** **CBSE SQP 2023**

(i) Why had the narrator mentioned the incident with the actress?

(ii) Select the correct option from those given in brackets to fill in the blank.
The harm done to the actress was a/an .... (well-planned act/unintentional act).

(iii) Complete the sentence with an appropriate explanation, as per the extract.

The writer uses the word 'uniform' to refer to the outfits of the department members because just like a uniform ....

(iv) Identify the textual clue that allows the reader to infer that the writer is sympathetic towards the professional fate of the actress. (Clue: a phrase)

(v) Select the option that completes the given sentence appropriately.

'Stages of worldly experience' in the given context would refer to ....

(a) good education to gain knowledge
(b) situations that require one to be street smart
(c) smaller, not so important roles in acting
(d) training in soft skills

(vi) Based on the above extract, choose the statement that is true for the legal advisor.

(a) He disliked the actress from the countryside.
(b) He acted after thinking through things carefully.
(c) He did not get well with others in the department.
(d) He was always dressed smartly.

Ans. (i) The narrator had mentioned the incident with the actress to highlight how the lawyer was an illegal advisor as he led to the end of the acting career of a young actress.

(ii) unintentional act

(iii) which is a common dress code for all, the dress worn by the employees of the make-up studio was nearly the same - loose khadi shirt and khadi dhoti

(iv) The phrase 'sad end' shows that the writer is sympathetic towards the professional fate of the actor.

(v) (b) situations that require one to be street smart

(vi) (c) He did not get well with others in the department.

5. Barring the office boys and a couple of clerks, everybody else at the Studios radiated leisure, a pre-requisite for poetry. Most of them wore khadi and worshipped Gandhiji but beyond that they had not the faintest appreciation for political thought of any kind. Naturally, they were all averse to the term 'Communism'. A communist was a godless man-he had no filial or conjugal love; he had no compunction about killing his own parents or his children; he was always out to cause and spread unrest and violence among innocent and ignorant people.

Such notions, which prevailed everywhere else in South India at that time also, naturally, floated about vaguely among the khadi-clad poets of Gemini Studios. Evidence of it was soon forthcoming. **CBSE Question Bank 2021**

(i) The people at the Gemini Studios has not the faintest appreciation for political thought. Why does the narrator say so?

(ii) Select the correct option from those given in bracket to fill in the blank.

The narrator mentions that the people at the Gemini Studios were .... (neutral/ inclined) towards Gandhiji's political ideology.

(iii) Complete the sentence suitably.

The narrator say leisure is a pre-requisite for poetry because ....

(iv) What Evidence is being talked about in the extract?

(v) Pick the option that uses the same figure of speech as 'A communist is a Godless man.'

(a) She is as determined as Gandhi when it is a fight against injustice.
(b) She is a Gandhi when she raises her voice against 'hinsa' or violence.
(c) She, like Gandhi, feels that the Earth is crying for deliverance.
(d) She lives a life of opulence and calls herself a follower of Gandhi.

(vi) Based on the extract, choose the correct option with reference to the two statements given below.

Statement I At Gemini Studios, the poets had a profound knowledge about Communists.

Statement II Communists were responsible for anarchy and discontent in the country.

(a) Statement I is true but Statement II is false.
(b) Statement I is false but Statement II is true.
(c) Both Statement I and Statement II cannot be inferred.
(d) Both Statement I and Statement II can be inferred.

Ans. (i) The narrator says so because he knows that the people at the Gemini Studios only believed what has been popular at the time. They did not have their own political thought.

(ii) inclined

(iii) in order to write poetry, one needs free time

(iv) The evidence talked of in the extract refers to the coming of Frank Buchman's Moral Re-Armament army, a kind of counter argument to Communism to the Gemini Studios.

(v) (b) She is a Gandhi when she raises her voice against 'hinsa' or violence.

(vi) (d) Both Statement I and Statement II can be inferred.

6. Then the poet spoke. He couldn't have addressed a more dazed and silent audience - no one knew what he was talking about and his accent defeated any attempt to understand what he was saying. The whole thing lasted about an hour; then the poet left and we all dispersed in utter bafflement - What are we doing? What is an English poet doing in a film studio which makes Tamil films for the simplest sort of people? People whose lives least afforded them the possibility of cultivating a taste for English poetry. The poet looked pretty baffled too, for he must have felt the sheer incongruity of his talk about the thrills and travails of an English poet. His visit remained an unexplained mystery. **CBSE 2024**

(i) Explain one inference that can be drawn from the line, "He could not have addressed a more dazed and silent audience".

(ii) Select the correct option from those given in brackets to fill in the blank.

The audience were .... (baffled/enthralled) by the poet's impressive speech.

(iii) Complete the sentence suitably.

The failure of the speaker to connect with the audience with reference to the extract is his ....

(iv) What information in the extract reveals the fact that the people have no exposure other than to their own circle ?

(v) Choose the correct option.
The reason for the bewilderment of the audience is

(a) unknown identity of the visitor.
(b) that the speaker had not been introduced to them.
(c) the visit of an English poet to a Tamil film studio.
(d) that they did not understand English.

(vi) By 'thrills and travails' the author refers to

(a) joy and happiness (b) interest and aspiration
(c) excitement and pain (d) shocks and surprises

Ans. (i) One inference that can be drawn from the given line is that the audience was overwhelmed by the unusual appearance of the poet as they could not understand what the poet was talking about.

(ii) baffled

(iii) complex language and inability to capture the attention of the audience.

(iv) The reaction of the audience on the unusual visit of the English poet in a Tamil film studio is an indication of their limited exposure. It implies that they are not much knowledgeable regarding English poetry and are focused only in their own cultural and linguistic space.

(v) (c) the visit of an English poet to a Tamil film studio

(vi) (c) excitement and pain

Short Answer Type Questions

1. Through the mention of Robert Clive's activities, how does the narrator bring out the spectacle of those in power?

Ans. The make-up department of Gemini Studios was in a building that was believed to have been Robert Clive's stable. So, the place which was good to become a make-up room in a film studio had been misused by the Britishers. Further, the fact that Robert Clive used to own several buildings indicates how those in power live a life of extravagant luxury.

2. Describe the make-up room of the Gemini Studios as described by the author.

Ans. The make-up room of the Gemini Studios looked like a hair cutting salon with incandescent lights. The lights, placed at all angles around half a dozen mirrors, made the room very hot.

3. 'A strict hierarchy was maintained in the make-up department.' Explain.

Ans. Strict hierarchy was maintained in the make-up department so that each make-up man was allotted his task according to his designation.

The chief make-up man attended the chief actors and actresses, his senior assistant attended the second hero and heroine, the junior assistant attended the main comedian and the office boy in the department did the make-up of the actors who played the crowd.

4. What advantage did the office boy think Subbu had?

Ans. The office boy thought that Subbu was in no way superior to him in talent or education. It was due to Subbu's birth in a Brahmin family that he had got a lead over him and helped him get better openings, opportunities and exposure. Thus, he had an advantage over the office boy.

5. Subbu was charitable and improvident, yet he had enemies. Why?

Ans. Subbu's good qualities were overlooked as his desire to please the Boss who was, the key to his success. This made him seem like a sycophant. His non-critical attitude was misconstrued as cleverness. So, he had enemies such as the office boy, all of whom blamed him for their failure in life.

6. What made the lawyer lose his job? What was funny about it?

Ans. The closing down of the Story Department by the Boss made the lawyer lose his job. The writer found this situation funny because he thought that this was perhaps the only instance in all human history where a lawyer lost his job because the poets were asked to go home.

7. What was the opinion of the khadi clad poets of Gemini Studios about Communism?

Ans. The khadi clad poets of Gemini Studios were against Communism as that was the prevailing political notion in South India. A Communist to them was a Godless man, had no filial or conjugal love, could unhesitatingly kill his parents or children and was always out to cause and spread violence and unrest.

8. Why do you think Stephen Spender visited Gemini Studios?

Ans. Stephen Spender was an anti-Communist, similar to the people at Gemini Studios. He had been invited by the Boss to talk about his journey into Communism and his return after being disillusioned with Communism.

9. What role did the canteen play at the Gemini Studios?

Ans. The canteen at the Gemini Studios played the role of giving leisure and entertainment to the employees as it supplied good coffee at all times of the day and for most part of the night. As Prohibition had been imposed by the government in Madras, meeting over a cup of coffee was rather a satisfying entertainment.

10. The boss did not know anything about Stephen Spender yet invited him to speak at Gemini Studios. How will you characterise the Boss in this regard?

Ans. The fact that the boss did not know anything about Stephen Spender yet invited him to speak at Gemini Studios tells us that he was a vain man. He like erudite and scholarly people and so, supported them without knowing anything about them.

11. The Boss of Gemini Studios had nothing to do with Spender's poetry but not with his 'God that failed'. Bring out the significance of this line.

Ans. This line is significant as the Boss had only invited Stephen Spender to Gemini Studios because he was a contributing author to the book 'The God that failed' which presented the failures of Communism.

He himself did not have any knowledge of Spender's background and so spoke about Spender only in general terms while introducing him to the employees of the Studios.

12. What kind of effect does Asokamitran's style of writing have on the reader? Competency Based

Ans. Asokamitran satirical style of writing has an underlying tone of humour which highlights the human foibles.

The description of the events and the people at the Gemini Studio makes the reader identify the common foibles in people present not just in the story but also in real life.

13. Discuss the significance of the make-up room in the chapter, 'Poets and Pancakes'. CBSE Question Bank 2021

Ans. The make-up room of the Gemini Studio is the central crux of the story. It is the setting which takes us towards the superficiality of the people in life and of the people in the studio. The people in the make-up studio only accept what is popular much like people in reality who accept popular things blindly.

14. "In all instances of frustration, you will always find the anger directed towards a single person openly or covertly...". Competency Based

Do you think it is right to direct our anger towards someone who is not responsible for the cause of anger? Justify.

Ans. No, I feel that it is not justified to direct our anger towards someone who is not responsible for the cause of anger. It shows that the person who does so needs someone to blame for his/her failures. Such a individual comes out as vain and undetermined.

15. The narrative presents how literature and cinema are deeply connected. Substantiate.

Ans. It is true to say that the narrative of Poets and Pancakes presents how literature and cinema are deeply connected. The title of the story itself, highlights this connection as poets are associated with literature and Pancake is the name of the make-up used in Gemini Studios. Further, many people working in the studios like the office boy, Subbu, the Boss and the narrator himself write prose or poetry. Moreover, the Boss is an editor of a popular Tamil weekly Ananda Vikatan. So, the café of his studio was a leisure place of many poets and the boss invites Stephen Spender for a speech.

16. In the story 'Poets and Pancakes', why does the narrator say that film-making was very easy with a man like Subbu around? Answer in 20–30 words. Competency Based

Ans. The narrator says that film-making was very easy with Subbu around because he was very creative and could come up with ideas in an instant. If the producer was not very happy with the original idea, Subbu would come up with many other suggestions for shooting the scene.

17. "...prose writing is not and cannot be the true pursuit of a genius. It is for the patient, persistent, persevering drudge with a heart so shrunken that nothing can break it..." Elucidate. Competency Based

Ans. The given statement challenges the traditional romanticised view of prose writing as a genre of genius writers. It presents a realistic picture of prose writing to be an art of patience and perseverance and not merely talent. By using phrases such as 'shrunken heart', there is an emphasis on the hardships and rejections faced by prose writers. Excellence in prose writing can be achieved only through discipline and consistent efforts. Prose writing is a challenging field which requires immense patience.

18. The narrator of 'Poets and Pancakes' writes the following line while describing the make-up department.

(Even the make-up department of the Gemini Studio had an 'office boy'!)

What does the exclamation mark indicate? What can you infer about the narrator's attitude towards make-up through this line? Answer in 40–50 words. Competency Based

Ans. The exclamation mark in the line indicates that the narrator was surprised to learn that the department had an office boy. I think this shows that the narrator looked down upon make-up and did not think it was as important as the other departments in cinema.

Long Answer Type Questions

1. The 'office boy' in the Gemini Studios attributes his inability to rise up the ladder in work to Subbu and the strict hierarchy followed in the film company of SS Vasan. However strict the hierarchy, our 'Action should speak more than words'. Hard work, honesty and sincerity of purpose should be the mantra to success. Justify. Competency Based

Ans. It is agreed that there is no shortcut to success. Only hard work, honesty and sincerity of purpose should be the key to success. However, instead of blaming others for our misfortunes, as the office boy was doing, we should face challenges head on. We should try to find solutions to our problems instead of evading them or brooding over our failures. In the story 'Poets and Pancakes', the office boy was not ready to accept his flaws or find out how to overcome hurdles in his path to success. He should have had passion for his job, whatever it may be.

Work should be worship and we should not to be deterred by division of labour. Instead, we must have the tenacity and determination to prove oneself, just as Subbu has achieved over the years. He has developed the qualities required for success due to which he has risen to the position of No. 2 at Gemini Studios, over the years.

2. There was a great deal of National Integration in the Gemini studios with the make-up department being headed by people from all parts of India in succession. The need of the hour in India is an idealistic situation where people are more tolerant towards each other to realise the dreams our founding fathers had dreamt of at the time of Independence. What role could the Youth of India play in this regard? Competency Based

Ans. The Youth of India can play an important role in this regard. For this, they need to become secular in spirit and more tolerant towards people pursuing other religions or faiths.

They should be more spiritual than religious meaning that they should just not blindly follow the rituals of the religion they profess but also understand the principles underlying the rituals. If the Youth of India work together in social causes by rising above the pettiness of their minds, they can succeed in building the nation that our founding fathers had dreamt of at the time of Independence.

All the Youth must be literate so as to become more tolerant and understanding. They can promote the values of compassion and love through street plays, music and dance (fine arts). For this, schools should promote national integration and patriotism in developing life skills.

Then only will we produce the India that is personified by the make-up department at Gemini Studios whose successive heads were from all parts of the country.

3. Identify any three literary devices used by the author in the line below from 'Poets and Pancakes' and analyse the effect each technique has on the reader. Answer in 120-150 words.

"This gang of nationally integrated make-up men could turn any decent-looking person into a hideous crimson hued monster with the help of truck-loads of pancake and a number of other locally made potions and lotions." Competency Based

Ans. In the given line from the text 'Poets and Pancakes', the author is referring to the make-up department of the studio. The use of the 'crimson hued monster' to refer to the actors with the makeup is an example of an imagery and a hyperbole.

The use of imagery helps the reader imagine how the actors would be looking while the hyperbole, adds humour and helps the author convey how ridiculous the situation was.

Another writing technique used in the given line is rhyming words which can be seen in the words 'potions and lotions'. This gives a certain rhythm to the lines while making the process of reading fun for the reader. The author also hyphenates some words in the lines (such as 'decent-looking'), rather than using a phrase (such as 'a person who looked decent'). This helps the author convey more information using fewer words. For a reader, this makes it easier to read through the information as it is concise.

4. Contrast the character of Subbu and the lawyer from the story 'Poets and Pancakes' with any three points of differences. Do you think the qualities of both the characters are equally important on a movie set? Justify your opinion in 120-150 words. Competency Based

Ans. Subbu and the lawyer from the chapter 'Poets and Pancakes' are very different individuals. Subbu is depicted as a spontaneous and creative individual, always generating new ideas, while the lawyer is characterised by his logical thinking. Subbu is also social and generous, frequently hosting guests at his home, contrasting with the lawyer's cold demeanour and tendency to be seen alone. Furthermore, Subbu is passionate and likely a follower of Gandhi, whereas the lawyer maintains a neutral stance. Both characters' qualities are crucial: Subbu's creativity addresses the artistic needs, while the lawyer's logical and objective approach ensures the movie runs smoothly without legal issues. This balance between creativity and objectivity is essential for the successful production of the film.

SELF ASSESSMENT TEST

Extract Based Questions

Read the extract given below and answer the questions that follow.

1. And there were copies of 'The Encounter' lying about in various degrees of freshness, almost untouched by readers. When I read the editor's name, I heard a bell ringing in my shrunken heart. It was the poet who had visited the Gemini Studios - I felt like I had found a long lost brother and I sang as I sealed the envelope and wrote out his address. I felt that he too would be singing the same song at the same time - long lost brothers of Indian films discover each other by singing the same song in the first reel and in the final reel of the film.

(i) What does the fact that the 'The Encounter lying about in various degrees of freshness' indicates?

(ii) Select the correct option from those given in bracket to fill in the blank.

The narrator was feeling .... (regretful/nostalgic).

(iii) Complete the sentence suitably.

The narrator was looking for 'The Encounter' because ....

(iv) I heard a bell ringing in my shrunken heart'. Comment.

(v) What is the author feeling in the extract?

(a) Excited (b) Outraged

(c) Flustered (d) Irritated

(vi) Stephen Spender is the .... of 'The Encounter'.

(a) author (b) editor

(c) founder (d) All of these

Short Answer Type Questions

Answer the following questions in 40-50 words.

1. Can you say that the narrator disliked the office boy? Substantiate.

2. The office boy states that Subbu was successful because he was a Brahmin. Do you agree? Give reason.

3. The Boss played at the hands of the Moral Rearmament Army. Comment.

4. What does the fact that the Tamil movies copied the sunrise and sunset scene of the 'Jotham Valley' indicate about the film industry?'

Long Answer Type Question

Answer the following question in 120-150 words.

1. The author has used gentle and subtle humour to point out human foibles and idiosyncrasies in the lesson 'Poets and Pancakes.' Elucidate.

07

About the Author

Christopher Silvester (1959-Present) was a student of History at Peterhouse, Cambridge. He was a reporter for Private Eye for ten years and has written features for Vanity Fair magazine.

▼ **YOUR STUDY GOALS**
- Chapter Sketch
- About the Characters
- Summary of the Chapter

▼ **YOUR PRACTICE GOAL**
- NCERT Folder
- Extract Based Questions
- Short Answer Type Questions
- Long Answer Type Questions

The Interview

Chapter Sketch

'The Interview' is an excerpt from the author's introduction to the 'Penguin Book of Interviews, An Anthology from 1859 to the Present Day'. The author expresses his views on the interview as a genre of communication. The chapter has two parts. The first part deals with the views of eminent people about the condemnatory aspects of the interview. The latter part reproduces an actual interview of Umberto Eco, who is being interviewed by Mukund Padmanabhan from 'The Hindu'.

About the Character

Umberto Eco He is an expert scholar in Semiotics (the study of signs) and a professor at the University of Bologna in Italy. His novel 'The Name of the Rose' sold more than 10 million copies.

Mukund Padmanabhan He is the interviewer who is from the newspaper 'The Hindu'.

Summary of the Chapter

The given chapter is divided into two parts. Part 1 is a general information presenting different views of prominent people regarding interviews. Part 2 is an interview itself.

Part I

About Interviews

Today, interviews have become a common aspect of journalism. Every person have read or heard an interview. Hence, different people have varied opinions about its uses, modes and advantages. Some people claim that it is a source of truth while others feel that in practice it is an art. Many celebrities despise interviews. They believe themselves to be victims of unwarranted intrusion into their lives and feel that it depreciates their personality.

Different Opinions

VS Naipaul is of the opinion that interviews injure people as they lose a part of themselves.

Lewis Carrol, the creator of 'Alice in Wonderland', never consented to an interview. His refusals for interviews helped him keep his fans, acquaintances and interviewers at bay. Later, he would narrate such experiences of his refusal with great satisfaction and amusement.

Rudyard Kipling hated interviews. His wife, Caroline, wrote in her diary that on 14th October, 1892 that their day was ruined by two reporters. Since then, he refused to give interviews. He considered them immoral, cowardly, a crime and an assault which is worthy of punishment. He did not respect the interviewee or the interviewer. However, Kipling himself interviewed Mark Twain a few years before this tirade against interviews.

HG Wells, an eminent science fiction writer, frequently gave interviews but in an interview in 1894, referred to 'the interviewing ordeal'. Forty years later, he interviewed Joseph Stalin, a Russian revolutionary.

Saul Bellow felt that interviewers created so much tension and pressure that he felt suffocated.

Summing Up

Despite its disadvantages, the interview is an excellent medium of communication. Denis Brian gives an elevated position to the interviewer because of his power and influence over the interviewee. He terms the interview as an expressive medium.

Part II

This part is an extract from an interview of Umberto Eco, who is being interviewed by Mukund Padmanabhan from 'The Hindu'.

Umberto Eco is a renowned scholar known for his ideas on Semiotics (the study of signs), literary interpretation and medieval aesthetics. He has written an array of works ranging from literary fiction, academic texts, essays, children's books and newspaper articles. He became popular due to his book 'The Name of the Rose'.

Eco's Secret

Mukund Padmanabhan, asks Umberto Eco how he could do all the things that he did. Umberto Eco replies that he has always been writing the same philosophical and ethical ideas in different genres. Eco discloses that he utilises the 'empty spaces' i.e. the shortest gaps between two different works, to write. That's the reason why he has produced so many works. He calls the 'empty spaces' 'interstices'.

Eco's Style of Writing

When the interviewer questions him about his playful and personalised style of writing, Eco replies that he learnt this writing style when he had presented his first Doctoral Dissertation in Italy. He had told the story of his research which impressed his Professor, who published his Dissertation as a book. This made Eco understand that he had to adopt the narrative style in all his works. This led him to become a novelist at the age of 50.

Eco remembers his friend Roland Barthes, an essayist, died frustrated before he could become a creative writer. Then, Eco mentions that he started writing novels by accident on a day when he had nothing to do. They catered to his taste for narration.

Eco-the Academician

Mukund Padmanabhan asks how Eco feels about people recognising him as a novelist although he is an academician with over 40 works in non-fiction. Eco tells him that he is not pleased as he belongs to the academic community and participates in academic conferences. He writes novels only on Sundays.

Success of 'The Name of The Rose'

Mukund asks Eco if he is surprised by the success of the novel, 'The Name of the Rose'. It is a serious novel that spins a detective yarn and ventures into metaphysics, theology and medieval history.

Eco says that he is not puzzled by its success. Only journalists and publishers are surprised as they believe that people "don't like difficult reading experiences". The people who bought his book do not want easy experiences. Then, Eco states that the medieval period to which this book belongs could have played a major role in its success.

For Umberto Eco, the success of the book is a mystery. His American publisher expected that the book won't sell more than 3000 copies in a country where no one has seen a cathedral or studied Latin hence, Eco believes that if he had written it at any other time, it might have not been a success.

Word-Meaning

common place	normal part
celebrities	famous people
unwarranted	unnecessary
diminishes	lowers stature
lionised	glorified
condemnatory	reproachful
perpetrated	carried out
thumbprints on his windpipe	giving a feeling of suffocation
serviceable medium	useful method
of moment	having importance
staggeringly	surprisingly
elevator	lift
depersonalised	formal
dissertation	thesis
hypotheses	proposed explanations based on limited evidence
academic	scholar
seminal	that which strongly influences later developments
yarn	lengthy story
metaphysics	philosophy concerned with abstract ideas
theology	the study of God and religious belief

Important Themes of the Chapter

The main theme of the chapter is the various perspective of an interview and the ethics associated with an interview. It presents a spectrum of opinions on interviews, reflecting people's various attitudes toward this journalistic practice. Some view interviews as valuable and essential, while others perceive them as invasive and detrimental. It also discusses ethical dimensions of conducting interviews, including debates about privacy, consent, and the potential impact on interviewees. The excerpt highlights concerns about the moral implications of interviewing, with references to it being seen as immoral or even criminal.

NCERT Folder

Think as you Read (NCERT Page 69)

1. What are some of the positive views on interviews? CBSE 2020

Ans. Interview is a genre that has become a common place of journalism within a span of about 130 years. It is an art that brings out truth and gives us vivid impressions of the interviewees. It is an excellent medium of communication.

2. Why do most celebrity writers despise being interviewed?

Ans. Most of the celebrities do not like giving interviews because they believe that interviews diminish them. Writers such as VS Naipaul feel wounded by interviews and that people lose a part of themselves in the process of an interview. Some others such as Rudyard Kipling condemn interviews as immoral, an offence, a crime and something vile and cowardly. Saul Bellow feels suffocated during interviews.

3. What is the belief in some primitive cultures about being photographed?

Ans. Some primitive cultures believe that if they are photographed, some part of their soul is robbed. Hence, they condemn photography and view it with suspicion.

4. What do you understand by the expression 'thumbprints on his windpipe'?

Ans. Saul Bellow compares interviews to 'thumbprints on the windpipe'. This refers to the fact that interviewers make the interviewees feel suffocated and uneasy during the course of an interview. Bellow feels that interviewers are strangulators while interviewees are their victims.

5. Who, in today's world, is our chief source of information about personalities?

Ans. Ever since interviews were invented over 130 years ago, this excellent medium of communication has become our chief source of information. As compared to the other sources of information (biographies, autobiographies and movies) interviews convey information in a fast, simple and effective way.

Understanding the Text (NCERT Page 73)

1. Do you think Umberto Eco likes being interviewed? Give reasons for your opinion.

Ans. Umberto Eco, the interviewee does not seem to dislike being interviewed. He gives long and elaborate answers to the questions posed by Mukund Padmanabhan. He answers all the questions in a straightforward, truthful and sincere way sharing his experiences with the world at large.

Nowhere, does he try to evade a question. He also smiles and shrugs during the interview which shows his interest. At no point during the interview do we feel that he is in a hurry to wind up the interview. Thus, he seems to like being interviewed.

2. How does Eco find the time to write so much?

Ans. Umberto Eco finds time to write so much in the small gaps between two tasks. He names these empty gaps as interstices which he utilises to do something productive.

3. What was distinctive about Eco's academic writing style?

Ans. Umberto Eco's style was distinctive because it is written in a narrative style in contrast to a regular academic style which is invariably depersonalised, dry and boring. Even his scholarly works have a certain playful and personal quality about them.

4. Did Umberto Eco consider himself a novelist first or an academic scholar?

Or Did Umberto Eco like to be identified as a novelist? Give reasons in support of your answer. CBSE 2024

Ans. Umberto Eco's primary work was in the academic field itself and he wrote novels occasionally, on Sundays only. He also mentioned that he participated in academic conferences over meetings of Pen Clubs and writers. He confirmed that he identified himself with the academic community. Thus, he considered himself an academic scholar first and then a novelist.

5. What is the reason for the huge success of the novel, 'The Name of the Rose'?

Ans. The reason for the huge success of the novel 'The Name of the Rose' is probably that it was a different kind of novel as it had a highly personalised narrative written in an unconventional style. It was a serious detective story which probed into metaphysics, theology and medieval history. All these topics interested readers. The author himself was mystified by its success and says that probably the novel was written at the right time; it may not have been such a success if it had come earlier or later.

Exam Pattern Questions

Extract Based Questions

Read the extracts given below and answer the questions that follow.

1. **Others, usually celebrities who see themselves as its victims, might despise the interview as an unwarranted intrusion into their lives or feel that it somehow diminishes them, just as in some primitive cultures it is believed that if one takes a photographic portrait of somebody then one is stealing that person's soul.**

VS Naipaul 'feels that some people are wounded by interviews and lose a part of themselves,' Lewis Carroll, the creator of Alice in Wonderland, was said to have had 'a just horror of the interviewer' and he never consented to be interviewed. **CBSE 2023**

(i) Choose the most appropriate option with reference to the given extract.

Most of the celebrities dislike being interviewed because ....

(a) it is sheer nonsense
(b) nobody reveals his/her inner-self
(c) it is sheer waste of time
(d) it is an unwanted intrusion in their lives

(ii) Complete the analogy with the word from the extract.

Light: Darkness :: .... : Refused

(iii) In primitive cultures being photographed implied ....

(a) announcing victory
(b) soul has been stolen
(c) saving a memory for posterity
(d) becoming popular

(iv) From the given extract, we know that .... never agreed to be interviewed.

(a) Lewis Carroll (b) VS Naipaul
(c) TS Eliot (d) Charlie Sheen

(v) In the given extract, the word 'diminish' most nearly means ....

(a) deepens (b) disappoints
(c) lessens (d) languishes

(vi) In the given extract, the writer indicates that most people .... interviews.

(a) celebrated (b) read
(c) gave (d) despised

Ans. (i) (d) it is an unwanted intrusion in their lives
(ii) Consented (iii) (b) soul has been stolen
(iv) (a) Lewis Carroll (v) (c) lessens
(vi) (d) despised

2. **"Why do I refuse to be interviewed? Because it is immoral! It is a crime, just as much of a crime as an offence against my person, as an assault, and just as much merits punishment. It is cowardly and vile. No respectable man would ask it, much less give it."**

(i) From the kind of response towards interviews, do you think that the speaker had a bad experience with the interviewers?

(ii) Select the correct option from those given in bracket to fill in the blank.

The attitude of the speaker of these lines towards an interview was .... (applauding/depreciative).

(iii) Complete the statement with an appropriate explanation.

The speaker's statement about the interview is ironical because ....

(iv) What does the expression 'merits punishment' mean here?

(v) What drawbacks of the 'interview' did his wife point out?

(a) It was an assault on the individual
(b) It was a crime
(c) It was an immoral act
(d) All of the above

(vi) The general experience of the authors regarding interviews is that of ....

(a) amusement (b) harassment
(c) satisfaction (d) anger

Ans. (i) Yes, I think that the speaker had a bad experience with the interviewers as his wife mentions in her diary that on 14th October, 1892 their day was 'wrecked by two reporters from Boston'.

(ii) depreciative

(iii) although he states that he does not find interviews to be respectable he himself took an interview later on.

(iv) The given sentence indicates that the interviewers should be condemned and punished.

(v) (d) All of the above

(vi) (b) harassment

3. Saul Bellow, who has consented to be interviewed on several occasions, nevertheless once described interviews as being like thumbprints on his windpipe. Yet despite the drawbacks of the interview, it is a supremely serviceable medium of communication. "These days, more than at any other time, our most vivid impressions of our contemporaries are through interviews," Denis Brian has written. "Almost everything of moment reaches us through one man asking questions of another. Because of this, the interviewer holds a position of unprecedented power and influence." **CBSE Question Bank 2021 Modified**

(i) How would you describe Denis Brian's opinion on interviews?

(ii) Select the correct option from those given in brackets to fill in the blanks.

Dennis Brain's view on interview is in .... with that of VS Naipaul. (contrast/complementary)

(iii) Complete the sentence suitably.

The use of the word 'serviceable' implies that interviews are ....

(iv) 'Interviews had been called as thumbprints on windpipe'. Explain.

(v) According to Saul Bellow, interviews are like thumbprints on his windpipe. What emotion might best describe such an image?

(a) Sadness (b) Frustration
(c) Pain (d) Fear

(vi) Denis Brian states that the interviewer occupies a position of power and influence as

(a) everything reaches us through one man asking questions of another.
(b) the interview is a supremely serviceable medium of communication.
(c) our most vivid impressions of our contemporaries are through interviews.
(d) interviews are like thumbprints on the interviewee's windpipe.

Ans. (i) Denis Brian's opinion on interviews can be described as of approval. He finds interviews to be a useful medium through which we get to know more about people.

(ii) contrast

(iii) useful

(iv) Saul Bellow calls interviews to be thumbprints on windpipe because interviews suffocates an interviewee.

(v) (c) Pain

(vi) (a) everything reaches us through one man asking questions of another.

4. Umberto Eco Aah, now that is more difficult to explain. I have some philosophical interests and I pursue them through my academic work and my novels. Even my books for children are about non-violence and peace...you see, the same bunch of ethical, philosophical interests.

And then I have a secret. Did you know what will happen if you eliminate the empty spaces from the universe, eliminate the empty spaces in all the atoms? The universe will become as big as my fist. **CBSE 2025**

(i) Complete the following suitably.

Eco suggests that his books for children also share his ethical interest because they are about .... (violence/peace).

(ii) Complete the following suitably

Umberto Eco's philosophical interests are .... in his academic work and novels, making them interconnected.

(iii) Select the textual option that is closest to indicating how his philosophical interests are represented.

(a) Aah, now that is more difficult to explain.
(b) I have a secret.
(c) I pursue them through my academic work and my novels.
(d) The universe will become as big as my fist.

(iv) What does the following line from the extract showcase?

"The same bunch of ethical, philosophical interests".

(a) Separation (b) Interconnectedness
(c) Isolation (d) Division

(v) "I work in empty spaces."

Choose the option that most accurately captures Eco's idea of empty spaces.

(a) Management of time (b) Integration of work
(c) Management of space (d) Tasks of a writer

(vi) What according to Umberto Eco will happen if all the empty spaces are eliminated from the universe?

Ans. (i) peace (ii) present

(iii) (c) I pursue them through my academic work and my novels.

(iv) (b) Interconnectedness

(v) (a) Management of time

(vi) According to Umberto Eco, if all the empty spaces are eliminated from the universe, the universe will shrink to the size of his fist.

5. "So in a way I reached only a small percentage of readers. But it is exactly these kinds of readers who don't want easy experiences. Or at least don't always want this."

I myself, at 9 pm after dinner, watch television and want to see either 'Miami Nice' or 'Emergency room'.
I enjoy it and I need it. But not all day.

(i) Who is 'I' referred to in these lines?

(ii) Select the suitable word from the extract to complete the following analogy :

Reached : Verb :: .... : Emphatic pronoun

(iii) Complete the sentence with an appropriate explanation, as per the extract.
The speaker concludes "I reached only a small percentage of reader's" because ....

(iv) Why does the speaker say the given lines?

(v) What does the author mean by 'easy experiences' in reading?

(a) Some humourous reading material like comics, etc.
(b) Horror stories which keep you engaged
(c) Reading material which is entertaining and easy to understand
(d) Reading of newspapers, magazines, etc.

(vi) Why does the author love to watch TV after 9 pm?

(a) To listen to important news
(b) To relax
(c) To entertain himself
(d) Both (b) and (c)

Ans. (i) 'I' in the given extract refers to Umberto Eco.

(ii) Myself

(iii) 10 million copies is small number compared to worldwide readers

(iv) The speaker says the given lines as an answer to the question asked by his interviewer Mukund Padmanabhan who had asked him about the theme and readership of his book 'The Name of the Rose'.

(v) (c) Reading material which is entertaining and easy to understand

(vi) (d) Both (b) and (c)

Short Answer Type Questions

1. What drawbacks of interviews have been pointed out by Lewis Carroll?

Ans. The drawbacks of interviews which have been pointed out by Lewis Carroll are that the interviews lionises or glorifies people. This make people including other interviewers, fans, etc. come after him which he does not want.

2. How do we know that Lewis Carroll was triumphant in his success of not giving interviews?

Ans. We know that Lewis Carroll was triumphant in not giving interviews because afterwards he would tell the stories of his success in silencing all such people with much satisfaction and amusement.

3. Why did Rudyard Kipling dislike being interviewed? CBSE 2020

Ans. Rudyard Kipling disliked being interviewed because two interviewers had spoiled his interview in Boston. In addition to this, Kipling considered interview to be immoral. Another reason was that it was an assault on a person and an offence against him.

4. What evidence from the text reveals that Rudyard Kipling did not walk the talk? CBSE 2024

Ans. Although Kipling expressed his hatred towards the act of interviewing quite openly, his actions were not consistent with his words. Kipling degraded the act of interviewing as an 'assault' but he had himself perpetrated such an 'assault' on Mark Twain only a few years before. Thus, Kipling did not walk the talk.

5. What is the variety of writing that Umberto Eco has produced?

Ans. Umberto Eco has produced a large variety of writings which include his ideas on Semiotics (the study of signs), literary fiction, academic texts, essays, children's books, newspaper articles and finally detective novels.

6. What is the one thing that Umberto Eco is convinced that he is doing through all his variety of writing? Why is he convinced about it?

Ans. Umberto Eco is convinced that he is pursuing his philosophical interests through his academic work and his novels. He is convinced about it because, as he says, even his books for children are about non-violence and peace which are part of his ethical, philosophical interests.

7. Explain the concept of 'interstices' in our lives, as given by Umberto Eco.

What does Umberto Eco mean by the concept of 'interstices' in out lives? CBSE 2020

Ans. Umberto Eco explained that we have a lot of empty spaces of time in our lives which he calls 'interstices'. For instance, if we are waiting to meet someone, we are 'free'. This is an interstice or an empty space. He is able to be a prolific writer because he works during these empty spaces.

8. What is the advantage of writing novels as mentioned by Umberto Eco?

Ans. As mentioned by Umberto Eco, the advantage of writing novels is that he is able to reach to a larger audience which would not be possible with his scholarly writings.

9. What did the publisher think of 'The Name of the Rose'?

Ans. The publisher loved the book 'The Name of the Rose' but didn't expect to sell more than 3000 copies in a country such as the USA where nobody has seen a cathedral or studied Latin.

10. How does the author's writing style in 'The Interview' affect the reader's understanding of the story? CBSE SQP 2024

Ans. The author's writing style in 'The Interview' deeply affects the reader's understanding of the story. In the story, the author often blends a conversational tone with introspective moments. The use of direct dialogues with reflective commentary not only makes the interactions more dynamic and engaging but enhances the reader's insight into the complexities of personalities and themes being explored.

11. Why do you think Christopher Silvester describes the viewpoints of other writers and authors when discussing the concept of an interview? Support your opinion with reference to any one writer.

Ans. Christopher Silvester describes the viewpoints of other writers and authors when discussing the concept of an interview to show how the views about interviews vary across people. While for common people interviews are an effective medium of communication, for authors and writers it is a vile crime. Take for example, Rudyard Kipling who finds that interviews are so vile that the interviewers should be punished.

12. How would you evaluate Mukund Padmanabhan as an interviewer? Mention at least two qualities he displays in his interview, supported by textual evidence.

Ans. Mukund Padmanabhan comes out to be a sensible and a logical journalist who knows not to exasperate a writer. As an interviewer, he talks about things that interests the interviewee and even asks his questions in an orderly manner.

13. Christopher Silvester shares authors' reservations about interviewing. Bearing that in mind, would you interview a writer of your choice? If so, what would you pay particular attention to in interviewing the said writer? Competency Based

Ans. If I had an opportunity I would interview JK Rowling, the author of the Harry Potter series. While doing do, I would keep a number of things in mind.

I would make sure that the interviewee is comfortable and would prepare questions that interest her. I would avoid going into the personal lives of the author and would focus on her professional outlook and works.

14. In 'The Interview', we learn that Kipling strongly condemned interviews, yet he had previously interviewed Mark Twain. In 20-30 words, state a possible reason for such a contradictio Competency Based

Ans. In 'The Interview', it is shown that Rudyard Kipling hated the process of interviews very much. But he had previously interviewed Mark Twain. This contradiction can be due to many reasons. One possible reason could be that Kipling made an exception for Mark Twain. It is also possible that he may have developed a hatred for interviews after he interviewed Mark Twain himself. Conflicting beliefs are a part of human nature and Rudyard Kipling is a fine example of this.

15. Consider there are six billion people on this planet. 'The Name of the Rose' sold between 10 to 15 million copies. So in a way I reached only a small percentage of readers.

How does Umberto Eco's perspective on the readership of his novel 'The Name of the Rose' reflect his personality? Answer in 20–30 words based on 'The Interview'. Competency Based

Ans. Umberto Eco's perspective on the readership of 'The Name of the Rose' shows that he is self aware.

He is mindful of the vast number of potential readers that his novel did not reach. Even so, Eco is a world famous author and the acknowledgment of his limited reach is a true sign of humility.

16. Explain why Umberto Eco said, "I started writing novels by accident". CBSE 2025

Ans. Umberto Eco said, "I started writing novels by accident", because he initially focused on academic writing and semiotics. His transition to fiction was unplanned—he wrote 'The Name of the Rose' for personal satisfaction without expecting it to become a bestseller. His love for storytelling eventually led him to continue writing novels.

Long Answer Type Questions

1. 'What impression do you form about Umberto Eco as a scholar and writer on the basis of 'The Interview'?

Ans. On the basis of the information given in the lesson 'The Interview', we get to know that Umberto Eco is a professor at the University of Bologna in Italy. He is a scholar in Semiotics (the study of signs). He likes to attend academic meetings and loves giving interviews, unlike other famous writers mentioned in the chapter. He does literary interpretation, writes academic text, children's books, newspaper articles and novels. The novels are written on Sundays, as he says that he started writing his first novel at the age of 50 years when he found one day that he had nothing to do. He has written 40 papers on scholarly works of non-fiction and five novels. He has a narrative style which is informal and playful. His research work has the qualities of a creative and narrative style. His first novel, 'The Name of the Rose', brought a lot of fame to him and a large readership, so that he came to be known as a novelist, although he wanted to be known as an academician.

2. Imagine that you are Christopher Silvester. You have been invited to a seminar series titled – 'Ethics and Techniques of Interviewing'. The organisers would like you to speak about the challenges of conducting interviews, and skills interviewers must have in order to conduct good and ethical interviews. Based on your reading of 'The Interview, Part I and II', draft your speech. Include relevant details from the text in support of your answer. Competency Based

Ans. Good morning to one and all present here. I am very pleased to be standing here at the seminar titled 'Ethics and Techniques of Interviewing' to be able to tell you all about how an effective medium of communication can be a course of distrust for many. We all are aware that interviews are one of the major sources of getting to know about our favourite people today. Be it film stars, writers, singers or any other public personality, interviews have become a must. But do you know that the process of taking an interview is not always smooth. Sometimes, in out hurry to get good trending data we, as interviewers, cross our boundaries and make the interviewee so uncomfortable that they stop giving interviews altogether and change their perception about it.

Hence, we must be careful about how we conduct good and ethical interviews. Remember, focus on getting the interviewees comfortable. Either take an appointment or pre-inform the interviewee about the interview. Do not enter his/her personal life or interfere in it. Further, the question asked should not be vain. They must interest the interviewee as well. These few things can prove to be a boon to take a successful interview.

Thank you

3. Mukund Padmanabhan was gifted the 'Penguin Book of Interviews - An Anthology from 1859 to the Present Day' edited by Christopher Silvester, after interviewing Eco. He shared his thoughts on his personal blog exploring his own concerns about interviewing a distinguished writer like Eco, followed by an evaluation of the interview in light of his reading. As Mukund Padmanabhan, write a blog about it. Competency Based

Ans. **Exploring Interviews**

It was a fantastic week for me for I got to read a book that had been on my list for a long time. 'Penguin Book of Interviews - An Anthology from 1859 to the Present Day' edited by Christopher Silvester was something that had blown my mind away given the fact that I successfully interviewed Umberto Eco. I did not for once feel that a distinguished writer like Eco was irritated at the questions I was asking. In fact, the interview went smoothly.

One reason for this was my approach. I think approach is very essential to any interview. If an individual interferes in any person's life or asks questions that are not at all interesting to the interviewee then, the person is bound to have a bad experience. I believe that the people who hated interviews have had some bad experiences with interviewers. Thus, we have to remember that we need to follow certain rules for a smooth, successful and good interview.

4. Imagine you are Mukund Padmanabhan from the 'The Hindu' (The Interviewer) and you interviewed M. Hamel, after he finished delivering the last lesson. (The Last Lesson)

Write a paragraph on Hamel's views on individual responsibility and nationalism. Competency Based

Ans. In my interview with M. Hamel, following his significant delivery of the last lesson, his views on individual responsibility and nationalism were deeply profound. Hamel emphasised the importance of individual accountability in preserving one's cultural heritage and national identity. He lamented the complacency of society, attributing the decline of language and culture to neglect. According to Hamel, each individual bears a responsibility to uphold and cherish their cultural heritage, regardless of external circumstances or political upheavals. He believed that nationalism moves beyond mere loyalty to a government or flag; it is rooted in a deep-seated commitment to preserving one's language, traditions and values.

Hamel's impassioned plea for individual responsibility and nationalism resonated deeply, serving as a reminder of the enduring significance of cultural preservation amidst the tumult of modernity.

Mukund Padmanabhan

SELF ASSESSMENT TEST

Extract Based Questions

Read the extracts given below and answer the questions that follow.

1. "Almost everything of moment reaches us through one man asking questions of another. Because of this, the interviewer holds a position of unprecedented power and influence."

(i) Do you think that the speaker supports taking interviews?

(ii) Select the correct option from those given in bracket to fill in the blank.

.... (interviewer/interviewee) is at the superior position.

(iii) Complete the sentence suitably.

The given words are ....

(iv) Why does the interviewer hold the position of power?

(v) The given statement can be a part of which mode of communication?

(a) Discussion (b) Speech on TV (c) Interview (d) All of these

(vi) What does the expression 'Everything of the moment' refer to?

(a) All types of information (b) All types of questions

(c) Author's reaction to a specific question (d) None of these

2. "It is a marked departure from a regular academic style - which is invariably depersonalised and often dry and boring. Have you consciously adopted an informal approach or is it something that just came naturally to you?"

(i) State the context of the given extract.

(ii) Select the correct option from those given in bracket to fill in the blank.

The speaker .... (lauds/denigrates) the listeners writing style.

(iii) Complete the sentence appropriately.

The term 'marked departure' indicates ....

(iv) Briefly explain the common writing style.

(v) What is the speciality of Umberto Eco's Literary writing?

(a) Highly philosophical (b) Dramatised

(c) Full of narrative style (d) Full of figures of speech

(vi) The concerned author 'Umberto Eco' teaches in which university?

(a) Oxford University, London (b) University of Bologna, Italy

(c) Cornell University, USA (d) None of these

Short Answer Type Questions

Answer the following questions in 40-50 words.

1. What reaction did Umberto Eco get from a professor when he presented his Doctoral Dissertation?

2. What does Umberto Eco say about journalists and publishers?

3. What did Rudyard Kipling's wife has to say about Kipling's attitude towards interviewers?

4. Did the fact that most people thought of Umberto Eco as only a novelist bother him? Why?

Long Answer Type Question

Answer the following question in 120-150 words.

1. 'The Name of the Rose' was predicted to be not be able to become popular in America. However, this prediction comes out to be incorrect. Substantiate. How does Eco justify the success?

08

About the Author

AR Barton is a modern writer who lived in Zurich and writes in English. He has authored many stories like 'Going Places' which are mainly concerned with the problems of the stage of adolescence like fantasising and hero worship.

▼ **YOUR STUDY GOALS**

- Chapter Sketch
- About the Characters
- Summary of the Chapter

▼ **YOUR PRACTICE GOAL**

- NCERT Folder
- Extract Based Questions
- Short Answer Type Questions
- Long Answer Type Questions

Going Places

Chapter Sketch

In his story Going Places, Barton explores the theme of adolescent fantasising and hero worship through the character of Sophie, a young teenage girl from a lower middle class family. Sophie is a daydreamer. Her family and friends try to stop her daydreaming and help her from time to time, but she keeps on building castles in the air. When reality hits her, all her dreams appear to be shattered. The author has thus, emphasised the aspirations and ideals of the modern young generation and at the same time highlights the pain of unfulfilled promises and unrealised dreams.

About the Characters

Sophie She is a highly ambitious lower middle-class adolescent girl living in a world of dreams and fantasy.

Jansie She is Sophie's close friend and very practical about their status. She is also a gossip monger.

Danny Casey A talented football player who is a local hero, idolised by Sophie.

Geoff He is the hardworking elder brother of Sophie who is a sports enthusiast and confident of his sister's desires and fantasies.

Sophie's father He is hardworking, practical man who wants to provide better facilities for his family.

Summary of the Chapter

Daydreamer Sophie

Sophie was returning home from school with her friend Jansie, when she told her about her dream of owning a boutique. She said that she would become a manager to save the money needed for the boutique. However, Jansie, being practical, told Sophie that her dreams require a lot of money and are not realistic. She further added that they would work in the biscuit factory. Sophie remained unbothered by Jansie and kept on talking about being an actress or a fashion designer.

Sophie's Family

Sophie entered her house talking about money with Jansie. Her father was eating and her mother was doing household chores when her younger brother Derek mocked her. Sophie felt sad and went to her brother, Geoff.

Geoff was working on a part of his motorcycle in another room. He worked as an apprentice mechanic and was a quiet person. Sophie was jealous of his silence. She often thought of the places he went and wished that someday Geoff would take her with him. She imagined riding the motorcycle with him.

Meeting Danny Casey

Suddenly, Sophie told Geoff about her meeting with Danny Casey, an Irish sports star. Geoff doesn't believe her. So, she described that she met him while window shopping at the Royce. She told Geoff that the meeting with Casey was a chance encounter. She wanted his autograph for Derek but neither of them had a paper or pen. So, they talked and then, decided to meet next week. Casey promised to give her an autograph then.

After Geoff was finally convinced with Sophie's description, he shared it with their father. Her father got angry and warned Sophie that one day she would land herself in trouble because of her wild stories. Later, Sophie informed Geoff of her date with Danny Casey but Geoff refused to believe her.

Jansie- The Gossip Monger

On Saturday, Sophie, Derek and their father went to see a match played by the United. After the match, when Sophie met Jansie, she was surprised by the fact that Jansie knew about the meeting with Casey. As a result, she felt irritated with Geoff for talking about her secret to others as she knew Jansie would tell her secret to everybody. However, she was relieved to know that Jansie has no idea about the date.

Sophie's Dream Shattered

Sophie was now at the canal waiting for Danny Casey. While waiting, she imagines Casey coming along the river. She imagines her excitement. However, when after some time she does not see Casey, she realises that her date with Casey was just her imagination. Hence, she becomes sad and miserable as she thought of how she would explain this to her family. She knew Geoff would be disappointed and others would doubt her. She doesn't want to live with the burden of the truth.

Sophie Keeps on Dreaming

However, Sophie does not give up her dream. She once again dreams of meeting Casey at Royce. She asks for an autograph. But they don't have a pen. Sophie is so into her fantasising that she fails to differentiate her dream from reality. She keeps waiting in the arcade for a long time, remembering Casey's voice and eyes.

Word-Meaning

boutique	—	a small shop selling fashionable clothes or accessories
Mary Quant	—	a Welsh fashion designer and British fashion icon
natural	—	person having an inborn talent for a particular task or activity
earmarked	—	destined for working
huh	—	an expression showing scorn or disagreement
shepherd's pie	—	a dish of minced meat under a layer of mashed potato
incongruity	—	unsuitability
exotic	—	unusual, belonging to a foreign country
cape	—	a short, sleeveless cloak
arcade	—	a covered passage with shops along the sides or a mall
chastened	—	humbled
unawareness	—	ignorance
grunt	—	a harsh sound to express disgust or discontentment
grimaced	—	frowned, made a facial expression suggesting disgust

amber glow	—	honey-yellow coloured light
prodigy	—	a young person with exceptional qualities or abilities
inquisition	—	inquiry, cross-examination
nosey	—	curious about other people's affairs
gawky	—	awkward, ungraceful
chuffed	—	very pleased
misery	—	unpleasant and disbelieving person
row	—	quarrel
wharf	—	dock, harbour
solitary elm	—	single elm tree
pangs of doubt	—	feelings of uncertainty
resignation	—	giving up
freckled	—	covered with light brown patches or marks
shimmer	—	shine with a soft, wavering light
gazelle	—	a small, slender deer
ghost past	—	pass through like a ghost
lumbering	—	moving in a slow, awkward way
eruption	—	outbreak
approbation	—	praise or appreciation

Important Themes of the Chapter

Adolescent Hero-Worship The story portrays adolescent hero-worship through protagonist Sophie's admiration for a young football prodigy named Danny Casey. Her fascination with Casey borders on obsession blinding her to the reality of his fame and the unlikelihood of their developing a significant relationship. Sophie's character illustrates how adolescents idealise their idols, projecting their fantasies and desires onto them.

Fantasising Sophie's vivid imagination and tendency to construct elaborate fantasies define her character. Her dreams reflect her desire to escape the confines of her working-class life. Sophie's encounter with Danny Casey becomes a focal point of her fantasies, highlighting the power of imagination to provide solace and inspiration in the face of adversity. It also highlights the importance of dreams and aspirations in the lives of adolescents, serving as a means of coping with the challenges of adolescence and envisioning a brighter future.

Relationships The story also focuses on relationships among family members, particularly Sophie's strained relationship with her father. It also explores Sophie's complicated bond with her brother Geoff and her friendship with Jansie. These relationships shape the characters' aspirations, perceptions and interactions with each other and the world around them.

Family-Friends Dynamics Sophie's family's socio-economic status shapes their outlook on life and reactions to her aspirations. Her desire for support and validation is met with doubt. Trust and confidentiality are essential to her, revealing her need for autonomy.

NCERT Folder

Think as you Read (NCERT Page 79)

1. Where was it most likely that the two girls would find work after school?

Ans. The two girls, Sophie and Jansie, were most likely to find work in the local biscuit factory. This was so because they belonged to the lower middle class and could not go for higher studies after school. Hence, they could not get good well-paying jobs.

2. What were the options that Sophie was dreaming of ? Why does Jansie discourage her from having such dreams?

Ans. Sophie was dreaming of opening a boutique. When Jansie told her that it would require a lot of money, she would say that she would become a manager till then to save the money for her boutique. She also hoped of becoming an actress.

Jansie discouraged Sophie from having such dreams as she was a practical girl. She knew that Sophie and herself were from lower middle-class families and so would only be able to work in the local biscuit factory.

Think as you Read (NCERT Page 81)

1. Why did Sophie wriggle when Geoff told her father that she had met Danny Casey?

Ans. Sophie wriggled when Geoff told their father that she had met Danny Casey because she knew her father would scold her for having such wild fantasies. She knew that he would not believe and would be angry with her.

2. Does Geoff believe what Sophie says about her meeting with Danny Casey?

Ans. Geoff finds it hard to believe the story of Sophie's meeting Danny Casey. He knew that her stories were never true and he couldn't believe this one also.

However, we can say that Geoff might have believed her story partially, because he tells about it to Jansie's brother Frank.

3. Does her father believe her story?

Ans. Sophie's father does not believe Sophie's story at all and dismisses it as another of her wild fantasies. Further, he warned Sophie that such made up stories will land her in trouble some day.

4. How does Sophie include her brother Geoff in her fantasy of her future?

Ans. Sophie includes her brother Geoff in her fantasy of her future by imagining herself riding behind Geoff on his motorcycle to go to the unknown places he visits and the world rising to greet them with applause.

5. Which country did Danny Casey play for?

Ans. Danny Casey was a young soccer player who played for Ireland. He was a popular athlete because he played really well. His technique was a blend of innocence and Irish genius.

Think as you Read (NCERT Page 85)

1. Why didn't Sophie want Jansie to know about her story with Danny? **CBSE 2020**

Ans. Sophie didn't want Jansie to know about her meeting with Danny Casey because Jansie could not keep a secret. The moment she knew of someone's secret, the whole neighbourhood would get to know of it. Sophie also didn't want this meeting to reach her father's ears or else she would be in trouble.

2. Did Sophie really meet Danny Casey?

Ans. No, Sophie never really met Danny Casey. She has just seen Danny Casey on the field when she went to watch the team United play a football match. There, she was one of the spectators and could see Casey playing but only from a distance.

3. Which was the only occasion when she got to see Danny Casey in person?

Ans. The only occasion when Sophie got to see Danny Casey in person was when she and her family went to watch a football match of their team, United. Sophie was sitting amongst the spectators and could see her hero Casey only from a distance while he played the match.

Understanding the Text (NCERT Page 85)

1. Sophie and Jansie were class-mates and friends. What were the differences between them that show up in the story?

Or Compare and contrast Sophie and Jansie, highlighting their temperament and aspirations.

Or Jansie is just as old as Sophie but she is very different from her. Bring out the contrast between the two friends, citing relevant instances from the story, 'Going Places'.

Ans. Although Sophie and Jansie were classmates and intimate friends, both of them had an altogether different approaches towards life.

Sophie is a dreamer who always lives in a make-believe world of her own. She always imagines that she will have a successful career as a boutique owner, store manager, actress or fashion designer. She also imagined that the famous footballer Danny Casey would date her. She even went to the extent of waiting beside the canal for him. After he did not turn up, she realised that this was only her dream. Even then, she is lost in her dream world becoming sad that Danny did not come.

In contrast, Jansie's feet are grounded in reality. She knows that they have been earmarked for working in the biscuit factory and accepts her fate. Hence, she does not indulge in fantasising and hero-worship like Sophie. She is also a gossip monger who pokes her nose into other's affairs.

2. How would you describe the character and temperament of Sophie's father?

Or Draw a character sketch of Sophie's father.

Ans. Sophie's father has the character and temperament of a typical working class man. He is the sole provider of the family. We first meet him as a coarse, ill-mannered man stuffing shepherds pie into his mouth, wearing his dirty and sweaty vest.

He is a practical person who never leaves the harsh world of reality. He wants Sophie to step out of her dream world and tells her that her habit of making up stories is going to land her into trouble some day.

He goes to the pub to celebrate something as frivolous as a football match. In spite of being the head of an impoverished family with many mouths to feed, we never see him indulging in self-pity or cursing his fate. Instead, he enjoys life to the fullest by making a weekly pilgrimage to watch the local football match.

3. Why did Sophie like her brother Geoff more than any other person? From her perspective, what did he symbolise?

Ans. To Sophie, her brother Geoff symbolised liberty from her dull, drab, monotonous and impoverished existence. He had left school three years ago and was working away from home as an apprentice mechanic. She imagined that he met many exotic and interesting people.

She wished in her heart of hearts that she could be admitted more deeply into her brother's affections and that some day he might take her with him.

She even imagined herself and Geoff to be a part of that glamorous world.

Sophie liked Geoff because he was a man of few words. He patiently listened to her stories about meeting the sports icon Danny Casey although he suspected it was not true. Still he gave her the impression that he had believed her. This made Sophie adore him more than she did any other member of her family.

4. What socio-economic background did Sophie belong to? What are the indicators of her family's financial status?

Ans. Sophie belonged to a lower middle class socio-economic background. There are many indicators that point towards this status. The first indicator is Jansie and Sophie's conversation about them working after finishing school. Sophie longed for a good life but Jansie knew that they were both destined to become workers in the local biscuit factory. When Sophie mentioned her ambition to own a boutique, Jansie told her to first buy a 'decent house' to live in before buying a boutique. The second indicator is her father's face still grubby and sweaty after a day's hard work. Third, she observes her mother stooping over the sink. The small room was steamy from the stove and cluttered with the dirty washing piled up in the corner.

Fourth, her brother Geoff was an apprentice mechanic. Fifth, they travelled by bus to watch their team United play a football match. Last, on her way back home from the solitary place where she spent time in the evening sometimes, outside the pub, she passed her 'father's bicycle' propped against the wall. All these details point towards their lower middle class status.

Talking about the Text (NCERT Page 85)

1. Sophie's dreams and disappointments are all in her mind. Discuss.

Or Sophie lives in a world full of dreams which she does not know she cannot realise. Comment.

Ans. It is true to say that Sophie's dreams and disappointments are all in her mind. Sophie lives in a make-believe world- a world full of dreams- which she does not know she cannot realise. She always imagines that she will have a successful career as a boutique owner, store manager, actress or fashion designer. Even though, her friend, Jansie always used to remind her of their reality, she never listened. Sophie comes face to face with her reality when she imagines that Danny Casey had promised to meet her near the canal. However, he does not show up. This is because the meeting with Danny Casey and the so-called date were all a figment of her imagination. However, Sophie never realises how her imagination is affecting her sense of reality.

Sophie dreams big and believes that they will be fulfilled even though she had faced disappointment. She does not accept or realise that her dreams are far away from her reality and their fulfillment is an almost impossible thing.

2. It is natural for teenagers to have unrealistic dreams. What would you say are the benefits and disadvantages of such fantasising? Discuss.

Or Teachers always advise their students to dream big. Yet, the same teachers in your classrooms find fault with Sophie when she dreams. What is wrong with Sophie's dreams?

Ans. Dreaming is a necessary part of one's life. Without dreams, there will be no aims and aspirations in our lives.

As teenagers, each one of us set some goals in life. To reach those goals, we start daydreaming and fantasising about unrealistic things. This is what happens with Sophie too. Her dreams are unrealistic and she views the world with rose-coloured glasses.

Her longing for earning a large amount of money forces her to dream of opening a boutique, become an actress or a fashion designer. Such unrealistic dreams which are not within our reach can be damaging to our personality as unrealistic goals can lead to depression, low self-esteem and suicidal tendencies.

Thus, dreams are a part and parcel of our lives. We cannot do without them but we must remember that if we go overboard with them, they may have a negative effect on our personalities.

Exam Pattern Questions

Extract Based Questions

Read the extracts given below and answer the questions that follow.

1. "Or an actress. Now there's real money in that. Yes, and I could may be have the boutique on the side. Actresses don't work full time, do they? Anyway, that or a fashion designer. You know something a bit sophisticated". And she turned in through the open street door leaving Jansie standing in the rain. "If I ever come into money I'll buy a boutique". "Huh, if you ever come into money ... if you ever come into money you'll buy us a blessed decent house to live in, thank you very much."

Sophie's father was scooping shepherd's pie into his mouth as hard as he could go, his plump face still grimy and sweat-marked from the day.

"She thinks money grows on trees, don't she Dad?" Said little Derek, hanging on the back of his father's chair. Their mother sighed. **CBSE 2023**

(i) **Sophie wants to become an actress to**

(a) become famous (b) to earn money

(c) to support her father (d) to compete with Jansie

(ii) **Jansie wanted Sophie to spend her money on**

(a) her marriage (b) her career

(c) to open a boutique (d) buying a house

(iii) **Sophie is daydreaming about ....**

(iv) **The phrase 'money grows on trees' indicates that Sophie ....**

(v) **Sophie's mother's sigh is one of**

(a) regret (b) delight

(c) relief (d) helplessness

(vi) **Complete the following sentence appropriately.**

From the extract, Jansie comes across as a .... person.

Ans. (i) (b) to earn money

(ii) (d) buying a house

(iii) becoming an actress and opening a boutique

(iv) is not very practical

(v) (d) helplessness

(vi) practical

2. **"She thinks money grows on trees, don't she, Dad?" said little Derek, hanging on the back of his father's chair. Their mother sighed. Sophie watched her back stooped over the sink and wondered at the incongruity of the delicate bow which fastened her apron strings. The delicate-seeming bow and the crooked back. The evening had already blacked in the windows and the small room was steamy from the stove and cluttered with the heavy-breathing man in his vest at the table and the dirty washing piled up in the corner. Sophie felt a tightening in her throat. She went to look for her brother Geoff.**

(i) **Why did Sophie's mother sigh?**

(ii) **Select the correct option from those given in bracket to fill in the blank.**

It could be inferred that Sophie's mother was fatigued and burdened. We reach this inference because of .... (her sigh/her posture).

(iii) **Complete the sentence appropriately.**

"Sophie felt a tightening in her throat." Sophie is feeling ....

(iv) **What can be we make out about the financial condition of the family from the extract?**

(v) **Choose the correct option about Sophie's parents based on the extract given above.**

(a) Sophie's parent's marriage was an example of harmony and affection.

(b) Sophie's relationship with her parents was warm and friendly.

(c) Sophie's mother was subdued while her father was detached.

(d) Sophie and her brother didn't like to stay with their parents.

(vi) **Choose the option that supports the contention coming through Derek's dialogue, "She thinks money grows on trees, don't she, Dad?".**

(a) Derek thought his sister to be unreasonable at times.

(b) Derek had no faith in Sophie's abilities to open a boutique.

(c) Derek thought of his sister as someone who was not realistic.

(d) Derek was not at all happy about Sophie's habit of day dreaming.

Ans. (i) Sophie's mother sighed because of the dreamy tendencies of her daughter.

(ii) her sigh

(iii) anxious and uneasy

(iv) From the given extract, we can make out that the family lived in a impoverished condition. They belonged to the lower middle class and had very little money.

(v) (c) Sophie's mother was subdued while her father was detached.

(vi) (c) Derek thought of his sister as someone who was not realistic.

3. **On Saturday they made their weekly pilgrimage to watch United. Sophie and her father and little Derek went down near the goal — Geoff, as always, went with his mates higher up. United won two-nil and Casey drove in the second goal, a blend of innocence and Irish genius, going round the two big defenders on the edge of the penalty area, with her father screaming for him to pass and beating the hesitant goalkeeper from a dozen yards. Sophie glowed with pride. Afterwards Geoff was ecstatic.**

(i) **Who joined his friends higher up the stairs?**

(ii) **Select the correct option from those given in bracket to fill in the blank.**

Their visit to the match was like a 'weekly pilgrimage' refers to .... (love for a fixed routine/similar feelings of devotion).

(iii) **Complete the sentence appropriately.**

'Sophie glowed with pride.' Her pride is the result of ....

(iv) **How did the 'United' perform in the match?**

(v) **Based on the following statements, choose the correct option.**

Assertion "Geoff, as always, went with his mates higher up."

Reason I Geoff was not very close to his family and lived in his own world.

Reason II Geoff was rude and indifferent towards everyone around him and didn't care about anyone at all.

(a) Reason I and Reason II both can be inferred from the assertion.
(b) Reason I can be inferred but Reason II cannot be inferred from the assertion.
(c) Reason I cannot be inferred but Reason II can be inferred.
(d) Reason I and Reason II both cannot be inferred.

(vi) **Choose the option listing the situation in which one would be 'ecstatic'.**

(a) Going to an old age home and listening to them share stories from the past.
(b) Being seated next to your favourite pop singer during a short flight.
(c) Going to a dog show and losing your pet there.
(d) Coming home and finding that there are 11 messages from your Principal in your email inbox.

Ans. (i) Geoff joined his friends higher up the stairs.
(ii) similar feelings of devotion
(iii) being an avid fan and her sense of closeness with Danny
(iv) The United won the match by two-nil.
(v) (b) Reason I can be inferred but Reason II cannot be inferred from the assertion.
(vi) (b) Being seated next to your favourite pop singer during a short flight.

4. **There was a wooden bench beneath a solitary elm where lovers sometimes came. She sat down to wait. It was the perfect place, she had always thought so, for a meeting of this kind. For those who wished not to be observed. She knew he would approve.**

For some while, waiting, she imagined his coming. She watched along the canal, seeing him come out of the shadows, imagining her own consequent excitement. Not until some time had elapsed did she begin balancing against this the idea of his not coming.

(i) **Why was Sophie waiting at that location?**

(ii) **Select the correct option from those given in brackets to fill in the blank.**

Sophie is feeling .... (flustered/excited) at the prospect of him liking the place.

(iii) **Complete the sentence suitably.**

'He' did not come because ....

(iv) **How does Sophie come to realise the reality?**

(v) **What is the wooden bench beneath a solitary elm symbolic of ?**

(a) Peacefulness
(b) Isolation
(c) Distant and lonely
(d) Lovers' point

(vi) **Why would he approve of that place?**

(a) It was the perfect place
(b) People could not be observed here
(c) The bench was very comfortable
(d) It was safe from wild animals

Ans. (i) Sophie, in her imagination, had setup a date with Danny Casey. So, she was waiting for him at the canal.
(ii) excited
(iii) the entire event of him promising to come was a part of Sophie's imagination
(iv) Sophie had been waiting for Casey for a long time. When he did not come, she came to realise that the date was a fantasy and not a reality.
(v) (d) Lovers' point
(vi) (b) People could not be observed here

5. **Now I have become sad, she thought. And it is a hard burden to carry, this sadness. Sitting here waiting and knowing he will not come I can see the future and how I will have to live with this burden. They of course will doubt me, as they always doubted me, but I will have to hold up my head remembering how it was. already I envisage the slow walk home, and Geoff's disappointed face when I tell him, "He didn't come, that Danny". And then he'll fly out and slam the door.**

(i) **Why do you think Geoff would slam the door?**

(ii) **Select the correct option from those given in brackets to fill in the blank.**

The fact that Sophie is predicting her family's reaction shows that she is .... (anticipating their reactions/feeling embarrassed).

(iii) **Complete the sentence suitably.**

The 'burden' here refers to ....

(iv) **Do you think Sophie's sadness is justified?**

(v) **What is hard for Sophie to carry?**

(a) Jansie's friendship
(b) Casey's indifferent attitude
(c) The sadness of not meeting Danny
(d) Her father's anger

(vi) On the basis of the extract, choose the correct option with reference to the two statements given below.

I. Sophic idolised Danny Casey.

II. Sophie disliked her family.

(a) I can be inferred from the extract but II cannot

(b) I cannot be inferred from the extract but II can

(c) I is true but II is false

(d) II is the reason for I

Ans. (i) Geoff would slam the door because of his anger. He would be angry at Danny Casey was not keeping his promise to his sister.

(ii) feeling embarrassed

(iii) the fact that Casey's date with her was just her imagination and not her reality

(iv) Yes, I find Sophie's sadness to be justified because as a young teenage girl she was deeply engrossed in her imagination. So, when the realisation of her reality struck her, she becomes sad.

(v) (c) The sadness of not meeting Danny

(vi) (a) I can be inferred from the extract but II cannot

6. **And afterwards you wait there alone in the arcade for a long while, standing where he stood, remembering the soft melodious voice, the shimmer of green eyes. No taller than you. No bolder than you. The prodigy. The innocent genius. The great Danny Casey.**

And she saw it all again, last Saturday - saw him ghost past the lumbering defenders, heard the fifty thousand catch their breath as he hovered momentarily over the ball, and then the explosion of sound as he struck it crisply into the goal, the sudden thunderous eruption of exultant approbation.

(i) Who is 'the prodigy' in the extract?

(ii) Select the suitable word from the extract to complete the following analogy:
Glitter : Shimmer :: Sweet ....

(iii) Complete the sentence with an appropriate explanation, as per the extract.
The given extract is significant because ....

(iv) Do you think Sophie would stop dreaming about Danny Casey?

(v) Where did Sophie had to wait alone?

(a) Along the canal (b) In the arcade
(c) At the Royce (d) In the biscuit factory

(vi) Why did she hear the fifty thousand of people catching their breath?

(a) To have the glimpse of the shimmer of green eyes

(b) To listen to the melodious voice

(c) Due to hovering of Danny Casey momentarily on the ball

(d) Due to Sophie coming to the ground

Ans. (i) 'The prodigy' in the given extract is a young football player named Danny Casey.

(ii) Melodious

(iii) In this extract we explicitly come to know that Sophie had been imagining her meeting with Danny Casey. She had only seen Casey while watching the matches.

(iv) No, I do not think that Sophie would stop dreaming of Danny Casey due to her intensified hero-worship, high imagination and her ritual to go watch the match played by Casey every week.

(v) (b) In the arcade

(vi) (c) Due to hovering of Danny Casey momentarily on the ball

Short Answer Type Questions

1. **'Soaf, you really should be sensible!' What does Jansie's advice to her friend Sophie reveal about their friendship?** **CBSE 2024**

Ans. Sophie aspires to grand endeavours like owning a boutique or pursuing careers in acting or fashion design, which demand significant resources and experience, neither of which she possesses. Jansie advises Sophie to control her aspirations, urging her to adopt a more practical approach and abandon her lofty dreams. This interaction reveals that despite their differences, their friendship is based on honesty and concern for one another's well-being.

2. **'Jansie, knowing they were both earmarked for the biscuit factory, became melancholy'. What inference about Jansie's character is drawn from the above line?** **CBSE 2024**

Ans. The given lines tell us that Jansie is more realistic and practical in life. She knows that big ambitions cost heavy investments, something their working-class status could not afford. Their reality would be limited to the biscuit factory. Hence, she makes the given statement to Sophie.

3. **Why was Sophie jealous of Geoff's silence?**

Ans. Sophie was jealous of the fact that Geoff never spoke much which made him a mystery. She always pondered over the areas of his life which he never talked about. His world remained a fascination for her. She felt that when he was not speaking, his mind was away at some unknown place and so, she was jealous of him.

4. **Did Geoff keep up his promise? How do you know?**

Ans. Geoff didn't keep his promise to Sophie. She told Geoff about her meeting with Danny Casey at the Royce's and requested him not to tell anyone about it. However, Geoff told this to Frank who in turn told his sister, Jansie.

5. **Why do you think Sophie is attracted to Danny Casey?**

Ans. Sophie is attracted to Danny Casey because of veracious reason. First, she idolises him because of his popularity, look and celebrity status. Second, somewhere Sophie finds that Danny's status would help alleviate her poverty and help her realise her professional dreams.

6. Why did Sophie dream of having a boutique after leaving school? CBSE 2025

Ans. Sophie dreamed of having a boutique after leaving school because she wanted an exciting and glamorous life beyond her modest background. She was ambitious and often indulged in fantasies about success and fame, imagining herself as a fashion entrepreneur despite having no concrete plans to achieve it.

7. What thoughts came to Sophie's mind as she sat by the canal?

Ans. Sophie was waiting for Danny Casey, sitting by the canal. In the beginning, she imagined him coming and even began to fantasise his actions and dialogues. However, after some time, when he did not turn up, reality hit her and she became sad. She thought that her family would never believe her. She also thought that Geoff would be disappointed.

8. What did Sophie imagine about her meeting with Danny Casey at the arcade?

Ans. Sophie imagined that she met the United football player, Danny Casey, at the Royce arcade. She asked him for an autograph but neither of them had a pen. Then, they began talking about the clothes in the shop. Casey promised to meet her again next week.

9. The story is written in a manner that it makes it difficult to point out clearly if Sophie met Danny Casey or not. Suggest possible reasons for such writing.

Ans. The story is written in a manner that it makes it difficult to point out clearly if Sophie met Danny Casey or not. The reason behind is to highlight how intensely young children and teenagers start hero-worshipping their idols.

10. Sophie flits from one dream to another. What trait of her character is brought out by this action?

Ans. Sophie was a dreamer who enjoyed creating her own fantasy world using her own imagination. She wanted to change her working class status by pursuing the ambition of a fashion designer or an actress. She also wanted to date a young football prodigy. This shows that Sophie was immature and lived in her own unrealistic world. She chose to ignore the reality of her economic background and lived in a fantasy world.

11. "Sophie felt a tightening in her throat. She went to look for her brother Geoff." In the light of this quote, discuss the relationship Sophie shared with Geoff.

Ans. The given sentence indicates that Sophie liked her brother Geoff more than any other person in the world. She could open her heart to him. She knew that Geoff was the person who would share her dreams.

Geoff spoke very little and his silence always troubled Sophie very much. But Geoff was always the first with whom she always shared her secrets. She had a strong faith in Geoff. Like every other sister she dreamt of riding behind her brother in their attractive dresses, to places where people would welcome and praise them.

She wanted to be more affectionate with her brother. Sophie saw in her brother Geoff, her moral supporter. To Sophie, Geoff was bold, smart, tall, promising and helpful. He recognised and respected his younger sister's emotions and aspirations well. She was certain that he would never let her down.

12. Why did Sophie long for her brother's affection?

Ans. Sophie longed for her brother's affections because she was jealous of her brother's silence and wanted him to confide in her. She thought he knew about things and had been to places she had never been to and this fascinated her. She longed to know more about these things from her brother and thus, craved for his affection, hoping that he would then take her to those places with him.

13. In the story, 'Going Places', what do Sophie and Geoff's reactions to the United match reveal about each of them? Answer in 40-50 words. Competency Based

Ans. Geoff watched the game and felt happiness that his favourite team had won the match. He watched the match as a fan. On the other hand, Sophie watched the match for her favourite player - Danny. The happiness and pride she felt was for Danny, not the team. The different loyalties and interests of the siblings are shown through their reactions to the match.

14. 'Going Places' is an interplay between reality and the dream world. Elucidate. Competency Based

Ans. The story 'Going Places' is an interplay between reality and the dream world. It highlights the contrast between one's aspiration and the harsh reality of life. Sophie's dream of opening a boutique and becoming an actress is a mere dream, considering her family's financial status. Her desire to escape her existence leads her to imagining her meeting Danny Casey, reflecting the negative effects of fantasising life.

15. How does Sophie plan to get the kind of money she wanted for her boutique? CBSE 2025

Ans. Sophie dreams of opening a boutique but lacks the financial means. She imagines acquiring the money through unrealistic means, such as becoming a manager, an actress, or even a fashion designer, rather than taking practical steps to achieve her goal.

Long Answer Type Questions

1. "I can see the future and now I will have to live with this burden," says Sophie. Discuss the statement in the light of the chapter 'Going Places'.

Ans. Sophie always lived in a make-believe world of her own. It was probable that in the course of her wishful thinking she imagined that Danny Casey had promised her a date. Nobody in the family believed her. However, she went to her favourite haunt to meet Casey who did not show up.

This made her realise that Geoff had been right. Still she was under the compulsion to insist that she had really met Danny Casey.

She would never be able to tell about her family, "they're wrong to doubt me".

She was filled with sadness because her life would not undergo the transformation she had imagined. The glamour of the exotic world she dreamt of was not within her reach. This was a burden that she found difficult to come to terms with and carry.

2. Contrast Sophie's real world with her fantasies.

Or Sophie is caught between the world she lives in and the world she wants to live in. Elucidate.

CBSE Question Bank 2021

Ans. The story 'Going Places' is a journey into the dream world of the protagonist, a school girl named Sophie, who drifts from one dream to another. Sophie finds the reality of her life too harsh to accept. She belongs to a lower middle class family where nobody encourages her to dream of better prospects. Still, she dreams of owning the best boutique, becoming a manager in some store or at other times becoming an actress or a fashion designer.

In reality, the pitiable condition of her life does not let her venture into such sophisticated professions. However, in her dream world, she visits Royce's arcade, meets Danny Casey - the sports icon, and even fixes up a date with him.

It's all in her mind but she considers it true and actually waits for him to show up at a specified spot and time. The flight of her imagination is such that it flits from one dream to another and from one place to the other.

3. Imagine Sophie's father finds out about Sophie's going to the canal to meet Danny Casey which leads him to think that she has lied to everyone about the whole affair. He is infuriated and prohibits Sophie from going anywhere except to school. As Geoff, write a diary entry disapproving of your father's punishment by citing your reasons for being sympathetic to Sophie. (You may begin this way)

Competency Based

Monday, 2nd September, 1940 9 p.m.

I cannot get myself to stand with father in his tirade against Sophie. Sure, she is not the most…

CBSE Question Bank 2021

Ans. Monday, 2nd September, 1940 9 p.m.

Dear Diary,

I cannot get myself to stand with father in his tirade against Sophie. Sure, she is not the most incredulous and illogical girl. She is a typical teenager who is hero – worshipping Danny Casey. I understand that sometimes she goes overbroad but this does not mean we can stop her from living her life.

Dad's decision of prohibiting her from going anywhere but school is not correct. I do not feel it is the way to deal with Sophie. I believe that it is just a stage that all of us face in our life. She will grow out of it and realise for herself how wrong she had been. There is no need to punish her like that. I have to talk to dad about it.

Geoff

4. Imagine Sophie meets Danny Casey after several years. Write a dialogue exchange between them where Sophie explains what that meeting means to her.

CBSE Question Bank 2021

Ans. **Sophie** Danny Casey. Am I dreaming? Ofcourse, I am.

Danny No, you are not dreaming. It is indeed me.

Sophie I am so sorry. I am surprised that such a successful player is standing in my boutique.

Danny Why? Can't I enjoy a normal life?

Sophie Ofcourse, you can! To be honest, it is funny that some years back I would have been imagining meeting you and so on.

Danny Oh really!

Sophie Yes, Just like any other teenager I hero worshipped you. Not that I do not appreciate you now, but now its different. I know how to keep reality and dreams apart.

Danny Good for you I guess.

Sophie Anyways, do you like something in the boutique?

Danny I am going to bring my mother here. The collection is good and her birthday is coming up. Help her with whatever she wants. It's a request.

Sophie Always. Don't worry.

Danny Thanks, Bye!

5. How do the characters of Sophie from 'Going Places' and Subbu from 'Poets and Pancakes' compare and contrast in terms of their aspirations, constraints, and the pursuit of their dreams? **CBSE SQP 2024**

Ans. Each one of us has dreams and we all face different circumstances that hinder our dreams. We can state the same with reference to two characters from the stories that we have read- 'Going Places' and 'Poets and Pancakes'.

Sophie in 'Going Places' dreams of owning a boutique or becoming a fashion designer. However, she faces financial limitations. Her family is poor and thus, her dreams seems to be unattainable until and unless Sophie remains determined to achieve her goals, showing persistence and creativity in her pursuits.

Subbu in 'Poets and Pancakes' aims to succeed in the film industry as a poet, actor and contributor to Gemini Studios. However, he faces challenges in the form of criticism for his perceived flattery, overshadowing of his literary achievements by his success in films.

However, we see Subbu's dedication to his craft and ability to adapt to various roles within Gemini Studios, which reflects his unwavering determination to work towards achieving his dream.

In both the cases, we see that while both Sophie and Subbu share aspirations for success in their respective fields, they encounter different constraints and demonstrate distinct approaches in pursuing their dreams.

6. 'Their mother sighed. Sophie watched her back stooped over the sink and wondered at the incongruity of the delicate bow which fastened her apron strings.'

The prose selection, 'Going Places' includes this telling comment about Sophie's mother. In 'Aunt Jennifer's Tigers', we are told that - 'The massive weight of Uncle's wedding band, Sits heavily upon Aunt Jennifer's Hand.'

Imagine a conversation between Sophie's mother and Aunt Jennifer. Create this exchange with reference to the two extracts given above.

You may begin the conversation like this ...

Sophie's mother Your embroidery is so beautiful. Do you love tigers? **Competency Based**

Ans. **Sophie's mother** Your embroidery is so beautiful. Do you love tigers?

Aunt Jennifer Yes, I do. They reflect what I have always wanted in life. My art is my means to express my deep-down desires and feelings.

Sophie's mother Oh, that is amazing! You are so lucky to have time to give to your art. I, on the other hand, don't have any time for myself. In fact, I find the 24 hours of the day less to complete my daily chores. All my time is spent in taking care of my husband and my three children.

Aunt Jennifer Don't feel bad because my life is same as yours. My husband hates my embroidery and I don't get to do it much often as I also have to take care of the daily needs of my husband and children. It is as if I do not have any other identity other than being a wife or a mother.

Sophie's mother You know what hurts more is the fact that our families don't consider us important. We don't have any say in the family matter and they even don't take us out to enjoy anything that the rest of the family does. I'll give you an example- they all went to witness Danny Casey's football match while I was to stay at home. No one even asked me if I wanted to go.

Aunt Jennifer What is even worse is the fact that there is no likelihood of any change in our status. One statement against the servility that we do and we will be branded as immoral women.

Sophie's mother True!

7. It is good to dream big, but one must have concrete plans and determination to turn dreams into reality. Comment with reference to 'Going Places'.

Ans. It is true to say that it is good to dream big, but one must have concrete plans and determination to turn dreams into reality. Sophie was a dreamer who created her own fantasy world using her fertile imagination. She displayed her urge to transcend her status from a working class girl to a higher level of sophistication by pursuing her dream to become an actress, a fashion designer, a manager or a boutique owner. But she needed to have concrete plans, determination and perseverance to realise her dreams, instead of just fantasising about what she wanted to become. She should understand her reality that she is from a middle class working family.

Initially, she would face many difficulties because of her poor financial condition but after she starts working, she should save her earnings and try to improve her education so that she could take up better jobs. This requires her character to be determined and hard-working, instead of being just a daydreamer that she is now. Gradually, she can raise her status to the level when she would be able to attract successful people such as Danny Casey, the famous footballer.

8. Every teenager has a hero/heroine to admire. So many times they become role models for them. What is wrong if Sophie fantasies about Danny Casey and is ambitious in life?

Ans. The statement that every teenager has a hero/heroine to admire is true. As teenagers, we all have role models or people who we idolise. Same is the case for Sophie a young teen girl from a middle class background. She had unrealistic dreams. She felt that she would become either a boutique owner, shop manager, actress or a fashion designer.

Like every young girl, Sophie also had a strong desire of knowing the unknown, seeing the unseen and even dating famous people like Danny Casey. So, she visited the perfect place for lovers and sat on the solitary wooden bench under the tree waiting for Danny but there was no sign of him.

This kind of fantasising is dangerous as it takes one away from reality. It can lead to depression among teenagers, as their life's ambitions are not fulfilled. This is not to say that it is not wrong to be ambitious in life. However, being over-ambitious like Sophie leads to failure and frustration in life. Hence, one should set practical goals in one's life.

9. Mention two points that the story 'Going Places' teaches us about celebrity culture and worship. Answer in 100-120 words. **Competency Based**

Ans. The story 'Going Places' illustrates how imagination can impact reality.

Firstly, Sophie fantasises about meeting Danny Casey and ends up lying to herself, her family, and friends. This shows how celebrity worship can lead to dishonesty and obsession.

Secondly, Sophie's belief in her fantasy leads her to an isolated place for a fake meeting with Casey, putting herself at risk of danger.

Imagination can make life more interesting, but it also has downsides. Being careless in real-life situations because of fantasies can lead to serious and lasting consequences. The story warns about the dangers of letting imagination take over reality.

SELF ASSESSMENT TEST

Extract Based Questions

Read the extract given below and answer the questions that follow.

1. Here I sit, she said to herself, wishing Danny would come, wishing he would come and sensing the time passing. I feel the pangs of doubt stirring inside me. I watch for him but still there is no sign of him. I remember Geoff saying he would never come, and how none of them believed me when I told them. I wonder what will I do, what can I tell them now if he doesn't come? But we know how it was, Danny and me-that's the main thing. How can you help what people choose to believe? But all the same, it makes me despondent, this knowing I'll never be able to show them they're wrong to doubt me.

(i) Are Sophie's family members really wrong to doubt her?

(ii) Select the correct option from those given in bracket to fill in the blank.

The given extract indicates that Sophie had .... (blurred the lines between dreams and reality/a mental breakdown)

(iii) Complete the given sentence.

Sophie getting worried about ....

(iv) Do you think Sophie is aware that meeting Danny was just her imagination?

(v) What was Sophie feeling while waiting for Danny?

(a) Dizziness (b) Doubt

(c) Elated (d) Enthralled

(vi) What did Sophie remember at that point of time?

(a) Her father's disbelief (b) Jansie's advice

(c) Casey's promise (d) Geoff saying he would never come

Short Answer Type Questions

Answer the following questions in 40-50 words.

1. Why was Sophie's first choice of job after completing her school? How did she hope to succeed in her aim?

2. Why doesn't anybody believe in Sophie's dreams?

3. Why did Jansie discourage Sophie from entertaining thoughts about the sports star, Danny Casey?

4. Describe briefly Sophie's 'meeting' with Casey at Royce's arcade.

5. Why did Sophie choose a canal to meet Danny Casey for a date?

Long Answer Type Questions

Answer the following questions in 120-150 words.

1. According to you, should Sophie have continued her dream or should she have stuck to the path that had already been chosen for her? Justify your choice in detail.

2. You are Sophie. You return home after the match and realise that you have wasted so much time in your dreams. You decide to write a diary entry about the experience and what a waste daydreaming is. Write the diary entry.

01

My Mother At Sixty-Six

About the Poet

Kamala Das (1934 - 2009) is recognised as one of India's foremost poets. Her works are known for their originality, versatility and the indigenous flavour of the soil. She has published many works in English and Malayalam under the name 'Madhavikutty'. She has written on many diverse topics including women's issues, childcare and politics.

YOUR STUDY GOALS

- Central Idea of the Poem
- Explanation of the Poem

YOUR PRACTICE GOAL

- NCERT Folder
- Extract Based Questions
- Short Answer Type Questions
- Long Answer Type Questions

Central Idea of the Poem

The poem written in lyrical idiom captures the feelings of coming to terms with a parent's ageing, the fear of loss and the attempt to hide these emotions with a smile. The poet is going back to her home when she realises that her mother had grown old and might die soon. Witnessing her mother's frailty, symbolised by her ashen face, triggers a wave of emotions - from denial to fear and eventually resignation. Despite the vibrant scenes outside the car window, the poet's attention is drawn to the inevitable passage of time and the fragility of life.

Explanation of the Poem

Stanza 1

"Driving from my parent's
home to Cochin last Friday
morning, I saw my mother,
beside me, doze, open mouthed, her face
ashen like that of a corpse"

Exp. The poet had gone to visit her parents' home. Last Friday, she was returning to her home in Cochin. On her way to the airport, she noticed her mother sleeping beside her in the car. Her mouth was open and her face was pale and lifeless, just like a dead body.

Stanza 2

"and realised with pain
that she was as old as she
looked but soon
put that thought away, and
looked out at young
Trees sprinting, the merry children
spilling out of their homes"

Exp. The poet was alarmed by the sudden realisation that her mother had grown old. It was a reality she found hard to accept. So, to take her attention away from the disturbing thought, she looked outside the car.

She saw that, the young green trees appeared to be running in the opposite direction. She also saw a group of children rushing out of their homes to play.

The image of the young sprinting trees and the children represent youth which was full of life and energy. Both these images present a sharp contrast to the old and ill mother sitting beside the poet.

Stanza 3

"but after the airport's
security check, standing a few yards
away, I looked again at her, wan,
pale as a late winter's moon"

Exp. After reaching the airport and passing through security check, the poet again looked at her mother who was standing a few yards away from her. Her mother looked lifeless and dull like a late winter's moon.

The image of 'a late winter's moon' emphasises the poet's mother's old age and impending death.

Stanza 4

"and felt that
old familiar ache, my childhood's fear,
but all I said was, see you soon,
Amma, all I did was smile and smile
and smile ..."

Exp. Once again, the poet was pained to see her mother in this condition.

As she was going away and leaving her mother, her old familiar pain-her childhood fear that she would lose her mother, suddenly came back to her. So, she tried to hide her emotions behind her smile. She did not want to reveal her feelings to her old mother, so instead she bade her farewell with a smile. She gave hope to her mother and herself by saying that they would meet again and kept on smiling.

Word-Meaning

doze	—	sleep lightly
ashen	—	very pale with shock, fear or illness
corpse	—	a dead body
spilling out	—	rushing out
wan	—	pale and giving the impression of illness or exhaustion
ache	—	pain

Literary devices used in the Poem

- **Tone** Observant, reflective and sad
- **Rhyme Scheme** Free verse
- **Enjambment** The entire poem is written as a single sentence punctuated by commas.
- **Simile**
  Stanza 1 'her face ashen like that of corpse'
  Stanza 3 'as a late winter's moon'
  Both of these expressions indicate the old age and lack of vitality in the poet's mother.
- **Personification**
  Stanza 2 'young Trees Sprinting' (indicates that the trees seem to be moving in the opposite direction of the car)
- **Imagery**
  Stanza 2 'young Trees Sprinting and merry children spilling' (presents a young and energetic image that stands in contrast to the old and weak mother)
- **Repetition**
  Stanza 4 'smile and smile and smile' (to emphasise on the reassurance given by the poet)

NCERT Folder

Think it Out (NCERT Page 91)

1. What is the kind of pain and ache that the poet feels?

Or What familiar ache and childhood fear did Kamala Das feel?

Ans. The pain and ache that the poet feels is an old familiar pain indicating that the pain had been felt by the poet before in her life. This pain is related to the fear of loss and separation from her mother.

2. Why are the young trees described as 'sprinting'?

Ans. The young trees are described as sprinting because they appear to be moving in the opposite direction of the car in which the poet is traveling to the airport. Further, such a description conveys a sense of vitality and energy. It is highlighting the difference between the swift energy of youth and the more measured, steady pace of later life.

3. Why has the poet brought in the image of the merry children 'spilling out of their homes'?

Or Why has the poet mentioned 'merry children spilling out of their homes' in the poem?

Ans. The poet has used this imagery to bring out the contrast between children, who are energetic and full of life, and her mother, who is old, pale and lifeless.

4. Why has the mother been compared to the 'late winter's moon'?

Or Why does Kamala Das compare her mother to a late winter's moon?

Ans. The poet has compared her mother to a late winter's moon to emphasise that her mother's face looks dull and colourless due to her old age. Just as a 'late winter's moon' looks hazy and appears to lack brightness and lustre due to mist and fog, similarly, the poet's mother, who is now old, looks pale and devoid of exuberance.

5. What do the parting words of the poet and her smile signify?

Ans. The poet's parting words, 'See you soon, Amma' and her smile signify hope and assurance, not only to herself but also to her mother, that they will meet again.

Exam Pattern Questions

Extract Based Questions

Read the extract given below and answer the following questions that follow.

1. **Driving from my parent's**
home to Cochin last Friday
morning, I saw my mother,
beside me,
doze, open mouthed, her face
ashen like that
of a corpse and realised with pain
that she was as old as she
looked but soon
put that thought away…

(i) What is the significance of comparing the mother's face to that of a corpse?

(ii) Choose the option that displays the same literary device as in the given lines of the extract.

her face
ashen like that
of a corpse …

(a) Just as I had this thought, she appeared and…

(b) My thoughts were as heavy as lead that evening when …

(c) I think like everyone else who…

(d) I like to think aloud when …

(iii) Complete the following suitably.

The poet ……………… the inevitability of fate that was to dawn upon her mother.

(iv) Select the correct option from those given in bracket, to fill in the blank.

The given poem can be said to be .... (an argument/ a recollection)

(v) Choose the option that applies correctly to the two statements given below.

Assertion The poet wards off the thought of her mother getting old quickly.

Reason The poet didn't want to confront the inevitability of fate that was to dawn upon her mother.

(a) Assertion can be inferred but Reason cannot be inferred.
(b) Assertion cannot be inferred but Reason can be inferred.
(c) Both Assertion and Reason can be inferred.
(d) Both Assertion and Reason cannot be inferred.

(vi) Why did the poet put the thought away?

Ans. (i) By comparing the mother's face to that of a corpse, the poet highlights the old age and the fact that her mother is nearing death.

(ii) (b) My thoughts were as heavy as lead that evening when ...

(iii) didn't want to confront

(iv) A recollection

(v) (c) Both Assertion and Reason can be inferred.

(vi) The poet put the thought away because she could not stand the pain that was associated with the thought.

2. **I saw my mother,**
beside me,
doze, open mouthed, her face
ashen like that
of a corpse and realised with
pain that she was as old as she
looked but soon
put that thought away and
looked out at Young
Trees sprinting, the merry children spilling
out of their homes, **CBSE 2023**

(i) Identify the phrase that indicates youthful energy.

(ii) Which thought is the poet trying to put away?

(a) Missing the flight
(b) Fear of losing her mother
(c) Leaving her mother behind
(d) Reaching Cochin

(iii) The poet's mother is described as 'open mouthed' because ....

(a) she is curious
(b) she is surprised
(c) she was dead
(d) she was dozing

(iv) Complete the following analogy.
Children spilling : Metaphor :: .... : Personification

(v) The sight of the trees and the children helped the poet ....

(vi) In the given extract, the phrase 'realised with pain' indicates the poet's

(a) anxiety (b) desperation
(c) troubled past (d) ill-health

Ans. (i) 'Trees sprinting, the merry children spilling'

(ii) (b) Fear of losing her mother

(iii) (d) she was dozing

(iv) Young Trees

(v) divert her mind from the sad and melancholy thoughts her mind had started thinking.

(vi) (a) anxiety

3. **.... but soon**
put that thought away, and
looked out at Young
Trees sprinting, the merry children spilling
out of their homes, but after the airport's security check,
standing a few yards away, I looked again at her, wan, pale
as a late winter's moon and felt that old
familiar ache, my childhood's fear, **CBSE 2024**

(i) Select the correct option.
The impact of 'merry children' on poet's mind ....

(a) caused anxiety
(b) created a sense of longing
(c) brought comfort
(d) reminded her of her own childhood

(ii) The tone of the poet expressed in the above lines is

(a) sadness and helplessness
(b) excitement and eagerness
(c) appreciation and gratitude
(d) anger and anxiety

(iii) The words 'wan, pale' indicate the mother's ....

(iv) Complete the following sentence appropriately.

The poet looked at her mother again to ....

(v) Explain one inference that can be drawn from the line 'felt that old familiar ache'.

(vi) 'Put that thought away'. What is the intention of poet that can be inferred from the above line?

Ans. (i) (a) caused anxiety

(ii) (a) sadness and helplessness

(iii) old and sickly appearance.
(iv) observe her after the airport's security check.
(v) The poet came to the realisation of her mother's old age and imminent death which caused her to feel the pain of loss and separation from her mother.
(vi) The poet's intention was to put away the painful thought of her mother's ageing and declining health and the possibility of losing her mother.

4. **"But after the airport's**
security check, standing a few yards
away, I looked again at her, wan, pale
as a late winter's moon."

(i) Why did the poet look at her mother again?

(ii) Mother's face has been compared to
(a) full moon brightness
(b) late winter's moon and its paleness
(c) young children
(d) young tree

(iii) Answer in one word.
The figure of speech used in the lines 'pale as a winter's moon' is ....

(iv) Select the correct option from those given in bracket to fill in the blank.
The reason of mother's pale face is .... (mother's depleting energy/mother's stress)

(v) On the basis of the extract, choose the correct option with reference to the two statements given below.
1. The poet is in a dilemma.
2. The poet wants to look at her mother.
(a) (1) can be inferred from the extract but (2) cannot
(b) (2) can be inferred from the extract but (1) cannot
(c) Both (1) and (2) can be inferred from the extract
(d) (2) is the reason for (1) and can be inferred from the extract

(vi) What do you think the poet is feeling in the extract?

Ans. (i) The poet looked at her mother's face again to bid her good bye.
(ii) (b) late winter's moon and its paleness
(iii) Simile
(iv) mother's depleting energy
(v) (b) (2) can be inferred from the extract but (1) cannot
(vi) The poet is feeling sad and painful in the extract.

5. **but after airport's**
security check, standing a few yards
away, I looked again at her, Wan, pale
as a late winter's moon and felt that old
familiar ache, my childhood's fear
but all I said was see you soon, Amma.
All I did was smile and smile and
smile... **CBSE 2023**

(i) Choose the correct option. In the above extract, the narrator feels
(a) satisfied (b) fearful
(c) nostalgic (d) regretful

(ii) Identify the word in the extract that means colourless.

(iii) Complete the following analogy correctly.
She sang like a bird : Simile :: All I did was smile and smile and smile : ....

(iv) Read the following statement and choose the correct option.
1. The poet had gone through the security check.
2. She did not want to look at her mother.
(a) (1) is true but (2) is false
(b) (1) is false but (2) is true
(c) Both (1) and (2) are true
(d) Both (1) and (2) are false

(v) What childhood fear is the poet referring to?

(vi) Fill the blank with appropriate words with reference to the extract.
Pale as a winter's moon suggests ....

Ans. (i) (b) fearful
(ii) Pale
(iii) Repetition
(iv) (a) (1) is true but (2) is false
(v) The childhood fear referred to by the poet is the fear of losing her mother forever.
(vi) lack of youth energy and fading away of life.

Short Answer Type Questions

1. **What are the feelings of the poet about her aged mother with reference to the poem 'My Mother at Sixty-Six'?** **CBSE 2023**

Ans. In 'My Mother at Sixty-Six', the poet feels a deep sense of concern and sorrow for her aging mother. Describing her as 'ashen' and 'pale' the poet expresses fear of losing her. The contrast between youthful vitality and her mother's frality evokes love.

2. Why does Kamala Das try to put away the thoughts of her ageing mother?

Ans. Kamala Das finds it hard to accept the fact of her mother is growing old as it brings back her childhood fear of losing her mother forever. She makes a deliberate effort to drive or put away such thoughts by looking outside the car at the sights passing by.

3. What were the poet's feelings at the airport? How did she hide them?

Or **What were Kamala Das' fears as a child? Why do they come back when she is going to the airport?**

Ans. During her childhood, Kamala Das was insecure about losing her mother just as all young children often are. The same old feelings come back to haunt her when she sees her mother's pale and lifeless face. She is tortured by the fact that she may not see her alive again. She hides her feelings by smiling.

4. What is the significance of the word 'but' in 'but all I said was, see you soon, Amma? CBSE 2023

Ans. The word 'but' in this context is used to emphasise the contrast between the narrator's thoughts and feelings and the words she actually said. The narrator is reflecting on their mother's age and how it made her feel sad, but despite this, she still manages to put on a brave face and say, 'see you soon, Amma'.

5. In the last line of the poem, 'My Mother at Sixty-Six', why does the poet use the word 'smile' repeatedly?

Ans. In the last line of the poem, the poet has repeatedly used the word 'smile' to mask her painful feeling of parting from her mother. She also wanted to reassure her mother of hope and happiness by smiling in front of her.

6. 'See you soon Amma.' How are these words contrary to the speaker's emotions? CBSE 2024

Ans. The poet's comforting words and smile starkly contrast with the childhood fear felt by her. They signify a conscious effort to conceal deeper emotions. The poet hides her doubts regarding her mother's declining health which makes her fear the separation. The statement showing assurance and cheer attempts to hide the underlying anxiety and concern.

7. The pain of separation is expressed both literally and metaphorically in this poem. Elucidate. CBSE Question Bank 2021

Ans. The pain of separation in 'My Mother at Sixty-Six' is one of physical separation since the poet was leaving her mother in Cochin while catching flight. The metaphorical separation is one that the poet fears. She fears an eternal separation from her mother because of her impending death.

8. Comment on the tone of the poem with references to 'My Mother at Sixty-Six'. CBSE Question Bank 2021

Ans. The tone of this poem is predominantly pensive and sorrowful. The poem starts with an observing tone wherein the poet suddenly notices that her mother looks as old as she is. Then comes the sad, sombre and anxious realisation that her mother is growing old and frail.

Hence, to distract herself, the poet turns away from her mother to look at the trees and the children. Then, the poet looks at her mother again at the airport which increases her sadness and there is an intense emotional connection between her and her mother.

The poem ends on the note of acceptance, reassurance and concealment.

9. Imagery was an effective literary device to bring out the contrast between the 'merry children' and mother. Comment. CBSE Question Bank 2021

Ans. Yes, Imagery was an effective literary device to bring out the contrast between the 'merry children' and mother. In the poem, the poet looks away from her mother's face in the car to see through the window children rushing out of their homes.

The contrast is all the more sharper since the poet has juxtaposed two vastly different images - old age and childhood - right next to each other.

10. State the common issue faced by most of the aged in the current times, with reference to the poem, 'My Mother at Sixty-Six'. Competency Based

Ans. In the present day world, there are many maladies that afflict the older population of the world. In this fast paced life, our elders have to face the absence of supporting presence. They suffer from loneliness when children move away for better education and employment opportunities. This malady is depicted by Kamala Das in *My Mother At Sixty Six*. The poet has to leave her mother alone in her old age when she is nearing death due to her other responsibilties and commitments.

11. Interpret the use of visual imagery by Kamala Das in her poem to depict the passage of time. CBSE SQP 2024

Ans. Kamala Das' poetry 'My Mother at Sixty-Six' consists of many instances of imagery. One such imagery is of her aging mother which is described as 'pale as a late winter's moon'. This image conveys the fragility and the inevitability of ageing along with the physical changes brought by time. With this image, it evokes a sense of gentle and serene decline rather than abrupt decay.

12. The poem 'My Mother at Sixty-Six' touches upon the transient nature of life. Comment.

Ans. It is true to say that the poem 'My Mother at Sixty-Six' touched upon the transient nature of life. The rapid movement of the trees and the cheerful children spilling out of their homes contrast the mother's ageing appearance. This contrast highlights how life moves swiftly, and youthful energy contrasts with the reality of ageing.

13. What is the significance of the ellipses (....) at the end of the poem?

Ans. The ellipses at the poem's end are significant as they create a sense of open-mindedness and leave the poem unresolved. The poet ends the poem with a series of ellipses after repeating the word 'smile' three times, indicating that the poet's emotions are complex and difficult to express fully in words. The ellipses suggest that there is more to be said or felt. Further, it allows for a sense of universality. It leaving room for interpretation of the reader's own emotions and experiences related to ageing, mortality, and their relationship with their parents.

14. How does the poem present the theme of unspoken emotions in the poem 'My Mother at Sixty-Six'?

Ans. The poem 'My Mother at Sixty-Six' touches on the theme of unspoken emotions. The speaker notices her mother's ageing, yet she doesn't vocalise her feelings of concern or sadness. The poet chooses to leave her feelings of pain unsaid, perhaps because the emotions are too overwhelming or because the relationship between the poet and her mother is deeply personal and cannot be fully conveyed through words alone.

15. Justify the statement below with reference to the poem 'My Mother at Sixty-Six' in 40-50 words. 'Being conscious of our mortality helps us cherish our moments with each other.'

Ans. It is true to say that being conscious of our mortality helps us cherish our moments with each other. Our awareness of our mortality makes us truly appreciate the people and things in our lives. In the poem, the poet talks about her fears of losing her mother which is an inescapable truth of life. The awareness of this fact, however, must have made her cherish the time that she spent with her mother even more.

16. In the poem 'My Mother at Sixty-Six', the poet hides her emotions from her mother. Do you think it was right of her to do so? Explain your answer in 40-50 words.

Ans. I think it was right of the poet to bid good-bye to her mother with a smile on her face as there was no point in upsetting her mother with her own emotions as she was leaving. As adults, we need to realise when to express our emotions and when not to.

Long Answer Type Questions

1. Analyse the concept of losing our dear ones on account of old age in the context of the poem.

Ans. The poem 'My Mother at Sixty-Six' brings out the natural complexities of the human mind and the natural fear of losing our parents, which is common to the hearts of all humans. Ageing is an indispensible part of human life which we have to accept, irrespective of the pain it cultivates in our hearts.

This pain and its acceptance has been aptly presented by Kamala Das in her poem 'My Mother at Sixty-Six' wherein the sudden realisation of the poet's mother's old age pains her. The poet realises that her mother is growing old and would die soon when she sees her sleeping in the car. The realisation brings pain which is unbearable for the poet and she tries to distract herself. In the end, she accepts the reality of her mother's impending death and the separation.

Just like the poet, we also must accept the reality of mortality of our parents, albeit with pain and immense sorrow.

2. Imagine the mother gets to know of the poet personal fears. Write a letter, as the mother, telling the daughter why she must not dwell on these fears.

You may begin this way.

Pallipuram Cochin, Kerala

22nd August, 60

My dear Kamala

I am writing to you because when you left me at the airport, I felt something wasn't right. Judging by how little you spoke that day ....

....(continue)......
....

With love

Amma **Competency Based, CBSE Question Bank 2021**

Ans. 22nd August, 60

My dear Kamala

I am writing to you because when you left me at the airport, I felt something wasn't right. Judging by how little you spoke that day, I was worried about what was making you anxious.

After much thinking, I now know that you are worried about me, my health and my impending death. Sweetheart, both of us know that whoever is born must die. I am a mortal and would have to be separated from you.

But remember that I will always love you. So why waste your time and worry with such fears. Let's spend the time we have together with much fun and frolic. I know, my saying this would not reduce your stress, but worry not, your mother will forever be with you.

With love

Amma

3. Imagine you are the poet's friend. Write a dialogue exchange between yourself and the poet where the latter confides in you about her fears and asks for your advice. What would your advice be –to face her fears, to ignore them or something else? Competency Based

Ans. **Poet** I am worried this was the last time I saw my mother. Just the thought of this separation is unbearable to me. What if I am not there with her when she dies? What will I do without her?

- **Friend** Kamala, relax! I know your fears. Trust me, I had felt the same. But look at me now, I have accepted the reality and to tell you the truth she is alive and you still have some time to spend with her.
- **Poet** But we will be separated!
- **Friend** Kamala, that is the reality of life. Everyone must die one day. We need to accept this truth and make the most of the time we have with our friends and family. Your worries, Kamala, would not go away but it would hamper the time you have left with her. So why worry?
- **Poet** I guess you are right. Mom also wrote the same thing to me. I cannot promise obviously but I will try.

4. Khalil Gibran has said, "And ever has it been known that love knows not its own depth until the hour of separation."

Both Franz and the poet are emotionally overwhelmed at the thought of separation. Comment with reference to 'The Last Lesson' and 'My Mother at Sixty-Six'. Competency Based

Ans. Khalil Gibrans's statement stands true for both Franz, the young boy in 'The Last Lesson' and the poet, Kamala Das, of 'My Mother at Sixty-Six'.

For Franz, his teacher the M. Hamel was a strict and cranky man. He does not really like the man and is often scared of him. He prefers to stay out rather than attending his lesson. However, when he gets to know that M. Hamel would be leaving the village the next day, his opinions for his teacher changed. He felt deep regard and love for the man who used to teach him.

The poet, Kamala Das loved her mother. However, her emotional attachment to her mother becomes intensified as she realises that she would soon be separated from her mother. She had felt the pain of separation before too but this time, the pain is unbearable. Hence, at the airport, her love shines through in her attempt to reassure her mother of meeting soon.

SELF ASSESSMENT TEST

Extract Based Questions

Read the extract given below and answer the following questions that follow.

1. Driving from my parent's
home to Cochin last Friday
morning, I saw my mother,
beside me,
doze, open mouthed, her face ashen like that
Of a corpse and realised with pain
that she was as old as she looked ....

(i) Why was her mother's face looking like that of a corpse?

(ii) What did the poet notice about her mother?

(a) She was growing old.
(b) She was not beautiful.
(c) She slept like a dead person.
(d) All of these

(iii) Complete the sentence suitably.
The poet was leaving the house of ....

(iv) Select the correct option from those given in bracket to fill in the blank.
The poetic device used in the line - 'ashen like that of a corpse' - is .... (simile/metaphor).

(v) Fill in the blank appropriately.
The reference to 'corpse' implies ....

(vi) Read the assertion and the reason below, with reference to the given extract.

Assertion 'My Mother at Sixty-Six' is a touching and introspective poem by Kamala Das.

Reason She reflects on her mother's ageing and mortality during a car journey from her parent's home to Cochin.

(a) Both the assertion and the reason are true, and the reason is the correct explanation of the assertion.
(b) Both the assertion and the reason are true, but the reason is not the correct explanation of the assertion.
(c) The assertion is true, but the reason is false.
(d) The assertion is false, but the reason is true.

Short Answer Type Questions

Answer the following questions in 40-50 words.

1. 'My Mother at Sixty-Six' presents emotional conflict. Do you agree? Substantiate your answer.

2. The poet does not directly mention the fear of her mother's death and yet she is successfully able to convey the same through different poetic techniques. Discuss.

3. Bring out the contrasting images in the poem.

Long Answer Type Question

Answer the following question in 120-150 words.

1. Bring out the significance of the smile of the poet as she bade farewell to her mother.

02

Keeping Quiet

About the Poet

Pablo Neruda (1904-1973) is a pen name of a famous Chilean poet and diplomat. He won the Noble prize for Literature in 1971. He used green ink for writing his personal symbol for desire and hope. Neruda has written in a variety of styles, which include surrealist poems, historical epics, political manifestos, a prose autobiography and passionate love poems. His poems often explored themes of love, nature, politics, and human experience.

▼ **YOUR STUDY GOALS**

- Central Idea of the Poem
- Explanation of the Poem

▼ **YOUR PRACTICE GOAL**

- NCERT Folder
- Extract Based Questions
- Short Answer Type Questions
- Long Answer Type Questions

Central Idea of the Poem

Keeping Quiet is a Spanish poem which was published in the collection 'Extravagaria' in 1958. In 1974, it was translated into English. The poem focuses on the importance of introspection, stillness, and unity in the face of the chaotic and often destructive nature. Neruda advocates for a moment of silence and contemplation, during which individuals pause their activities and refrain from speaking to connect with themselves and each other on a deeper level. Through this pause, he suggests that people can gain insights into the human condition, foster empathy, and find solace in simply being alive. The poem emphasises the need to break free from the relentless pursuit of progress and to embrace the inherent beauty and interconnectedness of all life.

Explanation of the Poem

Stanza 1

"Now we will count to twelve
and we will all keep still.
For once on the face of the Earth
let's not speak in any language,
let's stop for one second,
and not move our arms so much."

Exp. The poet directly addresses the readers and urges each of us to count up to twelve and then be quiet. He wants a moment of silence on the Earth when no language is spoken and there is no movement. It is interesting to note here that the poet had specifically used the number 12 as it is often associated with completeness and wholeness in various cultures. There are 12 months, 12 zodiac signs and 12 hours on a clock face. By instructing the readers to 'count to twelve,' the poet may suggest a sense of totality, encompassing the entirety of existence.

Further, these lines indicate a sense of shared or collective participation to foster a sense of unity. The reference to language indicates that in that moment of silence, there will be no mis-communication between people and no harsh words will be spoken. In addition, the reference to 'arms' can refer to both hands and weapons indicating that the poet wants to stop violence.

Stanza 2

"It would be an exotic moment
without rush, without engines,
we would all be together
in a sudden strangeness."

Exp. The poet feels that such a moment of silence would be an unusual and exciting one. There will be no hurry, no sound of machines or usual noise and activity. It will be a strange and unfamiliar moment with stillness all around. In this unusual period, the bonds of humanity will get stronger.

Stanza 3

"Fishermen in the cold sea
would not harm whales
and the man gathering salt
would look at his hurt hands."

Exp. In this moment of inactivity, the fisherman would not be catching fish. Hence, the whales in the sea will be safe. This idea is suggestive of the thought that human beings would not destroy nature. The man who gathers salt will be able to tend to his wounded hands for which he had no time earlier. Thus, both nature and humans will be able to recover from their wounds, indicating a positive change.

Stanza 4

"Those who prepare green wars,
wars with gas, wars with fire,
victory with no survivors,
would put on clean clothes
and walk about with their brothers
in the shade, doing nothing."

Exp. The poet now speaks of those who wage wars against humanity or environment. He refers to wars of all kinds, including the use of chemicals or poisonous gases. According to him these wars cause a lot of death and destruction. Even though, one side wins in a war, nobody is left to celebrate this victory.

So, he advises the men who wage wars to stop their activity, shed their clothes stained with the blood of humanity, put on new clothes and walk with their brothers. The poet implies that the war-torn world should be replaced by one with an atmosphere of peace, brotherhood and harmony.

Stanza 5

"What I want should not be
confused
with total inactivity.
Life is what it is about;
I want no truck with death."

Exp. The poet clarifies that though he is advocating the need for silence, his advice should not be confused with total inactivity. He does not want any association with death. According to the poet, life is meant to be lived and experienced but with occasional pauses of introspection.

Stanza 6

"If we were not so single-minded
about keeping our lives moving,
and for once could do nothing,
perhaps a huge silence
might interrupt this sadness
of never understanding ourselves
and of threatening ourselves with death."

Exp. The poet further advises that people should stop being self-centred and selfish. For one moment they should not think of keeping their lives moving, meeting their ends or fulfilling their duties. The poet believes that the huge silence, which will arise from such a moment, will only serve to help the people. It will help them introspect and overcome their sadness of failing to understand themselves. According to him, people threaten themselves with death by their activities. In such a situation, this moment of silence will give them time to understand themselves as well as their actions in a better manner.

Stanza 7

"Perhaps the Earth can teach us
as when everything seems dead
and later proves to be alive.
Now I'll count up to twelve
and you keep quiet and I will go."

Exp. The poet feels that the Earth can enlighten us and guide us on how this silence will help us. He wants us to observe that there is some activity under apparent stillness. For instance, a seed appears to be 'dead' in the soil. However, after sometime huge fruit-bearing trees are 'born' from these seeds.

Finally, the poet thinks that he has said what he intended to. Now he wants us to keep quiet while he is counting to twelve, after which he will leave.

Word-Meaning

exotic	— unusual and exciting	confused with	— mistaken for
engines	— machines	inactivity	— not doing anything
strangeness	— unusual moment	want no truck	— refuse to deal with
green wars	— wars against nature or environment	single-minded	— thinking about or focusing only on one thing
in the shade	— under the trees		

Literary devices used in the Poem

- **Tone** Contemplative, meditative and optimistic
- **Rhyme Scheme** Free verse
- **Anaphora** *Stanza 1, lines 4 and 5* 'let's not speak in any language, let's stop for one second,'
- **Alliteration**
  Stanza 1 Lines 1 and 2 'we will' (repetition of 'w' sound)
  Stanza 2 Line 9 'we would' (repetition of 'w' sound) Line 10 'sudden strangeness' (repetition of 's' sound)
  Stanza 3 Line 14 'his hurt hand' (repetition of 'h' sound)
  Stanza 4 Line 18 'clean clothes' (repetition of 'c' sound)
  Stanza 6 Line 26 'So single-minded' (repetition of 's' sound)
- **Repetition**
  Stanza 2 Line 8 'without rush, without engines'
  Stanza 4 Lines 15 and 16 use of the word 'wors'
- **Enjambment**
  Stanza 5
  Stanza 6 Line 29-32 'perhaps a huge silevce ...... threatening ourselves with death'.
- **Irony** *Stanza 4 Line 17* 'victory with no survivors'

NCERT Folder

Before you Read (NCERT Page 92)

1. What does the title of the poem suggest to you? What do you think the poem is about?

Ans. The title of the poem suggests the importance of silence. The poem is about the importance of quiet introspection so that we can understand ourselves as well as our actions and their impact in a better manner.

Think it Out (NCERT Page 93)

1. What will counting upto twelve and keeping still help us achieve?

Or **Why does Pablo Neruda want us to count till twelve and keep still?**

Ans. Counting up to twelve and keeping still will help us get some time to stop all our normal activities and self-introspect our actions. This will help us change our destructive ways and promote brotherhood among men.

2. Do you think the poet advocates total inactivity and death?

Ans. No, the poet does not advocate total inactivity and death. He clarifies that his concept of silence has no relation with death. According to him, life is meant to be lived to the fullest. He just wants the inhuman and destructive activities to stop.

3. What is the 'sadness' that the poet refers to in the poem?

Ans. The poet refers to the sadness that arises from the failure to understand ourselves. Today, we are so engrossed in achieving materialistic success that we have no time to introspect about our actions and their consequences. Hence, we often end up hurting ourselves and which results in sadness.

4. What symbol from nature does the poet invoke to say that there can be life under apparent stillness?

Ans. The poet uses nature as a symbol to explain his idea that there can be life under apparent stillness. An example from nature is the Earth itself as when everything seems dead, later proves to be alive.

Exam Pattern Questions

Extract Based Questions

Read the extract given below and answer the following questions that follow.

1. **For once on the face of the Earth**
let's not speak in any language,
let's stop for one second,
and not move our arms so much.
It would be an exotic moment
without rush, without engines,
we would all be together
in a sudden strangeness.

(i) What is the poet propagating through the given lines?

(ii) Margaret Atwood said, "Language divides us into fragments, I wanted to be whole." Choose the option that correctly comments on the relationship between Margaret Atwood's words and the line from the above extract – "let's not speak in any language".

(a) Atwood endorses Neruda's call to not speak in any language.
(b) Atwood justifies Neruda's request to not engage in any speaking.
(c) Atwood undermines Neruda's intent to stop and not speak in any language.
(d) Atwood surrenders to Neruda's desire for silence and not speak in any language.

(iii) Complete the following suitably.

The poet uses the word 'let's' to ....

(iv) Select the correct option from those given in bracket to fill in the blanks.

The poet has employed words like 'exotic' and 'strangeness' because .... (it highlights the importance of everyone being together suddenly for once/it emphasises the frantic activity and chaos that usually envelops human life.)

(v) Read the assertion and the reason below, with reference to the given extract.

Assertion The poet wants everyone to stop speaking.

Reason Not speaking would avoid any miscommunication and hard words.

Choose the correct option regarding their relationship.

(a) Both the Assertion and the Reason are true, and the Reason is the correct explanation of the Assertion.
(b) Both the Assertion and the Reason are true, but the reason is not the correct explanation of the Assertion.
(c) The Assertion is true, but the Reason is false.
(d) The Assertion is false, but the Reason is true.

(vi) What do we mean by 'arms' in the given extract?

Ans. (i) Through the given lines, the poet is propagating the need for peace and brotherhood.

(ii) (a) Atwood endorses Neruda's call to not speak in any language.

(iii) (b) invite readers as part of the poem's larger call to humanity.

(iv) it emphasise the frantic activity and chaos that usually envelops human life.

(v) (a) Both the Assertion and the Reason are true, and the Reason is the correct explanation of the Assertion.

(vi) The word 'arms' in the given extract can refer to general movement and chaos in the world. It can also refer to the use of weaponry.

2. **"It would be an exotic moment**
without rush, without engines,
we would all be together
in a sudden strangeness.

(i) Why will the moment be strange?

(ii) Pick phrases that portray 'exotic moment' in the poem.

1. Fisherman would not harm whales.
2. Salt gatherers would not have hurt hands
3. Victory with no survivors
4. People would walk around with their brothers
5. I want no truck with death

(a) 1, 2 and 4 (b) 2, 3 and 5
(c) 1, 2 and 5 (d) Only 1 and 2

(iii) Complete the sentence suitably.

The moment will be exotic because ....

(iv) **Select the correct option from those given in bracket, to fill in the blank.**

The reference to 'without rush, without engines' indicate the ....(monotony/ busyness) of everyday life.

(v) **Read the assertion and the reason below, with reference to the given extract.**

Assertion The contrast between 'without rush' and 'without engines' juxtaposes the usual hurry of modern life with the idea of tranquillity.

Reason The idea of being 'together' emphasises unity, while 'sudden strangeness' evokes a shared yet surreal experience.

Choose the correct option regarding their relationship.

(a) Both the Assertion and the Reason are true, and the Reason is the correct explanation of the Assertion.
(b) Both the Assertion and the Reason are true, but the Reason is not the correct explanation of the Assertion.
(c) The Assertion is true, but the Reason is false.
(d) The Assertion is false, but the Reason is true.

(vi) **Does the poet propagate total inactivity when he says 'without rush, without engines'?**

Ans. (i) The moment will be strange because in our everyday lives we do not have a moment of silence or quiet. There is chaos all around which will not be there in the moment of silence.

(ii) (a) 1, 2 and 4

(iii) it will bring a break from the usual noise and activity

(iv) busyness

(v) (b) Both the Assertion and the Reason are true, but the Reason is not the correct explanation of the Assertion.

(vi) No, the poet does not propagate total inactivity as he himself later states in the poem that he does not want people to confuse his thoughts of being silent with total inactivity. He wants people to be silent to introspect.

3. **"Fishermen in the cold sea**
would not harm whales
and the man gathering salt
would look at his hurt hands."

(i) **What does the poet expect of the fisherman?**

(ii) **How 'Keeping Quiet' is going to help the man who works as 'Salt gatherer'?**

(a) He will get time to take care of his wounded hands.
(b) He will not work as 'salt gatherer'.
(c) He will introspect about the type of work he does.
(d) None of the above

(iii) **Fill in the blank appropriately.**

The tone of the poet in the given extract is ....

(iv) **Select the correct option from those given in bracket, to fill in the blank.**

The expression 'the man gathering salt' symbolises .... (labour and human toil/exploitation of nature)

(v) **Read the Assertion and the Reason below, with reference to the given extract.**

Assertion 'Fishermen in the cold sea' evoke a harsh environment.

Reason This sets the scene for the subsequent transformation.

Choose the correct option regarding their relationship.

(a) Both the Assertion and the Reason are true, and the Reason is the correct explanation of the Assertion.
(b) Both the Assertion and the Reason are true, but the Reason is not the correct explanation of the Assertion.
(c) The Assertion is true, but the Reason is false.
(d) The Assertion is false, but the Reason is true.

(vi) **What does the expression 'hurt hands' imply?**

Ans. (i) The poet expects the fishermen to participate in his suggestion of being quiet and introspecting and stop killing whales in the sea.

(ii) (a) He will get time to take care of his wounded hands

(iii) hopeful and optimistic

(iv) labour and human toil

(v) (b) Both the Assertion and the Reason are true, but the Reason is not the correct explanation of the Assertion.

(vi) The expression 'hurt hands' imply the destruction that humans have caused to them selnes and the mature in their pursuit of their selfish desires and greed.

4. **Those who prepare green wars,**
wars with gas, wars with fire,
victory with no survivors,
would put on clean clothes
and walk about with their brothers
in the shade, doing nothing. **CBSE SQP 2024**

(i) **What is a common outcome of all the wars described?**

(ii) **What does the imagery of 'walking about with their brothers in the shade' primarily represent?**

(a) The readiness for further conflicts.
(b) A return to normal activities post-conflict.

(c) A moment of unity and peaceful reflection.
(d) The physical environment of a typical war zone.

(iii) Complete the following suitably.

The putting on of 'clean clothes' by the warmongers, symbolises ....

(iv) Select the correct option from those given in bracket, to fill in the blank.

The excerpt tells us that the speaker .... (condemns/glorifies) the destructive nature of modern warfare.

(v) Read the Assertion and the Reason below, with reference to the given extract.

Assertion The poet advocates for 'doing nothing' as a way to prevent the devastation of war.

Reason 'Doing nothing' refers to a time for stopping any action for a few moments.

Choose the correct option regarding their relationship.

(a) Both the Assertion and the Reason are true, and the Reason is the correct explanation of the Assertion.
(b) Both the Assertion and the Reason are true, but the Reason is not the correct explanation of the Assertion.
(c) The Assertion is true, but the Reason is false.
(d) The Assertion is false, but the Reason is true.

(vi) How can the message in the excerpt, about the outcome of wars be applied to promote peace?

Ans. (i) A common outcome of all the wars that are described in the given lines is the gaining of victory without any survivors on any side.

(ii) (c) A moment of unity and peaceful reflection.

(iii) a moment of pause and reflection which presents the possibility of transformation wherein they embrace a peaceful existence.

(iv) condemns

(v) (b) Both the Assertion and the Reason are true, but the Reason is not the correct explanation of the Assertion.

(vi) The message of peace presented in the extract can be applied by global leaders and communities to work toward more sustainable and peaceful solutions. They can advocate for non-violent or peaceful resolutions and negotiations in contemporary conflicts. They can also be used to promote dialogue and understanding over aggression and warfare.

Or Select the line/s that suggests the following **CBSE 2025**

(i) The so-called victors of the wars are indifferent to the consequences of their actions.

(ii) What does the imagery of 'green wars' not represent in the extract?

(a) Environmental conflict
(b) Harmful destruction
(c) Sustainable peace
(d) Continuous deforestation

(iii) Complete the following suitably.

'Clean clothes' here refers to ....

(iv) Choose a word from the brackets to complete the following suitably Phrases like 'victory with no survivors' illustrate the .... (irony/satire) in the situation where those claiming victory actually achieve nothing of true value.

(v) Read the Assertion and the Reason below with reference to the given context.

Assertion The poet criticises the superficial actions of those involved in conflicts.

Reason The actions described are meant to highlight the futility and destruction of wars.

Choose the correct option

(a) Both the Assertion and the Reason are ture and the Reason is the correct explanation of the Assertion.
(b) Both the Assertion and the Reason are true, but the Reason is not the correct explanation of the Assertion.
(c) The Assertion is true, but the Reason is false.
(d) The Assertion is false, but the Reason is true.

(vi) What is the message that you would give to the warmongers based on the given extract?

Ans. (i) The line that suggests the victors of wars are indifferent to the consequences of their actions is 'Victory with no survivors'.

(ii) (c) Sustainable peace

(iii) a symbolic renewal of conscience and a fresh start, free from the stains of war and destruction

(iv) irony

(v) (a) Both the Assertion and the Reason are true, and the Reason is the correct explanation of the Assertion.

(vi) Message to warmongers is wars bring destruction, not true victory. Instead of engaging in violence, they should embrace peace, coexistence, and harmony. True progress lies in building, not destroying.

5. **"What I want should not be Confused**
with total inactivity.
Life is what it is about;
I want no truck with death."

(i) What is life about according to the poet?

(ii) What should not be confused with 'total unproductivity'?

(a) Putting on clean clothes
(b) Stopping wars
(c) Practicising to keep still and quiet
(d) Relaxing for a while

(iii) Fill in the blank appropriately
The use of double quotation in the extract indicates that ....

(iv) Identify the phrase from the extract, that suggests the following
No association with death as life is to be lived fully
Stillness and inactivity for few minutes is different from death.

(v) Read the Assertion and the Reason below, with reference to the given extract.

Assertion The line break after 'confused' emphasises this distinction.

Reason The syntactical break and enjambment create a pause that allows readers to consider the contrast between the two concepts.

Choose the correct option regarding their relationship.

(a) Both the Assertion and the Reason are true, and the Reason is the correct explanation of the Assertion.
(b) Both the Assertion and the Reason are true, but the Reason is not the correct explanation of the Assertion.
(c) The Assertion is true, but the Reason is false.
(d) The Assertion is false, but the Reason is true.

(vi) Complete the following analogy correctly by choosing the correct option from those given in bracket (What/Truck).
Confusion : Uncertain : : Relation : ....

Ans. (i) According to the poet, life is something that is to be lived and experienced with brief pauses of introspection.
(ii) (c) Practicising to keep still and quiet
(iii) the poet is speaking to someone
(iv) Life is what it is about I want. No truck with death
(v) (a) Both the Assertion and the Reason are true, and the Reason is the correct explanation of the Assertion.
(vi) Truck

6. **If we were not so single-minded**
about keeping our lives moving,
and for once could do nothing,
perhaps a huge silence
might interrupt this sadness
of never understanding ourselves
and of threatening ourselves with death. **CBSE 2025**

(i) Select the phrase from the above extract that suggests the following
The ceaseless activity in our daily life.

(ii) What does the imagery of 'single-mindedness' not represent in the given extract?

(a) Flexibility
(b) Unwavering determination
(c) Dedication
(d) Persistent efforts

(iii) Complete the following suitably.
In the line, 'might interrupt this sadness', the phrase this sadness refers to ....

(iv) The poet has used phrases like 'never understanding ourselves' to illustrate .... (irony/humour) in continuous movement without reflection.

(v) Read the Assertion and the Reason below with reference to the given extract.

Assertion The poet emphasises the need for productive reflection.

Reason Purposeless and continuous movement leads to sadness and existential threats.

Choose the correct option from the following.

(a) Both the Assertion and the Reason are true, but the Reason is not the correct explanation of the Assertion.
(b) Both the Assertion and the Reason are true, and the Reason is the correct explanation of the Assertion.
(c) The Assertion is true, but the Reason is false.
(d) The Assertion is false, but the Reason is true.

(vi) State in one sentence what advice you would give to people who are always busy.

Ans. (i) The phrase that suggests 'the ceaseless activity in our daily life' is 'keeping our lives moving'.
(ii) (a) Flexibility
(iii) the emptiness and lack of self-awareness caused by continuous, unreflective activity
(iv) irony
(v) (b) Both the Assertion and the Reason are true, and the Reason is the correct explanation of the Assertion.
(vi) My advice to people who are always busy– Take time to pause, reflect, and embrace moments of silence to truly understand yourself and find peace.

7. "Perhaps the Earth can teach us
as when everything seems dead
and later proves to be alive.
Now I'll count up to twelve
and you keep quiet and I will go".

(i) Where does the poet go?

(ii) What is the significance of 'Keeping Quiet'?
(a) Very peaceful atmosphere
(b) No involvement in harmful activities
(c) Establishing peaceful coexistence
(d) All of the above

(iii) Complete the following sentence.

The poet uses conversational style and personal pronouns or 'you', 'we' and 'I' because ....

(iv) Select the correct option from those given in bracket, to fill in the blank.

These lines introduces the Earth as a .... (example/teacher).

(v) Read the Assertion and the Reason below, with reference to the given extract.

Assertion The metaphor of 'everything seems dead/and later proves to be alive' underlines the theme of transformation, aligning with the idea of stillness leading to new perspectives.

Reason Neruda wants to continue the poem by urging the reader to continue in silence as he departs, leaving them to reflect on the poem's message.

Choose the correct option regarding their relationship.
(a) Both the Assertion and the Reason are true, and the Reason is the correct explanation of the Assertion.
(b) Both the Assertion and the Reason are true, but the Reason is not the correct explanation of the Assertion.
(c) The Assertion is true, but the Reason is false.
(d) The Assertion is false, but the Reason is true.

(vi) What message does the poet give in the extract?

Ans. (i) The poet enters the moment of self introspection and goes to be silent.
(ii) (d) All of the above
(iii) he wants us to be friendly with whole mankind
(iv) teacher
(v) (c) The Assertion is true, but the Reason is false.
(vi) The poet wants to give a message that there is life even in the moment of total inactivity. This moment of total inactivity leads one to grow and become a better version of oneself.

Short Answer Type Questions

1. Which is the exotic moment that the poet refers to in 'Keeping Quiet'?

Ans. The poet refers to the moment of stillness and quietness as an exotic moment because it will initiate peace and brotherhood. There would be no movement, no talk, no activity and consequently, no violence.

2. Why does one feel 'a sudden strangeness' on counting to twelve and keeping quiet?

Ans. The sudden strangess of counting to twelve and keeping quiet in 'Keeping Quiet' arises from the disruption of routine and the stillness it creates. This pause forces a reflection on the busy, often chaotic, nature of life, making the act of silence feel unfamiliar.

3. How would keeping quiet affect life in and around the sea?

Ans. Keeping quiet would promote peace and harmony in the sea and its surrounding. It would allow marine life to thrive undisturbed, while humans reflect and reconnect with nature. The stillness would reduce noise pollution, fostering a healthier ecosystem and encouraging a deeper appreciation for the sea's fragile beauty.

4. What is Pablo Neruda's complaint against fishermen? CBSE 2024

Ans. Pablo Neruda's complaint against the fishermen is that they are failing to grasp the serene silence of the ocean. They are exploiting nature and disrupting the beautiful silence by their noisy endeavours.

5. What are the different kinds of wars mentioned in the poem? What is Neruda's attitude towards these wars?

Ans. The poet writes about wars against humanity and nature. Green wars, wars with poisonous gases and wars with fire are the kinds of wars mentioned in the poem. Neruda's attitude towards war is one of rejection. He feels that such wars may bring victory but there are no survivors to celebrate the victory.

6. How would humanity benefit if people maintained silence? CBSE 2025

Or What will possibly be the effect of keeping quiet?

Or How, according to Neruda, can keeping quiet change our attitude to life?

Ans. Humanity would benefit if people maintained silence because it would encourage self-reflection, mutual understanding, and peace.

Continuous activity and noise create stress and conflict, while moments of stillness allow people to connect with themselves and others, leading to a more compassionate and thoughtful society.

7. 'Life is what it is all about.' How is keeping quiet related to life?

Ans. Keeping quiet does not mean complete inactivity but stillness and quietness to introspect on what we are doing. This means stopping our normal day-to-day activities to reflect on our actions. Thus it is related to life, although this may not be visible outwardly.

8. 'There is life under apparent stillness'. Explain. **CBSE 2023**

Ans. The given phrase means that even when everything seems inactive and almost still, there is some activity in the background that shows that everything is alive. In other words, 'stillness' is not death but a time wherein activity happens in the background to promote positive development.

9. What, according to Pablo Neruda in the poem 'Keeping Quiet', is the lesson that we should learn from Mother earth? **CBSE 2023**

Ans. According to Pablo Neruda in the poem 'Keeping Quiet', the lesson that we should learn from mother earth is to remember that there is activity and positivity in the apparent stillness. He states that just like a seed that remains in a latent state but soon germinates into a plant, we can also learn many things during the moment of silence and retrospection.

10. How is the Earth a source of life when all seems dead on it?

Ans. In the poem 'Keeping Quiet', the Earth is a source of life because it is never in a state of total inactivity even when there is silence all around. Nature continues to work even when everything is still and silent.

11. In a world that is constantly running after 'more' chasing the next new thing, would it be fair to think of Neruda's call as merely a fanciful idea?

Ans. In a world that is constantly running after more, Neruda's idea would resonate with the people. Silence and stillness are therapeutic for the chaos that plagues modern life. In a place where yoga and meditation are becoming popular, Neruda's idea would be readily accepted.

12. The world has become a global village and people across boundaries, nationalities and communities are now connected to one another. With the advancement of technology, and the advent of social media, do you think that the task of keeping quiet, as envisaged by Neruda, has become easier or more complicated? Justify your stance. **Competency Based**

Ans. It is precisely because we are more connected than ever before that the task of keeping quiet has become more complicated. Earlier, it was possible to divide day and night activities but now everything is on for twenty-four hours whether that is the media or the internet. Keeping quiet is necessary but also more difficult at this time.

13. Give two Reasons why, according to Pablo Neruda, is 'keeping quiet' essential to attaining a better, more peaceful world. (Keeping Quiet) **CBSE SQP 2023**

Ans. For Pablo Neruda, 'Keeping Quiet' is essential to attaining a better and more peaceful world because silence makes us introspect and reflect upon our exploitative actions. It helps us better understand ourselves and what we want. It also enables us to realise that many of our mindless actions are only harming us and not giving us happiness.

14. The poem 'Keeping Quiet' centres around transformation and renewal. Substantiate. **Competency Based**

Ans. The poem 'Keeping Quiet' centres around transformation and renewal. It implies that a moment of silence and inactivity can lead to personal and global transformation. By interrupting the busyness of life, a 'huge silence' might lead to a deeper understanding of ourselves and a break from the cycle of misunderstanding and conflict.

15. What does the poet mean by 'green wars' in the poem 'Keeping Quiet'? Answer in 20–30 words. **Competency Based**

Ans. Through the given phrase, the poet refers to man's destruction of the environment and the Earth's green cover, specifically trees and forests.

16. Adi is constantly on his phone updating his life on social media to increase the number of followers he has.

What advice would Pablo Neruda give to Adi based on the poem 'Keeping Quiet'? Answer in 20-30 words. **Competency Based**

Ans. The poet Pablo Neruda would advise Adi to take a break from social media and put his phone aside. Just like he states in his poem 'Keeping Quiet', Neruda would urge Adi to spend some time with himself in solitude and learn to listen to his own voice, rather than the voice of the thousands of people online. Such introspection could lead Adi to identify the important things in life and move away from the fabrications of the social media.

17. How can Earth play the role of a teacher according to Pablo Neruda? **CBSE 2025**

Ans. According to Pablo Neruda, Earth plays the role of a teacher by demonstrating the power of stillness and renewal. Just as the Earth appears lifeless in winter but regenerates in spring, humans too can pause, reflect, and rejuvenate their lives through introspection and silence.

Long Answer Type Questions

1. What kind of an imaginary and ideal world does the poet visualise?

Ans. The poet longs for a calm, quiet and peaceful world, devoid of all forms of violence, as he visualises 'togetherness' of the people in a moment of silence and peace. According to the poet, this moment will give us time in silence for self-introspection. It will bring in a moment when we can spiritually attain our moral self through a moment of meditation.

This moment will bring an end to all destructive activities in the world. The fishermen will not be killing whales and the men gathering salt will have time to rest their injured hands. Environmental degradation will come to an end. The warmongers will be silenced in a moment of brotherhood to meditate and cleanse their souls. The poet hopes that it will be an ideal world where man will be able to come out from his self-centred attitude to gain moral peace.

2. It could be said that the poem 'Keeping Quiet' presents the poet's philosophy for a different kind of world.

If you were asked to highlight elements of Neruda's vision that resonate in your specific social, political and cultural context, which three main ideas would you engage with? Use relevant textual details to support your analysis. Competency Based

Ans. Pablo Neruda imagines a beautiful world in which silence and stillness becomes a regular part of one's life and which increases understanding of oneself and reduces environmental conflict and war. Neruda's vision can be adopted into a social, political and cultural context in the following ways.

The first is Neruda's suggestion of keeping quiet which can be adopted into the social context of a school curriculum.

Students can devote thirty minutes of silence in a week which could be spent in a library or meditation hall. They would be taught to be still and silent under any circumstances.

Second, Neruda's suggestion of stillness can be suggested to political parties who can incorporate them into their political doctrine.

Third, at a cultural level, stillness and silence can be adopted at a grassroots level movement starting with Stillness Clubs (where people go to stay still and be silent) for the public which can then be replicated in companies and neighbourhoods. Ideally, stillness and silence should be taught at home and from there, it should spread all over the world.

3. The last two years of school tend to be about planning for life after school. This can be motivating, overwhelming or encouraging for some and stressful for others. Write a diary entry recording your thoughts on the following

Neruda's ideas in 'Keeping Quiet' as a guide in this situation.

Thinking differently about your decisions with reference to Neruda's 'Keeping Quiet'. Competency Based

Ans. Wednesday, 6th November, 20XX 9:00 p.m.

Dear Diary,

I reflected on something today. This reflection did not come out of the blue. It came about deliberately after reading the poem 'Keeping Quiet' by Pablo Neruda. In the poem, the poet promoted stillness and quietness for self reflection. Now, you know how I have been confused about my future career and life. So, I decided to follow the technique suggested by Neruda. And it worked.

I locked myself in the study and just thought what I liked doing, whether I will be able to make my life in the field that I like and how will I go about it. It took me some days of research and thinking.

But now I have a solution. I want to pursue hotel management and convert our old ancestral haveli into a hotel for business. I know the decision will not be met with optimism but I have thought about it as well. Now, I will take your leave.

XYZ

4. Wars with gas, war with fire.
Victory with no survivors. (Keeping Quiet)

Pablo Neruda in the above lines, highlights the futility of war. Gandhi also brought about the change in the plight of the Champaran sharecroppers through Civil Disobedience and Non-Violence.

Write an article on the 'Importance of Peace' and the right way to resolve issues. Competency Based

Ans. **Importance of Peace**

by XYZ

In a world rife with conflict and turmoil, the significance of peace cannot be overstated. Pablo Neruda's 'Keeping Quiet' highlights the value of tranquillity and reflection in fostering harmony among humanity. Similarly, Mahatma Gandhi's transformative approach to the plight of Champaran sharecroppers exemplifies the efficacy of non-violent resistance in resolving disputes.

Peace serves as a catalyst for progress, allowing individuals and societies to channel their energies towards constructive endeavours. By advocating for Civil Disobedience and Non-Violent protest, Gandhi facilitated social change while upholding the principles of justice and compassion.

The path to peace requires humility, empathy, and a commitment to dialogue and understanding. It entails transcending differences and embracing shared humanity. By eschewing violence and embracing peaceful means, individuals can forge lasting resolutions to conflicts, fostering a world characterised by harmony, justice and mutual respect.

5. Why has the poet of 'Keeping Quiet' mentioned the concept of death? Justify with any two Reasons whether the thought of death helps people live a meaningful life or not. Anwer in 120–150 words. Competency Based

Ans. In the poem 'Keeping Quiet', the poet mentions the concept of death and says that we never understand ourselves because we keep threatening ourselves with death. He feels that due to our awareness of our mortality and our impending death, we are in a mad rush of activity. We always want to do something or the other and never take the time to reflect on our lives. Thus, we become 'single-minded' to keeping ourselves alive going until we are alive.

I think thinking about death can help us lead a meaningful life. It forces us to prioritise things that are important to us and let go of things that are not. So, one can let go of trivialities that do not serve any long term benefit. It also makes us appreciate everything around us even more as we understand that we are mortal and will one day cease to exist. However, I also understand that death can cease to be a good motivator and make one anxious.

6. It could be said that the poem 'Keeping Quiet' presents the poet's philosophy for a different kind of world.

If you were asked to highlight elements of Neruda's vision that resonate in your specific social, political and cultural context, which three main ideas would you engage with? Use relevant textual details to support your analysis. Competency Based

Ans. Pablo Neruda imagines a beautiful world in which silence and stillness become a regular part of one's life, which increases understanding of oneself and reduces environmental conflict and war. Neruda's vision can be adopted into a social, political and cultural context in the following ways.

The first is Neruda's suggestion of Keeping quiet can be adopted into the social context of a school curriculum.

Students can devote thirty minutes of silence in a week which could be spent in a library or meditation hall. They would be taught to be still and silent under any circumstances. Second, Neruda's suggestion of stillness can be suggested to political parties who can incorporate them into their political doctrine.

Third, at a cultural level, stillness and silence can be adopted at a grassroot level movement starting with Stillness Clubs (where people go to stay still and be silent) for the public which can then be replicated in companies and neighbourhoods.

Ideally, stillness and silence should be taught at home and from there, it should spread all over the world.

SELF ASSESSMENT TEST

Extract Based Questions

Read the extract given below and answer the following questions.

1. Those who prepare green wars,
wars with gas, wars with fire,
Victory with no survivors,
would put on clean clothes
And walk about with their brothers in the shade,
doing nothing.

(i) What does the expression "put on clean clothes" imply?

(ii) The purpose of the given stanza is to ....

(a) condemn exploitation
(b) visualise an ideal world
(c) blame someone
(d) All of these

(iii) Complete the sentence suitably.

The line 'victory with no survivors' means that ....

(iv) Select the correct option from those given in bracket, to fill in the blank.

The poet .... (devalues/criticises)wars due to its death and destruction.

(v) Read the Assertion and the Reason below, with reference to the given extract.

Assertion The lines highlight the devastating nature of inevitable conflicts.

Reason The poet contrasts violence and conflict with the peacefulness of doing nothing, suggesting that such moments of stillness are valuable.

Choose the correct option regarding their relationship.

(a) Both the Assertion and the Reason are true, and the Reason is the correct explanation of the Assertion.
(b) Both the Assertion and the Reason are true, but the Reason is not the correct explanation of the Assertion.
(c) The Assertion is true, but the Reason is false.
(d) The Assertion is false, but the Reason is true.

(vi) What would the poet state if the content of the given lines were to be a part of a speech?

Short Answer Type Questions

Answer the following questions in 40-50 words.

1. What does Neruda mean by 'an exotic moment without rush' in his poem, 'Keeping Quiet'?

2. 'Keeping quiet' protect our environment. Justify.

3. Which images in the poem 'Keeping Quiet' show that the poet condemns violence?

4. Explain the significance of number 12.

Long Answer Type Question

Answer the following question in 120-150 words.

1. Critically comment on the themes present in the poem.

03

A Thing of Beauty

About the Poet

John Keats (1795–1821) was a revered English Romantic poet whose works epitomised the era's emotional intensity and aesthetic beauty. He is known for his vivid and sensory descriptions of nature and his exploration of human emotions and experiences. He was a master of language and used a range of poetic techniques to create rich, complex and beautiful poems.

▼ YOUR STUDY GOALS

- Central Idea of the Poem
- Explanation of the Poem

▼ YOUR PRACTICE GOAL

- NCERT Folder
- Extract Based Questions
- Short Answer Type Questions
- Long Answer Type Questions

Central Idea of the Poem

The poem 'A Thing of Beauty' is part of John Keats' longer work, 'Endymion: A Poetic Romance'. The poem celebrates beauty's everlasting and uplifting power. Keats asserts that beauty brings perpetual joy and tranquillity to humanity. It never fades but grows in loveliness over time, offering a peaceful refuge for pleasant dreams and good health. Despite life's challenges and darkness, beauty remains a constant source of solace, connecting individuals to the Earth and inspiring noble qualities. Natural elements like the Sun, moon, trees and daffodils exemplify this enduring beauty, as do stories of grandeur and inspiration. Keats portrays beauty as an infinite source of refreshment, pouring divine nourishment onto humanity, ultimately conveying the message of beauty's eternal significance in enriching and inspiring human life.

Explanation of the Poem

Stanza 1

"A thing of beauty is a joy forever
Its loveliness increases, it will never
Pass into nothingness; but will keep
A bower quiet for us, and a sleep
Full of sweet dreams, and health, and quiet breathing."

Exp. The poet speaks of the permanent nature of beautiful things which bring us eternal joy. Their loveliness keeps on increasing and never fades away. The sight of beautiful things is stored in our memory forever. They give us peace, just like a quiet shady place gives us a sleep full of sweet dreams. A sound sleep results in the good health of our body and mind as it provides us tranquillity and mental peace.

Stanza 2

"Therefore, on every morrow, are we wreathing
A flowery band to bind us to the Earth,
Spite of despondence, of the inhuman dearth
Of noble natures, of the gloomy days,
Of all the unhealthy and o'er-darkened ways
Made for our searching: yes, inspite of all,
Some shape of beauty moves away the pall
From our dark spirits."

Exp. When we wake up the next morning after a sound sleep, all the beautiful memories of our sweet dreams help us to strengthen our bond with Earth. That is why the poet feels that every morning we prepare a wreath of flowers that binds us to Earth more strongly.

According to the poet, life is full of trials and tribulations, lost faith, hopelessness, sadness and disappointments, which result from our own doings. We harm ourselves by following unhealthy and wicked paths. However, inspite of all this, some wonderful sights of beauty remove all sadness and anxieties, bringing about hope and optimism in our lives.

Stanza 3

"Such the sun, the moon,
Trees old, and young, sprouting a shady boon
For simple sheep; and such are daffodils
With the green world they live in; and clear rills
That for themselves a cooling covert make
'Gainst the hot season; the mid forest brake,
Rich with a sprinkling of fair musk-rose blooms;"

Exp. The poet now goes on to list the objects of beauty. He says that the Sun, the Moon, old and young trees which provide shade to sheep, the daffodils, the greenery surrounding them, the cool and clear streams which provide respite in the heat of summer and the bushes growing in the forest with musk-roses blooming amidst them, are all eternal sources of joy and pleasure.

Stanza 4

"And such too is the grandeur of the dooms
We have imagined for the mighty dead;
All lovely tales that we have heard or read;
An endless fountain of immortal drink,
Pouring unto us from the heaven's brink."

Exp. The poet adds on further to his list. According to him, there is beauty even in death. He finds beauty in imaginary stories people have made about our dead ancestors who were deemed as heroic and mighty. Accordingly, all the lovely tales that we have heard can also be placed among things of beauty, as they have a sublime effect on the human spirit. All beautiful things are like an endless fountain from the heavens, sent by God himself, so that mankind may enjoy these precious gifts.

Word-Meaning

pass into	—	change or turn into
nothingness	—	an insignificant or worthless thing
bower	—	a pleasant shady place
morrow	—	morning
wreathing	—	weaving or forming into a wreath
spite	—	malice, ill will
despondence	—	disappointment, dejection
darkened	—	evil, bad
pall	—	covering, shroud or cloth spread over a coffin
dark	—	gloomy
spirits	—	souls, temperaments
daffodils	—	bright yellow flowers
rills	—	small streams
covert	—	shelter or covering
brake	—	dense undergrowth of ferns or other bush
rich	—	enriched, made beautiful
musk-rose	—	a wild rose with large white musk-scented flowers
blooms	—	flowers

Literary devices used in the Poem

- **Tone** Optimistic, contemplative and celebratory.
- **Rhyme Scheme** aabbc
- **Alliteration**
  Stanza 2, Line 9 'noble nature' (repetition of 'n' sound)
  Stanza 3, Line 16 'simple sheep' (repetition of 's' sound)
  Stanza 3, *Line 18* 'cooling covert' (repetition of 'c' sound)
- **Anaphora**
  Stanza 2, Lines 9 and 10 'Of noble natures, Of all the unhealthy ...'
- **Metaphor**
  Stanza 1, Line 4 'A bower quiet for us' (calmness of a bower is compared to a calming effect of beautiful things on us)
  Stanza 2, Line 6 and 7 'wreathing a flowery band' (beautiful things bind us to the Earth)
  Stanza 3, Line 16 'simple sheep' (can refer to innocent people)
  Stanza 4, Line 24 'endless fountain of immortal drink' (beauty as bestowed by heavens or Gods)
- **Imagery** Every line in the poem contains image of beauty.

NCERT Folder

Think it Out (NCERT Page 96)

1. List the things of beauty mentioned in the poem.

Ans. The poet, John Keats, lists many things of beauty. All objects of nature including the Sun, the moon, old and young trees, daffodil flowers, small streams with clear water, masses of ferns and blooming musk-roses. Further, according to the poet, the tales of our heroic and mighty ancestors are also a thing of beauty are things of beauty as they all add joy to our life.

2. List the things that cause suffering and pain.

Or What, according to Keats, causes a pall over our spirits? CBSE Term II 2022

Ans. According to Keats, there are many things that cause us suffering and pain. Malice, disappointment, lack of noble qualities and our unhealthy and evil ways all give birth to many troubles and sufferings.

3. What does the line, 'Therefore, are we wreathing a flowery band to bind us to earth' suggest to you? CBSE Term II 2022

Ans. The act of "wreathing/a flowery band to bind us to the Earth" suggests how people naturally seek out and celebrate beauty as a way to stay connected to the natural world. The 'flowery band' symbolises humanity's connection to the natural world and its beauty. By adorning themselves with this metaphorical band, people affirm their bond with the Earth and the beauty it offers.

4. What makes human beings love life in spite of troubles and sufferings? CBSE Term II 2022

Ans. Human beings love life in spite of all the troubles and sufferings they face because of all the things of beauty which surround them. These things remove our despondent state and allow us to enjoy the beauty of nature.

5. Why is 'grandeur' associated with the 'mighty dead'?

Or In the poem 'A Thing of Beauty', how is grandeur connected with the mighty dead? CBSE 2023

Ans. 'Grandeur' is associated with the 'mighty dead' because the revered individuals from history or mythology are remembered for their impressive or majestic qualities, often attributed to their achievements, deeds or the impact they had on society. The stories and legends around these people often portray them in a grand or noble light, elevating them to a status of reverence and admiration. Therefore, the association of grandeur with the mighty dead reflects the perception of their remarkable and awe-inspiring attributes.

6. Do we experience things of beauty only for a short moment or do they make a lasting impression on us?

Or How is a things of beauty a joy forever?

Ans. Things of beauty make a lasting impression on us because they are a source of pleasure and motivation forever. The happiness they give never fades away but keeps on increasing.

7. What image does the poet use to describe the beautiful bounty of the Earth?

Ans. The poet uses the image of a 'bower' to describe the beautiful bounty of the Earth. This metaphor conveys the idea of beauty providing a tranquil refuge or shelter for individuals, filled with sweetness, health and peace.

A bower typically refers to a leafy shelter in a garden or wooded area, suggesting a serene and natural environment abundant with beauty.

By invoking this image, Keats emphasises beauty's nurturing and comforting qualities in the natural world.

Exam Pattern Questions

Extract Based Questions

Read the extracts given below and answer the following questions.

1. "A thing of beauty is a joy forever
Its loveliness increases, it will never
Pass into nothingness; but will keep
A bower quiet for us, and a sleep
Full of sweet dreams, and health, and quiet breathing."
Therefore, on every morrow are we wreathing a flowery band to bind us to the Earth CBSE 2025

(i) By the phrase 'joy forever' the poet refers to things

(a) that make people extremely happy.
(b) that are a feast to eyes.
(c) that are a constant source of happiness.
(d) that are beautiful but transient.

(ii) Choose the correct option.

By using the expression 'never pass into nothingness' the poet states that nature's beauty will create a .... (lasting/temporary) impression on man's mind.

(iii) How does Keats make it evident that there is a link between man's wellness and nature's beauty?

(iv) Read the Assertion and the Reason below with reference to the given extract.

Assertion Keats states that man derives strength and inspiration from the beauty of nature.

Reason Nature gives physical, emotional, and mental solace to man.

Choose the correct option regarding their relationship.

(a) Both the Assertion and Reason are true, and the Reason is the correct explanation of the Assertion.
(b) Both the Assertion and Reason are true, and the Reason is not the correct explanation of the Assertion.
(c) The Assertion is false, but the Reason is true.
(d) The Assertion is true, but the Reason is false.

(v) Select one phrase from the extract which implies that man wants to continue his life on this earth despite innumerable problems.

(vi) Complete the following sentence.

'A sleep full of sweet dreams' implies ....

Ans. (i) (c) that are a constant source of happiness.

(ii) lasting

(iii) Keats makes it evident that there is a link between man's wellness and nature's beauty by describing how beautiful things provide a sense of peace, health, and quiet breathing, offering relief from life's struggles.

(iv) (a) Both the Assertion and Reason are true, and the Reason is the correct explanation of the Assertion.

(v) The phrase that implies man wants to continue his life on this earth despite innumerable problems is 'a flowery band to bind us to the Earth'.

(vi) peace, comfort, and a life free from worries and troubles

2. Therefore, on every morrow, are we wreathing
A flowery band to bind us to the earth,
Spite of despondence, of the inhuman dearth
Of noble natures, of the gloomy days,
Of all the unhealthy and o'er darkened ways
Made for our searching: yes, in spite of all,
Some shape of beauty moves away the pall
From our dark spirits. CBSE Question Bank 2021

(i) What makes our life full of inhuman dearth?

(ii) Pick the option that is NOT an example of 'unhealthy and o'er darkened ways.'

(a) A person who is egoistic and looks down upon others.
(b) A person who seeks God's help for all his problems.
(c) A person who uses evil ways to deceive others.
(d) A person who is corrupt and manipulative.

(iii) The poet says that we wreath a flowery band that binds us to Earth.

He means to state that nature's beauty fills man with ......

(iv) Select the correct option from those given in bracket to fill in the blank.

The 'flowery band' symbolises humanity's connection to the natural world and its beauty. By adorning themselves with this metaphorical band, people .... (affirm/applaud) their bond with the earth and the beauty it offers.

(v) Based on the poem, choose the correct option with reference to the two statements given below.

Statement 1 The Earth without the beautiful things is a place full of despair and unpleasantness.

Statement 2 The ornate band created by human beings; ushers hope in their lives.

(a) Statement 1 is true but Statement 2 is false.
(b) Statement 1 is false but Statement 2 is true.
(c) Both Statement 1 and Statement 2 can be inferred.
(d) Both Statement 1 and Statement 2 cannot be inferred.

(vi) What does 'noble natures' include?

Ans. (i) According to the poet, we ourselves make our lives full of inhuman dearth due to our selfish and self-centered nature.

(ii) (b) A person who seeks God's help for all his problems.

(iii) a spirit of living

(iv) affirm

(v) (c) Both Statement 1 and Statement 2 can be inferred.

(vi) The 'noble natures' include selflessness, enthusiasm and judiciousness.

3. "Therefore, on every morrow, are we wreathing
A flowery band to bind us to the Earth,
Spite of despondence, of the inhuman dearth
Of noble natures, of the gloomy days,
Of all the unhealthy and o'er-darkened ways
Made for our searching. **CBSE 2024**

(i) Which of the following themes is best represented in the given extract?

(a) The Beautiful Things in Nature
(b) Things that Cause Unhappiness
(c) The Immortality of Human Beings
(d) The Early Morning Fragrance of Flowers

(ii) State whether the given statement is True or False, with reference to the extract.

The paths we follow are often not worthy of our noble nature.

(iii) Complete the following sentence appropriately.

We wreathe for ourselves a flowery band every morrow because ....

(iv) The use of the word 'dearth' creates a powerful image of ....

(v) Based on the rhyme scheme in lines 4 and 5, which of the following words will rhyme with 'days' and 'ways'?

(a) Craze
(b) Pays
(c) Haste
(d) Waste

(vi) The lack of punctuation at the end of line 3 in the extract is to

(a) create a sense of continuity and flow that connects it with the fourth line.
(b) encourage the reader to understand grammar.
(c) forewarn the reader of gloomy days ahead.
(d) keep us connected to this Earth.

Ans. (i) (a) The Beautiful Things in Nature

(ii) True

(iii) it help us remain attached to the Earth and the nature, just like how a wreathe binds all the flowers.

(iv) lack of noble values

(v) (b) Pays

(vi) (a) creates a sense of continuity and flow that connects it with the fourth line.

4. A thing of beauty is a joy forever
Its loveliness increases, it will never
pass into nothingness :but will keep
A bower quiet for us, and a sleep
Full of sweet dreams, and health and quiet and breathing.
Therefore, on every morrow are we wreathing
A flowery band to bind us to the earth;
Spite of despondence, of the inhuman dearth
Of noble natures, of the gloomy days,
Of all the unhealthy and o'er darkened ways Made
for our searching. **CBSE 2023**

(i) Keats defines beauty as

(a) transient
(b) eternal
(c) illusionary
(d) short lived

(ii) 'Will keep a bower quiet for us' means all of the following, EXCEPT

(a) create a peaceful, shady place
(b) provide shelter
(c) will decrease noise pollution
(d) nature's canopy

(iii) On the basis of the extract, choose the correct option with reference to the two statements given below

1. Beautiful things uplift the soul.

2. Beauty is everchanging.

Codes

(a) 1 can be inferred from the extract but 2 cannot.
(b) 2 can be inferred from the extract but 1 cannot.
(c) Both 1 and 2 can be inferred from the extract.
(d) Both 1 and 2 cannot be inferred from the extract.

(iv) The things that cause unhappiness are

1. lack of noble nature	2. old tunes
3. dull days	4. calm mind
5. a flowery band	6. strong relationships

Choose the most appropriate option.

(a) 1 and 2
(b) 1 and 3
(c) 4 and 5
(d) 3 and 6

(v) Complete the analogy. Do not repeat from used example.

Flowery band : Metaphor :: .... : Noble nature

(vi) According to the poet, every morrow we are ....

Ans. (i) (b) eternal

(ii) (c) will decrease noise pollution

(iii) (a) 1 can be inferred from the extract but 2 cannot.

(iv) (b) 1 and 3

(v) Alliteration

(vi) wreathing a band of flowers to help us stay connected to the Earth.

5. "Such the Sun, the Moon,
Trees old and young, sprouting a shady boon
For simple sheep; and such are daffodils
With the green world they live in; and clear rills
That for themselves a cooling covert make
'Gainst the hot season.'

(i) Which of these provide joy and respite in the hot season?

(a) Shades of trees in forests
(b) Daffodils
(c) Clear water streams
(d) Both (a) and (c)

(ii) Identify the phrase from the extract that suggests the following

'All living beings'

(iii) Describe the role of clear rills.

(a) Cool and clear streams
(b) Cooling shelter
(c) Flowing in green surroundings
(d) Getting away our thirst

(iv) Complete the following analogy. Do not use the same example.

Sprouting a shady boon : Consonance : :
.... : Alliteration

(v) On the basis of the extract, choose the correct option with reference to (1) and (2) given below.

(1) Poet is a nature lover.

(2) Nature has healing quatities.

(a) (1) is true (2) is false
(b) (2) is true (1) is false
(c) (2) is the reason for (1)
(d) Both (1) and (2) are true

(vi) Fill in the blank appropriately.

The function of daffodils as in mentioned in the extract is ....

Ans. (i) (d) Both (a) and (c)

(ii) 'simple sheep

(iii) (b) Cooling shelter

(iv) Cooling covert/Simple sheep

(v) (d) Both (1) and (2) are true

(vi) to beautify the Earth and it lively

6. We have imagined for the mighty dead;
All lovely tales that we have heard or read;
An endless fountain of immortal drink,
Pouring unto us from the heaven's brink.

(i) Who are 'mighty dead'?

(ii) The phrase 'immortal drink' refers to ....

(a) blessings of our ancestors
(b) the teachings of nature
(c) a life giving force
(d) the beauty of heaven

(iii) Complete the sentence suitably.

The poem concludes with a powerful image of beauty as an 'endless fountain' of ....

(iv) Select the correct option from those given in brackets to fill in the blank.

In the concluding couplet, Keats uses the metaphor of a fountain to describe beauty. He portrays beauty as a continuous and eternal source (endless) of something spiritually .... (constructive/ enriching).

(v) **Read the Assertion and the Reason below, with reference to the given extract.**

Assertion The metaphor suggests that beauty nourishes the soul, akin to an everlasting flow of divine elixir.

Reason Keats continues the metaphor by depicting beauty as flowing from the very edge or brink of heaven itself.

Choose the correct option regarding their relationship.

(a) Both the Assertion and the Reason are true and the Reason is the correct explanation of the Assertion.
(b) Both the Assertion and the Reason are true, but the Reason is not the correct explanation of the Assertion.
(c) The Assertion is true, but the Reason is false.
(d) The Assertion is false, but the Reason is true.

(vi) **Comment on the concluding couplet of the poem.**

Ans. (i) 'Mighty dead' refers to revered individuals from history or mythology who are celebrated for greatness. Their stories and legends often portray them in a grand or noble light, elevating them to a status of reverence and admiration.

(ii) (c) a life giving force

(iii) inspiration and sustenance

(iv) enriching

(v) (b) Both the Assertion and the Reason are true, but the Reason is not the correct explanation of the Assertion.

(vi) In the concluding couplet of the poem, Keats uses the metaphor of a fountain to describe beauty in it. He portrays beauty as a continuous and eternal source of something spiritually enriching. This metaphor suggests that beauty nourishes the soul, akin to an everlasting flow of a divine elixir. This imagery also suggests that it originates from a celestial realm. The phrase 'pouring unto us' reinforcing the idea of its continuous and generous outpouring.

Short Answer Type Questions

1. How does a thing of beauty provide shelter and comfort? CBSE 2022 Term II

Ans. A thing of beauty provides shelter and comfort in many ways. It is like a bower, a place under the shade of a tree where we can rest. The small streams of cool and clear water, and the green forests around make it a comfortable place for us to rest. Thus, it gives us sweet dreams, peace and joy.

2. How would man suffer in the absence of beauty?

Ans. In the absence of beauty, man would suffer from sorrow and despair. It would be difficult for him to bounce back and he would have nothing to look forward to or draw strength from. Beauty lifts the pall of sadness and rejuvenates him. It lifts his spirit and fills his life with liveliness and hope.

3. What does a thing of beauty do for us? CBSE 2015

Ans. A thing of beauty adds endless joy to our life and helps us to come out of sadness and hopelessness. The memory of such a thing gives us everlasting happiness. It not only provides a pleasant and quiet place to relax but also makes life worth living in spite of despondence, inhuman dearth of nobel natures, gloomy days, unhealthy and over darkened ways.

4. 'And such too is the grandeur of the dooms; we have imagined for the mighty dead.' Explain the inference you can draw from the phrase 'mighty dead'. CBSE 2024

Ans. 'The mighty dead' refers to individuals renowned for their courageous and noble acts. Their legacies persist through tales and legends, serving as a wellspring of inspiration and beauty. Their virtuous lives promise eventual reward, symbolised by the 'grandeur' awaiting them on doomsday or judgement day, as acknowledgement of their noble deeds.

5. If you were given an opportunity to share your perception of beauty, what would you say? Explain. CBSE Question Bank 2021

Ans. Beauty for me is found in moments of peace and connection-whether in nature's tranquility, a kind gesture, or the simple, quiet joys of life. The concept of beauty can be different for everyone. One can even find beauty in the unwanted weeds or the humming of the bees if wanted.

6. 'Beauty is best left undefined.' Support your position on this statement with your rationale, coupled with ideas in the poem. Competency Based

Ans. It is true that beauty is best left undefined because the concept of beauty is unique for everyone. There are so many concepts, ideas and sources of beauty that is cannot be conceptualised or defined under one quality or aspect. One concrete thing that can, however, he said about beauty is that it is permanent and healing.
It never dies away but it brings peace, happiness, and joy in lives of people.

7. Artists, singers and musicians have a different perception of beauty as compared to people who are in other professions. Comment. Competency Based

Ans. It is true that the concept of beauty differs for each individual. An artist can experience the feelings associated with beauty while looking at a scenery which can act as an inspiration to them. In contrast, for singers or musicians beauty can be achieved with perfect melody which brings a peak experience or epiphany. Beauty is something that we perceive and respond to.
It brings a kind of experience, an aesthetic that is a response to the thing's representational qualities, whether it is man-made or natural.

8. **Rationalise why Keats uses the metaphor 'an endless fountain of immortal drink' in his poem, 'A Thing of Beauty'.** CBSE SQP 2023, CBSE 2022 Term II

Ans. Keats uses the metaphor 'an endless fountain of immortal drink' in his poem 'A Thing of Beauty', to state how all things of beauty are just like the immortal drink of the gods that flow continuously and never die. Further, just as the endless fountain of immortality is an elixir of life, similarly things of beauty are constant in providing everlasting joy, motivation and bliss in our lives.

9. **Comment on the tone of the poem 'A Thing of Beauty'.**

Ans. The tone of 'A Thing of Beauty' is optimistic, contemplative and celebratory. In the poem, Keats approaches the subject of beauty with a sense of wonder and reverence. He deeply appreciates the beauty he describes and its power to uplift and inspire the human spirit. While acknowledging life's challenges, the tone remains hopeful, suggesting that beauty can alleviate darkness and despair.

10. **Keats employs rich imagery to evoke a sense of beauty's diverse manifestations and its profound effects. Substantiate.**

Ans. Keats employs rich imagery to evoke a sense of beauty's diverse manifestations and its profound effects. The poem uses various symbols, including the Sun, the moon, trees, daffodils, clear rills and musk-rose blooms. These symbols represent the interconnectedness of nature, the comfort it provides, and its role in nourishing the human spirit.

11. **Keats celebrates the enduring, transformative and healing power of beauty. Comment.**

Ans. In 'A Thing of Beauty', Keats celebrates the enduring, transformative, and healing power of beauty in its various forms-both in the natural world and in stories that capture the essence of human experience. The poem emphasises that encountering beauty can offer solace, comfort, and a connection to something larger than oneself, ultimately contributing to a more enriched and meaningful life.

12. **What role does imagination play in the poem?** Competency Based

Ans. Imagination plays a role in the poem by highlighting the beauty of reality and imagination. The 'lovely tales' and 'grandeur of the dooms' represent the imaginative aspect of beauty that captivates the human mind and transcends ordinary existence.

13. **'And such too is the grandeur of dooms.' How can 'grandeur of dooms' be impressive and inspiring according to Keats?** CBSE 2025

Or **Rich with a sprinkling of fair musk-rose blooms.**
And such too is the grandeur of the dooms
Why is the grandeur of the dooms being compared to musk-rose blooms in 'A Thing of Beauty'? Answer in 20–30 words. Competency Based

Or **How is beauty seen in the grandeur of the dooms?** CBSE 2025

Ans. Keats describes the grandeur of dooms as impressive and inspiring because even in death, noble souls leave behind a legacy of bravery and greatness. Their sacrifices and struggles become eternal, inspiring future generations to find beauty in their actions and the lessons they impart.

14. ***A thing of beauty is a joy for ever:***
Its loveliness increases; it will never
Pass into nothingness; but still will keep
A bower quiet for us,

Why does the poet refer to 'a bower' in these lines from 'A Thing of Beauty'. Answer in 20-30 words. Competency Based

Ans. A 'bower' refers to a quiet leafy shelter away from the noise and turmoil of life. The poet refers to 'a bower' because just like beautiful things, bowers provide comfort and safety to those who take shelter under its leafy roof.

Long Answer Type Questions

1. **'A thing of beauty is a joy forever.' This is what John Keats says in the poem. Do you think in the present times of acute stress and violence, proximity to beautiful things can lead man to everlasting happiness? Discuss.** Competency Based

Or **In what way do the things of Beauty leave a lasting impression on us?** CBSE 2022 Term II

Ans. A thing of beauty gives us permanent happiness. When we look at objects of beauty, we feel happy and the lasting impression that such objects leave on our mind continues to give us pleasure even when they are no longer in our sight. In the present times of acute stress and fears, the objects of beauty attain even greater significance. When our mind is anxious and troubled, the very sight of beautiful things often comes as a relief and provides us comfort and happiness for the moment.

Appreciating beautiful things is like appreciating God who has bestowed them upon mankind as a gift so that we can derive happiness and solace from them. Proximity to beautiful things brings us closer to the creator in whom lies the ultimate power to grant us relief from all anxieties and troubles.

Therefore, it is sure to bring everlasting happiness at all times.

2. You are a blogger who loves to record travel stories. You recently visited a picturesque location and you were enamoured by its beauty. Pen down the post for your blog giving vivid descriptions of the natural beauty of this place. Supplement your writing with Keats' ideas about beauty. **CBSE Question Bank 2021**

Ans. Keats had correctly said that 'a thing of beauty is a joy forever'.

I really felt it yesterday when I was trekking across the Himalayan ranges.

My group leader wanted to take us to a hidden location near our base. Initially, we were suspicious but soon came across something so picturesque that its beauty cannot be expressed in words. The detour from the occasional trekking took us to a lakeside where innumerable birds had flocked to drink water.

The small lake in the middle of the forest surrounded by wild flowers and daffodils flowing in the wind is an image I can never forget. The clear water was shining as the sun was almost overhead us.

The majestic view filled me with pleasure and all the tiredness we felt faded almost instantaneously. The peace and serenity of the place was almost non broken except for the occasional cooings and chirrups of the birds. How I wish I could have stayed there longer if not forever, away from the rush of modern life.

3. How does Keats' poem, 'A Thing of Beauty' appeal richly to the senses, stimulating the reader's inner sight as well as the sense of touch and smell? Write your answer in about 120-150 words. **CBSE SQP, CBSE 2022 Term II**

Ans. It is truly said that Keats' poem, 'A Thing of Beauty' appeal richly to the senses stimulating the reader's inner sight as well as the sense of touch and smell. His descriptions allow for a deeper perception of the imaginary.

Everything he says in his poems can be converted into a life-like experience allowing the reader to experience exactly what he wants to convey.

In the poem, Keats establishes his idea of beauty in everything around us with powerful imagery and word play. The cooling comfort of the bower, the dancing daffodils in its green environment, the babbling stream and the mid-forest brake with the musk rose blooms evoke our imagination.

As readers, we can imagine ourselves in such a setup with sense of hearing, touch and smell. We can hear the sounds of the scene, smell the flowers and even feel like we are in the middle of nature.

Even the stories of mighty ancestors and the doom that befalls them appeals to our intellect as we can relate to the innumerable stories we have read or heard.

The endless fountain may be an allusion of the fountain of youth. One can imagine the fountain as rain that falls on our planet. Thus, Keats poetic descriptions presents beauty that appeals to our senses and gives delight.

4. ..... but will keep
A bower quiet for us.
Perhaps the Earth can teach us
as when everything seems dead
and later proves to be alive.

Based on ideas from 'Keeping Quiet' and 'A Thing of Beauty', as President of Eco Club of your school, draft a speech on the importance of preserving nature for the benefit of mankind.

You may begin like this.
Good morning to one and all!
After reading both the poems, I strongly believe …………….. **Competency Based, CBSE 2024**

Ans. Good morning to one and all!

After reading both the poem titled 'Keeping Quiet' by Pablo Neruda and 'A Thing of Beauty' by John Keats, I strongly believe in the importance of preserving nature for the benefit of mankind. Nature, as well know, has often been associated with healing qualities. It brings peace, solace and calmness to one and all while teaching us to take a breather between tasks to grow effectively. The poems present exactly these aspects of nature.

The poem 'A Thing of Beauty' shows how nature heals us from the modern world full of negativities. It keeps a 'bower' quiet for us to relax and enjoy our surroundings. The serenity of the bower heals us not just physically but also mentally.

The poem 'Keeping Quiet' teaches us that there is life under apparent stillness. Earth shows us how a seed takes times to grow into a sapling. When a seed is sown, it seems that no activity is going on and the Earth is dead. However, in reality, the seed is maturing to become sapling. Just like the Earth, we also need to be still and relax to grow and work for our survival.

Thus, by preserving nature, we are preserving not only our planet but also ourselves all the while becoming a better version of ourselves.

Thank You.

5. The poem 'The Thing of Beauty' embodies Romantic ideals by celebrating the sublime in nature and art and the individual's emotional and imaginative experiences. Comment. **Competency Based**

Ans. The poem 'A Thing of Beauty' falls under the genre of Romantic poetry. It exhibits characteristics of Romanticism, such as an emphasis on emotion, nature, imagination and subjective experience. The poem reflects the Romantic belief in the power of nature and beauty to inspire and elevate the human soul.

(i) **Beauty and Permanence** The poem revolves around the enduring quality of beauty. Keats suggests that true beauty is everlasting, bringing joy and solace to individuals regardless of time and circumstance.

(ii) **Nature's Influence** To exemplify beauty, Keats uses natural elements like the Sun, moon, trees and flowers. Nature is depicted as a source of inspiration and a means of connecting with the eternal.

(iii) **Human Response to Beauty** The poem explores how humans respond to beauty, portraying it as a balm for the soul. Keats suggests that beauty can counteract negativity and uplift human spirits.

(iv) **Escapism and Imagination** Beauty serves as a means of escape from the hardships of life. The idea that beauty can create a 'bower quiet' and a 'sleep / full of sweet dreams' indicates its role in providing an alternate, more positive reality.

(v) **The Power of Art** Through the reference to 'lovely tales that we have heard or read,' the poem highlights the role of literature and art in conveying beauty and inspiration. These creations are portrayed as avenues through which beauty is shared and experienced.

In essence, 'A Thing of Beauty' explores the relationship between beauty, nature, human emotion and the enduring impact of aesthetic experiences. Keats elevates the idea of beauty to a spiritual and transformative force that enriches human existence.

6. In the poem 'A Thing of Beauty', the poet has mentioned several attributes of beautiful things. Write about one beautiful thing/ relationship/experience from your life and describe any two of its attributes. Answer in 100–120 words. **Competency Based**

Ans. In the poem 'A Thing of Beauty', the poet has mentioned several attributes of beautiful things. According to the poet, all beautiful things have an everlasting goodness and they have the power to heal.

The most beautiful gift in my life is the relationship that I have with my mother. I have understood what unconditional and everlasting love is from my mother. Despite all of my ungratefulness and shortcomings, she never ceases to support and love me. In fact, it's in my moments of desolation that she comforts me all the more.

It's this unconditional love that heals and strengthens me from all of my mental and emotional afflictions. The love of a mother is healing to the soul and my mother's love nourishes my soul. It is my most powerful thing of beauty.

7. Why are things of beauty not fleeting pleasures, according to the poet of 'A Thing of Beauty'? How does this relate to the imagery of 'an endless fountain of immortal drink'? Answer in 100–120 words. **Competency Based**

Ans. Beautiful things are not fleeting pleasures because the poet suggests that a thing of beauty brings endless joy. Its beauty never fades; it only becomes more beautiful with time. Whenever we are sad or disappointed, it is a thing of beauty that heals and comforts us.

The poet considers all things of beauty as an endless fountain of immortality. This means that all the beautiful things in our world will always remain beautiful and continue to give us joy forever.
They do not provide temporal happiness. Just as water gives life to earth, beautiful things inspire human beings to live.

8. 'Nature is the best companion to man.' In the light of above quote, analyse the themes of 'A Thing of Beauty' and 'Keeping Quiet'. **CBSE 2025**

Ans. Both 'A Thing of Beauty' by John Keats and 'Keeping Quiet' by Pablo Neruda emphasise nature's role as man's best companion, offering beauty, peace, and wisdom.

In 'A Thing of Beauty', Keats highlights how nature provides endless joy and solace. The beauty of trees, clear streams, and the sun serves as a refuge from life's hardships, nurturing both physical and emotional well-being. Keats believes that nature's beauty is eternal, offering an escape from despair and negativity.
Similarly, in 'Keeping Quiet', Neruda presents nature as a teacher that guides humanity toward introspection and harmony. He urges mankind to pause, reflect, and learn from nature's stillness. By observing nature's quiet cycles, humans can understand the importance of coexistence, peace and self-awareness.

SELF ASSESSMENT TEST

Extract Based Questions

Read the extract given below and answer the following questions.

1. A thing of beauty is a joy forever
Its loveliness increases, it will never
Pass into nothingness; but will keep
A bower quiet for us, and a sleep
Full of sweet dreams, and health, and quiet breathing.
Therefore, on every morrow, are we wreathing
A flowery band to bind us to the Earth

(i) Why do we need sweet dreams, health and quiet breathing in our lives?

(ii) Choose the option that displays the same poetic device as used in the first line of the extract.

(a) I'm as happy as I can be.
(b) Life is a roller coaster ride.
(c) Nature is God's gift to us.
(d) The dazzling divas enchanted all.

(iii) Complete the sentence suitably.

When the poet says that 'a thing of beauty' will never pass into nothingness, he means that it is ....

(iv) Select the correct option from those given in brackets, to fill in the blank.

The phrase 'a bower quiet' indicates .... (serenity/morality)

(v) On the basis of the extract, choose the correct option with reference to the two statements given below.

1. We are surrounded by beautiful things.

2. Beautiful things provide us joy.

Codes

(a) 1 can be inferred from the extract but 2 cannot.
(b) 2 can be inferred from the extract but 1 cannot.
(c) Both 1 and 2 can be inferred from the extract.
(d) 2 is the reason for 1 and can be inferred from the extract.

(vi) How does the poet bring out the healing quality of nature in the given lines?

Short Answer Type Questions

Answer the following questions in 40-50 words.

1. Comment on the allusion to classics and historical legends.

2. How does the poem describe the lasting nature of beauty?

3. The poem connects beauty with immortality. Elaborate.

4. What are the qualities of a thing of beauty according to the speaker?

Long Answer Type Questions

Answer the following questions in 120-150 words.

1. Justify the title of the poem 'A Thing of Beauty'.

2. Do we experience things of beauty only for short moments or do they make a lasting impression? Explain. **CBSE 2023**

04

About the Poet

Robert Frost (1874-1963), an iconic American poet, masterfully captured nature's essence and the human experience through his verses. Frost's distinct style blends simplicity with profound meaning, using rural settings to delve into universal truths.

YOUR STUDY GOALS

- Central Idea of The Poem
- Explanation of the Poem

YOUR PRACTICE GOAL

- NCERT Folder
- Extract Based Questions
- Short Answer Type Questions
- Long Answer Type Questions

A Roadside Stand

Central Idea of the Poem

The poem 'A Roadside Stand' revolves around rural struggle and urban neglect, critiquing the urban-rural disparities. It highlights societal neglect, unfulfilled promises, and rural isolation, contrasting urban affluence with rural hardship. The poem portrays the desperation of rural folk who run a roadside stand, hoping for city money to improve their lives. However, they often face indifference or exploitation from passing urbanites. The poem also reflects on the longing for relief from suffering, whether the rural dwellers' longing for economic stability or the speaker's contemplation of the ultimate release from pain. It explores economic inequality, societal neglect and the yearning for a better life.

Explanation of the Poem

Stanza 1

The little old house was out with a little new shed
In front at the edge of the road where the traffic sped,
A roadside stand that too pathetically pled,
It would not be fair to say for a dole of bread,
But for some of the money, the cash, whose flow supports
The flower of cities from sinking and withering faint.
The polished traffic passed with a mind ahead,
Or if ever aside a moment, then out of sorts

At having the landscape marred with the artless paint
Of signs that with N turned wrong and S turned wrong
Offered for sale wild berries in wooden quarts,
Or crook-necked golden squash with silver warts,
Or beauty rest in a beautiful mountain scene,
You have the money, but if you want to be mean,
Why keep your money (this crossly) and go along.

Exp. On the roadside, there is an old house which has an extended shed. This shed is extended towards the edge of the road so that the fast moving vehicles speeding by may notice and stop there to buy the food and refreshments sold there. This shed made a pitiable sight. It seemed desperate and in need of financial help or money so that the rural folk could sustain themselves.

The poor feel that the money the rich spend to adorn their gardens with flowers can be used to better the lot of the less privileged. But the rich people passed by without paying any attention to the shed. If anyone cared to stop, it was only due to the irritation at the paint and decor that spoiled the picturesque scenery of the area. Also, the shed had a board on which the word STAND was painted such that the letters S and N were written in reverse displaying the illiteracy and carelessness of the local people.

This shed sold wild berries in wooden boxes and gourds with twisted necks. Besides these things, the place also offered a stay in the scenic surroundings. The poet then mentions that the poor feel that the rich who passed by the place had the money but had no desire to spend it. They wanted to keep the money with themselves.

Stanza 2

The hurt to the scenery wouldn't be my complaint
So much as the trusting sorrow of what is unsaid:
Here far from the city we make our roadside stand
And ask for some city money to feel in hand
To try if it will not make our being expand,
And give us the life of the moving-pictures' promise
That the party in power is said to be keeping from us.

Exp. The poet does not want to accuse the rural folk of marring the beauty of the landscape. He is more worried about the untold pain suffered by the people belonging to the countryside. These people have installed a roadside stand so far away in the countryside just to earn some hard cash. They long to have a comfortable lifestyle as depicted in movies. They hope against hope that the city citizens may fulfill the promise of giving them economic independence that the party in power is not providing them.

Stanza 3

It is in the news that all these pitiful kin
Are to be bought out and mercifully gathered in
To live in villages, next to the theatre and the store,
Where they won't have to think for themselves anymore,
While greedy good-doers, beneficent beasts of prey,
Swarm over their lives enforcing benefits
That are calculated to soothe them out of their wits,
And by teaching them how to sleep they sleep all day,
Destroy their sleeping at night the ancient way.

Exp. It is in the news that these rural people are to be relocated to places where they will have all comforts. They will enjoy privileges of the theatre and the local store just like their urban counterparts. These people will be so busy in enjoying these comforts that they will have no time to think about themselves or fight for their rights.

However, in the garb of benefits that they will provide, the city people will exploit them. Later, these privileged people will easily forget the promises they made, leaving these poor people more impoverished. Further, the changes introduced by the city people would make the rural people less aware and active. As a result, the rural folk would not only be impoverished but would also lose their traditional ways of life and values.

Stanza 4

Sometimes I feel myself I can hardly bear
The thought of so much childish longing in vain,
The sadness that lurks near the open window there,
That waits all day in almost open prayer
For the squeal of brakes, the sound of a stopping car,
Of all the thousand selfish cars that pass,
Just one to inquire what a farmer's prices are.
And one did stop, but only to plow up grass
In using the yard to back and turn around;
And another to ask the way to where it was bound;
And another to ask could they sell it a gallon of gas
They couldn't (this crossly); they had none, didn't it see?

Exp. The poet is very disturbed and feels very helpless when he sees their childish longing for money which is never fulfilled. These people keep their windows open all day as if in prayer waiting desperately and uselessly for someone to stop at the stand. Out of thousands of cars passing by, just one stopped only to inquire the prices of things sold there. Another stopped just to use the backyard of the place to reverse their car. Another car stopped just to inquire about the directions for where it wanted to go. The fourth stopped to know if they could sell them a gallon of gas (petrol).

The farmer grumbles in an angry manner that they could see for themselves that it was not sold there.

Stanza 5

No, in country money, the country scale of gain,
The requisite lift of spirit has never been found,
Or so the voice of the country seems to complain,
I can't help owning the great relief it would be
To put these people at one stroke out of their pain.
And then next day as I come back into the sane,
I wonder how I should like you to come to me
And offer to put me gently out of my pain.

Exp. Finally, the poet bemoans that lack of financial independence and economic progress in rural life. As a result, there is a collective dissatisfaction and complain regarding the lack of improvement in the countryside. The poet strongly feels that the countryside people should be freed from the pain of poverty and deprivation. Next morning, when the poet gains his senses, he wonders what if someone else thinks in the same manner for him so that he is gently relieved from his pain and agony of seeing the miserable condition of these people.

Word-Meaning

pathetically pled	—	pitifully begs
dole	—	donation
polished traffic	—	well off and sophisticated city dwellers who pass by
artless paint of	—	poorly painted
quarts	—	containers
crook-necked	—	twisted-necked
silver warts	—	silver lumps on them
hurt to the scenery	—	harm caused to the natural scenery
trusting sorrow	—	The rural people trust their rich brothers in cities to help them, but feel sad when their trust is breached by the city people through their indifference.
moving-pictures	—	films
beneficent beasts of prey	—	Men in power are beasts of prey in the garb of benefactors. They exploit common people for their vested interests.
selfish cars	—	selfish owners of the cars

Literary devices used in the Poem

- **Tone** Reflective and melancholic
- **Rhyme Scheme** The poem is not in free verse but has no set rhyme scheme
- **Metaphor** The stand is a metaphor for economic challenges, serves as a plea for support from the urban population.
  Stanza 2, line 17 'trusting sorrow' (indicates the trust and hope of the rural folk)
- **Alliteration** *Stanza 1, Line 3* 'pathetically pled' (repetition of 'p' sound)
  Stanza 3 Line 27 'Greedy good doers' and 'Beneficent Beasts' (repetition of 'g' and 'b' sounds)
- **Transferred epithet** *Stanza 1, Line 7* 'polished traffic' (the word polished actually refers to the city folk)
  Stanza 4, Line 37 'selfish cars' (the word 'selfish' is used for city people)
- **Oxymoron** *Stanza 3 Line 27* 'Greedy good doers' and 'Beneficent Beasts'
- **Personification** *Stanza 1, Line 3* 'A roadside stand that too pathetically'

NCERT Folder

Think it Out (NCERT Page 99)

1. The city folk who drove through the countryside hardly paid any heed to the roadside stand or to the people who ran it. If at all they did, it was to complain. Which lines bring this out? What was their complaint about?

Ans. The following lines bring out the complaining attitude of the city people who drove by the shed in the countryside.

'............. then out of sorts'

At having the landscape marred with the artless paint.

'Of signs that with N turned wrong and S turned wrong'.

The complaint of these passers-by was that the artless paint was spoiling the pristine beauty of the landscape. They were displeased that the board out there had signs of N and S pointing in the wrong directions. Moreover, they were critical of wild berries being sold in wooden containers.

2. What was the plea of the folk who had put up the roadside stand?

Ans. The folks who had put up the roadside stand wanted the passers-by to stop and buy the berries or the squash which they were selling. They wanted some ready cash, with which they could improve their lot and better their miserable lives.

3. The government and other social service agencies appear to help the poor rural people, but actually do them no good. Pick out the words and phrases that the poet uses to show their double standards.

Ans. The government and the party in power were least interested in the welfare of these poor rural people. Even the social service agencies were doing nothing for them.

They did things only to fulfill their own vested interests. The words and phrases which show their double standards are 'greedy good doers', 'beneficent beasts of prey', 'swam over their lives', 'enforcing benefits', 'calculated', 'to soothe them out of their wits.'

4. What is the 'childish longing' that the poet refers to? Why is it 'vain'?

Ans. 'Childish longing' literally means to want and wait for something without putting logic on it. The longing is, in a way, innocent. By using this phrase, the poet refers to the longing of the people running the roadside stand who are always waiting for prospective customers.

They keep their windows open to attract customers and become sad when nobody turns up. They hope that some car will stop there but their wait goes in 'vain' when they see that people come either to turn their cars or to ask where the way goes.

5. Which lines tell us about the insufferable pain that the poet feels at the thought of the plight of the rural poor?

Ans. The poet intensely feels that all the miserable pain from which the poor rustics suffer must be removed at one stroke. The following lines express his feelings.

'I can't help owning the great relief it would be,
To put these people at one stroke out of their pain'.

Exam Pattern Questions

Extract Based Questions

Read the extracts given below and answer the following questions.

**1. The little old house was out with a little new shed
In front at the edge of the road where the traffic sped
A road side stand that too pathetically pled
It would not be fair to say for a dole of bread.
But for some of the money, the cash, whose flow supports
The flower of cities from sinking and withering faint.**

CBSE 2024

(i) Which of the following expressions has the same literary device as used in

"A roadside stand that too pathetically pled".

(a) All the world's a stage.
(b) I wandered lonely, as a cloud.
(c) The brutal wind bullied the tree.
(d) And life is too much like a pathless wood.

(ii) Select the option that aptly conveys the poet's point of view with reference to the above extract.

The roadside stand is put up with the purpose to

(a) display fruits
(b) to stop the traffic
(c) to do business
(d) to interact with city people

(iii) What do you infer about the people, who put up the roadside stand from the phrase 'would not be fair to say for a dole of bread'?

(iv) Complete the following sentence with reference to the extract.

The word 'pathetically' reflects the .... condition of the roadside stand.

(v) State whether the following statement is True or False.

By 'Flower of Cities', the poet refers to the garden in cities.

(vi) Based on the rhyme scheme, evident in lines 1-4, which word would rhyme with line 2?

(a) Part (b) Fled (c) Seen

Ans. (i) (c) The brutal wind bullied the tree.

(ii) (c) to do business

(iii) From the phrase 'would not be fair to say for a dole of bread', it can be inferred that the people who put up the roadside stand were not begging but were selling something to earn money to buy some food.

(iv) the desperate and sad

(v) False, The term 'Flower of Cities' symbolises the prosperity and richness of city life, not referring to an actual garden.

(vi) (b) Fled

2. In front at the edge of the road where the traffic sped,
A roadside stand that too pathetically pled,
It would not be fair to say for a dole of bread,
But for some of the money, the cash, whose flow supports
The flower of cities from sinking and withering faint.
The polished traffic passed with a mind ahead,
Or if ever aside a moment, then out of sorts
At having the landscape marred with the artless paint
Of signs that with N turned wrong and S turned wrong

CBSE 2023

(i) What is the tone of the poet in the extract?

(a) Optimistic
(b) Resigned
(c) Sympathetic
(d) Indifferent

(ii) With reference to the given extract, what harm has been caused by the 'artless paint'?

(iii) The city is compared to ....

(a) a landscape (b) signs of N and S
(c) a flower (d) a dole of bread

(iv) The roadside stand is ....

(a) at the edge of the road (b) marred with artless paint
(c) like the flower of cities (d) well-maintained

(v) What type of expectations do the stand owners have from the city dwellers who come there?

(vi) Complete the analogy with a word from the given extract.

Donate : Contribute : : Dying : ....

Ans. (i) (c) Sympathetic

(ii) The 'artless paint' of the roadside stand harms or disrupts the beauty of the landscape.

(iii) (c) a flower

(iv) (a) at the edge of the road.

(v) The stand owners wanted the city dwellers to stop and buy their wares so as to enable them to earn some extra money for a decent living.

(vi) Withering

3. "Offered for sale wild berries in wooden quarts,
Or crook-necked golden squash with silver warts,
Or beauty rest in a beautiful mountain scene,
You have the money, but if you want to be mean,
Why keep your money (this crossly) and go along."

(i) What is the meaning of 'beauty rest in a beautiful mountain scene'?

(ii) What articles are 'offered for sale' at the stand?

(a) Wooden containers of wild berries
(b) Golden squash or gourd
(c) Paintings of mountain scenery
(d) Both (a) and (b)

(iii) Complete the sentence appropriately.

The phrase 'this crossly' is given in brackets to ....

(iv) Select the correct option from those given in bracket to fill in the blank.

The poor people of the roadside stand feel .... (dejected and angry/cheated and irritates) when city people decline to buy anything.

(v) On the basis of the extract, choose the correct option with reference to the two statements given below.

1. The rural people hoped to earn some money from the roadside stand.

2. For the rural people, the people belonging to the city are mean and miserly.

(a) (1) can be inferred from the extract but (2) cannot.
(b) (2) can be inferred from the extract but (1) cannot
(c) Both (1) and (2) can be inferred from the extract
(d) (2) is the reason for (1) and can be inferred from the extract

(vi) What qualities of the offered articles make then unfit for sale?

Ans. (i) The given expression indicates that the roadstand owners were selling even the beautiful scenery by allowing the city folk a place to stay.
(ii) (d) Both (a) and (b)
(iii) highlight and emphasise on the cruel nature of city people.
(iv) dejected and angry
(v) (c) Both (1) and (2) can be inferred from the extract
(vi) The qualities of the articles offered at the stand were considered unfit for sale because they were grown in wildness and did not look polished.

4. **"The hurt to the scenery wouldn't be my complaint
So much as the trusting sorrow of what is unsaid:
Here far from the city we make our roadside stand
And ask for some city money to feel in hand
To try if it will not make our being expand,
And give us the life of the moving-pictures' promise
That the party in power is said to be keeping from us."**

(i) Identify the phrase from the extract, that suggests the following.
The scenes of upliftment and financial betterment that are seen in films and movies.

(ii) What was the promise made by the government?
(a) To give a lavishing home to local people of the village
(b) To provide basic drinking and water facility
(c) To provide subsidy to the poor
(d) To give a comfortable life to the poor people

(iii) Fill in the blank appropriately.
In the extract, 'hurt to the scenery' implies ....

(iv) Select the correct option from those given in bracket, to fill in the blank.
The roadside stand is set in a seemingly simple setting as a .... (microcosm/symbol) that reflects more prominent societal and economic themes.

(v) Read the Assertion and the Reason below, with reference to the given extract.

Assertion 'A Roadside Stand' powerfully conveys the conflict between city and country life, economic differences, and the desire for understanding and help.

Reason The poem uses vivid images, contrasting themes, and a thoughtful voice.

Choose the correct option regarding their relationship.
(a) Both the Assertion and the Reason are true and the Reason is the correct explanation of the Assertion.
(b) Both the Assertion and the Reason are true, but the Reason is not the correct explanation of the Assertion.
(c) The Assertion is true, but the Reason is false.
(d) The Assertion is false, but the Reason is true.

(vi) Do you think that the promise made by the government was fulfilled?

Ans. (i) Moving pictures promise
(ii) (d) To give a comfortable life to the poor people
(iii) harm caused to the natural scenery
(iv) microcosm
(v) (b) Both the Assertion and the Reason are true, but the Reason is not the correct explanation of the Assertion.
(vi) No, I do not think that the promise made by the government was fulfilled.

5. **It is in the news that all these pitiful kin
Are to be bought out and mercifully gathered in
To live in villages, next to the theatre and the store,
Where they won't have to think for themselves anymore,
While greedy good-doers, beneficent beasts of prey,
Swarm over their lives enforcing benefits
That are calculated to soothe them out of their wits,
And by teaching them how to sleep they sleep all day,
Destroy their sleeping at night the ancient way.** **CBSE 2025**

(i) The expression 'It is in the news' suggests
(a) it is good news for the roadside stand owners
(b) an important decision has been taken by the government
(c) the roadside stand owners have protested against the government
(d) that the news was not there in the newspaper

(ii) Read the Assertion and the Reason below, with reference to the given extract.

Assertion The poet complains that the rural people are exploited by the people in power.

Reason The rural people reposed blind faith in the false promises of the people in power.

Choose the correct option regarding their relationship.

(a) Both the Assertion and the Reason are true, and the Reason is the correct explanation.
(b) Both the Assertion and the Reason are true but the Reason is not the correct explanation of the Assertion.
(c) The Assertion is false, but the Reason is true.
(d) The Assertion is true, but the Reason is false.

(iii) Complete the following suitably

In the line "that revolted to soothe them out of their wits," the phrase soothe them out of their wits refers to ....

(iv) Bring out the irony in the expression 'they won't have to think for themselves'.

(v) Select the correct option

The poet uses the expression "greedy good-doers" to (criticise/appreciate) the intention of the powerful people.

(vi) Complete the following suitably.

The tone of the poet in the above extract is ....

Ans. (i) (b) an important decision has been taken by the government.
(ii) (a) Both the Assertion and the Reason are true and the Reason is the correct explanation.
(iii) deceiving the rural people by giving them false hopes and making them dependent on the so-called benefits
(iv) The irony in the expression 'they won't have to think for themselves' is that while the move is presented as a relief for the rural people, it actually takes away their independence, making them passive and completely dependent on the authorities.
(v) criticise
(vi) sarcastic and critical

6. While greedy good-doers, beneficent beasts of prey,
Swarm over their lives enforcing benefits
That are calculated to soothe them out of their wits, And
by teaching them how to sleep they sleep all day, Destroy
their sleeping at night the ancient way. CBSE SQP 2024

(i) Select the phrase that suggests the following.

The so-called aids are not offered out of genuine care or consent but are imposed in a controlling and perhaps unwelcome manner.

(ii) What does the imagery of 'swarm' not represent in the given extract?
(a) Coordinated help
(b) Overwhelming force
(c) Discomfort and chaos
(d) Neglect of individual needs

(iii) Complete the following suitably.

In the line, 'destroy their sleeping at night the ancient way,' the phrase 'the ancient way' refers to ....

(iv) Select the correct option from those given in bracket, to fill in the blank.

The poet has used phrases like 'greedy good-doers' and 'beneficent beasts of prey' to illustrate the .... (irony/satire) in the situation where those claiming to help the rural poor actually impose self-serving and detrimental actions on them.

(v) Read the assertion and the reason below, with reference to the given extract.

Assertion The poet criticises the way the rural poor are treated by benefactors, suggesting it instills ambition.

Reason The interventions are overwhelmingly calming and lead to a loss of critical thinking among the rural poor.

Choose the correct option regarding their relationship.
(a) Both the Assertion and the Reason are true and the Reason is the correct explanation of the Assertion.
(b) Both the Assertion and the Reason are true, but the Reason is not the correct explanation of the Assertion.
(c) The Assertion is true, but the Reason is false.
(d) The Assertion is false, but the Reason is true.

(vi) State in one sentence, what cautionary advice your address to the rural poor from the extract, is most likely to include.

Ans. (i) Enforcing benefits
(ii) (a) Coordinated help
(iii) the traditional and longstanding sleeping patterns and night time rituals that have been part of the rural community's lifestyle for generations.
(iv) irony
(v) (d) The Assertion is false, but the Reason is true.
(vi) The cautionary advice my address to the rural poor is most likely to include the following words.
Be careful/wary of involvements by outsiders that might appear benevolent. In the long run, they take away your freedom/autonomy and dull your critical thinking abilities.

7. Sometimes I feel myself I can hardly bear
The thought of so much childish longing
in vain, The sadness that lurks near the open window
there.
That waits all day in almost open prayer.

For the squeal of brakes, the sound of a stopping car,
Of all the thousand selfish cars that pass,
Just one to inquire what a farmer's prices are. **CBSE 2023**

(i) What is the sentiment expressed in the above extract?

(i) Remorse (ii) Regret
(iii) Empathy (iv) Disappointment
(v) Guilt

Choose the correct appropriate option.

(a) (iii) and (iv) (b) (ii) and (iii)
(c) (iv) and (v) (d) (i) and (v)

(ii) Identify the phrase in the extract that suggests 'innocent desires'.

(iii) The roadside stand owners pray for
(a) a relief from the heat
(b) free housing
(c) cars stopping
(d) benefits from pollution

(iv) Name the poetic device used in 'selfish cars'.

(v) State whether the given statement is True or False.

The people who have put up the roadside stand keep waiting for customers.

(vi) Fill the blank appropriately with reference to the extract.

'Squeal of brakes' implies ....

Ans. (i) (b) (ii) and (iii)
(ii) 'childish longings'
(iii) (c) cars stopping
(iv) Transferred epithet
(v) True
(vi) stopping of cars

8. Sometimes I feel myself I can hardly bear
The thought of so much childish longing in vain,
The sadness that lurks neat the open window there,
That waits all day in almost open prayer.
For the squeal of brakes, the sound of a stopping car,
Of all the thousand selfish cars that pass,
Just one to inquire what a farmer's prices are
And one did stop, but only to plow up grass
In using the yard to back and turn around;
And another to ask the way to where it was bound;
CBSE 2024

(i) Select the option that has the same literary device as in 'The sadness that lurks near the open window there'.
(a) Lucy moved across the room like a warship sailing into battle.
(b) Art washes away from the soul the dust of everyday life.
(c) The water-wraith was shrieking.
(d) The pen is mightier than the sword.

(ii) They prayed for the stopping of a car. When one car finally stepped, it brought .... to the people of the roadside stand.
(a) help (b) happiness
(c) disappointment (d) cash flow

(iii) Explain one inference that can be drawn from the line, '................. childish longing in vain'.

(iv) Complete the sentence appropriately.

The emotion of the poet reflected in the above extract is ....

(v) The expression 'selfish cars' suggests that ....

(vi) Based on the rhyme scheme evident in the last two lines of the extract, which word would rhyme with the last line?
(a) brass (b) reply (c) sound

Ans. (i) (c) The water - wraith was shrieking.
(ii) (c) disappointment
(iii) It can be inferred that the poet feels saddened by the road vendors' unfulfilled or unrewarded wish who wait in hopes that someone would stop at the roadside stand.
(iv) a sense of sadness and hopelessness
(v) the city people who drive cars don't have human characteristics just like the inanimate objects 'cars' and thus don't concerned themselves with the needs of the people at the roadside stand.
(vi) (c) Sound

9. No, in country money, the country scale of gain,
The requisite lift of spirit has never been found,
Or so the voice of the country seems to complain,
I can't help owning the great relief it would be
To put these people at one stroke out of their pain.
And then next day as
I come back into the sane, I wonder how
I should like you to come to me
And offer to put me gently out of my pain.
CBSE Question Bank 2021 Modified

(i) Who can help the rural people?

(ii) Pick the option that mentions elements justifying monetary aspect as the 'requisite lift of spirit'.

1. Confidence 2. Ego
3. Self-esteem 4. Status
5. Fame

(a) 1, 2 and 4
(b) 2, 4 and 5
(c) 1, 3 and 4
(d) 1, 3 and 5

(iii) The 'country money' contextually here refers to

(iv) Choose the option that correctly paraphrases the given lines from the above extract.

"I can't help owning the great relief it would be
To put these people at one stroke out of their pain."

(a) The poet wants to kill the impoverished people.
(b) The poet feels that death is better than living such a miserable life.
(c) The poet wants to eliminate poverty from the society.
(d) The poet states that it is important that these people become rich.

(v) Choose the correct option with respect to the two statements given below.

Statement 1 The poet is agitated and depressed.

Statement 2 The poet realises the futility of his thought about giving up.

(a) Statement (1) can be inferred but Statement (2) cannot be inferred.
(b) Statement (1) cannot be inferred but Statement (2) can be inferred.
(c) Statement (1) and Statement (2) can be inferred.
(d) Statement (1) and Statement (2) cannot be inferred.

(vi) Do you think that the poet blames the poor people for their lack of spirit to better their economic condition?

Ans (i) According to the poet, government, the city people and the influential people can help the rural people in bettering their conditions.

(ii) (d) 1, 3 and 5

(iii) meagre income earned by the countryside people.

(iv) (b) The poet feels that death is better than living such a miserable life.

(v) (b) Statement (1) cannot be inferred but Statement (2) can be inferred.

(vi) We cannot really state that the poet blames the poor people for their lack of spirit to better their economic condition. But he does bemoan the lack of such a spirit.

Short Answer Type Questions

1. Why does Robert Frost sympathise with the rural poor and is anguished at the plight of the stand owners?

Ans. The poet, Robert Frost, is anguished at the plight of the stand owner because they are not getting enough business, as the city cars donot stop at the stand to buy products. Even when they do, the passengers have their own selfish motives which donot help uplift the economic situation of the owner. Instead, it leaves them angry and disappointed.

2. What does the expression 'polished traffic' refer to? What does it reveal about city people? CBSE 2023

Ans. The expression 'polished traffic' refers to the cars and other vehicles that pass by the new shed at the edge of the road.

It reveals that city people are in a hurry and have little time to spare for the people living in the countryside. They are focused on their own lives and goals and do not help the poor country people who are in dire need of a little extra earning to better their life.

3. What are the two significant roles of money in the lives of the poor people?

Ans. In 'A Roadside Stand' money serves as a means of survival for the poor, enabling basic needs, and as a symbol of hope for escape or improvement. Though, ultimately it reflects societal indifference and exploitation by wealthier individuals.

4. What are the probable causes of the passing cars to stop near the roadside stand? CBSE 2020

Ans. The probable causes of passing cars to stop near the roadside stand are as follows

- To use the backyard of the place to reverse their car.
- To inquire about the directions for where they wanted to go.
- To know if the roadside seller could sell them a gallon of gas (petrol).

5. Near the end of the poem, why does the poet seek an unrealistic solution for the poor people's distress even though earlier he had blamed them for their 'childish longing in vain?'

Ans. The poet, unlike the greedy good-doers, genuinely wishes to get the poor people out of their pain, poverty and endless miseries. However, he is saddened by observing that there is no one to help them come out of their poverty. This helplessness drives the poet to seek an unrealistic solution for the poor people's misery.

6. Though money holds the same value everywhere, the poet draws a distinction between city money and country money. Elaborate. CBSE Question Bank 2021

Ans. Though money holds the same value everywhere, the poet draws a distinction between city money and country money. City money for the poet means living a life of luxury and fulfillment. However, country money is the money needed for survival.

7. The roadside stand and the moving cars are a contrast around which the entire poem is woven. Expound. CBSE Question Bank 2021

Ans. It is true that the roadside stand and the moving cars are a contrast around which the entire poem is woven. Throughout the poem, we are made to understand the conditions, hopes and desires of the roadside stand.

The owners of the roadside stand want money to earn their survival and hope for the city dwellers to help them. But in contrast to their hope are the moving cars in which the city dwellers come and show their cruelty and miserliness. They do not stop at the shop but when they do, they express irritation or have some other selfish motive. They overlook the pitiable condition of the stand and move on.

8. Comment on the significance of the symbol of the car in the poem. CBSE Question Bank 2021

Ans. In the poem, the moving cars are to be seen from two perspectives. They are a symbol of hope of getting money for survival for the rural people. The rural people want the cars to stop and buy their produce. This will earn them a livelihood. But, at the same time, they represent the cruelty and selfish attitudes of the city people who live a luxurious life in comparison to the rural people but do not have any kindness or compassion in them.

9. Does the poet reach a conclusive solution for the issue at hand? Discuss.

Ans. No, the poet does not reach a conclusive end in the poem. We, as readers, know that the poet identifies himself with the villagers and would want to be relived of the pain of poverty at once. But this is not the solution to the problem, he had posed in the poem.

10. Who does the poet accuse of having double standard in 'A Roadside Stand'? CBSE 2023

Ans. The poet accuses the so called benefactors- the government and other social service agencies of having double standard. He does so because these authoritative people deceive the poor rural people by giving them hope of doing something good and instead reap only personal benefits out of it. When time comes to meet the promise, they forget them or just fulfill self-motives.

11. Comment on the title of the poem.

Ans. The title 'A Roadside Stand' immediately establishes the central location of the poem. This seemingly simple setting becomes a microcosm that reflects more prominent, societal and economic themes. The stand represents the intersection between rural life and urban development, where the clash between tradition and progress is evident.

12. How does the narrative of the poem convey the speakers thoughts and emotions?

Ans. The poem is presented through the first-person narrative voice, allowing readers to intimately connect with the speaker's thoughts and emotions. The reflective tone emphasises the personal nature of the struggle and the deep contemplation of societal issues. This narrative choice draws readers into the speaker's perspective and encourages reflection on the themes.

13. What does the plea of the rural folk reflect?

Ans. The speaker conveys that the rural inhabitants who have set up the roadside stand are pleading for financial support. They seek 'city money' to improve their economic conditions, hoping it will expand their lives. The plea reflects a desire for a better quality of life, echoing the promises seen in 'moving-pictures', and suggests a frustration with the party in power, which is believed to withhold these promised benefits from the rural community.

14. How do the expressions 'greedy good-doers' and 'beneficent beasts of prey' convery irony in the poem?

Ans. The given expressions convey a sense of irony and scepticism, suggesting that the assistance provided by these entities may not genuinely benefit the rural people. Instead, the poet implies that the aid is driven by self-interest, portraying them as both exploitative and deceptive.

15. Critically comment on the tone of the poem.

Ans. The tone of the poem is a mixture of sadness, frustration, cynicism and reflection. The speaker contemplates the struggles and longing of the people at the roadside stand and contrasts them with the indifference of passing traffic. There's also a sense of bitterness and scepticism towards the plans of those in power.

16. How does the poet's contemplation of pain and relief relate to the broader human experience?

Ans. The poet's contemplation speaks to the broader human experience of grappling with suffering and the desire for relief. It touches on universal themes of empathy, ethical dilemmas, and the complexity of addressing profound pain personally and within communities.

17. How does the poet use the shift in perspective from one day to the next to convey his internal conflict?

Ans. The poet's shift from contemplating a drastic solution to questioning its morality the next day illustrates his internal conflict and the complexity of his feelings. It shows the tension between his empathy for the rural people and his recognition of the ethical implications of his thoughts.

18. In 20-30 words, suggest two ways to help the roadside owners in 'A Roadside Stand'. Competency Based

Ans. By setting up stalls, where more city people have access to their products, can help the rural folk get a place into a market where they could earn their livelihood in a better manner. Further, educating them can help to open up new avenues of earning a fair livelihood.

19. What is the complaint of the country folk against the 'party in power'? **CBSE 2025**

Ans. The complaint of the country folk against the 'party in power' is that the government promises to improve their lives but never fulfills those promises. They feel neglected and deceived as their roadside stands remain unnoticed, and they continue to struggle while urban development benefits only the wealthy.

20. Comment on the contrast brought out in the poem 'A Roadside Stand'. **CBSE 2025**

Ans. The poem highlights the stark contrast between the poor villagers, who desperately seek financial support through their roadside stand, and the wealthy urbanites, who remain indifferent to their plight. While the villagers long for economic upliftment, city dwellers pass by without acknowledging their existence.

Long Answer Type Questions

1. Robert Frost, brings out that progress and development is unequal between cities and villages leading to feelings of distress and unhappiness among the rural people. Comment with reference to 'A Roadside Stand'.

Ans. Robert Frost, in his poems, usually focuses on the theme of human tragedies and fears and their ultimate acceptance or their solution. In 'A Roadside Stand', he deals with the lives of poor deprived people of the villages with a clarity that is perceptive and at the same time portrays his deepest sympathies and his feelings of humanity.

In this poem, the poet describes the feelings of the owners of a roadside shed who seem to wait interminably for the motorists passing in their shiny cars, to stop and buy something from what has been displayed there for sale. They long for the cash that is a symbol of poverty alleviation in their lives of deprivation. However, it appears to be a vain hope because nobody buys anything.

The poet is outraged at the callous attitude of the government, the civic authorities and the social service agencies who appear to help them but actually end up harming them. The news says that these poor people are to be relocated to the vicinity of the towns and that they will be well looked after. However, the poet regards this as a great disservice to the people who will be thus robbed of their voices, their freedom and the ability to find solutions to their problems.

2. Imagine a car stops and actually buys from the roadside stand. Keeping in mind the reaction you think the peasants would have, write a diary entry as the farmer describing not only your immediate experience but also your after-thoughts on being able to earn 'city-money'. You may begin this way:

Wednesday, 2nd March XX 9 pm

We had an unexpectedly good day today!

Competency Based

Ans. Wednesday, 2nd March XX 9 pm

We had an unexpectedly good day today! After months, we made a sale. Somebody bought the entire produce. Before this, we all waited and waited everyday for someone to stop, someone to just buy something. But this never happened. People only stopped to ask for directions or some other thing. It's all changed today.

A burly looking man bought the entire harvest and even asked me to sell everyday's harvest to him. Initially I was shocked when he asked me to sell. Its unexpected for this never happened.

But I had to be quick and make a sale. Finally I had money in my hand. I could buy food, proper clothes and all other requirement for my family. The money I earned was enough for a few days. I am excited and hopeful that this day repeats and we are never out of money.

A thankful Farmer

3. Imagine a child from the farmer's family migrates to the city for their education. As the child, write back to your family telling them whether you would or would not want to turn into a city-person. Use the context of the poem 'A Roadside Stand' in mind to pen down this letter. **Competency Based**

You may begin this way

12, Davidson County

23rd January, 20XX

Dear mom

I have been thinking about the roadside stall lately. Now that I find myself surrounded by city-people all the time,

I think..............................

With love

Jennifer

Ans. 23rd January, 20XX

Dear mom

I have been thinking about the roadside stall lately. Now that I find myself surrounded by city-people all the time, I think that these city people are too haughty as you had said. They are always grumbling and irritated by ugly things. Just yesterday I heard a girl talking about our roadside stand. When I asked her perspective, all she did was complain. For her, her own needs and desires were important. She even had the audacity to call our stand useless. I was going to shout at her but realised that I am not like them and would never be like the city people. I will always help everyone financially and never be mean and cruel to anyone.

With love

Jennifer

4. A Roadside Stand is a social satire depicting the two contrasting worlds existing in society. Justify this statement with reference to the poem. CBSE 2023

Ans. 'A Roadside Stand' by Robert Frost is indeed a social satire that portrays the two contrasting worlds that exist in society. The poem is set in a rural countryside, where there is a roadside stand selling fruits and vegetables.

The poem describes the two types of people who stop at the stand: the wealthy and the poor. The first society described is of the wealthy people who stop at the stand. They are portrayed as superficial, materialistic and self-absorbed. They drive expensive cars, wear fancy clothes and have an air of superiority about them. They come to the stand not to buy fruits and vegetables, but to show off their wealth and social status. They do not care about the quality of the produce or the people who sell it. They are only interested in flaunting their wealth.

The second society, on the other hand, describe the poor people who stop at the stand. They are portrayed as hardworking, honest, and down-to-earth. They walk to the stand, wear simple clothes, and carry baskets to collect the produce. They come to the stand to buy food for their families and are grateful for what they can afford. They have a sense of community and solidarity with the people who sell the produce.

Through the contrast between the wealthy and the poor, the poem highlights the social and economic inequalities that exist in society. The wealthy are portrayed as shallow and self-centered, while the poor are portrayed as honest and hardworking. The poem is a criticism of the materialistic values that dominate modern society and a call for a return to simpler and more authentic ways of life.

5. The poem 'A Roadside Stand' have often been claimed to be a multilayered poem. Do you agree? Justify your stance.

Ans. I agree that the poem 'A Roadside Stand' is multilayered dealing with issue such as economic struggle, the effects of urbanisation, the conflict between tradition and progress, and the difficulties of social intervention. These issues are covered in the following manner

(i) **Critique of Urbanisation** Frost uses irony to criticise the effects of urbanisation. The 'polished traffic' (the busy city cars) moves quickly and without care. In contrast, the 'artless paint' on the commercial signs looks simple and out of place. While the traffic ignores the signs, the signs disrupt the natural landscape and show how rural beauty is being commercialised. This irony shows the loss of authenticity and connection to the land due to commercial interests.

(ii) **Economic Struggle and Power Dynamics** The poem talks about the economic problems that rural communities face due to urban influences. The phrase 'flower of cities' means the wealth and success of urban areas supported by money. The stand's request for 'some of the money' shows the big economic difference between city and country areas. The idea that the 'party in power' keeps promises of wealth from the rural people criticises political manipulation and economic inequality.

(iii) **Critique of Well-Intentioned Intervention** Frost criticises people who try to help with good intentions but end up imposing their ideas. The terms 'greedy good-doers' and 'beneficent beasts of prey' describe these people as forcing their ideas of progress on the rural community. This imposition reduces the villagers' independence and self-sufficiency. Thus, the helpers are making the villagers dependent and less active.

(iv) **Inner Conflict and Moral Dilemma** The speaker's internal conflict is a vital part of the poem. His wish to quickly end the villagers' suffering shows their compassion. However, taking such a drastic step also shows how morally complex the decision is. This conflict adds depth to the speaker's character and reflects the challenges of solving social problems.

Thus, using vivid imagery, irony and deep thinking the poem shows the complex relationships between people, their environment, and progress and encourages readers to think about how these factors affect individual lives and society as a whole.

6. 'A Roadside Stand' and 'Lost Spring' depict two contrasting worlds existing in society. Justify the statement with reference to the poem 'A Roadside Stand' and the text 'Lost Spring'.

You may begin this way

Social Satire in the two texts portrays two contrasting worlds that exist in society. Competency Based

Ans. Social satire in the two texts portrays two contrasting worlds that exist in society. In Robert Frost's poem 'A Roadside Stand', the stand symbolises resilience and independence in the face of economic hardship. Despite their modest means, the stand's owners show dignity and self-reliance, presenting a rustic charm that goes against societal expectations.

On the other hand, 'Lost Spring' by Anees Jung delves into the harsh realities of child labour and poverty in India. The story exposes the exploitation and deprivation faced by children like Saheb, who scavenge for a living amidst the grandoise of urban India. The stark juxtaposition of wealth and poverty highlights the systemic inequalities that persist within society..

While 'A Roadside Stand' celebrates the courage and determination of individuals to carve out a livelihood, 'Lost Spring' exposes the harsh realities faced by marginalised communities. Together, they offer a critical commentary on the different experiences and socio-economic disparities prevalent in society.

SELF ASSESSMENT TEST

Extract Based Questions

Read the extract given below and answer the following questions.

1. "The little old house was out with a little new shed
In front at the edge of the road where the traffic sped,
A roadside stand that too pathetically pled,
It would not be fair to say for a dole of bread,
But for some of the money, the cash, whose flow supports
The flower of cities from sinking and withering faint."

(i) What presumption does the given extract highlight about the city people?

(ii) Where was the new shed put up?

(a) Behind the house (b) In front of the house (c) Besides the house (d) At the door of the house

(iii) Complete the following suitably.
'The power of cities' refer to ....

(iv) Select the correct option from those given in brackets, to fill in the blank.
The figure of speech used in these lines, 'polished traffic' is .... (metaphor/ transferred epithet)

(v) Read the assertion and the reason below, with reference to the given extract.

Assertion 'A Roadside Stand' is a poignant symbol of the economic difficulties faced by the rural population.

Reason The stand's plea for money and the depiction of signs offering goods for sale highlight the struggle for financial stability.

Choose the correct option regarding their relationship.

(a) Both the assertion and the reason are true and the reason is the correct explanation of the assertion.
(b) Both the assertion and the reason are true, but the reason is not the correct explanation of the assertion.
(c) The assertion is true, but the reason is false.
(d) The assertion is false, but the reason is true.

(vi) What does the poet tell us about the power of money?

Short Answer Type Questions

Answer the following questions in 40-50 words.

1. What are the usual complaints made by the city men when they stop at the roadside stand?
2. Comment on the imagery and description used by the poet.
3. Analyse the 'childish longing' referred to by the poet with reference to the rural folk.
4. What emotion does the speaker express about the situation?
5. How does the poet convey the frustration of the people running the roadside stand? What deeper social commentary is Frost making through the depiction of the roadside stand?
6. How do the actions of the motorists reflect broader societal attitudes towards rural communities?

Long Answer Type Questions

Answer the following questions in 120-150 words.

1. What is expected to happen to the rural folk when they are relocated to live near the cities, as expected by the poet?
2. The poet sympathises with the rural folk and reflect their plight in the poem. Elucidate.

05

Aunt Jennifer's Tigers

About the Poet

Adrienne Rich (1929 - 2012) was an American poet, essayist and radical feminist. She was called one of the most widely read and influential poets of the second half of the 20th century. She is widely known for her involvement in contemporary women's movement as a poet and theorist. Her work is known for its unapologetic exploration of complex themes, including gender, identity and social justice. Rich's poetry often challenged societal norms and power structures, advocating for women's rights and equality.

▼ **YOUR STUDY GOALS**

- Central Idea of The Poem
- Explanation of the Poem

▼ **YOUR PRACTICE GOAL**

- NCERT Folder
- Extract Based Questions
- Short Answer Type Questions
- Long Answer Type Questions

Central Idea of the Poem

'Aunt Jennifer's Tigers' by Adrienne Rich is a short but powerful poem that explores themes of women's oppression, marriage and constraint within patriarchal societies along with the enduring strength of art.

Through the metaphor of Aunt Jennifer's embroidered tigers, the poem depicts her desire for freedom and empowerment, contrasted with her life of submission and fear under her husband's dominance. The tigers symbolise Aunt Jennifer's aspirations for strength and autonomy, which are unattainable in her marital reality. Adrienne Rich explores the tension between personal creativity and societal expectations, highlighting the struggle for women to assert themselves and find agency in a world that often limits their expression and stifles their individuality. Ultimately, the poem highlights the pervasive impact of gender inequality and the longing for liberation within oppressive structures.

Explanation of the Poem

Stanza 1

"Aunt Jennifer's tigers prance across a screen,
Bright topaz denizens of a world of green.
They do not fear the men beneath the tree;
They pace in sleek chivalric certainty."

Exp. Aunt Jennifer's tigers prance and move across a screen or panel. The poet describes them as bright-coloured like the shining golden-yellow jewel topaz. They are free inhabitants of the green forests and are not scared of the men standing under the tree. These tigers move about with grace, elegance and confidence.

Aunt Jennifer's tigers are not real or living tigers. They are images created by her on tapestry. Aunt Jennifer, who is held captive by the oppressive hand of a patriarchal society, creates in her art an alternate world of freedom. The tigers represent her dreams and her desire to be free from constant fear and oppression that govern her life. These majestic and fearless tigers also present a sharp contrast to Aunt Jennifer herself, who is bound by the constraints of married life.

Stanza 2

"Aunt Jennifer's fingers fluttering through her wool;
Find even the ivory needle hard to pull.
The massive weight of Uncle's wedding band;
Sits heavily upon Aunt Jennifer's hand."

Exp. In the second stanza, Aunt Jennifer appears to be creating beautiful images of the tigers by using wool. But she finds even the ivory needle quite hard to pull. She is so terrorised and tortured that her fingers are shaking. The uncle's wedding band seems heavy on her hand. It suggests that she feels burdened with her marital responsibilities.

Through this stanza, the poet wants to convey the fact that a woman is subjugated throughout her life. After marriage, she is burdened with so many responsibilities and expectations that marraige itself becomes a burden. This is also the reality of Aunt Jennifer's life.

Stanza 3

"When Aunt is dead, her terrified hands will lie
Still ringed with ordeals she was mastered by.
The tigers in the panel that she made
Will go on prancing, proud and unafraid."

Exp. In this stanza, the poet says that even death will not be able to release Aunt Jennifer from the trauma she had to undergo during her lifetime. Her life will be a story of her ordeals and the oppression that she was subjected to. However, the tigers created by her will be eternal. They will always be 'proud and unafraid.' Here we get a glimpse of an oft-quoted conventional theme in poetry that art endures beyond human life.

Perhaps, the poet wants to say that the women, who are creating these tigers, need to break their shackles and be unafraid like the tigers themselves. One more thing that can be inferred from the poem is that Aunt Jennifer, who for long has borne the miseries she was subjected to, now longs for freedom from dominance and male chauvinism.

Word-Meaning

prance	—	jump or move in a spirited manner
screen	—	here, the wall or the surface of the tapestry
topaz	—	a bright yellow precious stone
denizens	—	inhabitants
chivalric	—	brave and honourable
certainty	—	confidence
fluttering	—	moving with a light irregular or trembling motion
massive	—	heavy
wedding band	—	wedding pact, signifying marital duties
ringed	—	confined or tied up
ordeals	—	unpleasant or painful experiences
mastered	—	controlled
panel	—	flat board

Literary devices used in the Poem

- **Tone** Sympathetic
- **Rhyme Scheme** aabbccddeeff
- **Alliteration** *Stanza 2, Line 5* 'Fingers fluttering' (repetition of 'f' sound)
  Stanza 3, Line 12 'prancing proud' (repetition of 'p' sound)
- **Pun** *Stanza 3, Line 10* 'ringed' (refers to the wedding ring as well as a jail)
- **Symbols**
  'Aunt Jennifer' as symbol of all women
  'Tigers' as symbols of Aunt's desires and dreams, untamed free spirit
  'Wedding Band' as symbol of Patriarchal male domination, unhappy marriage
- **Transferred Epithet** *Stanza 3, Line 9* 'terrified hand' (Aunt Jennifer is herself terrified)

NCERT Folder

Think it Out (NCERT Page 96)

1. How do 'denizens' and 'chivalric' add to our understanding of the tiger's attitudes?

Ans. 'Denizens' means occupants of a particular place and 'chivalric' points to honour, bravery and fearlessness. These words characterise the tigers created by Aunt Jennifer. The tigers occupy their territory after much struggle and are very possessive about it. They live on their own terms and fear none, as they regard themselves to be superior in their domain.

These words choices underscore the tigers' confidence and comfort in their environment, mirroring Aunt Jennifer's desire for a similar sense of ownership in her life.

2. Why do you think Aunt Jennifer's hands are 'fluttering through her wool' in the second stanza? Why is she finding the needle so hard to pull?

Ans. Aunt Jennifer's hands and fingers are fluttering and she is finding the needle hard to pull because she feels afraid. She is so traumatised by the ordeals of her marital life and a male dominated society that she cannot even use the light-weight needle properly.

3. What is suggested by the image 'massive weight of Uncle's wedding band'?

Ans. The image of the 'massive weight of Uncle's wedding band' in the poem 'Aunt Jennifer's Tigers' suggests several things

Symbol of Oppression The wedding band symbolises Aunt Jennifer's oppressive marriage. Its 'massive weight' conveys that her marital obligations and the expectations of her role as a wife are burdensome and suffocating. It's as if the weight of the wedding band symbolises the weight of the traditional gender roles and societal expectations that she is forced to bear.

Power Imbalance The description of the wedding band as 'massive' implies a power imbalance within the marriage. It suggests that Uncle may have had a dominant or controlling role, contributing to Aunt Jennifer's feelings of constraint and subjugation.

Emotional Burden The 'massive weight' of the wedding band is a metaphor for the emotional burden that Aunt Jennifer carries due to her marriage. It suggests that the expectations and responsibilities associated with her role as a wife have become oppressive and suffocating.

Lack of Autonomy The weight of the wedding band implies a lack of autonomy and personal freedom. Aunt Jennifer may feel trapped and weighed down by her marital obligations, unable to fully express herself or pursue her desires.

In sum, the image of the 'massive weight of Uncle's wedding band' highlights the poem's theme: the suffocating and constraining nature of Aunt Jennifer's marriage and the societal expectations she grapples with. It symbolises her sense of oppression and her yearning for independence and self-expression.

4. Of what or of whom is Aunt Jennifer terrified with in the third stanza?

Ans. Aunt Jennifer is terrified of her husband or the male dominated society, who/which dominates her in her married life.

5. What are the 'ordeals' Aunt Jennifer is surrounded by, why is it significant that the poet uses the word 'ringed'? What are the meanings of the word 'ringed' in the poem?

Ans. The word 'ordeals' in the poem 'Aunt Jennifer's Tigers' refers to the challenges, difficulties, and hardships that Aunt Jennifer faced throughout her life, particularly in the context of her marriage and societal expectations. These ordeals could include the emotional and psychological burdens she endured as a result of her marital role and the constraints placed upon her as a woman in a patriarchal society. The word 'ordeals' signifies the struggles and oppression she experienced.

The poet's use of the word 'ringed' is significant for several reasons

Symbol of Confinement 'Ringed' implies that Aunt Jennifer was surrounded and confined by these ordeals. It suggests that she was encircled by the difficulties and constraints, unable to escape them. This word choice emphasises the suffocating nature of the challenges she faced.

Symbol of Entrapment 'Ringed' also conveys a sense of entrapment or being engaged, which aligns with the theme of Aunt Jennifer's constrained existence. It symbolises her lack of freedom and autonomy within the confines of her marriage and societal expectations.

Repetition of the Wedding Band The word 'ringed' also serves as a subtle play on words, linking to the 'massive weight of Uncle's wedding band' mentioned earlier in the poem. The repetition of the ring imagery reinforces the idea of the burden and oppression associated with her marital obligations.

In essence, the word 'ringed' highlights the theme of confinement, oppression and the emotional burdens that Aunt Jennifer endured. It signifies her struggle to break free from the constraints of her marriage and societal expectations, which is the poem's central theme.

6. Why do you think Aunt Jennifer created animals that are so different from her own character? What might the poet be suggesting, through this difference?

Or

For Aunt Jennifer, what do the tigers symbolise?

Ans. Aunt Jennifer created tigers, which are a symbol of strength, fearlessness and confidence. These are the qualities that Aunt Jennifer lacks in her own self. These tigers represent Aunt Jennifer's suppressed desires to become bold and fearless, and free from oppression.

The poet, uses this contrast to convey several possible suggestions.

Desire for Freedom Aunt Jennifer's creation of fearless and majestic tigers may symbolise her inner longing for freedom and independence. The stark contrast between her timid and oppressed persona and the mighty tigers highlights her yearning for qualities she might feel are missing in her life.

Artistic Liberation Through her art, Aunt Jennifer can express aspects of herself that she might find difficult to manifest in her everyday life. The act of creating these fierce tigers allows her to break free from the societal expectations and limitations imposed on her as a woman in a patriarchal society.

Sublimation of Desires The tigers in her art can be seen as a way for Aunt Jennifer to sublimate (control) her desires for strength and autonomy. She can channel her yearnings and frustrations through her artistic creation into something tangible and enduring.

Legacy of Independence The poet may also suggest that one can leave a lasting legacy of strength and courage despite adversity and constraint. The tiger's unafraid and proud demeanour in her art outlives her, serving as a testament to her enduring spirit and desire for a different life.

To conclude, the poet may be using the difference between Aunt Jennifer and her artistic creations to illustrate the power of art to express suppressed desires and seek personal liberation. It emphasises the potential for art to transcend the limitations of one's circumstances and leave a lasting legacy of individual strength and independence.

7. Interpret the symbols found in this poem.

Ans. There are many symbols found in the poem. Tigers are a symbol of strength and fearlessness. They are also symbolic of Aunt Jennifer's inner desire to be free from oppression. 'Ring' is another symbol which represents bondage. 'Wedding band' is a symbol of oppression. 'Aunt Jennifer' herself is a symbol of all women who are victimised.

8. Do you sympathise with Aunt Jennifer? What is the attitude of the poet towards Aunt Jennifer?

Ans. Yes, we sympathise with Aunt Jennifer. She represents those women who are victimised by the male dominated society. She feels oppressed as the rules of society do not allow her to express herself freely. The poet herself is very critical of the treatment given to Aunt Jennifer. So, she wants women to fight for their rights rather than being silent victims of oppression.

Exam Pattern Questions

Extract Based Questions

Read the extracts given below and answer the following questions.

1. "Aunt Jennifer's tigers prance across a screen,
Bright topaz denizens of a world of green.
They do not fear the men beneath the tree;
They pace in sleek chivalric certainty."

(i) How are Aunt Jennifer's tigers described?

(ii) Why are they described as denizens of a world of green?

(a) Because they eat the herbibores
(b) Because they are green in colour
(c) Because they live in dense green forests
(d) Because they are bright and beautiful

(iii) Fill in the blanks appropriately.
The tigers are not afraid of men because ....

(iv) Complete the following analogy correctly.
Assonance : Men beneath the true : : Rhyme scheme : ....

(v) On the basis of the extract, choose the correct option with reference to (1) and (2) given below.

(1) Aunt Jennifer is painting her tigers.

(2) Aunt Jennifer's creations reflect her deepest desires.

(a) (1) is true but (2) is false
(b) (2) is true but (1) is false
(c) (2) is the reason for (1)
(d) Both (1) and (2) cannot be inferred from the extract.

(vi) Identify the phrase from the extract that suggests the following.
They are yellow coloured enhabitants of forests.

Ans. (i) Aunt Jennifer's tigers have been described as bold, proud and self assured beings.
(ii) (c) Because they live in dense green forests
(iii) they are bold, fearless and symbol of strength
(iv) aabb
(v) (b) (2) is true but (1) is false
(vi) Bright topaz denizens of a world of green

2. Aunt Jennifer's tigers prance across a screen,
Bright topaz denizens of a world of green,
They do not fear the men beneath the tree:
They pace in sleek chivalric certainty.
Aunt Jennifer's fingers fluttered through her wool
Find even the ivory needle hard to pull.
The massive weight of the uncle's wedding band
Sits heavily upon Aunt Jennifer's hand. **CBSE 2023**

(i) Denizens of the world of green refer to
(a) huntsmen (b) Aunt Jennifer
(c) uncle (d) tigers

(ii) Choose the option that displays the same poetic device as used in the second line of the extract.
(a) Heart of stone (b) Trees sprouting
(c) Silver spoon (d) White murder

(iii) The men setting beneath the tree are ....

(iv) What quality of uncle can be inferred through these lines?
(a) Compassionate nature (b) Courageous
(c) Confident (d) Dominating

(v) The tigers in the extract are symbolic of
(a) creativity and courage
(b) confidence and gentleness
(c) cruelty and fear
(d) aggression and starving

(vi) Aunt Jennifer's tigers prance across
(1) the screen (2) the fields
(3) the embroidered tunic
(4) the cage
Which of the following is the most appropriate choice?
(a) (1) and (2) (b) (2) and (4)
(c) (1), (2) and (3) (d) (1) and (3)

Ans. (i) (d) tigers
(ii) (c) Silver spoon
(iii) courageous brave and strong
(iv) (d) Dominating
(v) (a) creativity and courage
(vi) (d) (1) and (3)

3. Aunt Jennifer's fingers fluttering through her wool
Find even the ivory needle hard to pull.
The massive weight of Uncle's wedding band
Sits heavily upon Aunt Jennifer's hand. **CBSE 2024**

(i) Which of the following themes is best represented in the given extract?
(a) The maturity of adulthood
(b) The glory of feminity
(c) Victim of male domination
(d) The superficial beauty

(ii) State whether the following statement is True or False, with reference to the extract.
Aunt Jennifer is nervous and traumatised because of the constraints of her marriage.

(iii) Complete the following sentence appropriately.
The fingers fluttering through her wool symbolise ....

(iv) The use of the words 'massive weight' creates a powerful image of ....

(v) Based on the rhyme scheme in lines 3 and 4, which words would rhyme with 'band' and 'hand'?
(a) Stand (b) Wind
(c) Bent (d) Tent

(vi) The heavy wedding ring is a source of
(a) joy
(b) freedom
(c) dignity
(d) burden

Ans. (i) (c) Victim of male domination
(ii) True
(iii) her oppressed mental condition
(iv) burden
(v) (a) Stand
(vi) (d) burden

4. Aunt Jennifer's fingers fluttering through her wool
Find even the ivory needle hard to pull.
The massive weight of Uncle's wedding band
sits heavily upon Aunt Jennifer's hand
when Aunt is dead, her terrified hands will lie.
still ringed with ordeals she was mastered by,
The Tiger in the panel that she made
will go on prancing, proud and unafraid. **CBSE 2024**

(i) 'Sits heavily upon Aunt Jennifer's hand.' Through the above expression the poet indicates
(a) Aunt Jennifer is happily married.
(b) Aunt Jennifer loves the tigers in the panel.
(c) Aunt Jennifer's unhappy married life.
(d) Aunt Jennifer's rich and luxurious life.

(ii) Select the option that has the same literary device as used in 'Still ringed with ordeals'.
(a) Leopards cannot hide in the jungle as they are spotted.
(b) Sun smiled happily on us.
(c) Her lovely voice was music to his ears.
(d) Life is like a box of chocolates.

(iii) Complete the following sentences with reference to the extract.

The tigers in the panel symbolise ....

(iv) State whether the statement given below is True or False.

"Find even the ivory needle hard to pull."

The above expression suggests that Aunt Jennifer is dying.

(v) Based on the rhyme scheme, evident in lines 1-2, which word would rhyme with line 1?
(a) Full (b) Sand (c) Bye

(vi) The use of the word 'fluttering fingers' in the extract suggest that the fingers of Aunt Jennifer are trembling. This creates an image of ....

Ans. (i) (c) Aunt Jennifer's unhappy married life
(ii) (c) Her lovely voice was music to his ears
(iii) Aunt Jennifer's desire to be free and fearless.
(iv) False, the expression means that Aunt Jennifer was subdued and suppressed in her marriage.
(v) (a) Full
(vi) fear and being oppressed

5. "When Aunt is dead,
her terrified hands will lie.
Still ringed with ordeals she was mastered by.
The tigers in the panel that she made
Will go on prancing, proud and unafraid."

(i) Read the statement given below.

Aunt Jennifer's plight is best explained by her hands, they hold both her freedom and the instrument of her imprisonment.

How would you explain the above statement, as per the extract?

(ii) Which of the following cannot be inferred from the given extract?
(a) Aunt Jennifer's tigers will keep her alive in everyone's memory.
(b) Aunt Jennifer feels oppressed and constricted in her marriage.
(c) Even in death, Aunt Jennifer cannot escape patriarchal subjugation.
(d) Aunt Jennifer's tigers prance as a lasting symbol of her desires.

(iii) Answer appropriately.
The theme associated with the extract is ....

(iv) Select the correct option from those given in brackets to fill in the blank.

The word .... (shuffling/strulting) does not reflect the movement implied by 'prancing'.

(v) On the basis of the extract, choose the correct option with reference to the two statements given below.

(1) Aunt Jennifer would not be free even after her death.

(2) Aunt Jennifer's desire of freedom would live through her art.

Codes
(a) (1) can be inferred from the extract but (2) cannot
(b) (2) can be inferred from the extract but (1) cannot
(c) Both (1) and (2) can be inferred from the extract
(d) (2) is the reason for (1) and can be inferred from the extract

(vi) What makes the tigers proud and unafraid?

Ans. (i) Aunt Jennifer knits her desires but is overpowered by the wedding ring she wears.
(ii) (a) Aunt Jennifer's tigers will keep her alive in everyone's memory.
(iii) 'With Art Lives the Artist'
(iv) shuffling
(v) (c) Both (1) and (2) can be inferred from the extract
(vi) The tigers are proud and unfraid because of their own self assured and fierce nature.

Short Answer Type Questions

1. Describe the tigers created by Aunt Jennifer.

Ans. Aunt Jennifer's tigers are bright yellow in colour. They are fearless and confident residents of dense green forests. The tigers represent strength, bravery and fearlessness. They are confident and graceful in their movements.

2. Explain the significance of the 'denizens pacing in sleek certainity' in the poem 'Aunt Jennifer's Tigers'? CBSE 2022 Term II

Ans. The reference to 'denizens pacing in sleek certainity' i.e. tigers is significant to contrast their nature to that of their creator-Aunt Jennifer.

The tigers are free, graceful, majestic, strong and confident as opposed to Aunt Jennifer who is weak, meek and submissive.

3. Why do you think Aunt Jennifer created animals that are so different from her own character? CBSE 2022 Term II

Ans. Aunt Jennifer created animals so different from her as a means of living an alternate life that is denied to her: a life that is proud, free, fearless and sure of itself. The tigers denote her yearning for power, freedom and fearless living. In this way, she faced the ordeals in her life.

4. How does the poet use the image of 'fingers fluttering through the wool' to highlight Aunt Jennifer's victimisation?

Ans. In the second stanza of the poem 'Aunt Jennifer's Tigers' the description of Aunt Jennifer's 'fluttering' hands can be interpreted as symbolic of her emotional and physical struggles within her marriage and the constraints of her societal role. Aunt Jennifer's 'fluttering' hands suggest nervousness, anxiety, or a lack of confidence. This could reflect her emotional state and the unease she experiences in her married life. 'fluttering' implies a sense of agitation, perhaps stemming from the pressures and expectations placed upon her as a wife.

5. What will happen to Aunt Jennifer's tigers when she is dead? CBSE 2013

Ans. The tigers created by Aunt Jennifer will keep on prancing even after her death, as she has created them on the tapestry. It shows that her longing for freedom from male domination will endure forever, even after she dies. Her art will forever state her struggle.

6. 'The tigers in the panel that she made
Will go on prancing, proud and unafraid'.
What is the tone of the poet reflected in the above lines? CBSE 2024

Ans. The tone of the poet reflected in the given lines is hopeful and empowered. As a means of designing an alternate life that is denied to her, she created animals that are different from her own character. A life that is proud, free and fearless is created through her art.

7. Aunt Jennifer's efforts to get rid of her fear proved to be futile. Comment.

Ans. The trembling hands of Aunt Jennifer because of the weight of the 'wedding band' show that she still is a victim of male chauvinism. Even her death won't free her from her ordeal as she will still be wearing the ring that symbolises her failed marriage.

8. How does Aunt Jennifer express her bitterness and anger against male dominance?

Ans. Aunt Jennifer is too terrified to openly resist the oppression that she is a victim of. So, she expresses her bitterness and anger against male dominance silently through her art. She creates tigers-animals that are symbolic of bravery, fearlessness and strength on her tapestry. The tigers she creates are wild and free from any kind of bondage.

9. What pictures of male chauvinism do we find in the poem, 'Aunt Jennifer's Tigers'?

Ans. In 'Aunt Jennifer's Tiger', we find the picture of male chauvinism through the presence of the 'wedding ring' which bound her to her dominating husband. Aunt Jennifer faced great hardships in her married life. She led a terrifying and oppressed life wherein she had never been free but a helpless victim of male chauvinism. Dominated and terrorised by her husband, Aunt Jennifer struggled for an existence within the deep conflicts of suppression.

10. Would you say that the poem ends on a note of hope? Justify your opinion. CBSE Question Bank 2021

Or Explain the irony at the end of the poem 'Aunt Jennifers Tigers'. CBSE 2022 Term II

Ans. I do not believe that the poem ends on a note of hope. The end talks about Aunt Jennifer's death and how ironically she will still be subdued by the patriarchal forces. This indicates that even death does not provide any relief to the Aunt. Her story, if remembered, would still be full of the struggles, burdens and responsibilities that she faced in life. Even though her art will exist to represent her dreams, wishes and desires, she herself would not be able to enjoy them.

11. "What knitting was to Aunt Jennifer; poetry was for Adrienne Rich". Do you agree? Comment with reference to the poem 'Aunt Jennifer's Tigers'. Competency Based

Ans. It is true that the act of knitting by Aunt Jennifer is similar to the act of writing poetry by Adrienne Rich. The act of knitting was the creative expression of Aunt Jennifer's talents through which she puts forward her desires, wishes and dreams.

Similarly, writing poetry is Adrienne Rich's creative expression through which she propagates her ideas, thoughts and beliefs.

12. Read the given quote. In your opinion, what silence does the poem 'Aunt Jennifer's Tigers' break? CBSE Question Bank 2021

Every poem breaks a silence that had to be overcome. —Adrienne Rich

Ans. The poem 'Aunt Jennifer's tigers' breaks the silence of women suppression and oppression in the male dominated society. It talks about how women, her talents, and her ideas are silenced by the patriarchal institutions of the society. Throughout the poem, the central character of Aunt Jennifer is silent. She cannot speak about the discrimination faced by her by the hands of her husband and her family. However, her artistic creation functions to break her silence. It loudly speaks what she wants.

13. Adrienne Rich chose to express her silent revolt through her poem, Aunt Jennifer's Tigers, just as Aunt Jennifer did with her embroidery. Explain. CBSE SQP, CBSE 2022 Term II

Ans. It is true that Adrienne Rich chose to express her silent revolt through her poem 'Aunt Jennifer's Tigers' just as Aunt Jennifer did with her embroidery.

Adrienne Rich, through her poem, criticises the traditional institution of marriage suggesting that it oppresses women. Aunt Jennifer as her subject is a victim of an unhappy marriage, under a domineering husband. She, just like Adrienne Riche, is also an artist who chooses embroidery to vent her angst. Art becomes their creative outlet as a form of protest against societal expectations.

14. What does Aunt Jennifer symbolise in the poem 'Aunt Jennifer's Tigers'? CBSE 2022 Term II

Ans. Aunt Jennifer, in the poem Aunt Jennifer's Tigers, is symbolic of all the females living a suppressed marital life. She represents all the females who are living a life of pain, misery, torture, oppression and humiliation under an authoritative husband in a male-dominated society.

15. How can we say that marriage was a compromise for Aunt Jennifer? Support your response with two justifications.

Ans. We can definitely say that Aunt Jennifer's marriage was a compromise for her because she was suppressed in her marriage. She couldn't live the way she wanted to or do what she wanted to.

She was burdened by her marital responsibilities and oppressed by her husband. The way the heaviness of the 'Uncle's wedding band' is presented and the way her hands shake while embroidering show that she was not happy in her marriage.

16. Can you understand Aunt Jennifer's Tigers as a narrative poem? Justify your stance. Competency Based

Ans. 'Aunt Jennifer's Tigers' can be categorised as a narrative poem. A narrative poem is a type of poem that tells a story, often with a straightforward plot, characters, and a sequence of events. In this case, the poem tells the story of Aunt Jennifer and her life, focusing on her artistic expression, her marriage, and the constraints she faces. It conveys a narrative about her experiences and emotions, making it more narrative in nature. While it also contains elements of lyricism, such as the use of vivid imagery and symbolism to express her inner thoughts and emotions, the narrative aspect of the poem is prominent, and it tells a story about Aunt Jennifer's life and struggles.

17. How does the poem address the theme of mortality/transience? Competency Based

Ans. The poem addresses the theme of mortality/transience by juxtaposing/contrasting Aunt Jennifer's fleeting existence with her artistic creation's enduring/lasting presence. Aunt Jennifer's struggles and fears are depicted as temporary, symbolised by her 'terrified hands,'which will eventually lie still in death. However, the tigers she creates outlive her, continuing to 'prance' proudly in the tapestry she leaves behind. This contrast emphasises that while individuals may be mortal and subject to the trials of life, their creations and legacies can endure beyond their lifetimes.

18. What does the poem 'Aunt Jennifer's Tigers' suggest about the kind of relationship Aunt Jennifer shares with her husband? Support your answer with evidence from the poem. Competency Based

Ans. The poem 'Aunt Jennifer's Tigers' suggests that there is unequal power distribution in aunt Jennifer's marriage. Aunt Jennifer is probably dominated by her husband and fears disobeying him. The poem mentions that, 'the massive weight of Uncle's wedding band' sits heavily upon Aunt Jennifer's hand', which implies that she feels oppressed by her husband. Further, 'Aunt's 'terrified hands'/'ringed with ordeals she was mastered by' indicates that she is suppressed in her marriage.

19. Bright topaz denizens of a world of green.
By referring to the tigers as 'bright topaz denizens' in the above line, the poet highlights their bold and confident nature.
Does this align with the description of the tigers in the rest of the poem? Justify in 20–30 words based on your understanding of the poem 'Aunt Jennifer's Tigers'. Competency Based

Ans. Yes, the reference to the tigers as 'bright topaz denizens' aligns with their bold and confident nature as depicted in the poem. The tigers are presented as being unafraid and sure of themselves throughout the poem. These creatures are brave to be themselves, secure in their own skin, not afraid of standing out, certain of themselves, proud and unafraid.

Long Answer Type Questions

1. Feminism refers to a collection of movements and ideologies that advocate women's rights and seeks to establish equal opportunities for women in all spheres. Discuss with reference to 'Aunt Jennifer's Tigers'. Competency Based

Ans. All of us live in a patriarchal society wherein a male is considered as superior to female. As a result, women have always been considered as subservient to men. They have had to suppress their desires and emotions. The poem 'Aunt Jennifer's Tigers' is the presentation of all such females. In the poem, the poet expresses the inner feelings of Aunt Jennifer. She is embroidering a motif comprising of energetic, fearless tigers moving freely around the bright greenery.

However, her life is the exact opposite of the tigers. She is living a life of submissiveness to her husband's command. Her acts are dominated by him and she fears him constantly. The wedding ring on her hand is a constant reminder that she belongs to her husband.

This torments her and it will not end until her death. Even after her death, the ring will remain on her hand and she will never be free. Feminism then emerged as a collection of movements and ideologies that advocate women's rights.

It seeks to establish equal opportunities for women in all spheres of life. Through this poem, Adrienne Rich is expressing her solidarity with the movement while presenting the pitiable conditions of women all over the world.

2. Imagine that Aunt Jennifer read the poem that Adrienne Rich wrote about her. After much contemplation, she decided to write a letter to her husband expressing her feelings and thoughts. Write a letter as Aunt Jennifer. Competency Based

Ans. Dear Husband,

You might be surprised why I am writing you a letter and not telling you this face to face but I am terrified of you reaction. Yes, I am terrified but this feeling is not new to me. I have always been terrified of you and your reaction to everything I do. When I got married to you, I expected a life of respect, equality and freedom. But my expectations were shattered bitterly. I was not given any freedom, not even to embroider which you very well know I love. Then, suddenly all the filial responsibilities were put on me and everyone expected me to excel in it.

You know I never thought I would be able to tell this to you out loud, but I had to. You know Adrienne Rich wrote about it all and that is what encouraged me to at least let you know the things I have gone through because of the social expectations. I do not blame you because I know you had no idea of how I felt but now after telling you all this, I expect you to support me.

Hoping that you understand me.

Yours lovingly

Jennifer

3. Comment on the various themes present in the poem 'Aunt Jennifer's Tigers'.

Ans. Aunt Jennifer's Tigers collectively create a narrative that explores the complexities of gender dynamics, personal expression, and the enduring legacy of women's struggles in a patriarchal society.

Gender Roles and Patriarchy The poem delves into the theme of gender roles and the impact of a patriarchal society on women. Aunt Jennifer's marriage is a source of constraint and oppression, symbolised by the heavy wedding band that weighs down her hand. The poem reflects on how societal expectations and traditional gender roles limit her autonomy and creative expression.

Artistic Expression and Escape Aunt Jennifer's creation of the tigers serves as a means of creative expression and a form of escape from the constraints of her marriage and societal expectations. The tigers in her art represent her desire for freedom and strength.

Legacy and Endurance The poem addresses the idea of legacy and endurance. Even after Aunt Jennifer's death, her art lives on, and the tigers in her tapestry continue to prance 'proud and unafraid.' This suggests that her spirit and desire for independence will outlast her and serve as an enduring testament to her inner strength.

Fear and Oppression The poem conveys Aunt Jennifer's fear and the oppression she experiences in her marriage. Her 'terrified hands' and the reference to 'ordeals she was mastered by' illustrate the emotional and psychological toll of her circumstances.

Freedom and Empowerment The tigers in the poem symbolise freedom and empowerment. They are unafraid and confident, in contrast to Aunt Jennifer. The poem highlights the stark contrast between her constrained life and the liberated spirit she expresses through her art.

4. Both the poems, ' My Mother at Sixty-Six and 'Aunt Jennifer's Tigers', delve into experiences of life. How do these poems bring out the internal conflict in each of the poem? CBSE 2025

Ans. 'My Mother at Sixty-Six' by Kamala Das and 'Aunt Jennifer's Tigers' by Adrienne Rich explore the internal conflicts experienced by women in different stages of life.

In 'My Mother at Sixty-Six', the poet struggles with the painful realisation of her aging mother's frailty. She observes her mother's pale, corpse-like face and feels an overwhelming fear of losing her. This internal conflict arises from her deep love and attachment, yet she suppresses her emotions, choosing to smile instead of expressing her sorrow.

In 'Aunt Jennifer's Tigers', the conflict is more about oppression and unfulfilled desires. Aunt Jennifer, trapped in a patriarchal marriage, finds solace in her art. The tigers she embroiders symbolise her suppressed courage and longing for freedom, contrasting with her own helplessness.

Both poems highlight the struggles women face—one dealing with inevitable loss, the other with lifelong oppression. Yet, through love and art, they find a way to cope with their internal conflicts.

5. Analyse the poems, 'A Roadside Stand' and 'Aunt Jennifer's Tigers' for the theme of inequality and its impact on the bearers. **CBSE SQP 2024**

Ans. In the world we live, we find that inequalities are commonplace. There are communities which bear the brunt of these inequalities. Two of such communities are presented in the poems 'The Roadside Stand' and 'Aunt Jennifer's Tigers'.

'A Roadside Stand' focuses on the economic disparities between rural and urban areas as well as lifetsyles. It depicts the struggles of rural individuals facing economic inequality and explores the loss of traditional ways of life due to modernisation and industrialisation. In doing so, it points out how the rural communities are exploited by those in power. As a result, they are struggling to make ends meet, leading to feelings of frustration and helplessness.

'Aunt Jennifer's Tigers' delves into the gender-based inequalities within marriage and society. It illustrates the oppression faced by Aunt Jennifer within her marriage. Through Aunt Jennifer, it reflects on the expectations and restrictions placed on women and explores the theme of domestic suppression and its impact on women's autonomy.

As such, both the poems present the people or bearers who face the psychological and emotional toll of their respective inequalities, resulting in a longing for freedom and empowerment. They are suppressed and are not free to do what they wish. However, despite their challenges, the bearers in both poems demonstrate a desire to assert themselves through small acts of defiance or dreams of liberation.

6. If Aunt Jennifer speaks to Pablo Neruda, the poet of 'Keeping Quiet' about her problems and constraints, would it be right for her to accept his response of introspection, reflection and silence? Write a letter to Pablo Neruda expressing her views. **Competency Based**

Ans. No, I do not think Aunt Jennifer would be right in accepting Neruda's response of introspection, reflection and silence as it would not help Aunt Jennifer in coming out of her fears. It would not help her in fighting for her rights and gaining her freedom from the oppression.

Dear Mr. Neruda

I hope this letter finds you well. I am Jennifer, a home maker and a suppressed woman under the patriarchal setup of marriage. Recently, I read 'Keeping Quiet' and couldn't help but write to you about how I am struggling so that you could help me find a way out of it. I have been married for a long time. I love my husband too but it is suffocating to live in a family where I have no voice. I am only good to fulfil the marital duties, take care of the house and the children, and have no life of my own. I can't even embroider which I love to do. I feel burdened by the ordeals of patriarchy. I do not want to live like this.

Please help me find peace.

Thanking you in advance.

Jennifer

7. After reading 'Aunt Jennifer's Tigers' and 'Going Places' you realise that Aunt Jennifer and Sophie's mother have been subdued by their respective husbands.

As a social activist you have to write an article in a newspaper on the need to empower women.

You may begin like this

Empowerment of women is very essential social reform. It needs to be accelerated for any nation to progress …… . **Competency Based**

Ans. Empowerment of women has been a theme deeply explored in literature, exemplified by characters like Aunt Jennifer from Adrienne Rich's 'Aunt Jennifer's Tigers' and Sophie's mother from Katherine Govier's 'Going Places'. These women showcase resilience and determination in the face of societal constraints.

Aunt Jennifer, depicted through her needlework, symbolises the silent struggles of many women, seeking solace and empowerment through artistic expression despite being confined by patriarchal norms. Her vivid imagery of tigers represents her desire for freedom and strength in a world where she feels powerless.

Similarly, Sophie's mother challenges traditional gender roles by encouraging her daughter to pursue her dreams, despite financial constraints. Her support empowers Sophie to aspire beyond societal expectations, fostering her independence and self-confidence.

Through these characters, literature illuminates the importance of supporting women's aspirations and agency, whether through creative outlets or familial encouragement. By acknowledging and amplifying women's voices and choices, society can truly empower women to achieve their full potential.

8. How have the descriptions of movement been used to contrast the differences between Aunt Jennifer and her tigers? Describe in 100-120 words based on your understanding of the poem 'Aunt Jennifer's Tigers'. Competency Based

Ans. In the poem, the descriptions of movement contrasts the differences between Aunt Jennifer and her tigers. Aunt Jennifer has been described as insecure, fearful and oppressed. Hence, her movements show her timidity and nervousness. Aunt Jennifer's fingers flutter and tremble, and her hands find even a tiny needle difficult to pull. Even her smallest actions are weighed down by the oppression she faces. These movements reflect her fearful and insecure nature. Her actions seems to be hesitant.

In contrast, the tigers are described as proud, noble and unafraid. Their respective movements have also been used to reflect these attitudes and qualities. The tigers prance, mirroring their joyful and fearless nature. They pace about confidently, certain of themselves and unafraid of the men around them. Their movements are sleek and self-assured.

9. 'Aunt Jennifer's Tigers' and 'A Thing of Beauty', can be read together to show the permanence and everlasting impact of art and of things of beauty. Comment. Competency Based

Ans. It is true that the poems 'Aunt Jennifer's Tigers' and 'A Thing of Beauty' show the permanence and everlasting impact of art and things of beauty. Both of these poems present lines which indicate that art forms and all things of beauty never lose significance. Even after the creator or the source of beauty is dead, the beauty is never lost. Its value increases with time.

In the poem 'Aunt Jennifer's Tiger's', Aunt Jennifer's expression- her embroidered tigers- will exist forever. Even after her death, her art work will continue to exist and speak of her struggles. This idea is furthered in the poem 'A Thing of Beauty' which deals with the everlasting beauty in its centrality. For Keats, beauty never goes away. It is forever present around us making us happy and bringing us peace.

10. Illustrate how symbols and images in the poem, 'My Mother at Sixty-Six and 'Aunt Jennifer's Tigers' enhance the reader's understanding of the characters' experiences and emotional landscapes. CBSE 2025

Ans. In 'My Mother at Sixty-Six', Kamala Das uses powerful imagery to depict the fleeting nature of life and the inevitability of aging. The comparison of the poet's mother to a 'late winter's moon' symbolises her frailty, faded vitality, and approaching death. The passing trees and sprinting children seen from the moving car contrast with the mother's stillness, emphasising the poet's fear of separation and loss. These images deepen the reader's empathy for the poet's silent sorrow.

Similarly, in 'Aunt Jennifer's Tigers', Adrienne Rich employs striking symbolism to highlight Aunt Jennifer's oppression and unfulfilled desires. The 'tigers prancing, proud and unafraid' represent strength, freedom, and defiance-qualities Aunt Jennifer lacks in her restrictive marriage. In contrast, the 'massive weight of uncle's wedding band' symbolises her burden and helplessness. The contrast between the bold tigers and the oppressed aunt intensifies the reader's understanding of her constrained life, making her plight deeply resonant.

SELF ASSESSMENT TEST

Extract Based Questions

Read the extract given below and answer the following questions.

1. Aunt Jennifer's finger fluttering through her wool
Find even the ivory needle hard to pull.
The massive weight of Uncle's wedding band
Sits heavily upon Aunt Jennifer's hand.

(i) How would you describe Aunt Jennifer based on the above extract? What do you as reader feel about Aunt Jennifer?

(ii) Which of the following is an example of an alliteration?

(a) Finger fluttering through the wool
(b) Upon Aunt Jennifer's hand
(c) Ivory needle hard to pull
(d) Massive weight of Uncle's wedding band

(iii) Complete the sentence suitably.
Uncle's wedding band sits heavily on Aunt Jennifer's hand because

(iv) The ivory needle used to embroider is .... (symbolic of/ in sharp contrast to) the difficulty in using it.

(v) Read the Assertion and the Reason below, with reference to the given extract.

Assertion The poet advocates for women to fight back against the patriarchal society.

Reason The aspect of patriarchal society focused on in the extract is marriage.

Choose the correct option regarding their relationship.

(a) Both the Assertion and the Reason are true, and the Reason is the correct explanation of the Assertion.
(b) Both the Assertion and the Reason are true, but the Reason is not the correct explanation of the Assertion.
(c) The Assertion is true, but the Reason is false.
(d) The Assertion is false, but the Reason is true.

(vi) Elucidate upon 'the wedding band' as a symbol of authority and oppression.

Short Answer Type Questions

Answer the following questions in 40-50 words.

1. Explain the transferred Epithet in 'terrified hands'.

2. How is the expression 'Hard to Pull the Needle' significant in presenting the emotional and physical burdens of Aunt Jennifer?

3. Aunt Jennifer deserves our sympathy. Elaborate.

4. How does the poem explore the themes of gender roles and power dynamics?

5. Why does Aunt Jennifer choose to depict tigers in her tapestry?

Long Answer Type Questions

Answer the following questions in 120-150 words.

1. Comment on the significance of the title of the poem. How does it impact our understanding?

2. Explain the stark difference in the death of Aunt Jennifer and the tigers prancing.

01

About the Author

Walter Braden 'Jack' Finney (1911-1995) was an American writer, mainly known for his contributions to the science-fiction genre. His most popular novels are 'The Body Snatchers' (1955) and 'Time and Again' (1970), although throughout his career he published nearly 50 novels that encompass the thriller and comedy genres. His works are characterised by their inventive concepts, meticulous attention to detail and exploration of the extraordinary within the ordinary.

▼ **YOUR STUDY GOALS**

- Chapter Sketch
- About the Characters
- Summary of the Chapter

▼ **YOUR PRACTICE GOAL**

- NCERT Folder
- Extract Based Questions
- Short Answer Type Questions
- Long Answer Type Questions

The Third Level

Chapter Sketch

'The Third Level' conveys that the life of modern man is full of insecurity, stress and worries and he is unable to cope with these challenges of a modern life. When he cannot cope with the harsh realities, he wants to escape into a fanciful world. He tries to find a level of existence that will provide him peace, happiness and tranquility. In the story, the modern man is Charley who reaches the 'third level' while taking the subway for his home. It presents how Charley looks for the third level again to escape and run away from the harsh realities of life. This third level is a mysterious world that is somewhere between our unfulfilled desires, expectations and dreams.

About the Characters

Charley A 31 year old daily commuter who accidently arrives at the third level of Grand Central Station and experiences a whole new world.

Louisa She is Charley's wife who was worried about her husband coming late.

Sam Charley's Psychiatrist and friend who serves as a proof for the existence of the third level at the Grand Central Station.

Summary of the Chapter

Waking Dream Wish Fulfillment

Charley feels that there are three levels at the Grand Central Railway Station. In reality, there are only two. He has discussed this with his psychiatrist friend, Sam Weiner. Sam felt that the narrator's experience is a waking-dream wish fulfilment. According to him, Charley is a modern man who is suffering from the modern day insecurities, anxieties and fears. So, he wants an escape from his stressful life. Sam added that the narrator's hobby of stamp collection is his 'temporary refuge from reality'. The narrator does not agree with this interpretation.

The Third Level

Charley came across the third level one summer night. In a hurry to get back home from his office, he decided to take the subway. As he was going to the subway, he got lost. He walked down a corridor and found himself at the third level at Grand Central Station!

The place that Charley reached was different. There were smaller rooms, fewer ticket windows and open-flame gaslights there. The information booth was made of wood and everybody at the station was dressed in the late 19th century fashion. To be sure, the narrator got a copy of a newspaper, 'The World' dated 11th June, 1894.

Desire to go to Galesburg

Charley went to the ticket window to get two tickets for Galesburg, Illinois. He wanted to go to this peaceful countryside of 1894 with his wife, Louisa. However, the clerk at the ticket counter did not accept his currency bills. Sensing trouble, the narrator ran away. Now, to get the tickets, Charley took three hundred dollars and bought the currency of 1890.

Charley, then, started looking for the third level but failed. After his wife pressured him, Charley stopped looking for the level and went back to stamp collecting. But after Sam's sudden disappearance, Charley and his wife got proof of the existence of the third level. So, they started looking for the third level again.

The Proof

One day, while looking at his stamp collection, Charley found a strange cover dated 18th July,1894 mailed to his grandfather's address in Galesburg. The envelope contained a letter for Charley by Sam, who confirmed the presence of the third level and advises him to keep looking for it.

Soon after, Charley found that Sam had bought eight hundred dollars' worth of old-style currency. This money was sufficient to set up a hay, feed and grain business which Sam dreamt of. Sam is a qualified psychiatrist but cannot go back to his profession in Galesburg of 1894.

Word-Meaning

stack	—	to put (things) in a usually neat pile
refuge	—	hiding place
gabardine	—	tough and tightly woven fabric
ducked	—	lower the head
arched	—	curved or vaulted
flickering	—	shining unsteadily
glint	—	shine
frowned	—	disapproval
glanced	—	a brief look
tremendous	—	huge
nodded	—	incline
fussing	—	fret
hay	—	grass that is cut and used as animal food

Important Themes of the Chapter

Escapism and Nostalgia 'The Third Level' by Jack Finney explores escapism, nostalgia and the allure of the past. Through the protagonist's discovery of a mysterious third level in Grand Central Station, the story delves into the desire to escape from the complexities and uncertainties of modern life. The protagonist's journey to a bygone era, represented by 1894, reflects a longing for simplicity, safety and a romanticised view of the past. The theme of nostalgia is further emphasised by the protagonist's friend's decision to remain in the past, highlighting the powerful pull of nostalgia and the quest for a simpler, more idyllic existence amidst the chaos of a contemporary society.

NCERT Folder

Read and Find out (NCERT Page 1)

1. What does 'The Third Level' refer to?

Ans. The Third Level is the third floor of the Grand Central Station as visited by Charley one day. In reality, this third level does not exist.

'The Third Level', then, can be said to be a symbol of a modern man's innermost desire to escape from the world full of tensions, war, insecurity and fear. It stands for man's pursuit for a life full of peace and tranquility in contrast to the materialistic and self-centered world of today.

Read and Find out (NCERT Page 5)

1. Would Charley ever go back to the ticket-counter on the third level to buy tickets to Galesburg for himself and his wife?

Ans. No, Charley couldn't go back to the ticket-counter on the third level to buy tickets to Galesburg for his wife and himself. This is because after the first visit, Charley never finds the corridor that leads to the third level at the Grand Central Station.

Read with Insight (NCERT Page 7)

1. Do you think that the third level was a medium of escape for Charley? Why?

Ans. The modern world is full of fear, insecurity, war, worry and stress. Man feels bogged down and helpless. He does not understand what to do and how to come out of adverse circumstances. So, he looks for a 'temporary refuge from reality'.

Charley, belonging to the twentieth century, faced the same dilemma of a modern man. Busy in the rut of life, he indulged in his hobby of stamp collection for some mental peace and tranquility. Undoubtedly, it was always in his subconscious mind to find a means of escape from the ironies and materialistic bent of the world. Moreover, he had an earnest desire for things 'pretty, nice and peaceful', as they were in his grandfather's time. Then when he meets his psychiatrist, he admits that 'everybody I know wants to escape'.

All these things combined together resulted in his flight of fancy to the third level. Sam, the psychiatrist also told him that his claim was 'a waking dream wish fulfillment'. Hence, we can say that the third level was a medium of escape for Charley.

2. What do you infer from Sam's letter to Charley?

Ans. Sam's letter was found in the oldest first day covers of Charley's grandfather. It was dated 18th July, 1894 and was written from Galesburg, Illinois. This means that Sam had found the third level and escaped. From this, we can infer that the third level did exist which encourages Charley and Louisa to continue searching for it.

3. "The modern world is full of insecurity, fear, war, worry and stress." What are the ways in which we attempt to overcome them?

Ans. The modern world, undoubtedly makes us frustrated, helpless and overworked. Our subconscious mind, thus, finds ways and means to escape tensions.

Depending on our upbringing, mindset and interests, people find novel ways to overcome such a sorry state of affairs. Most people find refuge in hobbies. The narrator, Charley, indulges in stamp collection to break the monotony of his life and use time productively.

Many turn to yoga, religion, spirituality, exercise, books, music and creative fields like painting and writing to overcome stress and find time for themselves.

These interests help reduce stress, anxiety and hopelessness associated with life. A positive energy exudes from the body making one calm, relieved and tranquil. Many health problems can be cured if we indulge in pleasurable activities.

4. Do you see an intersection of time and space in the story 'The Third Level'?

Ans. Yes, there is an intersection of time and space in the story. Time and space have been reduced to nothingness as all barriers related to them are broken. Charley bumps into the third level of 1894 and returns to the twentieth century. Similarly, Sam reaches Galesburg in 1894 and still can contact Charley in the twentieth century, which convincingly brings about an intersection.

5. Apparent illogicality sometimes turns out to be a futuristic projection. Discuss.

Ans. Some things in life do not have a valid explanation or scientific reason. The sudden discovery of the third level by the narrator and his earnest desire to live a peaceful and contented life at Galesburg is not open to justification. The disappearance of his psychiatrist friend Sam is equally perplexing.

Both these individual wish to escape from the insecurities and intricacies of life can turn out to be futuristic projections. They want to lead an easy going life, wayback in 1894 when no one had heard about world wars. This indicates that people's unhappiness in their present life can lead to frustration and eventually a virtual breakdown of emotions, relationships, organisations and systems in the future.

The other way of explaining this statement is that all inventions, sometimes or the other, have been termed illogical. The cell phones we use today were an improbability some years before, but today they have become a necessity. Who knows the idea of going back in time, travelling back and forth in time (as depicted in the story) would become possible one day!

6. Philately helps keep the past alive. Discuss other ways in which this is done. What do you think of the human tendency to constantly move between the past, the present and the future?

Ans. The time dimension is divided into the past, the present and the future. Our past shapes our present. Similarly, in the present, lie seeds of the future. Philately helps keep the past alive. In the same way, hobbies like coin collection, books on varied topics, archaeological excavations, monuments, relics from the bygone era, movies, paintings and even music prevent our glorious past from being lost.

The human tendency to constantly move between the past, the present and the future shows man's dissatisfaction with life and a need to rationalize. We hanker after something which we do not get. The present does not leave man satisfied. He longs for the past to come back and waits incessantly for something positive to turn up in the future.

Exam Pattern Questions

Extract Based Questions

Read the extracts given below and answer the questions that follow.

1. He said I was unhappy. That made my wife kind of mad, but he explained that he meant the modern world is full of insecurity, fear, war, worry and all the rest of it, and that I just want to escape. Well, who doesn't?

Everybody I know wants to escape, but they don't wander down into any third level at Grand Central Station. But that's the reason, he said, and my friends all agreed. Everything points to it, they claimed. My stamp collecting, for example; that's a 'temporary refuge from reality.' Well, maybe, but my grandfather didn't need any refuge from reality.

(i) Complete the following suitably.

When Sam gives the complete reason for Charley's unhappiness, he ....

(ii) Why did Sam's verdict make Charley's wife 'mad'?

(iii) Select the option that signifies the condition of people of the 'modern world' mentioned in the extract.

(i) unsure | **(ii) lazy**
(iii) offensive | **(iv) anxious**
(v) afraid

(a) (i) and (iii) | (b) (ii) and (v)
(c) (ii), (iii) and (iv) | (d) (i), (iv) and (v)

(iv) Why didn't Charley's grandfather need refuge from reality?

Ans. (i) clarifies that Louisa is not the reason behind it

(ii) When Sam suggests that Charley was unhappy, Louisa gets mad as she thinks that Charley is unhappy because of her.

(iii) (d) (i), (iv) and (v)

(iv) Charley's grandfather did not require any refuge from reality because he lived in the pre-war peaceful and simpler times. In those time, people had no insecurities and were not anxious.

2. Now, I don't know why this should have happened to me. I'm just an ordinary guy named Charley, thirty-one years old, and I was wearing a tan gabardine suit and a straw hat with a fancy band; I passed a dozen men who looked just like me. And I wasn't trying to escape from anything; I just wanted to get home to Louisa, my wife.

(i) Complete the sentence appropriately, with reference to the extract.

'This' refers to ....

(ii) When did 'this' incident take place?

(iii) The given lines show that the narrator, Charley

(a) fancied going to his old town
(b) was a very amiable man with a lot of friends
(c) wanted to lead a normal life with his wife
(d) had a great imagination

(iv) Why does the narrator say that he was not trying to escape from anything?

Ans. (i) seeing the non-existent third level

(ii) 'This' incident took place while the narrator was returning late from work.

(iii) (c) wanted to lead a normal life with his wife

(iv) The narrator says that he was not trying to escape from anything because his psychiatrist friend told him he was trying to escape the stress.

3. **Sometimes I think Grand Central is growing like a tree, pushing out new corridors and staircases like roots. There's probably a long tunnel that nobody knows about feeling its way under the city right now, on its way to Times Square, and maybe another to Central Park. And maybe — because for so many people through the years Grand Central has been an exit, a way of escape– maybe that's how the tunnel I got into... But I never told my psychiatrist friend about that idea.**

CBSE Question Bank 2021 Modified

(i) Complete the following suitably.

The given lines uses a literary device ....

(ii) Why does the narrator never tell his psychiatrist friend about his idea?

(iii) Charley decided not to tell his psychiatrist friend about his idea. Choose the option that reflects the reaction Charley anticipated from his friend.

(a) "That's such a lovely comparison. Why don't you become a writer, Charley?"

(b) "Oh Charley. It is so sad to see your desperation to run away! So very sad."

(c) "Maybe that's how you entered the third level. Who would have thought?"

(d) "You need help, my raving friend. You are way too invested in this crazy thought!"

(iv) "Grand Central has been an exit, a way of escape". Explain.

Ans. (i) named metaphor to make a comparison between the Grand Central Station and a tree.

(ii) The narrator would never tell his psychiatrist friend about his idea because he knew that his friend would call him unhappy.

(iii) (d) "You need help, my raving friend. You are way too invested in this crazy thought!"

(iv) The given line points out that the third level of the Grand Central Station is a figment of imagination that acts as a medium of escape for people like Charley who are stressed and anxious in their modern life.

4. **To make sure. I walked over to the newsboy and glanced at the stack of papers at his feet. It was The World and The World hasn't been published for years. The lead story said something about President Cleveland. I've found that front page since, in the Public library files, and it was printed on 11th June, 1894.**

I turned toward the ticket windows knowing that here – on the third level at Grand Central – I could buy tickets that would take Louisa and me anywhere in the United States we wanted to go. In the year 1894. And I wanted two tickets to Galesburg. **CBSE 2023**

(i) The newspaper that covered the lead story about President Cleveland was

(a) The Pioneer (b) The New York Times
(c) The World (d) The Times

(ii) The narrator wanted to buy tickets to ....

(iii) Which of the following in the extract most nearly means the opposite of 'stare'?

(a) Glance (b) Peek
(c) Ignore (d) Examine

(iv) Charley wanted two tickets because he wanted to go with

(a) Sam (b) Cleveland
(c) Louisa (d) the Psychiatrist

Ans. (i) (c) The World

(ii) Galesburg, Illinois of 1894

(iii) (a) Glance (iv) (c) Louisa

5. **Have you ever been there? It's a wonderful town still, with big old frame houses, huge lawns, and tremendous trees whose branches meet overhead and roof the streets.**

And in 1894, summer evenings were twice as long, and people sat out on their lawns, the men smoking cigars and talking quietly, the women waving palm-leaf fans, with the fire-flies all around, in a peaceful world. To be back there with the First World War still twenty years off, and World War II over forty years in the future... I wanted two tickets for that.

CBSE Question Bank 2021, Modified

(i) Complete the following suitably.

'tremendous trees whose branches meet overhead and roof the streets' contains two literary devices. They are ....

(ii) Who does 'you' refer to?

(iii) Imagine that the city of Galesburg is hosting a series of conferences and workshops. In which of the following conferences or workshops are you least likely to find the description of Galesburg given in the above extract?

(a) Gorgeous Galesburg: Archiving a Tourist Paradise

(b) Welcome to the Home you Deserve: Galesburg Realtors

(c) Re-imagining a Warless Future: Technology for Peace

(d) The Woman Question: The World of Women at Home

(iv) Describe the society represented in the above extract.

Ans. (i) imagery and alliteration

(ii) The reader

(iii) (c) Re-imagining a Warless Future: Technology for Peace

(iv) The society represented in the given lines is an upper class orthodox one.

6. The clerk figured the fate he glanced at my family hat band, but he figured the fare and I had enough for two coach tickets, one way. But when I counted out the money and looked up the clerk was staring at me. He nodded at the bills. "That ain't money mister" he said "and if your trying to skin me you won't get very far" and he glanced at the cash drawer beside him. Of course the money was old-style bill half again as big as the money was use nowadays and different looking. CBSE 2023

(i) Why did Charley ask for two tickets?

(ii) Complete the sentence by choosing the correct options.

When Charley offered money to the booking clerk, the latter stared at Charley because the booking clerk ....

(a) thought it wasn't money
(b) did not trust Charley
(c) thought Charley was trying to tease him
(d) thought that Charley had given him less money

(iii) Select the option that best describes Charley in this extract. He is

(a) a cheat (b) gullible
(c) an opportunist (d) an escapist

(iv) 'If you're trying to skin me' suggests ....

Ans. (i) Charley asked for two tickets because he wanted to go to Galesburg, 1894 with his wife, Louisa.

(ii) (a) thought it wasn't money

(iii) (d) an escapist

(iv) that the clerk thought that Charley was trying cheat him

7. 941 Willard Street
Galesburg, Illinois
18th July, 1894

Charley I got to wishing that you were right. Then I got to believing you were right. And, Charley, it's true; I found the third level! I've been here two weeks and right now, down the street at the Daly's, someone is playing a piano and they're all out on the front porch singing 'Seeing Nelly Home.' And I'm invited over for lemonade. Come on back, Charley and Louisa. Keep looking till you find the third level! It's worth it, believe me!

The note is signed Sam. CBSE 2023

(i) What was the feeling of Sam as conveyed in the letter? Choose the appropriate option in the context of the extract.

(a) Surprise (b) Doubt
(c) Excitement (d) Anger

(ii) What was Sam Weiner's initial reaction when Charley told him about the third level?

(a) Dismissal (b) Acceptance
(c) Wonderstruck (d) Puzzled

(iii) The phrase 'Charley, it's true' in the context of the extract implies which of the given options?

I. Sam is relaxed.
II. Charley had migrated with Louisa.
III. The existence of the Third level.
IV. Sam had met Charley's grandfather.

Options

(a) I and II (b) II and IV
(c) I and III (d) Only IV

(iv) Sam wrote the letter to Charley in order to ....

Ans. (i) (c) Excitement (ii) (a) Dismissal

(iii) (c) I and III

(iv) inform Charley of the existence of the third level and urge him to keep looking for it.

Short Answer Type Questions

1. What would you describe as your 'waking-dream wish fulfillment'? Explain. Competency Based

Ans. By the phrase 'waking dream wish fulfillment', the author wanted to talk of imaginative or fantastical situations through which Charley lived his dream or fulfilled his desire. My waking dream wish fulfillment will be to become a journalist who can travel the world and bring to light without any fear the reality of situations that people face in their day-today lives.

2. Does Charley agree that stamp collecting habit is a way of escapism? Why?

Ans. No, Charley doesn't agree with his claim of his pyschiatrist friend. Charley's grandfather was a stamp collector yet he was a happy man and he never ran away from reality. Another stamp collector was President Roosevelt.

3. Explain the metaphor Charley uses to describe the Grand Central Station.

Ans. Charley compared the Grand Central station to a huge tree which keeps on spreading its roots and branches all over. He makes this comparison because whenever he entered the Grand Central Station, he found new corridors, staircases and tunnels. Charley's comparison of

Grand Central Station to a tree emphasises its complexity and interconnectedness, with many paths leading to different destinations.

4. Why did the booking clerk refuse to accept the money offered by Charley? CBSE 2023

Ans. The booking clerk refused to accept the money offered by Charley as it was from a different time. In 1894, the currency used was different from that was usually used by Charley in his time.

5. Why did Charley run away from the third level?

Ans. Charley wanted to buy two tickets to Galesburg but the clerk at the station thought that his notes were fake. He thought that Charley was attempting to fool him. He warned him that he would call the police. Seeing that there was nothing good about police and jail in 1894 as well, Charley ran away.

6. 'My three hundred dollars bought less than two hundred in old style bills, but I didn't care'.

What prompted Charley to compromise on less value of money? CBSE 2024

Ans. Charley wasn't troubled by receiving less money because his immediate concern was the necessity of obtaining cash for his escape. In 'The Third Level', his priority lay in securing funds rather than the exact amount, demonstrating his urgency to leave the present reality behind and seek refuge in the mysterious third level of Grand Central Station.

7. Why was Charley fascinated with Galesburg? CBSE 2024

Ans. Charley was fascinated with and wanted to go to Galesberg, Illinois because he wants to go to a place away from the modern world which is full of stress, war, fear, etc. The Galesburg Charley wanted to visit was a world before the World Wars, when there was no violence and everybody lived in peace.

8. What work did Sam set for in Galesburg? Why?

or What would Sam have done in Galesbury for his living? Why?

Ans. Sam set himself up in a hay, feed and grain business because he could not continue his old profession in Galesburg. In 1894, everyone was happy and contented so no one needed a psychiatrist.

9. What role does Sam's letter play in the story? CBSE 2023

Ans. In the story, 'The Third Level', Sam's letter solidifies Charley's beliefs regarding the existence of the third level and the peaceful life during 1894, Galesburg.

10. At the beginning of the story, Sam is sceptical of Charley's discovery of the third level. By the end of the story, the reader is told that he found the third level and travelled back in time. How would Sam diagnose himself?

Ans. I believe that Sam had already diagnosed himself as one of the modern men who faced the difficulties, stresses, anxieties of modern life. Even if he had not diagnosed himself earlier, Sam would later diagnose himself as exhibiting the same urge to escape the anxious contemporary life as Charley did.

11. 'It's easy to judge others and give advice but much more difficult to apply it to ourselves.' Elaborate with reference to the character of Sam in 'The Third Level'.

Ans. The given statement is true with respect to Sam, the psychiatrist friend of the protagonist of the short story 'The Third Level'. In the story, Sam had explained Charley that he was dissatisfied and looking for an escape when he told the former about the third level. According to him, Charley wanted respite from the anxieties and fears of the modern world and thus found the third level. Interestingly, in the end, it is Sam who goes in search of the third level himself.

12. How would you evaluate Sam's character? Elucidate any two qualities, and substantiate with evidence from the text. CBSE Question Bank 2021

Ans. Sam, the psychiatrist friend of the protagonist is a typical city boy who himself faces the anguish, stress and anxieties of modern life. He is a loyal friend to Charley who made sure that his friend knew about the existence of the third level that he had been searching.

13. Interpret the significance of both literal and metaphorical journeys in the story, 'The Third Level'. CBSE SQP 2024

Ans. The story 'The Third Level' refers to both a literal and metaphorical journey. The literal journey involves Charley, the protagonist discovering a supposed third level at the Grand Central Station. The metaphorical journey is Charley's inner longing for a simpler, more reassuring past. These journeys are significant as they present the common or universal quest for happiness and fulfillment.

14. Louisa behaves like a perfect wife. Give evidence from 'The Third Level' in support of the above statement. CBSE 2024

Ans. In 'The Third Level', Louisa embodies the ideal wife by supporting her husband Charley's unconventional beliefs in the existence of a third level at Grand Central Station. Despite initial doubts, she listens empathetically and remains supportive as Charley becomes absorbed in his quest. Louisa's unwavering support and patience reflect her portrayal as a devoted and understanding partner.

15. How does 'The Third Level' blend fantasy with reality?

Ans. 'The Third Level' blends fantasy with reality by discovering a hidden subway station that connects to a parallel world from the past. Charley's exploration of this mysterious level blurs the lines between reality and fantasy, challenging his perception of time and reality.

16. **How does Charley describe himself?** CBSE 2025

Ans. Charley describes himself as an ordinary man who enjoys simple pleasures but has a tendency to escape reality through imagination. His fascination with the past and belief in the existence of the Third Level at Grand Central Station suggest his longing for a peaceful, nostalgic world free from modern anxieties.

17. **What was the shocking discovery made by Charley when he was going through the first day covers of his grandfather's collection?** CBSE 2025

Ans. While going through his grandfather's collection of first-day covers, Charley was shocked to find a letter addressed to him from his friend Sam. The letter was postmarked 18th July, 1894, from Galesburg, Illinois, proving that Sam had traveled to the past through the third level.

18. **Charlie's desperate attempt to find the third level reflects his frustration with the modern world. What aspects of the modern would have led to Charlie's frustration?** CBSE 2025

Ans. Charley's frustration with the modern world stems from its fast-paced, materialistic, and war-ridden nature. The pressures of daily life, stress and insecurity push him to seek an escape into an idealised past. The third level symbolises his longing for peace and simplicity, which he feels are missing in the present.

Long Answer Type Questions

1. **Describe briefly the scene at the third level of Grand Central Station as seen (or seemed to be seen) by Charley.** CBSE 2020

Ans. At the third level of the Grand Central Station, Charley noticed that there were fewer ticket windows and train gates and the information booth in the centre of the station was made up of wood and was old-looking. Everyone dressed like 1890's. The lights were dim and flickering.

He saw so many beards, side buns and fancy moustaches. He saw that a woman was wearing a dress with leg of mutton sleeves and a skirt to the top of her high buttoned shoes. He also saw a small currier and Ives locomotive with funnel shaped stack. Further, he saw the people used string-watches, long black sleeve protectors and big sized currencies. The trains ran on steam and coaches were smaller.

The last thing he noticed was that newspapers bore the date of 1894 and the lead story about the hundred year old America's President Cleveland.

2. **In the story 'The Third Level', Charley wanted to go to Galesburg, Illinois in the year 1894. If you had an opportunity to go to another time and place, where would you like to go? Why? How would Sam analyse your choice of alternate time and place?** Competency Based

Ans. If I had an opportunity to go to another time, I would love to go to the United Kingdom right before the Second World War. The lessons of the First World War were just being observed and everyone was trying to make sure that another war did not take place. There I would want to live in the countryside and go to the local school. Being in the countryside, the effects of the First World War was not so visible. Besides, food was in plenty because of the farm and vegetable gardens attached to the school. Clothing came from the village nearby. Going back there would satisfy my urge to study at an experimental school and get an all-round holistic education. Sam Weiner would analyse my wish as an urge to erase the regular humdrum of city life.

3. **Imagine that you come across Louisa's diary. What might you find in it about the third level? Compose at least one diary entry based on any of the events from the story, 'The Third Level'.** CBSE Question Bank 2021, Competency Based

Ans. Monday, 20th July 9 p.m.

Dear Diary

Charley is worrying me with all this third level drama. When he told me about it, I was shocked. For so many years we have been travelling from the Grand Central Station and never had we heard about its third level. I took him to his friend, Sam. And what he told me surprised me. Charley was not happy. Why was he not happy?

I really do not know what to do now? Even Sam is missing and Charley believes he is in 1894 Galesburg. How absurd is that? I have to talk to Charley about it and dissuade him from doing anything wrong.

Louisa

4. **Discuss the narrative techniques used by the author in 'The Third Level'. How do these techniques effectively convey the themes of escapism and nostalgia? Provide specific examples from the text to support your analysis.** CBSE SQP 2024

Ans. The author of the story 'The Third Level' uses various narrative techniques to effectively convey the themes of escapism and nostalgia.

The story is written from the first-person perspective of Charley, which creates an intimate and personal recounting of his experiences and thoughts. This allows readers to directly engage with Charley's desires and fears, making his longing for escape and the nostalgia for a simpler past more relatable. Charley gives a detailed description of his experiences at the third level, in 1894 and his discussion with his psychiatrist friend Sam. These descriptions not only build a believable world but also vividly paint the past, stressing the theme of nostalgia and the allure of escapism to a seemingly better and simpler time.

The story also uses the 'third level' as a symbol, representing not just a physical place but a mental escape into another time. It is a metaphor for the psychological refuge one seeks from the modern world's anxieties, underlining the theme of escapism.

5. Sam's letter to Charley is an interesting feature that adds to the theme of fancy and imagination. Comment.

Ans. From the reading of the story 'The Third Level', we can say that Sam's letter to Charley is an interesting feature that adds to the theme of fancy and imagination. Sam's letter was found in the oldest first day covers of Charley's grandfather. It was dated 18th July, 1894 and was written from Galesburg, Illinois. This means that Sam had found the third level and escaped. Although he diagonsed Charley's problem as an escape from the modern life, he himself had been bothered by the humdrum of modern existence and frustrations. In the letter, he asks Charley and Louisa to keep looking for the third level as 'It's worth it'.

The reader is not surprised by Sam's letter to Charley but instinctively questions how a letter was found in an old first-day cover in grandfather's collection. Charley feels puzzled when he realises that the letter was addressed to him and not to his grandfather although the address on the envelope was of his grandfather. Moreover, like the third level it is possible that the letter could be a figment of Charley's imagination. Thus, the letter gives an interesting angle to the story and makes the reader curious.

6. Charley plays a central role in exploring the story's themes and symbolises human longing for a romantic past. Elucidate with reference to Charley's character.

Ans. Charley is the protagonist of the story titled 'The Third Level'. He is portrayed as an ordinary thirty-one-year-old man leading a typical life, working in an office and living with his wife, Louisa in a bustling city. Despite his seemingly mundane existence, Charley's encounter with the mysterious third level at Grand Central Station sparks a profound curiosity.

Charley exhibits an inquisitive nature, which is evident in his exploration of the third level despite its enigmatic nature. His willingness to delve into the unknown and search for the third level demonstrates his adventurous spirit. However, it is his discovery of the third level which leads to self-discovery and exploration of themes such as escapism and nostalgia.

Charley's fascination with the third level stems from a desire to escape the complexities and uncertainties of modern life, suggesting a longing for a simpler, more idyllic existence. His quest to find the third level reflects a deep yearning for nostalgia as he seeks to connect with a past era of 1894. As the protagonist, he plays a central role in exploring the story's themes and symbolises human longing for a romantic past.

7. In the story 'The Third Level', Charley wanted to go to Galesburg, Illinois in the year 1894. If you had an opportunity to go to another time and place, where would you like to go? Why? How would Sam analyse your choice of alternate time and place? **Competency Based**

Ans. If I had an opportunity to go to another time, would love to go to the United Kingdom right before the Second World War.

The lessons of the First World War were just being observed and everyone was trying to make sure that another war like it did not take place. There I would want to live in the countryside and go to the local school.

Being in the countryside, the effects of the First World War were not so visible. Besides, food was in plenty because of the farm and vegetable gardens attached to the school. Clothing came from the village nearby. Going back there would satisfy my urge to study at an experimental school and get an all-round holistic education. However, Sam Weiner would analyse my wish as an urge to erase the regular humdrum of city life.

8. The story invites readers to reflect on their own desires for escapism and the interplay between dreams and reality.
Based on 'The Third Level', describe two adjustments you would need to make if you were to visit the third level of Grand Central Station, apart from dealing with the currency change. Answer in 100-120 words. **Competency Based**

Ans. If I were to visit the third level of Grand Central Station, I'd need to prepare beyond just currency changes. Dressing in late 19th-century fashion would be essential, including suits with specific lapel styles and appropriate hats. I'd have to adjust to gaslight instead of electric lights. Communication would be face-to-face, as smartphones and the internet wouldn't exist. Transportation would involve horse-drawn carriages and longer walks. Additionally, I'd need to manage with the limited goods and services of that time. Most importantly, understanding and adhering to the social norms and customs of the late 1800s would be crucial for blending in.

SELF ASSESSMENT TEST

Extract Based Questions

Read the extract given below and answer the questions that follow.

1. But I've never again found the corridor that leads to the third level at Grand Central Station, although I've tried often enough.

Louisa was pretty worried when I told her all this, and didn't want me to look for the third level any more, and after a while I stopped; I went back to my stamps. But now we're both looking, every weekend, because now we have proof that the third level is still there.

(i) Complete the following suitably.

"I've tried often enough" shows the narrator's ....

(ii) '........Because now we have proof' .....' what is the proof referred to in the extract?

(iii) "I went back to my stamps". This sentence means

(a) collecting post stamps
(b) looking for his granddad's post stamps
(c) preserving his granddad's post stamps
(d) working with post stamps

(iv) Why was Louisa worried?

Short Answer Type Questions

Answer the following questions in 40-50 words.

1. What is referred to as 'a temporary refuge from reality'? Why?

2. Why do you think Charley withdrew nearly all the money he had from the bank to buy old-style currency?

3. In his letter to Charley, Sam writes, '........... then I got to believing you were right?' What could have made Sam to believe?

4. Why was Charley not able to get to Galeburg again?

5. How did Sam reach Galesburg?

Long Answer Type Question

Answer the following question in 120-150 words.

1. The modern consumerist world is full of fear, insecurities, stress and wars. What are the ways in which we try to combat them? Answer with reference to 'The Third Level'.

02

About the Author

Ramaswamy Aiyer Krishnamurthy (1899 - 1954), better known by his pen name 'Kalki', was a Tamil writer, journalist, poet, critic and Indian independence activist. His writings include over 120 short stories, 10 novellas, 5 novels, 3 historical romances, editorial and political writings and hundreds of film and music reviews. He used his writings as a medium to voice his concerns about social inequalities, caste discrimination and political issues prevalent during his time.

▼ **YOUR STUDY GOALS**

- Chapter Sketch
- About the Characters
- Summary of the Chapter

▼ **YOUR PRACTICE GOAL**

- NCERT Folder
- Extract Based Questions
- Short Answer Type Questions
- Long Answer Type Questions

The Tiger King

Chapter Sketch

The story 'The Tiger King' is a satire on the pride and stubbornness of those in power. The writer takes us to the days of autocratic and strange kings, who spent their time in foolish pursuits. They flouted all laws and bent them to suit their selfish interests. The Maharaja of Pratibandapuram tried to believe what was written in his fate by killing a 100 tigers. His campaign of tiger-hunting was very successful. All his strategies and wise plans worked till he killed 99 tigers. But the hundredth tiger eluded him till his death. The irony of fate brings quite an unexpected end of the Maharaja. The hero who killed ninety nine tigers died due to a wooden toy tiger.

About the Characters

The Maharaja (Tiger King) He is a comical and eccentric character who behaves like an autocrat and kills tigers indiscriminately.

The Dewan He is the Maharaja's Chief Minister. He is not only supports the Maharaja in his decisions but also warns him of danger.

The Astrologer He is an Indian priest who predicts the Maharaja's demise. He is so confident of his prediction that he promises to remove his holy tuft if his prediction fails.

Summary of the Chapter

The Prophecy

The Maharaja of Pratibandapuram is often called 'Tiger King'. When he was born, the astrologers foretold that he would grow up to be a great warrior but one day he would have to meet his death due to a tiger. The child warned the tigers to beware of him. The crown prince grew taller and stronger day by day. Like other princes in India, the prince grew up like an Englishmen.

The Tiger Hunt

The Maharaja was crowned the king at the age of twenty, when the astrologer's prediction reached his ears. So, he went on a tiger hunt and killed his first tiger. When he showed his kill to the astrologer, he was told that he would be killed by the 100th tiger. The astrologer added that if the king would succeed in killing the hundredth tiger, the astrologer would cut off his tuft of hair, burn all his astrology books and become an insurance agent.

The Maharaja started his tiger hunt and banned tiger hunting in his kingdom. He further vowed to attend to all other matters only after killing a hundred tigers. In his quest, the Maharaja faced many dangers but each time it was the Maharaja who won.

Threat of Losing the Kingdom

Once the Maharaja was on the verge of losing his kingdom. He had refused to allow a high ranking British officer to hunt tigers. After much discussion with the dewan about the issue, they sent 50 diamond rings to the officer's wife. The Maharaja expected that she would choose one or two rings, but the lady kept the whole lot. The Maharaja lost money but his kingdom was saved.

Decision to Marry

The Maharaja's tiger hunts were very successful. Within ten years, he was able to kill seventy tigers. As a result, the tiger population became extinct in Pratibandapuram. The Maharaja, then, decided to marry a princess of a royal family with a large tiger population. He killed five or six tigers each time he visited his father-in-law. Soon, he had managed to kill ninety-nine tigers. Now, only one tiger remained to be killed.

The Maharaja's Anger

The Maharaja was unable to find the last tiger. Suddenly, there came the news that a tiger had been seen in a hillside village. The Maharaja was so happy that set out on the hunt at once. However, the tiger was not found. As a result, the Maharaja doubled the tax. When the dewan warned him against this decision, the Maharaja asked the dewan to resign.

Killing the 100th Tiger

The dewan, to save himself, decided to give up the old tiger that had been brought from the People's Park in Madras and kept hidden in his house. The dewan and his wife took the tiger to their car and left it in the forest in which the Maharaja had been hunting.

The Maharaja was delighted to see the hundredth tiger. He took careful aim and shot at the beast. Thinking that the tiger was dead, he asked other to bring the tiger to the captial. However, after the Maharaja left, the hunters realised that the tiger was still alive. It fainted by the shock of the bullet flying past it. They decided not to tell the Maharaja as they feared losing their jobs. So, one of the hunters then killed the tiger himself.

The Wooden Tiger

After achieving the feat, the Maharaja turned his attention to his child. It was his third birthday and he wished to give him something special. He went for shopping but couldn't find anything worthy enough. Finally, he spotted a wooden tiger and brought it for his son.

The wooden tiger was carved by an unskilled carpenter. Tiny slivers of wood stood up like quills all over it. One of the slivers pierced the Maharaja's right hand while he was playing with his son. He didn't mind it and pulled it out. The next day, an infection spread in his hand. In four days, it developed into a sore which spread all over his arm. Three surgeons from Madras operated on him, but were unable to save his life. Thus, the hundredth tiger took its revenge.

Word-Meaning

stuka bomber	—	A German dive-bomber and ground attack aircraft used in World War II
throw me off track	—	distract
beat a hasty retreat	—	to withdraw from a place very quickly
abode	—	residence
demise	—	death
swallowed hard	—	made an effort to control oneself, often because one is nervous
transfixed	—	motionless with wonder or astonishment
stupefaction	—	great astonishment
enunciated	—	uttered or pronounced clearly
growl	—	a low harsh sound of anger
hindsight	—	understanding of a situation or event only after it has happened
crown prince	—	a prince who is to inherit the throne
nanny	—	a woman employed to look after a child in its own home
court of wards	—	a legal body created to look after the upbringing of minor heirs and protecting their estates
tuft of	—	a bunch of hair growing from the back of an otherwise bald head
boar	—	wild pig
durai	—	(here) the British lord or officer
deliberations	—	long and careful discussions
duraisani	—	(here) the wife of the British officer
extinct	—	no longer in existence
harakiri	—	suicide
brandishing	—	waving a weapon in a threatening way
babble	—	talk rapidly in a foolish or confused way
fever pitch	—	a state of extreme excitement
tally	—	count or record
exemption	—	act of freeing from some obligation
wantonly	—	mischievously, playfully
flout	—	defy or disregard
catastrophic	—	disastrous
supplication	—	request
elation	—	great happiness
bafflement	—	confusion
whizzing	—	moving quickly
craftsmanship	—	art or skill in an occupation or trade
slivers	—	thin or narrow pieces
quills	—	sharp spines of a porcupine
suppurating	—	forming or discharging pus
sore	—	wound

Important Themes of the Chapter

Irony of Fate The theme of 'The Tiger King' contains the irony of fate, the pursuit of power and control, and the consequences of hubris (excessive pride or self-confidence). Throughout the narrative, the protagonist, the Maharaja of Pratibandapuram, strives to defy his predicted fate of death by a tiger through relentless tiger hunting. However, despite his efforts to control his destiny, he ultimately meets his demise unexpectedly and ironically, highlighting fate's unpredictability and human agency's limitations.

Satire on Power and Arrogance The story also explores themes of ambition, obsession and the consequences of unchecked power. Through the Maharaja's tragic fate, the narrative explores human agency's limitations and fate's inevitability. It serves as a cautionary tale about the consequences of hubris and the importance of humility in the face of life's uncertainties. Ultimately, 'The Tiger King' highlights the irony that sometimes, the harder one struggles against fate, the more firmly it traps them.

NCERT Folder

Read and Find Out (NCERT Page 8-13)

1. Who is the Tiger King? Why does he get that name?

Or How did the Tiger King acquire his name?

Ans. The Maharaja of Pratibandapuram was often referred to as the Tiger King. He got this name because when he was born, a prophecy was made that a tiger would be reason for his death. Hence, he was called the Tiger King.

2. What did the royal infant grow up to be?

Ans. The royal infant grew up to be crown Prince Jung Bahadur. He grew taller and stronger day by day. Like other princes of India, he grew up in a totally English atmosphere.

He drank the milk of an English cow, was brought up by an English nanny, tutored in English by an Englishman and saw nothing but English films. He grew up and became just like an Englishman in his ways.

3. What will the Maharaja do to find the required number of tigers to kill?

Or What was the reason for the Tiger King's sudden decision to marry?

Or What was the hidden agenda behind the Tiger King's marriage with the princess in the neighbouring state? CBSE 2023

Ans. The hidden agenda behind the Tiger King's marriage with the princess in the neighbouring state was to achieve his goal of killing a hundred tigers. Marrying a princess from a state with a large tiger population was one way to ensure that he had access to enough tigers to reach his goal. He had run out of tigers in his kingdom, and he needed to hunt thirty more tigers so as to prove the astrologer wrong.

Read and Find Out (NCERT Page 14-15)

1. How will the Maharaja prepare himself for the hundredth tiger which was supposed to decide his fate?

Ans. The Maharaja's anxiety reached a feverish pitch when there remained just one tiger to achieve the tally of a hundred. However, this last tiger was hard to be found as by this time the tigers went extinct even in his father-in-law's kingdom. Soon, there were reports of a tiger near a hillside village in his own state. The king set out on the hunt at once. He also exempted the villagers from paying taxes for three years as a reward.

2. What will now happen to the astrologer? Do you think the prophecy was indisputably disproved?

Ans. The king died and so no harm will come to the astrologer as there is nobody to question him. However, his prophecy was not disproved as the Maharaja was not able to actually kill a hundred tigers.

Reading with Insight (NCERT Page 17)

1. The story is a satire on the conceit of those in power. How does the author employ the literary device of dramatic irony in the story?

Ans. Dramatic irony is a literary device whereby the words and actions of the characters of a work of literature have an opposite meaning for the reader than they do for the characters. The author effectively uses the tool of dramatic irony in the story. For instance, after killing the first tiger, the Tiger King displays it ostentatiously in front of the astrologer. But the astrologer warns him to be 'very careful with the hundredth tiger'.

Having shot at the hundredth tiger, the king believed that it is dead. But the tiger had only fainted from the shock of the bullet flying past it. The irony comes into play when the king buys a wooden toy tiger for his son and gets injured from the slivers of wood. He dies due to an infection from the wooden sliver as he has been doomed to death.

2. What is the author's indirect comment on subjecting innocent animals to the wilfulness of human beings?

Ans. The author indirectly comments on subjecting innocent animals to the willfulness of human beings by portraying the Maharaja's obsession with tiger hunting. The Tiger King goes on a hunting spree and interferes with the course of nature by indulging in the heinous slaughter of tigers. Through this portrayal, the author criticises the arrogance and cruelty of humans who exploit and harm animals for their amusement or perceived superiority.

3. How would you describe the behaviour of the Maharaja's minions towards him? Do you find them truly sincere towards him or are they driven by fear when they obey him? Do we find a similarity in today's political order?

Ans. The behaviour of the Maharaja's minions towards him can be seen as driven by a combination of sincere loyalty and fear. While some may genuinely admire and support the Maharaja, others may obey him for fear of retribution or loss of status. One example of such a behaviour can be seen in the dewan. Although the dewan is Maharaja's adviser, he knows that going against him can have disastrous consequences. So, he arranges the Tiger King's marriage to a princess whose kingdom has a large tiger population. Later, he plants a tiger for the Maharaja to shoot just to save himself.

This dynamic reflects a common theme in political systems where individuals may feel compelled to align with those in power, either out of genuine loyalty or self-preservation.

4. Can you relate instances of game-hunting among the rich and the powerful in the present times that illustrate the callousness of human beings towards wildlife?

Ans. Instances of game-hunting among the rich and powerful illustrate human callousness towards wildlife. For example, trophy hunting expeditions, where wealthy individuals pay large sums of money to hunt and kill endangered animals for sport, highlight humanity's disregard for these creatures' lives. Additionally, destroying natural habitats for development or commercial interests further demonstrates humanity's disregard for the well-being of wildlife and ecosystems.

5. We need a new system for the age of ecology – a system which is embedded in the care of all people and also in the care of the Earth and all life upon it. Discuss.

Ans. Being the finest creation of God, man, on the basis of his intelligence, has dominated all other forms of life on Earth. In a bid to satisfy his innumerable needs, man has altered the symbiotic relationship between him and nature. Man's needs have changed into greed now. It is said, "The Earth has enough for man's need but not enough to satisfy his greed".

This has led to a dismal scenario in which we have to face problems like global warming, melting of polar ice-caps, receding glaciers, soil erosion, pollution, depleting forest cover and extinction of several species of flora and fauna.

It is important that at this critical juncture, we need a revolution to save our planet and its ecological heritage.

Thus, there is need for a new system for the age of ecology. This system should prioritise the well-being of all people and the Earth itself, recognising the interconnectedness of human societies and the natural world. It should promote sustainability, conservation and responsible stewardship of resources to ensure the health and vitality of ecosystems for future generations.

Exam Pattern Questions

Extract Based Questions

Read the extracts given below and answer the questions that follow.

1. "All those who are born will one day have to die. We don't need your predictions to know that. There would be some sense in it if you could tell us the manner of that death".

(i) Complete the following suitably.

The speaker of the above lines is ....

(ii) To whom the above lines are addressed to?

(iii) Which of the following can be attributed to the listeners of the given lines?

(a) Admiration (b) Wonder
(c) Pride (d) Respect

(iv) How old was the speaker when he spoke the above lines?

Ans. (i) the Tiger King

(ii) The given lines have been addressed to the astrologers who have come to meet the prince.

(iii) (b) Wonder

(iv) The speaker was ten days old when he spoke the above lines.

2. From that day onwards it was celebration time for all the tigers inhabiting Pratibandapuram. The State banned tiger hunting by anyone except the Maharaja. A proclamation was issued to the effect that if anyone dared to fling so much as a stone at a tiger, all his wealth and property would be confiscated.

The Maharaja vowed he would attend to all other matters only after killing the hundred tigers. Initially the king seemed well set to realise his ambition. **CBSE 2024**

(i) Select the correct option.

'... he would attend to all other matters only after killing hundred tigers.' This reflects Tiger King's

(a) courage (b) determination
(c) selfishness (d) kindness

(ii) **Complete the sentence appropriately.**
'From that day onwards it was celebration time for all the tigers'. The given statement is ironical in a sense ....

(iii) **' ... if anyone dared to fling so much as a stone at a tiger, all his wealth and property would be confiscated'. What trait of the king is reflected in the above line?**

(iv) **State whether the following statement is True or False.**

The King's ambition is to save people from the tigers.

Ans. (i) (b) determination

(ii) because the king initiated a ban on the hunting of tigers in order to safeguard them but it eventually ends in putting them in danger by hunting them himself.

(iii) It is reflected from the above line that the king is ruthless and strict with regards to rules and regulations. However, he diminishes the same strictness when it comes to himself.

(iv) False

3. **From that day onwards it was celebration time for all the tigers inhabiting Pratibandapuram. The state banned tiger hunting by anyone except the Maharaja. A proclamation was issued to the effect that if anyone dared to fling so much as a stone at a tiger, all his wealth and property would be confiscated.**

The Maharaja vowed he would attend to all other matters only after killing the hundred tigers. Initially the king seemed well set to realise his ambition.

Not that he faced no dangers. There were times when the bullet missed its mark, the tiger leapt upon him and he fought the beast with his bare hands. Each time it was the Maharaja who won.

CBSE Question Bank 2021, Modified

(i) **Complete the following suitably.**
The tone of the author when he says, 'it was celebration time for all tigers' is ....

(ii) **Why did the Maharaja want to kill tigers specifically?**

(iii) **On the basis of this passage, pick the option that enumerates the characteristics of the king.**

1. gullible	**2. arrogant**
3. willful	**4. aggressive**
5. apathetic	**6. scrupulous**

(a) 1, 2 and 6 (b) 3, 4 and 6
(c) 3, 5 and 6 (d) 2, 3 and 5

(iv) **What does the proclamation show us about the authority possessed by the Maharaja?**

Ans. (i) sarcastic

(ii) The Maharaja wanted to kill tigers specifically because of the prediction that he would be killed by the hundredth tiger.

(iii) (d) 2, 3 and 5

(iv) The proclamation show us that the Maharaja possessed immense power and the authority over the masses. No one disobeyed him for the fear of his anger.

4. **The Maharaja and the dewan held deliberations over this issue. As a result, a telegram was despatched forthwith to a famous British company of jewellers in Calcutta. 'Send samples of expensive diamond rings of different designs'.**

(i) **Complete the sentence appropriately, with reference to the extract.**
The 'deliberations' were essential because ....

(ii) **How many rings were received from the company?**

(iii) **To whom the rings were gifted?**
(a) Raja's wife
(b) Wife of the British officer
(c) Killer of the 100th tiger
(d) Dewan

(iv) **On which issue Maharaja and the Dewan were tensed?**

Ans. (i) if immediate action was not taken to resolve the situation, the Maharaja could lose his kingdom.

(ii) Fifty rings were received from the company.

(iii) (b) Wife of the British officer

(iv) The Maharaja and Dewan were tensed because they prevented the British officer from fulfilling his desire of hunting a tiger in their kingdom. Hence, they were in fear of losing the kingdom.

5. **The dewan went home convinced that if the Maharaja didn't find the tiger soon, the results could be catastrophic. He felt life returning to him only when he saw the tiger which had been brought from the People's Park in Madras and kept hidden in his house.**

(i) **Complete the sentence appropriately.**
The phrase 'life returning to him' here means ....

(ii) **Why was the tiger hidden in his house?**

(iii) **Which characterisitc can you associate with the Maharaja on the basis of the given extract?**
(a) Moody (b) Manipulative
(c) Amiable (d) Authoritative

(iv) Why was the dewan worried?

Ans. (i) resurrect things that are inactive

(ii) The tiger was hidden in the Dewan's house so that he could fulfill King's desire to kill the hundredth tiger.

(iii) (d) Authoritative

(iv) The dewan was worried because he might lose his job if the king's demand aren't met.

6. At midnight when the town slept in peace, the dewan and his aged wife dragged the tiger into the car and shoved it into the seat. The Dewan himself drove the car straight to the forest where the Maharaja was hunting. When they reached the forest, the tiger launched its satyagraha and refused to get out of the car. The Dewan was thoroughly exhausted in his efforts to haul the beast out of the car and push it down to the ground.

On the following day, the same old tiger wandered into the Maharaja's presence and stood as if in humble supplication, "Master, what do you command of me?" It was with boundless joy that the Maharaja took careful aim at the beast. The tiger fell in a crumpled heap. **CBSE 2025**

(i) How did the Dewan manage to take the tiger to the forest?

(a) The Dewan conceded to the tiger's satyagraha

(b) The Dewan pushed the tiger into the car and drove to the forest

(c) The Dewan hauled the tiger into the tent

(d) The Dewan persuaded the tiger into a humble supplication of the Maharaja

(ii) Choose the correct option.

The attitude of the Dewan in the above extract can be described as .... (negligent and reluctant/meek and servile)

(iii) Select one statement or expression from the extract that reflects the humorous writing style of the author.

(iv) State one reason for the 'boundless joy of the Maharaja'.

Ans. (i) (b) The Dewan pushed the tiger into the car and drove to the forest.

(ii) Choose the correct option

The attitude of the Dewan in the above extract can be described as meek and servile.

(iii) Select one statement or expression from the extract that reflects the humorous writing style of the author.

"Master, Maharaja's presence and stood as if in humble supplication, 'Master, what do you command of me'?"

(This exaggeration of the tiger bowing down humorously reflects irony and satire.)

(iv) State one reason for the 'boundless joy of the Maharaja'.

The Maharaja was overjoyed because he believed he had successfully killed his hundredth tiger and fulfilled his vow.

Short Answer Type Questions

1. What gave the astrologers the greatest surprise of their life while they were studying the horoscope of the ten-day old prince?

Ans. When the astrologers were studying the horoscope of the prince, the infant prince suddenly began to speak clearly and wisely. This miracle, of the ten-day old prince speaking, gave the astrologers the greatest surprise of their life.

2. What made the chief astrologer place his finger on his nose?

Ans. When the baby Maharaja was only ten days old, he opened his lips in speech and raised intelligent questions to the chief astrologer. He asked him about the manner of his death. This made the chief astrologer place his finger on his nose in wonder.

3. "I shall cut my tuft crop my hair short and become an insurance agent." Explain the context.

Ans. The given line is taken from the story 'The Tiger King'. The line is spoken by the astrologer who had told the Maharaja that he would be killed by the hundredth tiger. To prove the truth of his prediction, the astrologer makes the statement that he would leave astrology and become an insurance agent if his prophecy is not fulfilled.

4. What led the Maharaja to start out on the tiger hunt?

Ans. When the Maharaja was born, a prophecy was made that the reason of his death would be a tiger. The Maharaja wanted to prove the prediction wrong. After he killed the first tiger, the astrologer told him that he would have to kill a hundred tigers as according to the prophecy the hundredth tiger would cause his death. So, the Maharaja started out on a tiger hunt to save his life.

5. What sort of hunt did the Maharaja offer to organise for the high-ranking British officer? What trait of the officer does it reveal?

Ans. When the British official came with a request for a tiger hunt, the Maharaja offered to organise a boar hunt, a mouse hunt or even a mosquito hunt for him, but not a tiger hunt. The Maharaja was then informed that the official would even be happy to simply pose with the tiger's carcass for a photograph, while the Maharaja could do the actual killing. This shows the vanity and shallowness of the officer.

6. How did the 'duraisani' behave on receiving the gifts? CBSE 2023

Ans. When the 'duraisani' received the gifts of 50 rings from the Maharaja of Pratibandapuram, she behaved like a greedy woman who kept all of them which was not expected by anyone.

7. How did the Tiger King manage to retain his kingdom?

Or How did the Maharaja please a high-ranking British officer?

Or What did the Maharaja and Dewan do to avoid the danger of losing the throne? CBSE 2023

Ans. The Maharaja did not permit a high-ranking British officer to hunt tigers in his kingdom, due to which he displeased the officer and was in danger of losing his kingdom. To counteract this, he sent the officer's wife a selection of fifty diamond rings from which she could keep the one she liked. The lady kept all of them, thus, pleasing the officer and helping the Maharaja retain his kingdom.

8. Why did the Maharaja order the Dewan to double the land tax?

Ans. When the hundredth tiger was hard to find near the hillside village which had reported its presence, the angry Maharaja ordered the Dewan to double the land tax for that village in frustration and anger.

9. Why did the Dewan decide to give up his own tiger to be killed by the Maharaja?

Ans. The Maharaja refused to leave the forest until he had killed the last tiger. Many officers lost their jobs, and the Dewan feared that he too might lose his job. So, to save his job, the Dewan decided to give up the tiger he had hidden.

10. Did the Tiger King shoot the hundredth tiger? Give reasons for your answer.

Ans. When the Tiger King shot at the tiger, the bullet actually missed its target but the old tiger fainted from the shock of the bullet whizzing past it. So, although the tiger appeared to be dead, it was only unconscious. Thus, although the Maharaja thought he had killed the tiger, it was not so. Later, it was killed by one of the hunters accompanying the Maharaja.

11. How did the Tiger King celebrate his victory over the killing of the hundredth tiger?

Ans. When he thought that he had killed the hundredth tiger, his joy knew no bounds. The elated king returned to his capital and ordered his staff to bring the dead tiger in a grand procession. The tiger was buried and a tomb was erected over it.

12. Discuss the significance of the toy tiger in the climax of 'The Tiger King'. CBSE SQP 2024

Ans. The toy tiger holds a significant role in bringing in the climax of the story 'The Tiger King'. This wooden tiger stands in stark contrast to the dangerous live tigers the Maharaja had been hunting throughout his life. Its role in bring the Maharaja's death brings up the themes of irony and fate central to the story. It illustrates that despite human efforts to control or escape destiny, it can manifest in the most unexpected and trivial forms. The toy tiger symbolises the ultimate futility of the Maharaja's efforts and points to the folly of those who believe they can master fate through power or violence.

13. What did the Majaraja do to realise his ambition of killing hundred tigers? CBSE 2023

Ans. To realise his ambition of killing hundred tigers, the Maharaja did many things. He banned tiger hunting and even faced the danger of losing his kingdom when he refused to allow a British official to hunt tigers. He himself stayed in forests to kill the tigers. Further, he even married a princess of a state with great tiger population to fulfill his ambition.

14. Do you think the prediction made by the state astrologer was indisputably disproved? Give reasons in support of your answer. CBSE 2024

Ans. The prophecy made by the state astrologer cannot to be indisputably disproved as the king was ultimately killed by a tiger that was neither a real one nor the hundredth one. The weak, old and almost lifeless tiger that was the hundredth one escaped the king's bullet by fainting at the shock of the bullet whizzing past. It was the 'tiny little wooden tiger' from the toy shop that caused the death of Tiger King.

15. The manner of his (The Tiger King's) death is a matter of extraordinary interest. Comment.

Or How did the Tiger King meet his end? What is ironical about his fate?

Ans. The manner of the Tiger King's death is a matter of extraordinary interest because it is ironical that, although he killed 99 live tigers, a harmless wooden toy tiger caused his death. A tiny sliver of wood of the toy tiger pierced the Maharaja's right hand. It became infected and the Maharaja died due to the infection. Thus, his death was destined and he failed to survive the ominous prediction.

16. Do you think an author who includes several instances of satire in a story faces the risk of being too cynical? Explain.

Ans. No, I do not think that the instances of satire in the story face the risk of being too cynical. The satire in the story highlights the reality of the authority and power possessed as well as misused by influential people.

17. "Knowing too much of your future is never a good thing." In light of this quote, examine how knowing the future paved way for the king's end. **CBSE Question Bank 2021**

Ans. It is truly said that "Knowing too much of your future is never a good thing". This has been aptly shown in the story of 'The Tiger King'. The Maharaja since his childhood had been aware of his death from a tiger. When he gets to know about his death from the 100th tiger, the Maharaja gets on a killing spree. He kills 100 tigers and feels infallible. He feels that he had escape death and does not pay attention to the wound given by the 100th wooden tiger which ultimately leads to his death.

18. The Maharaja justified his actions based on the maxim: "You may kill even a cow in self-defence, so there would be no objection to killing tigers in self-defence." Do you think it is right to justify our actions in this way? Elaborate. **CBSE Question Bank 2021**

Ans. It is true that the Maharaja justified his actions based on the maxim: "You may kill even a cow in self-defence,' so there would be no objection to killing tigers in self-defence." However, in the case of Maharaja, self-defence is a fight against fate. Fate had destined for the Maharaja to die through the hands of a tiger.

So, the Maharaja decides to fight it not knowing that he cannot escape it however, he may try. In this attempt, he kills many innocent tigers which is not justifiable.

19. Comment on any one aspect of the writing style of the author, Kalki in 'The Tiger King'.

Ans. The author of the story 'The Tiger King', Kalki uses a conversational tone and a narrative style in his writings. His, 'The Tiger King' is exemplary of his satires of those in power. He uses humour, exaggeration and harmony to criticise the unnecessary exploits and unreasonable actions of the Tiger King.

20. What message does the story 'The Tiger King' give to the readers? **CBSE 2023**

Ans. Through the story 'The Tiger King', the author wants to give the message of the transience of life and power. The story essentially is a satire on the conduct of the people in power. It is found that rulers like the Tiger King are not interested and bothered about working for public welfare. Rather, they spend their time in foolish things.

21. The upbringing of the Maharaja and all other crown princes was greatly influenced by British culture. Why did this happen? Justify your answer in 40- 50 words with an example from 'The Tiger King'. **Competency Based**

Ans. The Maharaja and the other crown princes were heavily influenced by British culture in their childhood. They were attended by an English nanny and watched English films exclusively. The reason for such a heavy influence was the close relationship of the princely states with the British empire. Due to placing such heavy importance on imported values, they were distanced from their own culture and disvalued the words of prophets and scholars.

22. What did the hunters realise when they looked at the hundredth tiger? **CBSE 2025**

Ans. When the hunters looked at the hundredth tiger, they realised that it was still alive. The king had missed his shot, but no one dared to tell him the truth. To maintain the illusion of his success, the hunters killed the tiger themselves.

23. What did the Dewan do to procure the hundredth tiger for the king? **CBSE 2025**

Ans. To procure the hundredth tiger for the king, the Dewan arranged for an old tiger from the People's Park in Madras. Fearing the king's wrath, he brought the weak tiger in his car and released it in the forest where the king was hunting. This trick helped the king believe he had killed his hundredth tiger.

Long Answer Type Questions

1. The astrologers predict, "The child will grow up to become the warrior of warriors, hero of heroes, champion of champions ......".

In contrast to the above statement, the Tiger King's death is an anticlimax. Comment.

Ans. When the Tiger King was born, the astrologers predicted that the Tiger King would be valiant and courageous but "the child born under this star will one day have to meet its death." When the Tiger King grew up and got to know of this prophecy, he set out on a tiger hunt. From that day onwards, the tigers in the kingdom were under threat from the king himself. Just to disprove the prophecy and to prove himself powerful, the Maharaja started his ruthless slaughter of tigers.

The irony was that the Maharaja, who had bravely fought and killed ninety-nine tigers, lost his life because of a wooden inanimate tiger which he had brought as a birthday present for his son. A small splinter of wood from the crude toy injured him and infected his entire arm which led to his untimely death. Thus, the hundredth tiger avenged the death of all the other tigers.

It was, undoubtedly, a trick of fate and the cruelty of the Maharaja that led to such an anticlimax.

2. Imagine you are an ardent environmentalist who is involved in the Save the Tiger campaign. You have been asked to deliver a speech in a seminar related to your campaign and the need for the youth to be involved in such campaigns. Draft your speech. **Competency Based**

Ans. Good morning! My dear companions, I stand before you to speak on the topic – Save Tiger. Perhaps the most beautiful of God's creations are animals of the world. Among the most ferocious of these, is the proud tiger.

Tigers have become a very important issue all over the world presently. India is the home of about two third of the world's tiger population. Their reducing number has triggered the government authorities to awaken. While the government is already taking projects to preserve them, there is something that we as the typical public should do. The first thing what we can do is create awareness among people. We can increase the attention by creating leaflets, ads, advertising the cause on internet websites.

Secondly, we must stop the poaching. Even when the government has banned selling of tiger's skin, poaching, however, is still prevalent. Thirdly, our jungles are getting destroyed and that could be a significant cause why tigers are disappearing as they don't have a prper ecosystem to develop anymore. So, protecting jungles is also important. Saving Tiger is not only our duty but also our responsibility. We have to support the government in its projects for the protection of the tigers so that a healthy population of the tigers exists. If nature is responsible for our existence, we must take responsibility for its existence.

Thank you.

3. "Tiger population became extinct in the forests of Pratibandapuram." Tiger King is a typical example of man's dominance over nature. As a member of your school Eco Club, write an article for your school magazine on how man should follow the policy of 'Live and Let live'.

You may begin like this

The noblest principle, man should follow in his life is co-existence. **Competency Based**

Ans. The noblest principle, man should follow in his life is co-existence. Our world is a beautifully grand and diverse place resided by numerous species of flora and fauna. And yet, man, often led by ambitions, forgets the fundamental law of nature: co-existence. The Tiger King's story serves as a prime example of the perils of breaching this inherent principle.

As active members of our school's Eco Club, we must fervently advocate for the ethos of 'live and let live'. It is imperative to acknowledge that humans are but one strand in the intricate web of life, and our actions reverberate throughout the ecosystem. Our actions, like Maharaja's relentless hunting, can inflict irreversible damage on the ecosystem. The specialist term for such violation is biodiversity loss which encompasses not just the extinction of certain species but also disturbance in the equilibrium of life forms.

We must redefine our relationship with the natural world by learning to share our spaces and resources. Empathy, understanding, and respect are crucial for a harmonious relationship with nature and other species. By revering the natural world and fostering symbiotic relationships among humans, animals, and ecosystems, we can forge a path towards a sustainable future. Let us become stewards of the Earth, championing biodiversity, conservation and mutual reverence. Together, we possess the capacity to cultivate a world where all beings flourish in equilibrium and harmony.

Thank you

4. "Until then the Maharaja had given his entire time and energy to tiger hunting. He had no time to spare for the crown prince."

In the present times, we see people following their profession and running after money and neglect their children. As a professional counsellor, you address working parents, stressing the need to spend quality time with children. Take material from the story 'The Tiger King' to re-inforce your points of view.

You may begin like this

Spending time with children will boost their confidence .... **Competency Based**

Ans. Spending time with children will boost their confidence and give them a sense of security, love, and support, which is vital for their overall well-being. When children feel emotionally connected to their parents, it boosts their self-esteem, confidence and resilience. Knowing this and following this is very crucial in the current times wherein individuals become consumed by their professions, often overlooking the emotional needs of their children.

The narrative of 'The Tiger King' by Kalki Krishnamurthy serves as a poignant reflection of this modern-day dilemma where individuals prioritise career pursuits over familial obligations. This is seen in the Maharaja's fixation on tiger hunting at the expense of neglecting his relationship with his son, the crown prince. This neglect, driven by ambition and pursuit of personal glory, mirrors the contemporary phenomenon where.

Just as the Maharaja's neglected to tragic consequences in the story, modern instances of parental neglect can have profound impacts on children's well-being and development. 'The Tiger King' thus serves as a cautionary tale, urging individuals to strike a balance between professional ambitions and family responsibilities, recognising that true fulfillment lies not only in personal success but also in nurturing meaningful relationships with loved ones.

5. **'Your Majesty, I have two wives already. If I marry you .... (Tiger King)'**

No doubt it adds humour to the story. Humour always captures the mind of readers.

Taking ideas from the story 'The Tiger King', write an article on the 'Importance of Humour in Life'.

You may begin like this

Sense of humour helps us deal with problems of life and improves one's mental and physical health ....

CBSE 2024

Ans. Sense of humour helps us deal with the problems of life and improves one's mental and physical health. In 'The Tiger King', humour adds depth and resonance to the narrative, providing moments of relief amidst the serious themes of power and ambition. Humour serves as a coping mechanism, allowing characters and readers alike to navigate through difficult situations with ease and perspective.

Laughter has been shown to reduce stress, boost immune function and foster social connections. Moreover, humour enables us to approach challenges with creativity and resilience, turning setbacks into opportunities for growth. In our daily lives, a good laugh can alleviate tension, enhance communication and strengthen relationships. Embracing humour not only enriches our individual experiences but also fosters a more positive and compassionate society. As demonstrated in 'The Tiger King' humour is an essential ingredient for a fulfilling and well-rounded life.

6. **Comment on any one aspect of the writing style of the author, Kalki in 'The Tiger King'.**

Ans. The writing style of Kalki in 'The Tiger King' is known for its vivid and descriptive language. Kalki has a talent for painting pictures with words, creating vivid images in the reader's mind that bring the story to life. He has a keen eye for detail, and his descriptions of the natural world, characters and events in the story are rich and evocative.

One aspect of Kalki's writing style is his ability to create a strong sense of place. He sets the scene with vivid descriptions of the landscape and the environment, making the reader feel as though they are right there in the story. Whether he is describing 'the lush tropical forests of India' or 'the bustling streets of a city', Kalki creates a rich and immersive environment that draws the reader into the story.

In addition to his descriptions of place, Kalki also has a talent for capturing the emotions of his characters. He writes with empathy and compassion, and his characters feel real and relatable. He is able to convey the inner thoughts and feelings of his characters through their actions and dialogue, creating a deep and nuanced portrayal of the human experience.

Overall, Kalki's writing style is characterised by its vivid and descriptive language, its ability to create a strong sense of place, and its compassionate and empathetic portrayal of characters. These elements combine to create a rich and immersive reading experience that draws the reader into the world of 'The Tiger King'.

7. **Imagine you are an ardent environmentalist who is involved in the 'Save the Tiger' campaign. You have been asked to deliver a speech in a seminar related to your campaign and the need for the youth to be involved in such campaigns. Draft your speech.**

Competency Based

Ans. Good morning! My dear companions, I stand before you to talk about our compaign, 'Save Tiger'. Perhaps the most beautiful of God's creations are the birds and animals of the world. And among the most ferocious of these, is the proud tiger. Tigers have become a very important topic of interest and issue all over the world presently. India is the home of major wild tigers about 2/3 of the world population. Their reducing number has triggered the government authorities to awaken and take observe. While the government is already taking projects to preserve the tiger, there is something that we, as responsible humans have to do.

The first thing what we can do is create awareness among people. And, this program is even more essential when the focus is to preserve the tigers. We can increase the attention to Save Tigers' by creating leaflets, ads, advertising the cause on internet websites and the like.

Secondly, to preserve the tigers we must stop the poaching. Even when the government has banned the selling of tiger's skin and bodies, poaching, however, is still prevalent.

Thirdly, it's been found that our jungles are getting destroyed and that could be a significant cause why creatures like tigers are disappearing. Today, tigers don't have a proper ecosystem to develop and generate. So, protecting jungles is the next important phase. It is not possible to plant a forest but yes you can plant many trees.

Saving Tiger is not only our duty but also our responsibility. We have to support the government in its projects for the protection of the tigers so that a healthy population of the tigers exists.

We should know that when we ask something from nature, we must be ready to give something back. If nature is responsible for our existence, we must take responsibility for its existence.

Thank you.

SELF ASSESSMENT TEST

Extract Based Questions

Read the extract given below and answer the questions that follow.

1. He wished to give him some special gift on his birthday. He went to the shopping centre in Pratibandpuram and searched every shop, but couldn't find anything suitable. Finally, he spotted a wooden tiger in a toyshop and decided it was the perfect gift.

(i) Complete the following suitably.

The Maharaja, as a father, was ....

(ii) Why Tiger King wished to give a special gift?

(iii) The wooden tiger cost's about

(a) One annas (b) Two annas

(c) Five annas (d) Ten annas

(iv) Why did the Tiger King consider a toy tiger as the perfect gift?

Short Answer Type Questions

Answer the following questions in 40-50 words.

1. What anecdote is related to the Tiger King's birth?

2. Was the Maharaja's bid to save his kingdom successful? How?

3. Describe the upbringing of the royal infant.

4. When he was only ten days old, a prediction was made about the future of the Tiger King. What was ironic about it?

5. Even today so many among us believe in superstitions. An astrologer predicted about 'The Tiger King' that he would be killed by a tiger. He 'killed' one hundred tigers yet was himself 'killed' by a tiger. How did the superstitious belief 'prevail'?

6. What social commentary does the story offer regarding colonialism and power dynamics?

7. How does the Maharaja's relationship with his son symbolise his legacy and priorities?

Long Answer Type Questions

Answer the following questions in 120-150 words.

1. Attempt a character sketch of the Tiger King.

2. "Even though the Maharaja lost ₹ 3 lakh, he was still happy." Justify the statement.

03

Journey to the End of the Earth

About the Author

Tishani Doshi
(1975-Present) is an Indian poet, journalist and dancer. She has published six books of poetry and fiction. Her essays, poems and short stories have been widely appreciated. Her passion for dance made her lead dancer in the Chanderlekha troupe and she toured many countries performing on stages. She had travelled a lot and her most exciting travels include travel to Antarctica, Ethiopia, Bhutan, Mexico, Tanzania and Italy. She currently countributes to an Interivew series for The Hindu and Open Magazine.

▼ **YOUR STUDY GOALS**
- Chapter Sketch
- About the Characters
- Summary of the Chapter

▼ **YOUR PRACTICE GOAL**
- NCERT Folder
- Extract Based Questions
- Short Answer Type Questions
- Long Answer Type Questions

Chapter Sketch

This is an enlightening account of Tishani Doshi's visit to the coolest, windiest, driest continent in the world. She is hopeful that this vast expanse of ice will unlock many mysteries about the evolution of Earth. The chapter essentially presents her feelings regarding her experience in Antarctica.

About the Characters

The Narrator Tishani Doshi herself narrates her experience of Antarctica. From the chapter, we can gather that she is a thoughtful, adventurous, and enthusiastic woman who is full of life and excitement. She is cheerful about knowing Antarctica and is also thoughtful about the deteriorating condition of the Earth and warns readers about the same.

Summary of the Chapter

Going to Antarctica

The narrator went to Antarctica on a Russian research vessel named Akademic Shokalskiy, with a group of high school students. She started her journey from Madras, crossed nine time zones, six checkpoints, three water bodies and many ecospheres to reach her destination. When she reached her destinations, she felt relief and wonder.

Gondwana

The narrator tells us that six hundred and fifty million years ago, Antarctica was a part of a giant Southern supercontinent called Gondwana. At that time humans did not exist, the climate was warm and there was a huge variety of flora and fauna. After around 500 million years, Gondwana broke up and separated into countries.

Pristine Antarctica

The narrator was shocked to see Antarctica. There is no human life there and nothing to show that human life existed on this planet. She was surrounded by midges, mites, blue whales and limitless expanse of huge icebergs. There is twenty four-hour summer lights and silence, that is interrupted only by the breaking of an ice sheet or rocks.

Humans Damaged the Earth

Human beings have been on the Earth for about 12,000 years. In this span of time, we have changed the face of our environment for worse. As a result, we are damaging Mother Nature. We are limiting resources on the planet for other creatures. Increasing population has added to our woes. The average global temperature is rising and the blanket of carbon dioxide around the world is increasing.

There are many unanswered questions about climate change and the narrator is alarmed by them. In this debate, Antarctica has a major role to play. This is because as compared to other places it remains relatively 'pristine' and contains half-million-years-old carbon records trapped in its layers of ice.

Students on Ice Programme

The narrator works on the 'Students on Ice' programme which aims at studying the ecological processes in Antarctica. It takes school students on the trip of Antarctica to generate a new awareness and respect for our planet. The programme has been in operation for six years and is headed by a Canadian, Geoff Green. Earlier he used to take celebrities, and retired, rich curiosity seekers to Antarctica for money. However, soon he decided to take school students there. It was his firm belief that young minds could learn and act better about the potential hazards regarding the environment which our Earth faces. The programme was a success because children could see that the threat of global warming was real.

Phytoplankton

The visit taught the narrator that little changes in the environment can have big repercussions. The microscopic phytoplankton are nourishment for marine animals and birds in the region. Any more depletion in the ozone layer will affect the activities of these phytoplankton which will affect the lives of others in this region and the global carbon cycle. The phytoplankton leads us to conclude that if we take care of small things, the big things can be saved.

Overwhleming Experience

The narrator says that the experience of strolling on the ocean at Antarctica was a never-to-be-forgotten incident for all. At 65.55 degrees South of equator, the narrator and the students were told to get down. They put on Gore-Tex ice shoes and Sun glasses. On over 180 metres of salt water, there was one-meter-thick layer of ice.

The author is overwhelmed with the beauty of balance in play on our planet. She has many questions in her mind. Whatever be the answers to those questions, she is full of optimism about the teenagers who are full of idealism to save the Earth after having made the trip of Antarctica.

Word-Meaning

ecosphere	—	part of the atmosphere where it is possible to breath normally or planetary ecosystem including all the Earth's living organisms and their physical environment.	
expansive	—	open or unrestrained, vast	
flora and fauna	—	plant life and animal life	
thrive	—	prosper or flourish	
wiped out	—	killed or became extinct	
extinction	—	total disappearance	
mind-boggling	—	overwhelming extremely surprising and difficult to understand	
perspective	—	outlook	
microscopic	—	very small which can be seen through microscope only	
austral	—	related to Southern hemisphere	
ubiquitous	—	present everywhere	
consecrate	—	make sacred or bless	
prognosis	—	forecast or prediction	
ruckus	—	a noisy situation	

unmitigated	— complete or absolute	assimilate	— to become part of a group
pristine	— uspoilt, perfect	epiphanies	— manifestation of God or Divine
blase about	— to be indifferent to	wage	— squeezed
repercussions	— consequence or outcome	revelation	— disclosure
phytoplankton	— very small plants that float near the surface of water and on which sea creatures feed.		

Important Themes of the Chapter

Exploration and Adventure The excerpt centres around the author's expedition to Antarctica, one of Earth's most remote and inhospitable places. Through vivid descriptions and personal reflections, Doshi captures the awe and wonder of exploring unknown territories and encountering the pristine beauty of Antarctica's landscape.

Environmental Awareness and Conservation Doshi highlights the fragility of Antarctica's ecosystem and the urgent need for ecological conservation. She discusses the impact of human activities, such as climate change and pollution, on this remote continent and emphasises the importance of preserving its pristine environment for future generations.

Intricate Balance of Nature The story highlights the interconnectedness of all living beings and ecosystems on Earth. Doshi reflects on the complex balance of nature and how changes in one part of the world can have far-reaching effects on others. Through her experiences in Antarctica, she encourages readers to appreciate life's interconnected web and take responsibility for protecting the planet's biodiversity and natural resources.

Humanity's Relationship with Nature The narrative prompts readers to reflect on humanity's relationship with the natural world and the impact of our actions on the environment. Doshi emphasises the need for greater environmental stewardship and sustainable practices to mitigate the adverse effects of human-induced climate change and preserve the Earth's natural beauty and diversity.

NCERT Folder

Read and Find Out (NCERT Pages 19–20)

1. How do geological phenomena help us to know about the history of humankind?

Ans. It is the geological phenomena that truly lets us know about the history of humankind, as they present before us how things were and how they evolved and went to extinction.

2. What are the indications for the future of humankind?

Ans. Keeping the present condition in mind, the future of humankind is in dark and a matter of grave concern. Rapid growth of human population, limited resources and depletion of ozone layer due to disturbed global carbon cycle are severe warnings for humans as well as sea animals and birds of the region.

There are many reasons responsible for the present condition but severe and immediate attention can probably reduce the disaster if not cure it.

Reading with Insight (NCERT Page 23)

1. "The world's geological history is trapped in Antarctica." How is the study of this region useful to us?

Ans. The study of Antarctica is helpful to us because Antarctica preserves a wealth of geological data, including ice cores containing atmospheric gases and climate records that provide insights into Earth's past climates and environmental changes. By analysing Antarctic ice cores, scientists can study past climate variations, understand the causes of climate change, and predict future climate trends. Antarctica's unique geological features, such as its continental drift, glacial formations, and fossil records, offer valuable information about Earth's geological history, evolution, and biodiversity.

Studying Antarctica helps scientists understand global environmental processes, such as ocean circulation patterns, sea-level rise, and the dynamics of polar ecosystems, which are crucial for addressing contemporary environmental challenges and informing sustainable management practices.

2. **What are Geoff Green's reasons for including high school students in the 'Students on Ice' expedition?**

Or 'Students on Ice' is a programme that prepares global citizens. Discuss. **CBSE Question Bank 2021**

Ans. Geoff Green decided to include high school students in the expedition because he believes that at this stage, it would be easier for them to grasp things and realise the impact of nature in a more demonstrative manner. The idea is to foster a new understanding and respect for our planet. Inspiring educational opportunities could be discovered by them. Antarctica provided young students a perfect place to study the changes in the environment as these changes can have big repercussions. The entire expedition was a life changing experience for the young learners where they were taught to learn, absorb and act to become Global leaders.

3. **"Take care of small things and the big things will take care of themselves." What is the relevance of this statement in the context of the Antarctica environment?**

Ans. The statement "Take care of the small things and the big things will take care of themselves" is relevant in the context of the Antarctic environment because despite their simplicity and lack of biodiversity, Antarctica's ecosystems play crucial roles in global environmental processes. These include carbon cycling, nutrient recycling and maintaining ecological balance. Although seemingly insignificant, small organisms like phytoplankton form the foundation of Antarctic food webs and support the entire marine ecosystem. By prioritising the conservation and protection of tiny organisms and delicate ecosystems in Antarctica, humans can help preserve the health and stability of polar environments and mitigate the impacts of climate change on Antarctic biodiversity and ecosystems.

4. **Why is Antarctica the place to go to, to understand the Earth's present, past and future?**

Or Why is Antarctica the place to go to for the scientists today?

Or How can visit to Antarctica be an enlightening experience? Elaborate. **CBSE 2023**

If we want to study and examine the Earth's past, present and future, Antarctica is the place to go. Comment. **CBSE 2023**

Ans. Antarctica is the place to go to understand the earth's present, past, and future because its pristine environment and remoteness from human civilisation make it an ideal laboratory for studying natural processes, environmental changes and climate dynamics with minimal human interference. Antarctica's ice cores contain invaluable records of Earth's past climates, atmospheric conditions and environmental changes spanning hundreds of thousands of years. These records provide insights into past climate variations, natural disasters and geological events.

Scientists can better understand climate change drivers and impacts by studying Antarctica's geological features, ice sheets, and ecosystems, predicting future environmental trends, and developing strategies for mitigating global ecological challenges. Antarctica serves as a critical indicator of global environmental health and resilience, highlighting the interconnectedness of Earth's systems and the urgent need for international cooperation, scientific research, and sustainable management practices to address contemporary environmental issues and ensure the long-term viability of our planet.

Exam Pattern Questions

Extract Based Questions

Read the extracts given below and answer the questions that follow.

1. **My journey began 13.09 degrees North of the Equator in Madras, and involved crossing nine time zones, six checkpoints, three bodies of water, and at least as many ecospheres.**

By the time I actually set foot on the Antarctic continent I had been travelling over 100 hours in combination of a car, an aeroplane and a ship; so, my first emotion on facing Antarctica's expansive white landscape and uninterrupted blue horizon was relief, followed up with an immediate and profound wonder. **CBSE 2025**

(i) **Complete the following suitably.**

The passage suggests that the author's journey to Antarctica was ....

(ii) **Select the correct option from those given in brackets to fill in the blank.**

The author highlights the numerous challenges and difficulties to emphasise the .... (remoteness/proximity) of Antarctica.

(iii) **How does the mention of crossing multiple time zones, checkpoints, and bodies of water impact the writer?**

(a) Is excited by the adventure of travel

(b) Feels indifferent towards the journey

(c) Is surprised by the number of logistical obstacles

(d) Feels overwhelmed by the logistical challenges

(iv) **How does the description of the journey reflect the author's initial emotions upon arriving in Antarctica?**

Ans. (i) long, arduous and physically exhausting

(ii) remoteness

(iii) (d) Feels overwhelmed by the logistical challenges

(iv) The description of the journey reflects the author's initial emotions upon arriving in Antarctica by portraying a sense of relief after a strenuous trip, followed by awe and wonder at the vast, pristine landscape. The contrast between the exhausting journey and the breathtaking beauty of Antarctica heightens the author's appreciation of the continent's untouched majesty.

2. **To visit Antarctica now is to be a part of that history; to get a grasp of where we've come from and where we could possibly be heading. It's to understand the significance of Cordilleran folds and pre-Cambrian granite shields; ozone and carbon; evolution and extinction. When you think about all that can happen in a million years, it can get pretty mind-boggling. Imagine: India pushing Northwards, jamming against Asia to buckle its crust and form the Himalayas; South America drifting off to join North America, opening up the Drake Passage to create a cold circumpolar current, keeping Antarctica frigid, desolate, and at the bottom of the world.**
(Journey to the End of the Earth) **CBSE SQP 2024**

(i) **Complete the following suitably.**
The passage suggests that visiting Antarctica offers insight into geological processes and Earth's history by ....

(ii) **How does the author imply the role of geological knowledge in understanding the Earth's past and potential future changes?**

(iii) **The writer says, "When you think about all that can happen in a million years, it can get pretty mind-boggling."**
What is the most likely impact on the writer?

(a) Feels overwhelmed by the vastness of geological time scales.

(b) Is uneasy about the rapid pace of geological changes.

(c) Feels indifferent towards geological phenomena.

(d) Is surprised by the lack of significant geological events over a million years.

(iv) **How might understanding the geological processes mentioned in the passage help scientists in predicting and mitigating future environmental changes, particularly in polar regions?**

Ans. (i) Exploring Cordilleran folds, granite shields and environmental factors like ozone and carbon.

(ii) The author implies the role of geological knowledge in understanding the Earth's past and potential future changes by linking the geological events to Antarctica's environmental conditions.

(iii) (a) Feels overwhelmed by the vastness of geological time scales.

(iv) Understanding the geological processes mentioned in the passage helps the scientists in predicting and mitigating future environmental changes, particularly in polar regions by providing insights into how geological events impact polar regions and influence global climate patterns.

3. **You lose all earthly sense of perspective and time here. The visual scale ranges from the microscopic to the mighty: midges and mites to blue whales and icebergs as big as countries (the largest recorded was the size of Belgium). Days go on and on and on in surreal 24-hour austral summer light and a ubiquitous silence, interrupted only by the occasional avalanche or calving ice sheet, consecrates the place. It's an immersion that will force you to place yourself in the context of the Earth's geological history and for humans, the prognosis isn't good.** **CBSE Question Bank 2021**

(i) **Complete the sentence suitably.**
The 'visual scale' refers to ....

(ii) **Which of the following fits the category of 'microscopic to the mighty' out of the ones given below.**

1. **Trace of a skin cell: trace of a bird's egg**
2. **A grain of rice: field of wheat**
3. **A scoop of ice cream: an ice-cream cone**
4. **A drop of water: Pacific Ocean**

(a) 1 and 2 (b) 1 and 3 (c) 3 and 4 (d) 2 and 4

(iii) **Choose the option listing the elements that influences one to think of Earth's physicality.**

1. **Breakage of an iceberg from a glacier**
2. **Midges and mites**
3. **A regular seen avalanche**
4. **Summer light in the Southern hemisphere**

(a) 1 and 2 (b) 3 and 4 (c) 1 and 4 (d) 2 and 3

(iv) **How does the narrator feel in the given extract?**

Ans. (i) range of things one can see.

(ii) (d) 2 and 4

(iii) (c) 1 and 4

(iv) The narrator feels amazed to see the grandeur of the icy region.

4. **Human Civilisations have been around for a paltry 12,000 years - barely a few seconds on the geological clock. In the short amount of time, we've managed to create quite a rukus, etching our dominance over nature with our villages, towns, cities, mega cities. The rapid increase of human populations has left us battling with other species for limited resources and the unmitigated burning of fossil fuels has now created a blanket of carbon dioxide around the world, which is slowly but surely increasing the average global temperature.** CBSE 2024

(i) According to the view expressed by the author in the above extract, increase in global temperature is due to

(a) mega cities (b) human people
(c) burning of fossil fuels (d) limited resources

(ii) Complete the following sentence with reference to the extract.

Humans are criticised by the author for ....

(iii) According to the author, the relation between human population and resources is ....

(iv) 'In that short amount of time, we've managed to create a ruckus'. By 'ruckus' the author refers to ....

(a) movement (b) misunderstanding
(c) breach (d) commotion

Ans. (i) (c) burning of fossil fuels

(ii) unmitigated burning of fossil fuels which has resulted in the increasing average global temperature

(iii) one of conflict and inequity, as the rapid increase in the human population results in a struggle for limited resources.

(iv) (d) commotion

5. **Students on Ice, the programme I was working with on the Shokalskiy, aims to do exactly this by taking high school students to the ends of the world and providing them with inspiring educational opportunities which will help them foster a new understanding and respect for our planet. It's been in operation for six years now, headed by Canadian Geoff Green, who got tired of carting celebrities and retired, rich, curiosity-seekers who could only 'give' back in a limited way.**

With Students on Ice, he offers the future generation of policy-makers a life-changing experience at an age when they're ready to absorb, learn and most importantly act. CBSE Question Bank 2021, Modified

(i) Complete the sentence appropriately with reference to the extract.

The writer refers to the educational opportunities as 'inspiring' because ....

(ii) Which of the following would not be 'a life changing experience'?

(a) Being given the lead role in a play
(b) Going on an adventure trip
(c) Playing a video game
(d) Meeting a great leader, you admire

(iii) Select the most suitable title for the given extract.

(a) Adventure with a Mission
(b) Adventure – The Spice of Life
(c) The Wanderlust
(d) Students of the Future

(iv) Why does the writer refer to 'act' as more important than 'absorb' or 'learn'?

Ans. (i) these educational opportunities would motivate students to work towards the good of the planet by allowing them to observe first-hand that the planet needs to be respected and nurtured rather than abused.

(ii) (c) Playing a video game

(iii) (a) Adventure with a Mission

(iv) The writer believes that to 'act' is more important than to 'absorb' or 'learn' because having the right knowledge or understanding gets just half of the job done. It fails to have an impact till the theoretical knowledge is applied, practiced or put to use in our actions.

6. **The reason the programme has been so successful is because it is impossible to go anywhere near the South Pole and not be affected by it. It's easy to be blase about polar ice caps melting while sitting in the comfort zone of our respective latitude and longitude, but when you can visibly see glaciers retreating and ice shelves collapsing, you begin to realise that the threat of global warming is real.**

Antarctica, because of her simple eco-system and lack of biodiversity, is the perfect place to study how little changes in the environment can have big repercussions. CBSE 2024

(i) As per the given extract, the reason for the success of the programme is

(a) the participation of young students.
(b) the journey to Antarctica.
(c) the exposure to reality.
(d) it was impossible to go near South Pole.

(ii) Complete the following sentence.

The warning that can be inferred from the above extract is ....

(iii) State whether the statement given is True or False with reference to the extract.

Global warming is a threat to human survival.

(iv) Explain one inference that can be drawn from the line "It's easy to be blase about polar ice caps melting while sitting in the comfort zone".

Ans. (i) (d) it was impossible to go near South Pole.

(ii) that small environmental changes should not be neglected because it can lead to serious repercussions on a large scale.

(iii) True

(iv) Warnings and threats in distant lands may not have a bigger impact on people as it would when one experiences it with their own eyes. People tend to not comprehend the intensity of the effect it would cause on globally.

Short Answer Type Questions

1. How did Antarctica amaze the writer when she first saw it?

Ans. The writer was amazed to see the vastness and isolation of Antarctica. The white beauty of the place left her wonder struck. She wondered how there could have been a time when India and Antarctica were a part of the same landmass - Gondwana.

2. Antarctica is unlike any other place on Earth. Justify the statement. CBSE Question Bank 2021

Or

How is Antarctica different from the place you live in? CBSE 2020

Ans. Antarctica is different from all other places as there has never been a human existence on it. There is 24 hours austral light on the continent. The visual scale ranges from microscopic to the mighty phenomena. There are no trees, no bill boards, no buildings. Only vast stretches of ice can be seen all around.

3. What happened to Gondwana 650 million years ago?

Ans. Gondwana was a Southern super continent which existed 650 million years ago. But around the time when the dinosaurs were destroyed and the age of mammal got underway, the landmass was forced to separate into continents shaping the world globe much as we know it today.

4. 'And for humans, the prognosis is not good.' What is in store for humans, as per the above statement? CBSE 2024

Ans. The statement hints at an ominous future for humanity, indicating the dire consequences of environmental degradation. It suggests that humans face significant challenges and potential threats to their existence, particularly in the context of climate change and ecological crises. It underscores the urgent need for collective action to address these issues and ensure a sustainable future for generations to come.

5. What are phytoplanktons? How are they important for th Earth's survival?

Ans. Phytoplanktons is a single-celled grass that feed the entire Southern ocean's marine life. These micro organisms require a low degree of temperature for their survival.

But due to the overheating and depletion of ozone layers, their existence is threatened. The message for the humans is to take care of small things so that bigger issues or problems will fall in place.

6. What did Geoff Green switch over to? Why? CBSE 2023

Ans. Geoff Green switched from taking celebrities and rich retired people to Antarctica to taking high school students to one end of the world. The reason for this switch was that he wanted to provide the future policy makers the opportunity to develop the respect and understanding for the Earth. He wanted the students to experience how difficult it would have been for the Earth to sustain life by rising its temperature.

7. Tishani Doshi considered the programme 'Students on Ice' a success. Do you agree with her? Why/Why not? Competency Based , CBSE 2024

Ans. Yes, I agree with Tishani Doshi in considering the programme 'Students on Ice' a success. It is due to the fact that the school students could see the collapsing ice shelves and retreating glaciers with their own eyes which will help them to stay aware of the reality. Their young minds could learn and act better about the potential hazards that our Earth's environment faces.

8. How can you say 'Students on Ice Programme' was a step towards the future? CBSE 2024

Or What was the aim of the project 'Students on Ice'? CBSE 2025

Ans. The 'Students on Ice' initiative sought to equip high school students with environmental awareness by immersing them in Antarctica's extreme conditions. Geoff Green envisioned these students as pivotal in addressing global warming and ecological threats. By experiencing Antarctica's simplicity and vulnerability, students would gain insights into the interconnectedness of Earth's systems, preparing them to be responsible stewards of our planet's future.

9. 'With students of ice, he offers future generation of policy makers a life-changing experience ……'
What expectation of the narrator is reflected in the above line? CBSE 2024

Ans. The narrator anticipates that by participating in the 'Students on Ice' programme, students will undergo a transformative experience that will shape them into future policymakers. The expectation is that this immersive journey will not only provide students with valuable knowledge and insights but also instil in them a sense of responsibility and stewardship towards the planet, influencing their decisions and actions in the future.

10. **What prevented the 'Shokalskiy' from going further? What did the captain instruct the passenger to do?** CBSE 2023

Ans. The 'Shokalskiy' was prevented from going any further because it had wedged itself or one can say that the ship was stuck in a thick white sheet of ice between the peninsula and Tadpole island. The captain instructed the passengers to climb down the gangplank and walk on the ocean.

11. **For the narrator, spending two weeks in Antarctica is a challenge not only for the body but also the mind. Elaborate.** CBSE Question Bank 2021

Ans. It is true that spending two weeks in Antarctica was a physical and a mental challenge for the narrator. She has never endured such harsh cold conditions. The lack of human habitation and the low temperatures along with the self reflection made by the narrator, made the entire experience very enlightening but tiring.

12. **What are the significant features of the 'Students on Ice' programme?** CBSE 2023

Ans. The 'Students on Ice' programme aims to provide high school students with inspiring educational opportunities to take them to the end of the world and foster a new understanding and respect for our planet. The main goal of the programme is to inspire future generations of policy-makers to act on environmental issues, and the main benefit of participating is understanding the real threat of global warming.

13. **In 20–30 words describe one primary emotion felt by the speaker during her expedition to Antarctica in 'Journey to the End of the Earth'?** Competency Based

Ans. During her expedition to Antarctica, the speaker felt a distinct sense of awe about the cosmic nature of creation and the place of humanity in the vast history of this planet. She also felt excitement tinged with fear at witnessing nature in such a grand and unforgiving form.

14. **It is easier to measure and study the effects of climate change in Antarctica. Explain in 40–50 words with an example from 'Journey to the End of the Earth'?** Competency Based

Ans. The ecosystem of Antarctica is simple and not very diverse. Due to this, little changes in the environment can cause considerable impact that are noticeable. For example, if the phytoplankton, which is a microorganism, disappears, it will endanger the marine animals and birds in the entire world.

Long Answer Type Questions

1. **Based on the chapter, elucidate any three consequences that global warming will have on Antarctica.** CBSE Question Bank 2021

Ans. Scientists warn that a further depletion of the ozone layer will affect the lives of the sea-animals and birds of the region. It will also affect the global carbon cycle. The burning of fossil fuels has polluted the atmosphere. It has created a blanket of carbon dioxide around the world. It is increasing the global temperature which is visible at Antarctica when we see icebergs melting away.

It shows how minor changes in the atmosphere can cause huge effects. If the global temperature keeps on increasing the human race may be in peril. 'Students on Ice' is a programme which provides the students an ample opportunity to understand how global temperature can be a big threat to human existence.

It inculcates a new understanding in them. Geoff Green thinks that high school students are the future policy makers. They can help in saving the earth from ecological dangers and the effects of global warming.

2. **What is the significance of the title 'Journey to the End of the Earth'?**

Ans. The title assumes significance as the author travels to Antarctica, which is the southernmost part of Earth and almost appears at the end of it. This chapter is a memoir of the author's journey to Antarctica with high school students on board a Russian vessel.

The two poles North and South virtually signify two ends of the planet Earth. The journey takes the author across nine time zones, three water bodies three ecosystems and six check points, which implies that almost the whole of the planet has been travelled before one reaches to the end of it.

As Antarctica is at one end of the planet, it is without human existence; there is no sign of billboards or trees. It is a place far-far away from the crowd noise and pollution.

Thus 'Journey to the End of the Earth' is an apt title.

3. **What are phytoplankton? How are they important to our ecosystem?** CBSE 2020

Ans. Phytoplankton are microscopic plants that live in the Southern Ocean. These small plants are very important to the ocean and to the whole planet. These single-celled plants use the sun's energy to assimilate carbon and synthesise organic compounds. They are at the base of foodchain. They nourish and sustain the entire Southern Ocean's food chain. Many small fish and whales eat them. Then bigger fish eats the small fish and so, the food chain continues.

At some point in time we also get joined in this food chain. So, the energy of plankton becomes our energy too. But unfortunately these plants face extinction due to depletion of ozone layer. Scientists warn that a further depletion in the ozone layer will affect the activities of phytoplankton. This will affect the lives of all the marine animals and birds of the region and the global carbon cycle, as a whole. In this context there is no doubt that we have got to "take care of small things and big things will take care of themselves."

4. **The author of 'Journey to the End of the Earth' is Tishani Doshi who is now a famous poet and dancer. As the narrator, write a speech discussing the impact of the 'Students on Ice' programme on your life and writing.** Competency Based

Ans. **The Making of a Writer**

Dear audience members, I did not simply take to writing. Many experiences of my life forced me to pick up the pen and write about my experiences. One of these experiences had been of the 'Students on Ice' programme. I had never expected the programme to change the way I think and live life. The journey was tiring and challenging but was it worth it?

Yes, it was. When you are there, in the middle of the white ice with no human habitation, you realise how vain and futile we humans are. For our own selfish need, we are destroying our planet. I had seen it first hand- the reducing ice caps, the rising temperatures and so on. The experience of the journey left a huge mark on my life. Everything that I do has to be well- thought of. My writing had changed. I had become environmentally conscious and expect the same out of my reader.

Thank you

5. **Imagine you are the narrator writing to your parents back home telling them about your experience in Antarctica and how it is similar to that back home in some ways.**

Antarctica

2nd August, 20XX

Dear Mom

It is so different here. I can't post this letter but I write to capture these amazing moments I am spending here. Antarctica is...

With love CBSE Question Bank 2021

Ans. Antarctica

2nd August, 20XX

Dear Mom

It is so different here. I can't post this letter but I write to capture these amazing moments I am spending here. Antarctica is so mysteriously beautiful that words will fall short but I would not stop describing it. There is white ice sheet all around. You lose all earthly sense of perspective and time here.

The visual scale ranges from the microscopic to the mighty midges and mites to blue whales and icebergs as big as countries. Days go on and on and on in surreal 24-hour austral summer light, and a ubiquitous silence, interrupted only by the occasional avalanche or calving ice sheet, consecrates the place.

I hope I could bring you here someday.

With love

XYZ

6. **On returning home, Tishani Doshi writes her thoughts reflecting on how her decision to enrol for the 'Students on Ice' programme has been the single most important decision of her life that has completely transformed her.**

Imagine yourself to be Tishani and express these thoughts.

You may begin like this...

I can't thank my stars enough for having cashed in on the opportunity of ....

Ans. I can't thank my stars enough for having cashed in on the opportunity of a lifetime wherein I got the opportunity to visit Antarctica with the world famous 'Students on Ice' Programme. It was an experience completely different from any other - to visit a landscape that is not inhabited by humans and so still relatively pristine. The views, the weather and the extensive knowledge provided by expert scientists gave us deep insights into its ecosystem.

The landscape provided an insight into the Earth's past, present and the future. It made us delve deep into the threat faced by the environment and the Earth itself due to human's exploitative activities. I not only understood how our actions have been so selfish but also that little changes can have a major impact on our surroundings. Therefore, we need to take care of the small things and protect our environment as well as the Earth at all costs.

Overall, it was an eye opening experience which made me understand that everything on this Earth is interlinked.

7. **Justify the title of the story 'Journey to the End of the Earth' as a metaphor for devastating climate change. In 120–150 words, mention another reason for the title of the text.** Competency Based

Ans. It is true to say that the title 'Journey to the End of the Earth' is a metaphor given to the devastating climate change. The title literally assumes significance as the author travels to Antarctica, which is the Sourthern-most part of Earth and almost appears at the end of it. This chapter is a memoir of the author's journey to Antarctica with high school students on board, in a Russian vessel.

However, the journey of self reflection indicates that Antarctica's vulnerable ecosystem is affected first due to the changing climate.

The ecosystem of Antarctica is already collapsing due to global warming leading to the destruction of the planet.

This reflection contributes to the thematic exploration of the passage by highlighting the urgency of addressing climate change and the need for collective action to mitigate its effects. Through the narrator's introspection, readers are encouraged to consider the long-term implications of environmental degradation and the importance of adopting sustainable practices to safeguard the planet for future generations.

SELF ASSESSMENT TEST

Extract Based Questions

Read the extract given below and answer the following questions.

1. Students on Ice, the programme I was working with on the Shokalskiy, aims to do exactly this by taking high school students to the ends of the world and providing them with inspiring educational opportunities which will help them foster a new understanding and respect for our planet. It's been in operation for six years now, headed by Canadian Geoff Green, who got tired of carting celebrities and retired, rich, curiosity-seekers who could only 'give' back in a limited way. With Students on Ice, he offers the future generation of policy-makers a life-changing experience at an age when they're ready to absorb, learn, and most importantly, act.

(i) Complete the sentence appropriately, with reference to the extract.

The writer states that educational opportunities do 'exactly this. 'This' refers to ....

(ii) Which of the following would not be 'a life changing experience'?

(a) Getting into Oxford University
(b) Standing first in the International Olympiad
(c) Playing a role in local Ramayana
(d) Visiting a concert attending

(iii) Select the most suitable word that can be attached to the biven extract.

(a) Hopeful (b) Factual (c) Argumentative (d) Poetic

(iv) Write a short note on Geoff Greene and how he seems as a person.

Short Answer Type Questions

Answer the following questions in 40-50 words.

1. What was the objective of the 'Students on Ice' programme?'

2. Antarctica is the doorway to the past. Explain.

3. How is man responsible for creating a ruckus on this Earth in a short span of 12 thousand years?

4. What concerns does the author express regarding human impact on the environment, particularly in Antarctica?

5. In what ways does the author underscore the urgency of addressing climate change and environmental degradation?

Long Answer Type Question

Answer the following question in 120-150 words.

1. Human civilisations lack in Antartica is crucial for its beauty. Elucidate?

04

The Enemy

About the Author

Pearl Comfort Sydenstricker Buck (1892-1973) was an American writer and novelist, best known for 'The Good Earth', which won her the Pulitzer Prize in 1932. In 1938, Buck became the first American woman to win the Nobel Prize in Literature "for her rich and truly epic descriptions of peasant life in China" and her two memoir-biographies of her missionary parents. Pearl has published over seventy books: novels, collections of stories, biography and autobiography, poetry, drama, children's literature, and translations from the Chinese.

▼ YOUR STUDY GOALS
- Chapter Sketch
- About the Characters
- Summary of the Chapter

▼ YOUR PRACTICE GOAL
- NCERT Folder
- Extract Based Questions
- Short Answer Type Questions
- Long Answer Type Questions

Chapter Sketch

'The Enemy' is a short story based against the Second World War, specifically focusing on the war between Japan and America. Tension ran high in both nations with Japanese being extremely hostile to the Americans. The story centres around a Japanese doctor named Sadao and his wife Hana's moral dilemma when they find an injured American soldier near their home. Despite societal pressures, Sadao saves the soldier's life, sparking tensions in their household. Throughout the story, Sadao faces a dilemma where he has to choose between his allegiance to his country and his duty to save lives. When faced with the choice to hand over the soldier or dispose of him secretly, Sadao arranges for his escape.

Through the character of Sadao, the story explores themes of morality, duty, compassion, and the complexity of human relationships in times of conflict. It highlights the struggle between individual conscience and societal expectations and the blurred lines between loyalty to one's country and the universal value of human life.

About the Characters

Dr. Sadao He is an accomplished surgeon who resolves the conflict between his patriotic duty and his duty to save the life of people.

Hana Sadao's wife who helps her husband in operating on the American despite her physical discomfort.

Tom (the American) He is an American soldier, who has faced the tortures of the war.

The General He is a selfish old man, only wanting Sadao, so that he could recover from his illness.

Yumi and the other Servant They represent the general voice of the Japanese people who live a very traditional life. They are loyal to Sadao but also remember their boundaries and refuse to help the white man.

Summary of the Chapter

Dr. Sadao Hoki and His Family

Dr. Sadao Hoki was a famous Japanese surgeon and an accomplished scientist. He lived in a house on the Japanese coast. His father was a traditional man whose main concern was Sadao's education. He sent Sadao to America to complete his studies. He also inculcated in him values of patriotism and national loyalty.

When the Second World War started, Sadao was not sent with the troops because he was about to make a discovery which would render wounds entirely clean. Further, Sadao was required to ensure a successful treatment of the General.

Sadao met Hana in America at Professor Harley's house. He made sure that she was Japanese before marrying her. After Sadao and Hana had finished their studies, they returned to Japan and married according to the Japanese tradition.

The Prisoner of War

One night, Sadao and Hana were enjoying the view of the sea from their verandah when they saw a man coming out of the mists. When they reached the man, Sadao and Hana found that it was a white prisoner of war and he was wounded.

Sadao saw that a bullet wound had reopened and packed it with sea moss. After that, he wanted to throw the man back into the sea and Hana agreed. They knew that giving shelter to the enemy would get them into trouble. Sadao was torn between his moral duty as a doctor which urged him to save the dying man and his national duty which required handing him over to the army as a patriot. However, both Hana and Sadao finally decided to take the man home. They also decided to tell the servant that they would hand over the man to the authorities.

Taking Care of the White Man

Sadao and Hana carried the white man to Sadao's father's bedroom. The man was very dirty and needed to be washed. Hana suggested that Yumi, the governess, might wash him. However, Yuri refused and Hana had to wash him herself. Hana also realised that the other two servants were frightened at what Sadao had told them.

Soon, Sadao was ready to operate and told Hana that she would need to give anaesthetic to the man. Hana had never seen an operation and started vomiting, which made Sadao irritable as he couldn't help his wife. However, she was able to assist her husband in the operation. After some time, Sadao had finally succeeded in taking the bullet out. He was sure that the man would live in spite of his sufferings.

The Servant's Reaction

After the surgery, Hana had to take care of the man. The servant refused to go into the room where the white man was kept. They resented their decision to help the American soldier and talked about the consequences of harbouring an enemy. Soon after, they left their house. The white man was surprised to see Hana talk in English and revealed that his name was Tom.

Informing the General

On the day the servant had left, a messenger in official uniform came to Sadao's house. Hana was scared as she thought that he was there to arrest Sadao. However, the messenger had come to inform Sadao that the General needed him. Looking at Hana in distress, Sadao decided to get rid of the man.

Sadao told the whole episode to the General for whom Sadao was indispensible. So, the General promised Sadao that nothing would happen to him. He then planned to get the American soldier assassinated. He told Sadao that his private assassins would also remove the dead body.

Sadao's Escape Plan for Tom

After that meeting, Sadao spent three restless nights waiting for the assassins. But they didn't come. Finally, Sadao planned to get rid of the enemy himself. He told the escape plan to Tom. He had arranged a boat, food, drinking water and clothing for the young man and also gave him his own flashlight. He told Tom that he should flash the light two times if he needed something. Tom must do this only when the sun has set. He further added that Tom could find many fish to eat but he should eat them raw, lest the fire be seen. He also told Tom to wait for a Korean ship to escape.

Sadao's Dilemma

Sadao went to the General and informed him that the American had escaped. In reply, the General informed Sadao that he forgot about the prisoner. He further told Sadao not to leak out this information to anybody.

Back at home, Sadao remembered his days in America and the Americans he met there. He wondered why he could not kill Tom, his enemy.

Word-Meaning

outlined	—	marked on the outer edge
yonder	—	over there
render	—	make
wreathing	—	covering, surrounding
haori	—	a loose open-front Japanese garment usually worn over the kimono
kimono	—	a long, loose traditional Japanese robe with wide sleeves, tied with a sash
breaker	—	a heavy sea wave that breaks into white foam on the shore
spiked	—	covered with sharp points
tended	—	looked after
beachcombers	—	people who make a living by searching beaches for valuables and selling them
stanch	—	check or stop the flowing of
whole	—	not wounded or injured
matted	—	covered with mats
pallor	—	an unhealthy, pale appearance
nursery	—	a room in a house for special use of young children
resistance	—	refusal
rugs	—	thick woollen carpets
blond	—	light-coloured
ebbing	—	gradually decreasing
tokonoma	—	a recess or an alcove in a Japanese home for displaying a flower arrangement or pictures
alcove	—	a recess in the wall of a room
superficial	—	existing or occurring on the surface
retching	—	vomiting
flickers	—	fleeting
anatomy	—	study of the body structure of humans
cardinal	—	serious
incisions	—	cuts
guts	—	intestines
hypodermic	—	a syringe for injection
porcelain	—	a white translucent ceramic
bitter	—	feeling or showing hurt or pain
dragged on	—	was managed with difficulty or effort
pinching	—	breaking off, removing
wistaria vine	—	a climbing shrub of the pea family
condemned	—	blamed
assuage	—	lessen, make less intense
brusquely	—	bluntly, roughly
execution	—	the act of killing or carrying out death sentence against someone
assassins	—	persons who murder an important person for political reason
absolute state	—	a form of government which has absolute or unrestricted power
gosh	—	an expression of surprise
stubbly	—	with short rough growth
shaggy	—	having long, thick, unkempt hair
refrain	—	repeated idea or complaint
eaves	—	the part of a roof that meets or overhangs the walls of a building
pawnshop	—	cheap shop
dereliction	—	neglect
slatternly	—	dirty and untidy

Important Themes of the Chapter

Moral Dilemmas in Times of Conflict The story revolves around the complexities of morality, loyalty and humanity in times of war and conflict. It explores the internal conflict individuals face when their ethics clash with their societal obligations and national loyalties. The story delves into the moral dilemma of prioritising individual compassion and mercy over allegiance to one's country and duty. It also examines themes of forgiveness, redemption, and the transformative power of human connection across cultural and ideological boundaries. The story highlights the universal struggle to reconcile personal conscience with societal expectations, especially when moral choices have profound consequences.

Duty vs. Self-Interest The story delves into the conflict between duty and self interest through two different men representing two distinct expressions of self-interest. Sadao knows it is his patriotic duty to turn the American over to the authorities, but his compassion as a physician sworn to heal trumps that duty. On the other hand, General Takima avoids the expectations of duty to his country in order to overlook Sadao's dangerous decision because of his self-interest.

NCERT Folder

Read and Find Out (NCERT Pages 24-35)

1. Who was Dr. Sadao? Where was his house?

Ans. Dr. Sadao Hoki was a famous Japanese surgeon and scientist. He completed his study of medicine in America. He lived in a house which was built on the Japanese coast. The house was surrounded by pine trees.

2. Will Dr. Sadao be arrested on the charge of harbouring an enemy?

Ans. Dr. Sadao knew that he would be arrested if he gave shelter to an American in their house, as Japan was at war with America. The wounded man was an escaped prisoner of war who had escaped with a bullet in his body. Harbouring an enemy would mean being a traitor. If somebody complained, Dr Sadao could be arrested for treason.

3. Will Hana help the wounded man and wash him herself?

Ans. Yes, Hana would help the wounded man. As the man was in a very bad condition and needed to be washed before being operated on and her servant Yumi had refused to do so, Hana had to do it herself out of compassion for another human being.

4. What will Dr. Sadao and his wife do with the man?

Ans. Dr. Sadao and his wife Hana brought the wounded man to their house and helped him greatly. Sadao operated on him and saved his life by removing the bullet in his body.

Hana washed him and served him when none of their servants wanted to do so. Dr. Sadao finally even helped him escape to safety.

Read and Find Out (NCERT Pages 39-43)

1. Will Dr. Sadao be arrested on the charge of harbouring an enemy?

Ans. It was now unlikely that Dr. Sadao would be arrested on the charge of harbouring an enemy because the old General was being treated by him. If Sadao was arrested, there would be no one to operate upon the General in case of an emergency.

2. What will Dr. Sadao do to get rid of the man?

Ans. Dr. Sadao first waited for the General to get the man assassinated. But when that didn't happen for three days, he gave the man a boat with provisions and helped him escape to a nearby island. He instructed him to wait for a Korean fishing boat which would safely take him far from there.

Reading with Insight (NCERT Page 47)

1. There are moments in life when we have to make hard choices between our roles as private individuals and as citizens with a sense of national loyalty. Discuss with reference to the story you have just read.

Ans. There are times when we are faced with difficult choices in life. An individual is torn between his duty towards his motherland and the moral and ethical responsibility of helping a needy person when you can do so. This is the same dilemma that Sadao is confronted with. Patriotic citizens of Japan were expected to hand over an American prisoner of war at the time of the Second World War. But this is a short-sighted view of the situation. If we bring in the humanistic angle to this dismal reality, then it is a doctor's duty to save a human life. As a doctor, Sadao could not differentiate between an enemy and an ally.

Similarly, Hana, as a kind and compassionate human, cannot leave a wounded person to die. Both Sadao and Hana face a conflict but rise above it. They balance their obligations as private individuals with their responsibilities as citizens.

2. Dr. Sadao was compelled by his duty as a doctor to help the enemy soldier. What made Hana, his wife, sympathetic to him in the face of open defiance from the domestic staff?

Ans. Hana, Dr Sadao's wife, sympathises with her husband in helping the enemy soldier because she understands the ethical duty of a doctor to save lives regardless of nationality. Despite facing open defiance from the domestic staff and societal pressure, Hana supports her husband's decision out of compassion and a shared belief in the sanctity of human life. Her empathy and understanding strengthen their bond and illustrate the importance of standing by loved ones in difficult circumstances.

3. How would you explain the reluctance of the soldier to leave the shelter of the doctor's home even when he knew he couldn't stay there without risk to the doctor and himself?

Ans. Tom, the American prisoner of war, knew fully well that Dr. Sadao had saved his life, although, being Japanese citizens, they could have left him to fend for himself. He was aware of their empathy towards him. Moreover, he understood that their house was a safe haven for him because they had stayed in America and could communicate with him easily in English.

Additionally, the soldier may be hesitant to venture out alone into an unfamiliar and potentially hostile environment, preferring the relative safety of the doctor's care despite the dangers it poses to both of them. The soldier's reluctance to leave the shelter of the doctor's home despite knowing the risks reflects his vulnerability and fear of the unknown.

4. What explains the attitude of the General in the matter of the enemy soldier? Was it human consideration, lack of national loyalty, dereliction of duty or simply self-absorption?

Ans. The General's attitude toward the enemy soldier appears to be driven by a combination of factors. While he initially promises to have the soldier killed, he later forgets his promise due to his own health concerns and self-absorption. The General's actions stem from a sense of pragmatism, prioritising his well-being over his duty to eliminate the enemy. His wavering commitment reflects the complexities of human nature, where self-interest and personal considerations often influence decision-making, even among those in positions of authority. This does not mean he lacks human consideration or national loyalty.

5. While hatred against a member of the enemy race is justifiable, especially during wartime, what makes a human being rise above narrow prejudices?

Ans. While hatred against the enemy race may be justifiable in the context of war, individuals can transcend these prejudices by acknowledging the intrinsic worth and dignity of every human being. Rising above such narrow prejudices often requires empathy, compassion, and a recognition of shared humanity. These qualities along with the ability to see beyond surface differences enable individuals to empathise with others, fostering mutual respect and reconciliation even in times of conflict.

In this case, Dr. Sadao does not think twice before stopping the bleeding in the American soldier. He packs the wound with moss available on the seashore. It is his moral obligation to save a human being's life, although that human being is his enemy.

His sense of humanity and empathy does not allow him to differentiate between any man. He takes care of the wounded American in the same manner as he would have treated any other wounded man. Further, he is also worried that the life that he had saved is in danger.

6. Do you think the doctor's final solution to the problem was the best possible one in the circumstances?

Or Dr. Sadao emerges as a saviour of humanity. Substantiate your answer with evidence from the text. **CBSE 2023**

Or 'The Enemy' portrays the victory of humanity in a moment of crisis. Illustrate this fact through the actions taken by Dr. Sadao for the enemy soldier.

Ans. The doctor's final solution to the problem, allowing the enemy soldier to escape to a nearby island, may be considered the best option given the circumstances. When Dr. Sadao came across the prisoner of war, the first thing he did was to save his life. As a doctor, he fulfilled the moral and ethical obligation of saving a human life. Next, he proved himself loyal to his country by informing the General about the enemy soldier. When the General assured Sadao of sending private assassins to eliminate the American, Dr. Sadao felt restless and guilty of betraying the same person whose life he had saved.

After spending three sleepless nights waiting for the assassins who never came, he finally worked out a plan to let Tom, the American prisoner of war, escape.

By facilitating the soldier's departure, the doctor ensures the safety of himself and the soldier while avoiding potential repercussions from authorities. While the decision may not be ideal, it reflects the doctor's commitment to preserving life and minimising harm in a challenging situation. Further, this decision proves that even if two countries are at war, the religion of humanity does not change. Its basic principle is saving a human life, which Sadao does with success. In a way, Dr. Sadao echoes the author's views against war and the hatred that it generates between man and man. Through Dr. Sadao, the author conveys the message of universal brotherhood, peace and amity. It is the best solution to the problem.

7. Does the story remind you of 'Birth' by AJ Cronin that you read in Snapshots last year? What are the similarities?

Ans. 'The Enemy' shares similarities with 'Birth' by A.J. Cronin regarding the protagonists' ethical dilemmas and moral complexities. Both stories explore themes of duty, compassion and the inherent value of human life. They depict characters grappling with conflicting loyalties and navigating the moral grey areas of wartime situations. While the specific contexts and plot details may differ, the underlying themes of morality and human compassion resonate across both narratives.

8. Is there any film you have seen or novel you have read with a similar theme?

Ans. This story is based on a strong sense of duty, selflessness, humanitarian gestures and love for a fellow human being. A movie with a similar theme is, 'My Name is Khan', where the protagonist saves the lives of his friends from floods, guided by a strong sense of humanity and moral duty, without fearing for his own life.

Exam Pattern Questions

Extract Based Questions

Read the extracts given below and answer the following.

1. Sadao knew that his education was his father's chief concern. For this reason he had been sent at twenty-two to America to learn all that could be learned of surgery and medicine. He had come back at thirty and before his father died he had seen Sadao become famous not only as a surgeon but as a scientist. Because he was perfecting a discovery which would render wounds entirely clean, he had not been sent abroad with the troops. Also, he knew, there was some slight danger that the old General might need an operation for a condition for which he was now being treated medically and for this possibility Sadao was being kept in Japan.

(i) Complete the sentence suitably.

Sadao's father's role in his life is ....

(ii) Choose the correct option that best describes Sadao as a perfect son.

(a) Sadao went to America as desired by his father.
(b) Sadao returned to Japan before his father's death.
(c) Sadao gained fame as a doctor as well as scientist while his father was alive.
(d) Sadao stayed with his father and did not go abroad with the troops.

(iii) Why was Dr. Sadao not sent abroad?

(iv) For how many years did Sadao study in America?

Ans. (i) that he was very concerned about his education

(ii) (a) Sadao went to America as desired by his father.

(iii) Sadao was not sent abroad with the troops because he was working on a discovery.

(iv) Sadao studied medicine for 8 years in America.

2. The man moaned with pain in his stupor but he did not awaken.

"The best thing that we could do would be to put him back in the sea," Sadao said, answering himself. Now that the bleeding was stopped for the moment he stood up and dusted the sand from his hands.

"Yes, undoubtedly that would be best," Hana said steadily. But she continued to stare down at the motionless man.

"If we sheltered a white man in our house we should be arrested and if we turned him over as a prisoner, he would certainly die," Sadao said.

"The kindest thing would be to put him back into the sea," Hana said. But neither of them moved. They were staring with curious repulsion upon the inert figure.

CBSE Question Bank 2021 Modified

(i) Complete the following suitably.

Sadao and Hana cared about the soldier but ....

(ii) State one characteristics that describes Sadao and Hana in the passage.

(iii) Pick the idiom that best describes the situation in which Sadao and Hana were in.

(a) To be like a fish out of water
(b) Like water off a duck's back
(c) To be dead in the water
(d) To be in hot water

(iv) Why did Sadao suggest to put the man back into the sea?

Ans. (i) were worried about the consequences of being considerate.

(ii) Sadao: prudent Hana: suspicious

(iii) (d) To be in hot water

(iv) Sadao suggested to put the man back into the sea because the man was a prisoner of war who would anyhow die.

3. **"If I am able, are you?" Sadao asked.**

"No," Hana said, "But if you can do it alone..."

Sadao hesitated again. "The strange thing is," he said, "that if the man were whole I could turn him over to the police without difficulty. I care nothing for him. He is my enemy. All Americans are my enemy. And he is only a common fellow. You see how foolish his face is. But since he is wounded." **CBSE 2024**

(i) Complete the sentence appropriately

The dilemma faced by the couple was ....

(ii) What does Hana ask Dr. Sadao to do alone?

(a) Treat the wounded soldier

(b) Give him shelter in the outhouse

(c) Throw him back into the sea

(d) Hand him over to the authorities

(iii) Explain the expression.

'If the man were whole'.

(iv) Dr. Sadao says, 'All Americans are my enemy.' What character trait of Dr. Sadao does it reflect?

Ans. (i) whether to treat the wounded man or not

(ii) (c) Throw him back into the sea

(iii) The expression 'if the man were whole' means 'if he wasn't injured'.

(iv) Dr. Sadao's patriotism towards his nation, Japan is reflected in the given line.

4. **"The master ought not to heal the wound of this white man," he said bluntly to Hana. "The white man ought to die. First he was shot. Then the sea caught him and wounded him with her rocks. If the master heals what the gun did and what the sea did they will take revenge on us."**

(i) Complete the following suitably.

The white man belongs to ....

(ii) Which of the best summarises the speakers attitude towards the white man?

(a) Pity (b) Hatred

(c) Indifference (d) Disdain

(iii) Who is the speaker of the above lines?

(iv) Why the speaker didn't want the white man to live?

Ans. (i) USA

(ii) (c) Indifference

(iii) The Gardener is the speaker of the given lines

(iv) The speaker did not want the white man to live because to save him is against the law of nature.

5. **"It will be better for her to empty her stomach," he thought. He had forgotten that of course she had never seen an operation. But her distress and his inability to go to her at once made him impatient and irritable with this man who lay like dead under his knife.**

(i) Complete the following suitably.

The reason for the speaker's irritation with the 'man' is ....

(ii) Who in the speaker of the above lines?

(iii) Which of the following best summarises the reason for the operation?

(a) Gun wound

(b) Death of the nation's leading deplomat

(c) Fear of war

(d) Underlying illness

(iv) Why Hana reacted in a different way while the operation was going on?

Ans. (i) that Sadao had to help the man made him due to which he had to ignore his wife's distress

(ii) Dr. Sadao is the speaker of the given lines.

(iii) (a) Gun wound

(iv) It was unusual for her to see operation in person. So she reacted in a different way.

Short Answer Type Questions

1. **How did the writer indicate that Dr. Sadao's father was a very traditional and conventional man?**

Ans. The writer has very clearly indicated that Dr. Sadao's father was a very traditional and conventional man. Sadao didn't marry Hana until he knew she was Japanese because his father wouldn't have approved of her otherwise. The old man never let any foreign object even enter his room.

2. **Why was Dr. Sadao not sent to the battlefield?** **CBSE 2020**

Or Why was Dr. Sadao not sent abroad with the troops? **CBSE 2023**

Ans. Dr. Sadao had not been sent abroad with the troops into the battlefields because the General was being treated by him and he could trust no other Japanese surgeon. Secondly, Dr. Sadao was about to make an important discovery that would leave wounds entirely clean.

3. What was the servants' reaction to Sadao's decision of treating the American soldier ? CBSE 2024

Ans. The servants express shock and disbelief when Sadao decides to treat the wounded American soldier. Initially, they warn Sadao about the potential consequences of harbouring an enemy, fearing punishing actions from their own government. However, they ultimately comply with Sadao's decision, albeit reluctantly, demonstrating their loyalty to their master despite their reservations.

4. What efforts did Dr. Sadao and Hana make to save the American soldier? CBSE 2020

Ans. Dr. Sadao and his wife Hana brought the wounded man to their house and helped him greatly. Sadao operated on him and saved his life by removing the bullet in his body. Hana washed him and served him when none of their servants wanted to do so, as he was an enemy soldier. Dr. Sadao even helped him escape to safety.

5. In what context does Hana remember the cruel nature of General Takima? How does this connect with the tortures of war?

Ans. Hana remembered General Takima who used to beat his wife cruelly. She inferred that if he was so cruel with his wife, he would be extremely cruel with the American prisoners. This shows that during the war, the Japanese were very callous with the prisoners of war, torturing them until death.

6. 'Don't thank me too early', Sadao said coldly. What inference is drawn about Sadao's state of mind from the above line? CBSE 2024

Ans. Sadao's cold response, "Don't thank me too early," suggests a guarded and cautious demeanour. His tone implies a reluctance to accept gratitude prematurely, hinting at underlying reservations or apprehensions. This suggests that Sadao may be wary of potential consequences or complications arising from his actions, indicating a sense of caution and uncertainty about the future despite his outward display of generosity.

7. Why did Dr. Sadao treat the American soldier even though it was an unpatriotic act on his part?

Ans. It was Dr. Sadao's moral and ethical duty as a doctor to treat the ill, wounded or injured irrespective of the person's nationality. So, he treated the wounded American soldier, even though it would seem an unpatriotic act on his part.

8. On the seventh day after the American soldier was found by Sadao, two things happened. Why did Hana feel scared of the second?

Ans. The second event that occurred was a messenger from the General visiting their house. Hana felt scared, thinking that the servants had informed the authorities about them sheltering an enemy soldier. However, her fear was unfounded, as the messenger had only come to inform that the General was ill again and Sadao was required at his bedside immediately.

9. "I must get rid of this man for your sake". Said Dr. Sadao.

How will you describe Dr. Sadao as a husband with reference to the above line? CBSE 2024

Ans. The given lines demonstrate Dr. Sadao's love and care for his wife. It shows his commitment to his wife's safety by choosing to remove the injured American soldier concealed in their home, despite his medical oath. His decision reflects a dedication to safeguarding his wife from potential risks and prioritising their security above all other onsiderations.

10. Sadao's acceptance of the General's plan to assassinate Tom was counterproductive to having put him on the path of recovery. Substantiate with your reason/s.

Ans. It is true to say that Sadao's acceptance of the General's plan to assasinate Tom was counterproductive to having put him on the path of recovery. Dr. Sadao had not let the authorities know about him and had taken him home so that he could give the injured man medical attention. He had even operated on him. In this regard, getting him assasinated would put Sadao's efforts to save the man to waste. Thus, getting Tom assasinated would be same as letting the injured man die at the shore.

11. Why was Dr. Sadao not arrested on the charge of harbouring an enemy? CBSE 2020

Or Why did the General not order immediate arrest of Dr. Sadao who had sheltered a white man?

Ans. Dr. Sadao was not arrested on the charge of harbouring an enemy because the old General was being treated by Dr. Sadao. If he was arrested, there would be no one to operate upon the General in case of an emergency. Further, Dr. Sadao had informed the General about the presence of the American in his house.

12. Sadao and Hana have a moral compass which urges them to save the prisoner's life. Do we all need this moral compass? Why? CBSE Question Bank 2021

Ans. Yes, we all need a moral compass. By placing a moral compass in front of us we create a clear vision of the mental processes that point us in an ethical direction. This is all the more important in the modern world wherein we all have become selfish and self-centered. With moral compass, we will retain all those ethics and values that make us good.

13. Pearl Buck depicts the servants in a way to convey a message about Japanese people and culture. Support your answer with textual evidence.

Ans. Pearl Buck depicts the servants in a way to convey a message about Japanese people and culture. Japanese people are highly patriotic and love their duties.

The servants, though loyal to Dr. Sadao's family, left their jobs because their master had helped a prisoner of war, who was the enemy of the nation. Further, the reference to the way the servants work and follow the traditional methods is also symbolic of the Japanese culture.

14. The author has used 'blood' as a symbol in the story. Comment on its impact on the reader. CBSE Question Bank 2021

Ans. Blood is a central symbol of the story, most obliquely encapsulated in the narrator's assertion that "Blood is the best of fertilizers" as the cook allows the blood of a freshly killed bird to flow onto wisteria. The symbolism of 'blood' is expansive. Through the doctor's operating on both the American and Japanese soldiers, blood is situated as the unifier of humanity as its source cannot be determined on its own.

The quote above, however, also makes 'blood' symbolically representative of the poison of nationalistic pride that is passed along and 'fertilizes' things like racism and prejudice.

15. Sadao and Hana look upon their time in America with disdain due to the prejudice that they were subjected to. How does racial prejudice taint a person's soul forever? CBSE Question Bank 2021

Ans. It is true that Sadao and Hana look upon their time in America with disdain due to the prejudice that they were subjected to. Such behaviour leads to racial prejudices which taints a person's mentality forever. They are filled with bitterness and cannot think of any way of helping the other.

16. How do we know that Dr. Sadao was conscientious as well as loyal? CBSE SQP 2023

Ans. We know that Dr. Sadao was a conscientious as well as loyal individual because in the face of an adverse dilemma of choosing between his profession and his nation, he found a middle path. He remained true to his profession and saved the life of the Prisoner of War from the enemy nation. At the same time, he made sure that a Japanese authority knew about it. He informed the General about the prisoner and agreed to the plan of assassination.

17. In the story 'The Enemy', why do you think Sadao forbade the American from sharing any details about himself? Answer with a reason in 20–30 words. Competency Based

Ans. Sadao forbade the American from sharing any details about himself because he wanted to hand over the man to the Japanese police once he had recovered. So, he wished to see the man only as an enemy and did not wish to get emotionally attached to the man or know him as a person with qualities.

18. In 20–30 words, mention one character trait of the General with one example from the story 'The Enemy'. Competency Based

Ans. The General comes out to be a selfish character with an unusual sense of humour. We say this because when the General found out that Sadao had sheltered and cared for an American, his reason for not wanting to turn in Sadao was his concern for his own health. He protected Sadao out of self-interest and even made a joke about Sadao murdering him.

19. What was the dilemma faced by Sadao on seeing the prisoner of war? CBSE 2025

Ans. Sadao's dilemma on seeing the prisoner of war was a conflict between his duty as a doctor and his loyalty to Japan. He knew he should report the enemy soldier, but his medical ethics compelled him to save the wounded man's life. His internal struggle reflected his humanity and moral responsibility.

Long Answer Type Questions

1. What was the General's plan to get rid of the American prisoner? Was it executed? What traits of the General's character are highlighted in the lesson 'The Enemy'?

Ans. After getting to know about the presence of an enemy at Dr. Sadao's home, the General planned that his private assassins would take care of the whole matter; they would kill the enemy and even take his body away.

However, the General's plan was not executed. His assassins never arrived and Sadao, tired of the wait, helped the prisoner escape.

The General was so absorbed in his own illness that he had forgotten about the whole affair. He even wanted Sadao not to inform anybody about this, lest the General be charged with lack of patriotism or negligence of duty.

This shows that the General was a highly selfish man, being only concerned about his own safety and pride. He also didn't send Sadao to the battlefield where he could have saved the lives of thousands of soldiers, only because he himself needed Sadao's services.

2. What impression do you form about Dr. Sadao as a man and as a surgeon on your reading the chapter 'The Enemy'?

Ans. Dr. Sadao is a superb surgeon and human being. Sadao is a Japanese surgeon. He is well-educated and skilled in his profession. Sadao takes great pride in his medical abilities and is committed to saving lives regardless of the circumstances. He was about to perfect a discovery which would render wounds entirely clean. The General trusted him so much with his life that he was not sent with the troops.

He respected his father. It was his father's wish that he became a surgeon and Sadao fulfilled it. He married Hana according to his father's wishes. Dr. Sadao is a man of compassion.

When Sadao encounters the American prisoner of war, he faces a profound ethical dilemma. Despite knowing the risks to his safety and reputation, Sadao saves the prisoner's life, reflecting his deep-rooted dedication to his Hippocratic oath.

Further, Sadao feels responsible for ensuring the well-being of the prisoner. He navigates the delicate balance between his professional obligations and allegiance to his country. Sadao transforms as he confronts the complexities of wartime ethics and the human cost of conflict. His experiences challenge his preconceptions and force him to re-evaluate his values and beliefs.

3. Draw a character sketch of Hana on the basis of her role in the story.

Ans. Hana is Sadao's wife and shares his upbringing and education. She has experienced life in America and brings a perspective influenced by her time there. Hana demonstrates adaptability, having adjusted to life in both Japan and America. Exposure to different cultures gives her a nuanced understanding of societal expectations and human behaviour.

As the household mistress, Hana manages domestic affairs and supports Sadao in his professional endeavours. She is depicted as a caring mother and wife, prioritising the well-being of her family.

Hana faces a conflict of loyalties between her allegiance to her husband and her sense of duty to her country. She grapples with the implications of sheltering an enemy soldier and the potential consequences for her family and reputation. Throughout the story, she experiences internal turmoil as she navigates the moral complexities of wartime Japan. Her inner conflict reflects the societal tensions and ethical dilemmas prevalent during the era.

Despite her challenges, Hana is resilient and determined to preserve her family's integrity and navigate the turbulent political climate.

4. The influence of belief in traditions such as religion, family bonds, or patriotism can be used to develop narrative techniques like setting, motivation, sources of conflict, and pacing. Analyse how the writer has incorporated such influences to good effect in the story, 'The Enemy'. Support your answer with valid textual evidence. **CBSE SQP 2024**

Ans. It is true to say that the influence of belief in traditions such as religion, family bonds, or patriotism can be used to develop narrative techniques like setting, motivation, sources of conflict, and pacing. In the chapter, the writer had incorporated Japanese traditions and family bonds that influences Sadao's father's, Sadao's and Hana's actions and decisions. Sadao goes to America just to study medicine and returns. He marries Hana, a Japanese girl according to Japanese traditions. The story also shows how national loyalty and patriotism create tension and conflict. Sadao's duty as a citizen and as a doctor may conflict with his compassion towards the wounded soldier, highlighting the complexities of wartime allegiances. These traditions affect the themes as well as the characters of the story. The wartime setting amplifies the moral dilemmas faced by the characters and adds urgency to their decisions. These conflicts drive the narrative forward and heighten the tension. This tension reflects the characters' internal struggles and external conflicts which shape character motivations.

5. After having escaped from Japan with the help of Dr. Sadao, Tom (the prisoner of war) writes an article highlighting how Sadao's actions demonstrated the importance of humanity and living in harmony. **Competency Based, CBSE 2024**

You may begin like this

Humanity is a value that binds us together ....

Ans. Humanity is a value that binds us together irrespective of our nationalities, caste, creed, religion, etc. I had never thought I would ever be able to believe in humanity after being captured by the Japanese soldiers in the war. I had been tortured to an extent wherein death would have been better for me but they kept me alive in inhumane conditions. I thought I would die when I jumped from the ship into the waters. However, when I woke up, I was scared and shocked to find myself in a Japanese home. I was at the renowned Japanese Dr. Sadao's house. I also got to know that he had operated on me and saved my life. I was scared as I thought he would send me back to that hell. But he did no such thing. Infact, he helped my escape and well, here I am today alive and happy.

Whenever I think about Dr. Sadao, I am filled with the wonders of humanity. It made me realise how vain borders and wars are. In the end, we all are human who need to live together in peace and harmony so that everyone enjoys the life that they live. With this, I end this blog leaving you all to think about harmony and humanity. Hoping for a better and harmonious future!

6. After seeing off the enemy soldier, Dr. Sadao must have felt relieved. He was able to uphold the oath that he had taken as a doctor. Dr. Sadao made an entry into his daily diary explaining the dilemma faced by him and how he resolved it. Imagine yourself to be Dr. Sadao and express his thoughts.

You may begin like this

I was able to uphold the oath I had taken as a doctor....

Competency Based, CBSE 2023

Ans. Thursday, 10th October, 20XX 10:00 p.m.

Dear Diary

I was able to uphold the oath I had taken as a doctor while also maintaining the loyalty that I had for my nation. The recent days have been very depressing and stressful for me. I had to make a choice that could change everything.

On one hand, I had an injured man in need of medical attention and on the other, was my loyalty towards the nation. The injured man was an American prisoner of war, the enemy of the nation. If I were someone else, I know I would have informed the authorities or let the enemy die. But I am a doctor and my oath prevented me from ignoring the man. As a doctor, I had to save all lives irrespective of differences. But in saving the life, I would have gone against my nation. The choice was difficult for both of them would indicate a moral loss to me. So, I took the middle ground. I operated on the man and saved his life. Simultaneously, I informed the General of the situation hoping that he would help me retain my honour and do away with the man. The General promised help but nothing happened for a few days. So, I finally let the man escape.

The entire incident is irksome but I and my family are now safe, peaceful and tension free.

Sadao

7. Why did Sadao help the American prisoner to escape? What precautions did he want the man to take?

Or Dr. Sadao planned and helped the enemy soldier to escape. Comment.

Or How did Dr. Sadao plan the American prisoner's escape? **CBSE 2025**

Ans. Sadao's expertise in his profession and compassion as a human being were his most dominant personality traits. As a dutiful doctor, he could not have let the prisoner die of his injuries and so he saved his life. At the same time, he acted like a responsible citizen and informed the General of the presence of the enemy in his house. However, when the General's men did not come to kill the American, Sadao decided to save his life.

Dr. Sadao didn't want to throw him into the jaws of death again. So, he asked the young soldier to take his private boat at night. He should row in the cover of darkness to a little deserted island nearby. The young American could live there until he saw a Korean fishing boat pass by. Food, bottled water and two quilts were put inside the boat. If the food ran out, he could signal two flashes. He was not to signal in darkness because he could be seen. Thus, the young American came down into the darkness of the garden and escaped.

8. The servants of Sadao and Hana reflect a particular mindset of the general public in society towards the thinking of broad - minded human beings. Elaborate with the help of the story 'The Enemy'.

Ans. The servants of Sadao and Hana reflect the mindset of the poor, uneducated and narrow-minded section of society. They are frightened on hearing about the wounded American soldier in Sadao's house because they are worried about what will happen to them if the authorities discover that they had been helping an enemy soldier. They are not broad-minded like Sadao, who was more interested in saving a human being's life than reporting about his presence to the authorities.

The gardener was superstitious. So he felt that the soldier should die; if he was saved, the sea would take revenge on them. The maid, Yumi, refused to wash the wounds of the enemy soldier because she was angry with Sadao for putting the family in danger. The cook felt that Sadao was excessively proud of his surgical skills. That is why he operated on and saved the enemy soldier. Finally, the servants left Sadao's house, as they were afraid of the repercussions of helping enemy soldier. They could not understand Sadao's dilemma.

9. To choose between professional loyalty and patriotism was a dilemma for Dr. Sadao. How did he succeed in betraying neither?

Or Dr. Sadao faced a dilemma. Should he use his surgical skills to save the life of a wounded person or hand an escaped American prisoner of war over to the Japanese police? How did he resolve this clash of values?

Ans. Dr. Sadao was a modern, enlightened and educated Japanese surgeon who succeeded in maintaining a balance between his professional loyalty and patriotism in an admirable manner.

As Japan was at war with America, the white American soldier was considered as his enemy. As a patriotic citizen of Japan, Dr Sadao was duty bound to hand over the American soldier to the Japanese police. However, Sadao was a doctor and his duty towards his profession was to save a human life.

Dr. Sadao resolved the clash of values in a creative manner. He treated the American soldier by operating him to remove the bullet, thus fulfilling his duty towards his profession. Simultaneously, he informed the General about the presence of the American, thus fulfilling his patriotic duty towards his country.

10. The arrival of the prisoner destroy the peace of Sadao's home. Elaborate

Ans. The arrival of the prisoner does destroy the peace of Sadao's home. At the onset Dr. Sadao and his wife are anxious and confused whether they should save the wounded soldier who they know is an American. The servants in Dr. Sadao's house are against his decision of harbouring a soldier from the enemy's camp. Yumi refuses to wash the American soldier as he was a white man. The cook and gardener criticise Dr. Sadao and threaten to leave the house. Finally, all the servants leave.

Dr. Sadao's home and Hana, Dr. Sadao's wife, stands by him but is in constant terror. The messenger from the General frightens Hana. She fears her husband will be condemned as a traitor. Dr. Sadao himself is in a dilemma. Being a patriotic Japanese citizen he doubts the rightness of his act. It is only after the prisoner leaves that things start getting normal in Dr. Sadao's house.

SELF ASSESSMENT TEST

Extract Based Questions

Read the extract given below and answer the following questions.

1. He saw the flicker of terror on the young face that was still very pale. "Okay," the boy murmured. Evidently he was determined to say more. "I feel I ought to thank you, Doctor, for having saved my life."

Don't thank me too early," Sadao said coldly. He saw the flicker of terror again in the boy's eyes- terror as unmistakable as an animal's.

(i) Complete the sentence suitably.

The young boy was thanking Dr. Sadao for ....

(ii) Why the boy terrified with the words of Dr. Sadao?

(iii) Which of the following would not bring 'a flicker of terror'?

(a) Seeing a spider
(b) Breaking an expensive vase
(c) Scoring less marks than expected
(d) Getting an unexpected gift

(iv) Why do you think Sadao was talking coldly with the boy?

Short Answer Type Questions

Answer the following questions in 40-50 words.

1. How can you say that Sadao respected his father very much?

2. Why did Sadao decide to operate on the injured man?

3. Why did Sadao agree to get the white man assassinated?

4. How did Dr. Sadao perform his duty as a patriotic Japanese?

5. In what condition did Dr. Sadao find the American soldier at the seashore?

6. What role did the American professor play in bringing Hana and Sadao together?

7. Why did Dr. Sadao treat the American soldier even though, it was an unpatriotic act on his part?

8. Did Hana think the Japanese tortured their prisoners of war? Why?

Long Answer Type Questions

Answer the following questions in 120-150 words.

1. Dr. Sadao was more a dutiful doctor than a loyal citizen. Substantiate the statement by quoting suitable evidence from the story 'The Enemy.'

2. Explain the reactions of the servants in Dr. Sadao's house when he decided to give shelter to an enemy in the house.

3. What do you know about the white man from the story?

05

On the Face of It

About the Author

Susan Elizabeth Hill (1942-Present) is a critically acclaimed English novelist and short-story writer whose production first reached its peak in the late 1960's and early 1970's. She has authored numerous novels, collections of short stories, non-fiction and children's fiction as well as a respected reviewer, critic, broadcaster and editor. Her simply drawn novels examine the lives of small, sometimes eccentric people, who look for life and warmth in their often icy and sterile lives.

YOUR STUDY GOALS

- Chapter Sketch
- About the Characters
- Summary of the Chapter

YOUR PRACTICE GOAL

- NCERT Folder
- Extract Based Questions
- Short Answer Type Questions
- Long Answer Type Questions

Chapter Sketch

The play 'On the Face of It' beautifully yet grimly depicts the sad world of the physically impaired. It is not the actual pain or inconvenience caused by a physical impairment that trouble a disabled man but the attitude of the people around him. The story centers around two physically impaired people, Mr. Lamb with a tin leg and Derry with a burnt face, who strike a band of friendship. The play covers theory conversation and how Mr. Lamb is able to change Derry perspective and make him hopeful.

About the Characters

Mr. Lamb He is an old cripple who enjoys life despite his handicap.

Derry He is a 14 year old boy with one side of his face disfigured in an accident. Reclusive at first, he learns how to live from Mr. Lamb.

Derry's Mother She seems to be a loving mother. However, her over-protectiveness curbs Derry's freedom and joys.

Other people These are people who make rude comments on Derry's burnt face. They represent the apathetic nature of common masses to those impaired.

Summary of the Chapter

Mr. Lamb's Garden

The play begins in Mr. Lamb's garden. Derry enters the garden and walks slowly, thinking nobody is there. However, he is shocked when Mr. Lamb's warns Derry to not trip up on the crab apples. Derry tries to justify himself and but Mr. Lamb puts his fears at rest. He assures Derry that everyone is welcome in his garden. This angers Derry who replies that he is not afraid but people are afraid of him. He adds that he himself is afraid of himself because one side of his face got burnt as acid fell on it.

Philosophy of Perception

Mr. Lamb changes the subject, angering Derry more. He tells Mr. Lamb that he has changed the subject because he is also afraid of his burnt face just like other people. Mr. Lamb tells him to talk about it, but Derry has become upset. Derry is confused at Mr. Lamb's indifference and asks him if he is not interested in him. Mr. Lamb replies that he is interested in everybody. Then, he presents his first philosophy. He tells Derry that one plant is called a weed and the other a flowers because of perception.

Mr. Lamb's Impairment

Mr. Lamb tells Derry that one of his legs got blown off in a war and when he goes out, some kids call him 'Lamey-Lamb'. This doesn't bother him as he thinks that such a name suits him. To this, Derry says that Mr. Lamb could cover his tin leg with his trousers, and none would notice it or stare. But Derry could not cover his face.

Mr. Lamb reminds Derry of the tale of Beauty and the Beast to further his philosophy of perception.

However, Derry is filled with bitterness. He says that his face will always remain the same and that no one will kiss him. Only his mother kisses him on the other side of his face Mr. Lamb tries to reason with him, telling him to notice the beautiful things in the world and not care about his face.

Philosophy about Life

Derry narrates an incident where in he had heard two women talk mean things about his face. He is very hurt and calls it cruel. Mr. Lamb advises him not to believe everything that he hears. Hearing this, Derry thinks that Mr. Lamb is 'peculiar'. He further tells him that he came in the garden because he liked it. But he doesn't like being near people.

Mr. Lamb starts telling him a story about a man who locked himself inside a room as he was afraid to die. However, the man died because a picture fell off the wall on his head. Through this story, Mr. Lamb wanted to show Derry that one cannot hide oneself or shun society just because of some fear. One should enjoy life as it comes.

Derry is not Lost

Derry notices that there are no curtains on the windows of Mr. Lamb's house. Mr. Lamb replies that he is not fond of curtains and he likes to see the nature. Derry says that he likes to hear the rain falling on the roof. Hearing this, Mr. Lamb realises that Derry can become optimistic.

Insignificance of Name

Derry tells Mr. Lamb that even his family pities him. They feel that it would be difficult for him to get on in this world with a face like that. Mr. Lamb shows him that he can live his life easily like others do. When Derry asks Mr. Lamb if he has any friends, the old man tells him that everyone is his friend, even Derry. Derry is confused as Mr. Lamb doesn't even know his name. Mr. Lamb explains that names don't signify anything. To him, being friends doesn't mean that you should know all the details about a person. At this point, Derry chooses to tell him his name. He says it's Derek, but he wants to be called 'Derry' only.

'Watching, Listening, Thinking'

When Derry tells Mr. Lamb that he hates some people, the old man replies that hatred is more dangerous than the acid that burned his face. Derry narrates another incident about the time when he returned home after the accident. He heard someone say that he'd have been better in the hospital with others 'like him'. Mr. Lamb contradicts it which leaves Derry amazed. When he asks Mr. Lamb how he understands all these things, Mr. Lamb replies, 'Watching, listening, thinking'.

Becoming Derry's Friend

Mr. Lamb tells Derry that he can come and go in his house as he wishes. Derry tells Mr. Lamb that his friends would run away at seeing Derry's face. Mr. Lamb tells him that it is a 'risk' he has to take. He wants Derry to understand that he has to come out of his shell and shed his bitterness if he wants to live life to the fullest.

When Derry asks Mr. Lamb how he is going to get the apples down, Mr. Lamb assures him that over the years he has learned to deal with his handicap. Derry says that he could help him, but his mother won't allow him to come out once he gets home.

Transforming Derry

Mr. Lamb tells Derry that it is not Derry's mother but Derry's bitterness and hesitation that won't let him go out. Derry tries to give a reason but Mr. Lamb tells Derry that he could do anything if he chooses to. The power of choosing what one wants lies in one's own hands.

A small altercation takes place between them. Mr. Lamb says that Derry doesn't have the guts to fight the odds. His burnt face is just an excuse. Derry becomes infuriated and mocks the tin leg of Mr. Lamb. He promises to return to the garden.

Derry Chooses Himself

The second scene begins in Derry's house. He is fighting with his mother because he wants to return to Mr. Lamb, and his mother is not allowing him to go. She believes that Mr. Lamb is a strange man. But Derry insists that he wants to go as he wants to talk to Mr. Lamb about things which matter to him. His mother tells him to stay but Derry tells her that he hates it. His mother simply tells him that he is bound to say such awful things because of his face. Derry strongly replies that he doesn't care about his face anymore.

Derry is a Changed Person

The final scene shifts to the garden again. Derry reaches the garden to find Mr. Lamb lying on the ground. He has been trying to pick the apples off the tree when the ladder has slipped and he, alongwith it, has fallen on the ground. Derry tries to awaken him, but Mr. Lamb is probably dead. Derry has lost his only friend and he begins to cry. Mr. Lamb was able to do what he has been trying; he has taught Derry how to live.

Word-Meaning

crab apples	—	small wild apples with a sharp pungent taste
windfalls	—	fruits blown down from a tree or bush by the wind
scrump	—	steal (fruit) from an orchard or garden
jelly	—	a sweet or dessert made from fruits
give (me) a hand	—	help, assist
stuff	—	worthless matter
blown off	—	separated by a blow
lamey	—	a nickname for a lame person
monstrous	—	frightening
daft	—	crazy, foolish
dribble	—	to let saliva drip from the mouth
humm/hum	—	make a continuous murmuring sound
filing box	—	a box for keeping documents or files in order
make (all that) out	—	understand
thumping	—	falling down with a loud, dull sound
swishes	—	moves with a hissing sound

Important Themes of the Chapter

The Power of Human Connection and Empathy The central theme of 'On the Face of It' revolves around human connection, empathy, and understanding in overcoming prejudice, isolation, and adversity. The play delves into the unlikely friendship between Derry, a young boy with a disfigured face, and Mr. Lamb, an elderly man with a prosthetic leg, who meet in Mr. Lamb's garden. Despite societal judgements and personal insecurities, Derry and Mr. Lamb form a bond based on mutual acceptance, empathy, and companionship. Through their interactions, the play explores themes of compassion, resilience, the impact of physical appearance on social interactions, and the importance of finding solace and understanding in human relationships. 'On the Face of It' suggests that genuine connections can transcend external differences and provide healing and emotional support in adversity.

NCERT Folder

Read and Find Out (NCERT Page 48)

1. Who is Mr. Lamb? How does Derry get into his garden? CBSE 2022 Term II

Ans. Mr. Lamb is an old man who lives in a big house. He has no family. He lost one of his legs in an explosion in a war.

As Derry was walking past Mr. Lamb's garden, he felt the place was isolated. So, he got into the garden by climbing over the garden wall.

Read and Find Out (NCERT Page 54)

1. Do you think all this will change Derry's attitude towards Mr. Lamb?

Ans. Yes, I think Derry's attitude towards life itself will entirely change. Mr. Lamb will be able to show him the bright side of life. Derry will be transformed totally and develop a new understanding about his life. Accordingly, his attitude towards Mr. Lamb will also change and he will consider Mr. Lamb a true friend.

Reading with Insight (NCERT Page 61)

1. What is it that draws Derry towards Mr. Lamb in spite of himself?

Ans. Derry finds Mr. Lamb quite different from the other people he has come across till now. He is impressed by the old man's talk about beauty and the beast, pretty girls and the plain talk about how the world will change its attitude towards Derry. Mr. Lamb's concept of the world, friendship, not believing everything one hears, the story about the timid man who locked himself in, and the like, sound peculiar to Derry, but interest him. He understands the underlying message that Mr. Lamb has given him.

Derry is also drawn towards Mr. Lamb despite himself due to Mr. Lamb's genuine acceptance and interest in him. Despite Derry's initial resistance and fear of judgment, Mr. Lamb's non-judgmental attitude, willingness to listen, and genuine kindness create a sense of belonging and connection for Derry, which he may not experience elsewhere.

2. In which section of the play does Mr. Lamb display signs of loneliness and disappointment? What are the ways in which Mr. Lamb tries to overcome these feelings?

Ans. Mr. Lamb displays signs of loneliness and disappointment in Scene One, where he reflects on the fleeting nature of human connections and the tendency of people not to return. At the end of Scene One, when Derry promises to Mr. Lamb that he will return, as he rushes home, we hear Mr. Lamb telling himself, "We all know. I'll come back. They never do, though. Not them. Never do they come back". Thus, although Derry promises to come back, Mr. Lamb does not believe him. The words spoken by Mr. Lamb reveal his deepest feelings of loneliness.

Further, in scene one Mr. Lamb states that he spends most of his time watching, listening and thinking. When Derry asks him to name some of his friends, the old man is at a loss. These also show that he lacks human company.

To overcome these feelings, Mr. Lamb engages in activities he enjoys, such as tending to his bees and finding solace in nature. He is happy because the neighbourhood children come to his garden for stealing apples and pears.

3. The actual pain or inconvenience caused by a physical impairment is often much less than the sense of alienation felt by the person with disabilities. What is the kind of behaviour that the person expects from others?

Ans. The actual pain or inconvenience due to a physical impairment is often much less than the sense of alienation felt by the person with disabilities because it creates a feeling of loneliness in the physically disabled person. People in society make such a person realise that they are not liked and maintain a distance from them. A person with a physical disability like a tin leg or a burnt face can live a life of respect and honour if he/she is not ridiculed or pitied. If everyone else looks at such persons in a negative way, they can never break out of their seclusion from the world.

Such people expect respect understanding, acceptance and empathy from others.

Here, Mr. Lamb understands his situation and copes with it successfully, whereas Derry, who is only 14 years old, is not mature enough to cope with his predicament.

That is why he liked Mr. Lamb after meeting him for the first time. A person with a physical impairment expects a normal behaviour from others. He wants others to respect him instead of pitying him.

4. Will Derry get back to his old seclusion or will Mr. Lamb's brief association affect a change in the kind of life he will lead in the future?

Ans. Suffering from a physical impairment, Derry had become a pessimist. But after he met Mr. Lamb, he gradually began to see the bright side of life. He realised that, in the form of Mr. Lamb, he had found a true friend who has shown him the right approach towards life.

A brief association with Mr. Lamb boosted Derry's self-confidence and made him respect himself as he was. This new self-esteem brought about a major change in Derry and he told his mother that his looks do not matter. A change has certainly come about in Derry's attitude towards himself and towards life in general. It is unlikely that he will revert to his past secluded life, even with Mr. Lamb's probable death at the end of the story. In fact, he will now lead a more active life with the positive thoughts given to him by Mr. Lamb because Mr. Lamb was the person who taught him the correct approach to life.

How about... (NCERT Page 62)

1. Using your imagination to suggest another ending to the above story.

Ans. The above story can be changed slightly to end on a happy note. It can happen that Derry will make efforts to revive Mr. Lamb instead of weeping. Mr. Lamb regains consciousness, gets up with Derry's assistance and invites Derry to meet him regularly so that Derry can learn more about living a better life from him. Derry is overjoyed and promises to do so.

Exam Pattern Questions

Extract Based Questions

Read the extracts given below and answer the questions that follow.

1. Derry I'd not come to steal anything.

Mr. Lamb No, no The young lads steal... scrump the apples. You're not so young.

Derry I just ...wanted to come in. Into the garden.

Mr. Lamb So you did. Here we are then.

Derry You don't know who I am.

Mr. Lamb A boy. Thirteen or so.

Derry Fourteen. (Pause) But I've go to go now. Good-bye.

Mr. Lamb Nothing to be afraid of. Just a garden. Just me.

Derry But I'm not .... I'm not afraid. (Pause) People are afraid of me.... . CBSE 2024

(i) Why does Mr. Lamb feel that Derry has not come to steal?

(ii) Cite instances from the extract which show that Mr. Lamb is trying to put Derry at ease.

(iii) Choose the correct statement.

(a) Derry entered the garden as he was fascinated by the bees.

(b) Derry came to meet Mr. Lamb.

(c) They were well acquainted with each other.

(d) Derry entered as he wanted to see the garden.

(iv) People are afraid of Derry because ....

Ans. (i) It is because Derry is not as young as those lads who come to steal from the garden.

(ii) Mr. Lamb tells Derry that there is nothing to be afraid of in the garden and there's only him as a way to put Derry at ease.

(iii) (d) Derry entered as he wanted to see the garden.

(iv) of the way he looks

2. Aren't you interested?

You're a boy who came into the garden. Plenty do. I 'm interested in anybody. Anything. There's nothing God made that doesn't interest me. Look over there.... over beside the far wall. What can you see?

Rubbish.

(i) Complete the following suitably.

'Aren't you interested'? This line has been stated in the context of ....

(ii) Why Mr. Lamb is interested in anybody?

(a) Because he is friendly to others.

(b) Because he has a positive outlook in life.

(c) Because he loves to help others.

(d) Because he didn't want anybody to be in trouble.

(iii) What was the purpose of Mr. Lamb asking Derry to look at the far wall?

(iv) What is called 'rubbish'? Why?

Ans. (i) Derry's burnt face

(ii) (b) Because he has a positive outlook in life.

(iii) Mr. Lamb asked Derry to look at the far wall to make Derry understand the absurdity of his behaviour.

(iv) Weeds are called 'rubbish'. They are called so because people find them to be useless and something that destroys the beauty of all other plants.

3. **Mr. Lamb** Look, boy, look.... what do you see?

Derry Just....grass and stuff. Weeds.

Mr. Lamb Some call them weeds. If you like, then.... a weed garden, that. There's fruit and there are flowers, and trees and herbs. All sorts. But over there.... weeds. I grow weeds there. Why is one green, growing plant called a weed and another 'flower'? Where's the difference. It's all life.... growing. Same as you and me.

Derry We're not the same.

Mr. Lamb I'm old. You're young. You've got a burned face, I've got a tin leg.

Not important. You're standing there.... I'm sitting here. Where's the difference?

(i) Complete the sentence suitably.

The word .... describes Derry's tone when he says–"We're not the same"?

(ii) Which of the following represents Mr. Lamb's analysis of flowers and weeds?

(a) Comparison is an act of violence against the self.
(b) If you have a garden in your library, everything will be complete.
(c) One man's freedom fighter is another man's terrorist.
(d) The cosmos is within us. We are made of star-stuff.

(iii) Like the play, the given extract is a study in contrasts. What does Mr. Lamb seek to do by bringing up distinctions?

(iv) Mr. Lamb and Derry suffer from physical impairments. What are the impairments?

Ans. (i) gloomy

(ii) (c) One man's freedom fighter is another man's terrorist.

(iii) To highlight that labels are arbitrary and essentially reflect a common life experience.

(iv) Mr. Lamb's impairment is that he wears a tin leg. Derry's impairment is his burnt face.

4. **Derry** You're ... peculiar. You say peculiar things. You ask questions I don't understand.

Mr. Lamb I like to talk. Have company. You don't have to answer questions. You don't have to stop here at all. The gate's open.

Derry Yes, but...

Mr. Lamb I've a hive of bees behind those trees over there. Some hear bees and they say, bees buzz. But when you listen to bees for a long while, they humm. ... and hum means 'sing'. I hear them singing, my bees.

Derry But....I like it here. I came in because I liked it ..... when I looked over the wall.

Mr. Lamb If you'd seen me, you'd not have come in.

Derry No.

(i) List the playwright's purpose of using ellipses (…) in this extract.

(ii) Select the option that best describes Derry and Mr. Lamb in the extract.

(a) Derry: introvert; Mr. Lamb: friendly
(b) Derry: fearful; Mr. Lamb: domineering
(c) Derry: friendly; Mr. Lamb: weird
(d) Derry: open minded; Mr. Lamb: charming

(iii) Which of the following best summarises Mr. Lamb's attitude towards the bees?

(a) Beauty is being true to yourself.
(b) There is a kind of beauty in imperfection.
(c) Beauty is the promise of happiness.
(d) The beauty of the world lies in the details.

(iv) Derry says, "I came in here because I liked it ...." What was the one significant thing Derry might have liked about the place, as per the extract?

Ans. (i) The playwright's purpose of using ellipses (…) in this extract to show that the character is pausing to think about something.

(ii) (a) Derry: introvert; Mr. Lamb: friendly

(iii) (d) The beauty of the world lies in the details.

(iv) The statement by Derry that "I came in here because I liked it …" is significant in showing that Derry liked to stay away from the prying eyes of people.

5. **Derry** What do you do all day?

Mr. Lamb Sit in the sun. Read books. Ah, you thought it was an empty house, but inside, it's full. Books and other things. Full.

Derry But there aren't any curtains at the windows.

Mr. Lamb I'm not fond of curtains. Shutting things out, shutting things in. I like the light and the darkness, and the windows open, to hear the wind. **CBSE 2023**

(i) The description of the house indicates that Mr. Lamb ....

(ii) The experience 'does not like shutting things out, shutting things in' suggests Mr. Lamb's

(a) welcoming nature
(b) poverty-stricken existence
(c) lack of resources
(d) confused state of mind

(iii) **Mr. Lamb spends his time ....**

I. **reading books**

II. **cooking meals**

III. **shutting things out**

IV. **enjoying the beauties of nature**

Which of the following options are appropriate?

(a) I and IV (b) II, III and IV

(c) I and II (d) I and III

(iv) **On the basis of the extract, study the two statements I and II given below.**

I. **Mr. Lamb liked meeting people.**

II. **Mr. Lamb accepted life as it comes.**

Choose the most appropriate option.

(a) I can be inferred from the extract, but II cannot

(b) II can be inferred from the extract, but I cannot

(c) Both I and II can be inferred from the extract

(d) Neither I nor II can be inferred from the extract

Ans. (i) was an optimistic man who loved to read

(ii) (a) welcoming nature

(iii) (a) I and IV

(iv) (c) Both I and II can be inferred from the extract

6. Mr. Lamb Well that needn't stop you, you needn't mind.

Derry It'd stop them. They'd mind me. When they saw me here. They look at my face and run.

Mr. Lamb They might. They might not. You'd have to take the risk. So would they.

Derry No, you would, you might have me and lose all your other friends, because nobody wants to stay nearme if they can help it.

Mr. Lamb I've not moved.

Derry No ....

Mr. Lamb When I go down the street, the kids shout 'Lamey-Lamb'. But they still come into the Garden, into my house; it's a game. They're not afraid of me. Why should they be? Because I'm not afraid of them, that's why not. **CBSE 2023**

(i) **The kids tease Mr. Lamb but still come into his garden. Why?**

(ii) **Choose the best option that describes Mr. Lamb.**

(a) Headstrong (b) Pessimist

(c) Negligent (d) Positive

(iii) **Choose the correct option with reference to the extract.**

What makes Derry tell Mr. Lamb that if he comes, others would stop coming?

(a) Mr. Lamb would not let others come.

(b) They would be surprised by Derry.

(c) Mr. Lamb will have to choose between him and others.

(d) Derry would flare up.

(iv) **What does Mr. Lamb mean by "They might, they might not"?**

Ans. (i) It is true that the kids tease Mr. Lamb but still come to his garden. This is so because the garden provides them open and safe place to play. Further, the crab apples may also seem to attract them.

(ii) (d) positive

(iii) (c) Mr. Lamb will have to choose between him and others.

(iv) Through the given phrase, Mr. Lamb wants to state that he does not care if people stop coming to his garden. He believes that his garden is open for all even Derry and if they choose not to come to the garden, it will not affect him.

Short Answer Type Questions

1. What kind of garden does Mr. Lamb have? Why does he like it?

Ans. Mr. Lamb's garden has flowers, fruit trees as well as a place for rearing bees.

He likes the garden because it keeps him busy. He spends his entire day looking after the plants, breaking the crab apples from the trees and making jam out of them.

2. Why does Mr. Lamb leave the gate of his house always open? **CBSE 2020**

Ans. Mr. Lamb always keeps his gate open because he always wants visitors to come to his house. Mr. Lamb resided alone in a big house and liked to meet and talk to people. He was warm and welcoming. He had a positive outlook towards life and believed that everything that belonged to him, belonged to everyone.

3. Why does Mr. Lamb say to Derry, "So you are not lost, are you? Not altogether?"

Ans. Mr. Lamb makes this remark when Derry mentions that he too enjoys the sound of falling rain. He makes the remark to change Derry's negative approach towards life. The lines boost Derry's self-confidence and fill him with positivity.

4. Mr. Lamb and Derry were both suffering from similar problems. Comment.

Ans. It is true that Mr. Lamb and Derry were both suffering from similar problems. They both were physically impaired by the virtue of which they both were alienated from the society. However, they both react differently to their conditions. While Mr. Lamb accepts it, Derry becomes a pessimist.

5. How did Mr. Lamb's conversation and company change Derry's desire to isolate himself from the world? CBSE 2022 Term II

Ans. Mr. Lamb tried to remove the baseless fears of Derry by pointing out the nature and its wonders. He tells Derry about how his negative thoughts destroyed him and will continue to destroy him. He highlights the importance of perspectives and optimism. All of these bring a change into Derry.

6. How is the Derry we meet at the beginning different from the Derry at the end ?

Ans. Derry in the beginning of the play 'On the Face of it' is a withdrawn and a defiant person. He is filled with negativity and miserable as well as pitiable. But by the end, we find a positive change in Derry. The meeting with Mr. Lamb has given him a direction and purpose of life. He is now free from his old complexes.

7. Why did Derry go back to Mr. Lamb's garden even after opposition? CBSE Questions Bank 2021

Ans. Derry decided to go back to Mr. Lamb's garden even after opposition from his mother because for the first time someone had not judged him for his injured face. Instead, Mr. Lamb had inspired Derry to overcome his disability by adopting an optimistic outlook on life. The teachings and advices given by Mr. Lamb impacted Derry to tread the path showed by him, and thus, he returned to Mr. Lamb.

8. "It is not merely age but experience that counts." With reference to any one example from the text, comment on how Derry found Mr. Lamb different from other adults he had encountered? CBSE Question Bank 2021

Ans. Derry is a pessimist. His negative attitude towards the world is a result of the negative outlook of people towards him. People around him have always made him feel inferior and ugly. Even his parents reflect a similar attitude. In middle of such experience, Mr. Lamb provides him a new approach to things because he himself had experienced such behaviours in his life.

Based on his experience, he tells Derry that it is the perception of an individual that matters. He teaches him the importance of being positive and also about now he needs to believe in his own self. He tells him that he should not hate others and that hatred is worse than acid because it burns the inside.

9. Imagine that Mr. Lamb had not fallen off the ladder at the end. Recalling his conversation with the bees, do you think Derry's return might have changed him as much as he had changed Derry? Elaborate. CBSE Question Bank 2021

Ans. Yes, I think that Derry's return would have changed Mr. Lamb if he had not fallen off the ladder at the end. Derry is so impacted by Mr. Lamb's words that he decides to visit Mr. Lamb again. This would have taken the old man from loneliness to a happy companionship.

Mr. Lamb liked company which he did not enjoy but with Derry he would have someone to talk to, tell his experiences to, share his joys with and enjoy his life. Most importantly, the old man will have a purpose to hand over his philosophy of life to Derry and inspire him to find out what he wants to be.

10. How do you think Derry's mother contributes to his sense of alienation and isolation? (On the Face of It) CBSE SQP 2022 Term II

Ans. It is truly said that Derry's mother contributes to his sense of alienation and isolation. By stating this, we cannot ignore that she as a mother is aware of how the world treats her son. She also feels over protective for him. However, she comes at fault when she fails to understand her son's longing for companionship. Unknowingly, she treats him with a sense of pity and robs him of his dignity by perpetually treating him like a helpless victim. This pushes Derry further into alienation and isolation.

11. What made Derry extremely self-conscious? CBSE 2022 Term II

Ans. Derry had become extremely self conscious due to the remarks and comments he had recieved from others regarding his handicap. One side of Derry's face is disfigured and scarred due to acid burns. When people see his face, they make mean remarks which had affected Derry and made him a pessimist as well as extremely self conscious. As a result, he had become a recluse.

12. Do you think Derry's mother is protective of him? Justify your opinion with textual evidence. CBSE Question Bank 2021

Ans. Though Derry's mother is given little characterisation in the play, in the little she exists, she comes out as simultaneously overprotective and not understanding of her son. She knows that the world would not be kind to her son and is worried for him.

Her protectiveness only becomes visible when she forbids him from returning to Mr. Lamb's house for all the bad things she had heard of him. But at the same time, she herself contributes to his isolation by keeping him home. She treats him like a helpless victim with a sense of pity that robs him of dignity and adds to her son's pessimism.

13. When Mr. Lamb tells Derry that, while some describe the sound that the bees make as 'buzzing', to him it seems they are singing. What character trait of Mr. Lamb is brought to light? Why?

Ans. The fact that Mr. Lamb tells Derry that while some describe the sound made by bees as 'buzzing' but to him they seem to be singing shows that Mr. Lamb was an optimistic person. He only saw the positive side of things and ignored all negativity.

14. Why does Derry not like being with people? CBSE 2023

Ans. Derry did not like being in the company of other people and remained isolated because he hated the pitiful and curios stares that were directed towards him. He felt that everybody was afraid of his appearance and stayed with him out of compulsion. He also does not like when people talk about his disfigured face.

15. How does Mr. Lamb try and convince Derry that there is no essential difference between them? CBSE 2023

Ans. In the story 'On the Face of It', Mr. Lamb tries to convince Derry that there is no essential difference between them by engaging him in a conversation and finding common ground. Mr. Lamb tells Derry that he, too, has been 'scarred' in life and has faced challenges. He talks about his own experience of being burned in a fire and how it changed his life. Mr. Lamb also emphasizes the importance of looking beyond the surface level and seeing people for who they are on the inside. He tells Derry that "everybody's the same when you come down to it, in their hearts and souls." Through this conversation, Mr. Lamb tries to build a connection with Derry and show him that they are not so different after all.

16. How does Susan Hill subtly portray a blend of pessimism and optimism in 'On the Face of It'? CBSE SQP 2024

Ans. Susan Hill very subtly portrays a blend of pessimism and optimism in 'On the Face of It' through the medium of its two characters- Derry and Mr. Lamb. Both Derry and Mr. Lamb are disabled but present an opposite view of life. Derry holds pessimistic view due to his disfigured face. In contrast stands, Mr. Lamb who depicts an optimistic view of life, suggesting the possibility of emotional survival despite physical and social barriers.

17. How does Mr. Lamb's attitude towards Derry differ from others?

Ans. Mr. Lamb treats Derry with genuine acceptance and interest, contrasting sharply with the fear and avoidance Derry faces from society. His kindness and openness create a unique bond that transcends Derry's appearance.

18. What role does the garden play in the relationship between Derry and Mr. Lamb? How does Derry's return to Mr .Lamb's garden reflect his internal struggle?

Ans. The garden serves as a sanctuary where Derry and Mr. Lamb connect on a deeper level. It symbolises acceptance and understanding, offering them a space free from judgment and prejudice.

Derry's return symbolises his yearning for acceptance and belonging despite societal pressures. It highlights his desire to defy expectations and embrace genuine connections, even when facing rejection.

19. How do themes of resilience and human connection emerge from the play?

Ans. The play explores themes of resilience as characters confront adversity and societal prejudice. It highlights the transformative power of human connection, emphasising the importance of acceptance, empathy, and understanding in overcoming barriers to belonging.

20. How does Derry's journey throughout the play reflect the universal human desire for connection and acceptance?

Ans. Derry's journey mirrors the universal human longing for connection and acceptance in a world that often judges based on appearances. His pursuit of belonging highlights the inherent need for companionship and understanding.

21. How does 'On the Face of It' challenge traditional notions of beauty and acceptance?

Ans. 'On The Face of It' challenges traditional notions of beauty by portraying characters like Derry, whose physical appearance is undesirable, yet they seek acceptance and understanding. It prompts reflection on the deeper qualities that define human worth beyond appearances.

22. Mr. Lamb from 'On the Face of It' says the following lines.

Or Why is one green, growing plant called a weed and another 'flower'? Where's the difference. It's all life. .. growing. Same as you and me.

Or Why does he compare a weed to a flower? What effect is it intended to have on Derry? Explain in 20–30 words.

Competency Based

Ans. Mr. Lamb compares a weed to a flower to show that what society parameters of defining 'ugly' and 'pretty' are baseless and devoid of logic. Things that may essentially be the same, such as growing plants cannot be logically divided into weeds and flowers based on one's preferences. In this way, Mr. Lamb intended to challenge Derry's rejection of himself based on his appearance. He wanted to comfort Derry and bring him out of his dejection.

23. How does Mr Lamb's dislike of curtains symbolise his views on life and people? Describe based on your understanding of the text 'On the Face of It' in 20–30 words. Competency Based

Ans. Mr Lamb's dislike of curtains symbolises the fact that he didn't like shutting things in or out. Similarly he didn't like isolating himself or pushing people away. He was open to meeting all kinds of people which is further proved by his congenial and warm treatment of Derry.

24. What overall impact did Derry's mother seem to have on him? Support your answer with evidence from the play 'On the Face of It' in 40–50 words. Competency Based

Ans. Derry's mother seemed to have a negative impact on Derry. Her excessive focus on Derry's scar probably caused him to view his own self in a negative sight and lead to his self-rejection. He had overheard her worrying about his future, and he felt that she only showed him affection because it was her duty to do so.

Long Answer Type Questions

1. Discuss the relevance of the title 'On the Face of It'.

Ans. The title of the play 'On the Face of It', seems somewhat odd and awkward at first.

However, it is related to the central thematic concern that sometimes people may be quite different from what they appear to be at first. Mr. Lamb appears to be a secretive, mysterious, lonely, lame old man who lives all alone. But in the story, he appears to be a gentle, kind, generous and considerate person who helps Derry in overcoming his fears, obstacles, complexes and inhibitions.

In a similar way, Derry seems to be a introvert who hates people because of his ugly face. He is withdrawn and defiant. However, as the story move on, one finds out the Derry is not completely pessimistic and his pessimism results from the way the world has treated him.

Both Mr. Lamb and Derry undergo a transformation Mr. Lamb gets a companion in Derry and Derry find a mentor and guide in Mr. Lamb. On the face, it may seem that their age might hinder their companionship. However, their circumstances bring them closer.

2. Mr. Lamb died just as soon as Derry was beginning to feel positive about life. Do you think that this would bring about a setback in his life? Give reasons for your answer. CBSE 2020

Ans. I don't think that Mr. Lamb's death would bring a setback in Derry's life. Mr. Lamb plays an instrumental role in changing Derry's attitude to life. Suffering from a physical impairment, Derry had become a pessimist.

But after meeting Mr. Lamb, he gradually began to see the bright side of life. He realised that, in Mr. Lamb, he has found a true friend who has shown him the right approach towards life. A brief association with Mr. Lamb boosted Derry's self-confidence and made him respect himself as he was.

This new self-esteem brought about a major change in Derry and he told his mother that his looks do not matter. A change has certainly come about in Derry's attitude towards himself and towards life in general.

It is unlikely that he will revert to his past secluded life, even with Mr. Lamb's probable death at the end of the story. In fact, he will now lead a more active life with the positive thoughts given to him by Mr. Lamb, because Mr. Lamb was the person who taught him the correct approach to life.

3. Derry mentions two kinds of responses people often have to justify misfortune, one "Look at all those people who are in pain and brave and never cry and never complain and don't feel sorry for themselves"; and secondly, "think of all those people worse off than you."
Far from comforting him, these empty words only agitate him.
In both cases, one's sense of self is derived from others and how they live their lives.

(i) How far might looking at others itself be the cause of suffering?

(ii) In what way can people, especially children, be empowered to face their challenges without the spectre of comparison? CBSE Question Bank 2021

Ans. (i) Looking at others can easily become the cause of suffering simply because of the comparison we make with others. Others suffering and even betterment can make one feel dejected and alienated. This is exactly what happens with Derry.

While some people feel sorry for Derry because of his burned face, others alienate him for being different from other people. Due to such comparisons one becomes prone to a pessimistic attitude, low self-esteem, lack of confidence, desolation and withdrawal.

(ii) People, especially children can be easily empowered to face their challenges without any spectre of comparison by simply considering all of them as equals irrespective of their genders, disabilities etc. With right opportunities, genuine concern and no differentiation everyone should be given a chance to prove themselves.

A person with any physical impairment can live life with respect and honour, if he is not ridiculed. He/she expects empathy rather than sympathy. The feeling of sympathy and pity is just a constant reminder of the disability which should be avoided. In the play, Mr. Lamb, as an adult, is able to cope with such problems, but Derry falls into the pit of seclusion and pessimism. It is only when he finds an equal optimistic approach without judgement that he undergoes a change.

4. Mr. Lamb stands as a symbol of optimism and hope. Support your answer with examples from the text. CBSE 2023

Ans. In the story Mr. Lamb represents a symbol of optimism and hope. He constantly tries to convince Derry that there is no essential difference between them and that they are both human beings with the same potential for goodness.

Mr. Lamb's hope for a better future is also evident in his conversation with Derry about the potential for peace and understanding between people of different backgrounds. He believes that by getting to know each other, people can overcome their differences and live together in harmony.

Furthermore, Mr. Lamb's attitude towards life is a symbol of hope and optimism. He does not let his circumstances get him down and always looks for the good in every situation. He is hopeful that Derry will eventually come around and see things from his perspective.

Thus, Mr. Lamb's character represents a symbol of hope and optimism in the story. His unwavering faith in humanity and his hope for a better future are evident throughout the story, and serve as an example of how one can maintain a positive attitude even in the face of adversity.

5. 'Mr. Lamb Lord boy, you've got two arms, two legs and eyes and ears ....
You could get on better than all the rest. Optimism is the best tool to face challenges in life'.
Imagine you are Mr. Lamb. You want to give a motivational speech to a group of differently abled students urging them to be positive in their approach to life. Write the speech on the behalf of Mr. Lamb.
Competency Based, CBSE 2024

You may begin like this

Hello! Dear Students! Believe in yourself. Nothing is impossible.

Ans. Hello, esteemed students! I implore you to embrace your capabilities and believe in your innate potential. Despite the challenges posed by our circumstances, remember that nothing is unachievable with determination and resilience. Life may present obstacles, but it is our response to adversity that defines our character. Instead of dwelling on limitations, focus on your strengths and the boundless possibilities that lie ahead. Each of you possesses unique talents and abilities waiting to be unleashed upon the world. Embrace a positive mindset, for it is the foundation upon which success is built.

Look at me, I have a tin leg. Yet, I have my own beautiful world, my garden. It is different yet complete, just like each one of us. Do not let the world define your disabilities, instead show the world what you are capable of.

Together, let us strive for greatness and prove that with perseverance, there are no limits to what we can achieve. For only the sky is your limit. Life will always be beautiful, it just depends on our perspective of looking at things.

Thank you.

6. 'Derry Oh no, because if I don't go back there, I'II never go anywhere in this world again'.
Derry later realises that the decision taken at that moment helped him to come out of shell. As Derry, write a diary entry expressing your happiness and thanking your stars for the right decision taken.
Competency Based, CBSE 2024

You may begin like this

I was so fortunate to be able to be decisive at the right moment ....

Ans. Friday, 18th March, 20XX

I was so fortunate to be able to be decisive at the right moment that today, I find myself overwhelmed with gratitude and joy as I reflect on it. When I uttered those words to my mother - "Oh no, because if I don't go back there, I'll never go anywhere in this world again" - I had no idea how profoundly they would shape my future.

Looking back now, I realise that returning to face my fears at Mr. Lamb's garden was the catalyst for my personal growth and liberation. Confronting my anxieties head-on has allowed me to break free from the confines of my self-imposed limitations and emerge from my shell. I am filled with a sense of empowerment and renewed purpose, knowing that I have taken control of my life and embraced the opportunities that lie ahead. I am deeply thankful for the courage and conviction that guided me to make the right decision.

Today marks the beginning of a new chapter in my journey, and I am eager to embrace it with open arms.

Derry

7. Imagine you are Derry speaking at the funeral of Mr. Lamb highlighting Mr. Lamb's optimism and the change he brought about in your attitude towards life.
Competency Based, CBSE 2024

You may begin like this

Dear Friends,

I will be eternally grateful to Mr. Lamb ....

Ans. Dear Friends

I will be eternally grateful to Mr. Lamb for if I had not met him, I would have never realised what a fool I had been. For the large part of my life after my accident, I had felt that people were scared of me. I paid a lot of attention to what other people said for me. As a result, I had felt that I was not enough for even my mother. Hence, I became an introvert and anti-social child.

All of this changed when I met Mr. Lamb. Mr. Lamb helped me see that my accident did not define me and that I did not need to pay attention to what others think of me. He taught me to be confident of myself and that I am just as important as others. His optimistic attitude had filled a pessimist like me with an optimistic attitude towards life.

8. Examine the characters of Derry and Mr. Lamb in the context of the themes of alienation and loneliness in the story 'On the Face of It'. **CBSE 2022 Term II**

Ans. One can find a lot of affinity between the characters, Derry and Mr. Lamb, in the story 'On the Face of it'. Both of them suffer from a physical affliction. However, their attitude towards the afflictions is very different.

In Derry's case, his face is burnt by acid, so he suffers from a sense of inferiority complex and has a negative attitude towards life. People are scared of him and he tries to alienate himself. He is defiant and withdrawn. He does not trust people and thinks that no one will ever love him except his mother. He can't face the stare of the people.

On the contrary, Mr. Lamb does not allow his disability to come in his way. He develops a positive attitude and accepts it as it comes. Though children tease him by calling 'Lamey-Lamb', he does not mind. He keeps his door always open. People visit him and he gives toffees to the children. He has friends everywhere. He sits in the sun to read books. He grows weeds, plants, flowers and fruits. He believes in living life to the fullest.

9. Mr. Lamb calls Derek his friend while Derek refuses his affirmation. Would you consider their relationship with each other as friendship? Support your answer with reference to the instance(s) from the text.

Ans. Although Mr. Lamb calls Derek his friend, Derek refuses his affirmation. I would still consider their relationship with each other as friendship. This is simple because during the interaction with Mr. Lamb, Derek seems to develop a bond with him. Mr. Lamb's positivity, optimism, maturity and persistence impresses Derek. Mr. Lamb calls Derek his friend and also says that there are friends everywhere. He accepts Derek with all his imperfections. This makes Derek open up to him and he finds his company appealing. Derek states to Mr. Lamb that his condition has made him bitter due to people's bad behaviour and treatment towards him. Mr. Lamb's words have an impact on Derek and he overcomes issues that held him back.

Even though Derek does not affirm his friendship with Mr. Lamb openly, Mr. Lamb's words inspired trust in him. Later, he gets back to Mr. Lamb's garden just because he wanted to spend time with him. This is only due to the fact that he considered Mr. Lamb his friend.

10. Both Derry and Lamb are victims of physical impairment, but much painful for them is the feeling of loneliness. Comment.

Or The lesson, 'On the Face of It' is an apt depiction of the loneliness and sense of alienation experienced by people on account of a disability. Explain.

Ans. It is true to say that 'On the Face of It' is an apt depiction of the loneliness and sense of alienation experienced by people on account of a disability. Mr. Lamb and Derry both were victims of physical impairment. Mr. Lamb had an artificial leg made of tin and Derek had a scarred face. Undoubtedly, both had suffered humiliations in life on account of their handicaps.

One such humiliation came in the form of social rejection which led to loneliness and a sense of alienation experienced by Derry and Mr. Lamb on account of disability. It is not their disability which pains them but the rejection, the harsh words and treatment given to them by others that brings them pain.

Derry suffered from severe negative complexes because of his burnt face. He became a pessimistic loner as people got scared and stayed away from him. So, he indulged in self-pity and was always suspicious of the intention of others. His anger and frustration made him withdrawn.

Mr. Lamb, on the other hand, was a loner who craved for company and acceptance. Though outwardly he was an always jovial, outgoing and optimistic, he was an extremely sensitive person.

11. Mr. Lamb is a complex and empathetic character whose presence enriches the thematic exploration of friendship, acceptance, and resilience in 'On the Face of It'. Elaborate.

Ans. It is true to say that Mr. Lamb is a complex and empathetic character whose presence enriches the thematic exploration of friendship, acceptance, and resilience in "On the Face of It."

Mr. Lamb is an old man with a prosthetic limb. However, his character attracts us to him.

Mr. Lamb exudes warmth and empathy in his interactions with Derry and others who enter his garden. He demonstrates genuine concern for Derry's well-being and seeks to create a welcoming environment where individuals feel accepted and understood.

Mr. Lamb exhibits resilience and adaptability. He refuses to be defined by his disability and embraces life with optimism and zest, evident in his love for gardening and beekeeping. He encourages Derry to embrace his individuality and find solace in their shared experiences, fostering a sense of belonging and acceptance.

Mr. Lamb possesses a wealth of wisdom and patience from a lifetime of experiences and observations. He imparts these valuable lessons to Derry about resilience, empathy, and the importance of embracing life's uncertainties with grace and humility.

Mr. Lamb emerges as a symbol of hope and redemption, offering Derry a glimpse of kindness and compassion beyond societal prejudices and superficial judgments. His friendship with Derry serves as a beacon of light in the darkness, inspiring both characters to confront their fears and embrace the beauty of human connection.

12. How did Derry's character evolve from the beginning to the end of the play 'On the Face of It'? Describe in 100–120 words with ideas and examples from the play. **Competency Based**

Ans. Derry transformed from being hostile and lonely to becoming more open and hopeful. Initially, Derry avoided others, feeling that everyone was repulsed by his appearance. He feared cruel remarks and being shunned, resenting the empty platitudes people offered him.

However, his interaction with Mr. Lamb was different. Mr. Lamb engaged him in an unprejudiced and tolerant conversation, which intrigued Derry. When Mr. Lamb shared his own experiences with impairment and ridicule, Derry felt a sense of kinship with him. He even grew out of his fear and defied his mother's wishes by helping Mr Lamb.

Mr. Lamb's philosophical outlook on life and people had a significant impact on Derry, helping him understand the difference between living with fear and without it. By the end, Derry wanted to embrace a hopeful life despite the inevitable challenges he would face, inspired by Mr. Lamb's wisdom and acceptance.

13. In the story 'On the Face of It', Derry's responses suggest that other people have attempted to comfort him unsuccessfully about his face. However, Mr Lamb's words have a different impact on Derry. In 120–150 words, analyse Mr Lamb's approach and the effect that it has on Derry. **Competency Based**

Ans. In 'On the Face of It' , Mr. Lamb's approach to Derry is significantly different from the way others have tried to comfort him. While others may have offered pity or superficial reassurances, Mr. Lamb treats Derry with genuine respect and acceptance. He doesn't focus on Derry's disfigurement but instead engages him in meaningful conversation, encouraging him to look beyond his physical appearance and see his own worth.

Mr. Lamb shares his own experiences and perspectives, showing that physical imperfections don't define a person's value or potential. This empathetic and philosophical approach helps Derry to begin seeing himself in a new light. Mr. Lamb's words empower Derry, instilling a sense of self-worth and optimism that he hadn't felt before. This shift in Derry's mindset highlights the profound impact of authentic human connection and understanding in overcoming personal insecurities and challenges.

14. Compare and contrast the characters of Mr. Lamb and Derry in the play 'On the Face of it'. **CBSE 2025**

Ans. In 'On the Face of It', Mr. Lamb and Derry represent contrasting perspectives on life despite both facing physical disabilities. Mr. Lamb, an elderly man with a tin leg, embraces life with optimism, refusing to let his impairment define him. He enjoys simple pleasures, welcomes visitors, and finds beauty in everything, demonstrating resilience and acceptance. He encourages Derry, a young boy with a burned face, to adopt a similar outlook.

Derry, in contrast, is initially withdrawn, bitter, and self-conscious due to his scars. He avoids social interactions, believing people judge him based on his appearance. He fears rejection and isolates himself, feeling unworthy of love or friendship. However, through his conversation with Mr. Lamb, he begins to rethink his perspective, realising that his scars do not define his worth.

15. Analyse the theme of optimism being the right approach to life in the play 'On the Face of It'.

Ans. In 'On the Face of It' by Susan Hill, optimism emerges as the right approach to life through the interaction between Mr. Lamb and Derry. Mr. Lamb, an elderly man with a tin leg, refuses to let his disability define him. He embraces life with positivity, keeping his doors open to everyone and enjoying nature's beauty.

Derry, a young boy with a burned face, initially sees himself as an outcast, believing that society judges him solely by his appearance. However, Mr. Lamb teaches him to focus on inner strength rather than external flaws. He encourages Derry to overcome self-pity and social fears, inspiring him to embrace life despite challenges.

The play conveys that optimism helps individuals rise above adversity. Mr. Lamb's philosophy—seeing the good in everything—proves that hope and confidence can change one's perspective, making life meaningful and fulfilling.

SELF ASSESSMENT TEST

Extract Based Questions

Read the extract given below and answer the questions that follow.

1. It's got nothing to do with my face and what I look like. I don't care about that and it isn't important. It's what I think and feel and what I want to see and find out and hear. And I'm going back there.

(i) Complete the sentence suitably.

Derry is willing to go to ....

(ii) Derry has transformed himself as .... person.

(a) positive (b) confident

(c) introvert (d) straightforward

(iii) What was the reason due to which Derry wants to return to that place?

(iv) What does Derry see when he returns to the garden?

Short Answer Type Questions

Answer the following questions in 40-50 words.

1. Why does Mr. Lamb say that names are not important?

2. Did Derry consider Mr. Lamb his friend? Why/Why not?

3. How does Derry's mother talk about Mr. Lamb?

4. How does Mr. Lamb overcome his feelings of loneliness?

5. How has Mr. Lamb kept himself open to everyone?

6. Why did Mr. Lamb help Derry?

7. Derry was amazed and attracted towards Mr. Lamb. Why?

8. How does 'On the Face of It' illustrate the impact of societal judgments on individuals with physical differences?

9. In what sense is the friendship between Mr. Lamb and Derry fruitful?

Long Answer Type Questions

Answer the following questions in 120-150 words.

1. Derry and Mr. Lamb both are victims of physical impairment but their attitudes towards life are completely different. Explain.

2. Derry sneaked into Mr. Lamb's garden and it became a turning point in his life. Comment.

3. Briefly analyse Derry's character as a complex and multifaceted character whose journey of self-discovery and resilience forms a central narrative arc in 'On the Face of It'.

06

Memories of Childhood

About the Authors

Gertrude Simmons Bonnin (1876 – 1938), with the pen name 'Zitkala-Sa', was a Native American writer, editor, musician, teacher and political activist. She wrote several works chronicling her youthful struggles with identity and pulls between the majority culture and her Native American heritage.

Faustina Mary Fatima Rani (1958–Present), with the pen name 'Bama', is a Tamil, Dalit feminist, teacher and novelist. She rose to fame with her autobiographical novel Karukku (1992), which chronicles the joys and sorrows experienced by Dalit Christian women in Tamil Nadu.

YOUR STUDY GOALS

- Chapter Sketch
- About the Characters
- Summary of the Chapter

YOUR PRACTICE GOAL

- NCERT Folder
- Extract Based Questions
- Short Answer Type Questions
- Long Answer Type Questions

Chapter Sketch

The chapter is divided into two parts, containing autobiographical episodes from the lives of two women from marginalised communities. The stories belong to their childhood and describes how they were treated by those in 'assumed' power or authority.

The first part by Zitkala-Sa is a chapter taken from her book 'American Indian Stories' and describes the oppression she faced at the Carlisle Indian School. Her hair, the symbol of her culture, was taken away from her.

The second part by Bama is an excerpt taken from 'Karukku'. It relates to her first experience with untouchability.

About the Characters

The Cutting of My Hair

Zitkala Sa She is a young girl who is taken to an English school away from her culture and land. She feels strange and powerless in the institute. Her dignity is stripped off with the cutting of her hair.

Judewin She is Zitkala-Sa's friend who warns her about the cutting of her hair. She seems to be a submissive girl who gives in to the injustice.

Other Native American Girls and Boys These are other children who have been displaced from their native lands and cultures. They depict how the white people forced many communities to accept their system.

The paleface women and other white people They are representative of the oppressive structures who forced other communities to forget their own cultures in favour of the white culture.

We too are Human Beings

Bama She is a young and innocent school going girl who observes her surroundings keenly. When she gets to know about untouchability, she had a strong reaction and decides to fight against it.

Annan He is Bama's older brother. Her tells Bama about untouchability and how she can overcome the stigma associated with it.

Other Characters Old man carrying the vadais as symbol of the stigma associated with untouchability. Others people represent those who belong to the 'higher caste'.

Summary of the Chapter

The chapters comprises two excerpts taken from different works of two different authors. These works are combined under a common theme of unjust treatment to marginalised communities.

I-The Cutting of My Hair

The Land of Apples

The story started with Zitkala-Sa remembering that her first day in the land of apples was unpleasant.

It was time for breakfast as the bell had rung. A white woman placed them in the line of girls who were marching into the dining room. The narrator noticed that they were Native American girls who wore tightly fitted clothes and had short hair. But she was feeling very uncomfortable in the school dress.

Eating by Formula

In the hall, a small bell was tapped and every student pulled out a chair from under the table. Zitkala-Sa did the same and sat down. But she was the only one sitting. Just as she began to rise, a second bell was rung and everybody sat down. Then, she heard a man praying while the students sat with their heads bent.

As Zitkala-Sa was glancing at the surroundings, she saw that a white woman was looking at her. After the man stopped praying, a third bell was tapped and everybody started eating with a knife and fork. However, Zitkala-Sa started crying.

Importance of Her Hair

Later, Judewin told Zitkala- Sa that the white woman was talking about cutting their long hair. The thought of having her hair cut was unacceptable to Zitkala. Her mother had taught her that in their society, short hair was worn by mourners and shingled hair by cowards.

Loss of Spirit

Judewin thought that the school people were strong and they would all have to allow their hair to be cut but Zitkala-Sa was ready to put up a fight. When Zitkala-Sa got the chance to escape, she went upstairs and hid under the bed in a large and dark room.

After some time, people started searching for her. Soon, she was caught and forcibly taken downstairs. She was resisting, kicking and scratching wildly. However, nothing worked. Finally, her hair was cut and Zitkala-Sa lost her spirit.

II-We too are Human Beings

The Entertaining Walk Home

The story starts with the narrator was a carefree child. She used to return home from school in thrity minutes as she loved observing the entertaining sights on the journey. She used to see the performing monkey, the snake charmer, the cyclist who kept pedalling for many days, the Maariyaata temple and the pongal offering being cooked outside it along with a political procession, puppet shows and stunt performances.

Encounter with Untouchability

One day, when Bama was returning home, she noticed an elder of her street, carrying a small packet of vadai holding it with a string. The narrator found this scene to be humorous and told about it to her elder brother Annan. She was laughing uncontrollably, but Annan didn't seem to be amused. Annan told her about untouchability. He told her that the upper caste people thought that if low caste people touched them or anything that belonged to them, they would be 'polluted'. That's why the elder was carrying the packet by its string. He added that because they were born into a low caste community, they were never given any honour, dignity or respect.

Annan's Advice

After hearing about untouchability, Bama got angry and wanted to rebel. However, Annan advised her to study hard and learn all that she could, because only education could help them refute all the indignities. These words made a deep impression on Bama. She studied hard and stood first in her class.

Word-Meaning

marginalised	—	made to feel unimportant, confined to the outer edge of society
mainstream	—	ideas, attitudes or activities that are shared by most people and, therefore, considered normal
dogma	—	rules laid down by authorities and unquestionably accepted
excerpt	—	extract
serrated	—	having a saw-toothed edge or margin
felicitous	—	appropriate
pun	—	a play on words, exploiting their different meanings
belfry	—	a bell tower
undercurrent	—	whisper
bedlam	—	a scene of great confusion and noise
paleface	—	white
shingled	—	closely cropped or cut
moccasins	—	soft leather shoes
immodestly	—	indecently
venture	—	have the courage to do or say anything
trial	—	a trying or difficult experience
whither	—	to what place
indignities	—	humiliating or abusive treatment
herder	—	a person who drives cattle
untouchability	—	practicing caste system
novelties	—	new and unusual things
oddities	—	strange things
spur (him) on	—	incite or stimulate
hunter gypsy	—	a member of a group of wandering hunters
lemur	—	a mammal resembling a monkey, but with foxy face and long tail
instruments	—	tools
harangue	—	deliver a long pompous speech
smart	—	pain sharply
savoury	—	with pleasing taste or smell
payasam	—	a sweet South Indian dish made by boiling rice with milk
iced lollies	—	ice cream on a small wooden stick
tread out	—	to press or crush beneath the feet
vadais	—	an Indian dish consisting of a ball made from ground pulses and deep-fried in oil
together	—	to collect with difficulty
run (these) petty errands	—	do small odd, insignificant jobs
appa	—	a term of address
thambi	—	fellow
community	—	here, caste
stripped of	—	deprived of
of (their) own accord	—	without being asked or forced

Important Themes of the Chapter

It is important to note here that both the excerpts deal with different themes that could be clubbed under social injustices. However, we will study these themes separately.

The Cutting of My Long Hair

Cultural identity, oppression, and resistance The story portrays the struggles of Native American children forced into assimilation at boarding schools and the traumatic experience of having their cultural identity stripped away.

Resistance and defiance The excerpt also highlights the themes of resistance and defiance in the face of oppression as Zitkala-Sa rebels against forced assimilation. The autobiographical account sheds light on the profound impact of colonialism and cultural assimilation on indigenous communities.

We too are Human Beings

Caste-based Discrimination The narrator vividly describes instances of untouchability and caste-based discrimination that she witnesses in her community. These incidents highlight the rigid social hierarchy and the dehumanising treatment of marginalised groups.

Social Injustice The excerpt portrays the systemic injustices faced by the Dalit community, including being relegated to menial tasks and denied basic dignity and respect due to their caste status.

Education and Empowerment The narrator's brother emphasises the importance of education as a tool for empowerment and social mobility. Education is presented as challenging societal norms and gaining respect and recognition.

Struggle for Dignity and Equality The narrator's reflections on the indignities faced by her community underscore their ongoing struggle for dignity and equality in a society marked by caste-based prejudices and discrimination.

NCERT Folder

Reading with Insight (NCERT Page 70)

1. The two accounts that you read above are based in two distant cultures. What is the commonality of theme found in both of them?

Ans. The common theme found in both accounts is the experience of marginalisation, discrimination and the struggle for dignity and identity within their respective cultures.

Zitkala-Sa's narrative reflects the oppression faced by Native American children in assimilationist boarding schools, where cultural practices were suppressed and identities were forcibly altered. Similarly, Bama's account illustrates the pervasive caste-based discrimination and social exclusion experienced by the oppressed in India, highlighting the dehumanising treatment and denial of fundamental rights based on caste identity.

Both narratives depict the profound impact of systemic oppression on individuals and communities and the resilience and determination to resist and assert their humanity and cultural pride despite adversity.

2. It may take a long time for oppression to be resisted, but the seeds of rebellion are sowed early in life. Do you agree that injustice in any form cannot escape being noticed even by children?

Ans. Yes, I agree that injustice in any form often does not escape the notice of children. Children are naturally perceptive and sensitive to fairness and equality from a young age. They have an innate sense of right and wrong and can quickly discern when something is unjust or discriminatory, even if they might not fully understand the situation's complexities. Children absorb information from their surroundings, which shapes their understanding of justice. Injustice affects them deeply, making them feel empathy for marginalised people and may motivate them to speak out or take action. Therefore, while children may not always have the vocabulary or understanding to articulate complex social issues, they are often aware of and affected by injustice in various forms. This awareness can plant the seeds of rebellion and resistance against oppression later in life.

Both Zitkala-Sa and Bama were school-going children when they witnessed rough treatment being meted out to themselves or to their community. Zitkala-Sa revolts and resists the school authorities with all her might because she does not want her hair to be shingled like that of a coward. Bama too realises the oppression that her community faces. She puts up a fight by bringing laurels to her community through her scholarly achievements. Thus, she proves that she is superior to the so-called upper castes.

3. Bama's experience is that of a victim of the caste system. What kind of discrimination does Zitkala-Sa's experience depict? What are their responses to their respective situations?

Ans. Zitkala-Sa's experience depicts the discrimination faced by Native American children in assimilationist boarding schools, where their cultural identity was systematically eroded. Forced to conform to Euro-American norms, Zitkala-Sa's traumatic experience of having her long hair forcibly cut symbolises the loss of Indigenous identity and autonomy. In response, she became a vocal critic of such institutions, advocating for the preservation of Native American culture and rights.

Bama's experience as a victim of the caste system reflects the pervasive discrimination and social hierarchy present in Indian society of the 90s. Subject to caste-based oppression, Bama highlights the indignities of untouchability and social marginalisation faced by her kind. Her writing challenges caste norms and advocates for social justice and equality. Zitkala-Sa and Bama respond to their situations with resilience and activism, seeking to dismantle oppression systems and affirm their communities' dignity and rights.

Exam Pattern Questions

Extract Based Questions

Read the extracts given below and answer the questions that follow.

1. The first day in the land of apples was a bitter-cold one; for the snow still covered the ground, and the trees were bare. A large bell rang for breakfast, its loud metallic voice crashing through the belfry overhead and into our sensitive ears.

The annoying clatter of shoes on bare floors gave no peace. The constant clash of harsh noises, with an undercurrent of many voices murmuring an unknown tongue, made a bedlam within which I was securely tied.

(i) Complete the sentence suitably.

Zitkala-Sa is an account of ....

(ii) Where was she?

(iii) 'Murmuring an unknown tongue' indicates ....

(a) innocence (b) mystery
(c) separation (d) disfamiliarity

(iv) What is the tone used by the author in the given extract?

Ans. (i) A Native American woman
(ii) She was in the land of apples.
(iii) (d) disfamiliarity
(iv) The given extract indicates a tone of resentment and anger.

2. I did not open my mouth to answer. Then the steps were quickened and the voices became excited. The sounds came nearer and nearer. Women and girls entered the room. I held my breath and watched them open closet doors and peep behind large trunks. Someone threw up the curtains, and the room was filled with sudden light. What caused them to stop and look under the bed, I do not know. I remember being dragged out, though I resisted by kicking and scratching wildly. In spite of myself, I was carried downstairs and tied fast in a chair. **CBSE 2024**

(i) Select the appropriate option.

'......... sounds came nearer and nearer' ....

(a) describes the increase in volume
(b) adds suspense and anxiety to readers
(c) reflects the thought of the speaker
(d) is a factual narrative

(ii) Complete the following sentence.

'Inspite of myself' suggests that the speaker was ....

(iii) What do you infer from the first line of the extract?

(a) It was her first day in school.
(b) She did not want to get caught.
(c) She was unprepared for the lesson.
(d) She preferred to be by herself.

(iv) State whether the statement given below is True or False.

The speaker hoodwinked the people looking for her.

Ans. (i) (b) adds suspense and anxiety to readers.
(ii) carried downstairs by force and she had no choice in the matter.
(iii) (b) She did not want to get caught.
(iv) True

3. I cried aloud, shaking my head all the while until I felt the cold blades of the scissors against my neck, and heard them gnaw off one of my thick braids. Then I lost my spirit. Since the day I was taken from my mother I had suffered extreme indignities. People had stared at me. I had been tossed about in the air like a wooden puppet. And now my long hair was shingled like a coward's! In my anguish I moaned for my mother, but no one came to comfort me. Not a soul reasoned quietly with me, as my own mother used to do; for now, I was only one of many little animals driven by a herder. **CBSE SQP 2024**

(i) Complete the following suitably.

Zitkala-Sa's description of her experience at the boarding school conveys a sense of abandonment through her portrayal of ....

(ii) List any one emotion that Zitkala-Sa experiences as her hair is being cut.

(iii) Select the suitable option to complete the following. The metaphor of being 'tossed about in the air like a wooden puppet' contribute to the reader's understanding of Zitkala-Sa's feelings of being ....

(a) forced to interact with others
(b) manipulated and controlled
(c) preached at and insulted
(d) made to exist like toy animals

(iv) In what ways does the imagery of her 'long hair shingled like a coward's' symbolise the erasure of Zitkala's cultural heritage and the imposition of Western norms?

Ans. (i) isolation and lack of support from others along with a loss of identity.

(ii) When Zitkala-Sa's hair was being cut, she felt anguished and a sense of loss.

(iii) (b) manipulated and controlled

(iv) The imagery of her 'long hair shingled like a coward's' symbolises the erasure and suppression of Zitkala's Indigenous cultural heritage by portraying the cutting of her hair as an act of cultural violence and the imposition of Western ideals of appearance and behaviour.

Or

(i) 'Then I lost my spirit'. Choose the option that does not refer to 'spirit'.

1. resolve	**2. energy**
3. determination	**4. indifference**
5. enthusiasm	**6. will power**

(a) 1, 2 and 5 (b) 2, 4 and 6
(c) 1, 3 and 6 (d) 3, 4 and 6

(ii) Choose the correct option with reference to the two statements given below.

Statement 1 The author had been subjected to humiliation when she was separated from her mother.

Statement 2 Nobody was able to ease her distress and empathise with her.

(a) Statement 1 is true but Statement 2 is false.
(b) Statement 1 is false but Statement 2 is true.
(c) Both Statement 1 and Statement 2 cannot be inferred from the passage.
(d) Both Statement 1 and Statement 2 can be inferred from the passage.

(iii) Why was shingling of hair so heartbreaking for the narrator?

(iv) How would you describe the author's tone when she says, "I was only one of many little animals driven by a herder"?

Ans. (i) (c) 1, 3 and 6

(ii) (d) Both Statement 1 and Statement 2 can be inferred from the passage.

(iii) The shingling of hair was heart-breaking because in the narrator's community , shingled hair was worn by cowards.

(iv) In the given line, the author's tone is dismal.

4. I cried aloud, shaking my head all the while until I felt the cold blades of the scissors against my neck, and heard them gnaw off one of my thick braids. Then I lost my spirit. Since the day I was taken from my mother I had suffered extreme indignities. People had stared at me. I had been tossed about in the air like a wooden puppet.

(i) Select the option that best describes the literary device used in the extract.

(a) Simile (b) Metaphor
(c) Allusion (d) Imagery

(ii) Complete the sentence suitably.

The narrators is feeling .... in the extract.

(iii) What were the extreme indignities faced by the speaker?

(iv) Why was the speaker crying?

Ans. (i) (a) Simile (ii) despair

(iii) The extreme indignities faced by the speaker included tight fitting clothes and shingling of her hair.

(iv) The speaker is crying because her long hair were shingled.

5. When I was studying in the third class. I hadn't yet heard people speak openly of untouchability. But I had already seen, felt, experienced and been humiliated by what it is. I was walking home from school one day, an old bag hanging from my shoulder. It was actually possible to walk the distance in ten minutes. But usually, it would take me from half an hour to an hour to dawdle along watching all the fun and games that were going on. All the entertaining novelties and oddities in the streets, the shops, and the bazaar.

CBSE 2023

(i) The narrator was humiliated because ....

(ii) The narrator dawdled along as she

(a) enjoyed looking at the various sights
(b) was getting late for school
(c) she didn't like going home
(d) she loved haggling and shopping

(iii) On the basis of the extract, choose the correct option with reference to the two statements given below.

I. The distance from school to home was very short.

II. She was feeling upset and so dawdling her way home.

(a) I can be inferred from the extract but II cannot
(b) II can be inferred from the extract but I cannot
(c) Both I and II cannot be inferred from the extract
(d) Both I and II can be inferred from the extract

(iv) The word 'novelties' in the passage most nearly means

(a) colourful trinkets
(b) wooden toys
(c) unique and interesting items
(d) expensive souvenirs

Ans. (i) of the practice of caste differentiation and untouchability.

(ii) (a) enjoyed looking at the various sights

(iii) (a) I can be inferred from the extract but II cannot

(iv) (c) unique and interesting items

6. I was walking home from school one day, an old bag hanging from my shoulder. It was actually possible to walk the distance in ten minutes. But usually it would take me thirty minutes at the very least to reach home. It would take me from half an hour to an hour to dawdle along, watching all the fun and games that were going on, all the entertaining novelties and oddities is the streets, the shops and the bazaar.

(i) Complete the sentence suitably.

'The entertaining novelties' as stated in the passage include ....

(ii) The word 'dwadle' as used in the extract means ....

(a) to push
(b) to walk slowly
(c) to delay deliberately
(d) to put off

(iii) Why did Bama take so much time to reach her home?

(iv) What can be gathered about the speaker from the given lines?

Ans. (i) a performing monkey, stunt performers and puppet shows among others.

(ii) (b) to walk slowly

(iii) Bama took so much time to reach her home as she seemed to stop at all stalls that fell between her school and home.

(iv) From the given extract, it can be gathered that the speaker can get easily distracted from things.

7. My elder brother was there. I told him the story in all its comic detail. I fell about with laughter at the memory of a big man, and an elder at that, making such a game out of carrying the parcel. But Annan was not amused. Annan told me the man wasn't being funny when he carried the package like that. He said everybody believed that they were upper caste and therefore must not touch us.

(i) Complete the sentence appropriately, with reference to the extract.

Annan was not amused because ....

(ii) What is 'story' referred to in the extract is about?

(iii) 'Making such a game' means ....

(a) making a show
(b) making it entertaining
(c) doing something nonsensical
(d) playing a game

(iv) What problem has been highlighted in the given extract?

Ans. (i) he knew the seriousness of the situation

(ii) The 'story' referred to in the extract is about the way in which the old man was carrying the food parcel

(iii) (b) making it entertaining

(iv) The problem highlighted in the extract is of discrimination based on the caste system.

8. When I heard this, I didn't want to laugh any more, I felt terribly sad. How could they believe that it was disgusting if one of us held that package in his hands, even though the vadai had been wrapped first in a banana leaf, and then parcelled in paper? I felt so provoked and angry that I wanted to touch those wretched vadais myself straightaway. Why should we fetch and carry for these people, I wondered. Such an important elder of ours goes meekly to the shops to fetch snacks and hands them reverently, bowing and shrinking, to this fellow who just sits there and stiffs them into his mouth. The thought of it infuriated me.

CBSE 2025

(i) 'I felt terribly sad'. The reason for the speaker's sadness is because it was an act of ....

(ii) Choose the correct option.

'The thought of it infuriated me' with reference to the above line, what do you think is the impact of the incident on the speaker?

(a) The speaker was sympathetic and helpless
(b) The speaker was angry and condemning
(c) The speaker was excited to see the incident
(d) The speaker was very impressed and motivated

(iii) Complete the sentence suitably.

I wanted to touch those wretched Vadais myself'

The above expression indicates the speaker's …………. .

(iv) Select the correct option from those given in brackets to fill in the blank.

The incident made the speaker realise that the discrimination was …….. . (dehumanising/elevating)

Ans. (i) discrimination
(ii) (b) The speaker was angry and condemning
(iii) defiance and urge to challenge the discriminatory practice
(iv) dehumanising

Short Answer Type Questions

1. How did Zitkala-Sa's first day in the land of apples begin?

Ans. Zitkala-Sa's first day in the land of apples was full of embarrassment and indignities. It was a bitter cold day and the ground was covered with snow. A large bell rang for breakfast and everybody moved towards the dining hall. The annoying clatter of shoes disturbed the place. Before entering the dining room, she was given tight fitting clothes which she found immodest. They took away the blanket wrapped around her and Zitkala-Sa felt embarrassed.

2. "I felt like sinking to the floor," says Zitkala-Sa. When did she feel so and why?

Ans. Zitkala-Sa felt like sinking to the floor because she was made to wear a new dress at school. Her shawl had also been removed. She was feeling ashamed of her body-clinging dress. Hence, when she was walking to the dining hall, she felt like sinking to the floor with shame at all the unfamiliar way of dressing.

3. Why was Zitkala-Sa in tears on the first day in the land of apples?

Ans. Zitkala-Sa was in tears on the first day in the land of apples because she was feeling sad about being taken away from her culture. Further, she was already embarrassed by the tight and uncomfortable clothes that she had to wear. Her situation became bad when everybody was following a certain order with the bells to begin to eat. Further, she did not know how to eat using knives and forks. All of these culminated in her feeling strange and sad, leading to her crying.

4. According to Zitkala-Sa what does 'eating by formula' mean?

Ans. According to Zitkala-Sa, 'eating by formula' meant following an eating-decorum in the dining room. At the sound of the first bell, the pupils drew a chair from under the table. All were seated when the second bell was sounded and when the third bell was tapped everyone started eating with forks and knives.

5. What was the terrible warning that Judewin gave Zitkala-Sa?

Or What did Judewin tell Zitkala-Sa? How did she react to it?

Or What did Judewin tell the narrator? What was the effect? **CBSE 2023**

Ans. Judewin warned Zitkala-Sa that she had overheard the white woman talking about cutting their long, heavy hair. Zitkala-Sa was horrified with the thought of getting her hair cut. Judewin further told her friend that they had to submit to the will of the authorities as they were strong. Zitkala-Sa reacted strongly and said that she would not give up without struggling.

6. Why did Zitkala-Sa resist the cutting of her hair?

Ans. Zitkala-Sa was terrified by the thought of having her hair cut because, in her community, shingled hair was worn by unskilled warriors who were captured by the enemy. Thus, it was a sign of cowardice. She decided that she would not go down without a fight.

7. How did Zitkala-Sa try to prevent the shingling of her hair?

Ans. When Judewin informed Zitkala that their hair would be cut short, Zitkala-Sa decided to escape. When no one was noticing, she crept up the stairs and found a large dark room to hide in. She hid under the bed farthest from the door.

8. How did Zitkala-Sa feel when her hair was shingled?

Ans. Zitkala-Sa felt anguished and ashamed when her long hair was cut. She missed her mother very much. No one could comfort her like her mother did. She was feeling like an animal driven by a herder.

9. Zitkala-Sa mentions the indignities she had to suffer as a child. How do such indignities break the morale of a child?

Ans. Ever since she was separated from her mother, Zitkala-Sa faced a number of indignities. People stared at her and she was tossed about in the air as if she were a wooden puppet. The ultimate insult came when her long dark hair was cut. It was then that she missed the comfort of her mother's presence. These events impacted Zitkala severely. Her spirit, courage and morale had been shaken and broken down.

10. What impact does the boarding school environment have on the narrator's emotional and psychological well-being, both during and after the incident of having her hair cut? Competency Based

Ans. The boarding school environment profoundly impacts the narrator's emotional and psychological well-being, exacerbating feelings of isolation, trauma, and cultural alienation. During the incident of having her hair cut, the environment fosters a sense of powerlessness and betrayal, intensifying her emotional distress. Post-haircut, the boarding school continues to serve as a site of psychological turmoil, where the narrator grapples with the aftermath of cultural erasure and loss. The oppressive atmosphere perpetuates feelings of alienation and invalidation, compounding her sense of displacement from her artistic roots and community. This experience leaves lasting scars on her psyche, contributing to feelings of disconnection and identity crisis that persist long after the traumatic event, highlighting the enduring impact of cultural oppression on indigenous individuals' emotional and psychological well-being.

11. Which activities of the people would Bama watch keenly in the bazaar?

Ans. The bazaar, on the way home, was always buzzing with activity. The snake charmer, street plays, puppet shows and stunt performance were a few interesting things going on there. Bama used to love all these things and would be attracted by them.

12. Describe the experience Bama had on her way back home which made her feel sad.

Ans. On her way back home, Bama saw an elder of her street carrying *vadais* for the landlord. The manner in which he carried the packet by holding its string made Bama laugh. She related this comic incident to her brother, Annan. However, he was not amused and he told Bama that the elder was behaving that way because people of their community were considered of low caste. This horrific truth made Bama sad.

13. Why did the landlord's man ask Bama's brother on which street he lived? What was the significance?

Ans. Annan was returning home from the library in the neighbouring village, when the landlord's man asked him his name. Then, he wanted to know where Annan lived. He asked this to ascertain Annan's caste because all the lower caste people lived in one area of the town.

14. How was Annan instrumental in Bama achieving success in life? CBSE 2025

Ans. Annan played a crucial role in Bama's success by making her aware of the discrimination faced by their community and encouraging her to focus on education as a means of empowerment. He advised her to study hard and excel academically, which motivated her to overcome societal barriers and achieve success in life.

15. The words that Annan spoke to me that day made a deep impression on me. What inference do you draw about the bond between Annan and Bama? CBSE 2024

Ans. The given lines show that Annan and Bama shared a deep and loving sibling bond. Annan knew that his sister was not aware of the harsh reality of their caste. So, he told her about the caste system and how it had demeaned their existence. He, as a loving brother, encouraged Bama to study hard to overcome the barriers of the caste.

16. How does Bama's narrative highlight the intersectionality of caste, gender, and religion?

Ans. Bama's narrative highlights the complex intersectionality of caste, gender, and religion in shaping the experiences of Dalit women within Tamil society. As a Tamil Dalit woman from a Roman Catholic family, she navigates multiple layers of marginalisation and discrimination, offering insight into the interconnected nature of oppression.

17. Bama's innocence was lost when she came face to face with the ugly truth of racial discrimination. Do you think children who have a difficult childhood become even more resolute than children who have a comfortable one? Competency Based

Ans. Bama's innocence was lost when she came face to face with the ugly truth of racial discrimination. Children like Bama become more resolute to change the situation and fight the oppressive forces that subdue them. Even though their childhood is difficult, they make sure that their adult life is not so and they face all challenges with more courage and resolution.

18. "Where there is oppression, there will be resistance." Comment on this statement with reference to the story. CBSE Question Bank 2021

Ans. It is true that "Where there is oppression, there will be resistance." We can see this from both the stories of Zitkala-Sa and Bama. Zitkala-Sa faces oppression in the new school where she is not only taken away from her mother but also made to wear tight uncomfortable clothes. Her resistance comes when she gets to know that her hair will be cut.

She fights, cries and resists any attempts to stop her oppression but to no avail. Bama, on the other hands, faces oppression in the form of caste biasness. She fights and resists this oppression with education.

19. In 20–30 words, mention one point of similarity and difference between Zitkala-Sa and Bama with reference to 'Memories of Childhood'. Competency Based

Ans. The stories of Zitkala-Sa and Bama present social evils present in the Indian Society. While reading these descriptions, one can find some similarities and differences between both women. While Zitkala-Sa and Bama belonged to marginalised communities and were victims of oppression, the cause of their oppression are different. Zitkala-Sa was a victim of cultural discrimination whereas Bama was a victim of class-based discrimination.

20. In 40-50 words, analyse the author's message in the context given below.

In the story 'We Too Are Human Beings', we first read about the old man carrying the parcel through the eyes of Bama and later understand the full context of the event when Annan explains it to her. Competency Based

Ans. By showing us the same event from the perspective of Bama and then Annan, the author is trying to show that children are innocent and do not discriminate. It is only the adults who practice it and consequently teach the children to do so too. Further, it highlights the stupidity of the practice of untouchability.

Long Answer Type Questions

1. For people like Bama, it is necessary to break the shackles that society burdens them with and come out triumphant. What should one possess or acquire to help one live without fear?

Ans. For people like Bama, who belong to a 'marginalised' caste, it is essential to possess or acquire the values of patience, perseverance, a determination to succeed by fighting against all odds and then live without fear. Then only can they necessarily break the shackles that society burdens them with and come out triumphant.

They must have patience and work hard to improve their lot. Bama did this by studying so well that she soon stood first in her class. She persevered and the result was that she made many friends due to her merit. She acquired the determination to succeed against all odds after her brother explained to her the reason why they were discriminated against.

This helped her to get motivated to show everybody that she was no less than them. Thus, she was able to succeed in life and live without fear in future.

2. Both Bama and Zitkala-Sa experienced the harsh reality of discrimination in their childhood. Instead of letting it pull them down, they both found a way to overcome it.

You wish to include a cameo* of both in your upcoming blog post.

As a part of the research, compare and contrast the experiences faced by the two and their response/s to these experiences, in 120-150 words. (Clue: Include the similarities and differences in the discrimination they faced - their feelings - determination to overcome - success)

***a short description that neatly encapsulates someone or something** Competency Based

Ans. When it comes to discrimination the story 'Memories of Childhood' clearly tell us the struggles faced by those discriminated. The stories of Zitkala-Sa and Bama hit our hearts as we read how they fight and stand up against the malady against humanity. The stories of Zitkala-Sa and Bama are stories of different forms of discrimination. While Zitkala-Sa was discriminated against because of cultural differences, Bama faced discrimination due to her caste.

Beside this differentiation, we can see many similarities between our two protagonists. Both of them come out as strong female figures who fought for what was right. Zitkala-Sa rebelled and refused to get her hair cut. She put up a strong fight, though had to give in finally. Similarly, Bama was enraged when she got to know that her elder was treated badly because of caste. She wanted to go and touch the packet of vadai to teach a lesson to the landlord. But was guided by her elder brother to calm down. He showed her the path to overcome discrimination.

Both Zitkala-Sa and Bama worked hard to excel in education to succeed as writers. They have written much against discrimination and evils of oppression, thus continuing the fight for justice for their communities.

3. Bama and Zitkala-Sa, though victims of a system that crushes their aspirations, are determined to break out. Comment. CBSE 2023

Or Both Bama and Zitkala-Sa were from marginalised communities. They challenged the system to bring dignity to their lives. Justify. CBSE 2023

Or The author vividly describes the trauma of Zitkala-Sa and Bama in 'Memories of Childhood'. Support with examples from the texts, to illustrate the prejudices that were present in society. CBSE 2025

Ans. It is true that both Bama and Zitkala-Sa, though victims of a system that crushes their aspirations, are determined to break out of the oppression that they face.

Zitkala-Sa faces oppression in the new school where she is not only taken away from her mother but also made to wear tight uncomfortable clothes. She fights, cries and resists the school authorities with all her might because she does not want her hair to be shingled like that of a coward.

Bama, on the other hands, faces oppression in the form of caste biasness. She fights and resists this oppression with education. She puts up a fight by bringing laurels to her community through her scholarly achievements. Thus, she proves that she is superior to the so-called upper castes.

4. Zitkala-Sa's character embodies courage, resilience, intellect, and a deep commitment to preserving Native American culture and advancing social justice. Comment.

Ans. It is true to say that Zitkala-Sa's character embodies courage, resilience, intellect, and a deep commitment to preserving Native American culture and advancing social justice. Zitkala-Sa, whose real name was Gertrude Simmons Bonnin, was a remarkable Native American woman, who exhibited strong determination and resilience from a young age. Despite facing immense challenges and cultural oppression, she remained steadfast in her commitment to preserving her Native American identity and heritage. Despite various challenges, she persevered with courage and resilience, using her voice and platform to raise awareness and advocate for change.

Zitkala-Sa had a deep connection to her Native American heritage and traditions. Her upbringing instilled in her a profound respect for her cultural beliefs, language and customs, which she courageously sought to uphold amidst the pressures of assimilation. Zitkala-Sa was a activist and leader who challenged stereotypes, combated prejudice, and empowered Indigenous peoples to reclaim their rights and cultural heritage through her writings and advocacy work.

5. Draw a character sketch of Bama on the basis of your reading of 'We too are human beings'.

Ans. Bama, the author and narrator of 'Karukku', is a resilient and introspective individual who navigates the complexities of caste-based discrimination and social injustice in her community.

Courageous and Resilient Bama confronts her community's injustices and indignities. Despite the challenges and discrimination, she refuses to accept the status quo.

Reflective and Observant Bama is thoughtful and observant of her community's social dynamics and power structures. She keenly observes the nuances of caste-based discrimination and reflects on its impact on her identity and sense of self-worth.

Driven by Education Education is a central theme in Bama's life. Motivated by her elder brother's advice, she recognises education as a pathway to empowerment and social change. Her dedication to academic achievement reflects her determination to challenge societal norms and break free from the constraints of her caste.

Empathetic and Compassionate Bama demonstrates empathy and compassion towards her community who endure similar experiences of discrimination and marginalisation. She shares their struggles and aspirations, advocating for their rights and dignity.

Bama emerges as a multifaceted and dynamic character whose resilience, empathy, and commitment to social justice profoundly impact readers. Her character embodies the struggle for dignity, equality, and empowerment in the face of entrenched social hierarchies and systemic oppression.

6. Do you think 'Memories of Childhood' is an appropriate title for the chapter? State YES or NO, along with a reason for your response in 100–120 words. **Competency Based**

Ans. Yes. In my opinion, the title of the story is very fitting to its subject matter. The chapter contains stories from Zitkala-Sa and Bama, both of whom had turbulent childhoods filled with injustice and violence. Their childhood memories are extremely important because not only are they a mirror of how discrimination and injustice can affect the mindset of an innocent child, these memories also shape their personalities and belief systems as they grew up.

Giving these painful remembrances the title of 'Memories of Childhood' is a stroke of mastery because the title evokes an image of happiness, joy and laughter. But the actual childhood instances of the writers are filled with violence, fear, and an attack on their authentic selves. This stark difference makes the stories of Zitkala-Sa and Bama even more impactful.

7. Untouchability is not only a crime, it is in human too. Why and how does Bama decide to fight against it? **CBSE 2025**

Ans. In Memories of Childhood, Bama, a young Dalit girl, becomes acutely aware of the inhumanity of untouchability when she sees an elderly man from her community carrying food for an upper-caste landlord in a degrading manner. She realizes that her people are treated as inferior solely due to their caste. This deeply impacts her, filling her with anger and a strong resolve to fight against this injustice.

Her brother's advice that education is the key to empowerment inspires Bama to excel in her studies. She understands that knowledge and awareness can help her challenge discrimination and uplift her community. Instead of accepting her marginalized status, she chooses to resist oppression by striving for academic excellence and encouraging others to do the same.

SELF ASSESSMENT TEST

Extract Based Questions

Read the extracts given below and answer the questions that follow.

1. I crept up the stairs as quietly as I could in my squeaking shoes,--- my moccasins had been exchanged for shoes. Along the hall I passed, without knowing whither I was going. Turning aside to an open door, I found a large room with three white beds in it. The windows were covered with dark green curtains, which made the room very dim.

(i) Complete the sentence suitably.

The given lines show that the speaker is ....

(ii) From whom was she hiding?

(a) Barber (b) Teacher (c) Bullies (d) Friend

(iii) Where did she hid herself?

(iv) Why did she crept up the stairs quietly?

2. How was it that these fellows thought so much of themselves? Because they had scraped four coins together, did that mean they must lose all human feelings? But we too are human beings. Our people should never run these petty errands for these fellows. We should work in their fields, take home our wages, and leave it at that.

(i) Complete the sentence suitably.

The narrator had just gotten to know about ....

(ii) The tone of the narrator in the extract is

(a) anger (b) vengeful (c) arrogant (d) sad

(iii) What is the cause of the narrator's feelings?

(iv) Do you think that the narrator's feelings are justified?

Short Answer Type Questions

Answer the following questions in 40-50 words.

1. Why was the white woman keeping an eye on Zitkala-Sa?

2. What was the news given by Judewin? How did they both react to it?

3. What does the cutting of Zitkala-Sa's long hair symbolise in the context of her Native American identity?

4. What role does the narrator's friend, Judewin, play in the story, and how does their relationship contribute to the theme of resistance?

5. What role does education play in Bama's journey of empowerment?

6. How does Bama's academic success impact her social relationships and community standing?

Long Answer Type Questions

Answer the following questions in 120-150 words.

1. How do the narrator's interactions with other Indian girls at the boarding school contribute to her understanding of cultural resilience and solidarity?

2. How did education shape the experiences and activism of Zitkala-Sa and Bama, and what role did it play in their efforts to challenge cultural oppression within their communities?

Assessment of Speaking & Listening Skills (ASL)

CBSE Examination Paper 2025

Sample Question Papers

ASL

Assessment of Speaking and Listening Skills

CBSE has clearly outlined the significance of Speaking and Listening Skills as a part of co-scholastic areas of achievement by every learner. Considering this, CBSE has formally introduced the Assessment of Speaking and Listening Skills with 10 marks allotted to it. Thus, Schools have to conduct ASL themselves as per the guidelines provided by the CBSE.

The ASL comprises two skill sets- Listening and Speaking Skills which are assessed throughout the year in student interactions and participation. Further, teachers can also organise special tasks and activities in the session for assessment purposes. The parameters for assessment are as follows

- Interactive competence (Initiation and turn taking, relevance to the topic)
- Fluency (Cohesion, coherence and speed of delivery)
- Pronunciation
- Language (Grammar and vocabulary)

So, let us prepare ourselves for the ASL properly.

Speaking Skills

Speaking skills have acquired a very important place as a communication skill with a number of sub-skills needed to be consciously developed among students. Some of the sub-skills are as follows

- Speaking intelligibly using appropriate word stress, sentence stress and intonation patterns.
- Narrating incidents and events, real or imaginary, in a logical sequence.
- Presenting oral reports or summaries; making announcements clearly and confidently.
- Expressing and arguing a point of view clearly and effectively.
- Taking active part in group discussions, showing ability to express agreement or disagreement, summarising ideas, eliciting the views of others and presenting own ideas.
- Expressing and responding to personal feelings, opinions and attitudes.
- Participating in spontaneous spoken discourse in familiar social situations.

Assessment Patterns

Generally, teachers assess this skill by organising like debates, extempore, speeches, etc. For the same, teachers would provide you any topic, primarily related to the literature prescribed in the syllabus.

Some of these topics include

- How to overcome fears
- Importance of Education in Developing Character

- The Impact of Social Media on Human Relationships
- Importance of Recreation and Physical Activity
- The Role of Youth in Environmental Conservation
- Netiquette
- Social Media Morality
- The Influence of Role Models on Young Minds
- India's Unemployment Issue
- India's Changing Face in the Space Exploration
- The advent of AI and Its effects
- Virtual Reality
- Online Education vs. Offline Education
- Learning Technology
- The Increasing Importance of Mental Health
- Maintaining Mental Well-being
- The Significance of Meditation in a Student's Life
- Value of Family in One's Life
- Impact of War on Society
- Various Facets of Bullying
- Digital Privacy
- Importance of Culture
- A World without Mobile Phones
- The Future of Electronic Vehicles
- The Double Burden on Modern Woman
- The Changing Face of News in the Digital Era
- The Importance of Soft Skills for Future Careers
- The Role of Diet in Mental and Physical Health
- The Rising Concern of Screen Addiction
- Should Artificial Intelligence Have Moral Boundaries?
- "Happiness is not Something Ready-made. It Comes from Your own Actions."
- "The only Way to Do Great Work is to Love What you Do."

The total administration time for the speaking assessment is approximately 10 minutes.

Speaking Skills Assessment (Sample Tasks)

TASK 1 : Netiquetee (Speech)

Netiquette is simply about good online manners - the rules that help us communicate politely and respectfully on the internet. Just like we have social etiquette in real life, netiquette makes digital interactions positive and considerate. One of the most important things is to be kind and respectful. Use polite language and avoid saying anything that could hurt someone's feelings. When talking in online discussions, listen to other people's opinions and respond thoughtfully, even if you don't agree with them.

Also, avoid typing in ALL CAPS, as it feels like shouting. Writing clearly with proper punctuation helps people understand your messages better. Privacy matters too. Be respectful of other people's personal information and don't share sensitive details without permission. If you're using someone else's work, like a photo or a quote, make sure to give them credit.

Another part of good netiquette is being prompt. Replying to messages and emails on time shows that you value other people's time. Lastly, never engage in cyberbullying or spread false information. If you see harmful behaviour online, report it and avoid contributing to negativity.

In the end, netiquette is about being thoughtful, responsible, and respectful online. By following these simple guidelines, we can help make the internet a safer and friendlier place for everyone.

TASK 2 : Online Education vs. Offline Education (Debate)

Online education has revolutionised the way we learn. It offers flexibility and convenience, allowing students to access lessons from anywhere in the world. You can learn at your own pace, which is great for those who need extra time or wish to advance faster. Additionally, online education provides a wide range of courses, enabling students to explore subjects that may not be available locally. The use of multimedia, such as videos and interactive quizzes, enhances the learning experience and makes it more engaging. With the internet, we can stay connected with classmates and teachers globally, offering an opportunity to learn from diverse perspectives.

While online education has its advantages, offline education has an edge when it comes to interaction and personal connection. In a physical classroom, teachers can gauge the students' understanding better through face-to-face communication and non-verbal cues. Students also benefit from peer interactions, which help in social development and teamwork skills. The structure of a traditional classroom, with set times for lessons and breaks, fosters discipline and focus. Furthermore, in offline education, access to resources such as libraries, labs, and immediate support from teachers makes it easier to dive deep into subjects.

Both online and offline education have their strengths. Online education offers flexibility and accessibility, making it ideal for self-paced learners or those with busy schedules. On the other hand, offline education provides a more traditional, structured environment with face-to-face interactions, fostering collaboration and discipline. Ultimately, the choice between online and offline education depends on the individual's learning style, preferences, and needs.

TASK 3 : How to Overcome Fears (Extempore)

We all feel scared sometimes. It's part of being human. Whether it's speaking in front of people, trying something new, or facing a tough situation, fear can sneak up on us. But the good news? We don't have to let it control us.

The first step is simple — admit that you're afraid. Don't try to hide it or push it down. Ask yourself, *What exactly am I scared of?* When you name your fear, it feels a bit less powerful. Next, take it slow. You don't have to do everything at once. If public speaking terrifies you, start by talking to a small group. Then build up to a bigger audience. Baby steps count. And don't forget your thoughts matter. Fear loves to trick you into thinking the worst. *Instead of worrying, What if I mess up? flip it to, What if I do great?*

One thing that helps a lot is breathing – deep, steady breaths. It's amazing how something so simple can calm your mind. Lastly, talk about it. Share your fears with someone you trust. Sometimes, just hearing someone say, *You've got this can make a big difference.* Remember, courage isn't about not being scared. It's about taking that first step, even when your heart is racing. Every time you face a fear, you grow a little stronger. And that's a win worth celebrating.

Listening Skills

The Listening skills section tests the student's ability to listen for basic interpersonal, instructional and academic purposes. It includes a number of sub-skills that include the following

- Listening for specific information
- Predictive listening
- Listening for pleasure
- Evaluative listening
- Listening for general understanding
- Inferential listening
- Intensive listening

Assessment Patterns

The listening skill assessment takes places in a language lab, which is the specific lab comprises individual equipments for each students. The equipment comprises a headset and audio recordings. Students are made to listen to those recordings and answer some questions. If there is no such equipment, the teacher would read a piece of literature. The topic of the audio recording can be anything.

General Instructions for Students

- You are not allowed to ask questions or interrupt the Examiner at any point.
- You will hear a set of recordings of the Listening Input.
- Each of the recordings will be played twice.
- You are required to answer a set of questions based on each of the Listening Inputs.
- After you have listened to the input, you will be given specified minutes to answer the questions on your worksheet.
- You may answer the questions on your worksheet while listening.

Listening Skills Assessment (Sample Tasks)

TASK 1

The given bar code or link contains an audio recording. Listen to the recording and answer the following questions.

TO LISTEN THIS TRANSCRIPT

Link https://www.esl-lab.com/intermediate/travel-airlines/

OR **Scan the Code**

Questions

1. **What is the number of this flight?**

   (a) 80 (b) 81 (c) 18

Ans. (c)

2. **How long is the flight?**

   (a) 2 hours, 4 minutes (b) 2 hours, 14 minutes (c) 2 hours, 40 minutes

Ans. (b)

3. **What is the local time in Seattle?**

   (a) 10 : 12 a.m. (b) 12 : 15 p.m. (c) 11 : 45 p.m.

Ans. (c)

4. **What is the current weather in Seattle?**

   (a) Sunny (b) partly cloudy (c) rainy

Ans. (a)

5. **At what gate will the plane arrive?**

   (a) 3 (b) 30 (c) 13

Ans. (c)

TASK 2

The given bar code or like contains an audio recording. Listen to the recording and answer the following questions.

TO LISTEN THIS TRANSCRIPT

Link https://www.esl-lab.com/intermediate/online-medical/

OR **Scan the Code**

Questions

1. **James thinks that he has ....**
   (a) a cold (b) the flu (c) a stomachache
2. **The woman thinks that James has a virus because ....**
   (a) his eyes are red (b) he has a high fever (c) his skin in a different color
3. **Where did the woman find information on this virus?**
   (a) on a medical podcast (b) in a medical journal (c) on a Web site
4. **James doesn't believe the information because it ....**
   (a) doesn't deal with his symptoms (b) is somewhat outdated and old
   (c) doesn't come from a qualified doctor
5. **According to the woman, James only has .... to life.**
   (a) a little over a month (b) about a week (c) a few days

TASK 3

The given bar code or link contains an audio recording. Listen to the recording and answer the following questions.

TO LISTEN THIS TRANSCRIPT

Link https://www.esl-lounge.com/student/listening/3L4-online-trouble.php

OR **Scan the Code**

Questions

1. **Jackie was surprised that David had problems placing his order.**
   (a) True (b) False (c) Don't know
2. **David needs to order the .... for his office.**
   (a) software (b) hardware (c) equipment
3. **Jackie gives him the .... discount even though he's not ordering online.**
   (a) 25% (b) 45% (c) 55%
4. **The Mac version is more expensive than the Windows version.**
   (a) True (b) False (c) Don't know
5. **Jackie tells David that the free microphones are usually not very good ....**
   (a) quality (b) quantity (c) quirkiness

TASK 4

The given bar code or link contains an audio recording. Listen to the recording and answer the following questions.

TO LISTEN THIS TRANSCRIPT

Link https://youtu.be/Gy69OZP04ws OR **Scan the Code**

Questions

1. Who would give money to charity?
2. Who would stop working?
3. Who would buy a big country house?
4. Who would study something creative?
5. Who would go travelling?
6. Who would give the money to family members?
7. Who would buy a horse?
8. Who would save some of the money for later?

TASK 5

The given bar code or link contains an audio recording. Listen to the recording and answer the following questions.

TO LISTEN THIS TRANSCRIPT

Link https://youtu.be/WkpHFzegBg8 OR **Scan the Code**

Questions

1. Someone killed James Carrington with ....
   (a) a gun (b) a knife (c) poison
2. Lucille was staying with her .... Joanna at the time of his death.
   (a) friend (b) aunt (c) daughter
3. On the afternoon of the 5th June, Lucille was buying ....
   (a) tea (b) medicine (c) clothes
4. She spent that afternoon ....
   (a) with Joanna (b) with James (c) alone
5. The neighbour, Mrs. Box, saw a woman wearing a ....
   (a) grey hat (b) coat (c) long dress
6. According to Mrs. Box, a man and a woman were .... in the house.
   (a) talking (b) fighting (c) arguing
7. Lucille ....
   (a) knew who James' lover was (b) had seen James with his lover once
   (c) didn't know who James' lover was
8. Lucille thinks that James' lover killed him ....
   (a) for money (b) because she found something in his pocket
   (c) because she was jealous

Rubric for ASL

CBSE has also provided a rubric which helps the teacher assess and grade a student's listening and speaking skill.

	1	2	3	4	5
Interaction	• Contributions are mainly unrelated to those of other speakers • Shows hardly any initiative in the development of conversation • Very limited and interaction	• Contributions are often unrelated to those of the other speaker. • Generally passive in the development of conversation.	• Develops interaction adequately makes however minimal effort to initiate conversation • Needs constant prompting to take turns	• Interaction is adequately initiated and developed • Takes turn but needs some prompting	• Initiates and logically develops simple conversation on familiar topics • Takes turns appropriately
Fluency & Coherence	• Noticeably/long pauses; rate of speech is slow • Frequent repetition and/or self-correction this is all right in informal conversation • Links only basic sentences; breakdown of coherence evident	• Usually fluent; produces simple speech fluently, but loses coherence in complex communication • Often hesitates and/ or resorts to slow speech • Topics partly developed; not always concluded logically	• Is willing to speake at length, however repetition is noticeable • Hesitates and/or self corrects; occasionally loses coherence • Topics developed, but usually not logically concluded	• Speaks without noticeable effort, with a little repetition • Demonstrates hesitation to find words or use correct grammatical structures and/or use correct grammatical structures and/or self-correction • Topics not fully developed to merit.	• Speaks fluently almost with no repetition and minimal hesitation • Develops topic fully and coherently
Pronunciation	• Frequent inaccurate pronunciation • Communication is severely affected	• Frequently unintelligible articulation • Frequent phonological errors • Major communication problems	• Largely correct pronunciation and clear articulation except occasional error	• Mostly correct pronunciation and clear articulation • Is clearly understood most of the time; very few phonological errors	• Pronounces correctly and articulated clearly • Is always comprehensible • Uses appropriate intonation
Vocabulary & Grammar	• Demonstrated almost no flexibility, and mostly struggles for appropriate words • Many Grammatical errors impacting communication	• Is able to communicate on some of the topics, with limited vocabulary. • Frequent errors, but self-corrects	• Is able to communicate on most of the topics, with limited vocabulary. • A few grammatical errors	• Is able to communicate on most of the topics with appropriate vocabulary • Minor errors that do not hamper communication	• Is able to communicate on most of the topics using a wide range of appropriate vocabulary, using new words and expressions No grammatical errors

Project Work

Apart from the specific skill test given above, CBSE also allots 10 marks to ASL based project work. This project work involves a project which can include an interview based project, an audio-visual data based project or a one-act play project. These project can be done by students individually or in a group.

Students have to plan and prepare the project throughout the academic session to given a presentation at the end of the year and answer the viva questions. Hence, the project work includes

(a) Project (b) Presentation (c) Viva Questions

Let us learn how to prepare for them to score well.

Themes of Project

CBSE mentions that the project can be inter-disciplinary in theme. The ideas/issues highlighted in the chapters/ poems/ drama given the prescribed books can also be developed in the form of a project. Students can also take up any relevant and age-appropriate theme. Some suggested themes include

- Voting Rights
- Technology Addiction
- Increasing Adoption of AI
- Role of a Mother in a Family
- Various Facets of Discrimination
- Evolving Food Tastes in my Neighbourhood
- Sports as a Career
- Travel to India- The Country of Magnificent Individuals
- Value of Mental Wellness
- Impact of War
- Hobbies-Changing Scenario
- Corona-Impact of Environment and Health Consciousness, etc.

Types of Project

As mentioned, CBSE has suggested 3 types of project that can be made

- Interview-based research
- An audio-visual data based
- One-act play project

1. Interview-Based Research

In this project, students can choose a topic on which to do their research. Then, they can read as much as they can about the topic. Then, they make questionnaire to be filled by at least 5-10 people around them or interview them. After the interviews are taken and the questionnaire are filled. They write an essay/ write up / report etc. up to 1000 words on his/her research and submit it.

Here is a sample of a questionnaire or interview questions and the essay.

Questionnaire: Evolving Food Tastes in My Neighbourhood
Demographics (Optional)

Age

☐ Under 18 ☐ 18-24 ☐ 25-34 ☐ 35-44 ☐ 45-54 ☐ 55+

Gender

☐ Male ☐ Female ☐ Non-binary/Other ☐ Prefer not to say

How long have you lived in this neighbourhood?

☐ Less than 1 year ☐ 1-3 years ☐ 4-10 years ☐ More than 10 years

Food Preferences and Trends

How would you describe the general food preferences in your neighbourhood?

☐ Traditional, home-cooked meals ☐ Modern, fusion cuisine

☐ Health-conscious (e.g., vegan, organic) ☐ Fast food and takeout

☐ Other (Please specify) ______________

Do you feel that food tastes have changed in your neighbourhood over the past 5-10 years?

☐ Yes, significantly ☐ Yes, somewhat ☐ No, not much ☐ Not sure

What factors do you think have influenced food tastes in the neighbourhood the most? (Select all that apply)

☐ Increase in international restaurants ☐ Growing awareness of healthy eating

☐ Popular food trends (e.g., keto, plant-based) ☐ Cultural influences from new residents

☐ Changes in economic factors (e.g., affordability of dining options)

☐ Other (Please specify) ______________

Are there any specific cuisines or types of food that have become more popular in your neighbourhood recently?

☐ Yes (Please specify) ______________ ☐ No ☐ Not sure

In your opinion, what food-related trend is currently most popular in your neighbourhood?

☐ Street food ☐ Plant-based or vegan options ☐ Fast casual dining

☐ International (e.g., Asian, Mediterranean) ☐ Health-conscious and organic options

☐ Other (Please specify) ______________

How often do you eat out or order food from restaurants or cafes in your neighbourhood?

☐ Every day ☐ Several times a week ☐ Once a week ☐ Once a month

☐ Rarely or never

What type of establishments do you prefer for eating out?

☐ Fine dining ☐ Casual dining ☐ Cafes or bakeries ☐ Fast food or takeout

☐ Street food vendors ☐ Other (Please specify) ______________

Local Food Scene and Impact

Do you believe that local restaurants and food businesses reflect the tastes of the community?

☐ Yes ☐ Somewhat ☐ No ☐ Not sure

What are some of the most popular food spots or restaurants in your neighbourhood?

____

Do you think there is a growing demand for more diverse or specific food options in your neighbourhood?

☐ Yes ☐ No ☐ Not sure

How important is sustainability (e.g., eco-friendly packaging, locally sourced ingredients) when choosing where to eat or what to buy?

☐ Very important ☐ Somewhat important ☐ Not important

☐ I don't consider sustainability when making food choices

Final Thoughts

What would you like to see more of in the food offerings in your neighbourhood? (Check all that apply)

☐ More international cuisine ☐ Healthier food options ☐ Vegan/plant-based options

☐ Family-friendly dining ☐ Affordable dining options ☐ Sustainable and locally sourced food

☐ Other (Please specify) ______________

Do you have any other comments or suggestions about food trends or changes in the neighbourhood?

____

____

Interview Questions

1. Can you tell me a little about yourself and how long you've lived in this neighbourhood?
2. How would you describe the general food culture or eating habits in this neighbourhood?
3. Do you feel like the food tastes in this neighbourhood have changed over the years? If yes, how so?
4. What kind of food do you typically enjoy eating in this area? Has that changed over time?
5. Have you noticed any new food trends emerging in your neighbourhood recently? If so, what are they?
6. In your opinion, what are the most popular types of food in the neighbourhood right now? Are there any specific cuisines or dishes that seem to be gaining popularity?
7. Do you think there is more variety in the types of food available now compared to a few years ago?
8. What factors do you think have influenced the evolving food tastes in your neighbourhood? (e.g., cultural influences, new businesses, economic changes)
9. Have you noticed an increase in demand for healthier or more sustainable food options? If so, in what ways?
10. What types of dining establishments or food spots are most popular in this area right now? Do you think the community's food tastes are reflected in the types of restaurants and food businesses here?
11. How has your personal food preference evolved since you've lived in this neighbourhood?
12. What do you think the future of food in this neighbourhood looks like? Are there any emerging trends you expect to see more of in the coming years?
13. What would you like to see more of in terms of food offerings or dining experiences in this neighbourhood?
14. Is there anything else you'd like to share about the food scene or food culture in the neighbourhood?
15. How can the community support or encourage positive changes in food preferences and trends here?

Report on Evolving Food Tastes in My Neighbourhood

Introduction

Food plays a central role in our lives, serving not just as sustenance but also as a key element of socialisation, culture, and identity. Over time, food preferences can change due to various factors such as cultural shifts, economic trends, and global influences. This report examines how food tastes have evolved in my neighbourhood, the factors driving these changes, and the impact these shifts are having on local dining and food culture. By analysing local trends and community responses, this report aims to provide insights into the dynamic food landscape in my area.

The Changing Food Landscape

Over the past decade, food tastes in my neighbourhood have evolved significantly. Historically, the neighbourhood was known for its classic comfort foods, often featuring hearty, traditional dishes passed down through generations. Local eateries typically offered home-cooked meals, with a focus on regional flavours and familiar, well-loved recipes. However, this traditional food culture has gradually given way to a more diverse and dynamic food scene, reflecting broader societal shifts and the influence of global food trends.

One of the most noticeable changes has been the rise of ethnic and international cuisines. Ten years ago, the neighbourhood had only a handful of international restaurants, mostly offering Italian, Chinese, and American fast-food options. Today, however, the culinary landscape has expanded significantly, with new restaurants and food vendors serving Mediterranean, Latin American, Middle Eastern, and Asian fusion dishes. This shift can be attributed to a growing interest in global flavours, as well as an influx of residents from different cultural backgrounds, each bringing their culinary traditions with them.

Key Factors Influencing Changing Food Tastes

Several factors have contributed to the evolving food tastes in my neighbourhood. These include demographic changes, economic influences, the rise of food trends, and increased awareness of health and sustainability.

Demographic Changes and Cultural Diversity One of the key drivers of the shift in food tastes is the changing demographics of the neighbourhood. Over the past few years, there has been an increase in the number of people from diverse cultural backgrounds moving into the area. As these new residents bring their food traditions and culinary preferences, local dining options have had to adapt. For example, the introduction of Mediterranean and Indian restaurants can be directly linked to an influx of people from those regions. This has led to a richer and more diverse culinary environment, where traditional dishes from around the world are now readily available and appreciated by both newcomers and long-time residents.

Economic Factors and the Rise of Food Entrepreneurs The local economy has also played a role in reshaping food tastes. The rise of the 'foodie' culture, supported by social media and food blogs, has created a demand for unique and novel dining experiences. As a result, there has been a boom in food startups and small, independent eateries. Many local entrepreneurs have capitalised on this trend, opening restaurants and food trucks that offer inventive, artisanal, or fusion dishes. This entrepreneurial spirit has not only brought fresh food concepts to the neighbourhood but also encouraged established restaurants to diversify their menus to cater to the changing tastes of consumers.

Health and Wellness Trends In recent years, there has been a noticeable shift towards healthier eating. The growing awareness of issues such as obesity, dietary restrictions, and food allergies has led many residents to prioritise healthier food choices. As a result, there has been an increase in the number of restaurants offering vegetarian, vegan, gluten-free, and low-carb options. Additionally, organic and locally sourced ingredients have become more popular, with consumers increasingly interested in the quality and sustainability of the food they eat. This health-conscious shift has also been fueled by social media influencers and fitness enthusiasts who promote clean eating and healthy lifestyles.

Sustainability and Ethical Eating Alongside the focus on health, sustainability has emerged as a significant factor in the evolving food landscape. Many residents are becoming more conscious of the environmental impact of their food choices. As a result, there has been a noticeable rise in demand for restaurants that serve sustainably sourced, ethically produced food. This includes organic produce, free-range meats, and seafood that is responsibly harvested. In addition, there is a growing trend towards zero-waste dining, with restaurants opting for compostable packaging, reducing food waste, and offering plant-based menu options as a more sustainable alternative to traditional meat-based dishes.

Emerging Food Trends in the Neighbourhood

Several food trends have emerged as particularly influential in my neighbourhood in recent years. Some of the most notable trends include

Plant-Based and Vegan Options Veganism and plant-based eating have moved beyond a niche lifestyle and have become mainstream in my neighborhood. Many local restaurants now offer extensive plant-based menus that cater to the growing demand for meat alternatives. Dishes like vegan burgers, plant-based sushi, and dairy-free desserts have become common offerings, even at non-vegan establishments. This trend is likely driven by both ethical concerns regarding animal welfare and environmental impact, as well as health-conscious consumers looking for cleaner, plant-based options.

Street Food and Casual Dining Street food has gained popularity in the neighbourhood, with food trucks and pop-up vendors offering affordable, quick, and flavourful meals. These vendors often specialise in international cuisines, providing an accessible way for people to try new and exotic dishes. The growing trend toward casual dining, where the focus is on high-quality, flavourful food without the formality of fine dining, has also contributed to this shift.

Health-Conscious Fast Food As traditional fast food chains face growing competition from healthier alternatives, a new wave of 'health-conscious fast food' has emerged in the area. These establishments focus on providing fast, affordable meals that are made with wholesome, minimally processed ingredients. Many of these businesses offer grain bowls, smoothie bowls, salads, and wraps, emphasising fresh vegetables, lean proteins, and nutrient-dense foods.

Fusion Cuisine Fusion cuisine, which combines elements from different culinary traditions, is another growing trend in the neighbourhood. Restaurants that experiment with blending diverse flavours and techniques are attracting attention from adventurous diners. For example, you might find Korean tacos, sushi burritos, or Mediterranean-style pizza. These inventive dishes allow residents to experience the best of multiple culinary worlds in a single meal.

Challenges and Opportunities

While the evolving food tastes in the neighbourhood present many exciting opportunities, there are also challenges to consider. The rapid diversification of food options has led to increased competition among local restaurants, making it difficult for some businesses to stand out. Additionally, as the demand for organic and sustainably sourced ingredients grows, it can be challenging for smaller, independent restaurants to keep up with the rising costs of these products.

On the other hand, the evolving food scene presents a wealth of opportunities for innovation and community engagement. New food trends open the door for creative entrepreneurs to develop niche concepts that cater to emerging consumer preferences. Furthermore, the neighbourhood's growing food diversity can help build stronger connections between residents of different cultural backgrounds, fostering a more inclusive and interconnected community.

Conclusion

The food tastes in my neighbourhood have evolved significantly over the past decade, driven by demographic changes, economic shifts, and global food trends. The rise of international cuisines, health-conscious eating, and sustainability concerns has transformed the local dining scene, offering a wider variety of dining options to cater to diverse tastes and preferences. As the food culture continues to evolve, it is clear that the neighbourhood will continue to embrace innovation while honouring its rich culinary traditions. With increased demand for ethical, healthy, and unique food options, there are many exciting opportunities for both consumers and food businesses in the years to come.

Sample Viva Questions

Some viva-based questions on this report are

1. Can you briefly summarise the main changes in food tastes in your neighbourhood over the past decade?
2. What are some of the key factors that have contributed to the evolution of food tastes in your neighbourhood?
3. How have cultural diversity and demographic changes impacted the food scene in your neighbourhood?
4. What role does social media and food bloggers play in the evolution of food tastes in your area?
5. In your report, you mentioned a rise in plant-based and vegan food options. Why do you think this trend has gained popularity in recent years?
6. Can you discuss any specific examples of restaurants or food establishments in your neighbourhood that focus on sustainable or organic offerings?
7. In your report, you mentioned the rise of street food. Why do you think street food has become so popular, especially in urban areas?
8. Do you think the neighbourhood's shift towards health-conscious fast food will continue to grow, or is it just a passing trend? Why?
9. You mentioned the increased competition among food businesses. How do you think restaurants can differentiate themselves in such a competitive environment?
10. How do you see the future of food tastes in your neighbourhood? Do you think the changes will continue, or will there be a shift back to more traditional food options?
11. Do you think the growing interest in sustainable food choices is driven more by consumer demand or by businesses trying to capitalise on a trend?
12. From your research and observations, which food trend do you think will have the most lasting impact on your neighbourhood in the next decade?

2. An Audio-visual Data Based

In this project, students can listen to podcasts/interviews/radio or TV documentary on a topic and prepare a report countering or agreeing with the speakers.

Here is a list of some podcasts, interviews and documentaries that a student can listen to.

Podcasts

- Ted talks
- Think Fast Talk Smart
- Reducing Human Impact on the Environment-Lauren Pettifer
- The Time of India Podcast
- Think School
- BBC Earth
- The Stories of Mahabharata

Shows, Videos and Documentaries

- Why go to mars- The Economist - https://youtu.be/ticaLyuePjA
- How to fuel the future- The Economist- https://youtu.be/_d325ohXLxE
- Susan Benett- The voice behind Siri- https://youtu.be/QP-iVhdXjPk
- The hidden underground city of Turkey- https://youtu.be/Wc7MgKMYN7s
- How languages become extinct? The Economist- https://youtu.be/Qr8QsNCe3C4
- The Ecocapsule- https://youtu.be/c6jbJwckH7o
- Interview with Lily Singh- https://youtu.be/Fwo7UW7c_8o
- Detox camps for internet addicts- https://youtu.be/YuT_RAugJu0

- Threat of War Between South Korea and North Korea- https://youtu.be/K0oAWBs9Ha0
- Planet Earth (2006) by BBC
- The Social Dilemma (2020)
- The White Tiger
- The True Cost of Fashion
- The Elephant Whisperers (2022)
- Cosmos: A Spacetime Odyssey (2014)
- Our Planet (2019)
- Period, end of sentence
- Cities of Sleep
- Writing with Fire (2021)

SAMPLE

You can access the Podcast titled Transform your fear into strength - Gautam Buddha from the bar code given below.

https://open.spotify.com/episode/0xyMzWaWj2kf75BJy2Uofc?si=cSSttCk8QbOZlBZhNX1KEw

Sample Essay

'Transform Your Fear into Strength' by Gautama Buddha

Fear is a natural human emotion that has been a part of our existence since the dawn of time. While it serves an essential role in survival, fear can often become a hindrance, limiting our growth and preventing us from living our lives to the fullest. Gautama Buddha, the founder of Buddhism, offered profound insights on how to overcome fear and transform it into a source of strength. His teachings emphasise the importance of self-awareness, mindfulness, and inner peace as pathways to conquer fear. This essay explores the essence of transforming fear into strength through the teachings of Buddha and how we can apply his wisdom in our modern lives.

Understanding Fear from a Buddhist Perspective

Buddha viewed fear not as an inherent part of our nature, but as a product of the mind and our attachments to worldly desires. According to him, fear arises from ignorance-the inability to see things as they truly are. This ignorance leads to attachments, expectations, and desires, all of which give birth to anxiety and fear. We fear losing what we love, being judged by others, or failing to meet our own standards. These fears are all connected to our sense of 'self'-an ego that we are desperately trying to protect.

One of Buddha's central teachings is the concept of 'impermanence' (anicca)-the understanding that all things are temporary. Fear often arises from our attachment to things that are fleeting. Buddha taught that by acknowledging impermanence, we can release our attachment to outcomes and the fear of loss. When we realise that all things, including life itself, are temporary, fear loses its power over us.

The Role of Mindfulness in Overcoming Fear

Mindfulness, or sati, is another key Buddhist practice that Buddha proposed as a way to transform fear into strength. Mindfulness is the art of being present in the moment, fully aware of our thoughts, feelings, and sensations without judgement. Fear often arises when we dwell on the past or worry about the future. We become trapped in our anxieties and forget to live in the present.

By practicing mindfulness, we learn to observe our fears without being controlled by them. Instead of reacting impulsively to fear, mindfulness teaches us to pause, breathe, and approach the situation with clarity and wisdom. When we are fully present in the moment, we begin to see fear for what it is-a mental construct, not a reality. This realisation allows us to approach fear not with resistance, but with acceptance, which weakens its grip over us.

Buddha also emphasised the importance of meditation as a tool for cultivating mindfulness. Through meditation, we can develop a deep awareness of our inner world and understand the root causes of our fears. Meditation helps calm the mind, reduce anxiety, and foster a sense of peace. By regularly meditating, we can shift our focus from fear to inner strength, gradually transforming our fearful thoughts into sources of empowerment.

Courage and the Path to Freedom

Buddha taught that fear is an obstacle on the path to enlightenment. To attain freedom from suffering, one must overcome the limitations of the mind, including fear. This requires cultivating courage, which Buddha described not as the absence of fear, but as the ability to act despite it.

In his famous teachings, Buddha emphasised that the 'middle path'-a path of moderation-was key to overcoming fear. This involves balancing our desires and actions, neither overindulging nor suppressing them. Fear often arises from extremes: extreme attachment to pleasure or avoidance of pain. By practicing moderation, we can learn to accept both joy and suffering, and in doing so, reduce the anxiety that arises from trying to control everything.

Buddha's teaching on compassion also plays a crucial role in transforming fear. Fear often comes from isolation, from feeling alone in our struggles. By cultivating compassion for ourselves and others, we can realise that we are not alone in our fear. Everyone experiences fear, and through empathy, we can connect with others and find strength in our shared humanity. Compassion softens the heart, making it less susceptible to fear and more open to love and courage.

Applying Buddha's Teachings in Modern Life

In our modern world, fear continues to manifest in many ways-fear of failure, fear of judgement, fear of loss, and fear of the unknown. Buddha's teachings remain highly relevant today, offering a roadmap for overcoming these fears and transforming them into sources of inner strength.

Embrace Impermanence Understanding that all things are temporary can help us release the grip of fear. Whether it's a difficult situation, a relationship, or a personal challenge, knowing that nothing lasts forever can bring comfort and perspective. This awareness helps us approach life's uncertainties with calm and resilience.

Practice Mindfulness In our fast-paced world, it is easy to become overwhelmed by fear. By practicing mindfulness-whether through meditation, deep breathing, or simply pausing to observe our thoughts, we can cultivate a sense of presence and awareness that weakens the power of fear. Mindfulness helps us confront fear without judgement, allowing us to take conscious, empowered action.

Build Courage Fear is natural, but courage is a choice. Buddha's teachings encourage us to take action despite fear, knowing that we are capable of overcoming obstacles. By embracing the discomfort that fear brings, we can build inner strength and resilience. Each step taken despite fear strengthens our capacity for courage.

Cultivate Compassion Fear often isolates us, making us feel separate from others. By practicing compassion-for ourselves and others–we can create connections that dissolve the barriers fear builds. Compassion nurtures understanding, reduces judgement, and opens the heart to greater courage.

Conclusion

Buddha's teachings offer profound wisdom for transforming fear into strength. By understanding the impermanent nature of life, practicing mindfulness, cultivating courage, and embracing compassion, we can gradually free ourselves from the grip of fear. Fear will always be a part of human existence, but through the lens of Buddha's teachings, we can learn to face it with equanimity and wisdom. In doing so, we transform fear into a powerful force that propels us toward greater growth, inner peace, and freedom. Fear, once a barrier to our potential, becomes a catalyst for our strength and enlightenment.

Sample Viva Questions

Some viva-based questions on this report are

1. Can you explain the Buddhist concept of fear? How does Buddha define fear in relation to the mind?
2. What is the relationship between ignorance and fear, according to Gautama Buddha?
3. Buddha talks about the impermanence of things. How does the understanding of impermanence help in overcoming fear?
4. What is the significance of the 'middle path' in overcoming fear and anxiety?
5. Can you give an example from your own life or current events where understanding impermanence helped reduce fear?
6. Do you think fear is a natural and necessary emotion for personal growth, or do you believe it is purely detrimental? Why?
7. How has your understanding of fear changed after learning about Buddha's teachings?
8. What specific Buddhist practice would you start with if you wanted to work on transforming your own fears into strength?
9. What do you think is the biggest obstacle in applying Buddha's teachings on fear in modern society?

3. One-Act Play Project

Another project that students can do is to create their own video/audio, after writing a script. While planning the one-act play project, a student has to keep the following things in mind

- Theme/topic of the audio/video
- What are the elements that need to be part of the script?
- What would be the duration?
- How would they present the script/report to the teacher, e.g. Can it be in the form of a narrative?

Remember, this is a team-based project. It will involve planning, preparation and presentation. There will be researching, discussion, writing the script, auditioning and ultimately producing the play.

Sample Script

Here is a sample of a script that students can use to make their once act play.

Characters

Aarav A school student, concerned about the environment.

Maya Aarav's friend, focuses on health and hygiene.

Teacher The class teacher, guiding the students.

Doctor A health expert discussing the pandemic's effects.

Environmental Activist A passionate advocate for environmental protection.

SCENE

(The stage is set as a classroom. Aarav and Maya are seated, along with several other students. The Teacher is standing at the front, ready to begin a discussion. There is a doctor and an environmental activist sitting on chairs, facing the children. There is a large poster on the wall that reads "Corona– A Wake-Up Call for Our Planet and Health.")

Teacher (Addressing the class) Good morning, everyone. Today, we are going to discuss something that has affected the entire world-COVID-19. It has not only changed our daily lives but has also impacted our environment and our consciousness about health. Let's start by hearing your thoughts one by one. Aarav, you start.

Aarav (excitedly) Sir, I've been reading about how the environment has actually benefited during the lockdown. With fewer cars on the road and industries temporarily shutting down, the air quality improved in many cities. I've even heard about wildlife returning to urban areas.

Doctor (Smiling warmly) Its true to say that The COVID-19 pandemic has certainly transformed how we think about our health. In the past, many people didn't take basic hygiene seriously. But the virus has shown us how easily diseases can spread if we don't take these precautions.

After seeing and suffering from the devastating impact of the virus, people have become more aware of their health. People are exercising more, eating healthier and being more conscious about their overall well-being. We've seen an increase in mental health awareness as well, as many people have struggled with isolation, stress and anxiety during lockdowns.

Aarav Dr. Gupta, what do you think the future holds for health consciousness after the pandemic? Will people continue to be this careful, or will things go back to how they were?

Doctor (thoughtfully) That's a great question, Aarav. There is hope that some of the habits we've developed during the pandemic-like wearing masks during flu season or regularly washing hands-will stick around. But we also need to stay vigilant, as the temptation to return to old habits can be strong. The key is to make these health-conscious behaviours a part of our everyday life.

Teacher Maya, what do you think about the impact of COVID?

Maya From a health perspective, the pandemic has made us much more conscious of cleanliness and hygiene. People are washing their hands more, wearing masks and sanitising everything. It's like we've realised how important these small actions are for our health.

Environmentalist I agree with you Maya. The pandemic has been a wake-up call for our environment, and we mustn't forget the lessons it's taught us. When human activity slowed down, we saw the environment healing. Air pollution levels dropped, rivers and oceans became cleaner, and wildlife began to reclaim spaces we had taken from them.

Maya (curious) That's amazing! So, you mean the environment benefited from the lockdown?

Environmentalist (nodding) Yes, absolutely! But, we must recognise that these positive effects were temporary. Once restrictions were lifted, pollution and environmental degradation started creeping back. The real question is Can we maintain this balance? Can we adopt habits that protect our planet while also focusing on our health?

Aarav (thoughtful) I think we need to rethink how we live. The pandemic showed us that small changes in our habits, like reducing unnecessary travel or using less plastic, can make a big difference in reducing our impact on the environment.

Environmentalist (smiling) Exactly, Aarav. Small steps make a big difference. If we all choose to live more sustainably-whether it's using public transport, conserving water, or reducing waste–we can protect the environment and our health at the same time.

The pandemic has taught us that we are all interconnected–with each other, with nature and with our health. Let's not wait for another crisis to remind us of this. Let's use what we've learned to build a healthier, more sustainable world.

Doctor (nodding) The journey towards better health and a cleaner environment starts with us. Every small action counts.

Teacher (concluding) So, remember, the lessons from COVID-19 aren't just about surviving a pandemic. They're about living consciously and responsibly. Let's commit to being more aware of our actions, making health-conscious choices, and protecting the planet for the generations to come.

(The students nod in agreement as the lights dim, and the play concludes.)

Sample Viva Questions

Some viva-based questions on this one act play are

1. Maya talks about health and hygiene. How do her concerns represent the shift in people's attitude toward health during the pandemic?
2. Do you think the play successfully addresses the idea of long-term environmental recovery following a global crisis like COVID-19? Why or why not?
3. Do you agree with the view that individual habits like reducing travel or using less plastic could have a significant long-term effect on the environment? Explain your answer.
4. How does the play suggest that young people, like the students in the classroom, can make a difference in shaping a more sustainable and healthy future?
5. What impact do you think this play would have on a young audience in terms of raising awareness about health and environmental issues?
6. If you were to perform this play in front of a large audience, how would you ensure the message about health and environmental consciousness reaches them effectively?
7. How do you think the play handles the theme of responsibility, both individual and collective, when it comes to the pandemic's effects on health and the environment?

Compilation of the Project

Now that we know about how to make the project, students should be aware of how to compile the project. This compilation comprises all the work that the students produce during the process of working on their ALS Project. It includes

- Cover page, with title of project, school details/details of students.
- Statement of purpose/objectives/goals
- Certificate of completion under the guidance of the teacher.
- Students Action Plan for the completion of assigned tasks.
- Materials such as scripts for the theatre/role play, questionnaires for interview, written assignments, essays, survey-reports and other material evidence of learning progress and academic accomplishment.
- The 800-1000 words essay/script/report.
- Student/group reflections.
- If possible, photographs that capture the positive learning experiences of the student(s).
- List of resources/bibliography

Presentation of the Project and Viva

Presenting your Class XI-XII project effectively is crucial to communicating your hard work and ideas clearly. Here are some tips to ensure that your presentation is successful

- **Understand your Project Thoroughly** You should know every detail of your project, from its objectives to the results and conclusions.
- **Anticipate questions** Think about possible questions that might arise during your presentation, and prepare clear, concise answers.
- **Grab attention** Begin with an interesting hook-an intriguing fact, a relevant question, or a personal story related to the project topic. Clearly state the problem or question your project addresses. This will set the context for your audience.
- **Follow a logical flow** Organise your presentation into clear sections-Introduction, Methodology, Results, Discussion, and Conclusion.
    - **Introduction** Briefly explain the topic, objectives, and significance.
    - **Methodology** Explain the methods or processes you followed to carry out the project.
    - **Results** Present the findings or outcomes in a concise and understandable way.
    - **Discussion/Conclusion** Discuss the implications of your results and summarise your conclusions.
- **Avoid unnecessary details** Focus on the most important aspects of your project. If something is too technical or detailed, explain it briefly or provide supplementary material.
- **Maintain eye contact** Make sure to look at your audience (or camera, if virtual) to establish a connection.
- **Stick to the time limit** Respect the time allotted for your presentation. Plan your content so it fits within the time frame.
- **Rehearse your presentation** Practice delivering your project multiple times. This will help you become familiar with the flow and build confidence. Present in front of friends or family members for feedback.
- **Stay calm during the Viva** Listen to each question carefully and take a moment to think before responding. Don't be afraid to ask for clarification if needed.

Rubrics for Assessment

Remember that CBSE has suggested some parameters and a rubric to assess students on their project. These include the following

- Quality of content of the project
- Adherence to the specified timeline
- Clarity of thoughts and ideas
- Contributions by group members
- Accuracy of information
- Content in respect of (spellings, grammar, punctuation)
- Creativity
- Knowledge and experience gained

Sample Rubric for ALS Project Work (For Theatre/Role Play/Oral presentation/Interview/Podcast)

Category	1	2	3	4	5
Time Limit	• Presentation is less than or more than 5 minutes long	• Presentation exceeded or less than specified time limit by 4 to 5 minutes	• Presentation exceeded or less than specified time limit by 3 to 4 minutes	• Presentation exceeded or less than specified time limit by 2 to 3 minutes	• Students/group adhered to the given time limit
Content/Script/Questionnaire	• Script is not related to topic or issue	• Well written script/ content shows little understanding of parts of topic	• Well written script/ content shows good understanding of parts of topic	• Well written script/ content shows a good understanding of subject topic	• Well written script/ content shows full understanding of subject topic
Creativity	• No props/costumes/ stage presentation lack-lustre	• Some work done, average stage set-up and costumes	• Well organised presentation, could have improved	• Logical use of props, reasonable work done, creative	• Suitable props/honest effort seen/ considerable work done/Creative and relevant costumes
Preparedness	• Student/group seems to be unprepared	• Some preparedness visible, but rehearsal is lacking	• Some what prepared, rehearsal is lacking	• Good preparedness, but need better rehearsal	• Complete preparedness/ rehearsed presentation
Clarity of Speech	• Lack of clarity in presentation many words mispronounced	• Speaks clearly, some words are mispronounced	• Speaks clearly 90% of the time/a few mispronounced words	• Speaks clearly and distinctly 95% of time/ few mispronounced words	• Speaks clearly distinctly 95% of time/fluency in pronunciation
Use of Props (Theatre/Role Play)	• Only 1/no relevant props used	• 1 to 2 relevant props used	• 2 to 3 relevant props used	• 3 to 4 relevant props used	• 4 to 5 relevant props used
Expression/Body Language	• Very little use of facial expressions facial/body language, does not generate much interest	• Little use of facial expressions and body language	• Facial expressions and body language are used to try to generate some enthusiasm	• Facial expression and body language sometimes generate strong enthusiasm with the topic	• Facial expression and body language generate strong enthusiasm with the topic
Portfolio-Presentation	• Inadequate and unimpressive	• Some what suitable and convincing	• Adequate and relevant	• Interesting, enjoyable and relevant	• Brilliant, creative and exceptional

CBSE
Examination Paper 2025

ENGLISH CORE

Time : 3 Hours **Max. Marks : 80**

General Instructions

Read the following instructions very carefully and strictly follow them.

1. This Question Paper has 13 questions. All questions are compulsory.
2. This Question Paper contains three sections— **Section A** Reading Skills, **Section B** Creative Writing Skills and **Section C** Literature.
3. Attempt all questions based on specific instructions for each part. Write the correct question number and part thereof in your answer sheet.
4. Separate instructions are given with each question/part, wherever necessary.
5. Adhere to the prescribed word limit while answering the questions.

Set-1

Section A : Reading Skills

[22 Marks]

1. Read the following passage carefully. **12m**

1. Having a sense of humour might mean having the ability to entertain other people by making them laugh, but it can also mean having a quick wit that is frequently employed to criticise other people with snide comments. Some might define the sense of humour as the ability to see humour in everyday life or as appreciating the cleverness of puns and other wordplay, and may think it entirely possible to possess a good sense of humour without ever having those around them become aware of it.
2. In any case, a sense of humour is a socially valued trait that almost all of us would prefer to have more, rather than less of-akin to the way that we think about intelligence or good looks. A person with an undeveloped sense of humour lacks a social skill that puts him or her at a severe disadvantage in the hurly-burly of everyday social life.
3. Freud thought of humour as an outlet for forbidden impulses, and philosophers ranging from Aristotle to Descartes believed that we are amused by something when it makes us feel superior to other people.
4. Evolutionary psychologists believe that humour, along with other creative abilities, such as art and music, evolved as an honest signal of intelligence and genetic quality. The value of such a skill in defusing tense, aggressive situations and in managing alliances and friendships should not be underestimated either.

5. Schmoozing with a bunch of new people at a cocktail party is an opportunity to engage in light hearted banter, and other people are grateful when someone is skillful enough to turn a stiff and awkward situation into fun. Cracking jokes, making witty remarks, and engaging in tongue-in-cheek observations about the social world can be like fishing for other minds that connect naturally with one's own. In other words, humour can be a device for connecting people who are operating on the same wavelength.
6. Observing the performance of other people in such situations tips you off as to who you might like to get to know better–and who might be best left behind, wallowing in indignation and blank stares. In short, a sense of humour is the Swiss Army Knife of social skills. Perhaps it is indeed a single instrument, but it contains an arsenal of tools–each exquisitely designed for a unique social purpose.

Answer the following questions, based on the given passage above.

(i) How does the author prove in Paragraph 1 that sense of humour is a double edged sword? (1)

(ii) Cite evidences from the passage to prove that sense of humour is a valuable tool to make someone's life better. (2)

(iii) Complete the following sentence suitably with reference to Paragraph 3. (1)

One significant advantage of humour is that it helps one ....

(iv) Provide one textual evidence with reference to Paragraph 5. How a good sense of humour can be a great ice breaker. (1)

(v) Select the correct option from those given in bracket to fill in the blank. (1)

According to evolutionary psychologists, people with a sense of humour can .... (trigger/lighten) tense situation.

(vi) Choose the correct option. (1)

"....humour can be a device for connecting people who are operating on the same wavelength."

By the phrase 'same wavelength' the author refers to

(a) people of age group.
(b) people who belong to same line of profession.
(c) people having similar interests and attitudes.
(d) people who are working in the same organisation.

(vii) Complete the analogy with one word from Paragraph 6. (1)

advantage : benefit :: .... : anger

(a) situation
(b) stare
(c) indignation
(d) arsenal

(viii) In the line perhaps "it is indeed a single instrument, but it contains an arsenal of tools......" What does the phrase 'arsenal of tools' refer to? (2)

(ix) Provide one textual evidence from the text which states lack of sense of humour may prove to be a handicap in one's life. (1)

(x) An undeveloped sense of humour shows lack of a social skill that puts him or her at a disadvantage. (1)

Choose the correct option (A) or (B) which reaffirms the idea conveyed in the above extract.

(a) Sense of humour elevates the status of a person in the social circle.
(b) People with sense of humour are not taken seriously in the society.

2. Read the following passage carefully. **10m**

1. This report presents findings from the Youth Aspirations in India Survey in which 5,764 youth between the ages of 15 and 30 were asked about their employment, education, and skilling aspirations.
2. Indian youth valued higher education. 50 percent of respondents aspire to attain a post-graduate degree, 24 percent a PhD, and 21 percent a bachelor's degree. Only 2 percent of respondents hope to attain a college or vocational diploma as their highest form of education.
3. Respondents have a strong preference for attaining higher education degrees. At the same time, there is an awareness of changing skills requirements and an interest in augmenting their skills. 76 percent of youth report being very interested in pursuing a skills development programme. 70 percent of youth identified more employment opportunities as the main motivation for wanting to pursue skills development training.
4. A study related to their job preference reveals their strong desire for job security and opportunities for career advancement. It is evident from the following data

Percentage	Preference
49	Public Sector
23	Private Sector
17	Entrepreneurship

5. In the context of technological adoption and digitisation, jobs and tasks, along with the competencies required to execute them, are changing. 86 percent of youth feel very or moderately up to date with changes in skills requirements. Yet, 39 percent of youth feel very prepared or prepared for their ideal job, while 16 percent of youth feel either not prepared or very unprepared for their ideal job.
6. Female respondents' education and employment aspirations match, if not exceed, those of male respondents. Yet, female respondents face discriminatory biases in hiring, have less paid work experience than their male counterparts, and face greater barriers in pursuing skills development opportunities. 60 percent of female respondents, for example, report having no paid work experience, compared to 54 percent of male respondents. In addition, 15 percent of female respondents report personal biases such as marital status, gender, age, or family background as a main barrier to employment compared to 9 percent of male respondents. While more female respondents report being very interested in participating in a skills development programme, only 19 percent have enrolled in a programme, compared to 26 percent of male respondents.

Answer the following questions, based on the given passage above.

(i) As per the survey, Indian youth is broadly focused on **(1)**

(a) skill development and entrepreneurship.

(b) private sector jobs and technology.

(c) higher education and career opportunities.

(d) vocational diploma and public sector jobs.

(ii) With reference to Paragraph 3, what is the latest trend among Indian youth in preparing themselves for the job market? **(1)**

(iii) With reference to the table, state one reason for entrepreneurship being the last preference among Indian youth. **(1)**

(iv) Cite two evidences from the text to show that gender bias is still a hindrance in the progress of women in society. (2)

(v) Complete the following sentence suitably. (1)

The driving force for the Indian youth to join a skill development programme is ....

(vi) Paragraph 5 uses words 'competencies' and 'adoption'. Classify the following sentences which talks about 'competency' and which talks about 'adoption'. (1)

Sentence 1 Ria embraced new technology to gain global market for her paintings.

Sentence 2 Ria displays her artistic skill through her paintings.

(vii) Cite two evidences from the text to show that Indian youth is adapting itself to the needs of the job market. (2)

(viii) Choose the correct option. (1)

The main road blocks to employment opportunities for females are

(i) lack of interest
(ii) marriage
(iii) lack of opportunities
(iv) over qualification
(v) family background

Codes

(a (i) and (ii)
(b) (iii) and (iv)
(c) (ii), (iii) and (v)
(d) (iv) and (v)

Section B : Creative Writing Skills (18 Marks)

Note: All details presented in the questions are imaginary and created for assessment purpose

3. Attempt **ANY ONE** of the two, (A) or (B) in about **50** words. (4)

A. Your school is organising a road safety awareness workshop for students of Class IX-XII. As the head boy of your school, draft a notice informing the students about the workshop. Include other necessary details. You are Ashna/Ashish. Put your notice in a box.

OR

B. Your school is organising an Inter-House Science Model-Making-Competition. As President of the Science Club, draft a notice to inform all House members from Class IX-XII about the competition and specify the number of registrations invited per house. Include other necessary details. You are Mitali/Mukesh. Put your notice in a box.

4. Attempt **ANY ONE** of the two, (A) or (B) in about 50 words. (4)

A. Draft an invitation card on behalf of the Principal of J.B. Bhatia Public School for the launch of 'Yoga for Life' programme in the school. Mention a compelling highlight of the programme along with other necessary details.

OR

B. You are Mrs. Savita Manjrekhar, a professor in English. You are invited to be one of the judges for the inter-school debate competition by the Principal of J.M. Public School, Cochin. Write a formal letter expressing your inability to accept the invitation.

5. Attempt **ANY ONE** of the two, (A) or (B) in 120-150 words. (5)

A. You are Ajay of 36, N.J. Colony, Pune. You read the given advertisement and wish to apply for the post advertised. Write this job application along with your bio-data.

> **Bloom Public School, Bhopal**
> **Requires**
>
> **Hockey Coach** Graduates with B.P.Ed degree preferred. Minimum 4 years experience.
>
> **Skills** Well versed in defence techniques, knowledge of physical and psychological performance development. Ability to foster team culture and promote sportsmanship. Prepare students for state/national championships.
>
> Write to The Principal, Bloom Public School, Bhopal

OR

B. Social literacy is increasingly recognised as a crucial 21st century skill for young individuals. Write a letter to the editor of a local daily discussing the benefits of providing social literacy education to children. Also, suggest effective ways to raise awareness about the importance of this education among parents. You may use some of the given cues along with your own ideas to draft the letter. You are a counsellor, Reena Sharma of 36, M.V. Apartments, Pune.

> - What is social literacy?
> - What is the role of school in imparting social literacy to young students?
> - What are the benefits of social literacy?
> - How is social literacy connected to career advancement?

6. Attempt **ANY ONE** of the two, (A) or (B) about in 120-150 words. (5)

A. Write an article on the commercialisation of festivals, analysing the reasons for commercialisation and its impact on the younger generation. You may use some of the given cues along with your own ideas. You are Vinita Yadav of XII B.

> - Impact of globalisation on celebration of festivals
> - Sanctity and essence of festivals
> - Role of Media in commercialising festivals
> - Suggest ways in which individuals and communities can work together to preserve tradition and culture in the celebration of festivals

OR

B. You are Suraj, reporter of The Times of India. You are sent to cover the Mango Festival organised at the farmer's market.

Write a comprehensive report detailing the activities at the festival. Include descriptions of the events, participation details, the overall impact of these activities on the local community

You may organise your report by following

Who — What — When — Why — How

Section C : Literature

(40 Marks)

7. Read the following extracts and answer the questions for **ANY ONE** of the given two, (A) or (B). (6)

A.

It is in the news that all these pitiful kin
Are to be bought out and mercifully gathered in
To live in villages, next to the theatre and the store.
Where they won't have to think for themselves anymore,
While greedy good-doers, beneficent beasts of prey,
Swarm over their lives enforcing benefits
That are calculated to soothe them out of their wits,
And by teaching them how to sleep they sleep all day
Destroy their sleeping at night the ancient way.

(A Roadside Stand)

(i) The expression 'It is in the news' suggests
(a) it is good news for the roadside stand owners.
(b) an important decision has been taken by the government.
(c) the roadside stand owners have protested against the government.
(d) that the news was not there in the newspaper.

(ii) Read the Assertion (A) and the Reason (R) below with reference to the given extract.

Assertion (A) The poet complains that the rural people are exploited by the people in power.

Reason (R) The rural people reposed blind faith in the false promises of the people in power.

Choose the correct option regarding their relationship.
(a) Both (A) and (R) are true, and (R) is the correct explanation of (A).
(b) Both (A) and (R) are true, but (R) is not the correct explanation of (A).
(c) (A) is true, but (R) is false.
(d) (A) is false, but (R) is true.

(iii) Complete the following suitably.

In the line "that are calculated to soothe them out of their wits", the phrase 'soothe them out of their wit' refers to ....

(iv) Bring out the irony in the expression 'they won't have to think for themselves'.

(v) Select the correct option from those given in bracket to fill in the blank.

The poet 'uses the expression 'greedy good-doers' to .... (criticise/appreciate) the intention of the powerful people.

(vi) Complete the following suitably.

The tone of the poet in the above extract is ....

OR

B.

If we were not so single-minded
about keeping our lives moving,
and for once could do nothing,
perhaps a huge silence
might interrupt this sadness
of never understanding ourselves with death.

Perhaps the Earth can teach us
as when everything seems dead
and later proves to be alive.
Now I'll count up to twelve
And you keep quiet and I will go. *(Keeping Quiet)*

(i) Complete the following suitably.

The poet uses the expression 'single minded' to refer to ....

(ii) Why does the poet refer to silence as a welcoming interruption?

(iii) Read the Assertion (A) and the Reason (R) below with reference to the given extract.

Assertion (A) The poet personifies Earth as a teacher.

Reason (R) We learn from the Earth that pausing doesn't mean the end.

Choose the correct option regarding their relationship.

(a) Both (A) and (R) are true, and (R) is the correct explanation of (A).
(b) Both (A) and (R) are true, but (R) is not the correct explanation of the (A).
(c) (A) is true, but (R) is false.
(d) (A) is false, but (R) is true.

(iv) Complete the following suitably.

By the expression 'keeping our lives moving' the poet refers to ....

(v) Choose the correct option.

The intention of the poet in the above extract is

(a) to make us aware of the importance of Earth.
(b) to criticise our single mindedness.
(c) to highlight the reason for our sadness.
(d) to highlight the importance of sustaining peace and silence.

(vi) What is the significance of the last line of the extract 'you keep quiet and I will go'?

8. Read the following extracts and answer the questions for **ANY ONE** of the given two, (A) or (B). **(4)**

A. When I heard this, I didn't want to laugh any more, and I felt terribly sad. How could they believe that it was disgusting if one of us held that package in his hands, even though the Vadai had been wrapped first in a banana leaf, and then parcelled in paper? I felt so provoked and angry that I wanted to touch those wretched Vadais myself straight away. Why should we have to fetch and carry for these people. I wondered. Such an important elder of ours goes meekly to the shops to fetch snacks and hands over reverently, bowing and shrinking, to this fellow who just sits there and stuffs them into his mouth. The thought of it infuriated me. *(Memories of Childhood)*

(i) 'I felt terribly sad.' The reason for the speaker's sadness is because it was an act of ....

(ii) Choose the correct option.

'The thought of it infuriated me' with reference to the above line, what do you think is the impact of the incident on the speaker?

(a) The speaker was sympathetic and helpless.
(b) The speaker was angry and condemning.
(c) The speaker was excited to see the incident.
(d) The speaker was very impressed and motivated.

(iii) Complete the sentence suitably.

'I wanted to touch those wretched Vadais myself.'

The above expression indicates the speaker's ....

(iv) Select the correct option from those given in bracket to fill in the blank.

The incident made the speaker realise that the discrimination was .... (dehumanising/elevating).

OR

B. **Mr. Lamb** When I go down the streets, the kids shout 'Lamey Lamb'. But they will come into the garden, into my house; it's a game. They're not afraid of me. Why should they be? Because I'm not afraid of them, that's why not.

Derry Did you get your leg blown off in the war?

Mr. Lamb Certainly

Derry How will you climb on a ladder and get the crab apples down, then?

Mr. Lamb Oh, there's a lot of things I've learned to do and plenty of time for it. Years. I take it steady. *(On the Face of it)*

(i) Complete the following suitably.

Years. I take it steady. The above line speaks of the speaker's ....

(ii) Derry, how will you climb on a ladder? What does Derry hint at in the above query?

(iii) "When I go down the streets, the kids shout Lamey Lamb."

The attitude of the speaker expressed in the above line is

(a) his habit of finding fault.

(b) he is timid and faint hearted.

(c) his acceptance of reality and positive attitude.

(d) his indifferent and careless attitude.

(iv) Fill in the blank suitably.

Mr. Lamb's handicap has not .... his attitude towards life.

9. Read the following extracts and answer the questions for **ANY ONE** of the given two, (A) or (B). **(6)**

A. Those were the days of mainly indoor shooting, and only five percent of the film was shot outdoors. I suppose the sets and studio lights needed the girls and boys to be made to look ugly in order to look presentable in the movie. A strict hierarchy was maintained in the make-up department. The chief make-up man made the chief actors and actresses ugly, his senior assistant 'second' hero and heroine, the junior assistant the main comedian and so forth. The players who played the crowd were the responsibility of the office boy. (Even the make-up department of the Gemini Studio had an 'office boy').

On the days when there was crowd-shooting, you could see him mixing his paint in a giant vessel and slapping it on the crowd players. The idea was to close every pore on the surface of the face in the process of applying make-up. *(Poets and Pancakes)*

(i) What does the writer mean by the phrase 'indoor shooting' in the first line of the extract?

(ii) Pick up one sentence from the extract that reflects the sarcastic tone of the writer.

(iii) The hierarchy in the make-up department puts the 'office boy' in the .... (lowest/top) rung of the ladder.

(iv) Complete the following suitably.

On the days when there was a 'crowd-shooting'. By the phrase crowd-shooting, the author refers to ....

(v) Choose the correct option.

".....mix his paint in a giant vessel and slapping it on the crowd players."

The choice of words like 'paint' and 'slapping' by the author reflects.

(a) author's intention to degrade the office boy's role in the make-up department.
(b) the office boy's lack of seriousness.
(c) author's sarcastic and humorous writing style.
(d) author's dislike of the office boy.

(vi) Choose the correct option.

What does the following line from the extract showcase?

"A strict hierarchy was maintained in the make-up department."

(a) The office boy took all the decisions in the make-up department.
(b) A system of ranks according to importance of work was followed.
(c) Everyone was given an equal share of work in the department.
(d) Nepotism was prevalent in the make-up department.

OR

B. My Last French Lesson! Why, I hardly knew how to write! I should never learn any more! I must stop there, then! Oh, how sorry I was for not learning my lessons, for seeking birds' eggs or going sliding on the Saar! My books, that had seemed such a nuisance a while ago, so heavy to carry, my grammar, and my history of the saints, were old friends now that I couldn't give up and M. Hamel, too; the idea that he was going away, that I should never see him again, made me forget all about his ruler and how cranky he was.

Poor man! It was in honour of this last lesson that he had put on his fine Sunday clothes, and now I understood why the old men of the village were sitting there in the back of the room. It was because they were sorry, too, that they had not gone to school more. It was their way of thanking our master for his forty years of faithful service and of showing their respect for the country that was theirs no more. *(The Last Lesson)*

(i) Choose the correct option.

What is the tone of the speaker in the expression "I hardly knew how to write.... how sorry I was for not learning my lessons"?

(a) Confused (b) Regretful
(c) Surprised (d) Happy

(ii) Choose the correct option.

The speaker refers to 'seeking birds' egg' and 'sliding on the Saar' as

(a) part of his routine (b) his daily routine
(c) source of distraction from learning (d) fun time with friends

(iii) What is reflected through the shift in the speaker's perception of his books through his expression of calling them his 'old friends' rather than considering them as 'nuisance'?

(iv) Select the correct option from those given in bracket, to fill in the blank.

"It was because they were sorry too...."

They were sorry for .... (not following the government order/not learning their language).

(v) What is inferred from the expression 'the country that was theirs no more'?

(vi) What does M. Hamel's ruler reflect about his image?

10. Answer **ANY FIVE** of the following six questions in 40-50 words each. $(5 \times 2 = 10)$

(i) "One of these days you're going to talk yourself into a load of trouble;" her father said aggressively. What do you learn about Sophie's father from these lines? *(Going Places)*

(ii) 'A thing of beauty is a joy forever.' Explain with reference to the poem. *(A Thing of Beauty)*

(iii) How did Franz plan to turn the commotion in the classroom to his favour? *(The Last Lesson)*

(iv) How do the expressions 'polished traffic' and a stand that 'pathetically pled' depict the contrasting worlds that co-exist in the poem 'A Roadside Stand'?

(v) 'What I want should not be confused'. What clarification does Pablo Neruda give to his readers? *(Keeping Quiet)*

(vi) "But the game he is watching so intently is out of his reach."
What are the factors that have made their game inaccessible to Saheb? *(Lost Spring)*

11. Answer **ANY TWO** of the following three questions in 40-50 words each. (2 × 2 = 4)

(i) What is so ironical about Sam reaching the third level?

(ii) What image of the Tiger King is revealed in the diamond ring episode?

(iii) "In that short time, we've managed to create quite a rukus." What does Tishani Doshi refer to by 'rukus'?

12. Answer **ANY ONE** of the following two questions in 120-150 words. (5)

A. 'Where there is a will, there is a way'. The above saying aptly describes the character of Douglas from 'Deep Water' and Mukesh from 'Lost Spring'. Compare and contrast their characters in terms of their courage, determination, and the pursuit of their goals.

OR

B. Kamala Das in 'Keeping Quiet' and Keats in 'A Thing of Beauty' depict nature as a source of inspiration and strength to man. Analyse both the poems in terms of the above perspective.

13. Answer **ANY ONE** of the following two questions in 120-150 words. (5)

A. The element of dilemma, between humanity and Patriotism elevates the character of Dr. Sadao in 'The Enemy'. Support your answer with evidence from the text.

OR

B. How did Tishani Doshi's visit to Antarctica as part of the Students on Ice Programme make her realise the importance of preserving the Earth? *(Journey to the End of the Earth)*

Set-2

(Only Uncommon Question from Set 1)

5. Attempt **ANY ONE** of the two, (A) or (B) in about 120-150 words. (5)

A. You are Nidhi of 42, M.G. Road, Gwalior. You read the given advertisement and wish to apply for the post advertised. Write job application along with your bio-data.

M.V. Public School, Shimla
Requires
Western Music Teacher

Qualification Graduate in music

Experience Min. 2 years in similar field

Skills

- Lesson planning, preparing students for competitions and performances.
- Organise school bands, orchestra and choir groups.
- Proficiency in computers and technology aided music.

Apply to The Principal, M.V. Public School, Shimla

OR

B. The rapid expansion of urban sprawl (the geographic extent of cities and towns,) is mainly due to the desire for increased living space. This urban sprawl comes with a cost of air pollution, water pollution, and disruption of environmentally sensitive areas. Write a letter to the editor of a National daily expressing your concern over the above issue and also suggest ways to improve the situation. You are Sonal of 14, A, R.P. Nagar, New Delhi. You may use the following cues along with your own ideas to compose the letter.

- What is urban sprawl?
- What is the long term impact of urban sprawl in over daily lives?
- How can effective urban design and planning reduce problems of urban sprawl?

6. Attempt **ANY ONE** of the two, (A) or (B) in about 120-150 words. (5)

A. In this competitive world, students are expected to excel in all fields like academics, sports, music, art, etc. The main reason for students to reel under stress is poor time management.

Write an article stressing on the need to develop the skill of time management. You may use the following cues along with your own ideas to compose the article. You are Seema of Class XII C.

- What is time management?
- Why are realistic goals important?
- Ways to prioritise tasks, minimise distractions.
- How to utilise technology effectively?

OR

B. You are Heena of Class XII E and a member of the school magazine editorial board. Write a comprehensive report on Republic Day celebrations held in your school. Include descriptions of the events, participation details and the overall impact of these activities on the school community.

You may organise your report by following

Who — What — When — Where — How

11. Answer **ANY TWO** of the following three questions in 40-50 words each. (2 × 2 = 4)

(i) What is the significance of the third level? *(The Third Level)*

(ii) 'Not at all', Sadao said. "It is inconvenient to have you here any longer." *(The Enemy)*
What image do you form of Dr. Sadao based on the above remark?

(iii) Mr. Lamb : ..... you thought it has an empty house, but inside it's full. What do these words tell you about Mr. Lamb? *(On the Face of It)*

12. Answer **ANY ONE** of the following two questions in 120-150 words. (5)

A. Gandhi said, "The real relief for them is to be free from fear." *(Indigo)*

Roosevelt knew when he said, "All we have to fear is fear itself." *(Deep Water)*

Analyse the status of share-croppers and plight of William Douglas in the light of the above statements.

OR

B. Sophie is an escapist and a dreamer. Franz loves to miss school. Analyse the result of both these characters as a result of their attitude towards life.

(Going Places and The Last Lesson)

13. Answer **ANY ONE** of the following two questions in 120-150 words. (5)

A. Derry in 'On the Face of It' is a victim of self-pity. Analyse Derry's behaviour in the light of the above statement.

OR

B. "....how little changes in the environment can have big repercussions" Tishani Doshi in 'Journey to End of the Earth' gives an awakening call for man. Analyse the theme of the lesson in the light of the above statement.

Set-3

(Only Uncommon Question from Set 1 & 2)

5. Attempt **ANY ONE** of the two, (A) or (B) in about 120-150 words. (5)

A. You are Swati of 35, Jyoti Apartments, Hyderabad. You read the given advertisement and wish to apply for the post advertised. Write this job application along with your biodata.

WE24 Media Network, Jaipur

Requires News Reporter

Qualification Graduate in Journalism or Mass Communication

Experience Min. 2 years in relevant field

Skills Communication skills, proficiency in computers, strong writing and research skills, in-depth knowledge of current affairs.

Write to The HR Manager,
WE24 Media Network,
12, J.M. Road, Jaipur

OR

B. Adolescent obesity is a growing concern in India. Too little activity and too many calories from junk food and sweetened drinks are the main contributors to obesity. Write a letter to the editor expressing your concern over the issue and suggest ways to prevent obesity among teenagers. You may use some of the cues along with your own ideas to draft the letter. You are Mohan Lal, 40, J.N. Colony, Pune.

- Causes of teenage obesity
- Solutions
  – Healthy eating
  – Active lifestyle
- Role of parents and schools in inculcating health awareness among students.
- Role of media in creating awareness.

6. Attempt **ANY ONE** of the two, (A) or (B) in 120-150 words. (5)

A. We are living in a stressful world which leads to many health issues like depression and anxiety. Medical researches have revealed that laughter gives relief from stress and it is suggested as an alternative therapy to promote well-being. Write an article for a Health Magazine on the therapeutic benefits of laughter therapy. You may use the cues given along with your own ideas to draft the article. You are Anmol.

- What is laughter therapy?
- What are the emotional and physical benefits of laughter?
- How does laughter bring people together?

OR

B. You are Pawan of XII B, student reporter of your school. Your school conducted the Zonal Football match finals in your school playground. Write a comprehensive report of the match including details of the participating teams, results and the highlights of the finals.

You may organise your report by following

Who — What — When — Where — Why — How

11. Answer **ANY TWO** of the following three questions in 40-50 words each. (2 × 2 = 4)

(i) How was Annan instrumental in Bama achieving success in life? *(Memories of Childhood)*

(ii) What was Charlie's vision about Galesburg as it was in 1894? *(The Third Level)*

(iii) Dr. Sadao had saved the life of the American soldier, but agreed to the General's proposal of sending assassins. What prompted Dr. Sadao to agree to the General's proposal? *(The Enemy)*

12. Answer **ANY ONE** of the following two questions in 120-150 words. (5)

A. 'Deep Water' and 'Indigo' bring out the importance of overcoming fear. Discuss the two texts with reference to the above statement.

OR

B. Franz from 'The Last Lesson' and the peddler from the 'Rattrap' learn from their mistakes. Discuss with reference to the above texts, the human tendency to make mistakes and learn from them.

13. Answer **ANY ONE** of the following questions in 120-150 words.

A. The world's geological history is trapped in Antarctica. Discuss with reference to the chapter 'Journey to the End of the Earth'.

OR

B. Bama and ZitKala-Sa have proven that education is the antidote to all social evils.

Analyse their characters in terms of their struggles and their will to win.

(Memories of Childhood)

ANSWERS

Set-I

1. (i) The author states that a sense of humour can be used to entertain and make people laugh, but it can also be employed as a sharp wit to criticise others with snide comments. This demonstrates its potential for both positive and negative impacts, making it a double-edged sword.

(ii) Given below are evidences to prove that a sense of humour is a valuable tool to make someone's life better

- "The value of such a skill in defusing tense, aggressive situations and in managing alliances and friendships should not be underestimated either." (Paragraph 4)
- "Humour can be a device for connecting people who are operating on the same wavelength." (Paragraph 5)
- "A sense of humour is the Swiss Army Knife of social skills. Perhaps it is indeed a single instrument, but it contains an arsenal of tools - each exquisitely designed for a unique social purpose." (Paragraph 6)

(iii) feel superior to other people

(iv) One textual evidence how a good sense of humour can be a great ice breaker is "Schmoozing with a bunch of new people at a cocktail party is an opportunity to engage in lighthearted banter, and other people are grateful when someone is skillful enough to turn a stiff and awkward situation into fun."

(v) lighten

(vi) (c) people having similar interests and attitudes.

(vii) (c) indignation

(viii) The phrase 'arsenal of tools' refers to the various social skills that a sense of humour provides, each designed for a unique social purpose, such as defusing tension, making connections, and engaging in social interactions effectively.

(ix) One textual evidence that states that lack of sense of humour may prove to be a handicap in one's life is "A person with an undeveloped sense of humour lacks a social skill that puts him or her at a severe disadvantage in the hurly-burly of everyday social life."

(x) (a) Sense of humour elevates the status of a person in the social circle.

2. (i) (c) higher education and career opportunities

(ii) The latest trend among Indian youth is a strong interest in skills development programmes to enhance their employability. 76% of youth reported being very interested in pursuing such programmes, with 70% identifying better employment opportunities as the main motivation.

(iii) Entrepreneurship is the least preferred option because it lacks job security and career advancement opportunities compared to public and private sector jobs, which are more stable and structured.

(iv) Two pieces of evidence from the text to show that gender bias is still a hindrance in the progress of women in society are

(a) "60 percent of female respondents report having no paid work experience, compared to 54 percent of male respondents."

(b) "15 percent of female respondents report personal biases such as marital status, gender, age, or family background as a main barrier to employment, compared to 9 percent of male respondents."

(v) the availability of more employment opportunities

(vi) **Sentence 1** Adoption

Sentence 2 Competency

(vii) Two pieces of evidence from the text to show that Indian youth is adapting itself to the needs of the job market are

(a) "86 percent of youth feel very or moderately up to date with changes in skills requirements."

(b) "76 percent of youth report being very interested in pursuing a skills development programme."

(viii) (c) (ii), (iii) and (v)

3. A.

ABC SCHOOL, Delhi
NOTICE

5th February, 20XX

ROAD SAFETY AWARENESS WORKSHOP

This is to inform all students of Classes IX-XII that our school is organising a Road Safety Awareness Workshop in collaboration with the [Traffic Police Department] to educate students about essential road safety rules and responsible commuting.

Date 12th February, 20XX
Time 11:00 am to 3:00 pm
Venue School Auditorium
Guest Speaker V. K. Singh, Traffic Police Officer

The session will include demonstrations, interactive discussions, and important road safety tips. Attendance is compulsory for all students. For any queries, contact the undersigned.

Ashna/Ashish
(Head Boy/Head Girl)

Or

B.

ABC SCHOOL, Noida
NOTICE

9th October, 20XX

INTER-HOUSE SCIENCE MODEL-MAKING COMPETITION

The Science Club is excited to announce an Inter-House Science Model-Making Competition for students of Classes IX to XII on 23rd October, 20XX from 11:00 am to 4:00 pm in the School Auditorium. This is a great opportunity to showcase your creativity and scientific skills!

Theme Space Science
Team Size Group (Max. 3-4 members)
Registrations per House 5 Teams

Exciting prizes for the best models!

Interested students must submit their names to their respective House Captains by 14th October, 20XX. For further details, contact the undersigned.

Mitali/Mukesh
(President, Science Club)

4. A.

J.B. BHATIA PUBLIC SCHOOL
cordially invites you to the launch of
'YOGA FOR LIFE' PROGRAMME
on 21st June, 20XX
at 11:30 am
in the School Sports Ground

Highlight of the Programme special interactive session on 'Yoga for Holistic Well-being' by renowned Yoga Guru XYZ.

Join us as we embark on a journey towards a healthier mind and body through the power of yoga! Your presence will truly encourage our students in embracing this transformative practice.

RSVP
R S Saxena
Principal, J.B. Bhatia Public School
011 - 2033XXXX

We look forward to your gracious presence!

Or

B. Savita Manjrekhar
Professor of English
XYZ Apartments
Delhi - 11XXXXX

10th August, 20XX

The Principal
J.M. Public School
Cochin

Subject Regret for Inability to Accept Invitation

Sir/Madam

I sincerely appreciate your kind invitation to be a judge for the Inter-School Debate Competition at J.M. Public School. It is indeed an honour to be considered for such a prestigious event that fosters intellectual discourse and critical thinking among students.

However, due to prior professional commitments, I regret to inform you that I will be unable to attend the competition as a judge. I truly value the opportunity and deeply regret my inability to participate.

I wish you and the participants great success in organising an engaging and thought-provoking competition. I look forward to future opportunities to collaborate with your esteemed institution.

Thank you for your understanding.

Yours sincerely
Savita Manjrekhar

5. A. 36, N.J. Colony
Pune - 411001

12th April, 20XX

The Principal
Bloom Public School
Bhopal - 462001

Subject Application for the Post of Hockey Coach

Sir/Madam

This is in response to your advertisement in the daily newspaper dated 10th April, 20XX for the position of Hockey Coach at Bloom Public School. With a strong background in coaching and a passion for nurturing young talent, I believe I would be a valuable addition to your esteemed institution.

I hold a Bachelor's degree in Physical Education (B.P.Ed.) and have over four years of experience coaching school and college-level hockey teams. My expertise lies in defensive strategies, physical conditioning, and psychological training to enhance player performance. Additionally, I have successfully trained teams for state and national-level championships, instilling teamwork and sportsmanship among players.

I am eager to contribute my skills to your school's sports programme and help students achieve excellence in hockey. Enclosed is my bio-data for your perusal. I would be grateful for the opportunity to discuss my application further in an interview.

Thank you for your time and consideration.

Yours sincerely
Ajay
(9836XXXXXX)
(ajay.hockey@gmail.com)
Enclosure Detailed Resume

RESUME

Name Ajay
Address 36, N.J. Colony, Pune - 411001
Phone 9836XXXXXX
Email ID ajay.hockey@gmail.com
Date of Birth 19th September, 1995
Nationality Indian

Educational Qualification

Name of the Exam	Name of the Institute	Year	Percentage/ GPA
B.P.Ed.	XYZ University	2019	79%
Bachelor's Degree	PQR University	2016	86%

Work Experience

- Hockey Coach ABC College, 2022-2024
- Assistant Coach XYZ Institute, 2020-2022

Key Skills

- Expertise in defensive techniques and strategic gameplay
- Strong knowledge of physical and psychological performance development
- Ability to foster team culture and promote sportsmanship
- Experience in training students for state/national championships

Achievements

- Led school teams to multiple district and state-level victories
- Trained players who represented at national-level tournaments
- Conducted sports workshops on strength training and injury prevention

Languages Known English, Hindi, Marathi
References Available upon request

Or

B. Reena Sharma
36, M.V. Apartments
Pune - 411001

12th January, 20XX

The Editor
The Times Daily
Pune

Subject Importance of Social Literacy Education for Children

Sir/Madam

Through the columns of your esteemed newspaper, I wish to draw attention to the increasing importance of social literacy as a crucial 21st century skill for young individuals. In today's rapidly evolving world, where communication, collaboration, and adaptability are key to success, social literacy plays a vital role in shaping responsible, empathetic, and socially aware citizens.

Social literacy refers to the ability to interact effectively with others, understand different perspectives, and navigate social situations with confidence and respect. Schools play a fundamental role in imparting social literacy by integrating values-based education, teamwork activities, conflict resolution techniques, and emotional intelligence development into their curriculum.

The benefits of social literacy are numerous. It enhances communication skills, fosters empathy, builds leadership qualities, and promotes inclusivity. These skills are essential not only in personal relationships but also in professional environments. Socially literate individuals are more adaptable, better team players, and excel in networking, which directly contributes to career growth and success.

However, there is still a lack of awareness among parents about the importance of social literacy in their children's education. To address this, schools and communities can take the following steps

(i) **Workshops and Seminars** Organise sessions for parents to highlight the role of social literacy in academic success, mental well-being, and career advancement.

(ii) **Parental Engagement Programmes** Encourage parents to participate in group activities, storytelling sessions, and social responsibility projects with their children.

(iii) **Social Media Campaigns** Utilise digital platforms to share success stories, expert talks, and interactive discussions on the impact of social literacy.

(iv) **Incorporating Social Skills in Education** Schools should introduce interactive learning methods like role-playing, debates, and collaborative projects to enhance students' social intelligence.

Investing in social literacy education will help children grow into well-rounded individuals who are compassionate, resilient, and ready to take on the challenges of the future. I sincerely hope that this crucial subject gains the attention it deserves.

Yours sincerely
Reena Sharma
(Counsellor)

6. A. **The Commercialisation of Festivals**

by Vinita Yadav, XII B

Festivals, once deeply rooted in culture and tradition, are increasingly becoming commercialised affairs. Globalisation has introduced new ways of celebrating, often influenced by consumerism and marketing strategies. Traditional customs are overshadowed by extravagant spending, brand promotions, and social media trends, reducing festivals to mere shopping events.

The sanctity and essence of festivals-family bonding, spiritual reflection, and cultural significance-are being diluted. The media plays a key role in this shift by aggressively promoting festival sales, luxury gifting, and lavish celebrations, making people, especially the younger generation, equate happiness with materialism.

To preserve the true spirit of festivals, individuals and communities must promote sustainable celebrations, encourage handmade products, and focus on cultural teachings. Schools and families should emphasise the historical and moral significance of festivals, ensuring that they remain a source of unity, tradition, and joy rather than just a commercial opportunity.

Or

B. **Mango Festival Brings Joy to the Farmer's Market**

by Suraj, Reporter, The Times of India

Pune, 21st March, 20XX

The annual Mango Festival was held at the Farmer's Market yesterday, attracting mango lovers from across the city. Organised by the State Agricultural Board, the festival aimed to promote local farmers and celebrate India's rich mango diversity.

The event featured over 50 mango varieties, including Alphonso, Kesar, Dasheri, and Langra. Farmers set up stalls offering fresh mangoes, mango-based delicacies, and organic products. Visitors enjoyed tasting sessions, mango-eating contests, and interactive workshops on mango cultivation.

The festival saw active participation from local farmers, traders, and food enthusiasts, boosting their sales and exposure. The event also highlighted sustainable farming practices and encouraged direct farmer-to-consumer connections.

The Mango Festival proved to be a delightful celebration of India's 'King of Fruits', providing economic benefits to farmers while preserving traditional agricultural heritage. The overwhelming response ensured the festival's continued success for years to come.

7. A. (i) (b) an important decision has been taken by the government.

(ii) (a) Both (A) and the (R) are true and the (R) is correct explanation of (A).

(iii) deceiving the rural people by giving them false hopes and making them dependent on the so-called benefits

(iv) The irony in the expression 'they won't have to think for themselves' is that while the move is presented as a relief for the rural people, it actually takes away their independence, making them passive and completely dependent on the authorities.

(v) criticise

(vi) sarcastic and critical

Or

B. (i) humans' constant pursuit of material progress and their obsession with relentless activity, without pausing to reflect on life and its deeper meaning

(ii) The poet refers to silence as a welcoming interruption because it provides an opportunity for self-reflection, allowing humans to break free from their constant pursuit of progress and understand themselves better.

(iii) (a) Both (A) and (R) are true, and (R) is the correct explanation of (A).

(iv) the ceaseless human tendency to engage in work, responsibilities, and worldly affairs without taking a moment to pause and reflect

(v) (c) to highlight the reason for our sadness.

(vi) The significance of the last line 'you keep quiet and I will go' is that the poet has conveyed his message and now leaves it to the reader to introspect and embrace silence, as true understanding comes from personal realisation rather than external instruction.

8. A. (i) discrimination

(ii) (b) The speaker was angry and condemning.

(iii) defiance and urge to challenge the discriminatory practice

(iv) dehumanising

Or

B. (i) patience and resilience

(ii) Derry's question hints at Mr. Lamb's physical limitation and challenges due to his disability. However, it also reflects Derry's curiosity and skepticism about how Mr. Lamb manages his daily tasks.

(iii) (c) his acceptance of reality and positive attitude.

(iv) affected

9. A. (i) The phrase 'indoor shooting' refers to filming inside a studio using artificial sets and lights instead of shooting in natural outdoor locations.

(ii) "I suppose the sets and studio lights needed the girls and boys to be made to look ugly in order to look presentable in the movie."

(iii) lowest

(iv) the scenes in the film that required a large number of extras or background actors

(v) (c) author's sarcastic and humorous writing style.

(vi) (b) A system of ranks according to importance of work was followed.

Or

B. (i) (b) Regretful

(ii) (c) source of distraction from learning

(iii) The shift in the speaker's perception of his books reflects his deep regret and newfound appreciation for education. What once felt like a burden now feels invaluable, as he realises the importance of learning only when it is too late.

(iv) not learning their language

(v) The expression 'the country that was theirs no more' refers to the loss of their homeland to the Prussians, meaning that the people of Alsace and Lorraine would no longer be able to learn or use their native French language freely.

(vi) M. Hamel's ruler reflects his strict and authoritative image as a teacher. It symbolises discipline, but by the end of the lesson, it also represents his deep commitment to teaching and his sorrow for the loss of the French language.

10. (i) Sophie's father is strict, realistic and dismissive of her fantasies. His aggressive tone suggests he is frustrated with Sophie's habit of daydreaming and making up stories. He worries that her unrealistic expectations might lead her into trouble one day.

(ii) The line 'A thing of beauty is a joy forever' expresses the idea that beautiful things provide everlasting happiness. Beauty, whether found in nature, art, or good deeds, has the power to uplift the human spirit, offering comfort, inspiration, and a sense of hope in times of distress.

(iii) Franz planned to take advantage of the noise and distraction in the classroom by slipping unnoticed into his seat. He was late for school and afraid of being scolded by M. Hamel, so he hoped the commotion would divert the teacher's attention from his tardiness.

(iv) The phrase 'polished traffic' represents modern urban prosperity, where vehicles glide smoothly, symbolising the privileged class. In contrast, 'a stand that pathetically pled' represents the struggles of rural people, as their simple roadside shops desperately seek attention but are ignored by the wealthy city dwellers.

(v) Pablo Neruda clarifies that 'keeping quiet' does not mean complete inactivity or idleness but rather a moment of introspection and peace. He urges people to pause, reflect, and reconnect with nature and themselves, fostering a sense of unity and understanding among humans.

(vi) Saheb cannot participate in the game because of economic disparity. He is a poor ragpicker, lacking resources and social status to afford a proper game like the wealthy children he watches. His dreams remain unfulfilled due to the harsh realities of poverty and class divide.

11. (i) The irony of Sam reaching the third level is that he initially dismissed Charley's belief in its existence. However, in the end, Sam himself finds the third level and chooses to stay there, proving that Charley was right all along. This twist highlights the theme of escapism and wishful thinking.

(ii) The diamond ring episode portrays the Tiger King as arrogant, manipulative, and extravagant. To avoid punishment for killing the hundredth tiger fraudulently, the Dewan cleverly gifts expensive diamond rings to the British official's wife. This reflects the king's corrupt ways and his desperate attempts to maintain power.

(iii) By 'ruckus', Tishani Doshi refers to the destruction and environmental damage humans have caused on Earth within a short span. Despite being a relatively new species, humanity has led to deforestation, climate change, and biodiversity loss, creating chaos for the planet and its ecosystems.

12. A. 'Where there is a will, there is a way' - A Comparison of Douglas and Mukesh

Both Douglas from 'Deep Water' and Mukesh from 'Lost Spring' exemplify the power of courage and determination in overcoming obstacles. Douglas, despite his traumatic childhood experience with water, refuses to let fear control his life. Through persistent effort and rigorous training, he conquers his phobia and regains his confidence. His determination and resilience showcase his strong will.

Similarly, Mukesh, a young boy born into a family of bangle makers, dreams of becoming a mechanic despite his oppressive circumstances. Unlike others in his community who accept their fate, Mukesh dares to challenge tradition and strives for a better future. His self-belief and unwavering focus highlight his strength.

Both characters face adversity, but their courage and pursuit of goals distinguish them. Douglas fights internal fear while Mukesh fights societal constraints, proving that determination leads to success.

Or

B. Both Pablo Neruda in 'Keeping Quiet' and John Keats in 'A Thing of Beauty' highlight nature's power to inspire and strengthen human beings.

In 'Keeping Quiet', Neruda urges humanity to pause and embrace silence, drawing inspiration from nature's calmness and ability to renew itself. He believes that by observing nature, people can find peace and unity, breaking free from conflicts and self-destructive tendencies. The Earth's cycles teach that stillness is not an end but a step toward growth.

Keats, in 'A Thing of Beauty', glorifies nature's beauty as a source of eternal joy. Elements like the sun, trees, and daffodils uplift the human spirit, providing hope and relief from sorrow. He views nature as a healing force, offering comfort and inspiration.

Both poets emphasise that harmony with nature leads to inner peace, strength and happiness, making life meaningful despite hardships.

13. A. Dr. Sadao, in 'The Enemy', faces a deep moral conflict between his duty as a patriotic Japanese citizen and his ethical responsibility as a doctor. When he discovers an injured American prisoner of war on the shore near his home, he is torn between turning him over to the authorities, as expected during wartime, and fulfilling his duty as a physician to save a human life.

Despite his loyalty to Japan, Dr. Sadao chooses humanity over patriotism, treating the enemy soldier with compassion and skill. However, his fear of being labelled a traitor forces him to consider handing the soldier over to the police. Eventually, he helps the soldier escape, demonstrating that his conscience and medical ethics prevail over nationalistic duty.

Dr. Sadao's dilemma elevates his character, making him a symbol of moral integrity and compassion, proving that true humanity transcends political and national boundaries.

Or

B. Tishani Doshi's visit to Antarctica as part of the Students on Ice programme was an eye-opening experience that reinforced the urgency of preserving the Earth. Antarctica, the world's coldest and most pristine continent, provided her with a glimpse into Earth's past, present, and possible future.

She witnessed the fragility of the ecosystem, where even slight changes in temperature could have devastating effects on ice caps, marine life, and global climate patterns. Seeing glaciers retreating and ice shelves collapsing due to global warming made her understand how human activities impact nature.

The visit emphasised the interconnectedness of all life forms and how melting Antarctic ice could lead to rising sea levels, threatening coastal regions worldwide. She realised that preserving Antarctica means preserving humanity's future, reinforcing the importance of sustainable living and environmental conservation.

Set-II

5. A. 42, M.G. Road
Gwalior

21st March, 20XX

The Principal
M.V. Public School
Shimla

Subject Application for the Post of Western Music Teacher

Respected Sir/Madam

This is in response to your advertisement in the daily newspaper dated 19th March, 20XX for the position of Western Music Teacher at M.V. Public School, Shimla. With a graduate degree in Music and over two years of teaching experience, I am confident in my ability to contribute positively to your institution.

I have a strong background in lesson planning, training students for competitions and performances, and organising school bands, orchestras and choir groups. Additionally, my proficiency in technology-aided music education and computer applications enables me to create engaging learning experiences for students.

I am passionate about nurturing young talents and fostering an appreciation for music. I am eager to bring my expertise to your esteemed school and contribute to its vibrant musical culture.

I have attached my bio-data for your consideration. I would be grateful for an opportunity to discuss my qualifications further.

Looking forward to your positive response.

Yours sincerely
Nidhi

Enclosure: Bio-data

Bio-Data

Name	Nidhi
Address	42, M.G. Road, Gwalior
Contact	958XXXXX29
Email	nidhi2025@gmail.com
Date of Birth	19th May, 1996
Nationality	Indian

Educational Qualifications

Name of the Exam	Name of the Institute	Year	Percentage/ GPA
Diploma in Western Music	ABC University	2017	77%
B.A. in Music	PQR University	2015	82%

Work Experience

- **Western Music Teacher**, XYZ School, Gwalior (2019 to Present)
- Designed and implemented music lesson plans.
- Prepared students for inter-school and national-level music competitions.
- Organised annual school music events and choir performances.

Skills

- Lesson planning and execution
- Organising school bands, orchestras, and choir groups
- Training students for competitions and performances
- Proficiency in technology-aided music education
- Knowledge of music software and computer applications

Languages Known

- English, Hindi

References

- Mia Mahant, Music Teacher, XYZ School
- Swati Kumar, Dept. Head, XYZ School

Or

B. 14, A, R. P. Nagar
New Delhi

22nd March, 20XX

The Editor
The Times of India
New Delhi

Subject Concern Over Rapid Urban Sprawl and its Environmental Impact

Respected Sir/Madam

Through the columns of your esteemed newspaper, I would like to express my deep concern over the rapid expansion of urban sprawl, which is leading to severe environmental degradation. Urban sprawl, the uncontrolled expansion of cities, is primarily driven by the demand for more living space. However, this growth comes at the cost of air and water pollution, deforestation, and the destruction of environmentally sensitive areas.

In the long run, urban sprawl increases traffic congestion, depletes natural resources, and reduces air quality, negatively impacting public health. To mitigate these issues, cities must adopt effective urban planning, including sustainable infrastructure, green spaces, and efficient public transport to reduce reliance on private vehicles.

It is crucial that authorities prioritise smart urban design to balance development with environmental conservation. Public awareness and government intervention can help curb the harmful effects of urban sprawl.

Yours sincerely

Sonal

6. A.

Time Management: A Key to Success

by Seema, Class XII-C

In today's competitive world, students are expected to excel in multiple fields, from academics to extracurricular activities. However, poor time management often leads to stress, anxiety, and declining performance.

Time management is the ability to plan and control how much time is spent on different activities. It helps students stay organised, meet deadlines, and reduce unnecessary pressure. Setting achievable goals is essential. Unrealistic expectations lead to frustration, while well-defined, practical goals keep students motivated and focused.

Creating a to-do list, setting deadlines, and avoiding distractions like social media can help students stay on track. Focusing on urgent and important tasks first ensures better productivity.

Using digital planners, reminders, and educational apps can assist in scheduling tasks efficiently. Technology, if used wisely, can be a great tool for time management.

By developing this essential skill, students can balance academics and personal life, leading to success and reduced stress.

Or

B.

Republic Day Celebrations at XYZ School

by Heena, Class XII-E

XYZ School celebrated the Republic Day with great enthusiasm and patriotism on 26th January, 20XX. The event began with the hoisting of the national flag by the Principal, followed by the national anthem. Students from various grades participated in a vibrant cultural programme that included patriotic songs, dances, and a skit highlighting India's journey to democracy.

The highlight of the event was the speech competition on the significance of the Constitution, where students eloquently expressed their thoughts. A march-past by the school's NCC cadets added to the patriotic fervour. Teachers and students also took a pledge to uphold the values of justice, liberty, and equality.

The celebrations instilled a deep sense of nationalism and unity among students. The event concluded with a heartfelt vote of thanks by the Head Boy, leaving the school community inspired and proud to be citizens of India.

11. (i) The Third Level in Jack Finney's story symbolises an escape from reality and a yearning for a simpler, stress-free past. It represents a psychological refuge for Charley who is troubled by the anxieties of modern life. The story explores the theme of time travel, nostalgia and human imagination.

(ii) Dr. Sadao's remark reflects his practicality and inner conflict between duty and humanity. Though he saves the American soldier out of compassion, he remains aware of the risks involved. His words indicate a firm yet reluctant detachment, showing his sense of responsibility, ethical dilemma and ultimate decision to let the prisoner go.

(iii) Mr. Lamb's words reflect his optimistic and philosophical outlook on life. Despite his physical disability and loneliness, he finds joy and meaning in everything around him. His belief that an 'empty house' is actually 'full' symbolises his ability to see beauty, hope, and companionship in solitude.

12. A. Both Mahatma Gandhi's and Franklin D. Roosevelt's statements emphasise that fear is the biggest obstacle to freedom and progress. This idea is reflected in the struggles of the Champaran sharecroppers and William Douglas in their respective situations.

The Champaran sharecroppers lived in constant fear of the British landlords, who exploited them through unfair agreements. Gandhi helped them realise that true relief would come from overcoming fear and standing up for their rights. His leadership gave them the confidence to resist oppression and demand justice.

Similarly, William Douglas, in 'Deep Water', suffered from a deep-seated fear of water due to a childhood incident. This fear crippled his confidence and limited his experiences. However, through determination and systematic training, he conquered his fear, proving that freedom from fear leads to personal growth and empowerment.

Both stories highlight that fear enslaves people, and overcoming it is the first step toward true liberation.

Or

B. Sophie from 'Going Places' and Franz from 'The Last Lesson' are caught in their own unrealistic worlds, leading to consequences that shape their understanding of life.

Sophie is an escapist and a dreamer, constantly weaving fantasies about meeting famous people like Danny Casey. She refuses to accept her family's working-class reality and aspires for a glamorous life. However, her inability to differentiate dreams from reality leaves her disappointed and disillusioned when her fantasies do not come true.

On the other hand, Franz loves to skip school and avoid studies, unaware of the importance of education. His carefree attitude changes when he realises that this is his last French lesson, as German will replace French in Alsace. This realisation fills him with regret, but it is too late to change the past.

Both characters fail to face reality in time-Sophie remains trapped in illusions, while Franz learns his lesson only when his chance is lost.

13. A. Derry, the protagonist in 'On the Face of It', is deeply affected by his facial disfigurement, which makes him a victim of self-pity. His burnt face becomes the center of his identity, and he isolates himself from society, believing that people only see him as ugly. He assumes that others pity or fear him, which leads to his own self-hatred and low self-esteem.

Derry's behaviour reflects his negative mindset. He avoids social interactions and believes he will always be unloved. However, his encounter with Mr. Lamb, an optimistic and kind-hearted man with a disability, helps him realise that his scars do not define him. Mr. Lamb teaches him that life is about how one perceives oneself, not how others perceive them.

Ultimately, Derry begins to break free from his self-pity, realising that he must face the world with confidence, rather than letting his fears control him.

Or

B. Tishani Doshi's Journey to the End of the Earth serves as an awakening call about the fragile state of our environment. Through her visit to Antarctica, she witnesses firsthand how small environmental changes can lead to significant consequences. The region, often considered the Earth's last untouched landscape, acts as a climate archive, revealing the past and predicting the future.

She highlights that rising global temperatures are accelerating the melting of glaciers, disrupting marine ecosystems, and threatening biodiversity. Even a slight increase in temperature can cause glacial melting, rising sea levels, and extreme weather events worldwide. The lesson warns that human activities, including deforestation, pollution, and carbon emissions, are pushing the planet toward irreversible damage.

Doshi emphasises that understanding and preserving nature is crucial for survival. Through her journey, she urges humanity to take responsibility for its actions and adopt sustainable practices before it is too late.

Set-III

5. A. 35, Jyoti Apartments
Hyderabad

22nd March, 20XX

The HR Manager
WE24 Media Network
12, J.M. Road, Jaipur

Subject Application for the Post of News Reporter

Sir/Madam

This is in response to your advertisement in the daily newspaper dated 20th March, 20XX for the position of News Reporter at WE24 Media Network, Jaipur. With a graduate degree in Journalism and Mass Communication and over two years of experience in the field, I believe I possess the necessary skills and expertise required for this role.

I have strong communication, writing, and research skills, along with proficiency in computers and current affairs. My experience in news reporting, content creation, and investigative journalism has prepared me to contribute effectively to your esteemed organisation.

I have attached my biodata for your kind consideration. I look forward to an opportunity to discuss my application further.

Yours sincerely
Swati

Bio-Data

Name	Swati
Address	35, Jyoti Apartments, Hyderabad
Contact	9559XXXXXX
Email	Swati1995@gmail.com
Date of Birth	28th February, 1995
Nationality	Indian

Educational Qualifications

Name of the Exam	Name of the Institute	Year
B.A. in Journalism & Mass Communication	ABC University	2016

Work Experience

- News Reporter XYZ Network, Hyderabad (2018 to Present)
- Researched and covered breaking news stories.
- Conducted interviews and wrote detailed reports.
- Produced content for digital and print media.

Skills

- Excellent communication and writing skills
- Strong research and investigative skills
- Proficiency in computer applications and media tools
- In-depth knowledge of current affairs

Languages Known

- English, Hindi

References

- Available upon request

Or

B. 40, J.N. Colony
Pune

22nd March, 20XX

The Editor
The Times Daily
Pune

Subject Rising Concern of Adolescent Obesity

Sir/Madam

Through the columns of your esteemed newspaper, I would like to express my deep concern over the growing concern of adolescent obesity in India due to poor dietary habits and lack of physical activity. Excessive consumption of junk food and sugary drinks, combined with a sedentary lifestyle, has led to severe health issues among teenagers.

To combat this, schools and parents must promote healthy eating habits and encourage physical activities. Schools should organise sports programmes, yoga sessions, and awareness campaigns. Parents must ensure home-cooked nutritious meals and regulate screen time. The media should actively discourage unhealthy food advertisements and create awareness about fitness and balanced diets.

A collective effort is essential to tackle adolescent obesity. Encouraging a healthy lifestyle today will ensure a healthier future for our youth. I hope this issue is highlighted for immediate action.

Yours sincerely
Mohan Lal

6. A.

The Healing Power of Laughter Therapy
by Anmol

In today's stressful world, mental health issues like depression and anxiety are on the rise. Laughter therapy is an effective alternative approach to promoting well-being. It involves deliberate laughter sessions to improve emotional and physical health.

Laughter triggers the release of endorphins, the body's natural feel-good chemicals, reducing stress and anxiety. It strengthens the immune system, improves blood circulation, and relieves pain. Emotionally, it helps individuals develop a positive mindset and enhances resilience against life's challenges.

Beyond health benefits, laughter fosters social connections. It breaks barriers, enhances communication and strengthens relationships. Shared laughter creates a sense of belonging and unity, making people feel more connected.

Incorporating laughter therapy into daily life-through laughter clubs, social interactions, or even watching comedy-can transform mental and physical health. A hearty laugh truly is the best medicine!

Or

B.

Zonal Football Match Finals: A Thrilling Showdown
by Pawan, Student Reporter (XII B)

The Zonal Football Match Finals were held on 21st March, 20XX in the school playground, witnessing an intense face-off between St. Xavier's School and Greenfield Public School. Football enthusiasts and supporters gathered in large numbers, creating an electrifying atmosphere.

The match kicked off with both teams displaying remarkable skill and teamwork. The first half remained goalless, with both sides fiercely defending their posts. However, in the second half, St. Xavier's scored the winning goal, securing victory with a 1-0 score.

The Principal and the Chief Guest, a former football player, awarded the winners with the championship trophy. The event showcased sportsmanship, dedication, and teamwork, inspiring young players to excel in football.

The match concluded with loud cheers and celebrations, marking another successful sporting event in our school's history.

11. (i) Annan played a crucial role in Bama's success by making her aware of the discrimination faced by their community and encouraging her to focus on education as a means of empowerment. He advised her to study hard and excel academically, which motivated her to overcome societal barriers and achieve success in life.

(ii) Charley envisioned Galesburg in 1894 as a peaceful, picturesque town with tree-lined streets, large houses, and sprawling lawns. He imagined people relaxing on their verandas, enjoying a stress-free life, reflecting his longing for an era of simplicity and security, free from the pressures of modern civilisation.

(iii) Dr. Sadao agreed to the General's proposal of sending assassins out of practical necessity and self-preservation. He was torn between his duty as a doctor and his loyalty to Japan. Fearing suspicion and repercussions, he outwardly complied but his conscience ultimately led him to help the prisoner escape safely.

12. A. For answer refer to Long Answer Question No. 4 on page no. 204.

B. For answer refer to Long Answer Question No. 6 on page no. 218.

13. A. Antarctica, the Earth's most pristine and remote continent, holds invaluable clues to the planet's geological past. In 'Journey to the End of the Earth', Tishani Doshi highlights how this icy landmass preserves evidence of ancient climatic and geological transformations. Millions of years ago, Antarctica was part of the supercontinent Gondwana, which gradually broke apart due to continental drift. Fossils, rock formations, and ice cores found here provide insights into Earth's past climates, biodiversity, and tectonic shifts.

The thick ice sheets of Antarctica store air bubbles from millions of years ago, helping scientists study past atmospheric conditions. These studies are crucial in understanding climate change and global warming, as Antarctica's melting ice directly impacts rising sea levels.

Thus, Antarctica serves as a time capsule, revealing Earth's history and warning us about the effects of human-induced climate change. Preserving it is essential for the future of our planet.

Or

B. Bama and Zitkala-Sa, in 'Memories of Childhood', highlight how education empowers individuals to overcome social discrimination and injustice. Both faced oppression but used education as a tool to fight back.

Bama, a Dalit girl, experienced caste discrimination in her village. She realised that knowledge was the key to breaking social barriers and worked hard in her studies, eventually achieving success. Education gave her the strength to challenge oppression and inspire others.

Zitkala-Sa, a Native American girl, was forced into a missionary school, where she faced cultural erasure and humiliation. Despite this, she pursued education, becoming a writer and activist advocating for Indigenous rights.

Both girls endured discrimination, humiliation, and struggle, yet their determination and pursuit of education helped them rise above injustice. Their stories prove that education is the most powerful weapon to challenge social evils and uplift marginalised communities.

SAMPLE QUESTION PAPER 1

A Highly simulated Sample Question Paper for CBSE Class XII

ENGLISH CORE

GENERAL INSTRUCTIONS

1. This question paper has **13** questions. All questions are compulsory.
2. This question paper contains **three** sections— **Section A** : Reading Skills, **Section B** : Creative Writing Skills and **Section C** : Literature.
3. Attempt all questions based on specific instructions for each part. Write the correct question number and part there of in your answer sheet.
4. Separate instructions are given with each question/part, wherever necessary.
5. Adhere to the prescribed word limit while answering the questions.

TIME : 3 HOURS ***MAX. MARKS : 80***

SECTION - A

[22 Marks]

Reading Skills

1. *Read the passage given below.* **12M**

1. Many of us believe that 'small' means 'insignificant'. We believe that small actions and choices do not have much impact on our lives. We think that it is only the big things, the big actions and the big decisions that really count. But when you look at the lives of all great people, you will see that they built their character through small decisions, small choices and small actions that they performed every day. They transformed their lives through a step-by-step or day-by-day approach. They nurtured and nourished their good habits and chipped away at their bad habits, one step at a time. It was their small day-to-day decisions that added up to make a tremendous difference in the long run. Indeed, in matters of personal growth and character building, there is no such thing as an overnight success.
2. Growth always occurs through a sequential series of stages. There is an organic process to growth. When we look at children growing up, we can see this process at work: the child first learns to crawl, then to stand and walk, and finally to run. The same is true in the natural world. The soil must first be tilled, and then the seed must be sowed. Next, it must be nurtured with enough water and sunlight, and only then will it grow, bear fruit and finally ripen and be ready to eat.
3. Gandhi understood this organic process and used this universal law of nature to his benefit. Gandhi grew in small ways, in his day-to-day affairs. He did not wake up one day and find himself to be the 'Mahatma'. In fact, there was nothing much in his early life that showed signs of greatness. But from his mid-twenties onwards, he deliberately and consistently attempted to change himself, reform himself and grow in some small way every day. Day-by-day, hour-by-hour, he risked failure, experimented and learnt from mistakes. In small and large situations alike, he took up rather than avoiding responsibility.

4. People have always marvelled at the effortless way in which Gandhi could accomplish the most difficult tasks. He displayed a great deal of self-mastery and discipline that was amazing. These things did not come easily to him. Years of practice and disciplined training went into making his successes possible. Very few saw his struggles, fears, doubts and anxieties, or his inner efforts to overcome them. They saw the victory, but not the struggle.
5. This is a common factor in the lives of all great people: they exercised their freedoms and choices in small ways that made great impact on their lives and their environment. Each of their small decisions and actions, added up to have a profound impact in the long run. By understanding this principle, we can move forward with confidence in the direction of our dreams. Often when our 'ideal goal' looks too far from us, we become easily discouraged, disheartened and pessimistic. However, when we choose to grow in small ways, taking small steps one at a time, performing it becomes easy.

Based on your understanding of the passage, answer the questions given below.

(i) According to paragraph, how do great people transform their lives? (2)

(ii) What does the line 'Chipped away at their bad habits' given in the passage mean? (1)

(iii) Complete the following sentence by choosing the correct option. (1)

Through the passage, the author had intended to state that ....

(a) big things, big actions and big decisions make a person great
(b) small actions and decisions are importatn in one's life
(c) overnight success is possible for all of us
(d) personal changes are not important.

(iv) How did Gandhiji become a successful leader? (1)

(v) How does the writer look at Gandhiji's life? (1)

(a) Idolisation (b) Objectively (c) Wonder (d) Both (a) and (c)

(vi) Provide one textual evidence to cite how distance from goals impacts us. (1)

(vii) What is the 'Universal Law of Nature' mentioned in the passage? (1)

(viii) Complete the analogy with one word. (1)

Calculatedly : Deliberately :: .... : Consistently

(a) Always (b) Invariably (c) Changing (d) Entirely

(ix) What is a common factor in the lives of a great people? How does it affect them? (1)

(x) What did Gandhi try to do after he was about 25 years old? (2)

2. *Read the passage given below.* **10M**

1. Politics and now Pollution keep Delhi forever in the news, but a third P (Population Growth) has gone missing from the discourse on the capital: population growth, which has soared during the last two decades, and its disastrous fallout.

   Already, India's capital city is the world's second most populous urban agglomeration. The future is even more frightening: a United Nations report released in mid-2018 says Delhi could be the world's most populous city by 2028 with 37.2 million people. That is eight million more in just 10 years.
2. According to the report called World Urbanisation Prospects 2018 by the Population Division of the UN Department of Economic and Social Affairs, the population of Delhi and its immediate neighbourhood is now estimated to be 29 million, second only to Tokyo with 37 million people. But Delhi will zoom past Tokyo, whose population is projected to decline to 36.8 million by 2028.

Will Delhi be worth living in? Can the city state of Delhi escape the pressures put on it by an ever expanding National Capital Region (NCR), which touches as far as Alwar now? Are we prepared at all for this population explosion?

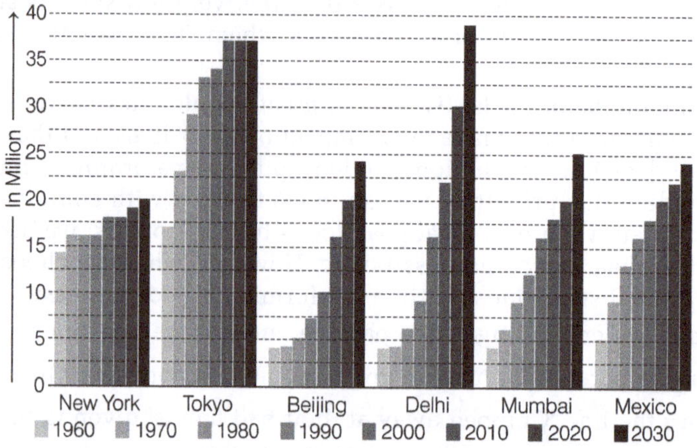

Projections for 2020 and 2030.

Population Growth in Major Global Cities

3. In a small office in Delhi's India Habitat Centre, a group of urban planners – all belonging to the National Institute of Urban Affairs (NIUA) – have just started collecting baseline data on land, housing, transport, environment, heritage, water, among others, for Master Plan for Delhi (MPD) 2041. "Our deadline for preparing the Master Plan is 2021. But unlike its earlier editions, it won't be a flat 20 year plan. This one will be divided into various achievables, say, for every five years," says Nilesh Rajadhyaksha, lead coordinator of MPD and urban specialist in NIUA.
4. The NIUA – an autonomous research and advisory body that comes under the Ministry of Housing and Urban Affairs – has been roped in by the Delhi Development Authority (DDA) to undertake this colossal strategy plan for Delhi 2041. The current master plan, MPD-2021, which was notified in 2007 and was prepared by an in-house team of the DDA, would expire in 2021.
5. The concern is that a sense of urgency to fix Delhi is missing. Many crucial elements of MPD-2021 still remain on paper, with just two years left for the plan to expire. AK Jain, former commissioner-planning in DDA and key architect of MPD-2021, gives a long list of what have not been implemented. The master plan talks about brownfield redevelopment of rehabilitation colonies such as Lajpat Nagar, Old Rajendra Nagar and Mukherjee Nagar, which were originally meant for Partition refugees. Nothing has been done on that front so far nor for the redevelopment of 45 resettlement colonies such as Ambedkar Nagar and Trilokpuri, which were developed during Emergency to rehabilitate slum dwellers. The rejuvenation of the Yamuna is also on the plan, but the river remains severely polluted in the Delhi stretch.

   Will Delhi be liveable? Jain is not very hopeful. He says Delhi won't be a highly liveable city even if the master plan is implemented in its entirety. "Delhi is part of the National Capital Region (NCR). So, Delhi's development can't happen in isolation," he explains.

Based on your understanding of the passage, answer the questions given below.

(i) Complete the sentence appropriately.

If the Master plan is implemented in its entirety, then .... (1)

(ii) "The concern is that a sense of urgency to fix Delhi is missing." With reference to this statement, select the correct inference from the following. (1)

(a) Delhi needs to be evacuated sooner or later

(b) The need to control population in Delhi is crucial

(c) The resources in Delhi needs to be readjusted according to its rising population

(d) Delhi's resources will extinguish soon

(iii) Why does the passage say that the future is frightening for the Indian capital city? What is the crucial issue regarding Master plans created for Delhi? (2)

(iv) Paragraph 5 includes words — 'concerns' and 'plans'. (1)

Classify the following sentences as 'concern' or 'plan'.

Sentence 1 The every expanding NCR region is becoming an overcrowded space due to increasing population.

Sentence 2 A strategy is being charted cut by collaborating with many government authories to make Delhi livable.

(v) Prateek lives in Noida while his best friend Akanksha lives in Alwar region. They had a debate on inclusion of regions in the ever expanding National Capital Region (NCR). (1)

Select the option that identifies the correct regions included in the NCR.

(a) NCR — Delhi, Alwar, Noida, Gurugram (b) NCR — Alwar, Noida, Rajasthan

(c) NCR — Delhi, Alwar, Uttar Pradesh (d) NCR — Delhi, Noida, Tokyo

(vi) Who did the Delhi Developmental Authority hire to look into the development of Delhi? (1)

(vii) Why does Jain says that Delhi will not be liveable? (2)

(viii) The urban planners are collecting data based on .... (1)

(a) heritage (b) land (c) transport (d) All of these

SECTION - B

Creative Writing Skills [18 Marks]

Note All details presented in the questions are imaginary and created for assessment purpose.

3. Attempt **Any One** from A and B given below. (4)

A. Every year in the central park of the city, a flower show is held in the month of February. Your school has received a circular from the District Collector inviting your students to visit it. Write a notice in about 50 words informing the students about the show and advising them to go and enjoy it. You are Navtej/Navita, Head Boy/Head Girl, Sunrise Public School, Surat.

Or

B. You are Divya, Secretary of the History Club of Saraswati Vidya Mandir School. Draft a notice in not more than 50 words informing the students about a proposed visit to some important historical sites in your city.

4. Attempt **Any One** from A and B given below. (4)

A. Your school is organising its Annual Day Function next month in one of the prestigious auditoriums of your city. Draft an invitation giving all the essential details. Do not forget to include necessary instructions against mobile phones and cameras. (50 words)

Or

B. You are Manoj /Manvi. You have been invited to attend a birthday party of your closest friend. Draft a reply accepting the invite in not more than 50 words.

5. Attempt **Any One** from A and B given below. (5)

A. You are Satish/Sarita of Class-XII. Write a letter to the Editor of a leading National Daily highlighting the unfriendly attitude of the staff of the 'Grameen Seva' transport buses. You can use the following clues. (120-150 words)

- Hundreds of people travel
- Never on time
- Causes immense chaos
- Problems while boarding
- Stops at random locations

Or

B. You are Parth/Prerna of M-114, Najafgarh, Delhi-110044. You would like to apply for the post of Marketing Manager in a reputed firm in Mumbai after reading an advertisement. Write a letter in 120-150 words applying for the job. Also, give your biodata. (120-150 words)

WANTED

Red Chilli Enterprises invites applicants for the post of the Marketing Manager in Mumbai. The applicant must have the required education from a reputed institute along with work experience. Fresher's can also apply. All interested candidates can send their application to the Public Relations Officer, Red Chilli Enterprises, Mumbai.

6. Attempt **Any One** from A and B given below. (5)

A. You are Shruti of Class XII-D. You are a member of the Environment Society of your school. Write an article on 'Reduce Environmental Pollution Through Education and Legislation'. You can take help from the following clues. (120-150 words)

- Environment getting destroyed due to pollutants and exploitation of natural resources
- Contamination of environment causes many diseases
- People need to be educated about using environment friendly items

Or

B. Aggressive driving has been a problem on our roads for a while and it seems to be only getting worse. Incidents of screaming, rude gestures and sometimes even violence are reported frequently on our roads, resulting into road rage. As Lalit/Lalita, a Staff Correspondent for 'The Times of India', write a report on one such incident of road rage witnessed by you with the help of the following clues. (120-150 words)

- A man fired a truck driver
- Shot missed saving the person
- The criminal was arrested
- Case of attempted murder

SECTION - C

Literature Textbooks

[40 Marks]

7. Read the given extracts and answer the questions for **any one** of the two given. (1 × 6 = 6)

A.

It would be an exotic moment
without rush, without engines,
we would all be together
in a sudden strangeness. *(Keeping Quiet)*

(i) What does the phrase 'without rush, without engines' mean? (1)

(ii) In the given passage, the poet promotes (1)

(a) peace (b) self-introspection (c) fraternity (d) All of these

(iii) Complete the sentence appropriately.

The use of the word 'sudden' indicates .... (1)

(iv) Select the correct option from those given in brackets, to fill in the blank. (1)

The poet wants peace and .... (calmness/calamity).

(v) Read the assertion and the reason below, with reference to the given extract. (1)

Assertion (A) the poet describes a moment "Without rust, without engines" to emphasise the rarity and peace of silence.

Reason (R) In the poem, the absence of human activity symbolises a temporary escape from industrialisation and disconnection, creating an unusual unity among people.

(a) Both (A) and (R) are true, and (R) is the correct explanation of (A).
(b) Both (A) and (R) are true, but (R) is not the correct explanation of (A).
(c) (A) is true, but (R) is false.
(d) (A) is false, but (R) is true.

(vi) Based on the given lines, mention which expression has used alliteration. (1)

Or

B.

The little old house was out with a little new shed
In front at the edge of the road where the traffic sped,
A roadside stand that too pathetically pled,
It would not be fair to say for a dole of bread,
But for some of the money, the cash, whose flow supports
The flower of cities from sinking and withering faint. *(A Roadside Stand)*

(i) Select the line that suggests the following. (1)

The deprived people with pitiless clarity were begging.

(ii) Who are referred to as 'the flower of cities'? (1)

(a) The kind hearted people (b) City dwellers
(c) Politicians (d) Journalists

(iii) Complete the sentence appropriately.

The poet uses the word 'pathetic' to .... (1)

(iv) Select the correct option from those given in bracket, to fill in the blanks.

The phrase 'too pathetically pled' means that by putting up the shed the owner was desperately .... (pleading/commanding to the rich city folks to stop at his stand. (1)

FULLY SOLVED

(v) Read the Assertion (A) and the Reason (R) below, with reference to the given extract. (1)

Assertion (A) The roadside stand in the poem seeks "some of the money, the cash" to prevent the rural people from "sinking and withering faint".

Reason (R) The stand owners are depicted as begging for survival resources because they cannot sustain themselves in a rural setting without external financial support.

(a) Both (A) and (R) are true, and (R) is the correct explanation of (A).
(b) Both (A) and (R) are true, but (R) is not the correct explanation of (A).
(c) (A) is true, but (R) is false.
(d) (A) is false, but (R) is true.

(vi) Where was the new shed put up? What was its purpose? (1)

8. Read the given extracts and answer the questions for **any one** of the two given. (1 × 4 = 4)

A. MR. LAMB Real one got blown off, years back. Lamey-Lamb, some kids say. Haven't you heard them? You will. Lamey-Lamb. It fits. Doesn't trouble me.

DERRY But you can put on trousers and cover it up and no one sees, they don't have to notice and stare.

MR. LAMB Some do. Some don't. They get tired of it, in the end. There's plenty of other things to stare at.

DERRY Like my face.

(i) Complete the following suitably.
People would stare at Derry's face because .... (1)

(ii) How does Mr. Lamb's attitude towards his disability differ from Derry's feelings about his own physical appearance. (1)

(iii) The writer uses the phrase. 'Real one' in the extract .... What do you think it refers to? (1)

(a) real hand (b) real leg (c) real thumb (d) real home

(iv) What other things do Mr. Lamb refer to which could be stared at? (1)

Or

B. Everyone stood transfixed in stupefaction. They looked wildly at each other and blinked. "O wise prophets! It was I who spoke." This time there were no grounds for doubt. It was the infant born just ten days ago who had enunciated the words so clearly. The chief astrologer took off his spectacles and gazed intently at the baby. "All those who are born will one day have to die. We don't need your predictions to know that. There would be some sense in it if you could tell us the manner of that death," the royal infant uttered these words in his little squeaky voice.

(i) Complete the following suitably. (1)

The story 'The Tiger King' is a work of fantasy because ....

(ii) What does the reaction of the people present reveal about their beliefs and expectations. (1)

(iii) Everyone was stupefied because .... (1)

Select the suitable option to complete the sentence above.
(a) they had seen a tiger
(b) they had come across an infant of only 10 days who was speaking fluently.
(c) the astrologer predicted something strange
(d) they saw a strange animal.

FULLY SOLVED

(iv) Identify and explain the literary devices used in line, Everyone stood transfixed in stratification. They looked wildly at each other and blinked." Discuss how it adds to the tone of the passage. (1)

9. Read the given extracts and answer the questions for **any one** of the two given. (1 × 6 = 6)

A. I heard M. Hamel say to me, "I won't scold you, little Franz; you must feel bad enough. See how it is! Every day we have said to ourselves, 'Bah! I've plenty of time. I'll learn it tomorrow.' And now you see where we've come out. Ah, that's the great trouble with Alsace; she puts off learning till tomorrow.

(i) Why would Franz by feeling bad? (1)

(ii) Select the correct option from those given in the bracket to fill in the blank. (1)

'Where we've come out' indicates that people of Alsace did not give .... (importance/ignorance) to learning French.

(iii) Complete the following suitably. (1)

The phrase 'puts off' suggests that ....

(iv) "She puts off learning till tomorrow." What does this line indicate about the people of Alsace? (1)

(v) Select the textual option that is closst to indicating a sense of procrastination. (1)

(a) 'I won't scold you ....' (b) 'Bah! I have plenty of time ......'
(c) That's great trouble with Alsace (d) You must feel bad enough

(vi) The story 'The Last Lesson' highlights which human tendency? (1)

(a) Chauvinism (b) Procastination
(c) Courage (d) Cowardice

Or

B. My American publisher said while she loved my book, she didn't expect to sell more than 3,000 copies in a country where nobody has seen a cathedral or studies Latin. So I was given an advance for 3,000 copies, but in the end it sold two or three million in the U.S.

A lot of books have been written about the medieval past for before mine. I think the success of the book is a mystery. Nobody can predict it. I think if I had written 'The Name of the Rose' ten years earlier or ten years later, it wouldn't have been the same. Why it worked at that time is a mystery.

(i) What does the American publisher say to Umberto Eco? (1)

(ii) Select the correct option from those given in bracket fill in the blank. (1)

The line 'Why it worked at that time is a mystery' indicates Eco's .... (surprise/shock)

(iii) Complete the following with a suitable reason. (1)

The author says that the success of the book is a mystery because ....

(iv) Explain the reason for the Eco's publisher's belief regarding the sale of his book. (1)

(v) Which is the correct description of 'The Name of the Rose'? (1)

(a) Detective Medieval mystery (b) Romantic Medieval drama
(c) Medieval religious novella (d) Detective thriller

(vi) Which quality can be associated with Umberto Eco? (1)

(a) Wise (b) Down to earth
(c) Egoist (d) Both (a) and (b)

10. Answer **Any Five** *of the following six questions in 40-50 words each.* (2 × 5 = 10)

(i) Why don't the people in Firozabad organise themselves into a cooperative? *(Lost Spring)*

(ii) 'The God That Failed' was the composition of six eminent men of letters. Describe. *(Poets and Pancakes)*

(iii) What are we single minded about? *(Keeping Quiet)*

(iv) Write about the poet's fear as a child. Why does it surface when she is going to the airport? *(My Mother at Sixty-six)*

(v) Explain what makes human beings love life inspite of all the troubles they face. *(A Thing of Beauty)*

(vi) How did the instructor 'build a swimmer' out of Douglas? (*Deep water*)

11. Answer **Any Two** *of the following three questions in 40-50 words each.* (2 × 2 = 4)

(i) Discuss what the Psychiatrist thought about Charley's stamp collection. Why did Charley not agree with him? *(The Third level)*

(ii) What are Geoff Green's reasons for including high school students in the 'Students on Ice' Expedition? (Journey to the end of the Earth)

(iii) Interpret the two significant things that happened on the seventh day in 'The Enemy'.

12. Answer **Any One** of the following two questions in about 120-150 words. (5)

A. Both 'Deep Water' and 'The Rattrap' explore themes of fear, transformation and the power of human resilience.

Compare and contrast the protagonists' struggles and eventual triumphs. How do these stories highlight the significance of overcoming obstacles and embracing kindness in one's journey? Discuss with relevant examples from both texts.

Or

B. The poems 'Keeping Quiet' by Pablo Neruda and 'A Thing of Beauty' by John Keats emphasise the importance of peace, introspection, and the beauty of life.

Compare and contrast how these poems convey the significance of inner peace and the appreciation of life's beauty in overcoming negativity and suffering.

13. Answer **Any One** of the following two questions in 120-150 words. (5)

A. As long as men are free to ask what they must; free to say what they think; free to think what they will and free to follow their religious beliefs – only then there exists democracy. What reforms can be advocated in order to avert the cruelties experienced by Zitkala-Sa and observed by Bama? *(Memories of Childhood)*

Or

B. Derry says "It's not what you look like; it's what you are inside." What are the qualities this sentence encourages people to have? *(On the Face of it)*

ANSWERS

1. (i) To transform their lives, great people approach their lives in a day-to-day-lives approach. They change and reform themselves slowly and believe in performing every day.

(ii) The line 'chipped away at their bad habits' means steadily gave up bad habits.

(iii) (b) small actions and decisions are important in one's life

(iv) Gandhiji became a successful leader by practicing a great deal of self mastery and discipline.

(v) (d) Both (a) and (c)

FULLY SOLVED

(vi) The distance from goals impacts the way we approach a situation. If the goal is at a greater distance, we become discouraged and pessimistic in our approach.

(vii) The Universal Law of Nature as mentioned in the passage is the organic process of growth.

(viii) (b) Invariably

(ix) A common factor in the lives of a great people is that they exercise their freedom and choices in small ways. This impacts their lives and environment in the long run of life.

(x) After Gandhiji turned 25, he deliberately and consistently tried to change, reform and grow to become a better version of himself.

2. (i) Delhi will not remain a highly liveable city as its resources will dwindle.

(ii) (c) The resources in Delhi needs to be readjusted according to its rising population.

(iii) The passage states that the future of Delhi is frightening because of its rising population. The crucial issue regarding the Master plans created for Delhi is that there is no urgency in implementing the plan to completion.

(iv) **Statement 1** concern

Statement 2 Plan

(v) (a) NCR — Delhi, Alwar, Noida, Gurugram

(vi) The Delhi Developmental Authority hired the NIUA to look into the development of Delhi.

(vii) Jain states that Delhi will not be a highly livable city because its development as a National Capital region means that it will initiate the development of other regions. This will lead to a further increase in population making it not liveable.

(viii) (d) All of these

3. A.

Sunrise Public School, Surat

NOTICE

11th February, 20XX

Flower Show in Central Park

This is to inform all the students that Mr. Salim Altaf, District Collector, has invited us to the flower show being held in Central Park from 14th February to 22nd February. The show timings are 11:00 am to 5:00 pm. Students may collect their entry passes from the undersigned by 12th February. All students and staff are recommended to enjoy the wide variety of flowers on display there.

Navita

(Head Girl)

Or

B.

Saraswati Vidya Mandir School

NOTICE

22nd September, 20XX

A Visit to Historical Sites

All students are hereby informed of a proposed educational visit to a few important historical sites in our city which is likely to be scheduled between the 28th September and the 30th September. Interested members of the club and all other interested candidates who want to visit historical places are required to pay 550 (inclusive of transport and snacks) during the zero period to the undersigned by 25th September. For further details, contact the undersigned.

Divya

(Secretary of History Club)

4. A.

The Management, Staff and Students of
Sarvodaya Senior Secondary School, Panchkula
cordially invite you to their

ANNUAL DAY FUNCTION

at 6:00 PM on Saturday, 4th December, 20XX

in State Auditorium, Sector 14, Panchkula

Shri Ishwar Chand

Secretary of Higher Education, Ministry of HRD, Government of India has kindly consented to be the Chief Guest.

RSVP
Sanjiv Khanna
Registrar
Ph. No. 88910XXXXX

Directions
- This card allows two persons only.
- Please be seated by 5:30 PM.
- The use of mobile phones and cameras is prohibited.

Or

B. 421, MIG Flats
Mayur Vihar, New Delhi

15th July, 20XX

Dear Raashi
I have received your invitation for your birthday party on 21st July, 20XX at 5:00 PM at Café Echoes. I am extremely happy to know that all our old friends are likely to be there. I would like to confirm my participation. Looking forward to the momentous occasion.

With love
Manoj/Manvi

5. A. 237/9 Venkat Colony
Vasant Nagar
Delhi - 110078

1st January, 20XX

The Editor
National Daily
New Delhi

Subject *Non-Cooperation of the Staff of 'Grameen Seva' Transport Buses*

Sir/Ma'am

Through the columns of your esteemed newspaper, I want to highlight the issues faced by daily commuters due to the non-cooperation of the staff of the 'Grameen Seva' transport buses.

We all know that hundreds of commuters travel daily in these buses. They face issues while boarding, alighting and purchasing tickets, all because of total inefficiency of the operating staff of these buses.

The buses never run on time and if queried about the reason, a rude answer is given. Buses stop at random points, rather than at designated stops which causes immense chaos and confusion amongst the waiting people as they have to run in either direction for boarding.

I had earlier complained to senior officials in the State Transport Authority (STA) highlighting the plight of commuters, but no response has been received from them so far. I hope the publication of this letter will act as a wake-up call for the STA officials to take suitable action and redress the commuter problems.

Thanking you

Yours sincerely

Satish

Or

B. M-114, Najafgarh
Delhi-110044

16th January, 20XX

The Public Relations Officer
Red Chili Enterprises
Mumbai

Subject *Application for the Post of Marketing Manager*

Sir/Ma'am

In response to your advertisement in the 'Hindustan Times' dated January, 20XX for the post of a Marketing Manager, I hereby offer my candidature for the same.

I possess requisite qualifications and experience fulfilling the conditions laid down in your advertisement. I have completed my MBA in Marketing Management from Indian Institute of Management Studies with 70% marks. I have also got one year working experience in XYZ Enterprises, Mumbai.

I am enclosing my detailed resume for your perusal. You may call me for an interview on any date as per your convenience. I shall be able to join my duties at one month's notice if appointed.

Thanking You

Yours sincerely

Parth

Enclosure: Resume

Resume

Name Parth
Father's Name Mr. Karan
Date of Birth 14th May, 1995
Address M-114, Najafgarh, Delhi-110044
E-mail pr123@gmail.com
Nationality Indian

Educational Qualification

Name of the Exam	Name of the Institute	Year	Percentage/GPA
MBA	IIMS	20XX	70%
B. Com (Hons)	Delhi University	20XX	76%

Hobbies Music, Reading, Photography
Languages Known Hindi, English, Spanish
Experience Currently working as an Marketing Manager at XYZ Enterprises
References Dr. Mohit Choudhary, Marketing Head in XYZ enterprises

6. A. **Reduce Environmental Pollution Through Education and Legislation**

by Shruti, Class XII-D

Our environment, whether it is the atmosphere, the water bodies or the land areas, is getting more and more polluted every day. To stop this trend, environmental protection has become a necessity today. The multiple factors destroying our environment include, various types of solid, liquid and gaseous pollutants as well as unhindered exploitation of natural resources.

FULLY SOLVED

All this is happening to support the ever growing population of the world and its growing needs. The contamination of the environment is also being linked to some of the diseases that are prevalent today. Yet, most people do not know about this problem. So, an awareness must be created urgently so that people can modify their activities suitably.

Environmental pollution is becoming an increasingly difficult problem that needs to be taken care of as soon as possible. In this regard, people can be educated regarding usage and disposal of certain items, legislations can be tailored for particular areas of the country, usage of environment friendly items can be promoted and so on.

It is high time that everyone knows that, if the current methods of handling the world's environmental problems continue, catastrophic consequences can follow for future generations. So, let's all take a pledge to contribute to this global cause and leave nature as a legacy for future generations.

Or

B. **Road Rage: Denied Right of Way While Driving, Man Opens Fire**

by Lalita, Staff Correspondent, The Times of India

Delhi

29th December, 20XX

In yet another incident of road rage, a man fired at a truck driver when he refused to let him overtake near ESI Hospital, Ring Road, on Tuesday night. Mahavir Singh Yadav (43), a resident of Delhi Cantonment, was arrested soon after the incident. In a written complaint to the police, truck driver Ishwar stated that he was returning home when a Maruti Swift car started honking at his truck from behind. The driver alleged that Yadav initially signalled him to stop.

When Ishwar showed no signs of doing so, he accelerated ahead of the truck and halted the car in front of it. Yadav then got off the car and allegedly fired at the truck driver. He missed the shot and Ishwar managed to escape. Upon crossing the Raja Garden flyover, he saw some traffic personnels and reported the matter to them. Soon, the Maruti Swift also reached the spot and Yadav alighted from the vehicle with the pistol still in his hand. He was immediately nabbed by the Traffic Police personnel. Identifying Yadav's firearm as a licensed pistol, police said a case of attempted murder has been registered against him.

7. A. (i) The given phrase means that in the moment of complete silence there would be no hurry to complete our activities. There will be no chaos or noise as no machine would be working in the movement.

(ii) (c) fraternity (iii) unexpectedness (iv) calmness

(v) (a) Both (A) and (R) are true, and (R) is the correct explanation of (A).

(vi) The expression Sudden strangeness has alliteration.

Or

B. (i) (b) They were not begging (ii) (b) City dwellers

(iii) emphasise the fact that the condition of the shed was most humble and that it presented a rather pitiable sight

(iv) pleading

(v) (b) Both (A) and (R) are true, but (R) is not the correct explanation of (A).

(vi) A little house at one side of the road was extended and a shed was added to it to put up a road stand. It was set up to attract passersby to buy things from them so that they could earn some money.

8. A. (i) he had burn marks on one side of his face which made him look hideous

(ii) Mr. Lamb's attitude twoards his disability is one of acceptance and resilience. He acknowledges that people might stare at his prosthetic leg, but he remains unbothered. This reflects his posetive outlook and ability to move beyond judgements. In contrast, Derry feels self–conscious and resentful about his facial scar, believering that it makes people stare and judge him negatively.

(iii) (b) real leg

(iv) Mr. Lamb refers to weeds, crab apples and spiders as things that could be stared at besides the legs.

Or

B. (i) as an infant of 10 days will never speak any language fluently

(ii) The people's reaction, as they stand in stupefaction reflects astonishment and possibly fear. Their belief in supernatural occurences and the authority of astrologes on matters of fate is evident.

(iii) (b) they had come across an infant of only 10 days who was speaking fluently.

(iv) The line uses imagery creating a vivid image of people frozen in shock, helping enablers visualise the intensity of the reaction. This amplifies the sense of awe and tension conveying astonished disbelief of onlookers.

9. A. (i) Franz would be feeling bad because he wanted to sho his command on French for the last time but he could not. Now, he would not be able to learn or use French.

(ii) importance

(iii) the inability to learn the mother tongue

(iv) The given lines indicates the careless attitude of the villagers of Alsace with respect to the learning of their mother tongue.

(v) (b) 'Bah! Ive plenty of time ....'

(vi) (a) Chauvinism

Or

B. (i) The American publisher told Umberto Eco that his books would not be loved by people as nobody has seen a cathedral or studies Latin.

(ii) surprise

(iii) it could not be predicted and he didn't know why it worked

(iv) Eco's publishers belief regarding the sale of his book was based on the fact that no one in America studied. Later on knew anything about cathedrals, the central aspects of the book.

(v) (a) Detective Medieval mystery

(vi) (d) Both (a) and (b)

10. (i) People in Firozabad cannot organise themselves into a cooperative due to the vicious circle of middlemen. They feel that if they try to get organised, they will be arrested up by the police, beaten and dragged to jail for doing something illegal. Moreover, there is no leader among them who can help them to get united.

(ii) 'The God That Failed' was a book that contained six separate essays of six renowned essayists about their journeys into communism and their disillusioned return. Those six distinguished writers were: Andre Gide, Richard Wright, Ignazio Silone, Arthur Koestler, Louis Fischer and Stephen Spender.

(iii) The poet of the poem 'Keeping Quiet' points out that we are single minded about keeping our lives moving at all costs and in the process lose sight of their goals. People only want fulfillment of ambitions and progress. Man is single-minded in his pursuit of wealth, supremacy and territorial acquisition.

(iv) As a child, the poet always suffered from a sense of insecurity and a fear of losing her mother. This childhood fear resurfaced while going to the airport when she looked at the pale and old face of her mother. She realised that her mother was ageing and she might lose her soon.

(v) Human beings love life in spite of all the troubles they face because of all the things of beauty which surround them. Things of Nature, stories of our ancestors and works of art and literature please us. They remove our despondent state and allow us to enjoy the beauty of things around us.

(vi) The instructor built a swimmer out of Douglas bit by bit. First, he put a belt round him and attached it securely to a pulley that ran on an overhead cable. For three months he was repeatedly made to go back and forth across the pool. Next, he was taught to put his face under water and exhale-inhale. Later he was made to kick with legs at the side of pool.

11. (i) The Psychiatrist thought that Charley's stamp collecting was a temporary refuge from reality. Charley did not agree with him because his grandfather, for whom life was nice and peaceful and who did not need refuge from reality, also collected stamps.

(ii) Canadian Geoff Green started the programme 'Students on Ice' for high school students to provide them most inspiring educational opportunities which would make them aware about the depletion of our ecosystem, create an understanding to save our planet as those teenagers still have an ideology to absorb, learn and most importantly act.

(iii) On the seventh day, two things happened. The first thing happened in the morning, when the servants left together with their belongings. In the afternoon, the second thing happened when Hana saw a messenger wearing official uniform come to their home. He came there to seek Dr. Sadao as the general was in pain and needed help.

12. A. Both 'Deep Water' by William Douglas and 'The Rattrap' by Selma Lagerlöf explore fear, transformation, and resilience.

In 'Deep Water', Douglas develops a deep fear of water after a near-drowning experience but overcomes it through perseverance and determination. His journey symbolises the triumph of courage over fear.

Similarly, in 'The Rattrap', the peddler initially leads a life of deception, believing the world is a trap. However, the kindness of Edla Willmansson transforms him, proving that compassion can change even the most hardened individuals. While Douglas fights a physical fear, the peddler battles moral weakness.

Both characters ultimately emerge stronger-Douglas conquers his fear through hard work, and the peddler redeems himself through kindness. These stories highlight that resilience and empathy can lead to personal growth and transformation, proving that overcoming obstacles and embracing kindness can bring profound change in one's journey.

Or

B. The mentioned poems highlight the importance of peace, introspection, and beauty in overcoming negativity and suffering. In 'Keeping Quiet', Neruda advocates stillness and silence as a means of self-reflection and unity, urging humanity to pause and embrace inner peace to heal the world's chaos. He believes introspection can lead to harmony and a deeper understanding of life.

On the other hand, Keats in 'A Thing of Beauty' finds solace in nature and art, portraying beauty as a source of eternal joy that helps overcome sorrow. He suggests that beautiful things, like nature and legends, provide comfort and renewal amidst life's hardships.

While Neruda emphasizes self-awareness and collective peace, Keats celebrates beauty's enduring power to uplift the human spirit. Both poets convey that reflection and appreciation of life's beauty can help overcome suffering and bring fulfillment.

13. A. Major reforms should be advocated in order to avert the cruelties experienced by Zitkala-Sa and observed by Bama. The reforms should include the values enshrined in the Constitution of India, but not actually followed by the majority of the population. These values are liberty, equality, fraternity and religious as well as ethnic tolerance. Then only will true democracy exist.

Zitkala-Sa experienced ethnic intolerance, as the white American settlers did not allow her to practice her customs and beliefs like keeping her long hair, eating without the use of cutlery and wearing a long dress. Instead, they forced her to follow their own customs of keeping short hair, wearing short dresses and using cutlery for eating. Thus, they inflicted cruelties on her.

Similarly, Bama observed the effects of discrimination of her caste in the case of the person carrying the package of eatables for their landlord. The members of their caste were not treated as equal to the landlord only because of their caste which is another form of cruelty.

Or

B. The sentence "It's not what you look like; it's what you are inside" encourages people to give more importance to the character and good qualities of other people than just to their appearance, as appearances can be deceptive. For instance, a man can look very smart by dressing well and grooming himself for a particular occasion, whereas in normal life he may be careless about his appearance.

So, is the case with Derry and Mr. Lamb. Mr. Lamb, as people know him is a lonely, crazy lame old man but in reality he is very kind, understanding and generous person who desires company. He loves all human beings without any discrimination and shows Derry the power of humanity.

Similarly, Derry appears to be an ugly, boy with a huge scar on his face whom no one loves or befriends. He is the object of other people's stares and ridicule. Yet this boy is very sensitive and kind hearted. He wants to love and be loved. Fortunately, he meets Mr. Lamb who transforms him with his healing touch.

So, this remark of Derry 'it's what you are inside' is true and may encourage people to have a warm and kind heart for others. It can also suggest that people should not get carried away by only outward appearances.

SAMPLE QUESTION PAPER 2

A Highly simulated Sample Question Paper for CBSE Class XII

ENGLISH CORE

GENERAL INSTRUCTIONS

1. This question paper has **13** questions. All questions are compulsory.
2. This question paper contains **three** sections— **Section A** : Reading Skills, **Section B** : Creative Writing Skills and **Section C** : Literature.
3. Attempt all questions based on specific instructions for each part. Write the correct question number and part there of in your answer sheet.
4. Separate instructions are given with each question/part, wherever necessary.
5. Adhere to the prescribed word limit while answering the questions.

TIME : 3 HOURS ***MAX. MARKS : 80***

FULLY SOLVED

SECTION - A

Reading Skills [22 Marks]

1. *Read the passage given below.* **(12)**

1. This is the largest Malay house on the peninsula. It is built of wood painted green and white with bold floral designs on a white background around some of the circular windows and a very large porch for followers to wait in, up a ladder of course.
2. Really the upper class of Malay houses show some very good work. The thatch of the steep roof is beautifully put on and between the sides of finely woven checked matting interspersed with lattice work and bamboo work, the shady inner rooms with their carved doorways and portieres of red silk, the pillows and cushions of gold embroidery laid over the exquisitely fine matting on the floors, the light from the half-shaded windows glancing here and there as the breeze sways the screens, there is an indescribable appropriateness to the region.
3. I waited for the elephant in a rambling empty house and Malays brought pierced coconuts, buffalo milk and a great bouquet of lotus blossoms and seed-vessels, out of which they took the seeds and presented them on the grand lotus leaf itself.

   Each seed is in appearance and taste like a hazel-nut, but in the centre, in an oval slit, the future lotus plant is folded up, the one vivid green seed leaf being folded over a shoot and this is intensely bitter.
4. The elephant at last came up and was brought below the porch of the house. They are truly ugly beasts, with their grey wrinkled, hairless hides, the huge ragged 'flappers' which cover their ears and with which they fan themselves ceaselessly, the small mean eyes, the hideous trunk which coils itself snakishly round everything, the formless legs, the piggish back, with the steep slope down to the mean, bare tail, features so unlike any other familiar and friendly beast.

5. Before I came out from England, I dreamt of *howdahs* and cloth-of-gold trappings, but my elephant had neither. In fact there was nothing grand about him but his ugliness. I dropped into one of two baskets on either side of his back from the porch, a young Malay lad dropped into the other and my bag was tied on behind with more ropes.
6. My ride was not comfortable. One sits facing forward with the feet dangling over the edge of the basket. This edge soon produces a sharp ache or cramp and, when one tries to get relief by leaning back on anything, the awkward rolling position is so painful that one reverts to the former position till it again becomes intolerable.
7. After we had travelled two hours, the baskets slipped down very dangerously and needed adjustment. We were forced to dismount while the pack was adjusted. Then, while the elephant was still sitting, the driver jumped on the elephant's back and giving me his hands hauled me up over the head, after which the creature rose gently from the ground and we went on our journey.
8. Soon the driver abandoned the elephant for a gossip and a smoke, leaving the animal to go its own way for a mile or more. The elephant turned into the jungle, where he began to rend and tear the trees and going to a mud-hole, he drew what water there was out of it and squirted it with a loud noise over himself and his riders, soaking my clothes with it. When he turned back to the road again, he several times stopped and seemed to stand on his head by stiffening his trunk and leaning upon it and when I hit him with my umbrella he uttered the loudest roar I ever heard. My Malay fellow-rider jumped off and ran back for the driver, at which the baskets both came down on my side of the elephant.
9. On the driver's return I had to dismount again and this time the elephant was allowed to go and take a proper bath in a river. He threw large quantities of clear water over himself and took up plenty more with which to cool his sides as went along. Thick as the wrinkled hide of an elephant is, a very small insect can still draw blood from it and so, like the water buffalo, he wisely plastered himself with mud from the river's edge for protection.

Based on your understanding of the passage, answer the questions given below.

(i) How does the author describe the elephant's act of putting mud on itself? Give the reason for this description. (1)

(ii) The author had previously regarded riding on an elephant as a luxurious means of travel. Comment. (2)

(iii) Complete the following sentence suitably. (1)

The writer has described the features of the elephant in paragraph 4 in order to highlight the ....

(a) friendly and active nature of elephants
(b) unfriendly nature of elephants
(c) Both (a and (b)
(d) None of the above

(iv) Why did the light in the inner room keep changing? (1)

(v) What expectation do you think the author had set for the elephant ride? (1)

(vi) The writer did not enjoy the elephant ride. (1)

Based on your reading of the passage, list the reasons for such an attitude.

(vii) List the two ways in which the Malay houses belong to the upper class of the region. (2)

(viii) Complete the analogy with ONE word from paragraph 2.

dark : shady :: moves : .... (1)

(a) cushions (b) bneeze (c) sways (d) carved

(ix) The writer would agree with the given statements based on paragraph eight, EXCEPT (1)
(a) The elephant did not like being hit.
(b) The speaker was not amused by the water thrown by the elephant.
(c) The driver of the elephant did not want the elephant to run away.
(d) The driver of the elephant needed to rest.

(x) How does the author compare his/her elephant to the one he/she dreamt of? (1)

2. *Read the passage given below.* (10)

1. A large majority of the elderly in India does not get long-term and palliative care, revealed a study conducted for the United Nations. The survey of more than 10,000 respondents across Northern, Southern, Western, Eastern and Central India during May-June 2018, showed that 62.1% of the elderly did not get such care. More than half of these people, 52.4%, said they primarily need traditional family support, says a study by Age well Research and Advocacy Centre.
2. Older people in India often face problems such as disability, restricted mobility, loneliness, poverty and lack of awareness on accessing old-term care. With a fast growing population of older people, the ever-increasing gap between generations and the fast and demanding lifestyle of young people, for a majority of older people, life is still a struggle for independence.
3. "According to 64% of elderly respondents, loneliness, marginalisation and isolation are the most critical issues faced by bedridden, elderly patients as they cannot visit, meet or interact with their relatives, friends and neighbours," said Himanshu Rath, founder of Agewell Foundation.
4. The elderly have to compromise and make adjustments in their lifestyle according to the wishes of the younger members of their families to ensure they are cared for, the study revealed. It highlighted that 67.6% of the elderly being taken care of their family members have to look after the children of the families. They have to perform tasks such as babysitting in return for proper care and support.
5. "Around 73.7% said they have to take care of the house and other properties of their younger family members to ensure long-term and palliative care in old age," the study report said. "Over 75% of respondents have to limit their personal social interactions as their family members direct them to do so, otherwise their family members can avoid providing their basic needs of food and medicines."Most elderly respondents (68.5%) said breaking up of the joint family system is one of the biggest factors for the challenges they face in getting long-term, palliative care.
6. Healthcare equipment such as wheelchairs, relief material such as adult diapers and care-giving service should be provided on a regular basis to destitute older people, who are bedridden and suffering from acute mobility issues, the report said.

   "Though providing long-term and palliative care to older persons comes in the purview of family responsibilities in India, it is observed that older persons, who are financially independent, have a high net worth or hold property entitlements, are treated comparatively well by their family members", said Rath.
7. "Managing home care for the elderly is a massive challenge as multiple service providers—nursing agencies, physiotherapists and medical suppliers—are small scale and unorganised and, therefore, provide incomplete care," he said. "In India, health insurance coverage is essentially limited to hospitalisation. The concept of geriatric care has remained a neglected area of medicine so far in the country."

Based on your understanding of the passage, answer the questions given below.

(i) Complete the following suitably. (1)

According to the study, long-term and palliative care comes under the purview of ....

(ii) Select the option that displays the most likely reason for stating that older people who live with family are no better. (1)

(a) they also suffer from loneliness

(b) they have no one who loves or cares for them

(c) they have additional burden of responsibility

(d) All of the above

(iii) List two essential requirements for older people suffering from mobility issues. (2)

(iv) The passage includes the words — 'challenges' and 'responsibility'. Classify the following sentences as challenge or responsibility. (1)

Sentence 1 Providing long term care to elders who are suffering from acute health issues.

Sentence 2 Managing home care for elderly is a massive challenge.

(v) Read the following. (1)

Sharanjeet is a 75 years old woman with acute arthritis. She lives with her family and is given good care. Mohan is an old man living with his extended family but he has to take care of the children in the house. Arindam, who lives in an old age home, is away from his family but is very comfortable and palliative care is given to him.

Select the option that best describes the situation of Sharanjeet, Mohan and Arindam.

(a) Sharanjeet — comfortable; Mohan — compromised ; Arindam — cared for

(b) Sharanjeet — compromised; Mohan — comfortable; Arindam — cared for

(c) Sharanjeet — cared for; Mohan — comfortable; Arindam — compromised

(d) Sharanjeet — comfortable; Mohan — cared for; Arindam — compromised

(vi) After reading the passage, what do you think is the primary need of all the elderly people in India? (1)

(vii) Based on the reading of the text, state a point to challenge the given statement. (2)

Joint Family System along with the need for private space has brought challenges to the long term elderly care.

(viii) What is the reason behind financially independent elderly being better off? (1)

(a) They have money of their financial cares

(b) They are treated with much more care and respect

(c) They are seen as one to be revered

(d) They have medical expenses

SECTION - B

Creative Writing Skills [18 Marks]

***Note** All details presented in the questions are imaginary and created for assessment purpose.*

3. Attempt **Any One** from A and B given below. (4)

A. As the honorary Director of an Old Age Home 'Tulasi', write a notice of appeal to be published in newspapers asking for donation of Man-Hours from general public. *(50 words)*

Or

B. As Principal of Vidya Niketan Public School, Raiganj, draft notice in not more than 50 words informing students of the change in school timings with effect from the 15th of November. State valid reasons for the change.

4. Attempt **Any One** from A and B given below. (4)

A. Nikhil/ Nikita has come out successful in the IIT entrance examination. He/she has decided to have a party with his/her friends. Write out an invitation giving details of venue, time and date. Do not exceed 50 words.

Or

B. You are Akshay/Aakriti. You have been invited to participate in a seminar on 'Fundamental Rights of Children', organised by the Lions Club of your district. Respond to the invitation by writing a letter to the Secretary of the Club. *(50 words)*

5. Attempt **Any One** from A and B given below. (5)

A. You are Sameer/Savita Arora. You have read an advertisement for the post of a Librarian. Write an application for the post. Also, give your Bio-data separately. *(120-150 words)*

> **VACANT**
>
> Wanted a smart, efficient professional librarian with proper education and a relevant work experience for a leading school library. Apply with complete bio-data within 10 days of the advertisement to the principal of Willows Public school, Meerut.

Or

B. Write a letter to the Editor of a National Daily expressing your concern on the deteriorating standard of living in your city. Give suggestions for improvement. You are Pratap/ Preeti of Kirti Nagar, Ghaziabad. You can use the following clues (120-150 words)

- Main road in a dug up condition
- Parks becoming garbage area
- Poor system of water supply
- Street lights not working

6. Attempt **Any One** from A and B given below. (5)

A. As the Sports Captain of your school, write an article in about 120-150 words for your school magazine emphasising the need of adventure sports in youngsters' lives. You are Rohit/Roshani. You can use the following clues

- Attraction towards exploring and experiencing the outdoors
- Help us in being strong, both in body and mind
- Prepare us to face the future challenges of life
- Lot of geographical diversity (mountains, hills, rivers, beaches etc) in our country

Or

B. Tourism plays an important role in improving the economy of a country. Write a report for your school magazine about the role of tourism and give suggestions how it can be improved. You are Aditi/Aditya. You can take help from the following clues (120-150 words)

- Economic development
- Employment
- Positive reviews
- Issues

SECTION - C

Literature

[40 Marks]

7. Read the given extracts and answer the questions for **Any One** of the two given. (1 × 6 = 6)

A.

"Aunt Jennifer's fingers fluttering through her wool
Find even the ivory needle hard to pull.
The massive weight of Uncle's wedding band;
Sits heavily upon Aunt Jennifer's hand." *(Aunt Jennifer's Tigers)*

(i) What do aunt Jennifer's fluttering hands through her wool tell us? (1)

(ii) What does the image 'massive weight of the wedding band' mean? (1)

(a) Wedding bond of hard married life
(b) Fatty structure of uncle
(c) Fatty body of aunty
(d) Heavy body of tiger

(iii) Complete the following suitably. (1)

Aunt Jennifer uses .... to express her repressed desires.

(iv) Select the correct option from those given in brackets to fill in the blanks. (1)

Aunt Jennifer is .... (brave/coward).

(v) Read the Assertion (A) and Reason (R) below, with reference to the given extract. (1)

Assertion (A) Aunt Jennifer's difficulty in pulling the ivory needle and the weight of uncle's wedding band symbolise her emotional and physical oppression.

Reason (R) The repetitive and burdensoms nature of Aunt Jennifer's task reflects her unability to escape the oppressive force of her.

(a) Both (A) and (R) are true, and (R) is the correct explanation of (A).
(b) Both (A) and (R) are true, but (R) is not the correct explanation of (A).
(c) (A) is true but (R) is false.
(d) (A) is false but (R) is true.

(vi) What do you, as reader, feel about Aunt jennifer? (1)

Or

B. *I saw my mother, beside me,*
doze, open mouthed, her face ashen like that of a corpse
And realised with pain
that she was as old as she looked but soon
put that thought away

(My Mother at Sixty-six)

(i) Select the phrase that suggests the following.

The poet's mother look like a corpse because of her old age (1)

(ii) What is the kind of pain and ache that the poet feels? (1)

(a) Losing her mother (b) Leaving her mother alone
(c) Headache (d) Children screaming at her

(iii) Complete the following suitably. (1)

"Her face ashen like that of a corpse" means that to the poet's mother's face was ....

(iv) The poetic device is used in the third and fourth lines of the extract is .... (simile/metaphor) (1)

(v) Read the Assertion (A) and the Reason (R) below, with reference to the given extract. (1)

Assertion (A) The poet tries to shift her thoughts away from her mother's appearance and again because it causes her distress.

Reason (R) The poet does not want to confront her own fears about mortality and separation from her mother, shocking instead to distract herself.

(a) Both (A) and the (R) are true, and (R) is the explanation of (A).
(b) Both (A) and (R) are correct, but (R) is not the explanation of (A).
(c) (A) is true, but (R) is false.
(d) (A) is false, but (R) is true.

(vi) Why did the poet put that thought away? (1)

8. Read the given extracts and answer the questions for **Any One** of the two given. (1 × 4 = 4)

A. "Not by you, but by someone who does not know him. I have my own private assassins. Suppose I send two of them to your house tonight or better, any night. You need know nothing about it. It is now warm – what would be more natural than that you should leave the outer partition of the white man's room open to the garden while he sleeps?"

(The Enemy)

(i) Complete the following suitably.

The General hatched the plan .... (1)

(ii) List the speaker's purpose behind getting the white man assassinated. (1)

(iii) The given lines indicate characteristic/s about the General. Pick the option that correctly states it/them. (1)

(a) Care and kindness (b) Ignorance and self-centeredness
(c) Humanist and patriotic (d) Both (a) and (c)

(iv) 'Not by you, but by someone who does not, know him.'

Why is there a need to assassinate 'him'? (1)

FULLY SOLVED

Or

B. Yes, I've taken the obvious step: I talked to a psychiatrist friend of mine, among others. I told him about the third level at Grand Central Station and he said it was a waking dream wish fulfillment. He said I was unhappy. That made my wife kind of mad, but he explained that he meant the modern world is full of insecurity, fear, war, worry and all the rest of it and that I just want to escape. Well, who doesn't? Everybody I know wants to escape, but they don't wander down into any third level at Grand Central Station. *(The Third Level)*

(i) Complete the following suitably. (1)

The third level, according to Charley, was ....

(ii) What does the psychiatrist explain to Charley? (1)

(iii) What is 'waking dream wish fulfillment' according to the psychiatrist in the lesson? (1)

(a) Charley's finding of a Third Level at Grand Central Station.

(b) Charley's realisation of his wish to visit Galesburg Illinois.

(c) Charley's escaping into his daydreaming everyday.

(d) Charley's post stamp collecting habit.

(iv) Why did the narrator go to a psychiatrist? (1)

FULLY SOLVED

9. Read the given extracts and answer the questions for **Any One** of the two given. (1 × 6 = 6)

A. The experience had a deep meaning for me, as only those who have known stark terror and conquered it can appreciate. In death there is peace. There is terror only in the fear of death, as Roosevelt knew when he said, "All we have to fear is fear itself." Because I had experienced both the sensation of dying and the terror that fear of it can produce, the will to live somehow grew in intensity. *(Deep Water)*

(i) Explain "All we have to fear is itself". (1)

(ii) Select the correct option from those given in brackets to fill in the blank. (1)

Roosevelt's .... (opinion/suggestion) on fear is that one should not fear death.

(iii) Complete the following suitably. (1)

The 'experience' in the context refers to ....

(iv) What happens after the fear of death is removed? (1)

(v) Identify the textual clue that allows the reader to infer that the writer has himself faced the terror. (1)

(vi) Select the correct option to fill in the blank. (1)

The effect of the experience was ....

(a) didactic (b) satisfying

(c) frustrating (d) undermining

Or

B. "I sometimes find a rupee, even a ten rupee note", Saheb says, his eyes lighting up when you can find a silver coin in a heap of garbage, you don't stops scrounging, for there is the hope of finding more. It seems that for children,garbage has a meaning different from what is means to their parents. For the children it is wrapped in wonder, for the elders, it is a means of survival. One winter morning I seen Saheb standing by the fenced gate of the neighborhood club, watching two young men dressed in white, playing tennis. "I like the game", he hums, content to watch it standing behind the fence. "I go inside when no one is around" he admits. "The gatekeeper lets me use the swing". *(Lost Spring)*

(i) What value does garbage hold for Saheb? (1)

(ii) Select the correct option from those given in the brackets to fill in the blank. (1)

'The gatekeeper lets me use the swing'. This line indicates that the gatekeeper was .... (kind/rude) towards Saheb.

(iii) Complete the sentence suitably. (1)

For the elders garbage is .... and for children it is ....

(iv) "There is hope for finding more." Explain with reference to the above extract. (1)

(v) What can't Saheb play the game? (1)

(a) He does not have membership
(b) The game is for upper class rich people
(c) Saheb was banned from the club
(d) None of these

(vi) Which emotion of Saheb is revealed in the phrase 'his eyes lighting up'? (1)

(a) Anxiety (b) Envy (c) Happiness (d) Greed

10. Answer **Any Five** of the following six questions in 40-50 words each. (2 × 5 = 10)

(i) Interpret how the peddler showed his gratitude to Edla? (The Rattrap)
(ii) What could be the reason of the shut of the story department?
(iii) Where did Gandhiji decide to go first and why? (Indigo)
(iv) How would man suffer in the absence of beauty?
(v) Explain why Aunt Jennifer creates animals that are so different from her own character? (Aunt Jennifer's Tigers)
(vi) Comment on the significance of the symbol of the car in the poem. (The Roadside Stand)

11. Answer **Any Two** of the following three questions in 40-50 words each. (2 × 2 = 4)

(i) Discuss the objective of the 'Students on Ice' programme? (Journey to the End of the Earth)
(ii) "I felt like sinking to the floor". Interpret why Zitkala-Sa said so? (Memories of Childhood)
(iii) The manner of his (The Tiger King's) death is a matter of extraordinary interest. Comment.

12. Answer **Any One** of the following two questions in 120-150 words. (5)

A. Aunt Jennifer's Tigers portrays a woman's silent resistance against patriarchal oppression through her embroidery. Meanwhile, Poets and Pancakes provides a satirical take on the film industry, exposing its pretensions and power dynamics.

Compare and contrast how these works highlight the challenges faced by individuals in expressing their creativity and identity in a restrictive environment. Discuss with relevant examples from both texts.

Or

B. In Indigo, Mahatma Gandhi says, "The real relief for them is to be free from fear." Similarly, A Roadside Stand by Robert Frost highlights the struggles of rural people who remain helpless due to societal neglect and false promises.

How do these texts portray the exploitation of the poor? What solutions do they suggest for their upliftment? Discuss with reference to the mentioned chapters.

13. Answer **Any One** of the following two questions in 120-150 words. (5)

A. Justify the title 'The Third Level'.

Or

B. What did Hana think of her husband as a surgeon and doctor in 'The Enemy'?

ANSWERS

1. (i) The author describes the elephant's act of putting mud on it as wise because the mud would save it from insect bites.

(ii) The author had previously regarded riding on an elephant as a luxurious means of travel because he dreamt of howdahs and cloth of gold trappings on the elephant.

(iii) (b) unfriendly nature of the elephant

(iv) The light in the inner room kept changing becuase of the winds that was swaying the screen.

(v) The author had an exciting expectation for the elephant ride.

(vi) The writer did not like the elephant ride because it was not only uncomfortable but also the elephant had thrown water all over them.

(vii) The two ways in which the Malay houses belong to the upper class of the region are

1. Pillows and cushions laid on the floor are embroidered with gold.
2. The inner rooms have carved doorways with red silk curtains on them.

(viii) (c) sways

(ix) (c) The driver of the elephant did not want the elephant to run away.

(x) The author dreamt of grandeur like howadahs and clotth-of gold trappings. But to his/her disappointment, his/her elephant had neither. There was nothing grand and showy about him but his ugliness.

2. (i) social responsibilities

(ii) (d) All of the above

(iii) The two essential requirements for older people suffering from mobility issues are wheelchairs and adult diapers.

(iv) **Sentence 1** Responsibility

Sentence 2 Challenge

(v) (a) Sharanjeet — comfortable; Mohan — compromised ; Arindam — cared for

(vi) Traditional family support is the primary need of all the elderly people in India.

(vii) The given statement is incorrect because while the need for private space has created the challenges in long term elderly care, the joint family system has always made sure that the elderly were well loved and cared for. In fact, it was the breaking up of the joint family system that initiated the problems in elderly care.

(viii) (b) They are treated with much more care and respect

3. **A.**

Tulasi : An Old Age Home

NOTICE

8th July, 20XX

Donate Time for a Noble Cause

The elders in our Old Age Home need your help. Come and spend time with them talking, walking, reading or playing. Utilise your time for this noble cause. For details and registration, please log on to our website www.Tulasi@yahoo.in or call us on this Toll Free number at 32773277.

Naveen Chawla

(*Honorary Director*)

FULLY SOLVED

Or

B. **Vidya Niketan Public School, Raiganj**
NOTICE

10th November, 20XX

Change in School Timings

All the students are hereby informed about a change in school timings from 15th November, 20XX.
The school will now start at 9:00 AM and end at 3:00 PM. In the past few years, it has been seen that winters are rather severe and it becomes quite difficult to start early due to the extreme cold weather and the dense fog. So, these new timings will be followed till further notice.

Thank you
Principal

4. A. D-42, Mayur Vihar
New Delhi

10th June, 20XX

Dear Pranavi/ Praveen
I am so excited to tell you that I have cleared the IIT entrance examination. On such a happy occasion, I would like to invite you to join me on 15th June 20XX at 6:00 PM at my residence in an intimate party to celebrate my success. All our old friends would be joining us.
Looking forward to seeing you.

Nikhil/ Nikita

Or

B. 25, RP Singh Marg
Meerut

5th July, 20XX

The Secretary
Lions Club, Meerut

Subject *Acceptance of Invitation*

Sir/Ma'am
Thanks for your invitation for a seminar on 'Fundamental Rights of Children' and your concern for the under-privileged children. I would like to utilise this opportunity to share my experience with other like-minded enthusiasts and experts.
I hereby confirm my participation in the seminar.

Yours sincerely
Akshay/ Aakriti

5. A. 67-B, Shanti Park
Meerut - 250004

18th February, 20XX

The Principal
Willows Public School
Meerut Cantonment - 250001

Subject *Application for the Post of Librarian*

Sir/Ma'am
Refering to your advertisement in 'Times of India' dated 20th February, 20XX for the post of a Librarian, I wish to apply for the same in your reputed institution.

FULLY SOLVED

I am currently working in a convent school as a Librarian and have earned respect from my seniors for my work.

I am enclosing my bio-data for your kind consideration. I shall be available for interview on any day at your convenience. If selected, I assure you of utmost devotion and sincerity. I hope for a favourable response from your side.

Thanking you

Yours sincerely

Savita Arora

Enclosed : Bio-data

Bio-data

Name	Savita Arora
Husband's Name	Mr. Jai Arora
Address	67-B, Shanti Park, Meerut - 250004
Phone	95621XXXXX
Email	savirora@gmail.com
Nationality	Indian

Professional Qualifications

Name of the Exam	Name of the Institution	Year	Percentage
M. Lib	Delhi University	20XX	76%
B. Lib	Delhi University	20XX	78%

Work Experience
- Worked in Dayal Public School, Delhi for 2 years as Asstt. Librarian
- Currently working with St. Ansle School, Meerut for the last 3 years as Librarian

Hobbies Reading classical literature, and watching old movies

References
- Shri Arun Lal, Principal, Dayal Public School, Delhi. Mobile No. 99886XXXXX
- Shri CK Gupta, Head Librarian, St. Ansle School, Meerut. Mobile No. 99666XXXXX

Or

B. 46/69, Kirti Nagar
Ghaziabad - 201008

20th July, 20XX

The Editor
National Daily
New Delhi

Subject Deterioration in Standard of Living

Sir/Ma'am

Through the columns of your esteemed newspaper, I would like to express my deep anguish about the deterioration in the standard of living in our colony so that the concerned authority can take suitable action.

The main road leading to this colony has been lying in dug up condition for years for unknown reasons. This road should be repaired on top priority. The water supply system is also in an alarming condition, as we get the supply for only one hour in a day and that too is not fit for drinking. The parks which were supposed to serve both the purpose of greenery as well as playgrounds for children appear more like a garbage area. Street lights are also not working.

With issues all around affecting the general living conditions, families have started moving out of this colony. If this exodus continues, soon very few families will remain in Kirti Nagar. We hope that the concerned authority will resolve these issues as soon as possible.

Thanking you

Yours sincerely

Preeti/Pratap

6. A.

The Need of Adventure Sports in Youngsters' Lives

by Rohit/Roshani

In the busy and hectic lifestyle of the present generation, everyone is attracted towards experiencing life outdoors and exploring unchartered territories. Therefore, the world today is going crazy about the newly emerging adventure sports. Adventure sports refers to activities like mountain biking, rock climbing, mountaineering, or kayaking, scuba diving, base jumping, and many more activities done in a variety of geographical diversity.

Known to teach people self reliance, teamwork and to leave their comfort zone, adventures sports helps to make us strong both in body and mind. These elements result in better health, improved self esteem and increased confidence that translates into all aspects of one's life. The emotional and physical benefits of adventure sports very impressively prepare us for future challenges of life.

The scope of adventure sports is great in a country like India where there is a diversity of geographical regions including mountains, hills, rivers, beaches etc. With all the facilities and proper rules-regulation, adventure sports have become a very important activity that must be introduced in the lives of youngsters who need to be prepared for a new future.

Or

B.

Tourism– Its Role and How It Can be Improved

by Aditya/Aditi

14th July, 20XX

Tourism plays a vital role in the economic development of any country. Tourism industry employs a large number of people, both skilled and unskilled. Every region is identified with its handicrafts, fairs, folk dances, music and people. Hotels, travel agencies and transport including airlines benefit a lot from this industry. It generates foreign exchange and promotes cultural activities. Infrastructure of the tourism destinations also gets better in order to maintain the standard as per the international levels of tourism.

However, in order to have positive reviews about the state of tourism in India, one should actively analyse the tourist trends and implement appropriate corrective measures wherever they are needed. Feedback from tourists visiting India should be taken into account. Issues like public transport, informational material, general safety and hygiene should match the international standards so that tourists do not leave with a bad impression. In order to increase the tourism potential, one needs to think beyond the simplistic sightseeing.

7. A. (i) Aunt Jennifer's fluttering hands through her wool tells us about the fear in her mind and the intensity of her suppression.

(ii) (a) Wedding band of hard married life

(iii) embroidery

(iv) coward

(v) (a) Both (A) and (R) are true, and (R) is the correct explanation of (A).

(vi) As reader, we feel sympathetic for Aunt Jennifer's condition. At the same time, we are angered by the oppressive nature of patriarchal society.

Or

B. (i) "... her face ashen like that of a corpse."

(ii) (a) Losing her mother

(iii) pale and lifeless

(iv) simile

(v) (a) Both (A) and (R) are true, and (R) is the correct explanation of (A).

(vi) The poet put that thought away because the thought was unbearable.

8. A. (i) to kill the white man

(ii) The speaker wanted to get the white man assassinated to keep Sadao safe from anything. He wanted Sadao to be safe so that he could perform the surgery.

(iii) (b) Ignorance and self-centeredness

(iv) There was a need to assassinate 'him' because he was an American prisoner of war.

Or

B. (i) third storey on the Grand Central station

(ii) The Psychiatrist explains to Charley that it was the result of stress and anxiety of his mind.

(iii) (a) Charley's finding of a Third level at Grand Central Station.

(iv) The narrator went to a psychiatrist because he went through an experience no one else did.

9. A. (i) The given phrase means that we need to be afraid of the idea of fear and how it affects us.

(ii) opinion

(iii) drowning in the YMCA pool and learning how to swim.

(iv) After the fear of death is removed, the will to live grow in intensity.

(v) (c) "The experience has a deep meaning for me, as only those who have known stark, terror and conquered can appreciate it."

(vi) (b) satisfying

B. (i) For Saheb, garbage is gold. It is a source of wonder and joy as well a means of survival.

(ii) kind

(iii) means of survival, treasure hunt.

(iv) The given line indicates that children like Saheb and other ragpickers keep on seconding the garbage dumps to look for something that could earn them money or livelihood.

(v) (b) The game is for upper class rich people.

(vi) (c) Happiness

10. (i) To show his gratitude to Edla, the peddler left a parcel containing a small rattrap with three ten kronor notes in it and a message with it. In the letter written by the peddler to Edla he promised to reform himself. He thanked her for her hospitality and for reposing faith in him.

(ii) The story department was comprised of many poets and writers and also a lawyer with them. The possible reason for the shutting down of this story department may be its uselessness or unbearable expenses or regular salary of the members and less output in return.

(iii) Gandhiji decided to go first to Muzzafarpur which was en-route Champaran. He didn't have any information about the problem in Champaran and had never heard of that place before. So, to obtain more detailed information about the problem in Champaran, he went to Muzzafarpur.

(iv) In the absence of beauty, man would suffer from sorrow and despair. It would be difficult for him to bounce back and he would have nothing to look forward to or draw strength from. Beauty lifts the pall of sadness and rejuvenates him. It lifts his spirit and fills his life with liveliness and hope.

(v) Aunt Jennifer creates tigers which are very different from her own character. Her tigers represent strength, fearlessness and confidence to express her longing of freedom and independence. She wants to get out of the bondage imposed by her husband if not in reality then at least symbolically. Her tigers express her hidden desires and unfulfilled wishes.

(vi) In the poem, the moving cars are to be seen from two perspectives. They are a symbol of hope of getting money for survival for the rural people. The rural people want the cars to stop and buy their produce. This will earn them a livelihood. But, at the same time, it represents the cruelty and selfish attitudes of the city people who live a luxurious life in comparison to the rural people but do not have any kindness or compassion in them.

11. (i) The objective of the 'Students on Ice' programme was to offer the future generation of policy makers a life changing experience at an early age. At this age, the students were willing to learn absorb the information and most importantly act. Mr. Geoff Green provided high school students an opportunity to understand and develop a respect for our planet.

(ii) Zitkala said so because she was made to wear a new dress at school and her shawl had been removed. She was feeling ashamed of her body-clinging dress which made her uncomfortable, uneasy and vulnerable. When she was walking to the dining hall, she felt like sinking to the floor with shame.

(iii) The manner of the Tiger King's death is a matter of extraordinary interest because it is ironical that, although he killed 99 live tigers, a harmless wooden tiger caused his death. Thus, his death was destined and he failed to survive the ominous prediction.

12. A. Both Aunt Jennifer's Tigers and Poets and Pancakes explore struggles of individuals trying to express their creativity in restrictive environments.

In Aunt Jennifer's Tigers, Aunt Jennifer, trapped in a patriarchal marriage, uses embroidery as a means of silent resistance. Her tigers symbolize strength and freedom, contrasting with her own oppressed existence. Despite her artistic expression, she remains burdened by societal constraints.

Similarly, Poets and Pancakes satirizes the rigid and pretentious nature of the film industry, where creativity is overshadowed by power dynamics and superficiality. The studio's hierarchical structure stifles genuine artistic freedom, making it difficult for individuals to express their true identity.

While Aunt Jennifer's oppression is personal and patriarchal, the film industry in Poets and Pancakes highlights institutional control over creativity. Both works reveal how societal structures suppress self-expression, yet art remains a tool for resilience and silent defiance.

Or

B. The mentioned chapters highlight the exploitation of the poor and their struggle for justice.

In Indigo, Gandhiji fights for the oppressed peasants of Champaran, who are forced to grow indigo and suffer under unfair British landlords. He realizes that their true suffering stems from fear and empowers them through self-reliance, legal awareness, and nonviolent resistance. His leadership helps them gain economic and social justice.

Similarly, A Roadside Stand portrays the plight of rural people who long for prosperity but are deceived by false promises of urban development. The poem criticizes the indifference of the wealthy, who ignore the struggles of the poor.

Both texts emphasise that real upliftment comes from awareness, self-sufficiency, and social justice. While Gandhi provides a practical path to empowerment, Frost urges compassion and genuine efforts to bridge the gap between the privileged and the marginalised.

13. A. The title 'The Third Level' is apt for the story that revolves around the third level of the Grand Central Station, New York. The story deals with the theme of insecurity, fear and war. The narrator, Charley longs for a serene and peaceful place like Galesburg. This makes him stray to a corridor at Grand Central Station that takes him into the past specifically the year 1894. The people, their attire, ambience, the platform, everything on the platform, locomotive, currency being used, the newspapers, magazines, etc., is old style. Only Charley is an exception in the setting.

This hallucination of Charley comes to an abrupt end when he has to flee from there in hurry to save himself from being caught by the cops. This experience is understood by his Psychiatrist friend as a way to escape the stresses he faces in life. However, Sam himself strays to the third level. He had somehow found the third level, had gone there and started a new business of hay, feed and grain. Hence, the entire story revolves around a third level making it an apt title for the story.

Or

B. Hana, the wife of Dr. Sadao believed that her husband was a highly professional surgeon and doctor. The fact that she assisted him in operating on an American prisoner of war shows how much confidence she had in his ability as a surgeon. She knew that if her husband believed that he will be successful in saving the American, then the American will live. She knew that Dr. Sadao would make sure that he knew everything about his patient before operating on him. Such was his perfection.

Hana was aware that her husband was passionate about his job and that he was sincere and diligent at it. Her belief in her husband is validated by the fact that she helps him treat and clean the wounded man even if it made her nauseous.

Hana supported her husband in his decision because she believed in him. Dr. Sadao's professional ability and his decisions filled Hana with a lot of respect for him as a doctor and surgeon.

SAMPLE QUESTION PAPER 3

A Highly simulated Sample Question Paper for CBSE Class XII

ENGLISH CORE

GENERAL INSTRUCTIONS

1. This question paper has **13** questions. All questions are compulsory.
2. This question paper contains **three** sections— **Section A** : Reading Skills, **Section B** : Creative Writing Skills and **Section C** : Literature.
3. Attempt all questions based on specific instructions for each part. Write the correct question number and part there of in your answer sheet.
4. Separate instructions are given with each question/part, wherever necessary.
5. Adhere to the prescribed word limit while answering the questions.

TIME : 3 HOURS ***MAX. MARKS : 80***

UNSOLVED

SECTION - A

Reading Skills

[22 Marks]

1. *Read the passage given below.* **(12)**

1. An urgent problem is now threatening libraries throughout the world. Their collections, which are crucial for diverse purposes as economic development, educational research and recreational pursuits are in danger of disintegration.
2. The problem is mainly due to one cause—the type of paper on which books have been printed for the past one and a half centuries. Until the 1850s, paper was produced from linen or cotton rags and proved to be relatively long-lasting. In the mid-19th century, however, the popular demand for paper and the commercial need for an economic method of production led to the use of mechanically ground wood pulp. Paper manufactured from wood pulp is highly acidic and therefore, inherently unstable. It contains lignin which causes paper to discolour and disintegrate.
3. Programmes are now being developed with two main aims in mind: on one hand, to improve the physical condition of library collections, especially by the process called 'mass deacidification' (to eliminate acid from the paper of published books and insert a buffer compound that will provide protection against future) and on the other, to transfer the contents of existing books to another medium.
4. Libraries will only be able to carry out these special tasks with the assistance of experts such as book conservators and high technology specialists. But, there is another group whose cooperation will be crucial, if the problem of decaying collections is to be arrested: the printing and publishing industries. The existing problem that of book collections already assembled in libraries is of vast proportions. It is intensified by the continuing use of acid-based paper in book publishing. The key issue is, how to preserve the books of the future, not simply those of the past.
5. If the future dimensions of the conservation problem are to be curbed, there will be a necessity of widespread adoption of paper which is of archival quality.

6. This change does not relate to a narrowly perceived need because the long-term preservation of library collections is important both for the overall social benefits they bring as well as for the special advantages they bestow on the printing and publishing industries.
7. In the first place, libraries are of critical importance to the well-being of citizens, since they provide the knowledge base of society. They contain the record of humanity, the accumulation of ideas and insights and discoveries on which social effort and progress are possible. The destruction of libraries would represent an immense cultural loss, a form of amnesia, which would affect every member of society.

Based on your understanding of the passage, answer the questions given below.

(i) According to the passage, linen or cotton rags were used as paper until the 1850's. Based on your understanding of the passage, state whether you promote going to back to using them as paper. Give reason for your answer. (1)

(ii) Comment on the importance of libraries referred to in the paragraph one. (1)

(iii) Read and complete the following sentence suitably. (1)

If the future dimensions of the conservation problem are to be curbed, there will be a necessity of widespread adoption of paper which is of archival quality ....

(iv) Why did the writer found the printing and publishing industries to be crucial to cause of protecting libraries? (1)

(v) Libraries can save their collections by .... (1)

(a) storing them in air-conditioned rooms
(b) laminating the pages
(c) creating a dust-free atmosphere in their premises
(d) widespread adoption of paper of archival quality

(vi) Why did the need to produce mechanically ground wood pulp arise during the mid-nineteenth century? (2)

(vii) List the two ways in which a book by Robert Frost could be saved from deterioration and loss. (2)

(viii) Complete the analogy with one word. (1)

conservation : knowledge base : : .... : cultural loss

(a) preservation (b) deacidification
(c) destruction (d) intensification

(ix) The writer would agree with the given statements based on paragraph 2, EXCEPT. (1)

(a) The paper produced from wood pulp is not everlasting.
(b) The paper produced from wood pulp is acidic in nature.
(c) The paper produced from wood pulp is still being produced.
(d) The paper produced from wood pulp is prone to discouloring.

(x) What would the destruction of libraries represent? (1)

UNSOLVED

2. *Read the passage given below.* **(10)**

Graduates in India feel let down by the education system's failure to equip them with the skills needed to become a success at work.

A recent study from Hindustan Times drew damning conclusions about the state of the Indian Education System and its effect on employability and career success amongst recent graduates, with both millennials and Gen Z'ers feeling their education did not significantly contribute to them landing their first jobs.

Young people are feeling out of their depth during the first few years of employment, the survey found. Crediting a deficit of industry links, lack of practical experience and inadequate career counselling at universities for the shortcomings in employability following graduation.

Aimed at assessing the efficacy of India's education system, the survey connected with 1,680 young professionals, men and women aged between 21 and 27. Those surveyed have been employed for three years or less, pursuing new-age careers – digital entertainment and media, retail, e-commerce, social media, digital advertising and media, and start-ups – in the six base metro areas: Mumbai, Delhi, Kolkata, Bengaluru, Hyderabad and Chennai.

Only 26 per cent of those surveyed felt their education contributed highly to their interpersonal management skills – a key trait needed for interviews and employment.

A problem with the relevance and timeliness of university curriculum was also highlighted with 74 per cent of respondents saying their college and university syllabus and courses are not updated regularly.

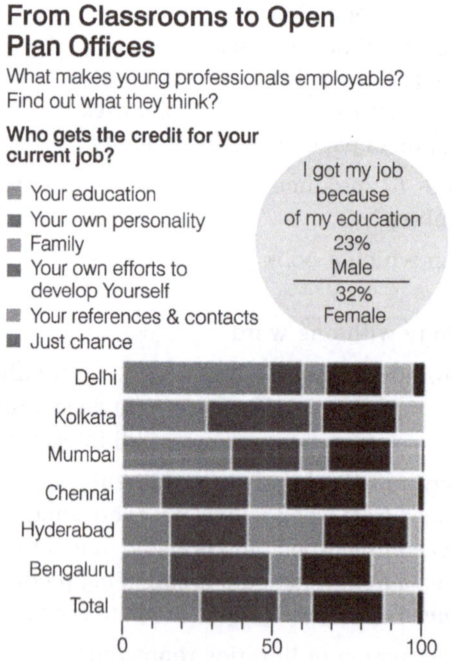

An overwhelming majority of graduates across India's major financial capitals – Mumbai (89 per cent), Kolkata (86 per cent) and Hyderabad (84 per cent) – felt they lacked the necessary practical experience, and blamed the deficiency on inadequate industry-academia linkages. Colleges also lack adequate career counselling services according to 79 per cent of respondents.

A historical focus on rote learning or memorising facts to be regurgitated is still prevalent in much of India's educational system and can lead to graduates attaining good grades but failing to pick up the skills needed for innovation or out-of-the-box thinking that is so vital in today's modern workplace.

Where some may lack in skills, however, they make up for in character with 26 per cent of millennials and Gen Z'ers feeling they secured jobs through the sheer power of their personalities alone.

A case was also made for self-development and taking it upon yourself to bridge the gap inadequate education has left, with 24 per cent of respondents believing personal initiatives to improve their skills paid off when it came to landing a job. Despite the negative outcome of the survey, founder of global learning company XSEED Ashish Rajpal told Hindustan Times the future isn't all bleak if the system can be overhauled at primary school level.

"Today we work with over a million children in over 3,000 schools and have visible evidence pointing that foundation for employability skills can be laid early at the elementary schooling stage," he says.

By encouraging children at a young age to engage with the world around them in order to gain a deeper understanding of the theory, they learn more practical real world experience and booster their communication skills and confidence to boot.

Based on your understanding of the passage, answer the questions given below.

(i) Complete the following suitably. (1)

Ashish Rajpal finds a solution in primary school level as ....

(ii) Select the option that displays one of the skills relevant to the present day employment. (1)

(a) Innovation
(b) Communication
(c) Collaboration
(d) All of these

(iii) Do you think the researchers of the study aimed to highlight the changes required in the Indian education system by pointing out the problems youth face in getting jobs? (2)

(iv) Classify the following statements 'suggestion' or 'prediction'. (1)

Statment 1 According to youth, educational institutes need to update and revise their curriculum to meet the needs of the present.

Statement 2 The future is not as all bleak if the system can be overhauled at primary level.

(v) Read the following. (1)

Pragati works as a HR Manager in a reputed publishing house. Her education is in English literature. She has good management and communication skills. Her role is characterised by creativity which is really good at she has no previous experience.

Select the option that identifies the correct factors for her employability.

(a) Education, skills, experience
(b) Education, skills, personality
(c) Efforts, family contacts, education
(d) Chance, personality, skills

(vi) Based on the reading of the text, state a point to challenge the given statement. (1)

By focusing on industry links, practical experience and career counselling, individuals will be wasting their resources and fall back in their studies.

(vii) Self development was also promoted to bridge the gap inadequate education has left. Give a reason for such a claim. (2)

(viii) What do Indian youngsters find about education system? (1)

(a) Provides wholesome factual knowledge.
(b) Does not have any role in employability.
(c) Does not promote professional skills.
(d) Is the best system in the world.

SECTION - B

Creative Writing Skills

[18 Marks]

Note *All details presented in the questions are imaginary and created for assessment purpose.*

3. Attempt **Any One** from A and B given below. (4)

A. While walking in a park in your neighbourhood you found a small plastic bag containing some documents and some cash. Write a notice in about 50 words to be put on the park notice board asking the owner to identify and collect it from you. You are Amar/Amrita

Or

B. You are Tanisha, the School Captain of Sarvodaya Kanya Vidyalaya, Delhi. You wish to call a meeting of the Students Council to discuss the measures to be taken to check the bursting of crackers in the school premises during Diwali time. Draft a notice inventing details in not more than 50 words.

4. Attempt **Any One** from A and B given below. (4)

A. M/s Shyam Lal & Sons are opening a new branch of their grocery store 'Galaxy Novelties' in Geetanjali Enclave, Dwarka, Delhi. The inauguration ceremony is fixed for Sunday, the 19th of October, 20XX at 11:00 AM. Prepare a draft of formal invitation letter for the purpose. (50 words)

Or

B. You are opening an exclusive parlour for ladies. Write an informal invitation, inviting your best friend for its inauguration not more than 50 words.

5. Attempt **Any One** from A and B given below. (5)

A. As the resident of 16 Shivpuri, Modinagar, write a letter to the Editor of a Local Daily regarding the long power cuts that your colony has to face every day and the resultant problems being faced by the residents. You can use the following clues. (120-150 words)

- Long power cuts
- Electrical appliances cannot be used
- Suffering due to heat and humidity
- Disrupts working hours (manpower)
- Disrupts study hours
- Harmful for health (heat stroke)

Or

B. Draft an application for the post of an accountant in Pioneers (Pvt.) Ltd. Co. Hyderabad in response to their advertisement that appeared in 'The Times of India' dated 1st August, 20XX. Prepare a biodata to be enclosed. You are Nipun/Aparna.

Join our Team as an Accountant

We're looking for an experienced individual to help manage financial records and ensure accuracy.

We offer

- Competetive Salary
- Professional growth
- Supportive environment

Apply now and be part of a dynamic team!

UNSOLVED

6. Attempt **Any One** from A and B given below. (5)

A. You were travelling by Chennai Express from Kollam Junction to Bhubaneshwar. In the early morning hours, 3 bogies of the train derailed and the train came to a grinding halt when it was nearing Bhubaneswar. All the passengers were awakened from their slumber to realise that their lives were in danger. Draft a report for a local daily using the visual clue. You are Neerja/Neerav, a Staff Reporter. (120-150 words)

Or

B. Teenagers today are getting hooked on to the latest gadgets. Write an article on 'The Advantages of Technology and its Adverse Effects'. You are Somya/Saurav Taneja. You can use the following clues. (120-150 words)

- Gadgets : Mobiles, iPods, computers
- Greater affluence : Easy availability
- Improved communication : Easy connectivity, faster information exchange, global vision.
- Impact on health : Sedentary lifestyle, obesity, eating habits
- Impact on academic performance
- Social impact

SECTION - C

Literature Textbooks [40 Marks]

7. *Read the given extracts and answer the questions for* ***any one*** *of the two given.* (1 × 6 = 6)

A.

Aunt Jennifer's tigers prance across a screen.
Bright topaz denizens of a world of green.
They do not fear the men beneath the tree;
They pace in sleek chivalric certainty.
Aunt Jennifer's fingers fluttering through her wool
Find even the ivory needle hard to pull.
The massive weight of Uncle's wedding band
Sits heavily upon Aunt Jennifer's hand.

(Aunt Jennifer's Tigers)

UNSOLVED

(i) What quality of Aunt Jennifer can be inferred from the given lines? (1)

(ii) Which of the following is an example of an alliteration? (1)

(a) Fingers fluttering through the wool
(b) Upon Aunt Jennifer's hand
(c) Ivory needle hard to pull
(d) Prance across the screen

(iii) Complete the following suitably. (1)

'..*Sits heavily upon Aunt Jennifer's hand'* implies that Aunt Jennifer ....

(iv) Select the correct option from those given in bracket to fill in the blank. (1)

The tigers are .... (fearless/cowardly), graceful and beautiful.

(v) Read the Assertion (A) and the Reason (R) below, with reference to the given extract. (1)

Assertion (A) Aunt Jennifer's tigers symbolise strength and fearlessness.

Reason (R) The tigers in the poem prance confidently and are unafraid of the men beneath the tree, unlike Aunt Jennifer who feels weighed down by societal expectations.

(a) Both (A) and (R) are true, and (R) is the correct explanation of (A).
(b) Both (A) and (R) are true, but (R) is not the correct explanation of (A).
(c) (A) is true, but (R) is false.
(d) (A) is false, but (R) is true.

(vi) How does the poet use Aunt Jennifer's struggle with the 'ivory needle' as a metaphor for her life? What inference can be made about her sense of control or power? (1)

Or

B.

Yes, in spite of all,
Some shape of beauty moves away the pall
from our dark spirits. Such the Sun, the Moon.
Trees old and young, sprouting a shady boon
For simple sheep; and such are daffodils.
With the green world they live in; and clear rills
That for themselves a cooling covert make
'Gainst the hot season; the mid forest brake,

(i) Select the phrase that suggests the following. (1)

Beauty in its various forms has the power to lift sadness or negativity from our minds and souls.

(ii) Which of the following is an apt title for the extract? (1)

(a) The Medicine of Nature
(b) Nature as a Magnum Opus
(c) Life full of Beauty and Hope
(d) Beauty Galore

(iii) Complete the following suitably. (1)

.... can be found in all aspects of nature.

(iv) Select the correct option from those given in the bracket to fill in the blank. (1)

When the poet says that *'Some shape of beauty moves away the pall away from our spirits'* he refers to .... (healing/destructive) power of nature.

(v) Read the Assertion (A) and the Reason (R) below, with reference to the given extract. (1)

Assertion (A) The poet believes that nature's beauty alternates the sorrows and 'pall' of human life.

Reason (R) Trees, both old and young, provide a sense of shade and comfort symbolising relief from hardships of life.

UNSOLVED

(a) Both (A) and (R) are true, and (R) is the correct explanation of (A).
(b) Both (A) and (R) are true, but (R) is not the correct explanationj of (A).
(c) (A) is true, but (R) is false.
(d) (A) is false, but (R) is true.

(vi) What message do the given lines highlight in the context of human suffering? (1)

8. Read the given extracts and answer the questions for **any one** of the two given. (1 × 4 = 4)

A. MR. LAMB Like a bomb only blew up my leg. There's worse things can happen. You can burn yourself away inside.

DERRY After I'd come home, one person said, "He'd have been better off stopping in there. In the hospital. He'd be better off with others like himself." She thinks blind people only ought to be with other blind people and idiot boys with idiot boys.

MR. LAMB And people with no legs altogether?

DERRY That's right.

MR. LAMB What kind of a world would that be?

(i) Complete the following suitably. (1)

The phase 'you can burn yourself away inside' means ....

(ii) Analyse Derry's frustration with the societal perception of people with disabilities. (1)

(iii) Select the option that best describes the stranger's belief regarding people like Derry? (1)
(a) That no one would love him and he would be alone forever.
(b) That he would not live for long and so should stay at home.
(c) That there should be a place where all people like him could stay together.
(d) That he should stop being a burden

(iv) Discuss the significance of Mr. Lamb's rhetorical question, "What kind of a world would that be?" (1)

Or

B. The Maharaja's anxiety reached a fever pitch when there remained just one tiger to achieve his tally of a hundred. He had this one thought during the day and the same dream at night. By this time the tiger farms had run dry even in his father-in-law's kingdom. It became impossible to locate tigers anywhere. Yet only one more was needed. If he could kill just that one single beast, the Maharaja would have no fears left. He could give up tiger hunting altogether. *(The Tiger King)*

(i) Complete the following suitably. (1)

The writer refers to the dreams of the Tiger King to highlight ....

(ii) How does the scarcity of tigers, even in his father-in-law's kingdom, add to the themes of the story? (1)

(iii) Select the most suitable title for the given extract. (1)
(a) Maharaja's Determination
(b) On the Way of Killing a Hundred Tigers
(c) The Selfish King
(d) Killing Other Creatures

(iv) Explain the irony in the Maharaja's desire to 'give up tiger hunting altogether' once he kills the hundredth tiger.

9. Read the given extracts and answer the questions for **any one** of the two given. (1 × 6 = 6)

A. Together they have imposed the baggage on the child that he cannot put down. Before he is aware, he accepts it as naturally as his father. To do anything else would mean to dare. And daring is not part of his growing up. When I sense a flash of it in Mukesh I am cheered. "I want to be a motor mechanic,' he repeats. He will go to a garage and learn. But the garage is a long way from his home. *(Lost Spring)*

(i) Why is daring not a part of the children of Firozabad? (1)

(ii) Select the correct option from those given in brackets to fill in the blank. (1)

The 'baggage' in the extract refers to .... (the bag of bangles/the job of bangle making).

(iii) Complete the following suitably. (1)

The writer states that the boys accepts bangle making as naturally as his father to state that ....

(iv) What metaphorical idea is represented by the phrase "is a long way from his home"? (1)

(v) Identify the textual clue that allows the reader to infer that Mukesh's dream will require determination and sincerity. (1)

(vi) Based on the above extract, choose the statement that is True for 'they'. (1)

(a) They are figures of authority
(b) They are scared of government
(c) They are suppressive
(d) Both (a) and (c)

Or

B. When I saw who it was, I said, "Excuse me, but aren't you Danny Casey?" And he looked sort of surprised. And he said, "Yes, that's right. And I knew it must be him because he had the accent, you know, like when they interviewed him on the television. So I asked him for an autograph for little Derek, but neither of us had any paper or a pen. So then we just talked a bit. About the clothes in Royce's window. He seemed lonely. After all, it's a long way from the west of Ireland. *(Going Places)*

(i) How does the speaker make 'he' believe in her words? (1)

(ii) Select the correct option from those given in the bracket to fill in the blank. (1)

He was surprised because he had not .... (expected/wanted) someone to talk to him.

(iii) Complete the following suitably. (1)

The given lines show that the speaker ....

(iv) Why was Danny unable to sign an autograph for Sophie? (1)

(v) Identify the line that suggests that Danny Casey missed his family and home. (1)

(a) And he looked sort of surprised.
(b) I asked him for an autograph.
(c) About the clothes in Royce's window.
(d) He seemed lonely.

UNSOLVED

(vi) What does the narrator's interaction with Danny Casey primarily reveal? (1)
(a) The narrator's admiration mixed with doubt about Danny's authenticity.
(b) A shared understanding between people from the same place.
(c) A moment of unexpected kinship due to a shared love of fashion.
(d) The narrator's nervousness and awe of someone famous.

10. *Answer **Any Five** of the following six questions in 40-50 words.* (2 × 5 = 10)

(i) What kinds of wars does Pablo Neruda mention in his poem? Describe each type of war and its effects.
(ii) In the story 'Rattrap' who was a keen observer, the ironmaster or his daughter Edla? Substantiate your answer with an example.
(iii) Interpret how M. Hamel appreciates his mother tongue. (The Last Lesson)
(iv) Explain the significance of the title 'My Mother at Sixty-six'.
(v) 'Garbage is gold for rag pickers'. Explain. (Lost Spring)
(vi) What do the symbols 'tigers', 'fingers' and 'ring' stand for in the poem 'Aunt Jennifer's Tigers'?

11. Answer **Any Two** of the following three questions in 40-50 words. (2 × 2 = 4)

(i) Describe Galesburg of 1894. (The Third Level)
(ii) Untouchability is not only a crime, it is inhuman too. Why and how did Bama decide to fight against it? (Memories of Childhood)
(iii) Why did Dr. Sadao did not throw the wounded man into the sea even though he was an enemy to his nation? (The Enemy)

12. Answer **Any One** of the following questions in 120-150 words. (5)

A. 'Bah! I've got plenty of time. I'll learn it tomorrow.' Franz was shocked when he heard that it was the last lesson and he hardly knew French, his mother tongue. Many of us find ourselves in similar situations and regret when all is over. Write with reference to the lesson 'The Last Lesson' from your text, the lesson learnt from this situation.

Or

B. Feminism refers to a collection of movements and ideologies that advocate women's rights and seeks to establish equal opportunities for women in all spheres. Discuss with reference to 'Aunt Jennifer's Tigers' and 'Going Places'.

13. Answer **Any One** of the following two questions in 120-150 words. (5)

A. Describe the efforts made by the Tiger King to achieve his target of killing a hundred tigers. (The Tiger King)

Or

B. How did Dr. Sadao rise above narrow prejudices of race and country to help a human being in need? (The Enemy)

